YOUR BRAIN IS A FILTHY LIAR
How Self-Deception Controls You and the Path to Freedom

Bizzie Gold

Published by Game Changer Publishing

Paperback ISBN: 978-1-967424-28-3
Hardcover ISBN: 978-1-967424-29-0
Digital ISBN: 978-1-967424-30-6

Printed in Canada

www.GameChangerPublishing.com

YOUR BRAIN IS A FILTHY LIAR

How Self-Deception Controls You
and the Path to Freedom

Bizzie Gold

TABLE OF
CONTENTS

FORE
WORD

Sitting in the theater, watching buildings explode in Fight Club's final moments, I felt my stomach turn. Not because of the destruction, but because, for the first time, I realized how easily reality could unravel. The fuzzy gray line between sanity and insanity stopped being an abstract concept and started to feel disturbingly close.

I'd spent significant time thinking about mental illness and psychosis throughout my childhood. And while I'd seen it dramatized in movies and felt its ripple effects in my own home, I always assumed people who struggled with their mental illness knew it deep down. That they were somehow hiding or compartmentalizing to avoid having to face it - but *knew* at some level. It never crossed my mind that someone could be completely oblivious to their own unraveling, living in a total different verson of reality while the rest of us are watching the train wreck from the outside.

If you haven't seen Fight Club, pause here. Go watch it. I'm about to spoil the twist, and you've had 26 years to catch up. No, I don't feel bad about ruining it for you.

Here's the kicker: the protagonist doesn't realize he's living as two people. His "friend," Tyler, isn't real—he's a projection of the protagonist's fractured mind. For 13-year-old me, sitting in that theater, this revelation wasn't just shocking—it was existential. My heart started pounding, my neck cramped up, and my mind raced to keep up. If this guy didn't know he was spiraling, how could I trust my own reality?

At the time, I was living at boarding school, a refuge far from my chaotic home life. It was the first time I'd experienced anything resembling peace. The daily panic attacks that had plagued me since the age of nine were finally starting to subside. For a few precious months, I could just exist—no fight or flight, no constant edge of survival. I was finally getting a taste of what it might feel like to be a normal kid.

But peace has never stayed in my life for long.

Just weeks before that fateful movie night, I'd made a decision that would permanently alter the trajectory of my mental state: I tried psilocybin mushrooms. It wasn't a choice I made lightly. Until then, I'd been the kid who parented everyone else, made sure my friends stayed safe at parties, and avoided anything that might impair my grasp on reality. But boarding school was a different world. The stressors that had defined my existence back home weren't there, and for the first time, I let my guard down.

Mushrooms were fun. Until they weren't.

My mind, already fragile and impressionable, became more malleable than I realized. I started noticing cracks in my perception—small ones at first, easy to dismiss. But when I walked into that theater to watch Fight Club, it was like someone took a sledgehammer to those cracks and blew them wide open.

The twist in Fight Club wasn't just a plot device. It was a direct confrontation of a question I hadn't dared to ask myself: What if I can't trust my own mind? If this character could live his life completely unaware of his own duality, there was nothing stopping me from doing the same. The thought was terrifying.

In the days and weeks that followed, I felt like I was walking a tightrope between logic and chaos. My mind became a battleground, a place where intrusive thoughts waged war against my desperate attempts to hold on to something concrete.

This unsettling moment marked the beginning of something bigger. It forced me to ask questions I couldn't unask: Why do we deceive ourselves? How can we be so blind to the truth of our own experiences? And, most importantly, can we learn to see it?

Spoiler alert: yes, we can. But the road to getting there isn't paved with the kind of clichés you'll find in most self-help books. This text isn't about "finding yourself" or going on a "healing journey." Screw that noise. Healing doesn't have to be a never-ending loop of revisiting your trauma and talking yourself in circles.

Here's the truth: most of us are stuck because we don't see the lies we're telling ourselves. Make no mistake—your brain is a filthy liar. It will do everything in its power to repeat patterns that sabotage your happiness, your relationships, and your goals. Why? Because those patterns are comfortable, familiar, and safe.

But safe doesn't mean good, peaceful, or successful.

The mental health industry has spent decades dancing around this truth. In fact, much of the industry actively feeds the deception through endless labels and therapy models that foster emotional codependency. But it doesn't have to be this way. You can learn to see through the lies. You can break free.

The process isn't comfortable. It isn't pretty. But it works.

That moment in the theater was the first step on a path I've been walking for twenty-six years. It set me on a relentless quest to understand the mechanisms of self-deception and, more importantly, how to dismantle them. Along the way, I've discovered that the truth isn't just liberating—it's a weapon. Once you learn to wield it, nothing can hold you back.

So, consider this book your training manual. It's not going to coddle you or sugarcoat the hard stuff. Instead, it will arm you with the tools you need to face your patterns of self-deception head-on.

By the end, you'll see your mind for what it is: a powerful instrument that's been working against you for far too long. And once you take control, you'll never see yourself—or the world—the same way again.

"Find out what you're afraid of and go live there."

- Chuck Palahniuk

CHAPTER 1

THE LIES YOU DON'T KNOW YOU TELL

Your brain, as remarkable as it is, functions like a master con artist. Day in and day out, it crafts stories, spins half-truths, and serves up carefully tailored illusions—all under the guise of keeping you safe. But let's get one thing straight: most of these distortions aren't about protection; they're about control—control over your perception of reality, your decisions, and ultimately, your outcomes. And the clincher? You rarely even notice it happening. This isn't a fluke, it's a symptom of your evolution, hardwired to prioritize emotional survival over logical clarity.

This covert sabotage is self-deception, and it's a universal feature of human cognition. Your brain filters, reframes, and edits reality to fit the narrative it believes will keep you comfortable—even when that narrative actively works against your best interests. It's why you rationalize procrastination as "waiting for the right moment," or dismiss red flags in relationships because "no one's perfect." While your brain might whisper sweet nothings about self-preservation or boosting your self-esteem, the reality is often far less flattering.

Self-deception keeps you locked in behaviors that directly conflict with what you claim to want, perpetuating cycles of frustration, avoidance, and stagnation. And here's the brutal truth: the lies you don't even realize you're telling yourself are the ones that cost you the most. This chapter is your invitation to examine these mental sleights of hand. It's not about blaming your brain—it's about outsmarting it.

What Is Self-Deception, Really?

Self-deception isn't the same as lying—not in the way you're used to thinking about it. Lying to others is a conscious choice; you know the truth and choose to obscure it. Self-deception, however, operates in the shadows. It's a subconscious process in which your mind selectively edits reality, filtering information to fit the narrative you've unknowingly committed to.

Evolutionary biologist Robert Trivers argues that self-deception evolved as a social advantage. By lying to ourselves, we're better able to convince others of our sincerity, creating stronger alliances and avoiding conflict. In the modern world, this evolutionary relic does more harm than good. Instead of fostering connection or survival, it often reinforces the very patterns that sabotage us.

Self-deception wears many masks, slipping seamlessly between rationalization and delusion. It's the justification of unhealthy habits ("I deserve this"), the denial of emotional realities ("It's not that bad"), or the blame-shifting that keeps you from owning your role in a problem ("They made me do it"). Self-deception subtly distorts your view of the world and your place in it. These distortions are not one-size-fits-all; they can skew overly negative or deceptively positive, with equally potent consequences.

A negative skew often looks like projecting fault onto others while ignoring your own role in the problem. For example, blaming your partner for relationship struggles without considering how your avoidance or criticism may contribute. This kind of self-deception creates a shield of false security but blocks the path to radical personal responsibility—the only real catalyst for change. On the flip side, self-deception can veer into dangerous overconfidence. Think of the adrenaline junkie who convinces themselves they can land an impossible stunt. Sometimes, that belief is enough to pull it off, but just as often, it ends in disaster.

At its core, self-deception taps into the powerful interplay between belief and behavior. When you buy into the lies your brain feeds you, they do more than color your perception, they steer your actions. Believe you're powerless, and you'll avoid the opportunities that could set you free. Believe you're invincible, and you may charge headfirst into ruin. This feedback loop of belief and action makes self-deception a self-fulfilling prophecy capable of shaping—or shattering—your life. Recognizing this dynamic is the first step toward reclaiming control from your brain's invisible hand.

The Science of Self-Deception

Research consistently shows that self-deception is both pervasive and persistent. Consider a study in Behavioral and Brain Sciences in which participants, incentivized to favor certain outcomes, unconsciously altered their judgments to align with the reward structure. They weren't intentionally lying—they genuinely believed their skewed interpretations. Self-deception doesn't announce itself or feel like a conscious choice. Instead, it rewrites your perception in real time, seamlessly integrating distortion into your decision-making.

Another study in Frontiers in Psychology explored how self-deception fluctuates with feedback. Negative feedback temporarily reduced self-deception, forcing participants to confront uncomfortable truths. But as soon as the opportunity arose, they returned to their old tricks, crafting narratives that protected their self-image. This cycle of suppression and resurgence is hardwired into our mental framework. This is not a passing glitch but a core feature of how we process and adapt to reality.

Self-deception offers a convenient escape hatch. Reconciling conflicting truths—like wanting to feel competent while knowing you've failed—requires significant mental effort. Instead of wrestling with that dissonance, your brain simplifies the equation by creating a version of reality that feels more palatable. This mental shortcut may reduce cognitive load in the moment, but it comes at a cost. The truth doesn't disappear just because you've ignored it—it lingers, shaping outcomes in ways that often leave you stuck, frustrated, or spiraling.

Despite the wealth of research, the mental health field has been slow to confront self-deception directly. Many practitioners seem hesitant to name it, perhaps fearing that addressing it too bluntly will alienate clients or disrupt therapeutic rapport. Instead, the focus often shifts to symptoms or surface-level behaviors, leaving the root cause untouched. The result? Clients who feel temporarily better but remain trapped in the same patterns, unable to break free from the lies their brains have convinced them to believe.

These studies and countless real-life examples make clear that self-deception isn't just a coping mechanism; it's a driver of human behavior. It shapes how we interpret feedback, make decisions, and even construct our identities. Left unchecked, it becomes a self-sustaining loop, where distortions reinforce the very beliefs and behaviors that caused them. The mental health field's reluctance to address this head-on is a missed opportunity to unlock true, lasting change.

The irony is that the very mechanism of self-deception that causes suffering also holds the potential for liberation. If belief can skew perception negatively, as when someone blames others for their problems, it can also fuel extraordinary feats, as when someone overcomes insurmountable odds because they believed they could. Addressed directly, self-deception can reshape your reality.

Understanding the science behind self-deception gives us the power to dismantle it. By identifying how it operates and why it persists, we can begin to question the stories we tell ourselves and the assumptions we make about the world. True healing begins when we stop running from these truths and start using them as the foundation for growth.

Ignore Self-Deception, Stay Stuck– The Choice Is Yours

Self-deception keeps you comfortable—and stuck. It's the reason you repeat patterns you swore you'd outgrown, avoid the hard conversations you know you need to have, and cling to habits that actively work against your goals. Self-deception is a masterful puppeteer, pulling invisible strings and keeping you locked in a performance that sabotages your potential.

Here's how self-deception sabotages progress:

- **It shields root causes.** You can't fix what you won't face. By redirecting blame or rationalizing failures, self-deception keeps the real issues out of sight.

- **It perpetuates harmful cycles.** Skipping the gym becomes "self-care," and procrastination becomes "waiting for the right moment." These justifications lock you into a loop of inaction.

- **It distorts self-perception.** Your brain convinces you that you're doing more than you are—or that your problems aren't as bad as they seem. Either way, meaningful change gets delayed.

- **It damages relationships.** The lies you tell yourself inevitably spill over, creating mistrust, projection, and conflict with others.

Confronting self-deception is not for the faint of heart. It demands you take a long, hard look at the narratives you've crafted. But this process,

14

as challenging as it is, holds unparalleled value. When you begin to strip away the layers of self-deception, you uncover a clearer picture of who you are and what's holding you back. This clarity becomes the foundation for transformation that isn't fleeting or performative, but deeply rooted in self-awareness and intentionality.

Facing your self-deception will feel like dismantling a safety net you've relied on your entire life. But what you'll come to realize is that it wasn't a safety net at all—it was a trap. Breaking free is uncomfortable, even painful at times, but the alternative is far worse: staying stuck in the same cycles, endlessly hoping for different results. The work is hard, but the reward—a life no longer tethered to self-imposed limitations—is more than worth it.

CHAPTER 2

THE MECHANICS OF SELF-DECEPTION

While everyone experiences self-deception, its manifestations are shaped by deeply ingrained subconscious patterns. Early experiences, unchallenged beliefs, and thought patterns form a blueprint for the particular flavor of lies your brain defaults to. These lies serve a purpose: they shield you from discomfort, reduce cognitive load, and maintain your internal narrative. But this so-called "protection" often comes at a premium.

Unfortunately, these distorted perspectives generate language that sounds like an excuse, justification, rationalization, or neutral observation—making them challenging to observe, confront, and oppose. To our brain, they are the truth, after all.

These narratives exist in the background of your mind for so many years that they start to feel like second nature. But hear me when I say this: they are not immutable. They can be unlearned—once you understand the mechanisms driving them. Let's break down the types of self-deception and put each mechanism into practical context. Once you understand how these operate, we can begin the process of observing the thoughts that keep you stuck in a survival-based loop.

Understanding the Mechanisms of Self-Deception

At its core, self-deception operates through a series of mental shortcuts and distortions that rewrite reality in ways that feel comfortable or justifiable. In psychology, a mechanism refers to the internal processes—cognitive, emotional, or behavioral—that drive how we think, feel, or act in response to certain stimuli. These mechanisms are often subconscious, operating beneath the surface of awareness, yet their patterns are predictable and consistent. Below, we'll explore the primary mechanisms that allow self-deception to thrive, pairing each with real-world examples and scientific insights to uncover their impact.

Cognitive Dissonance Reduction

When your beliefs or actions clash, your brain experiences discomfort. Rather than confront this dissonance, your brain takes the easy way out—it adjusts your narrative to align with your behavior. This can look like downplaying a mistake to preserve your self-esteem or convincing yourself that an undesirable outcome was actually for the best.

COVID Fog: When Beliefs Became Glass Houses

Like it or not, the COVID era of 2020 was a masterclass in cognitive dissonance on a global scale. Families were torn apart by conflicting beliefs, with some choosing complete isolation, while others dismissed precautions entirely. For many, their personal experiences didn't align with the overwhelming narratives being broadcast on the news. Instead of allowing these discrepancies to challenge their beliefs, many doubled down. They became angry, oppositional, and even took it upon themselves to police others, protecting their fragile glass house of belief from shattering under scrutiny.

Fast-forward to 2025: Much of the pandemic manipulation has come to light. Those who were once caught in the fog of cognitive dissonance now describe it as a haze that clouded their judgment, making it impossible to see what was right in front of them. Their actions weren't driven by malice but by their brain's desperate need to resolve the uncomfortable clash between belief and reality. Cognitive dissonance dictated their behaviors, reinforcing the very beliefs that kept them trapped.

Selective Attention and Memory

Your brain is a master at filtering reality to fit its chosen narrative. It emphasizes information that supports your beliefs and conveniently forgets evidence to the contrary. This mechanism explains why people stay in toxic relationships, holding onto selective memories of "the good times" while ignoring glaring red flags.

The Highlight Reel of Toxic Love

If you take a hard look at your relationship history, chances are you'll notice a pattern. The mechanism of selective memory is likely to blame. It's why so many of us seem to have a "type," even when that type consistently leads us into the same cycles of pain and disappointment. Our brain, eager to maintain comfort and avoid discomfort, conveniently forgets the moments of fear, betrayal, or hurt. Instead, it shines a spotlight on the fleeting good times—moments that feel so vivid and reassuring that they drown out the warning signs.

This mechanism rewrites the past. Imagine being lonely and reminiscing about an ex who, in reality, was toxic or even abusive. Suddenly, your brain starts replaying their kind words, the fun vacations, or the time they made you laugh uncontrollably. It conveniently edits out the fights, the mistrust, or the emotional scars they left behind. Before you know it, you're questioning whether they were really that bad, tempted to pick up the phone or reply to a text, convincing yourself that "this time will be different."

Selective memory is more than a psychological quirk; it's a survival mechanism. It allows us to hold onto the belief that things can get better, even when all evidence suggests otherwise. Without recognizing this pattern, it's easy to fall into the trap of rewriting history, repeating the same mistakes, and staying tethered to relationships that don't serve us.

Rationalization

Rationalization is your brain's way of smoothing over behavior that doesn't align with your values. It creates logical—but false—explanations to make your actions or inactions seem reasonable. Skipping the gym? "I needed to rest." Overspending? "I worked hard and deserved it." These justifications feel valid in the moment but keep you trapped in cycles of avoidance.

The Art of Justifying the Exception

Rationalization is one of the slipperiest mechanisms of self-deception because it often flies under the radar, cloaked in logic that feels perfectly reasonable. It's your brain's way of reconciling behavior or outcomes that don't align with your expectations, offering explanations that help you sidestep discomfort. The trouble is, these justifications—whether overly positive or catastrophically negative—keep you from confronting the real issues at play.

Take a negative skew, for instance: you're in the middle of a panic attack. Even though you've experienced this hundreds of times and know the symptoms by heart, you convince yourself that this one is different. This one is a heart attack. You rationalize the timing, the intensity, the sensations, telling yourself it must be an exception, not the rule. Instead of using the tools you know can help, you spiral into fear, reinforcing the cycle of panic and avoidance.

Now consider a positive skew. You underperform on a critical work project. Deep down, you know you weren't prepared. You stayed up too late, didn't put in enough effort, or failed to ask for help. But rather than face the reality of your lack of preparation, you tell yourself it was just an off day or that the project wasn't meant to succeed. This rationalization feels comforting in the moment, but it robs you of the chance to examine the behaviors that led to the outcome, leaving you vulnerable to repeating the same mistake.

Rationalization is a master of subtle sabotage. It cushions your ego and shields you from discomfort, but it also keeps you stuck. Whether it's catastrophizing or sugarcoating, this mechanism blinds you to the lessons embedded in your experiences—the very lessons that could propel you toward meaningful change.

Projection

Projection externalizes your discomfort by attributing your own thoughts, feelings, or insecurities to others. This mechanism shields you from self-reflection by turning the spotlight outward. For instance, accusing someone of being judgmental when, in reality, you're projecting your own critical thoughts.

The Mirror of Discomfort

We've all been there. You're in a relationship, and the dreaded question comes up: "Are you okay?" or "Is something wrong?" You pause, caught off guard, because the truth is, you've been quietly observing your partner subtly withdraw and go cold for the past 30 minutes. You've tried not to react, giving them space and hoping to sidestep a potential argument. But now they're questioning you, their tone tinged with frustration or suspicion.

Here's what's likely happening: your partner got stuck in their own head, trapped by a loop of negative self-talk or a faulty assumption. Maybe they convinced themselves you were annoyed with them or picking up on something they're insecure about. Instead of taking ownership of this internal dialogue, they unconsciously projected their discomfort outward. The result? Their withdrawal signals that something is wrong—but in their mind, you're the one with the problem.

Projection works like a mirror, reflecting your own unresolved thoughts and feelings onto someone else. It spares you from the hard work of self-reflection, but it also creates confusion and conflict. What could have been an opportunity for self-awareness becomes a misdirected accusation, leaving both partners feeling misunderstood and defensive. Breaking this cycle requires stepping back and asking the uncomfortable question: "Is this really about them, or is it about me?"

Confirmation Bias

Your brain loves to be right. Confirmation bias ensures that you seek out evidence to support your beliefs while dismissing or ignoring contradictory information. This mechanism is particularly insidious because it reinforces existing narratives, making it harder to challenge ingrained patterns.

Seeking What You Want to See

Confirmation bias is one of the most pervasive mechanisms of self-deception because it takes root so early in life. Between the ages of two and five, your brain begins to establish parameters about its environment—what feels safe, predictable, or true. These rules become the lens through which you view the world, and any challenge to them feels like a threat. Instead of pausing to examine the nuance, exceptions, or contradictions, your brain doubles down, seeking evidence that reinforces its original belief.

This mechanism plays out most dramatically in relationships. Imagine you've developed a belief that your partner can't be trusted. Whether this belief stems from past experiences, insecurity, or fear, it now shapes the way you interpret their actions. When your partner gets home late, forgets to respond to a text, or even seems distracted, your brain immediately flags it as evidence of their untrustworthiness. But here's the twist: could it be that when you felt suspicious, you unconsciously applied pressure—accusations, defensiveness, or passive-aggressive comments—that made your partner react in a way that seemed suspicious, even if they weren't actually doing anything wrong?

Confirmation bias is a self-fulfilling prophecy. By seeking out evidence to support your suspicions, you shape your environment to fit your narrative, often without realizing it. This mechanism reinforces mistrust and erodes the connection and safety you're craving. Breaking free requires stepping back and asking, "Am I seeing the full picture, or just the parts my brain wants to see?"

Minimization and Denial

Minimization downplays the significance of something painful or uncomfortable, while denial outright rejects it. These mechanisms keep you from fully confronting reality, whether it's the severity of a toxic relationship or the consequences of your own actions.

Gray vs. Black-and-White: The Tug-of-War Between Minimization and Denial

In relationships, minimization and denial often run the show, creating subtle but powerful dynamics that prevent growth and accountability. These mechanisms tend to correlate with specific Brain Pattern Types, which you'll explore in upcoming chapters. For now, it's important to understand that Brain Pattern Types usually cluster into one of these two mechanisms—rarely both.

Those who minimize tend to align with fawning or freeze protective responses. Minimization emerges when there's a desire to quickly reset and move on after conflict. For instance, if your partner says something hurtful, you might instinctively downplay its significance, thinking, It's not worth making a big deal about. This optimistic, "look on the bright side" attitude may feel constructive, but it often stems from dissociation or detachment. Minimizers live in shades of gray, where smoothing over discomfort feels safer than confronting it. This tendency may even lead to covering for a partner who leans on denial, allowing the cycle to persist.

On the other hand, denial tends to align with fight-or-flight responses. This mechanism avoids personal responsibility and protects one's self-concept. For those who lean on denial, everything is black and white—absolutes that simplify reality but erase nuance. If something feels exposing or vulnerable, denial swoops in to rewrite the narrative, shifting blame outward or reframing events to fit a more palatable story. Denial t protects the ego and shuts down meaningful introspection, leaving little room for growth.

These mechanisms often play off each other in relationships, creating an unbalanced dynamic. The minimizer subconsciously absorbs discomfort, covering for their denial-prone counterpart. Meanwhile, the denier rewrites history to align with their current mood, leaving the minimizer to navigate a fog of unresolved emotions. Understanding this interplay is key to breaking free from the loop—for you and your relationships.

Overconfidence and Optimism Bias

While positivity has its place, overconfidence and optimism bias can lead to risky or unrealistic decisions. Believing you're invincible—or that everything will "just work out"—prevents honest evaluation of the risks or effort required for success.

The Fine Line Between Confidence and Catastrophe

Overconfidence and optimism bias are fascinating because they highlight the complex relationship between belief and outcome. Sometimes, sheer belief can drive success—not because the person was prepared or deserved it, but because their confidence carried them through. Adrenaline junkies often embody this dynamic. These are the people who perform impossible feats, defying gravity and logic to walk away unscathed. It's not hours in the gym or meticulous preparation that set them apart—it's the perfect mix of recklessness and unwavering self-belief. Their confidence overrides fear and hesitation, allowing them to succeed where others might falter.

But here's the catch: overconfidence comes with immense risk. It's often built on shaky ground, where physical evidence or preparation doesn't align with the person's belief in their abilities. This disconnect isn't exclusive to extreme sports—it's a common thread in everyday life. Take the person who constantly procrastinates, ignoring looming deadlines until the last possible moment. Their optimism bias whispers, "You'll figure it out," convincing them to pull an all-nighter or cram weeks of work into hours. Sometimes they do pull it off—but at the expense of their health, well-being, and daily routine.

Even when overconfidence leads to success, it can wreak havoc. The athlete who barely survives the impossible stunt might pay for it later with injuries or burnout. The procrastinator who scrambles to deliver might earn praise but loses sleep and creates a cycle of self-induced stress. These mechanisms blur the line between brilliance and disaster, pushing people to accomplish the extraordinary while quietly setting the stage for potential collapse. Recognizing this pattern is key to finding a balance—leveraging belief when it serves you while staying grounded enough to avoid unnecessary risks.

Self-Handicapping

This mechanism sets up external excuses for failure before you even start. By procrastinating, under-preparing, or creating other obstacles, you ensure that, should you fail, you can blame the circumstances—not yourself.

The Rigged Experiment of Self-Sabotage

Self-handicapping is one of the most insidious mechanisms of self-deception because it operates seamlessly within the human experience. From a young age, our brains create rules about how to navigate the world. Rules forged between the ages of two and five tell us what to expect: "I'm not enough," "I'm too much," "I'll always be abandoned," or "I'm destined to fail." These narratives become the backdrop of our lives, and self-handicapping ensures they play out exactly as we feared.

Think of it like setting up a game where the rules are rigged from the start. Procrastinating on an important project, avoiding preparation for a big event, or overloading yourself with too many commitments ensures that failure feels inevitable. The whole time, you rationalize your choices: "I work better under pressure," or "It's not my fault I didn't have enough time." But underneath it all, you're creating the perfect storm for your worst fears to come true— fulfilling the belief that you're destined for disappointment.

This isn't about laziness or a lack of effort; it's about subconscious self-preservation. By setting up external excuses for failure, you protect yourself from confronting the deeper fear: that you're the problem. It's far easier to blame circumstances than to face the possibility that you might need to change. Self-handicapping feels like a safety net, but it's a trap, keeping you locked in cycles of avoidance and self-sabotage.

Breaking free requires seeing the pattern for what it is: a self-soothing illusion. By recognizing these self-imposed obstacles, you can start rewriting the rules your brain clings to and create a path where success is no longer sabotaged before it begins.

False Consensus Effect

The false consensus effect leads you to overestimate how much others share your beliefs or behaviors. This mechanism validates your choices by making them feel universal. If "everyone cheats a little," you don't feel as guilty about your dishonesty.

When "Everyone Does It" Becomes the Excuse

The false consensus effect makes harmful behaviors feel justified by convincing you they're universally accepted. One of the most glaring collective examples is the consumption of pornography. In today's society, it's everywhere: overtly sexualized advertising, suggestive content on social media, and endless access to explicit material. Despite its well-documented links to emotional dysregulation, addiction, and neurological issues, pornography is often rationalized with a simple justification: "Everyone does it." This belief allows people to sidestep uncomfortable questions about the impact of their habits, leaning on a perceived societal norm to shield themselves from accountability.

The same dynamic applies to marijuana use. What was once seen as a gateway drug is now widely normalized, celebrated even, in popular culture and everyday conversation. While legalization and destigmatization have opened the door for some legitimate medical uses, the pendulum has swung so far that the risks—especially for younger users—are ignored. Psychotic breaks, seizures, and other serious health consequences are on the rise, but the false consensus effect downplays these realities. "Everyone smokes weed" and, "It's natural" become the refrain, leading individuals to equate "normal" with "safe."

This mechanism operates quietly, validating choices by making them feel ubiquitous. But just because something is common doesn't mean it's harmless. The false consensus effect blinds us to the consequences of behaviors we'd otherwise question, keeping us locked into destructive patterns that feel justified. Recognizing this pattern requires challenging the assumption that what's popular is aligned with what's right—or what's best for you.

Emotional Reasoning

This mechanism relies on feelings rather than facts. If you feel unworthy, then it must be true. Emotional reasoning ensnares you in distorted narratives, where subjective emotions outweigh objective reality.

The Trap of Feeling as Truth

Emotional reasoning is one of the most important and widespread mechanisms of self-deception because it feels deeply personal and, therefore, true. The mental health space, along with many spiritual and consciousness communities, has unintentionally reinforced this trap. Clients are often taught to connect with their feelings, treating them as undeniable truths rather than signals to be examined. While feelings can provide valuable insights about your environment, they are far from infallible. More often than not, they are byproducts of self-deceptive thinking, prioritizing subconscious narratives over objective reality.

Take a moment to consider this distinction: feelings and facts are often at odds with one another. For example, you may feel unworthy of love, but that doesn't make it true. Emotional reasoning, however, leads you to accept the feeling as evidence, building an entire narrative around it. "I feel unlovable, so I must be unlovable." Every interaction or experience is filtered through this distorted lens.

One of the key distinctions this book seeks to make is that, while feelings have value, their purpose is to serve as clues—pieces of

26

a scavenger hunt guiding you to underlying patterns. Emotional reasoning will reinforce cycles of self-destruction, blooming from distortion rather than clarity.

Escaping this mechanism requires a willingness to question the validity of your feelings. Are they aligned with reality, or are they tied to an old, deceptive narrative? By stepping outside the spell of your emotional response, you can begin to see the error in your thinking and choose actions rooted in truth.

Fantasy and Escapism

When reality feels unbearable, fantasy offers an appealing escape. Whether through daydreaming, entertainment, or avoidance, this mechanism keeps you from engaging with the challenges of the present.

Lost in the Dream, Missing the Reality

Though they exist across all age groups, fantasy and escapism have become increasingly common among younger generations. For many, this pattern originates in childhood as a way to cope with a traumatic or unstable home environment—or a life that feels dull or monotonous. Daydreaming, storytelling, gaming, and constructing imaginary worlds offer a comforting refuge from pain or boredom. When this mechanism persists into adulthood, it begins to blur the line between aspiration and avoidance.

People who rely on this mechanism build elaborate dream scenarios or idealized goals in their minds, crafting a version of reality in which they have full control, masters of their own universe. Here's the catch: these imagined worlds rarely align with real life. When dreams don't materialize or fail to feel as fulfilling as they did in the mind, disappointment sets in. Worse yet, the time spent lost in thought or dreaming comes at the expense of engaging with physical reality. Without consistent, incremental actions, their goals remain just that—dreams. This creates a cycle of frustration and self-doubt, where reality never quite measures up and the pull of the imagined world becomes even stronger.

This mechanism feeds grass-is-greener thinking and FOMO. The mind, addicted to the pleasure of perfect scenarios and endless possibilities, struggles to stay present. Reality, with its imperfections and incremental progress, feels like a poor substitute for the vivid and flawless worlds crafted in the mind. Over time, this addiction to escape can erode the ability to connect with real life, sabotaging the actions and consistency needed to bring those dreams to fruition.

Recognizing the balance between imagination and reality can liberate you from this mechanism. While dreaming has its place, it must be paired with tangible, intentional action. The key is learning to anchor aspirations in the present moment, translating the beauty of the imagined world into the imperfect but rewarding process of building it step by step.

Self-Justification Through Comparison

Comparison offers a convenient way to justify mediocrity or harmful behavior. By finding someone worse off, you protect yourself from confronting your own shortcomings. "At least I'm not as bad as them" becomes the mantra of self-deception.

The Comparison Trap: Finding Comfort in "At Least I'm Better"

Self-justification through comparison is one of the most pervasive mechanisms, woven deeply into the fabric of contemporary society through platforms like social media. We scroll, compare, and contrast reflexively, often without even realizing it. This subtle but constant mental exercise seeps into every corner of life—relationships, personal goals, self-care, wellness, and beyond. Instead of confronting areas where we fall short or could improve, we lean on comparisons to justify inaction or mediocrity.

This mechanism influences even the most intimate parts of our lives, like dating. Subconsciously, some people choose partners they perceive as inferior in some way—less attractive, less successful, or less confident. This dynamic allows them to feel superior, believing they're less likely to face betrayal or infidelity. While this may provide temporary comfort, it often creates relationships built on imbalance and insecurity rather than genuine connection.

In other cases, comparison is used to rationalize harmful behavior or sheer laziness. Consider someone who avoids pursuing their health goals by thinking, At least I'm not as unhealthy as that person, or someone who justifies procrastination with, "I'm doing better than most of my coworkers." These comparisons might feel validating in the moment, but they ultimately rob you of the opportunity to hold yourself accountable and grow. The antidote to comparison is self-honesty—a willingness to confront patterns without leaning on someone else's shortcomings as a crutch. Only then can you step out of the shadow of "good enough" and into the light of radical personal responsibility.

Why Recognizing Self-Deception Matters

Recognizing the mechanisms of self-deception is the first and most crucial step toward escaping their grip. These aren't harmless quirks; they are deeply embedded patterns that actively shape your choices, relationships, and sense of self. Left unchecked, they foster avoidance, justification, and perpetual struggle.

Exposing these mechanisms requires confronting the lies you've built your life around and peeling back the layers of your own thinking. Discomfort is the price of clarity, and clarity is the foundation of change. By bringing these subconscious patterns into the light, you begin to reclaim control—aligning your actions with your intentions and making choices that reflect who you truly want to be, not just the narratives your brain has fed you.

This process isn't instant. It's a deliberate, often messy unraveling of the distortions that have shaped your life. But the reward is transformative: a future untethered from the distortions of the past, where your brain shifts from being a barrier to growth to becoming a powerful launch pad. This is where real progress begins—in exposing the lies we convince ourselves of with strategic and precise language. This is the process that sets us free.

CHAPTER **3**

WHEN BELIEF BECOMES A LIE

The Hidden Mechanisms of Self-Deception

Imagine self-deception as a clock whose face has been opened, exposing hundreds of small interconnected cogs—each doing its part to turn the hands. Self-deception operates beneath our conscious awareness because these smaller cogs work together to pull off the long con.

Yes, this entire process, puppet-mastered by your brain, is ultimately a con, a trick that leads to heartache, frustration, and conflict. The interconnected pieces of self-deception lead us to feel justified and secure in our choices, even when they ruin lives.

Some of you may see your mistakes as harmless when held up to someone struggling with addiction or abuse. But here's a harsh truth: this con impacts everyone. We all have something to gain from seeing the error in our brain's calculation of reality.

The Brain's Faulty Perception: The McGurk Effect

Revisiting the open-faced clock, let's examine the first small cog: belief. Belief is defined in the field of psychology as an internal mental state that is anchored to a premise that aligns with the perception of truth. In other words, it's a rule or sequence of language that passes your brain's lie detector test. What we believe to be true has incredible power to distort our perception of reality and, with it, our behavior.

Take, for instance, the McGurk Effect, a term coined in 1976 by Psychologists Harry McGurk and John MacDonald in "Hearing Lips and Seeing Voices." A groundbreaking experiment explored how the brain integrates sensory information. Participants were shown a video of a person articulating one syllable (like "ga") while a different syllable ("ba") was played in the audio track. When these conflicting cues were presented together, participants often reported hearing a completely different sound ("da"), revealing how the brain prioritizes and blends sensory inputs. This phenomenon, later dubbed "the McGurk Effect," showcased the brain's tendency to rewrite reality when sensory information doesn't align. In short: the McGurk Effect proves that your brain is a terrible judge of reality. When what you see (like lip movements) clashes with what you hear, your brain picks a fight with itself and spits out a hybrid perception that isn't real. It's a reminder that what you believe you're experiencing is often just your brain taking creative liberties with the truth.

Perceptual Set Theory: How Expectations Warp Reality

Perceptual Set Theory, part of an experiment conducted in 1955, demonstrates the power belief has to alter how we perceive reality. Psychologists Bruner and Minturn ran a deceptively simple experiment to expose how expectations warp perception. Participants were shown an ambiguous figure that could be interpreted as either the letter "B" or the number 13, depending on the context. When the figure appeared among letters, people saw it as "B," but when it was surrounded by numbers, their brains called it 13. The takeaway? Your brain doesn't just passively observe reality—it edits it on the fly based on what it expects to see.

Everyday Proof: When Memory and Perception Clash

Have you ever been in an argument with a loved one or friend who swears you said something you know you didn't say? Isn't it frustrating to know the truth but not be able to convince them? Have you been in a situation where you would swear you remember putting a certain item in your bag to bring to an appointment only to find out it isn't there? Belief is a primary puppet master in the world of self-deception. To a large extent, we believe what we perceive, and there isn't much wiggle room. As you can imagine, examining the origin and specific language of belief is one of the most important keys to our emotional freedom.

The Formation of Beliefs in Childhood

Beliefs are formed starting in early childhood. We enter the world akin to a blank slate. In my work, I typically lean on a Taoist concept of the Pu—an uncarved block. The block, formed by the innate structure of wood, evokes potential. Life experience will become the sculptor. Each experience becomes an input, carving the wooden block to reveal its eventual shape as a fully formed adult psyche.

In the earliest phases of life, when the child's psyche is still an uncarved block, it is primed for three primary functions. Curiosity prompts the child to explore its surroundings to learn about the world. Innocence blocks the ability to compare and contrast with thoughts like "This isn't as bad as last time." When innocence is intact, each carving of the block may be experienced as trauma. Even small but repetitive reactivity in an exhausted parent may be perceived as traumatic. The last function is love. A child arrives open to receiving love, not yet wounded by experience.

It is in these earliest years that we are at our most impressionable. The adult psyche is being sculpted daily, forming a series of beliefs about the world and our place in it. These beliefs become the foundation for our perception of reality—and self-deception. In childhood, we are largely powerless, guided by our caregivers' emotional responses, communication style, and ability to self-regulate. The beliefs we form are a byproduct of what we experience, the gaps of knowledge we fill in, and the faulty conclusions we draw. In many ways, when you are emotionally activated as an adult, it's your 8-year-old self that hijacks your consciousness.

Let's examine the beliefs we form through experience. Experience infers that multiple senses were engaged. Imagine a child accidentally spilling a bowl of cereal. In their mind, it's a simple mistake, but the parent's sudden outburst—yelling and sending them to their room—turns this small moment into something far more significant. The child, confused and hurt, internalizes the experience, their senses still buzzing with the memory of the crash, the yelling, and the sting of being isolated. From that point on, they form a belief—an outburst like this could come out of nowhere: "I should expect this as a possibility from now on." This belief sets them on edge, subtly reshaping their expectations and wiring their brain to anticipate more moments of unpredictable anger.

Beliefs formed through observation can be even more convoluted. A child is often missing the context of what they believe they are observing. A simple misunderstanding between parents could easily form a belief that Mommy and Daddy hate each other. If a child repeatedly witnesses similar exchanges, they might assume Mommy or Daddy will leave—even if this has never crossed the mind of the parents involved. Beliefs are assumptive. A simple conflict could easily spiral into an abandonment wound. If you're a parent reading this, don't worry. We will address in later chapters what you can do to help correct this and bring understanding.

We also generate beliefs from gaps in understanding. Children are often left to fill in gaps when adults don't provide the level of detail a child seeks. Think of a child continually asking, "Why?" A child's brain cognitively leapfrogs between interrelated thoughts in an attempt to formulate belief.

Unfortunately, adults don't tend to give the quality or quantity of answers a child seeks. In some cases, the adult may feel the information is too advanced or mature and declines to answer. There's only one problem: children won't just let it go. Their brain will try to figure it out on their own.

Think about a child who gets exposed to porn. In this instance, let's say the child is five. A parent is unlikely to explain with specificity what the child has just seen. They are likely to minimize it, make up a ridiculous story, or pretend it didn't happen. But the child did see it and is now trying to make sense of the visual input. Were they hugging? Playing doctor? A child will fill in the gaps using what they know. Beliefs formed from a child's limited understanding can be complicated to unravel.

There are two ways to stratify the formation of belief: intentionally and unintentionally. Religion, discipline, family, or ethnic culture all function as intentional inputs to formulate belief. These mechanisms are typically adopted to reinforce the belief. Consider the example of a Christian household. It is common for children raised in these environments to believe in the concept of heaven and hell. By contrast, I was raised in a Reformed Jewish household, where I never considered these concepts until I met friends who believed this in college. As you can imagine, I was shocked. Based on the way I had been raised, these ideas felt akin to believing in Santa Claus as an adult. aYet many children are raised with this foundational belief.

How might one concept create a cascade of additional beliefs? In many cases, the child begins to fear that their behavior will take them to hell. They begin to believe that they are inherently bad and become afraid to express themselves. By contrast, in my household, self-expression was held in high regard and never shamed.

You can see how intentionally ingrained beliefs might shift the trajectory of that child's life. After all, isn't that the point of intentionally passing on beliefs? Other examples include beliefs about the importance of academics, what behaviors are acceptable, and even how a culture or cultural attitude may be expressed. Often policed by social or spiritual sanctions, this intentional area of belief-formation can be challenging to overcome. We will specifically address the role religion and culture play in self-deception in a later chapter.

Unintentional beliefs are typically generated through observation, experience, and gaps in understanding. Parents or caregivers don't often tell a child to believe that no one can be trusted, yet many children end up with this belief due to the aggregate experience of observation, experience, and gaps in understanding. These beliefs can operate under the radar and can be more challenging to rewire than intentional because they feel real through some level of lived experience. They weren't passed down through a book or family tradition—they were lived and feel aligned with objective truth. The only problem is that they aren't objective truth at all. Remember when we discussed the inherent misalignment in power dynamics during childhood? You are the pinball in your parent or caregiver's game? We create these unintentional beliefs through lived experience in a game that wasn't set up by us. Eventually, we age out of the game, and we start our own life. Sadly, we take these beliefs with us and become the pinball in our game.

CHAPTER 4

THE
REALITY
DISTORTION
FIELD

It's time to descend into the abyss. For those of you who haven't yet asked hard questions about reality and existence, this chapter might feel jarring. I've been asking these questions in one form or another for as long as I can remember, so these topics feel slightly less destabilizing to me. Over the eleven years I've been in the field of mental health, I've worked with tens of thousands of clients and have seen firsthand how confronting these ideas can be challenging. Cognitive dissonance often blocks learning or receiving; accepting these truths could shake the very foundation of who you are.

To that, I say—good. That's why you're here. The only way out of your mental cage is through: breaking down the mechanics, spotting the errors, and stepping fully into the truth. Keep in mind, once we enter the realm of perception, truth may not be the warm blanket you want it to be. The truth is, reality—and how we construct our perception of it—isn't as solid or concrete as we like to believe. The moment we step out of the concrete, we enter the slippery, intangible, and gray aspects of what truly is.

The Brain's Need for Certainty Is a Trap

Let's not fear reality—let's embrace it. Our brain craves the concrete because it gives the illusion of control. But here's the irony: when we cling to control at all times, we actually confine ourselves within cycles of chaos.

To tackle this complex topic, we need to explore the function of perception, what parts of our body and consciousness we're using, and how we construct reality. It may not surprise you that this field of study is anything but settled in its understanding of these concepts. I'll do my best to break down common theories, as well as what I have experienced in my work over the last eleven years.

Defining Reality: Objective vs. Subjective

Let's begin with a working definition of reality. Reality is the sum of all that exists, both objectively and subjectively. It includes the external, measurable world independent of individual perception (objective reality), as well as the internal, personal experiences and interpretations shaped by belief, emotion, and cognition (subjective reality). Reality is both the concrete framework of the universe and the unique lens through which each individual experiences it. To understand how we, as human beings, perceive reality, we need to understand what it means to exist.

Experience: The Active Construction of Reality

Experience is more than a snapshot of the world around you—it's an active process that merges what you sense with how you move through it. Your sensory inputs (like sight, sound, and touch) give you the raw data of what's happening in your environment, while proprioceptive inputs—your internal awareness of body position and balance—help you understand how you fit into it all. When you climb a tree, for example, you're seeing the branches and feeling the bark, while knowing where your hand is without looking and trusting your body to keep you balanced. Experience is never just observation; it's a full-bodied interaction with reality that shapes how you perceive and respond to the world.

The Role of Differentiation in Perception

Beyond what you sense or how you move through the world, experience also includes a critical layer of differentiation. Differentiation is your brain's ability to draw boundaries between your internal experience and what's happening beyond yourself. It's what lets you

38

know where you end and the external world begins. Without it, your experiences would be a chaotic blur of sensations and emotions, leaving you unable to tell whether something is affecting you from the outside or your internal state is creating the chaos.

This concept starts with proprioception—your ability to sense your body's position and movement. Proprioception gives you a built-in understanding of your personal space, helping you feel the "edges" of your physical self. It allows you to know where your hand is without looking or how close someone is standing. These edges are psychological, too. Differentiation helps create a sense of safety and agency, which is essential for interpreting external interactions and responding effectively.

Differentiation allows you to filter external inputs. Imagine trying to hold a conversation with a friend in a crowded room. Differentiation helps your brain focus on your friend's voice and tune out the irrelevant noise. Without this ability, every sound would compete for your attention, making it nearly impossible to engage meaningfully with what's right in front of you.

This layer of differentiation is vital for understanding context and causality. It's how you know the heat you feel is coming from the coffee cup in your hand, not some spontaneous combustion of your palm. It's how you distinguish between an emotion that's yours versus one you might be absorbing from someone nearby. In short, differentiation is what grounds you in the reality of your experience while allowing you to make sense of the external world.

The Danger of Blurred Boundaries

When differentiation is underdeveloped, the lines between self and environment blur. This can lead to confusion, overwhelm, or distorted beliefs about cause and effect. Think of a child who hasn't yet fully learned to differentiate. They might confuse their parents' anger as their fault, even if it's directed at work or a financial snafu. Differentiation is the framework for experiencing reality with clarity and intention. It gives us the ability to interact with reality in an informed way.

Your Truth vs. The Truth: The Clash Between Objective and Subjective Reality

When we seek to understand the mechanisms by which we experience and define reality, we have to grasp the distinction between objective and subjective reality. Objective reality means that there is a physically occurring factual record that conforms to universally accepted principles outside of conscious awareness. The mention of a physical element is important, as it points to the dimension of this truth. When we describe something as having a physical record, we are describing the third dimension. If someone spills a glass of milk, there will be milk all over the floor. The milk on the floor is a physical record of the act of spilling milk.

Subjective reality, by contrast, is the version of the world that exists inside your head, shaped by your thoughts, emotions, beliefs, and past experiences. It's not about what's objectively true—it's about what feels true to you, even if it completely contradicts the physical factual record. In subjective reality, your perceptions act as filters, twisting and reshaping the external world to fit the story your brain wants to tell.

This means two people can live through the exact same event and walk away with wildly different interpretations because their internal frameworks color the experience. In subjective reality, your truth isn't the truth; it's your truth. It's the driving force behind how you see and interact with the world. A simple example is the perception of temperature. I like to take hot showers. What feels comfortable and soothing to me would not be the case for my husband. We both experience heat in subjective ways; therefore, "hot" is not a term that describes objective reality.

The key distinction between objective and subjective reality lies in their foundations. Objective reality is the world as it exists independently of your thoughts, feelings, or beliefs. It's measurable, verifiable, and consistent—gravity works whether you believe in it or not. Subjective reality, on the other hand, is entirely personal. It's shaped by how you interpret the world, influenced by your emotions, experiences, and beliefs. The line between the two is where things get messy: it's the point where your internal perception overlaps with external facts.

So, how do you know where the line is? You're reading this book, which means you're just chapters away from learning how to rewire your patterns. For now, let's put it this way: most of what you believe is objective reality is likely subjective and heavily influenced by self-deception. We're constantly using our senses to interpret what we see, experience, or feel—but we're doing this through faulty filters that don't want the same things we consciously want for ourselves. You want love, freedom, success, and happiness—your brain wants to know what comes next and to keep you locked in the repetitive cycles it understands.

The Multidimensional Nature of Reality

As if facing the blurred line between objective and subjective wasn't challenging enough, we also need to address multidimensionality. Let's briefly peek under the hood of multidimensionality, knowing that, as we expand our understanding of the building blocks in this book, we'll unpack this concept on a deeper level. Multidimensionality challenges our everyday understanding of reality by introducing dimensions beyond the three we navigate physically—height, width, and depth.

The fourth dimension, time, reveals how fluid our experience of reality can be. Time doesn't pass at the same pace for everyone; instead, it bends and stretches depending on emotional states, memories, and expectations. A joyful hour might feel like a fleeting moment, while an anxious minute can feel like an eternity. Or perhaps you've dabbled in marijuana or hallucinogens—time doesn't pass as it would for sober people. Our perception of time is as much a product of our internal world as it is an objective framework of the universe.

Beyond time, String Theory and other theoretical models propose the existence of higher dimensions—upward of eleven dimensions. The fifth dimension, for example, houses parallel realities or alternate versions of outcomes. These ideas push us to consider that the reality we perceive is only a fraction of what truly exists. While we only experience one version of events, the possibility of parallel experiences or alternate paths challenges us to think beyond the rigid, linear view of existence. This multidimensional lens invites us to see reality as a layered, interconnected web—some parts visible and tangible, others abstract and theoretical, but no less real in their influence.

But how could that be true if you only experience your personal reality? It's widely understood that the brain functions as a reducing valve, filtering and limiting what we perceive to construct a stable, manageable sense of reality. The brain receives approximately 11 million bits of information per second from all sensory channels but consciously processes only about forty to fifty bits. In doing so, it filters out over 99.999 percent of incoming data, narrowing reality to what it deems most relevant or aligned with its priorities. This filtering isn't random—it's guided by beliefs, emotions, and prior experiences. Our brain reduces the overwhelming complexity of multidimensional inputs into a simplified, coherent narrative that aligns with what we already think is true. This process offers stability, but it also creates blind spots, trapping us in a version of reality that conforms more to our expectations than to what might actually exist.

By examining the processes the brain uses to simplify and construct reality, we can begin to uncover the hidden dynamics that govern our perception and decision-making.

The Illusion of Stability: Why Perception Is Not Reality

Recognizing the malleable and subjective nature of perception is critical for facing self-deception head-on. Perception isn't the solid foundation we'd like it to be; it's a patchwork of beliefs, sensory inputs, and biases stitched together to create the illusion of stability. To heal, you must be willing to confront the fact that the "truths" you've relied on may not be truths at all.

If your perception of reality isn't real—if it's nothing more than an intricate illusion your brain has constructed—what happens when that illusion begins to crack?

CHAPTER 5

THE MIND BEYOND MATTER

Materialism's Death Grip on Psychology and Mental Health

Materialism is a cult-like belief system that has embedded itself into psychology and mental health, strangling our ability to see people as anything more than biological machines. Our human machinery plays a critical role in mental health, but to say that's where it ends is an oversimplification. If you're reading this book, you've already broached the idea that your brain is a filthy liar. Now, let's shatter the comforting lie that the mind can be reduced to a meat suit with neural circuits and chemical cocktails.

What Is Materialism?

Materialism is the philosophical belief that everything in existence, including thoughts, emotions, and consciousness, can ultimately be constrained to physical processes and interactions of matter. It's a framework that has driven much of modern science, with undeniable success in fields like physics and biology. But here's the problem: by insisting that all phenomena can be explained in purely material terms, it imposes a narrow lens that fails to account for subjective experience and deeper dimensions of reality.

Here's a question worth asking: can the tools of natural science—which measure and quantify the physical—ever truly explain something as intangible as love, the soul-shaking grief of loss, or the electrifying power of intuition? These experiences are undeniably real, yet they stubbornly resist the language of neurons and molecules. When we speak of the brain, are we merely describing an organ of tissue and electrical activity, or are we acknowledging it as a gateway—a portal—into something far more profound? Materialism would dismiss this possibility outright, but doing so ignores what so many intuitively feel to be true.

How Did We Get Here?

The rise of materialism began with a noble goal: to make psychology a "real science." In the late 19th century, psychologists like Wilhelm Wundt believed that focusing on observable and measurable phenomena would lend credibility to their field. Subjective experience—those messy, intangible aspects of human life—was pushed aside as irrelevant. This reductionist approach gained traction with behaviorists like John B. Watson and B.F. Skinner, who watered down human behavior to stimulus-response patterns. For them, if you couldn't observe, count, or condition it, it didn't exist. Consciousness, the very essence of human experience, was sidelined as an inconvenient afterthought.

Then came the medical model, which anchored psychiatry firmly within the framework of materialism. Mental health issues were rebranded as malfunctions of the brain, legitimizing psychiatry as a branch of mainstream medicine. The rise of psychopharmacology in the mid-20th century further entrenched this model, offering a biochemical explanation—and a pill—for nearly every form of distress. Depression? Here's an SSRI. Anxiety? Take a benzodiazepine. Trauma? Slap on a diagnosis and hope for the best. While profitable and efficient, this approach sacrificed depth and nuance, transforming mental health care into a conveyor belt of prescriptions.

By the late 20th century, cognitive neuroscience arrived with its arsenal of fMRIs and EEGs, bringing materialism into sharp focus. These technologies revealed the brain's electrical activity in unprecedented detail, reinforcing the belief that every thought, emotion, and behavior could be traced to physical processes. This narrative presented the brain as the sole architect of the mind, leaving little room for alternative explanations of human experience.

Materialists vs. Their Critics: A Clash of Worldviews

Materialism's dominance has been bolstered by influential proponents like Richard Dawkins, Daniel Dennett, and B.F. Skinner. Dawkins famously condensed life's complexity to "selfish genes," dismissing anything beyond material explanations as superstition. Dennett took it further, claiming that consciousness is an illusion created by neural processes. Skinner, ever the behaviorist, insisted that human behavior could be explained by conditioning, denying the existence of free will or subjective experience.

However, a growing cadre of critics has taken aim at materialism's blind spots. Philosopher David Chalmers coined the phrase, "hard problem of consciousness," pointing out that materialism fails to explain why physical brain processes produce subjective experiences. Biologist Rupert Sheldrake critiqued materialism as a dogma, proposing concepts like morphic resonance, which suggests that memory and behavior are influenced by non-material fields. Psychoanalyst Carl Jung championed the exploration of the unconscious, archetypes, and spirituality as integral to understanding the human psyche. Modern philosopher Bernardo Kastrup advocated for analytic idealism, which posits that consciousness, not matter, is the fundamental basis of reality.

What unites these critics is their willingness to acknowledge what materialists deny: that reality is far more complex than its physical components. They argue that materialism is a two-dimensional map trying to depict a multidimensional world. Truth, they contend, lies not in reducing everything to physical explanations but in expanding our understanding to embrace the mystery and richness of existence.

The Fallout of Materialism

The materialist paradigm has left a trail of harm in its wake, particularly in the realm of psychology and mental health. Limiting humans to their biological processes degrades the human experience. Emotional pain, under this framework, is viewed as a glitch in the system rather than a meaningful signal. Symptoms are treated like errors to be patched up with medication, rather than messages to be understood and explored.

This reductionist approach has turned mental health care into a prescription factory. Medications, while often life-saving, have become the default solution, masking deeper issues instead of addressing their roots. This dependency on a one-size-fits-all model not only neglects the unique contexts of individuals but undermines the potential for transformative healing. Patients are frequently left feeling powerless, believing that their brain chemistry is broken and they are passengers on a biochemical rollercoaster with no control over their destiny.

By focusing on materialism, the system has discouraged exploration of alternative treatment, perpetuating cycles of misdiagnosis and symptom suppression. Materialism also ignores the "hard problem" of consciousness: why and how subjective experiences arise from physical processes. Therapy models built on this shaky foundation are adept at managing symptoms but fail to address the deeper existential and spiritual dimensions of human suffering. The result is a mental health system that is effective at symptom suppression but woefully inadequate at fostering genuine healing.

A Way Out: Global Workspace Theory and Multidimensionality

Breaking free from the stranglehold of materialism requires a shift toward integrative and multidimensional approaches. Global Workspace Theory (GWT) offers a compelling alternative, viewing consciousness not as a mere byproduct of brain activity but as an emergent property of dynamic information integration. Global Workspace Theory argues that consciousness happens when information gets broadcast across the brain's unconscious systems, making coordinated thought and action possible. This perspective acknowledges that consciousness is more than the sum of its neural parts—it is the cohesive experience that arises from their interplay.

GWT provides a framework to see the brain as a dynamic interface—a system designed to process, integrate, and broadcast information across diverse networks. By doing so, it moves beyond the static, mechanistic views imposed by materialism. GWT validates the intuitive sense that consciousness is not confined to the physical brain but emerges through complex interactions that transcend its biological boundaries.

Materialism's narrow view leads to overmedication, misdiagnosis, and a culture of disempowerment, where patients feel defined by their conditions instead of empowered to address their deeper needs. The mental health crisis requires holistic approaches that respect the profound interplay of body, mind, and spirit.

For example, anxiety might indicate unresolved trauma, spiritual disconnection, or misalignment with life's purpose—insights that are inaccessible through materialist reductionism. Materialism's supposition that trauma is merely a neurochemical imbalance ignores the profound subjective reality of carrying emotional pain.

Therapists, researchers, and patients must champion models that honor the full spectrum of human experience. This means reclaiming consciousness as central to the conversation. Consciousness isn't a glitch in the system—it is the system. By centering it, we can move beyond the shallow waters of materialism and dive into the depths of what it truly means to be human.

A Paradigm Shift

Materialism has had its moment, but its reign as the dominant paradigm in psychology and mental health is coming to an end. While it has offered valuable insights into the physical mechanisms of the brain, its narrow focus has left us with an incomplete understanding of what it truly means to be human. By clinging to this outdated model, we have reduced individuals to malfunctioning machines, addressing symptoms without ever asking what those symptoms might be trying to communicate. Healing demands that we go beyond this reductionist framework to embrace the full complexity of human experience.

A new paradigm, built on frameworks like Global Workspace Theory and multidimensional approaches, offers the potential to bridge the gap between science and the deeper truths of existence. These perspectives honor the interconnectedness of biology, emotion, spirituality, and relationship. By viewing the brain not as the endpoint but as a gateway—a portal—into something larger, we can begin to understand consciousness as a dynamic, integrative force that transcends mere physical structures.

The goal isn't just to fix what's broken; it's to unlock the full potential of what it means to be alive. But by doing so, we open the door to a more expansive, compassionate, and effective approach to healing—one that respects the profound richness of the human experience.

CHAPTER **6**

SHATTERING THE COMFORTABLE LIE

If you've made it this far, you're already dipping your toe into something most people spend their entire lives avoiding. Confronting self-deception is terrifying—not because it threatens the reality you know, but because it threatens the reality you've built. The lies your brain tells are the scaffolding of your identity, your relationships, and the way you make sense of the world. Tearing that scaffolding down feels like stepping off a cliff, freefalling into the unknown.

This sensation, what I call reality vertigo, is the disorienting and often paralyzing experience of realizing the foundation you've been standing on isn't as stable as you thought. It's the gut-punch of cognitive dissonance, the dizzying awareness that what you believed was real may have been a carefully constructed illusion. And yet, this vertigo is the very thing you must push through if you want to heal. It's the threshold between the patterns that have held you back and the freedom to step into a reality that aligns with your conscious intentions.

The Brain's Comfort in Self-Deception

Your brain doesn't choose self-deception randomly—it clings to it because it feels predictable. Your brain's rules aren't crafted in adulthood; they're etched into your subconscious during childhood, when you're at your most impressionable and powerless. As a child, your parents or caregivers set the tone, creating a culture in a petri dish where you had to react and respond to the environment they controlled. The power dynamic was deeply skewed—they were the ones pulling the levers, while you were left to ricochet off their emotional states, communication styles, and ability (or inability) to regulate themselves.

In this chaotic game, your brain crafts rules to make sense of the stimuli it encounters. These rules turn into deeply ingrained beliefs: about the world, your place in it, and how you should respond to protect yourself. They become the framework for how you navigate life, embedding themselves into your subconscious so deeply that, when you finally leave your caregivers' environment, you don't even realize you've brought them with you.

In adulthood, these rules influence everything—who you trust (or don't), how you define love, and whether you believe you're capable or worthy. Worse, these rules lead you to set up faulty experiments that reinforce their validity. If you believe you're unlovable, you'll gravitate toward relationships that confirm it. If you think no one can be trusted, you'll unconsciously sabotage connections to prove yourself right. If you've been patterned to believe you must always be responsible because everyone else will let you down, you'll overextend yourself until you burn out, silently seething at those who "fail" you.

The irony is that these rules aren't real—they're the byproduct of a warped system designed to keep you safe in an environment you no longer live in. Your brain clings to these self-deceptions because they protect it from the discomfort of uncertainty. Breaking these rules feels like losing control, and your brain would rather loop in a cycle of predictable pain than risk stepping into the unknown.

The Comfort of the Cave: Why Your Brain Fears the Unknown

The brain loves familiarity, even when it's painful. It would rather replay heartbreak, isolation, or self-doubt—patterns it knows how to navigate—than face the uncertainty of charting new territory. Think about the movie The Croods, which follows a prehistoric cave family, led by a father who insists on staying inside their cave to protect them, venturing outside only himself, until his teenage daughter challenges his fears and pushes the family to explore the unknown. The father clings to the idea that the cave keeps them alive, hiding from the dangers of the outside world. To him, the cave represents security and predictability, though it's dark, cramped, and limiting. Allowing his family to step outside into the unknown feels unthinkable because it means confronting a world with risks he can't yet control.

Your brain operates in much the same way. It perceives the unfamiliar as a threat and works overtime to confine you to your metaphorical cave. The rules and patterns it learned in childhood—no matter how destructive—become the guideposts it uses to navigate life. Heartbreak? Your brain knows how to deal with that. Isolation? Familiar territory. Self-doubt? At least it's predictable. Stepping out into the unknown to oppose these patterns feels terrifying because it strips the brain of its safety net, forcing it to navigate a world without its well-worn map.

The irony is that the very pain your brain clings to isn't keeping you safe; it's keeping you stuck. Heartbreak feels safer than risking connection because the brain already knows the script: the ache, the tears, the slow rebuilding. Stepping into a healthy relationship, on the other hand, requires navigating uncharted waters. Who are you when you're not bracing for abandonment or betrayal? Isolation feels safer than vulnerability because there's no risk of rejection when you're alone. Self-doubt feels safer than confidence because there's no possibility of failure when you don't even try. These patterns, while familiar, are the cave walls your brain hides behind, convincing you that what's out there is worse than what's in here.

But here's the truth: the unknown isn't your enemy. It's your opportunity to collect evidence to disprove the beliefs you subconsciously hold dear. Stepping out of the cave might feel like leaping into darkness, but it's the only way to create a reality that aligns with your conscious desires instead of your subconscious fears. Your brain will fight you every step of the way, whispering that it's better to stay in the cave where things are predictable, even if they're miserable. But the world outside the cave isn't chaos—it's full of possibility. The question is, are you ready to leave the cave and face the unknown?

Facing Reality Vertigo: The Path Through Disorientation

Reality vertigo is what happens when the lies you've been living collide head-on with the truth you've been avoiding. It's the disorientation that comes with realizing that your personal narrative might be more tenuous than you thought. When you start pulling at the threads of self-deception, it doesn't just destabilize a single belief—it shakes the foundation of how you've made sense of the world and yourself for years.

This disorientation hits hardest when you're forced to confront your own role in the destruction. The heartbreak you've repeated, the opportunities you've sabotaged, the relationships you've let unravel—it all comes into focus as something you played a part in, consciously or not. That's a tough pill to swallow. Taking radical personal responsibility for your choices and mistakes means facing not just what others have done to you, but what you've done to yourself. At times, it might feel like a bad acid trip—your reality bending and twisting in ways that leave you questioning what's real and what's illusion.

But you can't heal without going through it. Reality vertigo is not the enemy; it's the gateway. Until you allow the walls of cognitive dissonance to come down, you'll keep spinning in the same web of limiting self-deception.

The good news? Once you step into the discomfort, the unraveling begins. You start to see the cracks in your old narrative, questioning long-held "truths" that no longer serve you. Every thread you pull reveals a deeper truth, and with each truth, you get closer to building a life that aligns with who you actually are, not who your brain convinced you to be. Yes, it's destabilizing. Yes, it's uncomfortable. But the freedom waiting on the other side of that vertigo is a reality worth fighting for.

Letting Go of "The Truth"

When we embark on the journey of healing, many of us assume it's about uncovering "the truth"—a definitive, concrete version of what happened, who's to blame, and why we are the way we are. But healing and the pursuit of the truth rarely walk the same path. I typically look my clients in the eye when I see them ruminating on a past event and say, "You can pursue healing, or you can pursue truth—but you can't pursue both at the same time."

The truth, as you've likely started to see, is far more slippery than we want to admit. What we believe is true is shaped by our perception, and what others believe is true is shaped by theirs. In the gray area where those perceptions clash, the answers we seek often dissolve into more questions.

Consider the example of an adult holding tightly to a narrative about something they believe their parents did to them. Perhaps the person believes their parent once abandoned them at a grocery store. When they brought it up - Mom vehemently denied it. But the memory and the stinging feeling in the body says otherwise. They might become obsessed with knowing the truth, replaying memories, gathering evidence, and enlisting siblings or friends as witnesses. Their efforts turn into a kind of detective work, piecing together stories and perspectives in hopes of arriving at a concrete answer. But here's the catch: every person they ask will have a different version of events. Each story will be filtered through the teller's own subjective reality, leaving the seeker with a handful of conflicting accounts instead of the clarity they crave.

I've seen this obsession play out over more than a decade of working with clients, and I can tell you with certainty: it's rarely productive. Instead of moving forward, people get stuck in the loop of their personal narrative, clinging to the need for a concrete answer before they feel they can heal. But the truth they're chasing often doesn't exist, at least not in the clean, objective form they want it to. Healing, by contrast, doesn't depend on knowing exactly what happened or who was right or wrong.

The fastest path to healing isn't found in hunting down the truth. It's found in letting go of the obsession to know it. The healing process often looks less like arriving at an answer and more like wading through gray areas and asking better questions. What do my patterns reveal about how I respond to pain? How do these responses impact my life and relationships? How can I change the way I show up now, regardless of the past? The answers to these questions don't lie in concrete truths, but in the actions you take to rewire your patterns. Healing isn't about tying up the loose ends of your narrative—it's about cutting them loose entirely.

CHAPTER 7

DISCOVERING BRAIN PATTERN TYPES

My entire life, I've had an inclination toward pattern recognition. If I paid attention to the not-so-subtle messages Instagram influencers try to drop on me these days, I'd suppose I'm neurodivergent or on the Autism Spectrum. I was born in 1985, when parents tried to avoid getting a diagnosis for fear of stigma—at least where I grew up. I was born in a typical East Coast family in Fairfield County Connecticut, where Ivy League education was a frequent topic of conversation as early as I can remember. School legacy seemed to be spelled out for me before I had a choice.

Academics, as you can imagine, were a pressure cooker in my household. I remember bringing papers I felt were surely "A" material to my father, only to have him rip it to shreds and tell me to get a thesaurus because I wrote "like a simpleton." In case the word simpleton is not in your vocabulary, it's a 17th-century word tied to the idea of "simple," naive, and lacking intelligence—a term that is both antiquated and sharply derogatory today. For what it's worth, I'm thirty-nine and have to be reminded to make language more accessible and practical. Thanks a lot, Dad.

From the time I was very small, I remember knowing the answers to things without being taught in a book. I recall hearing adult conversations and feeling emboldened to share my input or answers to the complex conversation topic as young as four. This emerging gift was a double-edged sword. The more I shared, the higher the standard my father set for me. There was only one glaring problem: this gift was not directly related to academic prowess, something I struggled with relative to my level of observed intelligence.

I recall struggling to complete homework. Reading books felt like an impossibility—I'd try, only to find myself waking from a deep sleep with no idea when I stopped reading. I was somehow able to pass exams by using the same emerging gift, to somehow intuit the answer. This worked particularly well when writing essays. I'd start writing and dip into what felt like a data stream about the story. It was as if I could access the story without having to read it. I could tap into the psyche of the characters to answer essay questions successfully.

But there was a major problem: my teachers knew I wasn't studying, reading, or doing my work. They assumed I was cheating. I remember going to my father, begging him to get me tested for ADD. I tried to explain that no matter how hard I tried to study, I just couldn't focus and would often just fall asleep.

This prompted a trip to a doctor's office on the Upper West Side of New York City. I found myself in a small room, with a Freud-like character, who I'll call Dr. M. Without any sort of introduction or context, Dr. M began reading me a story. I vividly remember my thoughts as I heard him read aloud the first sentence. I couldn't help but observe the man reading rather than listening to the words of the story. I evaluated his posture, the cadence of his speech, and even the small details around his office, but I couldn't seem to hear the story. It was as if he was reading in a frequency I couldn't quite hear. I knew I should listen, yet I couldn't. Then the dreaded question was posed: "Can you tell me as much about that story as you remember?" I stared helplessly. If he had asked me to deliver my psychological assessment of him, I could have done it. If he had asked me questions I shouldn't know about his personal history, likes and dislikes, I could have answered. But the story? I had nothing.

He then proceeded to say random number sequences, some as long as nine to ten digits. For what felt like hours, he asked me to recall the numbers back, start in the middle of the sequence, recall them in reverse, and so on. During this hours-long test, I was even required to eat my lunch in the room—surely to be observed. Finally, after hours of questions and interpreting Rorschach images and matrix problems, he said, "Remember that story I shared with you at the beginning of this test?" I quickly replied, "Yes." He asked if I could recall the story now.

To my complete shock, I could. How could I recall a story hours later when I failed to immediately after hearing it? This was one of the earliest sparks in my quest for understanding how the brain works and how we encode memory.

I left the test feeling overwhelmed and nervous—this test seemed to extend far beyond my initial request of being evaluated for ADD. About a week later, Dad called me over to share the results. To my complete and utter dismay, he delivered them in a cold, sarcastic tone: "You're a genius. So cut the shit and stop making excuses with your school work." I felt a rush of emotions. More than anything, I felt so frustrated I wanted to scream. My intelligence was never my concern. Simple tasks, that I now know to be tied to executive function, seemed so easy for some, yet for me, they were impossible. I felt confused and more aware than ever that something about the way my brain worked was not typical. For years, I continued to mask my struggle in public. My brain worked in a way that was inconsistent with my peers.

As an adult, I know there are other mechanisms at work beyond a potential Neurodivergent diagnosis. Many colleagues in my life would call it being a savant, a person who has exceptional abilities or access to information without having learned it in books. But these abilities carry paradox—unusual brilliance coupled with deficits or limitations. I have always had access to information that shouldn't be possible through the paradigm of natural sciences. Yet here we are.

To some extent, my entire life has felt like it has poised me to observe human interaction, categorize it, and demystify the complexities for those who would listen. My father would often remark that I was better than his therapist—a perfect blend of therapist and lawyer qualities. Ironically, he was right. The world I've uncovered over the last eleven years blends elements of three careers into one: a therapist, which I am not, although I do work in the mental health field; a lawyer, finding weakness and strength in the arguments formulated by our brains; and a detective, able to uncover the childhood origin of a behavior or habit.

I have carved out a niche in the mental health field that is both innovative and disruptive. My work questions the status quo and provides actionable insights into why our society has yet to meaningfully change our trajectory with mental health outcomes.

The Flaw in Client Self-Reporting

For decades, therapy has leaned heavily on self-reporting as its cornerstone. From Freud's psychoanalytic couch to modern talk therapy, the practice of asking clients to share their stories, recall memories, and describe their feelings has been the primary method for understanding and addressing psychological issues. Self-reporting puts the client's perception front and center, assuming it is both reliable and accurate.

Historically, this reliance stems from the belief that introspection and verbal expression are essential to uncovering hidden truths. Freud's free association technique, for example, depended on clients sharing whatever came to mind to access their unconscious thoughts. Over time, therapeutic methods have evolved, but the reliance on the client's own words and memories has remained foundational. Whether it's filling out questionnaires, recounting events, or identifying emotions, therapy often treats self-reported data as the starting point for change.

But here's the problem: you've already learned how unreliable your brain can be when it comes to discerning truth from lies.

Self-reporting is like asking someone to navigate a maze while wearing distorting glasses—and then expecting them to draw an accurate map of their journey. When you're asked to share your story or describe how something made you feel, you're not reporting from an objective viewpoint. You're speaking from behind the lens of your self-deception. This isn't intentional dishonesty; it's the result of years of subconscious distortions that shape how you perceive, process, and recount your experiences.

When you confront these harsh truths, however, you can begin to acknowledge the distortion and take the first step toward clarity. It's not about blaming yourself for wearing the glasses; it's about learning how to recognize their presence and start examining the prescription. What's been distorted? What patterns are clouding your vision?

The real work begins when we stop relying on the subjective narrative and instead focus on uncovering the objective patterns driving it. By learning to see through the lens of self-deception—or removing it altogether—you can finally address the root cause of your cycles and begin the process of meaningful change.

Data vs. Narrative: Seeing Beyond the Story

One of the biggest breakthroughs in my work came when I realized the need to separate data from narrative. Therapy, self-help, and even casual conversations about personal growth tend to fixate on the story—the emotional, subjective version of events we carry with us. But stories are slippery. They're shaped by perception, self-deception, and time, which makes them unreliable as a foundation for change.

Data, on the other hand, is concrete. It's factual, objective, and stripped of interpretation. Data doesn't care how you felt about what happened; it's simply what happened. For example:

"My parents lived in the same house until I was eight years old" is data.

"My father was a mean man" is narrative.

The distinction is critical. Data is consistent and measurable. Narrative is fluid, shaped by the emotional lens we use to make sense of the world. When we focus solely on narrative, we circle the problem without ever reaching the root. The story you tell yourself about your life might feel true, but it's often distorted by the same self-deception we've been unpacking.

The Birth of Pattern Recognition

Over the years, I began noticing patterns in the environmental factors and experiences my clients reported. When I stripped away the narrative and looked solely at the data—factual, objective details—a much clearer picture began to emerge.

For example:

- A client who experienced their parents' divorce at age six exhibited one set of behavior patterns.

- A client whose parents divorced when they were sixteen exhibited another.

- A client whose parents remained married but frequently fought displayed yet another set.

These details weren't about how the client felt about their parents' relationship or the stories they'd crafted about it. Instead, they were environmental markers—pieces of data that correlated directly with specific behavioral, emotional, and decision-making outputs later in life.

I spent years aggregating these patterns, working with thousands of clients to refine and expand this approach. What started as a series of observations turned into an in-depth system of historical data points. This data revealed predictable correlations between early-life experiences and the brain patterns that drive behavior. It was like uncovering a blueprint, a way to see the mechanics of a person's life without relying on the unreliable stories their brain told them.

This shift from narrative to data isn't just a tool for understanding your patterns; it's the foundation for dismantling them. And it all starts by asking: what's the data beneath the story I've been telling myself?

This distinction between data and narrative is a portal to uncovering the deeper forces that shape your thoughts, behaviors, and decisions. By focusing on objective truths, we peel back the layers of distortion and start to reveal the patterns that have been silently running your life.

But here's where it gets interesting: what if there was a way to map these patterns, understand their origin, and pinpoint how they influence every choice you make? The answers lie in the data you've carried with you all along—waiting for you to see it clearly for the first time.

CHAPTER 8

PATTERNS HIDDEN IN DATA

If you've ever been to therapy, chances are you've heard at least one (if not all) of these familiar questions: How did that make you feel? Tell me more about your childhood. What was your mother like? Why are you here today? And if you're anything like the countless clients I've worked with over the years, those questions probably left you feeling frustrated, maybe even a little annoyed. I still vividly remember sitting across from a child therapist when I was nine. My parents were shelling out $150 an hour for what amounted to me playing endless rounds of Battleship, while my therapist occasionally lobbed one of these vague, open-ended questions in my direction.

Whenever she did, my brain would light up with at least ten sarcastic (and probably rude) rebuttals, none of which I dared to say out loud. Instead, I'd just shrug and say, "I don't know." But the truth was, I did know. I could have answered her questions if I wanted to. Yet something about them felt wrong. It felt like she was asking me to do her job for her—as if the burden of digging for answers and making sense of my feelings was entirely on me. Even then, deep down, I had a sense that these weren't the right questions to ask.

Now, thirty-one years later, I have the proof to back it up: they weren't. Those questions didn't help me uncover anything meaningful or change the patterns driving my behavior. They were a placeholder for a process that was supposed to help, but never really did.

Nature vs. Nurture: A Mystery No More

The debate between nature and nurture in psychology often feels like an ongoing stalemate—a tug-of-war that leaves both professionals and laypeople wondering which side holds the most influence over our thoughts and behaviors. To this day, it's often framed as a great mystery, as though we're incapable of knowing exactly how these forces interact to shape the human experience. But in my work, I've found there's nothing particularly mysterious about it. In fact, when you examine the data, the roles of nature and nurture become surprisingly clear.

Over the last eleven years, I've meticulously tracked data points across a large and diverse population. These patterns reveal a consistent truth: environment (nurture) serves as the input system, feeding stimuli and experiences into our subconscious minds. These inputs—our childhood experiences, the way we were spoken to, our social environments—create a foundational framework that shapes our thoughts, behaviors, and reactions. Meanwhile, our nature—embedded in our DNA, biology, and even the intangible qualities of spirit—determines how we process, respond to, and integrate those inputs. It's a symbiotic relationship, not a chaotic unknown.

When viewed through this lens, nurture becomes the designer of the stimuli, while nature is the processing system. One dictates what comes in; the other determines how it's defined and responded to. This dynamic explains the predictability I've uncovered in behavior and thought patterns. By understanding both the environmental inputs and the inherent nature of a person's biology and brain, we can track and predict behavioral outputs with remarkable accuracy. It's not a guessing game; it's a matter of recognizing the interplay between these two forces.

The idea that nature versus nurture is still an unsolvable puzzle does a disservice to the progress we can make when we approach the issue with clarity and data. In my work, this clarity has culminated in a system called Brain Pattern Mapping. It bridges the gap between abstract theories and actionable insights by showing how nature and nurture work together to generate specific brain pattern types. Unlike traditional, narrative-based talk therapy, which often leaves clients stuck in subjective interpretation, Brain Pattern Mapping uncovers the intricate interplay between nature and nurture to reveal the patterns driving our behaviors.

Inputs Equals Outputs: Cracking the Code

Life operates on a simple, yet profound principle: input equals output. Whether it's the cause-and-effect of our decisions, the biological stimulus-response cycle, or even Newton's laws of motion, the concept is universal—every action has a reaction, every input a corresponding output. Yet, when it comes to our thoughts and behaviors, we often ignore this fundamental truth. Instead, we get lost in subjective narratives, blaming genetics or external circumstances for patterns we don't understand. But here's the reality: your behavior isn't random, and your thoughts don't exist in a vacuum. They're outputs, perfectly calibrated reactions to the inputs you've been fed over a lifetime. It starts in childhood, as early experiments with cause and effect shape the rules that govern your life.

Crying Over Spilled Milk: An Experiment Gone Wrong

A child approaches the world like a tiny scientist, driven by an innate curiosity to test, retest, and observe outcomes to create a rulebook for life. Imagine a young child eyeing a glass of milk on the table. The child stares at the liquid-filled glass, thinking, What will happen if I push it over The parents, intuitively sensing the child's curiosity, raise their eyebrows in a silent warning. The child interprets this new input—furrowed eyebrows—and pushes the glass anyway.

Milk spills onto the floor. The parents rush over, scolding, "No! We do not push the glass of milk over!" The child, a budding scientist, has conducted their first experiment and drawn these conclusions:

- Pushing a glass of milk causes it to spill.

- Furrowed eyebrows mean, "Don't do that."

- Disobeying furrowed eyebrows leads to being scolded.

But here's the twist—like any good scientist, the child knows one trial isn't enough. They need to confirm the result. The next day, the experiment continues. This time, the glass of milk sits on the same table, and Mom sees what's coming. She escalates the warning: "You better not push over that glass of milk." The child, now fully aware of the stakes, giggles and pushes it anyway. Milk spills. Mom's tone is sharper, and timeout follows.

Through this second test, the child adds to their conclusions:

- Pushing the glass still results in a spill.

- Mom now scolds me before I even act.

- Disobeying direct warnings gets me sent to timeout.

Yet the experiment isn't over. The child is driven to understand not just what happens to the milk, but also what happens next. Their brain craves clarity about the boundaries of their environment—and their role within it. So, the final experiment begins.

At dinner, both parents are watching. The child locks eyes with the glass. As their hand reaches out, both parents shout, "Don't you dare!" and lunge toward the table, just milliseconds too late. Milk spills again, and this time, the child cries.

From this third and final experiment, the child learns:

- Pushing the glass always results in spilled milk.

- Parents can predict my actions before I take them.

- Yelling and lunging feel scary.

- I don't like how this feels. I should stop spilling the milk.

In their quest to understand how liquids behave, the child has unintentionally stumbled onto a very different experiment: how people behave, and what that means for their sense of safety. What began as a simple test of cause and effect—milk spills when pushed—becomes a much deeper lesson about emotional cues, discipline, and perceived danger.

For the child, these moments aren't centered around "bad behavior" or "punishment;" they're meant to decode patterns in their environment. They begin to assign meaning to furrowed brows, vocal tones, and physical movement. While the parent may see discipline as an act of love and protection, the child's brain may register these moments as fear-inducing or unsafe. The child then encodes these results into their developing brain patterns—patterns that may still be influencing their thoughts and behaviors decades later.

Every child conducts thousands of experiments like this. Some are obvious, like the glass of milk, and others, much more subtle. They test the emotional waters of their environment, jump to conclusions, and adapt their behavior in an effort to feel safe. These experiments are the building blocks that shape how we think, act, and react throughout life.

The Web of Inputs and Outputs

Spilled milk is just one of countless input-output scenarios that take place every day, shaping the way we navigate our environment and perceive reality. From the moment we wake up, our brains are wiring themselves with rules based on the inputs we receive and the outputs we observe. For a child, these rules might start with something as small as a furrowed brow meaning, "Don't do that," or the realization that mistakes can provoke a scary reaction from a parent. Over time, these seemingly insignificant interactions form a complex rule set that becomes the framework through which we interpret the world.

Children come into this world as the Pu, unburdened by assumptions or biases. They are curious explorers, seeking only love, joy, and the maintenance of their innocence. They're not yet jaded by the world's complexities or the emotional baggage of adulthood. But from the moment they're thrust into the game of life—one governed by their parents or primary caregivers—they begin to internalize the world's rules. And for a child, anything that isn't experienced as loving, supportive of curiosity, or preserving their innocence can register as a trauma input. With no prior experiences to compare it to, the child has no buffer or context to soften the blow. Every adverse interaction becomes data, shaping their perceptions and wiring their brain patterns.

These early rules don't come solely from intentional teachings like religion or cultural norms—though those play a role. Many are born from the gaps in understanding and observation that occur during the day-to-day, often mundane, moments of childhood. A parent's expression, a tone of voice, or even a pattern of absence or neglect can create rules just as impactful as deliberate instruction. The result is an interconnected web of cause and effect that shapes who we become and, more importantly, how we perceive and define our reality. Though we tend to fixate on the big moments, it's the repetitive, adverse inputs that create the deepest and most ingrained outputs.

Many people believe their greatest challenges stem from a singular traumatic event or person—a betrayal, a breakup, or a failure later in life. But this perspective misses the mark. Those events are distractions, red herrings that pull focus from the true origin of our patterns. The roots of our behaviors and perceptions lie in the repetitive inputs of early childhood, when our brains are most malleable and eager to learn the rules of survival. These early experiences, unlike the dramatic stories we often cling to, aren't about narrative. They're about data. So, what kind of data should we be tracking, and why does it matter?

What Data Shapes a Brain Pattern Type?

When it comes to understanding Brain Pattern Types, the key lies in tracking the right data—objective, observable facts about a person's environment and experiences, not their subjective interpretations or emotional narratives. The factors that shape a Brain Pattern Type, of which there are over 200 that we track in Brain Pattern Mapping, can often be predicted by details like whether a child's parents were married or in a committed long-term relationship, how many siblings they had and their birth order, the presence of substance abuse in the home, and, crucially, the age at which they became aware of it. These are measurable data points that bypass the need for questions like "How did that make you feel?" or "Why do you think that happened?"

The insights extend further:

- Was there a religious structure in the home, and if so, what type?

- What were the delivery mechanisms of religious messaging?

- Was academic support consistent, and how did parents enforce discipline or set boundaries around poor performance?

- Did the household rely on physical discipline, and if so, how frequently and in what form?

Importantly, this data collection is not freeform; clients aren't asked to provide qualitative or subjective answers to these questions. Instead, they select from structured options—upward of five variations—to define or describe the quality of each factor. This ensures the data remains factual, repeatable, and free from the distortions of self-deception or emotional filtering, offering a precise framework to reveal the intricate web of inputs shaping behavior.

What I've discovered through years of mapping these patterns is that the "why" a client might provide in response to a therapist's question is rarely the truth. It's a byproduct of the output—their Brain Pattern Type—which is inherently distorted by self-deception. The brain skews its explanations to protect the client from pain, inconsistency, or the messy realities of their upbringing. This protective distortion means that traditional therapy questions relying on a client's subjective recall are inherently flawed. They attempt to access the truth through a lens that's already warped by the brain's need for self-preservation.

By tracking the right data, we bypass these distortions entirely. The story the client would tell themselves doesn't matter; the data tells the story instead. The factors that shape a brain pattern type are precise, measurable, and predictive, offering clarity that no amount of subjective storytelling ever could. And this is why understanding the data is essential: it cuts through the noise and reveals the patterns that truly dictate our thoughts, behaviors, and perceptions of reality.

Decode Your Brain: The Patterns Don't Lie

Your Brain Pattern Type isn't just a label—it's a key, unlocking the hidden mechanics behind your thoughts, behaviors, and perceptions. With 98.3 percent accuracy in predicting behavior, thought patterns, and decision-making, Brain Pattern Mapping offers unparalleled insight into why you respond to the world the way you do. It uncovers the patterns shaping your reality and provides a detailed timeline of the cascade of emotions and behaviors driving your daily life, showing you the precise path from input to output. As you continue through the rest of this book, understanding your Brain Pattern Type will allow you to customize the tools and strategies to your unique patterns, ensuring the most effective results. Are you ready to uncover the data that defines you? Turn the page, scan the QR code, and get started.

Scan the QR code to start Brain Pattern Mapping. This can customize your experience throughout the rest of the book and help you maximize the impact for your unique pattern of self-deception.

SCAN ME

CHAPTER 9

UNDERSTANDING BRAIN PATTERN TYPES

When you strip away the stories, the excuses, and the self-deception, what remains is the data—the raw, unfiltered input-output system that defines how you navigate the world. Brain Pattern Mapping breaks this system down into nine distinct components, each representing a critical piece of how your thoughts, behaviors, and decisions are shaped. It's a precise model that connects the dots between early childhood inputs, biological tendencies, and the cascading effects that define your perception of reality.

The nine-part system of Brain Pattern Mapping serves as both a diagnostic tool and a roadmap, revealing how nature and nurture converge to produce predictable patterns in behavior. These nine parts address the patterns housed in the most internal and private parts of our mind (2), the liminal space between where our thoughts trigger a biochemical reaction in the form of emotion (3), and our externally observable behaviors (4) – all functioning in a cyclical self-perpetuating system (9). Each point in the system corresponds to a key area of life— ranging from emotional regulation to interpersonal dynamics—and demonstrates the input-output relationship at play. For example, the environmental inputs a child receives, such as household structure, discipline style, or exposure to substance abuse, are processed through the lens of their innate nature, like temperament or genetic predispositions. Together, these factors create a pattern that not only defines their default responses but also governs how they approach decisions and relationships later in life.

One of the most critical aspects of Brain Pattern Mapping is understanding which components of the nine-part system are influenced by nurture—external, environmental factors—and which are rooted in nature, the biological and intrinsic makeup of the individual. Nurture-driven points focus on external influences like parental dynamics, sibling roles, or cultural norms. In contrast, nature-driven points tap into the internal operating system of DNA, emotional regulation, and even the spiritual aspects of identity. This interplay ensures that no single piece of the system exists in isolation. Instead, it's the relationship between these points that generates the full behavioral and emotional cascade.

These patterns drive the entirety of how you interact with the world. The nine points cluster into predictable cascades of behavior, thought, and decision-making, creating the framework for how you respond to inputs, perceive threats, or even approach opportunities. By understanding this system, you begin to see the predictability in what once felt chaotic. This is where Brain Pattern Mapping becomes a tool for transformation, not just observation.

The Three Layers of a Brain Pattern

A brain pattern can be visualized as a system of interconnected parts, each one generating or influencing the next—a continuous cycle of input and output. This system operates across three distinct layers: the internal, the liminal, and the external. Together, they represent the full spectrum of how inputs are processed and manifested in the real world. This forms the foundation of Brain Pattern Mapping. Each layer plays a specific role in the cascade of perception, emotion, and behavior, offering a complete picture of how our brains respond to the world around us.

The top layer, the internal, is entirely private—existing only within the mind. This is where the perception of reality, thought patterns, and assumptions take root. These are the silent narratives and judgments that no one else can see, which means there is no observable evidence in the physical world. For example, you might silently assume that someone is upset with you because of the way they looked at you, even though they've said nothing to indicate it. This assumption colors your perception of reality, but it remains invisible to others. It's in this layer where our internal distortions often begin, setting the stage for emotional and physical reactions.

The middle layer, the liminal, bridges the internal world and the external. It's the space where internal thoughts start to trigger emotional and chemical reactions within the body. While these responses might not always be fully externalized, subtle cues often appear. For instance, a person experiencing stress may notice their face flushing, their body temperature rising, or a slight shift in their facial expression. These signs are more observable than the purely internal layer but still lack the clarity of explicit action. This liminal space is where the body begins to prepare for the outputs that will take place in the next layer.

The bottom layer, the external, is where thoughts and emotions translate into fully observable physical behaviors. This is the realm of direct actions, reactions, and coping mechanisms that leave undeniable evidence in the physical world. Examples include openly communicating frustration, resorting to physical aggression, or engaging in flight-oriented coping strategies like abruptly ending a conversation, avoiding conflict, or even engaging in addictive behaviors. This layer is the final output of the brain pattern cycle, making the previously invisible and subtle processes fully visible.

By understanding these three layers and how they work together, we can see how internal inputs ripple through to external outputs, creating predictable cycles of thought, emotion, and behavior. Each layer offers unique opportunities for intervention, allowing us to disrupt patterns at their source and rewrite the cascade.

The Top Layer: Origin and Adaptive Source Belief Patterns

At the heart of the top layer lies the Origin Source Belief Pattern, a framework shaped by the environment during early childhood. This pattern is entirely nurture-driven, formed through repeated inputs from caregivers, family dynamics, and the broader environment. The Origin Belief acts as an assumption of what the child can expect from the world—a subconscious rulebook built to navigate safety, love, and connection. For example, a child raised in an environment where emotional warmth is inconsistent might develop the Origin Belief, "Love is conditional and can disappear at any moment." These assumptions are not consciously chosen; they're a survival mechanism, carved into the brain by the repetition of environmental cues.

Between the ages of six and twelve, the brain begins to refine its response to the world based on these foundational assumptions. This is where the Adaptive Source Belief Pattern takes shape. It is driven by nature—defined as genetic predisposition and the spiritual nature of humans as created beings with inherent uniqueness and destiny. While the Origin Belief establishes what can be expected, the Adaptive Belief answers what to do about it. Continuing the earlier example, a child who believes "Love is conditional" might adapt with the belief, "I must perform or please to keep love from disappearing." The Adaptive Belief is how the individual's spiritual and genetic nature responds to the environment, creating a strategy for navigating life based on their sense of purpose and distinctiveness.

As discussed in earlier chapters, the concept of the Pu, the uncarved block, provides a useful way to understand these layers. Between the ages of two and five, the environment repetitively chisels the block, carving the child's assumptions about the world. By age six to twelve, Adaptive Belief forms as the newly sculpted figure learns to exist in its environment, responding to the shape it has been given. This interplay between nurture and nature creates the foundation for how the individual perceives reality, navigates relationships, and makes decisions. Understanding these layers is critical to uncovering the hidden rules governing our thoughts and behaviors.

The Middle Layer: The Emotional Addiction Cycle

The middle layer of a brain pattern represents the critical transition between internal thoughts and external behaviors. This is where the Emotional Addiction Cycle comes into play—a three-part cascade of emotional responses that includes chemical and hormonal components, often accompanied by subtle physical signs like flushed skin, trembling, or temperature changes. These emotional reactions act as precursors to behavior; they generate the impulses that drive action. Deeply ingrained and instinctive, these responses form a constitutional pattern, meaning they are hardwired into the brain and will always be present. However, they can be intentionally rewired to reduce their intensity, volatility, or reactivity, providing individuals with greater emotional regulation and control.

An emotional addiction cycle always includes three distinct parts: Origin, Protective, and Escalating emotions. The Origin emotion is always rooted in fear—our most basic human instinct in response to the unknown. In some cases, the brain may immediately associate fear with a perceived shame stimulus, leading to a variation known as Fear of Shame. For example, a child who repeatedly experiences ridicule in moments of failure may subconsciously associate fear with the potential for humiliation. Whether it manifests as pure fear or Fear of Shame, the Origin emotion acts as the first spark in the emotional cascade.

From there, the cycle moves to the Protective emotion, the brain's instinctive strategy to guard against the perceived threat. This response typically falls into one of three categories: Anger, Anxiety, or a combination of Anger-Apathy or Anxiety-Apathy. For most people, the Protective emotion presents consistently, but rare cycles may include Apathy as a counterbalance. For instance, someone who typically responds with Anxiety might experience prolonged periods of Apathy every seventh or eighth cycle. True Apathy, however, is not the same as feeling disengaged or unfocused. It involves a complete shutdown of basic functioning, such as being unable to get out of bed, brush teeth, or perform simple self-care tasks. Brain fog or occasional withdrawal does not meet this threshold.

Finally, the cycle reaches the Escalating emotion, the stage where the person feels their protective strategies have failed. At this point, the brain shifts into survival mode, often pushing boundaries or rebelling against its typical patterns. For example, a person whose Protective emotion is Anxiety may escalate into Anger or Anxiety-Apathy, becoming uncharacteristically defiant or reckless in response to perceived chaos. However, when Anger serves as the Protective emotion, the cycle takes a different trajectory. Instead of escalating outwardly, the person is more likely to turn inward, ruminating on their perceived failures or falling into a state of hopelessness about the future. This inward collapse is often accompanied by an anxious spiral rather than external rebellion.

The emotional addiction cycle is predominantly driven by nature, aligning with the Adaptive Source Belief pattern. For instance, if Anger is an individual's Protective emotion, it will always remain part of their cycle, even after intentional rewiring. However, the intensity and reactivity of the Anger can be diminished, allowing the person to respond to triggers with greater control and less volatility. Understanding this cycle is critical because it highlights how emotions bridge the gap between internal thoughts and external behaviors, shaping the decisions and actions that define our lives. By addressing the middle layer, we unlock the ability to rewire the cascade of behaviors by directly rewiring our emotional triggers and the subsequent emotional responses that generate those behaviors.

The Bottom Layer: The Timeline Pattern

The bottom layer of a brain pattern system represents the most tangible aspect of our behavior—the actions and decisions that leave observable evidence in the physical world. At the heart of this layer is the Timeline Pattern, a structured sequence that helps us understand the type, quality, timing, and oscillation of behaviors within a set cycle. These patterns are not random; they are deeply ingrained and represent the cascade effect of behaviors generated by the emotional addiction cycle in the middle layer. A Timeline Pattern provides a roadmap to how our emotional responses manifest as actions, revealing the connections between what we feel internally and what we do externally.

Timeline Patterns are numerically categorized and defined by a pattern of oscillation, represented by the presence of +, -, +/-, or -/+ markers. These markers highlight the directionality and intensity of behavior within a cycle. For example, someone might confidently take a bold action (a + behavior) only to rapidly reverse course, smooth it over, or retreat entirely (a - behavior). This rapid shift in behavior reflects the underlying oscillation within their pattern. Similarly, these patterns can lead to impulsive actions—such as law-breaking or other high-risk behaviors—that occur in the early phases of a cycle, often without full awareness of their consequences. The individual might only recognize the lack of judgment or insight during the later phases, providing a clear snapshot of how behavior evolves across their Timeline Pattern.

A Timeline Pattern is a direct extension of the emotional addiction cycle. Each phase of the pattern corresponds to a specific output generated by the sequence of emotions: Origin, Protective, and Escalating. These phases play out as a repeating behavioral loop, showing how emotions like fear, anger, or anxiety translate into real-world actions. For example, an individual whose Protective emotion is Anger may exhibit impulsive, confrontational behavior during the early phases of their cycle. As the cycle progresses, they may oscillate into retreat or regret, but the behavior has already left its mark in the physical world. The ability to identify these patterns through numerical markers like + or - allows for precise tracking of when and how a person is most likely to act impulsively, retreat, or oscillate between the two.

Timeline Patterns are fixed—they do not change over time. They become fundamental to who we are, how we perceive the world, and what we feel justified, rational, or entitled to do. These patterns are deeply rooted frameworks that govern how we navigate the physical world, influenced by the sequence of emotions in our addiction cycle. Each individual's Timeline Pattern has four distinct phases, labeled as Primary, Secondary, Tertiary 1 and Tertiary 2, each corresponding to an output from their emotional addiction cycle. Understanding this layer provides crucial insights into how behavior cascades from emotional triggers, offering a clear map of the cyclical nature of human action and its relationship to the layers above.

The Glasses You Didn't Know You Were Wearing

Your Brain Pattern Map is a diagnostic tool that tells the story of where you've been and predicts where you're going. It reveals the inputs, history, and past experiences that have shaped your perception of the world. At the same time, it decodes the behaviors and choices you feel justified making, behaviors that are 100 percent impacted by self-deception—until now. With your Brain Pattern Map, you no longer have to wonder why you do what you do. It predicts and explains the patterns driving your thoughts and actions, allowing you to finally see through the lens of self-deception.

A brain pattern functions like a prescription for glasses, but until this moment, you've had no idea you were even wearing them. Your Brain Pattern Map doesn't just reveal that you've been looking at life through these lenses; it helps you decode exactly what the prescription distorts and skews. When you can identify the inputs that created these distortions, you can begin to rewire your brain and return to a clearer, more objective reality.

This isn't just about understanding your past; it's about rewriting your future. By learning to see through the deception and understanding what shaped your perception, you gain the ability to break free from the patterns that have held you back. The process starts here—with acknowledging the glasses you've been wearing and committing to the work of decoding their prescription. Only then can you step into a reality defined not by distortion but by peace, clarity, and collaboration.

CHAPTER 10

TRAPPED IN THE EQUATION

Source Belief Etiologies: Origin Source Belief

To understand the etiology of Source Beliefs, it is crucial to recognize their role in distorting perception and influencing behavior. A Source Belief acts as a lens through which we interpret reality, shaping our assumptions about situations and people. This lens is not neutral; it is deeply colored by early environmental inputs and the subconscious conclusions drawn from those experiences. These patterns are forged in childhood as adaptive mechanisms to survive perceived chaos, inconsistency, or lack. In adulthood, they often operate as blind spots, driving self-sabotage, emotional dysregulation, and behavioral loops that conflict with our conscious intentions.

As discussed in previous chapters, humans come into the world as the Pu—an uncarved block. Without context or nuance, every experience is new and devoid of prior meaning. From this blank slate, the brain begins its lifelong work of interpreting and organizing reality. All human beings arrive in life seeking to answer three foundational questions, which unfold sequentially. Each question builds upon the resolution of the previous one, and failure to adequately answer any of these questions results in the formation of an Origin Source Belief. These beliefs act as foundational rules for how the individual navigates the world but often distort the very outcomes they are meant to protect.

The Right to Exist: Life's First Question

As a child first enters the three dimensional world, the first question is more existential and intangible: Do I have the right to exist in a human body? A child's earliest exploration of this question centers on recognizing their right to exist as a distinct and sovereign being, unshaken by terror or chaos. This stage focuses on solidifying the fundamental right to exist, ensuring the child's sense of self remains intact and unthreatened by existential instability.

Chaos Origin Source Belief

If this need is not met, a Chaos Origin Source Belief forms. This belief typically arises in environments that are intensely abusive, neglectful, and—critically—unpredictable. Not all abusive or neglectful homes generate this pattern. The defining characteristic of Chaos patterns is a lack of observable cause and effect, leaving the child unable to form any coherent strategy to navigate their environment. This unpredictability induces an early existential crisis where life appears to be a cruel, purposeless joke. Consequently, the child adopts a nihilistic worldview encapsulated by the belief that "nothing matters or has a purpose."

The Chaos-pattern child stops striving and surrenders to the chaotic nature of their world. They often mimic the chaos they have experienced, perpetuating it in their own lives. A defining trait of this pattern is an inability to sustain consistent effort toward long-term goals. While raw talent may be present, it is rarely developed methodically. Chaos-pattern individuals frequently struggle with addiction, suicidal ideation, and deliberate self-sabotage. Their inability to maintain steady progress or a stable career is evident from childhood and persists into adulthood, reflecting the foundational instability of their early environment. Statistically, this pattern is rare, representing a small fraction of the population. However, its prevalence rises significantly within incarcerated populations.

Childhood Inputs That Can Generate a Chaos Pattern Type

- **Extreme neglect or abuse:** Caregivers are physically or emotionally absent or abusive without any consistency.

82

- **Unstable living environment:** Homelessness, or shifting between different caregivers like foster care or group homes.

- **Parental addiction or mental illness:** Exposure to substance abuse or untreated psychiatric conditions leading to erratic parenting.

- **Frequent disappearance of caregivers:** Sudden incarcerations, or extended absences without explanation.

- **Exposure to high levels of violence or trauma:** Witnessing domestic violence, community violence, or extreme household conflict.

- **Lack of basic safety and security:** Unreliable food, shelter, or protection from harm.

- **Dismissal or denial of reality:** Gaslighting or inconsistent narratives from caregivers, making the child question their own perceptions.

- **Early exposure to chaos as normal:** Growing up in an environment where unpredictability is the baseline, leading to a subconscious expectation that life is inherently unstable.

These inputs collectively shape a worldview where effort feels meaningless, trust is nonexistent, and chaos is the only certainty.

This Could Be Your Pattern If You:

- **Can't hold down a steady job.** You either quit impulsively, get fired for erratic behavior, or simply stop showing up when the structure feels too rigid.

- **Struggle with financial stability.** Overspending, impulsive purchases, ignoring bills, or going from periods of reckless spending to complete financial collapse.

- **Frequently end up in financial or legal trouble.** Bankruptcies, evictions, unpaid debts, or repeated run-ins with the law due to reckless decisions.

- **Engage with chaotic, reckless people.** You surround yourself with people who bring instability, drama, or danger, even when you know it's self-destructive.

- **Self-sabotage even when things are going well.** The moment life starts stabilizing, you unconsciously wreck it—quitting a job, ruining a relationship, or making a reckless decision.

- **Feel completely apathetic toward self-care and daily tasks.** Basic things like cleaning, cooking, or personal hygiene feel pointless or overwhelming, so they're neglected.

- **Fluctuate between extreme impulsivity and total shutdown.** Some days you engage in reckless behaviors with zero regard for consequences, while other days you check out entirely.

- **Have little regard for consequences or future planning.** You make decisions in the moment without thinking ahead, assuming things will either work out or crash and burn anyway.

- **See no real point in long-term goals or structured routines.** You struggle to envision a future because everything feels temporary, meaningless, or doomed to collapse.

- **Feel more comfortable in chaos than stability.** When things get calm or predictable, you either create instability or gravitate toward high-risk situations.

If this sounds like you, your brain may have been wired to expect instability as the norm, making self-destruction feel like the only predictable pattern.

The Search for Safety: Understanding the Rules

Once the question of existence is resolved, the human brain moves to the next lesson: Am I safe? This question builds on the understanding that one has the right to exist and is distinct from their environment. Now, the child seeks to understand the structure, rules, and patterns of their surroundings to feel secure. Many children struggle at this stage, as it is heavily influenced by the consistency and reliability of their caregivers.

Abandonment-Oriented Source Belief

The formation of an Abandonment-Oriented Source Belief does not necessarily require overt neglect or physical absence of a caregiver, although it certainly can. While overt traumas such as physical abuse, emotional neglect, or constant conflict in the home contribute to this pattern, it can often be more subtle or under the radar. A child may sense a parent's inability to be truthful or dependable, even when the outward appearance of home life seems polished and secure—a nice house, good clothes, strong academic performance, and other markers of stability. Unlike the Chaos pattern, Abandonment origin patterns emerge from a broader range of environmental conditions. The defining characteristic is a lack of trust in primary caregivers, which can stem from diverse factors and circumstances. Instead, it arises from environments marked by inconsistency and unpredictability. This could include caregivers who are emotionally dishonest, say one thing and do another, or engage in erratic or unsafe behaviors. For these children, safety becomes synonymous with predictability. The absence of predictable cause and effect forces them to develop hyperindependence, prioritizing self-trust over reliance on others. The brain concludes that delegating authority or placing trust in another person is inherently unsafe.

Childhood Inputs That Can Generate an Abandonment Pattern Type

- **Emotionally unavailable or inconsistent caregivers:** A parent may be physically present but emotionally disengaged, making affection, support, or validation unpredictable.

- **Unreliable or inconsistent nurturing:** Sometimes caregivers are loving and attentive, while other times they are distant, dismissive, or preoccupied - you didn't ever know what to expect.

- **Parents who say one thing but do another:** Frequent broken promises, inconsistent discipline, or behaviors that contradict verbal assurances create distrust.

- **Early responsibility for others' emotional states:** The child learns to suppress their own needs to manage or stabilize a parent's moods.

- **Fear of repercussions for expressing needs:** When seeking comfort, validation, or support, the child is met with irritation, withdrawal, or guilt-tripping.

- **Caregivers who are overly self-focused:** Narcissistic or emotionally immature parents who expect the child to cater to their emotions rather than the other way around.

- **Parental absence that is emotional, not just physical:** Even if a parent is home, they may be disengaged, preoccupied with work, social life, or their own struggles.

- **Early hyper-independence as a survival mechanism:** The child is expected to figure things out alone, discouraging reliance on others.

- **Early exposure to betrayal or broken trust:** Learning that people are unreliable through abandonment, infidelity in caregivers' relationships, or lack of protection in vulnerable moments.

These inputs shape a worldview where trusting others feels dangerous, self-sufficiency is survival, and connection is tied to obligation rather than security.

This Could Be Your Pattern If You:

- **Avoid asking for help.** You'd rather struggle alone than risk relying on someone who might let you down.

- **You struggle to trust other people's abilities and follow through.** You have a way of strategically supporting outcomes to make sure they turn out the way you want.

- **You only care about what others think if it starts to impact your financial well-being or security.** You don't naturally care what others think about you and even in the face of criticism or negativity, you can see behind the conflict at what's really going on.

- **You are extremely situationally aware.** Since childhood you've been aware of your surroundings and always know what could spiral out of control before it does.

- **You might miss relational cues because you're focused on tracking your external environment.** Conflict can arise in interpersonal relationships because your attention is not on the subtle relationship transactions as much as awareness of the big picture.

- **Your work or career life feels easier to manage and succeed than relationships.** You know where you stand in the work setting and the concrete structure of it feels easier to navigate than people's emotions—relationships can feel volatile or unwinnable.

If this sounds like you, your brain may have been wired to expect abandonment, making hyper-independence, overgiving, or emotional detachment feel like the safest way to exist.

The Need for Love: Seeking (or Avoiding) the Spotlight

If the child resolves the question of safety—trusting their caregivers and feeling secure in their environment—they progress to the next stage: Am I loved? At this stage, the focus shifts outward toward relational dynamics. Secure in their sense of safety, the child begins seeking love, validation, and acknowledgment from others. However, many rejection-oriented children, even when receiving attention, love, and validation, escalate their behaviors and become stuck in victim-centric thinking. This dynamic often leaves them in a toddler-like state of emotional reasoning, manifesting in two distinct ways: some actively seek attention to play out power dynamics, subconsciously setting up scenarios where others are destined to fail them, while others isolate, avoiding interaction due to assumptions that they will be embarrassed or dismissed. Both actions stem from unresolved relational insecurities. These children often become fixated on how others perceive them, leading to assumptions and projections about others' thoughts and feelings. This fixation traps them in a loop of relational power dynamics centered on control, attention, and validation. In many ways, this pattern reflects an emotionally immature reasoning process, carried forward into adulthood. Without the security of knowing they are loved for who they are, these individuals struggle to grow beyond their relational insecurities.

Childhood Inputs That Can Generate a Rejection Pattern Type

- **Stable, loving household with reliable caregivers:** Your parents were present, supportive, and provided a consistent home environment, making basic safety and love a given.

- **Parental trust was intact:** You generally believed your parents would do what they said and followed through on their commitments, reinforcing a sense of security.

• **No discipline or structure or highly structured, rule-oriented home:** Caregivers were either overly permissive, allowing you to act out without clear boundaries, reinforcing the belief that attention (good or bad) equaled love, or your household followed strict routines and expectations, where adherence to rules was expected but not always emotionally validated.

• **Perception of unconditional love, but craving more:** You knew your parents loved you. Seeking more love and pushing limits was coddled or fed into.

• **Encouragement of performance-based validation:** Praise was given for achievements (grades, sports, behavior) rather than intrinsic qualities, reinforcing the belief that success equals love.

• **Exposure to favoritism or social comparison:** Even in a supportive home, you may have felt compared to siblings, family members, or peers, driving a need to prove yourself.

• **Encouraged to be the "good child" or family representative:** You learned that pleasing others, being well-liked, or maintaining a public image was expected and reinforced.

• **Early exposure to social competition:** Whether through school, church, or cultural expectations, you were conditioned to seek approval and status in peer groups.

• **Family or community emphasis on reputation and honor:** Your value was tied to how well you upheld the family's social standing, behavior expectations, or moral image.

• **Religious or cultural standards that reinforced worthiness:** The idea that love, belonging, or divine favor was conditional on being morally, academically, or socially "good enough."

• **Fear of group rejection or judgment:** A deep concern about being excluded or shamed by religious, cultural, or community circles if you didn't meet expectations.

• **Perfectionism as a cultural or religious ideal:** The belief that anything less than excellence (in morality, academics, or behavior) meant failure or loss of worth.

• **Public vs. private identity split:** Learning early that there was a "correct" way to behave in public while suppressing emotions or struggles privately to avoid being seen as weak or problematic.

This Could Be Your Pattern If You:
Engaging Type (Seeks Attention to Avoid or Create Rejection):

- **Seek validation but never feel satisfied.** No amount of praise, reassurance, or attention fully quiets your self-doubt.

- **Feel exaggerated emotions and emotional instability.** Mood swings and emotional volatility are a part of how you react and respond to the world around you.

- **Focus on comparison or negativity when someone else is at the center of attention.** If the attention is on someone else you notice negative self-talk, comparison or judgment toward the other person.

- **Overanalyze social interactions for signs of approval or rejection.** A neutral response, delayed text, or lack of enthusiasm makes you spiral into self-doubt.

- **Read into what others are thinking or feeling.** You assume people's moods, tone shifts, or social cues are secretly about you, often imagining rejection where none exists.

- **Push people to prove their loyalty.** You create subtle tests, conflict, or impossible standards to see if others will abandon you or "fail" you.

- **Subconsciously cause rejection to confirm your fears.** You act out, push boundaries, or demand attention in ways that make people pull away, reinforcing your belief that rejection is inevitable.

- **Find yourself drawn to power dynamics in relationships.** You look to mentors or people who seem to be worth emulating. This tends to be fraught with push-pull dynamics where you end up comparing yourself and subconsciously looking to take them off their pedestal.

- **Hold grudges over perceived slights.** You keep score when people fail to meet your expectations, building up resentment and negativity in your mind.

Isolating Variant (Withdraws to Avoid Rejection But Still Fixates on It):

- **Push people away before they can reject you.** You create emotional distance, assume relationships won't last, or preemptively withdraw to avoid pain. This can present like feeling non-commital or not sure in early stages to justify pulling away.

- **Feel deeply wounded by perceived rejection, even minor instances.** A forgotten invitation, a friend choosing someone else, or lack of immediate attention feels devastating—even jokes and sarcasm can poke on your rejection wound.

- **Take things personally, even when they aren't about you.** You assume others' actions, moods, or decisions are a reflection of how they feel about you.

- **Read into what others are thinking or feeling.** You constantly assess facial expressions, body language, and tone for hidden meanings, often assuming rejection or disapproval.

- **Struggle to express emotions or needs openly.** You assume people won't care or that expressing your needs makes you weak or annoying.

- **Avoid asking for help or doing things in a way where you can be observed.** You convince yourself that asking for help or being observed will lead to ridicule or judgment.

- **Fear looking foolish, being embarrassed, or being caught off guard.** You avoid risks or new experiences in case you're judged, rejected, or don't perform perfectly.

- **Hold grudges over perceived slights but never address them.** Instead of resolving issues, you withdraw and keep a mental score of how others have hurt or disappointed you.

- **Feel like an outsider, even in groups where people have tried to include you.** You struggle with negative self-talk telling you that you aren't part of the group or acting the right way to be integrated.

- **Detach emotionally when relationships feel uncertain.** Instead of dealing with discomfort, you numb yourself, disengage, or slowly fade out of relationships.

If any of these patterns sounds familiar, your brain may have been wired to expect rejection as inevitable, making you either fight for attention and control or shut down to protect yourself from disappointment.

Unmasking Your Hidden Driver

Through these sequential stages, the formation of Origin Source Beliefs exposes how early environmental chaos, betrayal, or dysfunction hardwired your perception of reality. The uncarved block of the Pu didn't stand a chance against the hammer and chisel of your environment, shaping beliefs that now dictate how you stumble through existence, safety, and love. These beliefs may have kept you alive as a kid, but now they're the invisible hand strangling your growth as an adult.

Which of these Source Beliefs is running the show in your head? Be honest—it's already calling the shots, whether you like it or not. Do you feel like chaos is always waiting to strike? Does trusting anyone make your skin crawl? Or are you stuck playing out endless relational drama, chasing validation while setting up failure for everyone involved? If you haven't done your Brain Pattern Mapping session yet, what are you waiting for? Stop guessing and get the brutal clarity you need to move forward.

By unraveling the etiology of your Origin Source Belief, you rip the blindfold off and reclaim control over the unseen forces that have dictated your behavior. Yet, as the blindfold falls away, a new question arises: What fills the space left behind? The truth is, the beliefs etched into your mind during those early years don't simply vanish. They're met with resistance—or worse, reinforced—by the silent architect of your adaptive tendencies: your Adaptive Source Belief. How does this next layer of programming shape your responses, your defenses, and your sense of self? And more importantly, is it truly working in your favor, or has it become yet another unseen driver of chaos? To understand how you became who you are now, you must confront the reality of how your environment and internal responses unconsciously shaped the version of you that emerged then.

CHAPTER 11

THE REFLEXIVE MIND

The Adaptive Source Belief

In the intricate web of subconscious programming, understanding the Adaptive Source Belief is crucial to completing the picture. While the Origin Source Belief forms during the early years of life–shaped by repetitive environmental inputs between ages two to five–the Adaptive Source Belief emerges later, with full expression typically between ages six to twelve. This layer of the subconscious operates as a response mechanism, dictating how we react to the foundational assumptions instilled by the Origin.

To understand this distinction, imagine the Origin Source Belief as the uncarved block, or Pu from previous chapters. The environmental inputs during early childhood chisel and shape this block into a form, establishing the assumptions about how the world operates. The Adaptive Source Belief, determined by nature, represents how this newly sculpted form exists and responds in its world. It is influenced by genetic predisposition, epigenetic factors, and the spiritual uniqueness of humans as created beings.

The Formation of the Adaptive Source Belief

The Adaptive Source Belief arises as a person's innate nature responds to environmental inputs throughout their life, with key adaptive patterns often emerging around elementary-school age. Unlike the Origin Source Belief, which governs what we perceive and assume about the world, the Adaptive Source Belief is more closely tied to how we respond or react to those perceptions and assumptions. It is a byproduct of genetic and epigenetic predispositions, as well as the individual's spiritual or created uniqueness.

During this stage, the child's awareness broadens beyond the home, encountering external influences such as peers, teachers, and societal expectations. This expanded exposure allows the child to seek out new structures and situations in which to play out the foundational assumptions of their Origin Source Belief. As discussed briefly in previous chapters, self-deception often plays a critical role in tricking the individual into believing these new environments are similar to or the same as their childhood environments. In doing so, they assign new characters the same roles as primary caregivers or siblings. This self-deceptive pattern sets the stage for a faulty science experiment, where the individual distorts the variables or the way they perceive those variables in order to feel justified in playing out their Adaptive Source Belief Pattern.

Adaptive Source Beliefs: A Framework for Response

There are a set number of Origin and Adaptive Source Belief pairs that exist, each operating within a specific framework. The Origin Source Belief sets the stage by defining the foundational assumptions about the world, and in doing so, it inherently limits the responses a person believes they can choose from. This limitation isn't conscious but is driven by the subconscious programming established during early development. The Adaptive Source Belief emerges as a reaction to these assumptions, forming predictable patterns of response based on the perceived constraints of the Origin.

Once a Brain Pattern—comprising both Origin and Adaptive Source Beliefs—is formed, it becomes constitutional in nature. These patterns function like ruts in a well-worn road. Every interaction, decision, and experience reinforces the depth of the rut, making the pattern more ingrained with each passing day. The person's subconscious rules about the world begin to feel not just true but immutable, leaving little room for exceptions or alternative interpretations.

This entrenchment doesn't occur overnight. It is the cumulative result of years of repetition, where the brain's natural tendency is to seek familiarity and confirm its own assumptions. Left unchecked, the pattern continues to shape how the person engages with their surroundings, limiting their ability to recognize or seize opportunities for change.

Here's the inspiring reality: every day spent without addressing these patterns makes them harder to rewire, but the choice to act now holds immense power. The brain's plasticity—its ability to change and form new pathways—is waiting to be harnessed. The work may be challenging, but every step taken today loosens the grip of these subconscious patterns, paving the way for transformation.

Abandonment-Based Adaptive Source Belief Patterns

Abandonment-based Adaptive Source Beliefs present in two primary patterns: Control to Be Safe and Hold It All Together. Each of these patterns reflects distinct approaches to navigating the foundational assumptions of abandonment, shaped by how the individual's brain learned to compensate for a perceived lack of safety or reliability in their early environment.

Control to Be Safe

Control to Be Safe, as an Adaptive Source Belief, is a survival mechanism forged in response to the instability or unpredictability experienced during formative years. It is characterized by an unrelenting drive to create predictability and stability, often at the expense of emotional connection and adaptability. This pattern emerges not as a conscious choice but as a subconscious strategy to avoid the pain of perceived betrayal, abandonment, or chaos. Its defining feature is a pervasive belief that trusting others is inherently unsafe, leading to behaviors that prioritize control above all else. These behaviors manifest in one of three distinct subtypes: Overt Control, Covert Control, or Switch Control. Each individual's presentation remains consistent within their subtype, though Switch Control itself involves a deliberate oscillation between overt and covert strategies depending on the context or relationship.

For individuals presenting with Overt Control, the need for dominance is visible in nearly every interaction. Behaviors such as micromanaging, correcting others, or taking charge of situations are hallmarks of this subtype, often creating tension and alienation in relationships. In contrast, those with Covert Control adopt more subtle, behind-the-scenes tactics to achieve the same goal of maintaining control. These strategies might include people-pleasing, avoidance, or indirect manipulation, allowing them to avoid confrontation while still influencing outcomes. The Switch Control subtype is unique in its duality, as these individuals oscillate between overt and covert behaviors. However, this oscillation is not random—it is a calculated response to the demands of a particular relationship or situation, driven by the same underlying need to avoid vulnerability and preserve emotional safety.

What makes this belief so insidious is that the very behaviors designed to protect often create the outcomes they fear most. The obsessive need for control can lead to resentment, erosion of trust, and a disconnection from the spontaneity and joy that make relationships fulfilling. Regardless of subtype, each pattern leaves its own trail of conflict, heartbreak, and poor outcomes. The question that lingers is this: If these patterns were initially forged to protect, why do they so often leave destruction in their wake? And perhaps more importantly, how do you begin to break free from a belief so deeply ingrained it feels like a core part of your identity?

Overt Control Type

The Overt Control Type is characterized by direct and visible efforts to manage situations, often driven by a compulsion to ensure safety and stability. These individuals are quick to intervene, correct, or advocate, believing that their active involvement is necessary to maintain order. This pattern stems from a deep-seated belief that their presence and input are critical to achieving desirable outcomes. They often feel an inherent responsibility to "fix" or improve situations, which they perceive as otherwise chaotic or unsafe without their intervention.

Overt Control Types frequently struggle to see their actions through the lens of others, often unaware that their well-meaning behaviors may come across as controlling or overly critical. For example, their tendency to correct others or micromanage details is rooted in a genuine desire to help but is often misinterpreted as a lack of trust in others' abilities. This can lead to tension in relationships, as those on the receiving end may feel undermined or judged. Despite their intention to create stability, their actions can inadvertently breed conflict, reinforcing their belief that they alone can ensure order.

This compulsion to step in often leaves little room for flexibility, as Overt Control Types find it challenging to let go of outcomes or trust others to meet expectations. Their focus on ensuring fairness and justice can manifest as an inclination to advocate for themselves or others, frequently placing them at the center of disputes. While they are often motivated by a strong sense of responsibility and care, their inability to relinquish control or adapt to alternative approaches perpetuates cycles of frustration and conflict.

Thought patterns: Driven by a need to ensure safety and stability through direct actions and communication.

Behavioral traits: Actively manages people and situations through:

> • **Correcting and micromanaging:** Often perceived as criticism, even when motivated by helpful intentions.

> • **Advocating or fixing:** Compelled to speak up, often leading to conflict.

> • **Responsibility:** Believes others cannot match their capabilities, leading to anxiety and an overinflated sense of responsibility.

Key struggle: Struggles with timing, tact, and letting go of controlling outcomes, leading to frequent conflict despite perceiving good intentions.

Outcome: Controlling behaviors driven by a need to keep people safe (even from themselves) destabilizes relationships.

Covert Control Type

The Covert Control Type operates behind the scenes, avoiding direct confrontation while still seeking to shape outcomes and maintain control. This approach is often subtle, leveraging strategies like manipulation, people-pleasing, or avoidance to ensure their desired results. While their actions may appear passive or accommodating on the surface, the underlying intent is deeply rooted in a need to feel safe and in control of their environment.

These individuals often rely on indirect methods to influence others and create a sense of stability. For instance, they may use flattery, agreeableness, or small acts of service to gain favor or ensure outcomes align with their expectations. Avoidance is another key strategy, as they might deliberately steer clear of conflict or responsibilities they deem emotionally risky. This behavior often creates a sense of confusion for others, as the Covert Control Type's intentions are not always explicit, leaving their true motivations obscured.

At the core of this pattern is a fear of abandonment, which drives their preference for subtler forms of control. While they avoid overt confrontation, their behind-the-scenes strategies can still be manipulative, ensuring they maintain a sense of control without drawing attention to their actions—even if that means abandoning first. Over time, this pattern can lead to built-up resentment, as their efforts often go unnoticed or unappreciated. Despite their need for control, Covert Control Types may struggle with feelings of powerlessness, as their indirect methods rarely allow for the direct satisfaction of asserting their needs or boundaries.

Thought patterns: Shares similar underlying thoughts with overt control types but employs distinct strategies to achieve control.

Behavioral traits: Avoids direct confrontation and often manipulates situations to achieve desired outcomes. This may involve:

- **People-pleasing:** Adjusting behaviors to keep others happy while subtly guiding outcomes.

- **Avoidance:** Steering clear of conflict or responsibility, often destroying outcomes to maintain a sense of control.

- **Placating:** Saying or doing what others want to diffuse tension while remaining focused on personal goals.

Key struggle: Builds resentment over time and may become avoidant due to unaddressed issues and a lack of direct communication.

Outcome: Sneaky or manipulative behaviors can create relationship tension and frustration.

Switch Control Type

The Switch Control Type dynamically shifts between overt and covert strategies depending on the context, the people involved, or the perception of security in the relationship. This adaptability is often a subconscious mechanism to manage perceived risks in relationships or environments. In familiar or intimate settings, they tend to adopt overt control behaviors, feeling more confident to assert their needs and manage outcomes directly. In contrast, within professional or less familiar dynamics, they may revert to covert strategies, relying on subtle manipulation or avoidance to maintain control without drawing attention.

This pendulum-like behavior can create confusion and frustration for those around them. In one scenario, the Switch Control Type may seem assertive and decisive, while in another, they appear passive or evasive. This inconsistency complicates efforts to build trust, as their unpredictability makes it difficult for others to anticipate their responses or motivations. People often struggle to understand whether their behavior is rooted in genuine care or calculated self-preservation, which can lead to feelings of distrust or unease.

At the core of this pattern is an internal conflict between the desire for connection and the fear of vulnerability. In relationships where intimacy grows, the Switch Control Type may struggle with push-pull dynamics, oscillating between wanting to maintain control overtly and retreating into covert methods to protect themselves from abandonment or failure. This dual approach often leaves them feeling emotionally isolated, as neither strategy fully satisfies their need for safety or connection. Over time, their inability to settle into a consistent relational style can lead to strained relationships and a sense of internal instability.

Thought patterns: Combines elements of both overt and covert control types, dynamically shifting strategies based on context.

Behavioral traits: Alternates between:

- **Overt control:** Seen in close relationships where intimacy allows for directness.

- **Covert control:** Appears in professional or new relationships, employing subtle and indirect strategies.

Key struggle: May seem evasive or inauthentic due to the pendulum swing between approaches, creating confusion for others and making intimacy difficult to sustain.

Outcome: Push-pull behaviors in relationships, where deeper connection feels fraught with unpredictability.

Hold It All Together

Hold It All Together as an Adaptive Source Belief reflects a pattern of deep self-sacrifice and a pervasive inability to trust others' capabilities or emotional stability. This leads individuals to assume the role of mediator or peacekeeper, often suppressing their own needs and wants to stabilize the perceived needs of others. Unlike the Control to Be Safe pattern, which involves a clear awareness of an agenda or desired outcome, Hold It All Together individuals focus less on achieving specific outcomes and more on maintaining group harmony at any cost. This often results in placating or yielding to the most dominant voices in the room to avoid conflict.

This pattern is marked by an instinctual tendency to absorb responsibilities without explicit communication, avoiding any behavior that could be perceived as controlling or micromanaging. Instead of delegating or addressing issues directly, they silently take on tasks, believing others are emotionally incapable of handling criticism or feedback. Over time, this creates a dynamic where they feel burdened, resentful, and overworked, often leading to burnout.

As children, these individuals frequently took on the role of stabilizers in environments of conflict or instability, mediating between caregivers or shielding siblings from emotional upheaval. This early conditioning established the belief that their survival depended on prioritizing the emotional needs of others above their own. While their intentions are often noble, this pattern perpetuates cycles of self-neglect and dissatisfaction, as they continuously defer their own desires for the perceived greater good.

Thought Patterns:

- Suppresses personal wants and needs to stabilize group dynamics.

- Believes others are emotionally incapable of handling feedback or guidance.

- Views peacekeeping as essential to maintaining stability.

Behavioral Traits:

- Avoids direct confrontation and takes on responsibilities silently.

- Struggles with delegation, often stepping in to "fix" flaws or gaps.

- Placates aggressive or dominant individuals to maintain harmony.

Key Struggle: Consistently overcommits, neglects their own needs, and burns out while silently resenting everyone they're trying to help.

Outcome: Chooses short-term peace that overloads their plate or enables others.

Rejection Adaptive Source Belief Patterns

Rejection-based Adaptive Source Beliefs are rooted in fears of inadequacy and rejection, often fixating on how others perceive them or how they interpret being treated in various interactions. These patterns are driven by a deep need to secure validation and avoid rejection, leading individuals to closely monitor and influence external perceptions. Conflict in power dynamics is a hallmark of these patterns, with individuals often becoming entangled in struggles for approval, status, or recognition. Rejection types also frequently assume they will be blamed for something they didn't do or don't believe is their fault. However, this is an area where significant self-deception often occurs; they may unconsciously contribute to the situation, and project blame onto another person instead of acknowledging their own role.

A distinguishing feature of Rejection patterns is their classification into two key subgroups: self-trust rating and action-type. The self-trust rating, either positive (+) or negative (-), determines how individuals perceive their own capabilities and whether they lean on themselves or depend on external validation. Action-type defines how the individual navigates their rejection belief–either engaging or isolating. Engaging types actively seek out relationships, conflicts, or group dynamics, placing themselves at the center of power struggles or relational tensions. In contrast, isolating types assume negative outcomes are inevitable or that they will be blamed for failures, prompting them to avoid interactions and withdraw from opportunities.

These patterns create distinct behavioral loops that reinforce their underlying fears. Engaging types may become overly focused on gaining approval or asserting their presence in power dynamics, often exacerbating relational tensions. Meanwhile, isolating types may retreat entirely, forfeiting opportunities for connection or growth to maintain control over how they are perceived from a distance. Both strategies, though distinct, are rooted in the same core fear of rejection and the belief that their value is tied to how others perceive them.

Understanding these dynamics is essential to unraveling the complexity of Rejection Adaptive Source Beliefs. The interplay between self-trust and action-type not only defines how these patterns manifest but also provides insight into the specific challenges individuals face in breaking free from their cycles of rejection-driven behavior.

Control to Receive Love and Be Safe

Control to Receive Love and Be Safe as an Adaptive Source Belief reflects a need to manage external perceptions and control events to ensure emotional and situational security. This subtype mimics traits from the Abandonment – Control to Be Safe while blending with Rejection-based tendencies, forming a unique behavioral pattern. It combines the vigilance and micromanagement of Abandonment – Control to Be Safe with a Rejection-driven focus on attention and validation, often seeking these within relationships or group dynamics.

This pattern type is inherently risk-averse. These individuals avoid danger and take fewer chances, preferring consistent routines and structured environments. Control to Receive Love and Be Safe individuals lean toward predictable lifestyles, often resisting change to maintain stability and avoid uncertainty.

This dual nature allows them to balance fears of rejection with a strong desire for safety through control. They often approach tasks and relationships strategically, aiming to secure both love and emotional security, but this can lead to struggles with delegation and trust. Engaging subtypes assert themselves to secure validation in group settings, while isolating subtypes retreat to maintain control over outcomes and interactions. Both subtypes operate from a core belief that love and safety depend on their ability to predict and manage their environment effectively.

Thought Patterns:

- Preoccupied with how others perceive them and their actions.

- Seeks to minimize uncertainty by controlling outcomes and relationships.

- Blends Rejection-driven validation-seeking with Abandonment-driven safety behaviors.

Behavioral Traits:

- Micromanages tasks or relationships to prevent perceived threats or failure.

- Displays either isolating tendencies (avoiding interactions) or engaging tendencies (actively participating in conflict or relational struggles).

- Uses strategies like planning, vigilance, or manipulation to maintain control.

Key Struggles:

- Difficulty delegating tasks, often leading to overwhelm or burnout.

- Experiences tension in relationships due to perceived mistrust or controlling behavior.

- Internal conflict between seeking connection and fearing vulnerability.

Outcome:

- Short-term feelings of control at the expense of long-term relational satisfaction.

- Perpetuates cycles of mistrust and over-responsibility, reinforcing their fear of rejection and failure. Individuals with this pattern exhibit behaviors consistent with Control to Receive Love, emphasizing how others perceive and interact with them, but with a parallel drive to create predictability and stability reminiscent of Abandonment – Control to Be Safe. This dual nature enables them to navigate rejection fears while maintaining a sense of safety through control. They often approach tasks and relationships with a calculated strategy to secure both love and emotional security, which can lead to struggles with delegation and trust.

Control to Receive Love

Control to Receive Love as an Adaptive Source Belief revolves around managing how others perceive, label, or interact with them. These individuals are intensely focused on crafting favorable impressions, often tailoring their behavior or presentation to ensure they are seen in the best possible light. This pattern stems from a deep-seated fear of rejection and the belief that love and validation are conditional on their ability to control how they are perceived. Additionally, they often assume they will be blamed or shamed for something, whether or not it is within their control, further amplifying their need to manage perceptions.

This type can exhibit a positive adventurous streak, thriving on daring physical feats or sports. Their willingness to take bold actions can reflect a sense of courage and a drive for exploration and adventure. However, they may also struggle with impulsivity, particularly in areas like financial decisions, feeling the need to move on or free themselves, or other risk-centered behaviors. For Isolating types, this behavior may serve as an escape, providing a temporary reprieve from perceived pressures or obligations. In contrast, Engaging types are more inclined to pursue these actions for reputation or validation, seeking attention from peers or social media. While this daring nature can be exciting, it may also lead to self-centeredness, as they prioritize their own desires and interests over the needs or expectations of others. This can also lead to instability in relationships and career history with a variety of start-stop commitments.

The perception of obligation plays a significant role in this pattern, often fueling relational conflict. Responsibilities or expectations— real or imagined—may be interpreted as intrusive or burdensome, leading these individuals to become avoidant or non-committal. This avoidance is frequently driven by self-deception, as they reinterpret their obligations as conflicts with their autonomy or freedom. While they may seek pleasure or rewards, their focus on managing how they are perceived often overrides their ability to build mutually supportive relationships, leaving them isolated despite their outward engagement.

Thought Patterns:

- Preoccupied with managing how others perceive, label, or interact with them.

- Driven by a fear of rejection and the belief that love and validation are conditional.

- Assumes blame or shame for outcomes, whether or not within their control, amplifying their focus on perception management.

- May perceive commitment as obligation and seek to push away from it.

- Tends to project shame and blame into relational dynamics to justify desired actions.

Behavioral Traits:

- Exhibits an adventurous streak, thriving on daring physical feats or exploration.

- Struggles with impulsivity in financial decisions, risk-taking, or start-stop commitments in relationships or careers.

- Isolating types use bold actions as an escape, avoiding perceived pressures or obligations.

- Engaging types pursue validation and attention from peers or social media, often tied to reputation.

Key Struggles:

- Tendency to prioritize personal desires over the needs or expectations of others.

- Instability in relationships and careers due to avoidant or non-committal tendencies.

- Interprets responsibilities or obligations as burdens, leading to avoidance or self-deception.

Outcome:

- Short-term gratification through adventurous or impulsive behaviors, at the expense of long-term stability.

- Difficulty forming mutually supportive relationships due to self-centered focus on perception management.

- Cycles of isolation or superficial engagement, leaving them disconnected despite outward appearances.

Chaos – Rejection Adaptive Source Belief

The Chaos – Rejection Adaptive Source Belief is one of the most challenging patterns to navigate due to its foundational belief that life is inherently chaotic and without purpose. This belief stems from early childhood experiences where basic needs were not met, triggering an exaggerated escape mechanism in the brain. These individuals learn to dissociate from the pain of daily life, leading to extreme behaviors such as suicidal ideation, addiction, or self-sabotage. Unlike other patterns, this type struggles to generate momentum or develop the drive to overcome adversity, as their brain convinces them that there is no point in trying. Success and stability feel foreign and even unsafe to their brain, prompting self-destructive behaviors when things are going well.

This pattern often manifests as a cycle of chaos and destruction, with the individual sabotaging their own efforts to maintain the belief that life will never go their way. Despite raw talent or moments of success, they cannot sustain positive outcomes, as their brain defaults to chaos as a protective mechanism. This belief system significantly impacts their ability to cultivate a career, maintain relationships, or stay consistent in any area of life. The hallmark of this pattern is the constant question: "What's the point?"

The Adaptive Rejection belief further compounds the chaos, presenting with behaviors that actively obstruct success. These may include addiction, risky sexual behaviors, escapism, or self-sabotage through disorganization, poor time management, and conflict-prone communication. This ensures that the individual perpetuates the belief that life is rigged against them. However, the truth is that their chaotic behavior and inconsistency are the primary sources of destruction. Individuals with this pattern may attempt to escape it by leaning heavily into rigid structures such as Alcoholics Anonymous or Narcotics Anonymous, the military, or religious organizations, seeking external control to counterbalance their internal chaos.

Thought Patterns:

- Deep-seated belief that life is inherently chaotic and purposeless.

- Conviction that success and stability are unattainable or unsafe.

- Tendency to assume failure or sabotage outcomes as a way to feel safe in chaos.

Behavioral Traits:

- Engages in addictive behaviors, risky decisions, or escapism.

- Exhibits disorganization, poor time management, and inconsistent effort.

- Communication style often pushes buttons, leading to conflict and strained reputations.

Key Struggles:

- Difficulty maintaining momentum or consistency in career, relationships, or goals.

- Cycles of self-sabotage that reinforce feelings of chaos and hopelessness.

- Only able to maintain temporary consistency by dependency on external structures (e.g., AA, military, religion) to impose control

Outcome:

- Short-term reliance on external systems for stability, but difficulty sustaining personal growth.

- Self-fulfilling cycles of chaos that erode trust, reputation, and progress.

- Persistent belief that life is unfair, perpetuating a sense of futility.

You're Not Broken, You're Human

Reading about these Adaptive Source Beliefs may feel overwhelming, as though your behaviors or struggles have been laid bare. However, recognizing these patterns is not a declaration of being broken or hopeless—it is a turning point. Seeing yourself in these descriptions means you are steps away from understanding the self-deception that drives these behaviors. What if the very patterns you thought defined you were just the starting point for uncovering how your brain truly operates? And what if this isn't just your story—what if every one of the over 8 billion people on this planet fits into one of these categories, each navigating their own unique patterns?

CHAPTER 12

MAPPING THE SOURCE BELIEF SPECTRUM

The Foundation of the Source Belief Spectrum

At the heart of how you see and interact with the world lies our Source Belief Pattern—a deeply ingrained framework that drives our assumptions. This pattern operates as both filter and blueprint, shaping how you interpret situations and relationships, often unknowingly locking us into repetitive cycles of behavior. Whether it's the dynamics you create in your intimate relationships, the chaos you encounter in your workplace, or the ways you justify your choices, Source Beliefs are the invisible architects of our lives.

The Source Belief Spectrum is a tool to decode these patterns, offering a way to map the hidden mechanics of human behavior. It places all of humanity on a continuum defined by five primary variations, rooted in distinct belief systems: Abandonment, Rejection, and Chaos. Each variation emerges from a unique combination of early environmental inputs and the adaptive responses they shaped. By understanding your place on this spectrum, you can begin to unravel why certain relational and situational patterns seem to repeat endlessly in your life. This isn't limited to cultivating self-awareness—it's about recognizing the predictable ways in which self-deception distorts your perception of reality, driving behaviors that sabotage your goals.

What determines where you land on this spectrum? It's the interplay between your early environment and how your brain adapted to it. Data points like emotional availability, family structure, discipline style, and exposure to chaos all push you toward a specific Source Belief Pattern. These early experiences not only influence how you see yourself but also dictate the assumptions you make about others, creating a patterned lens through which you interpret all relational and situational dynamics. This patterned perception then shapes how you approach decision-making, conflict resolution, and even your capacity for trust.

Dimensions of the Source Belief Spectrum

The Source Belief Spectrum is defined by three core dimensions: situational awareness, relational awareness, and self-trust. Each dimension fluctuates depending on where an individual falls on the spectrum and which Source Belief Pattern drives their behavior.

As you move leftward from the spectrum's midline into the Abandonment patterns, situational awareness and self-trust tend to increase, while relational awareness decreases. This shift often corresponds with a heightened focus or level of comfortability on structure, work, and control. Individuals on this side of the spectrum perceive stability as something that must be actively created or maintained, often at the expense of relational dynamics. At the farthest left lies the Abandonment – Control to Be Safe Overt cluster, where heightened situational awareness and self-reliance dominate. However, within this group, some subtypes exhibit such an overwhelming degree of situational control that they may struggle to filter relevant information, leading to paranoia and fixating behaviors. This extreme variation, though rare, tends to emerge when an Abandonment – Control to Be Safe Overt subtype has isolated themselves for prolonged periods, cutting off external inputs that might otherwise help align their perspective with objective reality. Without these grounding influences, their perception becomes increasingly distorted, amplifying their fixation on control and further disconnecting them from the world around them.

In contrast, as you move rightward into the Rejection-oriented patterns, relational awareness increases significantly, while situational awareness and self-trust diminish. This shift often results in a fixation on external validation and an imagined concern with how others perceive them—preoccupations that are rarely grounded in objective reality and frequently stem from projection or deflection. These individuals tend to assign their internal fears onto others, unconsciously attributing blame or judgment. This relational focus fuels cycles of insecurity and conflict, leaving them highly attuned to interpersonal dynamics but at the expense of their own stability.

At the farthest right lies the Chaos – Rejection pattern. This group shares some behavioral characteristics with the far-left extremes, particularly in their difficulty anchoring to reality. However, their distortions are rooted in an existential crisis—a pervasive belief that nothing truly matters. This fundamental instability often drives them to relational conflict, as they frequently become dependent on others for survival, whether to be bailed out of jail, taken to rehab, or otherwise rescued from the consequences of their behavior. Unlike the far-left extremes, whose distortions stem from situational control, this group's instability is deeply tied to relational dynamics, amplifying their sense of disconnection and chaos. These individuals often engage in deliberate self-sabotage, creating chaos that not only disrupts their own lives but also brings disaster and problems to those around them. This behavior frequently generates relational conflict, as their actions strain trust and stability in interpersonal connections, perpetuating a cycle of chaos and perceived betrayal.

By understanding the interplay between situational awareness, relational awareness, and self-trust, we can illuminate not only the repetitive behaviors individuals fall into but also the predictable areas of life where conflict and chaos are most likely to arise. Placement on the spectrum provides clarity about how these dimensions interact, offering insight into the hidden architecture of human behavior.

The Spectrum's Paradox: The Mirror Effect

Placement on the spectrum also reveals an intriguing paradox: the Mirror Effect. Anywhere a person is placed on the spectrum, their equal and opposite counterpart—positioned the same distance from the midline on the opposite side—may present with behaviors that appear strikingly similar on the surface. For instance, a person on the left side of the spectrum may exhibit meticulous attention to planning and preparation, while their right-side counterpart demonstrates the same degree of attentiveness, but directed toward navigating social dynamics. Outwardly, their behaviors appear aligned, yet the internal motivations behind them diverge significantly.

Left-side individuals are often motivated by a deep-seated distrust in the natural unfolding of events and an inability to rely on others to follow through. As a result, they perceive the world as unpredictable and unsafe unless they take active steps to impose structure, maintain order, or act as the peacekeeper. This mindset heightens their situational awareness, as they are constantly scanning for potential disruptions or threats to the stability they seek to create.

Conversely, their right-side counterparts approach the world through an entirely different lens. They are driven by a need for external cues and validation from the people around them to shape their self-concept and define their role in the world. Lacking internal stability, they rely heavily on relational feedback to gauge their value and sense of security. This dependence on others for affirmation often leaves them vulnerable to emotional fluctuations, as their perception of themselves shifts with the dynamics of their interpersonal environment.

What truly distinguishes these counterparts is their perception of reality and the assumptions that drive their actions. While the behaviors may mirror one another, the underlying beliefs about the world and their roles within it are in direct opposition. This relativity has practical implications, particularly in therapeutic or clinical settings. Understanding the Mirror Effect and how perception drives behavior allows for targeted, effective interventions. Without this distinction, interventions risk addressing surface-level similarities rather than the root cause, leaving individuals trapped in cycles of self-deception. Recognizing these nuances ensures healing efforts align with the motivations and assumptions that truly need to be addressed, making the process more effective, efficient, and sustainable.

The Spectrum's Extremes: A Bridge Between Opposites

The Chaos-presenting Abandonment – Control Overt type provides a vivid illustration of how the spectrum can visually fold back on itself, creating overlap between extreme positions. At the farthest edges of the spectrum, behaviors that appear to be polar opposites can begin to resemble one another in outward presentation, even while being driven by entirely opposing forces.

For instance, while both may exhibit patterns of paranoia or distrust, the far-left individual's behavior is driven by an overwhelming need for situational control and order. In contrast, the far-right individual exists in a state of perpetual existential crisis, rooted in the belief that life is meaningless and that everything is part of a grand conspiracy. This deep sense of futility drives their paranoia, which manifests relationally not because of interpersonal instability itself, but due to patterns of willful self-sabotage and even law-breaking behaviors. These actions often create chaos and strain relationships, reinforcing their worldview that life's chaos is inevitable and nothing truly matters.

This phenomenon demonstrates that, in the extreme, you can go so far left in pursuit of order and control that you begin to exhibit the same chaos and disconnection that define the far right. The difference lies not in the behaviors themselves but in their underlying motivations. The left clings to control out of a desperate attempt to find safety, while the right rejects it entirely, believing life's instability is inevitable and pointless. These opposing perspectives underscore the importance of understanding not just what people do, but why they do it—an insight that is critical to unraveling the self-sabotaging patterns that dominate both extremes.

Understanding Your Position on the Spectrum

Your position on the Source Belief Spectrum serves as a roadmap to your history and a predictor of your future. Once your pattern type is plotted on the spectrum, it becomes clear how early environmental inputs and adaptive responses have shaped your worldview, relationships, and decision-making processes. Each pattern type has its own strengths and variances, meaning no two individuals with the same general pattern will present identically. For example, an Abandonment – Hold It All Together individual positioned near the line of Abandonment Control to Be Safe (Covert) may exhibit behaviors aligned with subtle manipulation and avoidance, creating interpersonal dynamics that revolve around de-escalating conflict while still maintaining a façade of stability. In contrast, someone with the same core pattern positioned more centrally on the spectrum may display a greater blend of traits from neighboring types, such as those found in the Rejection – Control to Receive Love and Safe cluster. This blending creates more fluidity in their behavior and relationships, but it can also introduce greater complexity in understanding their motivations and patterns of self-deception.

The position and strength of your Brain Pattern Type on the spectrum are influenced by a variety of data points. Early childhood experiences, such as the availability of emotional support, family structure, and exposure to chaos, all contribute to where you fall on the spectrum. Additionally, the degree of adaptive responses—how intensely your brain worked to counterbalance those early experiences—further defines the strength of your pattern. Someone positioned closer to the extremes of the spectrum will often display more rigid and predictable behaviors, as their worldview is heavily anchored in the need for control or validation. Meanwhile, individuals positioned nearer the midline tend to exhibit more flexibility and adaptability, often due to a more balanced set of early inputs or less extreme adaptive responses. This nuanced placement highlights the intersection between the past and the present, providing a clearer picture of why certain behaviors emerge and how they may evolve over time. Understanding this position not only demystifies the "why" behind your actions but also offers actionable insight into the "how" of rewiring these patterns for sustainable change.

The Circle of Complacency: Stability at a Cost

When your Brain Pattern Type places you within the center circle of the Source Belief Spectrum, your life tends to be defined by consistency, predictability, and a resistance to volatility. The center circle includes two specific subgroups: Abandonment - Hold It All Together from the left side and Rejection - Control to Receive Love and Be Safe from the right side. It's important to note that not all individuals within these broader pattern clusters fall into the center circle. The circle represents only those who are closest to the spectrum's midline, embodying the traits of stability and consistency without venturing into the extremes of their respective patterns.

These individuals typically lead steady, even mundane lives, characterized by routine and a lack of significant risk-taking. They are not natural seekers of excitement or creators of chaos, instead preferring to remain within the bounds of what feels safe and predictable. While this consistency can be a strength, it often crosses into complacency—a state of "good enough" where there is little striving for greatness or meaningful change. As a result, clients with a center circle Brain Pattern Type are unlikely to seek outside assistance unless their sense of stability is destabilized. Common triggers include life transitions such as experiencing an empty nest, navigating a midlife crisis, or losing the job they've relied on for decades. These disruptions challenge the foundations upon which they've built their lives, forcing them to confront the trade-offs of their longstanding aversion to change or risk.

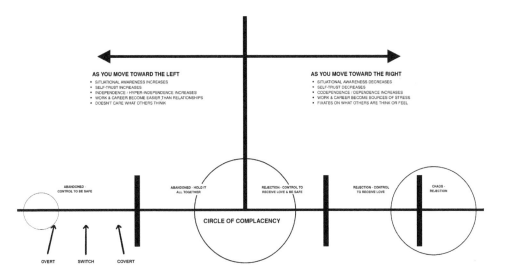

Pictured Above: Source Belief Spectrum Diagram

For instance, an Abandonment – Hold It All Together individual might have centered their life entirely around their children, only to feel a profound sense of loss and remorse once their kids grow up and move out. Without a career or other meaningful pursuits to fall back on, they may struggle to redefine their sense of purpose. Similarly, a Rejection – Control to Receive Love and Be Safe individual might remain in a dead-end job for decades, valuing the stability it provides over the opportunity for growth or fulfillment. If that job is suddenly lost due to layoffs or an unexpected retirement, the resulting upheaval can leave them feeling adrift and unmoored. These examples highlight how the patterns of center circle subgroups, while seemingly benign, can lead to significant emotional and practical challenges when the safety nets they've relied on are removed suddenly.

By understanding the dynamics of the center circle, it becomes clear how stability can sometimes come at a cost. These individuals may not face the overt chaos or volatility seen in other parts of the spectrum, but their avoidance of risk and change can lead to missed opportunities, unfulfilled potential, and emotional stagnation. Recognizing these patterns offers a chance to redefine stability—not as an end goal but as a foundation for growth and intentional action when life inevitably shifts.

A Balance of Opposites: How We Rewire & Repattern

When someone gains awareness of their Brain Pattern Type and its placement on the Source Belief Spectrum, the natural question arises: "Great, now what do I do about it?" Awareness, while transformative, is merely the starting point. The real work begins with rewiring—a neuroscientific process that employs pattern opposition to create balance. Rewiring is not about erasing the patterns that have shaped someone's life but about expanding their range of responses and moving them intentionally toward healthier, more adaptive behaviors.

As we progress through the remaining chapters of this book, we will explore the common themes of self-deception experienced by each pattern type and learn how to recognize the language of these distortions. This understanding is foundational for rewiring because it exposes the blindspots that have kept certain patterns locked in place. The ultimate goal, however, is not simply awareness but action. To create meaningful change, we must tailor interventions that counteract the brain's default tendencies, providing the individual with the tools to navigate their world in ways that were previously inaccessible.

When working within the framework of the spectrum, rewiring aims to achieve two primary goals:

1. **Expand dynamic range:** Help individuals move away from instinctive, repetitive, and out-of-pattern reactions by unlocking a variety of previously hidden responses. This increases their ability to adapt, rather than defaulting to the same patterns of behavior regardless of the situation.

2. **Shift toward the center:** Guide individuals closer to the spectrum's midline, where balance and stability are found—not by default but by design.

For individuals plotted toward the outer edges of the spectrum, this shift toward the center cultivates peace and stability, replacing the extremes of chaos, rigidity, or relational fixation with an intentional, measured approach to life. Ironically, for those naturally positioned in the Center Circle, the strategy is the reverse. These individuals must learn to step outside their comfort zones, take calculated risks, and break free from the complacency that has defined much of their lives. Pattern opposition for the Center Circle type involves shaking things up and exploring new aspects of themselves, such as likes, dislikes, passions, and purpose, which may have remained dormant due to their aversion to risk or change.

Through intentional rewiring, individuals not only learn to navigate life differently but also begin to embody a new, balanced version of themselves. For those moving toward the center of the spectrum, this process replaces the instability of their patterns with an enduring sense of peace and clarity. For the Center Circle type, it sparks an awakening of creativity, purpose, and self-discovery. In both cases, the goal is not merely to survive within the confines of one's patterns but to thrive through a deliberate and empowered way of living.

Tying It All Together: The Spectrum as a Path to Change

The Source Belief Spectrum offers a lens through which you can reexamine the behaviors, beliefs, and assumptions that have guided your life. Whether shaped by the chaos of the extremes or the stability of the center, every position on the spectrum reflects a unique interplay of perception and action, revealing your history and the trajectory of your future if left unchallenged.

Awareness of your Brain Pattern Type is the beginning of a journey, not its destination. True change requires expanding the range of responses available to you, stepping out of instinctive patterns, and embracing a balanced, intentional approach to life. For some, this means shifting away from extremes to find peace and stability. For others, it means disrupting the complacency of predictable routines to uncover passion, purpose, and a richer sense of self. In either case, transformation comes not from abandoning who you are but from unlocking new possibilities hidden behind the patterns that have defined you.

But what makes these patterns so stubbornly persistent? Why do we cling to beliefs and emotional responses that perpetuate cycles of self-deception and limit our potential? To truly break free, we must first understand the intricate connection between belief and emotion—and how this connection shapes the way we experience the world.

CHAPTER 13

THE SCIENCE OF BELIEF

Are you actively thinking, or does it simply populate without your input, leaving you to recognize it? That illusion of control you cling to—the belief that you are the master of your thoughts—is a clever lie your subconscious has crafted to keep you on autopilot. These subconscious beliefs, forged in the chaos of early childhood, don't just influence your reality—they dictate it. They are the silent architects whispering commands that steer your emotions, perceptions, and actions, all while you remain blissfully unaware. If that doesn't scare you, it should.

The Anatomy and Physiology of Belief

Your brain craves patterns and thrives on predictability. To survive, it relies on repetition to hard-code assumptions about the world, building neural pathways like well-trodden trails in a dense forest. The more you walk a trail, the clearer it becomes, until eventually, you don't even need to think about where it leads. This process, known as neuroplasticity, is both a gift and a curse. It allows you to learn and adapt, but it also means that once a belief takes root, it's not easily undone.

Consider a child ignored by their caregiver. Over time, this repeated experience embeds the belief, "I'm not worth paying attention to." Similarly, a child who is criticized after every failure may internalize the belief, "Failure makes me unlovable." On the other hand, a child who is only rewarded for their achievements learns to equate their value with their performance, forming the belief, "Love is conditional on my success." These beliefs don't fade into the background—they persist. Your brain doesn't care whether these beliefs are helpful or true; it only cares about efficiency, even when that efficiency leads to tragedy.

The Science Behind Belief Formation

The formation of beliefs is a complex interplay of neuroplasticity, emotional imprinting, and social reinforcement. Once a thought or experience repeats often enough, the brain starts building a dedicated neural pathway. These pathways are physical structures in your brain that grow stronger with each repetition. For instance, a child growing up in chaos may repeatedly reinforce the belief, "I need to control everything to feel safe." This belief, though initially protective, evolves into an anchor for hypervigilance and anxiety as they navigate adulthood.

Emotion adds another layer to this process. The stronger the emotional charge tied to an experience, the deeper the belief embeds itself. Your brain remembers pain, humiliation, and fear with precision, using these moments as lessons to avoid future harm. For example, a child who loses parental affection after failing at something feels the emotional sting of rejection, reinforcing the belief, "I am only lovable when I succeed." These emotional imprints become the cornerstone of their subconscious programming, shaping how they approach challenges and relationships.

As if this weren't enough, your Reticular Activating System (RAS) steps in to ensure that your beliefs are reinforced at every turn. The RAS is a filter in your brain that sifts through the endless stream of sensory input and prioritizes what aligns with your beliefs. If you believe people are untrustworthy, your RAS will highlight every betrayal or disappointment while conveniently ignoring acts of kindness. This creates a self-fulfilling prophecy, where your beliefs shape what you see and what you ignore, perpetuating the very narrative your brain has decided to maintain.

The Role of Society in Shaping Beliefs

Social influence further complicates the picture. Humans are wired for connection, which means we naturally adopt the beliefs of those around us. Mirror neurons, the part of the brain responsible for empathy and imitation, make it almost impossible to escape the influence of family, peers, and larger societal structures.

Take, for example, how accents subtly shift when you're around someone with a different way of speaking. If you've ever caught yourself mimicking a friend's accent or speech patterns after spending time with them, you've witnessed your mirror neurons in action. This subconscious mimicry shows how we adapt to those around us to create connection—often without realizing it. The same principle applies to belief systems: you unconsciously absorb the values and assumptions of those in your social sphere.

A child raised in a household where money equals self-worth internalizes, "My value depends on my financial success." Similarly, a child who observes their parents expressing love or connection only during arguments might internalize, "Love is tied to conflict." These societal and familial scripts become default settings, rarely questioned but constantly shaping behavior and choices.

In today's world, social media amplifies these dynamics, turning the influence of close-knit communities into a global phenomenon. The curated lives of influencers, the addictive validation of likes and followers, and the echo chambers of fandoms can all reinforce subconscious beliefs about worth, success, and identity. Mirror neurons play a significant role here, as they activate when we observe others, especially those we admire or aspire to emulate.

For instance, repeated exposure to curated content showcasing unattainable beauty standards can lead to subconscious comparisons. These mirror neuron-driven observations may contribute to distorted self-perceptions, reinforcing beliefs like, "I'm not attractive enough" or "I'll only be worthy if I look like them." This cycle can underpin issues such as body dysmorphia, where individuals fixate on perceived flaws in their appearance. Even when someone consciously understands that influencer content is edited or unrealistic, their subconscious beliefs may still internalize these standards as benchmarks for value or acceptance.

Religious and cultural influences add another layer to this dynamic. Historically, conformity has been a survival strategy deeply embedded in our ancestral reflexes. In tribal settings, the need to align with the group wasn't just about belonging, it was about staying alive. To deviate from group norms could mean ostracism, which, in environments where survival depended on communal resources and protection, was often a death sentence. Conformity ensured cohesion, cooperation, and mutual reliance, all critical for survival.

This reflex toward conformity may be linked to the role of mirror neurons, which are responsible for imitation and empathy. By enabling individuals to observe and replicate the behaviors of their group, mirror neurons likely played a key role in promoting alignment with social norms. This mirroring mechanism would have reinforced group cohesion, making individuals less likely to stray from accepted behaviors. While direct research on mirror neurons and conformity as a survival mechanism is still emerging, the interplay between our neural architecture and evolutionary pressures suggests that these neurons may have evolved, at least in part, to ensure we remain integrated within our tribes.

A person raised in a culture that prioritizes conformity and tradition may struggle with independent thought, internalizing concepts like, "Deviating from the norm means rejection." These influences, while sometimes offering structure and support, can also create limiting beliefs that are difficult to dismantle. In modern contexts, this ancestral reflex can manifest in behaviors like adhering to societal norms or fearing judgment for expressing individuality, even when survival is no longer at stake.

Whether it's through family, social media, or cultural traditions, these external forces shape our subconscious programming. They establish patterns that dictate how we interpret the world, interact with others, and measure our own worth—often without us realizing just how much power they hold.

But I Don't Actually Believe Those Things

This is the argument you might cling to: "I know those beliefs aren't real. I don't consciously think that way." But that's the very crux of the problem. The battle isn't between what you consciously believe and know to be true; it's between the subconscious beliefs you've absorbed over a lifetime and the conscious ideals you hold dear. And often, these two are in direct conflict.

Let's unpack this with an analogy. Imagine a dog whistle. When you blow the whistle, humans hear nothing, but dogs come running. The pitch is outside the range of human hearing, but that doesn't mean the sound doesn't exist. It's real, it's there, and it's influencing behavior—

just not in a way you can perceive. Your subconscious beliefs work the same way. From the moment you were born, you've been absorbing influences that shaped your belief systems. These inputs often operate below the threshold of conscious awareness, but they still shape your reality.

Subconscious beliefs form through processes deeply rooted in the brain's structure and function. The hippocampus, for instance, encodes memories and determines which experiences are stored as long-term reference points. Meanwhile, the amygdala assigns emotional weight to those memories, making them stick when tied to fear, shame, or joy. Over time, these encoded experiences form the foundation of your subconscious programming. While your conscious mind might dismiss a belief as illogical or outdated, your subconscious holds onto it, whispering it back to you in moments of vulnerability.

This is why you might tell yourself, "I know I'm smart," but still panic before a work presentation because of an ingrained belief that you're going to make a mistake and get in trouble. You might consciously believe in abundance but still hoard money and live in scarcity because your subconscious equates financial stability with survival. These conflicts aren't a matter of logic—they're a matter of programming.

The influences shaping your subconscious are everywhere: the tone of a parent's voice, the body language of a caregiver, the unspoken rules of your culture, and the emotional charge of significant events. They form a silent symphony, playing in the background of your life, altering your perception of reality without your consent or awareness. And until you acknowledge their presence and their power, they will continue to dictate outcomes in your life, no matter how enlightened your conscious mind claims to be.

Belief's Influence: Placebo and Nocebo

To truly grasp the power of belief, we need to examine it in action. The placebo effect is a phenomenon where patients experience real improvements in health after receiving a treatment with no active ingredients, simply because they believe it will work. This isn't wishful thinking but a rigorously studied scientific fact. In a 2001 meta-analysis published in The New England Journal of Medicine, researchers examined the effects of placebos across numerous clinical trials and found measurable, significant improvements in conditions ranging from pain management to depression. The mind's belief in healing triggered physiological responses, such as the release of endorphins and changes in brain activity, mirroring the effects of actual medication.

Consider the story of a patient given a sugar pill but told it was a powerful painkiller. The patient reported significant pain relief, despite the absence of any pharmacological intervention. The belief alone was enough to engage the brain's natural pain-relief systems. This is the placebo effect at work: the power of belief shaping the body's physical response.

On the flip side, the nocebo effect demonstrates the destructive power of negative belief. Just as belief in healing can elicit positive outcomes, belief in harm can cause real damage. Patients who expect adverse effects from a treatment often experience those effects—even when the treatment is a placebo. For example, participants in one study were told they might experience nausea as a side effect. Although the treatment was inert, a significant percentage of participants reported nausea. The nocebo effect shows that negative expectations can trigger stress responses, such as elevated cortisol levels, which in turn weaken the immune system and disrupt overall health.

One chilling example involves a man diagnosed with terminal cancer. His doctor told him he had three months to live. True to the prognosis, he died within the expected timeframe. But there's a twist: his autopsy revealed that the tumor was benign and non-lethal. So, what killed him? His belief in the diagnosis. This belief triggered a cascade of stress responses in his body, releasing cortisol and other hormones that wreaked havoc on his immune system, cardiovascular health, and overall resilience.

This isn't an isolated incident. The nocebo effect has been observed in numerous studies where patients who believed they were at risk for side effects from medications experienced those side effects, even when given a placebo. The power of belief is such that it can override physical evidence, dictating outcomes simply through the expectation of harm.

The Phenomenon of Psychogenic Death

The idea that belief can kill may sound like folklore, but the phenomenon of psychogenic death, sometimes referred to as "voodoo death," has been documented by researchers for decades. Walter Cannon, a renowned physiologist, coined the term to describe cases where individuals died simply because they believed they were cursed or doomed. The mechanism behind this isn't magic—it's the body's physiological response to extreme fear or stress.

When someone believes they are going to die, the fight-or-flight system activates. This response floods the body with stress hormones, increasing heart rate, blood pressure, and overall metabolic demand. While this response is designed for short-term survival, prolonged activation can be fatal. In cases of psychogenic death, the unrelenting stress overwhelms the cardiovascular and immune systems, leading to organ failure or sudden cardiac arrest.

Anthropologists have documented cases in tribal communities where individuals cursed by shamans withdrew from life entirely. Refusing food, water, and social contact, they effectively willed themselves to die. While this may seem distant from modern life, the underlying mechanisms are the same. Today, we see similar effects in cases of extreme grief, stress-induced heart failure, often called "broken heart syndrome," and even certain cases of unexplained sudden death. These examples underscore how deeply belief can penetrate the body, overriding physical resilience and turning perception into reality.

Now, let's pause here for those of you who might already be spiraling—Googling every symptom and diagnosing yourself with the latest exotic condition you stumbled across online. Relax. Yes, belief has power, but no, your brain isn't conspiring to doom you every time you stub your toe. The takeaway here isn't to panic; it's to be aware. Long-term fear, unchecked anxiety, and catastrophic thinking are what wreak havoc—not that one fleeting moment you thought you might have a cough. So, take a breath, and know that managing your thoughts is as critical for your health as exercise and nutrition.

How Beliefs Shape Reality

Beliefs can profoundly impact your physical health. The connection between your thoughts, emotions, and physiology is a well-documented phenomenon in the scientific and medical communities. Numerous studies have explored how emotional suppression, stress, and personality traits can manifest as physical health conditions over time.

One such area of research highlights the correlation between Type D personality traits and chronic health issues, including hypothyroidism and autoimmune conditions like Hashimoto's. Type D, or "distressed" personality, is characterized by two key traits: negative affectivity, a tendency to dwell on negative emotions like worry and sadness, and social inhibition, a reluctance to express emotions or opinions due to fear of judgment or rejection. These traits, studied extensively in psychological and medical literature, have been linked to dysregulation of the hypothalamic-pituitary-adrenal (HPA) axis and heightened inflammatory responses. A study published in the Journal of Clinical Endocrinology & Metabolism found that individuals with hypothyroidism often exhibit these traits, reporting higher levels of anxiety, emotional suppression, and dissatisfaction with health outcomes.

Let's distill Type D personality traits into something relatable: people-pleasing. Over a decade of working with clients, I've observed a striking trend—those who default to saying the "nice" or "polite" thing, overgive to their own detriment, suppress their true feelings, and ruminate on unresolved anger often present with physical symptoms like Hashimoto's or hypothyroidism. Beyond storing stress, the body reacts to it, translating emotional suppression into tangible physiological consequences.

Let's unpack additional aspects of the Type D personality trait example. The negative affectivity component fosters chronic stress and pessimism, while social inhibition amplifies emotional suppression, creating a perfect storm for physiological consequences. The body, unable to process these suppressed emotions effectively, shifts into a prolonged stress response, which compromises immune function and disrupts hormonal balance.

 However, over the years, I've seen countless clients who rewire behavior patterns like people pleasing not only get emotional relief but also a significant reduction in their physical symptoms. The body responds to a shift in neural and hormonal patterns, demonstrating the intricate relationship between belief, behavior, and biology.

Over time, beliefs and their associated behaviors carve out predictable physiological responses. Chronic anxiety from beliefs tied to unworthiness or scarcity can result in gastrointestinal issues, migraines, or even cardiovascular strain. Conversely, beliefs rooted in self-efficacy and resilience can create a cascade of positive physical outcomes, such as enhanced immune function and reduced systemic inflammation. These correlations are the body's way of mirroring the internal landscape.

The implications are clear: your beliefs can determine how your body operates, heals, or deteriorates. Recognizing these patterns is the first step toward breaking the cycle, offering not only emotional freedom but also a path to physical well-being.

CHAPTER 14

HOW YOUR BRAIN'S BELIEFS HIJACK YOUR EMOTIONS

Emotional Addiction: Breaking the Feedback Loop

As we've covered, belief systems are deeply rooted in the repetitive inputs you absorbed during early childhood. Subtle, adverse patterns—the ones that might not even register as traumatic—are often the most insidious in shaping your emotional addiction cycles. Even in cases where overt traumas occurred, the resulting emotional addiction patterns are more often the byproducts of repeated, nuanced inputs than of singular traumatic events.

Emotion, meanwhile, is your body's response to these filtered experiences. It exists as both a physiological and psychological reaction, directly linked to your belief system. Think of it this way: your beliefs are the input, and your emotions are the output. Together, they create a feedback loop where beliefs shape emotions, and emotions, in turn, reinforce those beliefs. If your belief system is rooted in fear, rejection, or chaos, your emotions will echo these states, feeding back into the belief system that generated them. This loop, left unchecked, becomes the foundation of your emotional addiction cycle.

The Messy Middle: Emotions, Moods, and States

Not all emotional experiences are created equal. While we often use phrases like "I'm moody" or "I'm feeling emotional" interchangeably, these distinct concepts operate on different levels of our experience. If we're going to dismantle your emotional addiction cycle, it's critical to differentiate between an emotion, a feeling, a mood, a state of being, and behavior. Without this clarity, you'll find yourself perpetually chasing symptoms while ignoring the root cause.

Emotion is a short-lived reaction chemically triggered by a perceived stimulus. It's a physical or mental state generated by neurophysiological changes, driven by a combination of neurotransmitters and hormones. Emotions are subjective, often disconnected from objective reality, and specific in their function. Think of them as sharp signals designed to guide your brain's next move: fear sharpens focus, anger motivates action, and anxiety reinforces hypervigilance. Though typically fleeting—lasting seconds to minutes—some emotional states can linger longer, leaving a significant imprint on your internal landscape.

Feeling emerges when you add a narrative to the raw data of an emotion, giving it additional meaning shaped by your subjective experiences and personal history. Feelings are the interpretative layer, where your brain blends emotion with personal context to influence how you react and what you believe about the experience. In this way, feelings create a bridge between the physiological response of an emotion and the cognitive understanding of its impact.

Mood is a more sustained emotional experience, lasting hours or days and subtly shaping your perception of reality. Unlike emotions, which are typically tied to specific triggers, moods are less immediate and more cumulative. Factors such as sleep quality, diet, and unresolved emotional patterns influence moods, making them quieter but no less impactful. If emotions demand your attention with sharp signals, moods operate in the background, subtly nudging your outlook and decisions.

State of Being represents a broader and more complex composite of feelings, physical sensations, and awareness that defines your overall experience of the present moment. Unlike the transient nature of emotions or moods, a State of Being encompasses longer-term patterns and cycles, providing the overarching context for how you perceive and interact with the world. It's less about what's happening to you in a given moment and more about the cumulative framework through which you interpret your reality.

Behavior is the outward response to an emotion or feeling, translating your internal experience into observable action. Whether it's a reaction, a choice, or a deliberate action, behavior bridges the gap between what's happening inside and how you interact with the external world. It's where the internal and external meet, often solidifying patterns that either perpetuate or disrupt your emotional cycles.

Why does this matter? Because mislabeling what you're feeling keeps you stuck. Calling a fleeting emotion a "state" or dismissing a pervasive state as merely a mood leaves you spinning in circles, unable to break free. The key to breaking the cycle lies in precision—developing the ability to identify and understand each layer of your experience clearly. Only then can you move toward sustainable emotional rewiring.

Emotional Mud: Why We Stay Stuck

If you've ever said you're "stressed," "tense," "overwhelmed," or "exhausted," you've experienced what I call Emotional Mud. This State of Being is an aggregate of emotions, moods, and states that lack clear differentiation. Add in descriptors like "defeated," and it becomes even harder to untangle what you're really feeling. Emotional Mud is the murky, sticky place where you're so bogged down by an undefined mix of sensations that no single emotion stands out, making it impossible to address the root cause.

Why is this a problem? Because Emotional Mud keeps you stuck. Without clarity, there's no path forward. You can't rewire patterns, break cycles, or make meaningful change when everything feels like one big, overwhelming mess. The mud must be cleaned off and examined to reveal what lies beneath. To overcome this, I use the concept of Emotional Sluicing. Sluicing is a method of separating valuable material from waste, often used in mining. Imagine running water over a pan of mud to reveal hidden gems or nuggets of gold. Emotional Sluicing works the same way. By intentionally sifting through your Emotional Mud, you can identify the core emotions driving your experience and separate them from the waste—the distractions, assumptions, and vague generalizations that keep you trapped.

Through this process, you'll uncover the "nugget of gold" that holds the key to your breakthrough. It's not about getting rid of the mud entirely but about learning how to process it effectively so that the valuable parts stand out. Emotional Sluicing helps you transition from overwhelm to clarity, allowing you to recognize which thoughts and actions align with specific emotions and where the clear transition markers are in your experience.

Emotional States: The Spectrum of Response

Welcome to the messy, vivid spectrum of emotional states. While it's easy to toss every emotional experience into one generalized bucket, the reality is far more nuanced. Each state serves a purpose, even when it feels destructive. Understanding these definitions is your first step toward breaking their hold and using them as tools rather than chains:

- **Fear:** A basic and intense emotional response to a perceived threat. Fear activates your survival instincts, sharpening focus and heightening awareness, often before logic can step in.

- **Fear-shame:** An intense emotional response to a perceived threat, with the added assumption that a shame stimulus will be attached to it. This compounds the fear with a self-focused dread of judgment or exposure.

- **Anxiety:** An emotional response that generally accompanies intrusive thoughts, creating a sense of tension and prompting you to plan or strategize excessively. Anxiety acts as a mental treadmill, keeping you moving but never arriving.

- **Anger:** An emotional response rooted in antagonism or the perception that something is unfair, unjust, or needs to be addressed. Anger demands action and often serves as a catalyst for change—if directed wisely.

- **Guilt:** A self-conscious emotional response that directly ties a negative outcome to an input you caused. Guilt isn't just about feeling bad; it's about ownership of impact.

- **Frustration:** An emotional response similar to anger but internalized rather than externalized. Frustration is the result of unmet expectations, leaving you simmering rather than boiling over.

- **Apathy:** An emotional state marked by an intense lack of interest in life, paired with little to no motivation to complete even basic daily tasks. Apathy is the emotional equivalent of hitting the pause button on engagement.

- **Sadness:** An emotional response characterized by the feeling of loss or disappointment, typically paired with replaying a memory or perceiving an injustice. Often confused with frustration, sadness tends to be more reflective and passive.

Each of these states offers a unique window into your belief system and emotional cycles. By understanding them, you'll start to see how they intertwine to form patterns that can either anchor you in dysfunction or become stepping stones toward intentional rewiring.

The Three Stages of Emotional Addiction

Your Emotional Addiction Cycle operates in three distinct but interconnected stages: Origin, Protective, and Escalating. Each stage builds upon the previous, creating a self-reinforcing loop that traps you in repeated patterns of thought, feeling, and behavior.

- **Origin Emotion:** This is the brain's immediate patterned response to any form of change, instability, or the unknown. For most, the Origin emotion is rooted in either Fear or Fear of Shame. These primal responses are automatic and instantaneous, acting as the first wave of reaction before conscious thought kicks in. The brain recognizes a stimulus and perceives it as a threat, even if the threat isn't objectively dangerous.

- **Protective Emotion:** Once the brain identifies the fear stimulus, it shifts into protective mode, determining what course of action to take. Protective emotions include Anger, Anxiety, or blended states like Anger-Apathy or Anxiety-Apathy. These emotional responses are the brain's way of strategizing, attempting to neutralize the perceived threat or stabilize the environment. Protective emotions are active and tactical, pushing you into action—but often without clear resolution.

- **Escalating Emotion:** When the protective strategies fail—when the fear stimulus remains unresolved or the situation worsens—the brain escalates into its final stage. Escalating emotions can manifest in rebellious or rule-breaking behaviors, as the brain attempts to take control in increasingly desperate ways. For those with Protective Anger, escalation often turns inward, resulting in cycles of rumination and paralyzing Escalating Anxiety. This stage represents the breaking point, where the emotional addiction loop becomes most destructive.

Recognizing these stages in your own emotional patterns is crucial. By identifying which stage you're in, you can begin to disrupt the cycle before it progresses, ultimately rewiring the belief system that keeps it alive.

Common Emotional Addiction Cycles

While every individual's patterns are unique, there are seven common emotional addiction cycles that emerge repeatedly:

1. Fear → Anxiety → Anger

2. Fear → Anger → Anxiety

3. Fear → Anger → Anxiety * Apathy

4. Fear → Anxiety → Anger * Apathy

5. Fear → Anxiety * Apathy → Anger

6. Fear → Anger * Apathy → Anxiety

7. Fear → Anxiety → Frustration

A Note on Apathy and Microcycles

As mentioned in previous chapters, apathy goes beyond feeling checked out or hopeless. It's an emotional state during which a person struggles with prolonged periods of being able to even manage basic self-care like brushing teeth or getting out of bed. Sure, Netflix binging may be part of the expression, but it needs to go beyond five seasons of your favorite show in bed to include an inability to function in daily life.

Typically, where we see apathy, it exists as a microcycle that doesn't occur every time. For example, someone with an Anger * Apathy cycle might express anger consistently, but every eighth cycle, they dip into apathy. This can happen when the person burns out emotionally, and the brain seeks a pendulum swing to offset the imbalance. Often, this pendulum aligns with moving from hyperarousal states to hypoarousal states as a form of resetting.

These cycles demonstrate how different emotional responses build upon one another, creating distinct but predictable patterns. By recognizing your dominant cycle, you can begin to understand the triggers, transitions, and escalation points that keep you stuck. This awareness is the first step in breaking free from these self-perpetuating loops.

Emotional Triggers and Presentations: Why Perception Matters

It's important to remember that each individual has unique reactions and triggers for every emotion. For instance, my fear might look like anger to someone who doesn't know me well. My fear is loud, externalized, and verbal, while my anger is quiet, introverted, and strategic. Without understanding the nuanced ways emotions can present themselves, it's easy to mislabel or misunderstand what someone is experiencing—or even misinterpret your own emotional responses.

Perception matters. The way an emotion manifests can depend on context, personal history, and the specific dynamics of the moment. Recognizing these variations is key to accurately identifying and addressing the root of your emotional patterns. This understanding allows you to create clarity, reframe reactions, and ultimately regain control over how emotions shape your behaviors and decisions.

Belief Constraints and the Chemistry of Perception

Beliefs act as gatekeepers, constraining the range of choices and possibilities your brain perceives. The way you perceive reality begins a cascade of chemical reactions in your body that elicits emotion. If you perceive something as dangerous, your body might trigger a heightened fear response. But here's the key: this perception isn't objective. What might provoke your Fear response could inspire or excite someone else.

Understanding this subjective nature of perception is critical. It highlights two key concepts:

1. **The encoding of memory is subjective:** Our perception of reality influences how we encode memories. These memories are far from objective—they are shaped by the lens of our beliefs and experiences. This subjectivity extends to our emotional responses, which become tied to the way these memories are stored and recalled.

2. **Triggers hold the keys to emotional freedom:** Subtle triggers, both external and internal, are often the driving force behind emotional responses. These triggers are rarely obvious. By identifying and understanding these triggers, we unlock the potential for long-term emotional freedom.

By examining how your beliefs shape your perception and how those perceptions ignite emotional responses, you begin to break free from the constraints that keep you locked in repetitive patterns.

The Role of Source Beliefs in Emotional Cascades

A person's Source Belief Origin and Adaptive play a pivotal role in generating the emotional cascade that perpetuates their emotional addiction cycles. The sequence begins when a person observes something in their environment that triggers fear—an emotional response originally patterned by the nurture and experiences of their early childhood.

This initial fear stimulus activates the Origin Source Belief, which alters the way the person interprets the world. It constrains their perception, shaping assumptions about situations, people, and outcomes. This distorted lens narrows the range of choices they perceive as viable, forcing them into a Protective Emotion. At this stage, the brain shifts into defensive mode, crafting strategies to manage the perceived threat based on the limitations imposed by the Origin Source Belief.

As the emotional cascade progresses, the Adaptive Source Belief is triggered, guiding the individual's actions. These actions often serve as a bridge between Protective Emotion behaviors and Escalating Emotion behaviors. The Adaptive Source Belief drives the behaviors that attempt to stabilize or control the situation, but when these efforts fail, the person escalates into more extreme emotional responses.

This interplay between Source Beliefs and the Emotional Addiction Cycle is the "middle layer" previously described in earlier chapters. It is the critical junction where beliefs and emotions merge to constrain perception, guide behavior, and reinforce the cycles that keep individuals stuck. Recognizing and addressing these patterns at their root is essential for creating meaningful and sustainable change.

CHAPTER 15

THE LANGUAGE OF EXCUSE

Language: Fueling Thought and Action

Have you ever spent the day intentionally taking notice of how often your brain observes your surroundings in a narrative way? If we could listen to every thought or observation that occurs in your mind, what would it sound like? These questions lead us to a pivotal realization: language is the fuel that powers how we understand and navigate reality. Imagine tuning into the constant stream of thoughts in your mind: I'm late. My boss is going to kill me. Why are my kids acting like this? Of course I had to spill my coffee. Sometimes, this internal monologue is humorous, other times harsh, and occasionally embarrassing. It reveals random, unrelated thoughts we know to keep to ourselves. Yet, even these scattered musings typically conform to a language structure, shaping our perception and response to the world around us.

Our brain uses systems of language much like a car uses gasoline to power its engine. Language structures fuel our thoughts and actions. Every observation we make, every behavior we choose, is profoundly influenced by the way our brain generates and interprets language. Without this internal structure, our thoughts would lack coherence, and our actions would lose direction.

How Language Shapes Perception

Consider the act of observing a red circle. For an English speaker, the brain might generate the thought, That circle is red. This sentence is the result of a cognitive process that integrates sensory input with prior knowledge and cultural understanding. For someone who speaks another language, the sentence structure might differ, such as Red, is that circle, reflecting the syntactical rules of their language. While the observation is the same, the structure alters the experience of it.

This difference underscores how language frames our perception of reality. Each language provides its speakers with a unique lens for interpreting the world. As written in articles discussing bilingualism, individuals fluent in multiple languages often experience "cultural frame switching," where behavior and perception shift depending on the language they are using. This demonstrates how language connects with cultural norms and influences how individuals interpret social cues and contexts.

Language structures also influence cognitive functions such as memory and attention. As noted in studies on color perception, speakers of languages with distinct color terminology perceive colors differently, showing how language can shape sensory experiences. In these instances, the speaker of that language would understand increasing levels of nuance or differentiation. This stratification would influence them to perceive the color in an expanded and unique way.

Anecdotal evidence further illustrates this connection. Many individuals report dreaming in a new language as they become fluent, an indication of how deeply the language integrates into cognitive and subconscious processes. This shift often coincides with changes in thinking patterns, behaviors, and emotional responses, reflecting the profound link between language and perception.

Fiction Meets Reality: Language and the Limits of Perception

There is no better movie to depict this concept than Arrival. The protagonist's journey to understand an alien language leads her to a groundbreaking revelation: the structure of the language rewires her brain, granting her the ability to perceive time non-linearly. This cinematic moment isn't just science fiction; it's a powerful metaphor for a real truth. More than a tool for communication, language is a framework that dictates how we experience, interpret, and interact with the world.

As we become fluent in new languages, whether human or hypothetical alien constructs, we expand our perceptual boundaries. Just as the protagonist of Arrival learns to see beyond linear time, we too can see beyond the limits imposed by our default linguistic structures when we challenge and rewire them.

Beliefs, Excuses, and the Structure of Language

Language guides how we interpret behaviors—our own and others'—and how we respond to them. When we form a belief, rationalization, or excuse, it's constructed from the building blocks of language. Excuses, in particular, are linguistic mechanisms that protect us from discomfort or challenge. They serve as barriers to growth by reinforcing patterns of avoidance and self-deception.

To change these patterns, we first have to call out the language structures that keep them alive. Take a moment to compare "This is too hard" with "I'm finding this challenging." The first one shifts responsibility away from the speaker, setting the stage for failure before the game even starts. The second leans into agency—our ability to own what we think, feel, and do, without the crutch of excuses. Agency isn't some woo-woo concept about self-empowerment; it's the gritty acknowledgment that we play an active role in our struggles. Dismantling these patterns means tearing apart the language we use to expose the fears and lies driving our behavior. When we stop hiding behind phrases that let us off the hook, we strip away the illusion of helplessness and face the hard truth: change only happens when we own it.

Throughout many years of teaching emotional repatterning seminars, I've relied on this analogy to highlight the importance of dismantling the strongholds our subconscious has over our lives. Most of you reading this book probably have a driver's license and a car. Many of you also have children. At the time of writing this book, I have four of my own.

Now, imagine your life is a car, but instead of you—at whatever age you are now—driving, it's eight-year-old you. You'd never hand over the keys to a young child, no matter how much you love or trust them. They'd make mistakes, put lives at risk, and wouldn't understand the rules of the road. And yet, that's exactly what you're doing when you act out of the instinct of your brain pattern.

In those moments, you move into the passenger seat and toss your childhood self the keys. That's what giving up agency looks like. You have the ability to stay in the driver's seat, but you need to learn the secret language and architecture required to stay in your seat.

Beliefs, Excuses, and the Structure of Language

Breaking down the language structures behind these mechanisms shows distinct patterns. Excuse structures often depend on absolutes and external forces, with words like "can't," "never," or "forced to" dominating the narrative. For instance, "I couldn't finish because my boss called last minute" shifts accountability away from personal action to external interference. The looming question, of course, is, "But what if this really happened? Is it still an excuse?" The answer is yes: something can function linguistically as an excuse and alter behavior while also being factually true. Excuses are less about whether the event occurred and more about how language frames inevitability or helplessness, redirecting accountability and shielding us from discomfort. The same facts, presented differently, wouldn't function as an excuse—for example: "I jumped on a call with my boss at the last second as I was leaving. Sorry I didn't finish." This version maintains the factual record while taking responsibility, demonstrating how subtle linguistic shifts can drastically alter perception and accountability.

Justification structures, by contrast, use conditional logic to present actions as necessary or inevitable, often relying on phrases like "had to," "because," and "the only option." For example, "I had to skip the meeting because I needed to take care of something urgent" reframes avoidance as practicality. Justifications often rely on reasoning that appears sound at first glance, appealing to external standards of logic, morality, or practicality to absolve the individual of accountability. This creates a sense of inevitability, as if no alternative course of action was possible.

Common justifications follow predictable patterns, framing actions as necessary or unavoidable while redirecting accountability. For example, "I had no choice but to work late; it's just what's expected in my job" reframes overworking as a necessity, deflecting responsibility for poor boundaries or prioritization. Similarly, "I didn't follow through because I didn't have enough information to make a decision" casts inaction as prudent caution, sidestepping the discomfort of indecisiveness. Emotional escalation is often justified with statements like, "I had to raise my voice; otherwise, they wouldn't have taken me seriously," rationalizing behavior as a necessary response to perceived disrespect. Even self-care can serve as a justification, such as, "I skipped my workout because I deserved to rest after such a long day," which blurs the line between compassionate choices and excuse-making. Finally, avoidance can be cloaked in assumptions about others' feelings, as seen in, "I canceled plans because they probably didn't really want to see me anyway," which uses imagined scenarios to validate withdrawal and avoid vulnerability.

While some justifications are directed outward, crafted to convince others that our actions were necessary or inevitable, others exist solely in thought form, designed to persuade ourselves. These internal justifications are particularly insidious because they create a self-deceptive loop: we believe our own rationalizations, allowing us to avoid uncomfortable truths about our choices and their consequences. By reinforcing this internal logic, we repeat patterns that sabotage progress.

While justifications may appear more reasoned than excuses, they serve the same underlying purpose: to validate behavior and maintain internal comfort by minimizing cognitive dissonance. The subtle difference lies in tone: a justification doesn't just explain behavior—it defends it, convincing both the speaker and the listener that the action was unavoidable or even virtuous. By doing so, justifications insulate us from self-reflection, reinforcing patterns of avoidance and self-deception.

Rationalization takes the concept of justification a step further, operating as a cognitive distortion in which a person retroactively constructs a logical explanation for behavior driven by emotion or subconscious motives. Unlike justifications, which often serve to preemptively defend an action, rationalizations are primarily reactive, seeking to make sense of choices after they've been made. These often involve elaborate reasoning or appeals to broader principles, using phrases like, "If you think about it, this actually benefits everyone," or "It wasn't ideal, but it's better than the alternative." The goal is not just to validate the action but to present it as aligned with higher ideals, effectively masking the true emotional or subconscious drivers behind the behavior.

Common rationalizations can be identified by their tendency to overcomplicate or intellectualize decisions to obscure accountability. For instance, someone might rationalize avoiding conflict by saying, "I didn't bring it up because I wanted to keep the peace," when the real motivation was fear of confrontation. Similarly, "I spent the extra money because I deserved to treat myself after such a tough week" reframes impulsive spending as an act of self-care, avoiding deeper questions about financial discipline. Rationalizations often lean on broad, seemingly virtuous principles, such as, "If you think about it, this actually helps everyone in the long run," which casts a self-serving decision as altruistic. Another common example is, "It wasn't ideal, but it's better than the alternative," which downplays poor choices by presenting them as the lesser of two evils.

While rationalizations may seem harmless or even well-reasoned on the surface, they are a powerful mechanism of self-deception. By retroactively assigning logic to emotionally or subconsciously driven decisions, they shield us from uncomfortable truths about our motivations and patterns. This makes them particularly dangerous because they create a false sense of clarity, convincing us that we are acting rationally when we are simply justifying instinctive or habitual behavior.

Like excuses and justifications, rationalizations manipulate language to protect underlying fears, insecurities, or resistance to change. However, their intellectualized nature can make them harder to recognize, both for the person using them and for others. To dismantle these patterns, we must first become aware of how rationalizations obscure the emotional drivers behind our choices, enabling us to confront and rewire the behaviors they defend.

Shaping Behavior Without Your Permission

Defining excuse, justification, and rationalization requires understanding how each operates as a linguistic mechanism to protect us from discomfort or challenge. An excuse is an explanation designed to avoid responsibility or accountability, often relying on external factors to deflect blame. Phrases like, "I didn't have a choice," or "It's not my fault," are common examples that use language to create a sense of inevitability or helplessness. A justification, by contrast, is a reason presented to make a questionable action seem acceptable, aligning it with perceived moral, social, or logical standards. Statements such as "I had to because…" or "Anyone would have done the same," illustrate how language frames actions as pragmatic or necessary.

Rationalization takes this further, operating as a cognitive distortion where a person retroactively constructs a logical explanation for behavior driven by emotion or subconscious motives. These often involve elaborate reasoning or appeals to broader principles, using phrases like, "If you think about it, this actually benefits everyone," or "It wasn't ideal, but it's better than the alternative." Together, these structures reveal how language is manipulated to protect underlying fears, insecurities, or resistance to change. Before we can dismantle these patterns, we need to define the key terms and examine their language structures:

- **Excuse structures:** These often rely on absolutes and external forces to relinquish responsibility. Words like "can't," "never," or "forced to" dominate, creating a sense of inevitability or helplessness. For example, "I couldn't finish because my boss called last minute" redirects focus from personal accountability to external interference.

- **Justification structures:** These use conditional logic to present actions as necessary or unavoidable. Phrases like "had to," "because," and "the only option" are common. For instance, "I had to skip the meeting because I needed to take care of something urgent" frames the decision as pragmatic rather than avoidant.

- **Rationalization structures:** These often include elaborate reasoning that obscures the true motivation. Complex sentence constructions, qualifiers like "if you think about it," and appeals to broader principles are prevalent. For example, "If you consider the long-term benefits, my decision actually makes a lot of sense" adds layers of logic to disguise emotional or reactive motives.

To change these patterns, we must first recognize the language structures that sustain them. For example, consider the difference between "I can't do this" and "I'm choosing not to do this" or even "I can't do this" and "I am scared of what happens if I do this." The first statement shifts responsibility away from the speaker, while the second acknowledges agency. Dismantling these structures involves dissecting the language we use to uncover the hidden beliefs and fears that drive our behavior.

THE
LANGUAGE OF
SELF-DECEPTION

CHAPTER 16

THE WORLD THROUGH ABANDONMENT'S LENS

At the heart of abandonment-oriented patterns is a lack of trust in people's ability to follow through, keep their promises or stick around. This distrust drives you to rely almost entirely on yourself, creating a hyperindependence that reinforces the belief that, if you don't handle it or guide someone along in the process, it won't happen. While this self-reliance can make you highly strategic and situationally aware, it also keeps you stuck in cycles of control, avoidance, and emotional distance. Your brain convinces you that self-trust is safer than relying on others, but that safety comes at the cost of deeper connection and vulnerability.

These patterns may look different on the surface, but they're all rooted in the same fear: being let down, left behind, or abandoned altogether. Whether it's the overt micromanagement of Abandonment – Control to Be Safe (Overt), the quiet manipulation of Abandonment – Control to Be Safe (Covert), the shifting strategies of Abandonment – Control to Be Safe(Switch), or the self-sacrificing tendencies of Abandonment – Hold It All Together, each is a strategy your brain has developed to avoid the pain of unmet expectations. This chapter isn't designed to assign blame—it's meant to help you notice the patterns for what they are. Only by recognizing how these behaviors play out in your thoughts, language, and actions can you start to question whether they're really working for you.

Abandonment – Control to Be Safe (Overt)

Even if you feel like you're helping or protecting, chances are you often receive feedback that you're controlling, aggressive, or lacking tact. Your Brain Pattern type creates a constant sense of urgency, making it almost impossible to resist pointing out mistakes, errors, or potential disasters. Out of all the patterns, yours may be the most misunderstood. Your brain shields you from recognizing your controlling or nagging tendencies by convincing you they're necessary—after all, if you didn't step in, things would fall apart, right?

And therein lies the problem. Your brain operates in absolutes, living in black and white with little room for gray. It struggles with nuance, rarely allowing space for other perspectives or opinions. At its core, your pattern is rooted in an inherent lack of trust and faith in others' ability to follow through, do what they say, or meet your standards. And let's be honest—your standard is the only one you truly see as right, even though "right" in this context is entirely subjective. Your brain naturally scans for errors and instinctively moves to correct them, often without pausing to consider timing or the impact on the person being criticized.

Your communication style is at the forefront of your Brain Pattern-driven behavior, often creating tension and conflict despite your intention to help. What others perceive as impulsive or lacking a filter may feel, to you, like honesty or helpfulness. This is the self-deception trap at work. Your brain tricks you into destructive communication cycles that come across as controlling, aggressive, and impulsive, often lacking tact. These patterns also hinder your ability to thrive in collaboration, practice delayed gratification, and cultivate patience. This doesn't have to remain your reality—it's about to change.

The Illusions of Control: Self-Deception Themes for Abandonment – Control to Be Safe (Overt)

The Abandonment – Control to Be Safe (Overt) pattern thrives on an unshakable belief that without your intervention, everything will spiral into chaos. You see control as a duty, a non-negotiable. And yet, despite your best efforts to keep everything running smoothly, you're constantly met with resistance, labeled as aggressive, overbearing, or even controlling. It's maddening. You're not trying to dominate—you're just trying to make sure things don't fall apart. But here's the problem: your perception of necessity isn't lining up with how others experience you, and that's the deception running the show.

This brand of self-deception locks you into a black-and-white reality where you're the only one who can keep things from going sideways. Hyper-vigilance keeps you scanning for risks, convincing you that if you don't step in, disaster is inevitable. Your sense of justice is absolute. You believe you see things as they really are, and any pushback feels like incompetence or recklessness. But the harder you push, the more you isolate yourself, proving your own worst fears: that no one else can handle things, leaving you with no choice but to double down. And just like that, the cycle tightens, reinforcing your pattern while limiting your ability to trust others, adapt to new approaches, and ultimately step out of the control loop.

Breaking free doesn't require letting go of your strengths—it calls for seeing where self-deception warps your reality. What feels like responsibility to you may feel suffocating to others. What seems like efficiency to you might read as rigidity to someone else. The more you recognize these disconnects, the more you can refine your approach, without sacrificing the structure and dependability that make you you.

- **Micromanagement:** Over-involvement in others' tasks, driven by the belief that only you can handle things correctly.

- **Hypervigilance:** A constant state of scanning for potential risks, making the need for control feel urgent and inescapable.

- **Justification for over-management:** The belief that if you don't intervene, everything will inevitably go wrong, further reinforcing your need to step in.

- **Black-and-white thinking:** Your brain frames situations as absolute, unable to see nuance or adapt to different perspectives. Things are either right or wrong, with no room for gray areas or alternative approaches.

- **Justice-centric conviction:** A strong internal compass for what feels "right" or "fair," which can lead to frustration or even anger when others' ideas or opinions conflict with this sense of justice. You often fail to recognize that your perspective is subjective rather than objective truth.

- **Blindspot for collaboration:** You struggle to acknowledge that multiple ways to accomplish a task or approach a situation can be equally valid. This blindspot makes it difficult to step back, concede, or genuinely collaborate with others, perpetuating your cycle of control.

- **Overidentification with responsibility:** You equate your value with how much you can carry, leading to an inability to delegate. You believe being overwhelmed is a sign of strength, reinforcing the cycle of control.

- **Preemptive resentment:** You assume others will let you down before they even get the chance, leading you to take on responsibilities before they can fail, which breeds silent frustration and exhaustion.

- **Perceived burden of competence:** You feel that because you are capable, you have an obligation to step in, even when it's not your responsibility. The more competent you are, the heavier the weight you carry, reinforcing a self-imposed pressure to always be in control.

The Words That Trap You: Excuses, Justifications, and Rationalizations of Abandonment - Control to Be Safe (Overt)

Each pattern type operates within specific language structures, and for the Abandonment - Control to Be Safe (Overt) pattern, this language centers around control, accountability, and obligation. You don't just see yourself as someone who takes charge—you see it as your responsibility, the thing that keeps everything from falling apart. The words you use to justify your actions are the scaffolding of your belief system. Phrases like "I'm just trying to help" or "If I don't do it, it won't get done right" don't feel like excuses to you—they feel like reality. But in truth, they serve as reinforcements for a self-deception loop that keeps you locked into patterns of micromanagement, hyper-vigilance, and distrust.

These justifications create a false sense of necessity, making it feel like stepping back isn't an option. The more you assert control, the more you believe it's required, and the more others push back, the more convinced you become that no one else is capable. What feels like responsibility to you often reads as control to those around you, leading to frustration and conflict. The phrases below are indicators of the deeper patterns driving your behavior. Recognizing them is the first step toward loosening their grip.

Micromanagement:

- **"I'm just trying to help."**

  Forcing unsolicited support as a socially acceptable entry point for control.

- **"They don't see the mistake they are about to make."**

  Inserting yourself preemptively to prevent others from making decisions without your oversight.

- **"If I don't do it, it won't get done right."**

  Micromanaging under the assumption that your way is the only correct way.

- **"I have to step in, or this will end badly."**

  Escalating urgency to justify taking control of situations that aren't yours.

- **"I'll just do it myself to save time and hassle."**

  Dismissing others' efforts to maintain control and avoid collaborative friction.

- **"They don't understand how to do it properly. I have to step in."**

  Invalidating others' competence to keep yourself in the dominant role.

- **"It's just common sense. This has to be done my way."**

  Positioning your rigidity as logic and dismissing alternatives as ignorance.

- **"I'm the only one who sees the truth here, and someone needs to point it out."**

  Appointing yourself as the enforcer of reality, regardless of whether anyone asked you to.

- **"They're making a mistake, and it's my job to correct it. If I don't, who will?"**

  Assigning yourself unsolicited responsibility to maintain a sense of control and purpose.

- **"I'm just holding them accountable. This isn't about me being controlling; it's about fairness."**

  Using moral authority to justify intrusive behavior and override others' autonomy.

- **"This is going to spiral out of control if I don't do something."**

  Creating imaginary emergencies to rationalize your need to tep in and take over.

- **"People just don't see it—if they did, they'd understand why my way is best."**

  Invalidating differing perspectives to legitimize your control as superior judgment.

- **"It's not about me being right. It's about making sure it gets done."**

  Masquerading control as efficiency to avoid relinquishing power.

Justice-Centric Thinking:

- **"What they just said doesn't add up—it has to be a lie."**

  Treating inconsistency as deliberate deception to justify interrogation or confrontation.

- **"If I don't speak up, they're going to get away with this."**

  Assuming personal responsibility as the sole enforcer of truth and consequence.

- **"Why are they acting like this is okay? Clearly, it's wrong."**

  Projecting your moral code onto others and demanding public accountability.

- **"They didn't ask me because they knew I'd call out what's wrong."**

  Believing your critical perspective is feared or avoided because it threatens hidden agendas.

- **"If I let this slide, it'll just keep happening to other people."**

  Using imagined ripple effects to legitimize stepping into situations that weren't yours.

- **"There's no way they didn't know what they were doing—they did this on purpose."**

  Defaulting to malicious intent to maintain control over the narrative.

- **"How could they 'accidentally' forget? They're obviously lying."**

  Interpreting forgetfulness as strategy to justify confrontation.

154

- **"They're covering something up. No one makes that kind of mistake unless it's deliberate."**

  Assuming deception where ambiguity exists to maintain a clear villain in the story.

- **"People don't just 'make mistakes' like that—it's clearly calculated."**

  Erasing the possibility of human error to fuel a control-based correction loop.

- **"They're pretending it's a mistake because they don't want to admit the truth."**

  Reading emotional dishonesty into situations to justify your authority to expose it.

- **"If I don't call them out, they'll think they've gotten away with it."**

  Believing silence is complicity and confrontation is the only path to justice.

- **"It's not a coincidence—they knew exactly what they were doing."**

  Assigning intent to preserve the illusion of control over unpredictable people.

- **"That 'slip-up' was way too convenient to be an accident."**

  Framing error as evidence to fuel a narrative of deliberate manipulation.

- **"They're lying to save face, and I'm not going to let it slide."**

  Taking on the role of truth enforcer to maintain dominance in the dynamic.

- **"I know when someone's guilty, and they're trying way too hard to act innocent."**

  Trusting your gut over facts and demanding punishment based on instinct.

- **"Nobody forgets something that important unless they're trying to hide something."**

  Interpreting omission as strategic concealment to avoid letting go of control.

- **"I can feel it—they're just trying to dodge accountability."**

  Using intuition as irrefutable proof to justify inserting yourself into resolution.

- **"If I don't confront them, they'll keep lying and think I'm too blind to notice."**

  Viewing confrontation as necessary for maintaining respect, power, and protection.

Lack of Trust:

- **"If I don't handle it, we're screwed. Simple as that."**

  Operating from survival urgency to justify total control over outcomes.

- **"I can't trust anyone else to get it right, no matter how many times they promise."**

  Filtering promises through past betrayals to maintain full control.

- **"They'll fail, and I'll be left holding the bag. I can't afford that."**

  Anticipating collapse to stay ahead of disappointment and avoid vulnerability.

- **"No one understands the stakes like I do. If I let go, everything will fall apart."**

  Positioning yourself as the only competent adult to justify overfunctioning.

- **"Even when people say they'll help, they never follow through."**

  Using past unreliability as evidence that control is always the safer option.

- **"It's not paranoia if I've been burned before."**

  Wearing past pain as armor to rationalize chronic distrust and micromanagement.

- **"People might mean well, but they're not reliable when it really matters."**

  Downplaying others' intentions to legitimize doing everything yourself.

- **"Trusting others always feels like setting myself up for disappointment."**

    Framing delegation as emotional risk to avoid surrendering control.

- **"I'd rather stay stressed out doing it myself than risk someone else screwing me over."**

    Choosing self-imposed burden over shared responsibility to maintain safety and certainty.

Seeing the World Through Control: Observation Patterns of Abandonment – Control to Be Safe (Overt)

The Abandonment – Control to Be Safe (Overt) pattern interprets the world through a lens of hyper-vigilance, where even minor mistakes or inefficiencies feel urgent and overwhelming. The idea of letting things unfold naturally seems not just irresponsible but outright dangerous. Your brain is constantly scanning for potential failures, convinced that if you don't intervene, chaos will follow. This relentless observation fuels an endless loop of control—because the more you step in, the more you reinforce the belief that your presence is the only thing keeping things from falling apart. Over time, this pattern makes it nearly impossible to trust others, as every hesitation, misstep, or deviation from your preferred approach serves as "proof" that they are unreliable, incapable, or careless.

Beyond avoiding catastrophe, your vigilance is rooted in efficiency, precision, and maintaining a sense of order. Even when a situation isn't dire, you find yourself stepping in to correct, optimize, or refine. You see inefficiencies where others see acceptable variation. You anticipate failures before they even have a chance to happen, often assuming the worst and acting preemptively. What feels like responsibility to you can feel like suffocation to those around you, creating tension in relationships and reinforcing your frustration that no one seems to care as much as you do. This cycle of observation, intervention, and frustration keeps you locked in a self-reinforcing loop where trust becomes impossible, and the burden of control becomes inescapable. This might be your pattern if:

- You tend to notice small mistakes or inefficiencies everywhere, making it difficult to let others handle things without stepping in.

- When observing others, you often assume they'll fail or won't follow through unless you intervene.

- You feel a persistent urge to monitor or double-check tasks, even when they're not your responsibility.

- You find yourself preemptively identifying potential problems, often jumping to conclusions about outcomes before they happen.

- You see yourself as the most reliable person in any situation, which reinforces your tendency to take over.

- People's hesitation, confusion, or mistakes tend to stand out to you as proof that you need to step in.

The Cycle of Control: How the Abandonment – Control to be Safe (Overt) Pattern Keeps Itself Alive

The Abandonment – Control to Be Safe (Overt) pattern perpetuates itself through a relentless cycle of behaviors that reinforce the need for control and validation, locking you into a self-deception loop that feels impossible to break. Over-management is the centerpiece of this pattern—you can't resist stepping into others' responsibilities, critiquing, or redoing tasks to meet your impossibly rigid standards. Your unrelenting sense of accountability drives you to enforce rules and structures that aren't even necessary, all while demanding perfection and strict adherence to your way of doing things.

If that weren't bad enough, this pattern trains everyone around you to fail. Your constant need to control, paired with the speed at which you criticize or correct, leaves people feeling like they're walking on eggshells, unsure how to meet your standards. Over time, they might disengage entirely, believing nothing they do will ever meet your expectations. This passivity reinforces your belief that only you can maintain control, perpetuating the cycle and keeping you stuck in the exhausting role of enforcer. Common behaviors include:

- **Preemptive intervention:** You step in before a problem even occurs, reinforcing the belief that without you, things would go wrong.

- **Overloading responsibility:** You take on more than you should, reinforcing the idea that you are the only competent one.

• **Dismissing others' input:** You assume others' suggestions or methods are flawed, making collaboration nearly impossible.

• **Reinforcing distrust:** Each time you micromanage or take over, you prove to yourself that others are incapable, further justifying your actions.

• **Creating learned helplessness in others:** The more you intervene, the less others take initiative, reinforcing your belief that they can't handle things.

• **Internalizing stress:** You convince yourself that being overwhelmed is just the cost of making sure things are done "right."

• **Justifying control as fairness:** You tell yourself that you're just holding people accountable or ensuring things are done properly, masking the deeper need for control.

• **Building resentment:** You become frustrated that no one else seems to step up, failing to see how your interventions prevent them from doing so.

• **Ignoring when things go well without you:** Any success that happens without your control is overlooked, while failures are used as proof that your intervention is necessary.

• **Inducing hesitation and mistakes in others:** Your hyper-vigilance and controlling nature cause others to walk on eggshells, making them more prone to hesitation and mistakes out of fear of criticism or negative feedback. This then reinforces your belief that people are always making mistakes and need your intervention.

Abandonment - Control to Be Safe (Covert)

The Abandonment - Control to Be Safe (Covert) pattern is a master of disguise, hiding its need for control under the surface while still pulling the strings. If you find yourself avoiding direct confrontation while subtly steering situations to align with your preferences, this may sound familiar. You don't see yourself as controlling—after all, you're not barking orders or micromanaging. Your brain convinces you that staying behind the scenes keeps you safe while still ensuring you get what you want. Instead of openly asserting yourself, you manipulate outcomes through indirect means, ensuring that things still go your way while maintaining plausible deniability.

Unlike its overt counterpart, this pattern thrives on subtlety. A passive-aggressive comment here, a well-timed withdrawal there— your influence is quiet but persistent. But more often than not, you don't even need to be passive-aggressive—you're far more likely to let others believe they're getting their way while covertly guiding them toward your preferred outcome. You may use charm, flattery, or people-pleasing to soften resistance, making others feel like they are in control while you are the one actually pulling the strings. Being direct or transparent feels too risky, so you speak in half-truths, subtly redirect conversations, or frame situations in ways that make others unknowingly choose what you wanted all along.

The Abandonment – Control to Be Safe (Covert) pattern thrives on indirect methods of maintaining control, often giving the appearance of compliance or alignment with others while secretly working to push their own agenda. This pattern doesn't rely on overt displays of control but instead masks disagreement or frustration, pretending to be on the same page while manipulating outcomes behind the scenes. Rather than openly expressing opposition, this type may make it seem like they're fully supportive or capable of handling the situation, all the while steering things toward their preferred outcome—sometimes even making it seem like the other person's idea.

A key feature of this pattern is an inability to honestly own feelings of upset or disagreement. Instead of confronting conflict directly, they rely on passive-aggressive behaviors, subtle guidance, or strategic withdrawal to ensure things go their way. Ghosting becomes a distinct mechanism within this pattern, serving as a preemptive strike to regain control when situations feel uncertain or overwhelming. By disengaging entirely, they detach before things can go wrong, convincing themselves they're avoiding drama or emotional fallout. This withdrawal is not an absence of control but rather a strategic move to reset the dynamic or remove themselves from perceived failure, reinforcing the belief that their quiet influence is the only thing holding everything together.

This pattern also involves strategic placating, offering just enough agreement or validation to keep people feeling comfortable, while ensuring they ultimately do what you want. You aren't avoiding conflict because you want harmony; you're avoiding direct confrontation because it might expose your control tactics. On the surface, you might appear agreeable, easygoing, or even accommodating, but beneath that exterior is an unwillingness to trust others to handle things without your influence. Letting go feels like losing control, so instead, you shape situations through calculated disengagement, strategic silence, or carefully chosen words that steer people exactly where you want them to go without them realizing it.

Another hallmark of this pattern is ghosting, your preemptive strike against anything that feels uncertain or headed toward conflict. Detaching is a way to maintain control by pulling away before things can turn against you. You tell yourself it's about protecting your energy, but the truth is your withdrawal is a manipulative strategy. It may feel less forceful than overt control, but the belief driving it is the same: if I don't find a way to control this, everything will fall apart.

The result is a behavior cycle that prioritizes indirect control, preserves the appearance of cooperation, and reinforces the belief that manipulation and avoidance are necessary to prevent chaos. Below are the unconscious patterns that fuel this cycle and keep it running:

Self-Deception Themes:

• **Passive Control:** You manipulate or indirectly guide others to align with your desires, ensuring things go your way without overtly stepping in.

• **Strategic compliance:** You let others believe you're on board while subtly influencing the outcome to fit your agenda.

• **Selective transparency:** You share just enough truth to avoid suspicion but hold back key details that might give others real autonomy in decision-making.

• **Self-protection:** You use passive-aggressive or subtle methods to ensure things go your way while maintaining the illusion of being hands off.

• **Emotional masking:** You pretend to be fine with things that actually bother you, pushing down frustration instead of addressing it directly.

• **Building resentment:** You act as though everything is fine while internally keeping score, letting anger build until you withdraw entirely or sabotage the situation.

- **Inability to trust:** You prefer to handle tasks on your own but disguise this belief by subtly pushing others to take action while still keeping control.

- **Avoidance and ghosting:** Instead of taking direct action, you withdraw and disengage, convincing yourself that you're avoiding conflict or emotional fallout. This "ghosting" behavior is a form of preemptive control by detaching before things can go wrong.

- **Shifting responsibility:** You make others feel like they are in control while subtly pulling the strings behind the scenes.

- **Rewriting reality:** You tell yourself that your avoidance or manipulation isn't about control—it's just about "keeping things smooth" or "not making a big deal out of things."

- **Withholding discomfort:** You avoid expressing dissatisfaction, allowing others to believe things are fine when you are actually unhappy or disagree.

The Quiet Trap: Excuses, Justifications, and Rationalizations of Abandonment – Control to Be Safe (Covert)

Honesty—especially the direct kind—isn't exactly your strong suit. The language of your thoughts often convinces you that your actions are selfless or for the benefit of others, but underneath, they're still centered around quietly pushing your own agenda. Your brain works hard to avoid the discomfort of vulnerability or direct confrontation by framing manipulation, avoidance, and passive control as helpful or necessary. This internal dialogue keeps you from owning your true motivations, letting you believe you're protecting others or maintaining peace when, in reality, you're just steering things toward your desired outcome.

The language of the Abandonment – Control to Be Safe (Covert) pattern is subtle yet powerful, designed to maintain the illusion of being hands-off while still exerting control. This language often disguises control as helpfulness, guidance, or self-reliance. On the surface, phrases like "I'm just offering suggestions" or "I'll let them think they're in charge" sound reasonable, even considerate. But beneath the surface, they reinforce the belief that others are incapable while simultaneously justifying your need to manipulate outcomes behind the scenes.

Thoughts like, "I'm not telling them what to do, I'm just offering suggestions," or, "It's better if I step away now to avoid the drama," feel logical. But these justifications often mask the fact that you're still trying to control the situation in a way that doesn't make you look controlling. Your brain tricks you into believing you're acting for others' sake when you're really safeguarding your own comfort or ensuring things go your way.

This covert language allows you to rationalize behaviors that subtly steer situations to align with your preferences. It convinces you that you're simply being pragmatic or avoiding conflict, even as it perpetuates your inability to trust others and let go of control. Recognizing these patterns in your internal dialogue is critical because the way you speak about your actions—whether to yourself or others—is a direct reflection of your Brain Pattern's grip on your behavior. Once you start identifying these excuses, justifications, and rationalizations, you can begin breaking the cycle and exploring healthier, more collaborative approaches.

Excuses: Masking Control as Protection

- **"I'll step back and let this play out until they see they should have done it my way."** Withdrawing strategically to let failure reinforce your perspective.

- **"I already know how this is going to play out. There's no point in sticking around for the drama."** Using disengagement as a means of control.

- **"I can see the end coming and it's not going to be pretty. Better to leave before things go sideways."** Withdrawing early to avoid responsibility for outcomes.

- **"I've already seen this before. If I don't bail now, I'll be stuck cleaning up the mess later."** Justifying avoidance as self-protection.

- **"I don't want to deal with the emotional fallout, so I'm just going to step away now before it gets messy."** Avoiding emotional discomfort by preemptively cutting ties.

- **"If I don't abandon this now, I'm going to be the one left holding the bag. I'm protecting myself by cutting ties."** Using self-preservation as justification for sudden withdrawal.

Justifications: Framing Control as Helpfulness

- **"I'll just ask them questions and play it cool until they see my approach is the best path forward."** Using indirect influence rather than openly asserting opinions.

- **"Maybe if I ask the right questions and get them thinking my way, they'll do it the way that I want."** Influencing through subtle suggestions rather than direct assertion.

- **"I'll just show them the 'right' way without telling them what to do."** Influencing behavior while maintaining the illusion of non-involvement.

- **"I'll guide the conversation until they come to the conclusion I wanted them to reach all along."** Shaping discussions to subtly lead others toward predetermined conclusions.

- **"If I subtly point out the flaws in their approach, they'll realize my way is better without me having to say it outright."** Steering perceptions by planting doubt rather than openly debating.

Rationalizations: Reframing Control as Pragmatism

- **"They aren't capable of hearing my opinion or agreeing with me so I'll just do it in secret and deal with the fallout if it comes to that."** Operating covertly rather than confronting disagreement directly.

- **"It's not worth arguing over—I'll just quietly fix it later when they're not paying attention."** Letting mistakes happen while planning to correct them later without discussion.

- **"I'll agree with them for now, but I know I'll end up doing what I think is best in the end."** Giving the illusion of cooperation while still planning to do things your way.

- **"They'll realize I was right eventually, so there's no point in wasting energy trying to convince them."** Opting out of discussion while still expecting validation later.

Language of Excuses, Justifications, and Rationalizations:

Passive Control:

- "I'll just ask them questions and play it cool until they see my approach is the best path forward."

  Using subtle redirection to lead others toward your desired outcome without overt confrontation.

- "They aren't capable of hearing my opinion or agreeing with me so I'll just do it in secret and deal with the fallout if it comes to that."

  Undermining consensus by acting independently under the guise of necessity.

- "I'll step back and let this play out until they see they should have done it my way."

  Withdrawing strategically to let failure reinforce your perspective.

- "It's not worth arguing over—I'll just quietly fix it later when they're not paying attention."

  Avoiding visible conflict while maintaining control behind the scenes.

- "I'll agree with them for now, but I know I'll end up doing what I think is best in the end."

  Performing compliance to avoid pushback while secretly planning to override the decision.

- "They'll realize I was right eventually, so there's no point in wasting energy trying to convince them."

  Letting time and consequence validate your position without having to defend it directly.

Manipulative Guidance:

- "I'll just show them the 'right' way without telling them what to do."

  Using demonstration as disguised control to avoid being seen as bossy or overbearing.

- **"Maybe if I ask the right questions and get them thinking my way, they'll do it the way that I want."**

  Disguising persuasion as curiosity to covertly guide others toward your preferred outcome.

- **"They aren't capable of handling this on their own, I'll pretend to let them do it but fix things quietly behind them."**

  Performing delegation while silently undoing or correcting others' efforts to preserve control.

- **"I'll guide the conversation until they come to the conclusion I wanted them to reach all along."**

  Orchestrating agreement while maintaining the illusion of collaboration.

- **"If I subtly point out the flaws in their approach, they'll realize my way is better without me having to say it outright."**

  Using passive critique to control direction while avoiding direct disagreement.

- **"They think they're in control, but I'll steer things behind the scenes to make sure it goes my way."**

  Maintaining dominance through hidden influence while letting others believe they're leading.

Lack of Trust:

- **"It's easier to just do it myself than have to try and deal with conflict or emotions."**

  Choosing quiet control over discomfort to avoid emotional exposure or pushback.

- **"I'll just do it myself so I don't have to fix it later."**

  Taking over tasks preemptively to avoid cleanup and confrontation.

- **"I don't want to seem like I'm controlling, so I'll let them think they're in charge and come up with backup plans quietly."**

  Masking control with deference while secretly preparing for failure.

- **"I'll let them take the lead, but I'll have a backup ready for when it inevitably falls apart."**

Pretending to relinquish control while staying two steps ahead to protect yourself.

• **"It's better to stay quiet and let them think they've got it handled—I'll step in with my plan when things go wrong."**

Waiting in silence with a solution, ready to regain control without ever openly challenging authority.

• **"They don't realize how bad this could get, so I'll just prepare my own solution for when their idea fails."**

Anticipating disaster to justify secret planning and hidden control.

Avoidance and Ghosting:

• **"I already know how this is going to play out. There's no point in sticking around for the drama."**

Using predicted failure as an excuse to disengage before vulnerability is required.

• **"I can see the end coming, and it's not going to be pretty. Better to leave before things go sideways."**

Withdrawing early to avoid emotional risk while maintaining control over the narrative.

• **"I've already seen this before. If I don't bail now, I'll be stuck cleaning up the mess later."**

Preemptively exiting to dodge responsibility and protect your energy.

• **"It's not worth the effort. They won't get it, and I'll just get frustrated. I'm saving myself the headache."**

Rationalizing withdrawal by framing others as incapable of change or understanding.

• **"I don't want to deal with the emotional fallout, so I'm just going to step away now before it gets messy."**

Avoiding confrontation by ghosting under the guise of emotional self-protection.

• **"I can't keep giving myself to this situation. I'll end up drained and empty. It's better if I just detach."**

Framing detachment as a healthy boundary to justify emotional disconnection.

- **"It's easier to move on and be free than deal with this."**

  Equating freedom with control to avoid emotional entanglement and complexity.

Learning to recognize the patterns in your internal language is a critical step in the rewiring process. For the Abandonment – Control (Covert) type, these thoughts often revolve around passive control, manipulative guidance, lack of trust, and avoidance. You might catch yourself thinking, I'll let them think they're in charge, or, It's easier if I stay quiet and fix it later. These phrases feel logical, even protective, but they're part of the architecture your brain uses to keep you stuck. Right now, the goal isn't to change these thoughts—it's to observe them. In the coming chapters we learn to dismantle and rewire. Pay attention to how your brain rationalizes your actions and convinces you to avoid discomfort or vulnerability. The clearer you become about how these thoughts show up, the more prepared you'll be to rewire the way you respond.

The Invisible Scorekeeper: Observations of Abandonment – Control to Be Safe (Covert)

For the Abandonment – Control to Be Safe (Covert) pattern, observations are rarely neutral. Your brain is constantly scanning the actions and behaviors of others, not to openly intervene but to quietly justify your need for indirect control. Unlike overt patterns, your observations lean toward subtle judgment and behind-the-scenes strategizing rather than direct confrontation. You may silently catalog mistakes, notice inefficiencies, or anticipate failures, all while preparing backup plans to clean up the mess without drawing attention to yourself. Frustration builds as you watch others make choices you don't agree with or take credit for successes you feel you quietly orchestrated. You tend to view others' independence or decision-making as risky, quietly reinforcing the belief that your indirect influence is essential to prevent things from falling apart. These patterns keep you stuck in a cycle of avoidance and quiet control:

- You notice when others seem uncertain or inefficient, silently cataloging their mistakes to confirm your belief that they need your guidance.

- You often find yourself anticipating problems, not by stepping in openly but by quietly preparing to "clean up" behind the scenes.

- You interpret others' hesitation or failure as proof that your influence, even if indirect, is essential.

- You feel a quiet sense of frustration when people don't take the approach you think is best, even if you never voice it directly.

- You notice when others take credit for successes you feel you engineered from the background, fueling resentment and reinforcing your belief that being overt isn't worth the trouble.

- You tend to view others' independence or decision-making as risky, quietly strategizing how to mitigate the fallout if they fail.

- You notice when someone's behavior seems unstable or untrustworthy, and you start making plans to protect yourself or run away.

The Covert Cycle: How Behaviors Reinforce the Abandonment – Control to Be Safe (Covert) Pattern

The Abandonment – Control to Be Safe (Covert) pattern sustains itself through behaviors that prioritize control and self-preservation while avoiding vulnerability and direct conflict. Manipulation and dishonesty often play a central role, with this pattern type saying what they think the other person wants to hear while subtly steering the situation toward their own agenda. Rather than openly addressing concerns or expressing their truth, they rely on indirect comments, guilt-tripping, or emotional pressure to get their way. This creates a dynamic where the other person may feel betrayed, lied to, or blindsided when the truth eventually surfaces, often leading to cycles of conflict and chaos.

When the tension escalates, the Abandonment – Control to Be Safe (Covert) type typically already has backup plans in place, ready to move on without fully engaging in resolution. Their truth and vulnerability were never truly on the line, as they had been carefully holding themselves at a distance from the start. Whether through ghosting, passive withdrawal, or cutting ties, these behaviors reinforce the belief that deep engagement or direct confrontation is too risky. Below are the key behaviors that perpetuate this pattern, keeping the cycle of manipulation, avoidance, and indirect control alive.

Perpetuating Behaviors:

- **Subtle manipulation:** Using indirect comments, guilt-tripping, or emotional pressure to push others into making decisions they want, while not openly controlling them.

- **Passive withdrawal:** While appearing hands-off, they end up doing things themselves, using passive methods to get others to back down or align with their approach.

- **Avoidance of direct confrontation:** Steering clear of direct conflict, preferring to subtly manipulate situations behind the scenes.

- **Strategic disengagement:** Choosing to disappear or disengage emotionally before things can get difficult, often leaving others confused or frustrated without any closure.

- **Cutting ties first:** Rather than seeing things through to a resolution, they emotionally distance themselves, convincing themselves they're doing everyone a favor by "leaving them to it."

- **Running from conflict:** Avoiding any real confrontation or the potential for disappointment by avoiding situations or relationships that might require them to engage deeply.

- **Justifying detachment:** Using self-deceptive language to rationalize that disengaging is for the "greater good" or is the only logical choice, rather than facing potential failure, judgment, or emotional risk.

Breaking free from the Abandonment – Control to Be Safe (Covert) pattern starts with an honest look at the subtle ways you've learned to navigate relationships and maintain control. The quiet manipulation, avoidance, and fallback plans may feel like self-protection, but they ultimately keep you in cycles of distrust, hidden agendas, and emotional distance. Moving forward, your challenge is to catch yourself in the act—to notice when you're avoiding direct honesty, steering situations from the sidelines, or withdrawing before things get uncomfortable. These patterns thrive in the shadows of your awareness, and bringing them into the light is the first step toward disrupting them.

Abandonment – Control to Be Safe (Switch)

This pattern was built in childhood, when you learned how to adjust how much of your personality or truth to reveal depending on the perceived situation or relationship. The Abandonment - Control to Be Safe (Switch) pattern isn't about adaptability; it's about survival. As a child, you figured out that safety came from reading the room, sensing what was expected, and molding yourself accordingly. Over time, this ability to switch became second nature. Now, you don't think of yourself as controlling—if anything, you believe control wouldn't even be necessary if people just did their part. You see yourself as flexible, someone who "adjusts" to different situations, but in reality, you shift between control styles based on who's around and what's at stake. To you, it feels like self-preservation. To others, it feels like inconsistency, manipulation, or deception. They thought they knew you—until they didn't.

This pattern plays out in three primary ways: Contextual Switching, Relational Switching, and Security-Based Switching:

- **Contextual Switching:** This type changes control styles depending on the environment. You might be overtly directive in one setting—like work, where you micromanage, issue directives, and intervene directly—while taking a covert approach in relationships, where you give the illusion of agreement while silently harboring resentment. Or, the reverse might be true: you start off agreeable and hands-off in a new job or relationship, only to shift into overt control once you feel secure enough to assert dominance. The setting dictates the switch, but the underlying belief remains the same: you wouldn't have to do this if others were capable of handling things correctly.

- **Relational Switching:** This type changes over time within the same relationships. You may begin interactions in covert control mode, seemingly easygoing, accommodating, even deferential. But as the relationship or role solidifies, so does your confidence in exerting overt control. The closer someone gets, the more comfortable you feel dictating, structuring, and making decisions without leaving room for negotiation. This can happen in romantic relationships, friendships, or even professional roles. You start as the "team player" but shift to the one calling the shots once you feel secure in your position. To you, this transition feels natural— proof that you trust the relationship or role enough to be your "real" self. To others, it feels like a bait-and-switch.

- **Security-Based Switching:** This type shifts control styles based on perceived emotional or situational security. Early on, you may operate from a place of covert control—letting others take the lead, appearing agreeable, or staying under the radar. But once you feel secure in your role, relationship, or status, overt control surfaces. This can be seen in career settings, where someone starts off appearing cooperative and adaptable, only to become increasingly rigid, directive, or controlling once their job security solidifies. The same applies to relationships, beginning as the ideal, go-with-the-flow partner, only to reveal a more controlling nature once commitment is established. This switching is subconscious, but it stems from the belief that security grants permission to assert more control.

The result of these shifts is often confusion and mistrust from those around you. To others, this pattern can feel inconsistent or manipulative–like they're being played or misled. A partner, friend, or colleague may feel they've gotten to know one version of you, only to feel blindsided when your behavior changes. While this switching may feel like self-preservation or practicality to you, it often leaves others unsure of who you really are, creating cycles of conflict, mistrust, and emotional distance.

The irony? While you're shifting between control styles to maintain security, you're creating the very instability you're trying to avoid. People don't trust inconsistency. The more you switch, the more those around you feel like they're being played–unsure which version of you is real. That cycle of mistrust reinforces the fear that made you start switching in the first place. But the truth is, real control doesn't come from switching tactics. It comes from understanding why you feel the need to switch at all.

Self-Deception Themes of Abandonment – Control to Be Safe (Switch)

- **Control as adaptability:** You believe that shifting between control styles is simply adjusting to circumstances rather than a subconscious way to maintain control and emotional safety.

- **Perceived necessity of shifting:** You justify control switches as a response to others' incompetence or instability rather than recognizing them as ingrained habits.

- **Emotional risk management:** You use control shifts as a strategy to manage emotional risk, ensuring that exposure is minimized until security is established.

- **Illusion of flexibility:** You frame control shifts as proof of flexibility, when in reality, they serve as a method to maintain authority without detection.

- **Shifting identity:** You convince yourself that both control styles are authentic aspects of your personality rather than an adaptive response to fear and uncertainty.

- **Control through perceived agreement:** You believe that initial compliance or agreeableness isn't manipulation, even when it leads to a later shift into overt control.

- **Defensive justification:** You minimize the impact of control shifts by focusing on external factors and blaming situations or people rather than internal patterns.

- **Strategic withholding:** You hold back honesty, emotions, or decisions early on to maintain influence later when you can assert control more directly.

- **Security-based dominance:** You see increased control as a privilege earned through security rather than recognizing it as a shift in self-perception and behavior.

- **Avoidance of accountability:** You dismiss concerns from others about inconsistency by framing their reactions as overreactions rather than acknowledging your shift in control styles.

- **Overt control as socially acceptable:** You believe that overt control in professional settings is justified or even rewarded, reinforcing the pattern of switching between covert and overt control styles.

These patterns of thinking shape how others experience you. One moment you seem easygoing and agreeable, and the next, you're suddenly asserting authority, taking charge, or making decisions without consulting anyone. To you, these shifts feel like the appropriate response to changing circumstances. To others, it feels like they never really knew you in the first place. This leaves them walking on eggshells, unsure of which version of you they're going to get.

Recognizing these self-deception themes is the first step toward breaking the cycle. The thoughts you use to explain your shifts reinforce the pattern, keeping control at the core of your interactions while convincing you that you're just doing what's necessary.

Double-Edged Words: Language of Excuses, Justifications, and Rationalizations in Abandonment - Control to Be Safe (Switch)

The way you explain your behavior—both to yourself and others—perpetuates this pattern. You don't think of yourself as someone who switches control styles; you see yourself as someone who simply responds to the reality of different situations. You believe you're adjusting to what's needed, when in reality, you're reinforcing a cycle that keeps control at the center of your interactions. Each switch feels logical in the moment, even justified. After all, wouldn't everything run more smoothly if people just handled things correctly?

These rationalizations protect you from confronting the truth: that your shifting approach is about maintaining control while avoiding the discomfort of owning that need. The brain is brilliant at coming up with reasons to justify behavior, and in this case, the justifications serve to obscure the pattern rather than reveal it. The more you convince yourself that your shifts are necessary, the harder it becomes to recognize that they're actually feeding the very instability and distrust you want to avoid.

Excuses: Masking Control as Adaptability

- **"I'm just adjusting to what's needed."** Framing the control switch as responsiveness rather than a subconscious mechanism for maintaining control.

- **"At work, I can be direct because they can handle it. But in relationships, I have to be careful."** Rationalizing why control shifts based on perceived emotional risk.

- **"They can't handle the truth, so I'll share it with them in small pieces to test the waters."** Using selective honesty as a way to manage how much control you exert.

- **"I don't want to scare them off by being too strong too soon."** Concealing overt control early in relationships or roles but planning to assert it later.

- **"I'll just see how things play out before I step in."** Appearing flexible while internally waiting for the moment to shift into overt control.

- **"They don't need to know everything just yet."** - Withholding key information as a way to manage emotional risk and maintain control.

174

• **"I can be myself in this setting, but I have to be strategic in that one."** Believing that switching control styles is simply adjusting to different environments rather than avoiding discomfort.

• **"It's not my fault people respond differently to different sides of me."** Blaming external circumstances instead of recognizing the internal pattern.

• **"I don't want to take over, but someone has to make sure things don't fall apart."** Framing the shift into overt control as a necessity rather than a subconscious habit.

Justifications: Framing Control as Necessary

• **"If I started off being too direct, they wouldn't listen to me."** Believing covert control is a prerequisite to exerting overt control later.

• **"I only take control when I know I can do it better."** Rationalizing the switch as situationally required, rather than recognizing it as a pattern.

• **"I just mirror what's needed in the moment."** Framing inconsistency as adaptability rather than a method of maintaining control.

• **"They need to earn my full honesty."** Using perceived security as the deciding factor for when to shift from covert to overt control.

• **"If I seem too strong at first, they'll push back. I have to ease them into it."** Justifying strategic withholding of control as a way to ensure influence.

• **"They'll thank me later."** Convincing yourself that shifting control styles is for others' benefit, rather than a personal need.

• **"I wouldn't need to shift if people just handled things correctly."** Blaming others for the control switch instead of recognizing the underlying fear driving it.

• **"I don't take control unless I have to."** Minimizing how often control is exerted by focusing on perceived necessity rather than recognizing the pattern.

• **"If I don't step in now, things will get out of hand."** Justifying overt control as a protective measure, ignoring the pattern of switching.

Rationalizations: Reframing the Shift as Logical

- **"I'm not controlling, I just have different sides to me."** Justifying the inconsistency in behavior as a natural personality trait rather than a strategic shift.

- **"I don't actually change—I just react to what's needed."** Reframing switching behavior as adaptability instead of control.

- **"People think I'm inconsistent, but I'm just adjusting to reality."** Avoiding accountability for the impact of control shifts by blaming external circumstances.

- **"I have to control things differently in different settings. That's just how the world works."** Viewing shifting control styles as necessary rather than a subconscious pattern.

- **"If people just handled things better, I wouldn't have to adjust so much."** - Blaming others for the need to switch between covert and overt control.

- **"They didn't ask, so I didn't lie."** Convincing yourself that omitting key information isn't deception.

- **"I'll just ask them questions and play it cool until they see my approach is the best path forward."** Using indirect influence rather than openly asserting opinions.

- **"If I subtly point out the flaws in their approach, they'll realize my way is better without me having to say it outright."** Steering perceptions by planting doubt rather than openly debating.

- **"They'll realize I was right eventually, so there's no point in wasting energy trying to convince them."** Opting out of discussion while still expecting validation later.

The Watchful Mind: How Abandonment - Control to Be Safe (Switch) Observes and Adjusts

The way you observe the world around you directly influences how and when you shift between control styles. You're constantly scanning, cataloging, and assessing what version of yourself feels safest to present. These observations reinforce the belief that shifting control styles is necessary rather than recognizing it as a pattern that keeps you stuck. Your ability to read a situation quickly may feel like a strength, but in reality, it's the mechanism that feeds the cycle of inconsistency.

Observations differ based on environment and stages of relationships or roles. In professional environments, overt control may feel justified, even expected. In personal relationships, the need for security often leads to more covert methods. Over time, as confidence grows, the shift into overt control can happen without conscious awareness, leading to confusion in those around you. Recognizing when and how you switch control styles begins with understanding the observations that trigger these shifts.

In Professional Environments (Overt):

- You notice inefficiencies, delays, or mistakes and feel compelled to step in, believing no one else will fix them.

- You anticipate failure or missed opportunities in others, often preparing to intervene before things go off track.

- You focus on measurable outcomes and feel frustrated when others don't meet your standards, reinforcing the belief that overt control is necessary.

- You may see yourself as the "only one" capable of handling the situation, justifying micromanagement or direct involvement.

In Personal Relationships (Covert):

- You observe emotional instability or unpredictability in others, convincing yourself it's safer to manipulate from the sidelines.

- You notice when others seem overwhelmed or incapable, subtly stepping in to guide outcomes without being overt.

- You feel hyper-aware of brewing conflict, often withdrawing or strategizing to avoid emotional fallout.

- You catalog emotional reactions or inconsistencies in others to justify covert control, telling yourself you're "just keeping the peace."

Key Observations for Early vs. Late Stages

Early Stages (Covert):

- You notice subtle emotional cues in others, trying to gauge their reactions and determine how much you can reveal without risking judgment.

- You carefully assess the situation for signs of instability, strategizing ways to influence outcomes without appearing controlling.

- You catalog others' behaviors, storing observations that you may later use to justify future decisions or disengagement.

- You hold back direct comments or opinions, preferring to appear agreeable while testing how others respond.

Late Stages (Overt):

- You stop filtering your thoughts or actions, becoming more direct in expressing your opinions or taking control of situations.

- You focus on others' perceived flaws or inefficiencies, feeling justified in stepping in or taking charge.

- You feel emboldened by the security of the relationship or environment, leading to less concern about emotional fallout from your actions.

- You may justify bluntness or micromanagement as honesty or efficiency, even if it creates conflict.

Recognizing how your focus shifts between overt and covert strategies is the first step toward breaking the cycle and creating more balance in how you engage with others.

Two Faces of Control: How Behaviors Perpetuate the Abandonment – Control to Be Safe(Switch) Pattern

The Abandonment – Control to Be Safe (Switch) pattern thrives on behaviors that feel logical or necessary in the moment but ultimately keep you locked in cycles of control and avoidance. These behaviors differ drastically depending on the setting—overt in professional environments and covert in personal or intimate relationships. While this switching may seem like a practical way to navigate different areas of life, it often leads to inconsistency, mistrust, and frustration for those around you. The duality can leave others confused about who you really are, especially when your behavior shifts from one extreme to another depending on the emotional stakes.

Taking ownership of these behaviors requires honesty about how your actions might feel justified to you but have unintended consequences for others. Whether it's micromanaging in your career or emotionally withdrawing in relationships, these patterns are strategies your brain has developed to avoid risk while maintaining control. The challenge is to notice when these behaviors surface and recognize the toll they take, not just on your relationships but on your own ability to connect authentically. By observing these patterns, you can begin to disrupt the cycle and create a more consistent, balanced way of engaging with the people and situations in your life.

Perpetuating Behaviors:

- **Over-management in career:** In professional settings, you often take charge, micromanage, and feel justified in your actions, believing that overt control is the only way to ensure success. This approach tends to become more pronounced as you gain experience and feel more secure in your position. Early on, you may adopt a more covert approach—observing, quietly planning, and waiting until you feel safe enough to step into overt control.

- **Emotional withdrawal in relationships:** In intimate relationships, you tend to withdraw emotionally, ghost, or use passive-aggressive tactics to maintain covert control. This behavior is especially common in the early stages of a relationship, when you're gauging how much vulnerability or honesty you can safely reveal. Once the relationship feels secure, your behavior may shift toward overt control—micromanaging the relationship dynamics or being overly blunt and direct.

- **Inconsistent control across contexts:** You manage control differently depending on the environment, handling work and personal life—or even different stages within the same setting— in vastly different ways. This inconsistency often leaves others confused or frustrated, particularly in relationships where your early covert behavior clashes with your later overt tendencies. People may struggle to trust you or feel emotionally safe, unsure of who you really are or how you truly feel.

- **Tactical disengagement in intimate settings:** In romantic or deeply personal contexts, you may create physical or emotional distance when you perceive emotional risk or fear of being hurt. This disengagement is often strategic, allowing you to maintain control by limiting your vulnerability while observing how others react. Over time, the lack of trust and safety caused by your switching behavior reinforces cycles of mistrust and emotional distance. Eventually, you may justify disengaging entirely, believing you're freeing yourself from a toxic dynamic without realizing you've been a significant part of creating it.

Breaking the Cycle: Finding Consistency in the Abandonment – Control to Be Safe (Switch) Pattern

You shift between overt and covert strategies to maintain control and avoid emotional risk, believing it keeps you safe. But what feels like protection to you often creates confusion, mistrust, and frustration for those around you. Others may struggle to pin down who you really are, questioning whether the version of you they're interacting with is the real one. This duality isn't just exhausting—it reinforces the very patterns you want to escape. The more you shift, the more you justify either disengaging or taking over to "fix" what feels broken, unaware of how your own behavior contributes to the instability you're trying to control.

Taking ownership of these behaviors means recognizing that the strategies you rely on—whether micromanaging at work or emotionally withdrawing in relationships—are deeply ingrained patterns meant to shield you from discomfort. But real security comes from facing the discomfort of direct honesty and consistent engagement. When you stop justifying these shifts as necessary and start acknowledging how they impact others, you create the possibility of stability, trust, and emotional authenticity in your relationships and environments. Your ability to switch has helped you survive, but now it's keeping you stuck.

Abandonment – Hold It All Together: The Fixer, the Overthinker and Emotional Pack Mule

If you're reading this and thinking, I don't need this section. I'm fine. Let's move on, congratulations—you're already proving how well the Abandonment - Hold It All Together pattern runs your life. Beyond keeping the peace, you duct-tape every crack in the wall, even if the foundation is crumbling beneath your feet. You're the one who believes you can juggle your responsibilities, everyone else's emotions, and the weight of the world—while telling yourself you'll deal with your own needs later. Spoiler alert: "later" never comes.

Let's be real for a moment. You pride yourself on being the strong one, the dependable one, the person who can hold it all together. But here's the catch: your self-deception game is Olympic-level. You convince yourself that others are capable of managing their own chaos while quietly cleaning up their messes behind the scenes. You tell yourself you can handle everything—until you can't. You've mastered the art of avoiding your own emotional truths by staying laser-focused on everyone else's needs. And if conflict or confrontation starts brewing, you're ready with a half-truth or a strategic dodge to keep the peace. But the more you try to hold everything together, the more things fall apart—especially for you.

This isn't about shaming you; it's about helping you recognize how your patterns of self-sacrifice, over-optimism, and hyper-independence keep you stuck. If you're ready to stop carrying everyone else's emotional baggage while pretending you're fine, this section is your invitation to drop the facade, unpack your self-deceptions, and take a hard look at what's really driving your behavior. Common behaviors include:

- **Overgiving as identity:** You believe you are destined to be a giver and it doesn't matter that you are neglecting yourself in the process. It's all in a day's work.

- **Chaos as adaptability:** Believing that your ability to adapt to any situation and be flexible is essential and being seen as flakey is just one of the costs.

- **Lack of boundaries as loyalty:** Seeing saying yes to everything as a sign of commitment or duty even though it leads to burnout and accidentally letting others down.

- **Time blindness and overcommitment:** Convincing yourself that you can take on just one more thing, despite overwhelming evidence that you're already stretched too thin.

- **Fixer mentality:** Believing you can solve any problem, even when the situation seems untenable. After all, you always pull it off.

- **Blind optimism:** Maintaining faith that things will work out, even when past patterns suggest otherwise, leaving you open to being taken advantage of.

181

- **Unintentional enabling:** Attracting and accommodating people who rely on you to manage their lives, often at your own expense.

- **Emotional chameleon:** Constantly scanning the needs of others and adapting yourself to meet them, leaving little room for your own wants and needs.

- **Lack of self-preservation:** Dismissing personal needs and comforts in favor of making sure others are okay first.

- **Burnout as a way of life:** Viewing exhaustion and burnout as the cost of doing business rather than a sign of imbalance.

- **Humor as a coping mechanism:** Using sarcasm and self-deprecating humor to mask how overwhelmed or trapped you feel, blow off steam or share truth.

- **Mediation as a necessity:** Believing that your involvement is necessary to keep the peace, even when it means sacrificing your own well-being.

- **Resignation to overload:** Accepting that your life will always be overfull and chaotic, rather than challenging the belief that you have no choice.

- **Sacrificing for peace:** Believing that if you hold everything together for others, you will eventually find peace. Hint: It's not likely.

- **Managing others' emotions through truth filtering:** Believing that others aren't capable of handling their emotions if faced with direct honesty. You know exactly what you want to say, but you scan for whether they can handle it or if they need a slow-dripped version of the truth.

- **Avoidance of delegation and detail work:** Viewing delegation as inefficient because explaining details or hand-holding feels like more effort than simply taking over. Avoidance, delay or procrastination of precision tasks like bill paying, scheduling, or paperwork because they feel tedious or unimportant compared to other responsibilities.

These self-deceptions keep you in a constant cycle of overextending, overgiving, and over-functioning, leaving you vulnerable to being taken advantage of, burned out, and constantly exhausted. Because you prioritize keeping the peace and making sure others feel secure, you often slow-drip the truth or withhold key information, setting up situations where others later perceive you as dishonest or unreliable–even though you were trying to protect stability. This pattern creates a perception of flakiness, inconsistency, or even deception, despite your best intentions.

By filtering, compartmentalizing, and managing others' emotions for them, you unconsciously manipulate people and outcomes while convincing yourself that you're just avoiding conflict. This approach prolongs toxic cycles and enables unhealthy dynamics, reinforcing the very instability you are trying to prevent. True stability doesn't come from holding everything together for others–it comes from allowing yourself to let go, set boundaries, and engage with honesty rather than strategic omission. Recognizing these patterns is the first step toward creating boundaries, preserving energy, and learning that true stability doesn't come from holding everything together–it comes from allowing yourself to let go.

The Excuses That Keep You Overloaded and Overwhelmed

The language you use to justify your actions might seem harmless. But if you constantly find yourself overextended, exhausted, and carrying responsibilities that aren't yours, these aren't just passing thoughts; they are deeply ingrained patterns that keep you stuck. The Abandonment - Hold It All Together pattern thrives on self-sacrifice, avoidance, and emotional compartmentalization. Whether you're telling yourself "They'll figure it out–I believe in them" or "I'll just get through this moment and deal with the rest later," these justifications allow you to prioritize everyone else's needs while ignoring your own limits.

This internal language convinces you to say "yes" when you should say "no," to suppress your emotions to maintain harmony, and to take on more than you can realistically handle. But these justifications reinforce a cycle that leads to disconnection from your own needs. The result? You end up feeling trapped, stretched too thin, and unsure why you can't seem to break free from the same dynamics.

Every time you hear these excuses surface, *ask yourself*: Is this really about keeping things together, or am I avoiding the discomfort of setting boundaries? By confronting these automatic justifications, you can begin to challenge the stories your brain tells you and take back control.

Excuses: Avoiding Boundaries and Personal Limits

- **"They'll figure it out—I believe in them."** Trusting others to change or improve without accountability, keeping you in cycles of over-functioning while waiting for people to rise to the occasion.

- **"They are just going through it right now. It's going to be ok."** Dismissing recurring issues as temporary setbacks, absorbing the fallout rather than addressing the real problem.

- **"If I just give them more time, they'll figure it out."** Justifying inaction by convincing yourself the situation will naturally resolve, even when history suggests otherwise.

- **"I don't need to step in; they'll get it on their own, eventually."** Framing avoidance as trust when it's really about dodging discomfort or conflict.

Time Management Struggles

- **"Ugh, this laundry is going to take forever. I'll do it later."** Underestimating how long tasks take, leading to repeated procrastination and last-minute stress.

- **"I can get this work project done really quick, then get home for dinner on time."** (Spoiler alert: no, you can't) Overestimating efficiency, leaving yourself rushed and overwhelmed.

- **"I'll figure it out. I always pull it off somehow."** Relying on last-minute problem-solving instead of creating realistic plans, reinforcing a cycle of crisis management.

- **"I do my best work under pressure."** Romanticizing procrastination instead of recognizing it as a pattern that leads to unnecessary stress and exhaustion.

Conflict Avoidance

- **"I can't tell them the truth—they won't be able to handle it."** Assuming others will emotionally collapse if confronted, leading to habitual filtering or sugarcoating.

- **"It's easier to just tell them what they want to hear."** Prioritizing momentary peace over long-term clarity, allowing dysfunction to persist.

• **"I'll just keep the peace for now. I'll deal with the consequences later."** Avoiding confrontation until the problem grows too big to ignore, reinforcing cycles of suppression and resentment.

• **"If things get any worse, it'll be too stressful. I'll just deal with it for now."** Convincing yourself that absorbing discomfort is easier than facing immediate tension.

Justifications: Framing Overgiving as Strength

Hyper-Independence

• **"I'm fine. I've got this."** Convincing yourself that asking for help is a burden, even when you're overwhelmed.

• **"It's faster just to do it myself."** Avoiding delegation because guiding someone else feels frustrating or inefficient.

• **"People count on me to handle things. It's faster if I just do it myself."** Prioritizing efficiency over long-term delegation, assuming that getting it done quickly is more important than teaching someone else how to do it.

• **"I don't have time to slow down and explain everything."** Avoiding teaching or guiding others because it feels tedious.

Self-Sacrifice and Overgiving

• **"I just have to get through this moment, then I'll rest."** Believing stress is temporary, when the cycle of overgiving keeps repeating.

• **"I can handle it. Might be stressful, but I've got this."** Convincing yourself that enduring stress is necessary to keep everything together.

• **"I don't really have time, but I'll figure it out."** Habitually overloading your plate, assuming you'll make it work somehow.

• **"They need me—I can't just walk away."** Feeling obligated to stay in depleting situations, even when leaving would be healthier.

• **"I don't want to let anyone down."** Prioritizing others' expectations over your well-being.

• **"If I don't help, who will?"** Assuming full responsibility for others rather than allowing them to manage their own needs.

- **"I'll take care of it first, and I'll rest later."** Pushing off self-care indefinitely in favor of taking care of others.

- **"If I don't say yes, they'll think I don't care."** Associating love and loyalty with always being available, even at your own expense.

- **"They need me more than I need to rest."** Framing exhaustion as a necessary sacrifice rather than a warning sign.

- **"I always find a way—I can stretch myself just a little more."** Underestimating the impact of chronic over-functioning while assuming you can handle just one more thing.

Rationalizations: Making Self-Sacrifice Seem Necessary

Avoidance of Delegation and Detail Work

- **"If I have to help too much, I might as well just do it myself."** Viewing delegation as inefficient because explaining details feels like more effort than taking over.

- **"It's just easier if I do it."** Taking over tasks not for credit, but because it feels faster and less frustrating.

- **"I'll handle it for now; they'll figure it out eventually."** Avoiding proper guidance and letting people fail rather than investing time in their success.

- **"Details don't matter as much as getting things done."** Justifying a reactive approach instead of creating structure.

- **"I can always fix it later if something goes wrong."** Assuming mistakes can be corrected after the fact rather than prevented through proactive planning.

Compartmentalization and Emotional Hiding

- **"If I tell them X, it'll set them off. I'll wait for a better time."** Delaying honesty out of fear of an emotional reaction, reinforcing secrecy.

- **"They can't handle this right now. I'll just figure it out on my own." Taking on unnecessary emotional labor instead of letting others manage their own challenges.

• **"It's easier to just go along with things than to risk upsetting them."** Prioritizing harmony over authenticity, even at the cost of long-term clarity.

• **"They can only handle part of the truth, so I'll tell them the rest later."** Withholding the full picture to control emotional fallout.

• **"I just can't handle any more stress right now, so I'll keep this to myself."** Avoiding necessary conversations to manage personal overwhelm, often making issues worse.

• **"People don't really want to hear about my struggles anyway."** Rationalizing emotional avoidance as consideration for others when it's really about self-protection.

• **"They rely on me to be strong. If I break, everything will fall apart."** Framing emotional suppression as necessary rather than recognizing it as unhealthy.

• **"If I act like everything is fine, eventually it will be."** Using emotional masking to maintain control rather than facing underlying issues directly.

The language of the Abandonment – Hold It All Together pattern isn't just about avoiding conflict or keeping the peace—it's how you set yourself up for failure. Every time you borrow from a future that never seems to arrive, willfully ignore red flags, or convince yourself that "you'll figure it out later," you're adding to the load that eventually leaves you exhausted, resentful, or even physically sick. These justifications allow you to keep overloading your plate, ignoring the reality of your own limits while believing you're holding everything together. The truth is, the more you rely on this internal dialogue to push through, the more unsustainable your patterns become. Recognizing this language is about seeing the cracks in the foundation so you can stop the cycle before it breaks you.

Burning the Candle at Both Ends While Holding the Match

If you're someone who thrives on juggling too much while pretending you're perfectly fine, welcome to the world of Abandonment – Hold It All Together. You're the person who says "yes" to everything, thinking you can manage it all, only to end up resentful, overwhelmed, and clinging to your last shred of sanity. Sure, it might feel noble to be the one everyone relies on, but your plate isn't just full; it's overflowing. And yet, you're still balancing dessert. The problem? You're so focused on keeping the peace and managing others' needs that you're completely ignoring your own, and eventually, something's gotta give. Spoiler alert: it's going to be you.

The behaviors that keep this cycle alive don't feel destructive in the moment—they feel like survival. But over time, all that over-giving, procrastinating, and emotional compartmentalizing leaves you drained, frustrated, and maybe even wondering why no one seems to appreciate all you do. Here's the hard truth: the burnout you're experiencing is a direct result of habits that you can't fix with another to-do list or a promise to "just get through this week." The good news? Once you start seeing how these behaviors work against you, you can begin to make changes that won't leave you collapsing under the weight of everyone else's baggage.

Perpetuating Behaviors: Abandonment - Hold It All Together

- **Overloading your plate:** You take on too many responsibilities, believing that saying "yes" to everyone will keep the peace, but ultimately, you burn out. You tend to ignore your limits, assuming you can handle more than you realistically can.

- **Resentment without boundaries:** You secretly feel drained and unappreciated but struggle to voice your feelings due to fear of conflict. Instead of expressing resentment openly, you cope with humor, sarcasm, or internal "WTF" moments, feeling trapped in your own generosity.

- **Compartmentalizing emotions:** You don't fully engage with your own emotions or detach from your needs, often without realizing it. This isn't intentional avoidance, but rather a reflexive act—you're so focused on the needs of others that you become unaware of your own feelings. Others may perceive you as stoic or detached, a trauma response that stems from constantly managing the emotional landscape of the group.

- **Procrastination and time blindness:** You misjudge how long tasks will take, leading to disorganization, last-minute panic, and unfinished work. You believe you will "somehow" make it work, relying on past moments of crisis management rather than developing sustainable time structures.

• **Avoidance of real confrontation:** You use white lies, withhold the full truth, or filter information to avoid difficult conversations, especially with those you believe can't handle emotional complexity. You convince yourself that you are keeping the peace, but this only delays resolution and deepens instability in relationships.

• **Over-responsibility for group dynamics:** You constantly scan and adapt to the emotions of those around you, believing it's your job to keep things harmonious. Your own needs become secondary to managing the emotional landscape of others, leading to emotional exhaustion.

• **Self-sabotaging optimism:** You convince yourself that you'll figure things out "somehow" or that everything will magically fall into place, even when all evidence suggests otherwise. This blind optimism leads to procrastination, over-promising, and ultimately falling short—reinforcing your belief that you're failing despite your efforts.

• **Fear of letting others down:** You say "yes" to requests or responsibilities, not because you want to, but because you fear disappointing others. This need to maintain approval fuels your tendency to overextend yourself, even when it's to your own detriment.

• **Avoidance of delegation and detail work:** You believe "If I have to help too much, I might as well just do it myself." Instead of delegating, you silently take over tasks because it feels faster and easier than guiding someone through them. This habit leads to burnout and keeps others dependent on you.

• **Unintentional enabling:** You attract and accommodate people who rely on you to manage their lives because you resist setting boundaries. This cycle leaves you depleted while reinforcing the belief that others need you to function.

• **Truth filtering and emotional withholding:** You decide how much of the truth someone can handle and slow-drip honesty to avoid destabilizing situations. This reinforces your belief that others are too fragile to handle difficult conversations.

- **Burnout as a baseline:** You live in a near-constant state of exhaustion but convince yourself that it's normal. When you do rest, you feel guilty or anxious, worrying that things will fall apart without you.

- **Control disguised as helpfulness:** You convince yourself that you're just being helpful when in reality, you are controlling outcomes by preemptively managing responsibilities or smoothing over problems before they arise.

Letting Go Without Letting It All Fall Apart

If reading this feels like being gently roasted by someone who knows you all too well, good. The Abandonment – Hold It All Together pattern thrives on your ability to convince yourself you're "fine" while quietly carrying everyone else's emotional baggage. Sure, you've mastered the art of doing too much and pretending it's sustainable, but you're exhausted, and, deep down, you know it's not working. The more you try to hold everything together, the more things slip through the cracks—your health, your boundaries, your peace of mind.

Here's the thing: you're not stuck in this pattern because you're lazy or incapable. Your overachieving, hyper-motivated side has kept this cycle alive. The good news? That same energy can get you out of it. You're more than capable of creating boundaries, saying "no," and letting people figure out their own messes for once. The first step is realizing that holding it all together isn't a badge of honor; it's a recipe for burnout. So, what if you let go, just a little? The sky won't fall, but your load might just get lighter. Isn't it about time?

Observations: How You See the World Through Holding It All Together

Your brain is constantly scanning for who needs what, adjusting to meet the unspoken needs of others before they even have to ask. You've trained yourself to anticipate instability, stepping in where things seem likely to fall apart. Whether it's in relationships, work, or social dynamics, you feel an almost reflexive need to fill in the gaps, smooth over tension, or prevent disaster before it happens. This hyper-awareness of who's struggling, who's overwhelmed, and what might go wrong makes you indispensable—and exhausted.

You don't just notice what needs to be done; you catalog emotional reactions, anticipate logistical failures, and assess when and how to insert yourself in ways that will keep things running. While this ability to stay ahead of the chaos makes you feel in control, it also reinforces your belief that if you don't do it, no one else will. Over time, this becomes a self-fulfilling cycle, where people expect you to step up and handle things, further entrenching your role as the one who holds it all together.

Key Observations of the Abandonment – Hold It All Together Pattern

Hyper-Awareness of Others' Needs

- You instantly recognize when someone is overwhelmed, stressed, or floundering and feel compelled to step in.

- You scan for emotional shifts in others, automatically adjusting your approach to keep interactions smooth.

- You predict when someone might fail or drop the ball, stepping in before they even realize they need help.

- You feel responsible for maintaining harmony in social or work settings, even when no one has explicitly asked you to.

Anticipating and Managing Chaos

- You notice inefficiencies, gaps, or potential disasters long before others do.

- You often feel like you're the only one thinking ahead while everyone else just reacts.

- You see yourself as the buffer that keeps things from spiraling out of control in family, friendships, or work environments.

- You catalog small red flags or inconsistencies in behavior, storing them for later reference in case they develop into something bigger.

Over-Adapting to Keep the Peace

- You are hyper-aware of unspoken expectations and shift your behavior to meet them, even if it's exhausting.

- You notice when someone seems emotionally unstable and instinctively adjust how much truth or stress you expose them to.

- You anticipate who will be resistant or reactive and find ways to repackage honesty in a way they can handle.

- You delay speaking up about things that bother you because you assume others won't handle it well.

Silent Workload Absorption

- You take on extra responsibilities without announcing it—not because you want credit, but because it feels more efficient than delegating.

- You downplay how much you are actually doing, assuming others either wouldn't care or would see it as unnecessary stress.

- You hesitate to delegate because explaining it feels like more work than doing it yourself.

- You track dozens of loose ends in your head, ensuring nothing slips through the cracks, even if it's exhausting.

The Illusion of Holding It All Together: Why You're Actually Falling Apart

These observations shape how you move through the world—always scanning, always adjusting, always preparing for what might go wrong. You've trained yourself to anticipate instability, to step in before the cracks become visible, and to ensure that no one else has to carry what you believe only you can handle. While this makes you highly dependable, it also reinforces your role as the one who takes on more than they should. The more you notice and absorb, the more others come to expect it from you, and over time, your ability to manage chaos becomes a trap—one that deepens your exhaustion and frustration while keeping everyone else comfortable at your expense.

But here's the truth: letting go doesn't mean letting everything fall apart. The world won't crumble if you stop over-functioning, and the people around you are more capable than you give them credit for. Learning to step back makes you free—free to set boundaries, free to prioritize yourself, and free to recognize that your worth isn't measured by how much you endure. You don't have to hold it all together to be valued. The challenge now isn't taking on more; it's trusting that you don't have to. While this makes you highly dependable, it also reinforces your role as the one who takes on more than they should. The more you notice and absorb, the more others come to expect it from you, deepening your exhaustion and frustration. Recognizing how you see and respond to the world allows you to question which responsibilities are truly yours and where you might be over-functioning at your own expense.

While this ability to stay ahead of the chaos makes you feel in control, it reinforces your belief that if you don't do it, no one else will. Over time, this becomes a self-fulfilling cycle, where people expect you to step up and handle things, further entrenching your role as the one who holds it all together.

Trust Issues: Are They the Problem, or Are You?

At the heart of every abandonment-driven pattern lies the same core struggle: trust. Whether your pattern manifests as overt control, subtle manipulation, or cycles of over-giving, the underlying belief is consistent—others can't be relied on. They won't follow through. They won't keep their word. They won't stick around.

When you operate from this belief, your brain is running a program designed to prove itself right. It scans for inconsistencies, catalogues disappointments, and conveniently ignores evidence that contradicts its assumption. It's not just that you expect others to fail you—you unconsciously create conditions that make failure the most likely outcome.

Consider this: is the other person actually untrustworthy, or are they responding to the unspoken cues you're giving them? Does your lack of trust bring out their best qualities or their worst?

Abandonment patterns are a self-fulfilling prophecy. The fear of being left compels behaviors that push people away. The belief that others will take advantage fuels over-giving, setting up resentment when they inevitably take what's offered. The assumption that no one will meet your needs justifies control, making true partnership impossible. And when the pattern completes its loop, you walk away with "proof" that you were right all along—people are unreliable, ungrateful, incapable of love. But what if that proof is just another illusion built by your brain?

This isn't just about trust issues. It's about the system of language that keeps you locked in cycles of pain, rationalizing behaviors that sabotage your deepest desires. If you don't question that system, you won't change your behavior. And if you don't change your behavior, you'll keep proving your worst fears right.

So before we move forward, *ask yourself*: What if the problem isn't just who you trust—but how you think about trust in the first place?

CHAPTER **17**

THE PUSH AND PULL OF REJECTION

If rejection runs your subconscious programming, your mind is constantly scanning for relational cues—who's noticing you, how they're responding, and what their reactions mean about your worth. Unlike other patterns that focus on controlling tangible outcomes, yours fixates on social dynamics, unspoken hierarchies, and subtle shifts in behavior. The problem? Your perception isn't reality. It's a projection, shaped by your own insecurities and subconscious fears. You tell yourself you're simply reading the room, but in reality, you're overanalyzing, assuming, and frequently misinterpreting. Instead of taking people's words and actions at face value, you insert meaning, look for subtext, and assign rejection where none may exist. The more you engage in this loop, the more disconnected you become from what's actually happening, stuck in a cycle of doubt, assumption, and emotional exhaustion.

This rejection-driven loop tends to split into two major patterns, rooted in different self-deceptions. One version stems from low self-trust, where you believe you are not enough—not smart enough, not capable enough, not worthy enough—and that, eventually, people will figure it out. You hesitate to put yourself in situations where you might fail, struggle, or expose your limitations. Instead of trusting your own instincts, you look for someone else to guide the way. You may latch onto mentors, hierarchies, or authority figures, believing they have the answers you can't generate on your own. Their approval or direction becomes your security, reinforcing the belief that without external validation or structure, you wouldn't know what to do.

For some, this struggle with self-trust is compounded by cultural or religious programming that has trained them to distrust their own inner voice entirely. If you fall into this category, it's likely that from a young age, you were taught that your natural instincts, desires, or opinions were wrong—or even dangerous. Over time, you learned to comply with the moral, religious, or societal standards imposed upon you, even if they conflicted with what felt true internally. You may not even realize this internal conflict exists anymore because the conditioning has been so deep. But the underlying issue isn't that you lack the ability to think critically or trust yourself—it's that you've been tricked into believing that self-trust itself is dangerous, selfish, or flawed. The result? You find safety in compliance, following established rules or seeking external guidance because stepping outside of that structure feels like stepping into the unknown without a lifeline.

The other version of rejection-based self-deception has a significant level of self-trust yet assumes others won't see you as you truly are. You believe you're competent, capable, and intelligent, but you assume that if you express yourself fully, you'll be ridiculed, shamed, or dismissed. Your fear stems from being misunderstood or misrepresented. You assume that no matter how clear you are, people will twist your words, project their own biases onto you, or fail to grasp what you actually mean. Instead of people-pleasing, you may take the conflict-prone route, preemptively defending yourself before anyone has the chance to reject or misjudge you. You brace for impact, assuming that others will diminish or challenge you, so you put up walls, assert dominance, or push back before they even get the chance. But in trying to prevent rejection, you create resistance. The more you defend, the more people feel the need to push back, reinforcing the very dynamic you were trying to avoid.

No matter which version of rejection runs your life, the core issue remains the same: you are exhausting yourself trying to control how others see you. Whether you are performing for approval, adhering to external standards to feel safe, or fighting to be perceived correctly, your energy is spent managing perception instead of living authentically. And here's the hard truth—in the effort to prevent rejection, you actually guarantee it. Instead of forming real, secure relationships, you remain trapped in a cycle where rejection—real or imagined—becomes the defining force in your interactions.

Rejection – Control to Receive Love and Be Safe: Losing Yourself in the Pursuit of Love and Safety

Your self-deception is rooted in the need to gain security, love, and approval through compliance, performance, and doing the "right" thing. Whether you lean toward people-pleasing or conflict-prone tendencies, the underlying motivation remains the same: you prove your worth by aligning with expectations—whether they're imposed by others or self-created. It's not just about being liked; it's about being seen as obedient, reliable, or capable. This relentless drive for validation often turns into a self-imposed standard that's impossible to maintain, leaving you trapped in cycles of overwork, over-analysis, or emotional burnout.

Your relationship with self-trust shapes how this pattern plays out. If you struggle with self-trust, you likely look outward for guidance, relying on feedback, hierarchy, or external structure to feel safe. You may find yourself second-guessing decisions, seeking approval before taking action, or avoiding conflict to maintain stability. Because you don't fully trust your own instincts, you default to whatever authority—whether cultural, religious, or personal—you've been conditioned to follow. Over time, this can make it difficult to separate who you actually are from the roles and expectations you've been taught to uphold. You may comply, not because you genuinely believe in the rules, but because questioning them feels dangerous—like stepping into unknown territory without a map.

Even if you have strong self-trust, this pattern can still take hold. In fact, self-trust positive individuals often use their confidence to double down on compliance, performance, or control when their sense of security feels threatened. If you lean toward people-pleasing, you might push yourself to exceed expectations, ensuring you're seen as "perfect" or "good enough." If you lean conflict-prone, you may justify asserting control, standing your ground, or challenging others in the name of doing what's "right." Either way, the same underlying mechanism is at play—you're managing relationships through external validation, making sure you're seen the way you want to be seen.

No matter where you fall on the self-trust spectrum, the core themes remain the same: an over-focus on obedience, external validation, and relational performance. Whether you over-identify with others' needs, fear rejection, or tie your worth to your ability to "do the right thing," these tendencies reinforce the cycle of self-neglect and external dependence.

The Cost of Pleasing: Self-Deception Themes for People-Pleasing Type

If you're the people-pleasing type, your fixation on others' needs isn't as selfless as you'd like to believe. It's a strategy—a way to sidestep your own unresolved fears. You've convinced yourself that catering to others will keep rejection at bay, but all it does is separate you from your own instincts and needs. You're so focused on gaining approval that you've forgotten what it even feels like to trust your own judgment.

Your fear of rejection and conflict runs deep, driving you to suppress your own needs, desires, and opinions. For you, approval equals love or safety. But the price of that so-called approval is constant second-guessing and a dependency on others to validate or agree with your decisions. When uncertainty strikes, you freeze. Instead of taking self-directed action, you run through a mental checklist of what is "appropriate" or what others would approve of, or you defer to others entirely, making yourself a magnet for outside influence.

An opinion that goes against the grain? Forget it. You're the type who says "yes" even when the disgust with the idea is visceral. But it's your duty, isn't it? Each time you convince yourself that pleasing others is the key to being liked or avoiding conflict, you reinforce the belief that your worth is tied to performance and compliance. The result? Exhaustion and resentment. Worse still, your identity crisis leaves you increasingly vulnerable to societal and peer pressure, not to mention a dwindling sense of purpose beyond duty.

This pattern type is also extremely susceptible to intrusive thoughts. Outside influences—whether from content consumption, religious messaging, or that random story you heard from a friend—trap you in fear-based narratives. You're constantly overthinking worst-case scenarios, hypervigilant to any sign of disaster, and clinging to control as if it's your only weapon against chaos. Instead of breaking the cycle, you double down on anxiety, reinforcing the patterns that keep you spinning in place:

• **Over-identification with others' needs:** You are highly dependent on external validation and struggle to trust your own instincts, focusing intensely on others' needs and emotions. You believe that, by aligning with others and pleasing them, you will gain approval and avoid rejection. This causes you to neglect their own needs and to disregard their internal sense of what feels right or wrong.

• **Fear of rejection and conflict:** A deep fear of rejection and disapproval drives you to avoid conflict at all costs. You suppress your own needs, desires, and opinions to please others, convinced that peace equals love or safety. Your lack of self-trust means you second-guess your decisions and rely on others' reactions for guidance.

• **Freeze response and external influence:** When faced with uncertainty, you freeze or become susceptible to outside influence. Your fear of conflict or rejection prevents you from taking action, leaving you vulnerable to others' expectations or fear-based messaging. You struggle to trust yourself and instead rely on external cues to guide their decisions and behavior.

• **Seeking feedback and validation:** Rather than trusting your own instincts, thoughts, or plans, this type tends to seek constant feedback, validation, or assistance from others. You are more focused on what others think or how others feel about your actions, reinforcing their lack of self-trust. This pattern prevents you from taking independent action and often causes you to second-guess yourself in situations where you should trust your own judgment.

• **Fear of uncertainty and over-overseeing:** You fear how things will unfold without your oversight. You often ask questions, double-check, or seek feedback repeatedly, believing that you need to control the process to prevent failure. Your fear drives you to project worst-case scenarios and makes it difficult for you to think practically or calmly about how to proceed. Your anxiety around potential outcomes keeps you in a state of hypervigilance, focused on avoiding disaster rather than thinking rationally.

• **Inability to set boundaries:** Your lack of self-trust leads to difficulties setting or maintaining boundaries. You often agree to things you don't want to do, overcommit, and allow others to take advantage of your time and energy. You convince yourself that saying "yes" is necessary to be liked or avoid conflict.

• **Self-Worth tied to performance or compliance:** You often tie your sense of self-worth to how well you perform for others or how compliant you are with others' needs and expectations. This leads to overcompensating behavior where you push yourself too hard in an attempt to meet external demands, further neglecting your own well-being and sense of self.

• **Over-identification with intrusive thoughts:** You are easily overwhelmed by intrusive thoughts. Highly susceptible to outside influences, you may find it challenging to separate yourself from the thoughts. This pattern type has a strong correlation with Pure OCD and some presentations of Gender Dysphoria where the thoughts present as fear-based intrusive thoughts. This is common with fear-based intrusive thoughts about sexuality as well.

The Fight for Fairness: Self-Deception Themes for Conflict-Prone Type

If you fall into the conflict-prone type, your life likely feels like a constant war zone—not just with others, but with yourself. While fairness and justice might seem like your driving forces, the truth is often simpler: your brain is addicted to finding fault. You're perpetually fixated on what you don't have, what could be better, or how things should've gone differently. This relentless dissatisfaction taints your view of the world, leaving you stuck in a victim mindset. You don't just feel wronged by life; you're convinced someone else is pulling the strings— even if they have no idea they've been cast in your internal drama.

Your brain loves to pit people against you. It scours interactions for fault, blame, or the slightest hint of justification to lash out, pull away, or reinforce your sense of being wronged. The kicker? Most of the time, these battles exist only in your mind. You weaponize assumptions about how others think or feel, projecting your own fears and insecurities onto them as if they were objective truths. This projection fuels conflict and keeps you locked in a loop of alienation and frustration, all while the other person may have no idea there's even a problem.

This pattern also blinds you to your own role in perpetuating the chaos. While you're busy pointing fingers, you fail to see how your own thoughts, behaviors, and assumptions pull the strings of your downfall.

Your lens of victimization creates self-fulfilling prophecies: you expect others to wrong you, so you act defensively or aggressively, ensuring the conflict you feared becomes reality.

Intrusive thoughts only pour gasoline on the fire. You replay scenarios, ruminate on worst-case outcomes, and spiral into overthinking about perceived slights. Instead of letting go, you cling to control, convinced it's the only way to avoid disaster. This constant hypervigilance keeps you on edge, making even minor issues feel like battles that must be fought and won.

You're also prone to believing that "something different" is the solution to all your problems. A new job, a new city, a fresh start—you convince yourself that change will fix everything. But no matter where you go, you take your unresolved issues with you. Reality rarely measures up to the idealized version in your head, leaving you disappointed and ready to start the cycle all over again.

Adding to the chaos is your tendency to assume ill intent. Instead of opening yourself to a new perspective or collaborating to understand what's really going on, you'd rather believe you've been wronged. It's easier to lean into blame than to risk vulnerability. Challenges to your perspective feel like personal attacks, so you dig in deeper, reinforcing your own narratives of victimization.

Grudge holding and rigid boundaries are your self-deceptive tools of self-preservation. You convince yourself that these boundaries are necessary to protect yourself, but they often serve to replay your victim narrative and push others away. By keeping people at arm's length and holding onto past offenses, you ensure your isolation while reinforcing the idea that others can't be trusted. These behaviors deepen your cycle of alienation and keep you stuck in conflict.

In the end, the real conflict isn't with others—it's with yourself. Common behaviors include:

- **Justice-centric thinking:** You tend to act based on your perception of fairness, often fixating on right and wrong. This can lead to defensiveness and difficulty understanding others' perspectives, frequently leaving you feeling wronged or overlooked in situations where the other person may not even see an issue.

- **Perpetual dissatisfaction and idealization:** You're constantly dissatisfied with the way things are, believing that something better, different, or new will fix your problems. Whether it's a new job, city, or opportunity, you idealize change without addressing the patterns you carry with you, ensuring the same issues resurface.

• **Fear of being taken advantage of:** A deep fear of being exploited or seen as weak drives you to assert control over situations, often through confrontation or criticism. While this gives you confidence in your actions, it can also isolate you, as you may overlook the complexities of others' emotions or circumstances.

• **Projection and blame:** You frequently project your fears and insecurities onto others, assuming ill intent or wrongdoing. This habit creates internal conflicts that others may not even be aware of, as you assign blame or motives that reflect your own unresolved fears rather than objective reality.

• **Resistance to vulnerability and collaboration:** Challenges to your beliefs or perspective often feel like personal attacks. Instead of opening yourself to new viewpoints or seeking collaborative solutions, you dig in deeper, reinforcing conflict and alienating yourself from others.

• **Intrusive thoughts and overthinking:** Your mind is a battleground of worst-case scenarios and perceived slights. Intrusive thoughts about potential outcomes or minor issues escalate your anxiety, driving a need for control and leading to impulsive or defensive reactions.

• **Addiction to control:** You cling to control as a way to manage your internal chaos, overanalyzing situations and often blowing minor issues out of proportion. This hypervigilance keeps you stuck in a state of anxiety and prevents you from letting go of inconsequential matters.

• **Self-fulfilling victimization:** Your defensive or aggressive behaviors often provoke the very reactions you fear, reinforcing your belief that others are out to get you. By failing to see your role in creating conflict, you perpetuate cycles of victimhood and alienation.

• **Assumption of ill intent:** You're quick to believe others are intentionally wronging you or acting against your best interests.

This makes it easier to lean into blame rather than risk the vulnerability required to understand what's truly happening.

• **Difficulty seeing different perspectives:** Strong in your own beliefs, you struggle to consider others' viewpoints. This inability to step outside of your perspective fosters conflict and keeps you locked in patterns of misunderstanding and strained relationships.

• **Grudge holding and rigid boundaries:** You convince yourself that your boundaries and grudges are tools of self-preservation, but in reality, they perpetuate your victim narrative. By pushing people away and holding onto past offenses, you reinforce your own isolation and deepen the cycle of alienation.

The Stories You Tell Yourself to Stay in Control

For those with the Rejection – Control to Receive Love and Be Safe pattern, your internal dialogue is your strongest weapon—and your biggest trap. Whether you lean toward conflict-prone tendencies or people-pleasing behaviors, the excuses and justifications you tell yourself create a sense of control while keeping you stuck. These thoughts might feel logical or righteous, but they're often just a way to avoid confronting the deeper truth: you don't trust that things will turn out okay unless you manage them.

If you're conflict-prone, your internal language is all about fairness, justice, and asserting your perspective. You tell yourself that speaking up, standing your ground, or calling out what's wrong is the only way to protect yourself or others. If you're more people-pleasing, your justifications focus on keeping the peace, avoiding conflict, and being agreeable—even when it costs you your own needs. Both approaches stem from the same fear: that if you loosen your grip, you'll lose love, safety, or stability. Recognizing these thought patterns isn't easy, but it's the first step toward dismantling the false sense of control they create—and reconnecting with what's real.

People-Pleasing: A Reflex, Not a Choice

If you're caught in the People-Pleasing Variant, these thoughts might hit you in one of two ways—or maybe a messy combination of both. For some, it feels like you're constantly striving, bending over backward to meet expectations, prove your worth, or earn approval. You go above and beyond because deep down, you're convinced you need to be seen as capable, reliable, or indispensable to keep rejection at bay.

For others, this variant centers around obligation. People-pleasing feels automatic, like a reflex. You're not trying to be exceptional; you're just doing what you think you're supposed to do. The focus isn't on excelling but on keeping things calm and avoiding conflict, disappointment, or guilt.

No matter how it shows up for you, the same thread runs through it all: you're not really putting others' needs first—you're protecting yourself. Being liked or approved of feels like a shield against rejection, ostracism, or shame. Maybe you're hustling for validation, or maybe you're playing it safe and staying small to avoid rocking the boat. Either way, this pattern is about survival.

Below is a list of common thoughts that pop up when this pattern takes over. As you read through them, notice what feels familiar. Are you striving, complying, or both? Don't judge yourself; call out these reflexive patterns for what they are: mental traps you can actually escape once you start spotting them.

Excuses, Justifications, and Rationalizations in Rejection - Control to Receive Love and Be Safe

Your brain doesn't just run rejection-based patterns—it defends them. Whether through excuses, justifications, or rationalizations, your subconscious works overtime to keep you in familiar cycles by making inaction, compliance, or control seem logical, necessary, or even virtuous. Depending on whether you are people-pleasing or conflict-prone, and whether you struggle with self-trust or rely on external validation, these thought loops will take on different variations.

Excuses

- **"I can't say no—what if they get upset with me?"** You anticipate a negative reaction before it even happens, assuming that asserting your own needs will lead to rejection.

- **"I don't want to make the wrong decision and let everyone down."** You avoid making a choice until someone else confirms you're on the right path, reinforcing the belief that you can't trust yourself.

• **"I don't want to upset them, so I'll just go along with what they want."** You tell yourself you're keeping the peace, but in reality, you're avoiding discomfort at the expense of your own boundaries.

• **"What if this isn't good enough? I need to ask someone for feedback."** You outsource decision-making to avoid the responsibility of trusting your own judgment.

• **"I don't want to mess this up—I'll ask for advice or do more research first."** You delay action under the pretense of preparation, but it's really about avoiding failure.

• **"If I speak up, they'll think I'm being difficult or selfish."** You hesitate to assert yourself because you assume others will misinterpret your intentions.

• **"What if they don't like me anymore after this? I should just keep quiet."** Your need for relational security overrides your ability to be honest or take action that aligns with your own needs.

Justifications

• **"I should do this because it's what a good person would do."** You use morality as a shield to avoid addressing your real motivation: fear of rejection.

• **"I need to ask for help because I don't want to get it wrong."** Instead of trusting yourself to navigate uncertainty, you rely on others to confirm your choices.

• **"I need to check in with someone to make sure I'm doing this right."** You've convinced yourself that guidance is necessary, when in reality, you're avoiding the discomfort of self-reliance.

• **"It's easier to just do it their way than to argue or explain myself."** You justify compliance as practicality, when in reality, you're dodging the discomfort of asserting your own needs.

• **"I feel bad even asking for time to figure this out—I should already have the answer."** You equate needing time or space to process as failure, reinforcing the belief that you're not enough.

• **"They'll be so disappointed if I don't do this right."** You frame your actions as a way to protect others from disappointment, when in reality, it's about protecting yourself from feeling unworthy.

207

Rationalizations

- **"How can I be sure this is the right way? I should double check."** You tell yourself you're being thorough, but you're really avoiding the discomfort of making a decision on your own.

- **"Ugh. I'm supposed to know this—what is wrong with me?"** You turn frustration inward, reinforcing the belief that if you were truly competent, you wouldn't need help.

- **"If I don't do this perfectly, everyone will think I'm a failure."** You assume any imperfection will result in rejection, even when no evidence supports this belief.

- **"I shouldn't need help—why can't I just figure this out on my own?"** You resist asking for support, equating self-sufficiency with worthiness.

- **"I should have thought of this earlier—why am I always behind?"** You fixate on what you should have done instead of moving forward, keeping yourself in a loop of self-criticism.

- **"I feel like I'm always falling short, no matter what I do."** You reinforce the belief that no amount of effort is enough, keeping yourself in a cycle of striving and self-doubt.

No matter how your rejection-based self-deception presents itself, these thought loops keep you locked in the same cycle—one where you either avoid action out of fear, justify compliance as necessary for approval, or rationalize behaviors that reinforce your own insecurity. Your brain is running an outdated survival script, convincing you that aligning with expectations, proving yourself, or controlling how you're perceived will somehow guarantee love, safety, or validation. But the reality is, every time you let these thoughts dictate your choices, you strengthen the very pattern that keeps you feeling overlooked, misunderstood, or at odds with the people around you.

For some, this pattern is reinforced by deeply ingrained cultural, religious, or moral conditioning that has trained you to distrust your own instincts entirely. If you grew up in an environment where strict rules dictated right from wrong, you may have been taught that your own inner voice—your preferences, opinions, or desires—was unreliable, dangerous, or even sinful. Over time, you learned to override your own instincts in favor of what you were told was "correct." If you were praised for obedience, you may have internalized the idea that security and love come from compliance rather than authenticity. If this has been your experience, your rejection-based self-deception is rooted in the fear of who you might become if you stopped following the rules. The assumption that deviation equals failure, punishment, or rejection can leave you deeply disconnected from your true self, questioning what's real and what's simply conditioning.

This pattern also distorts how you see yourself and others, creating a reality based on assumption rather than truth. You might believe people expect more from you than they actually do, that they are silently judging your every move, or that they will inevitably reject you the moment you fail to meet an unspoken standard. If you're conflict-prone, you likely assume others are trying to control, challenge, or dismiss you, leading you to become preemptively defensive, argumentative, or resistant. If you're more people-pleasing, you may assume that without constant validation or compliance, you will be abandoned or seen as unworthy. In both cases, you react to a rejection that hasn't actually happened—yet in doing so, you create the very rejection you fear. You push people away, become difficult to truly connect with, or exhaust yourself trying to prove something that was never in question.

Recognizing these patterns in real time is the first step to breaking free. Your worth isn't something you have to prove, and your security doesn't come from perfectly managing how you're perceived. The real work is about recognizing when your brain is distorting reality and refusing to let that distortion dictate your behavior. Every time you catch yourself making an excuse, overexplaining, seeking unnecessary validation, or bracing for disapproval before it even happens, you have an opportunity to challenge the pattern. The more you interrupt these cycles, the less control they have over you, and the more freedom you gain to act from a place of self-trust instead of fear.

The Internal War: How Your Mind Twists Reality to Justify Conflict

If you're conflict-prone, your mind interprets, distorts, and personalizes them before you even realize what's happening. These rarely feel like self-deception; rather, they feel like truth. You see patterns where there may be none, assume motives based on your emotions, and take disagreement as an attack on your character. The moment your feelings get hurt or you feel exposed, you flip into retaliation mode, justifying your reaction as necessary self-defense.

This pattern creates a self-fulfilling prophecy. The more you assume people are trying to embarrass, control, or disrespect you, the more you react as if it's true—which, in turn, makes people defensive, dismissive, or withdrawn. The outcome? You end up experiencing the very rejection, disrespect, or isolation you were afraid of in the first place.

Read through the thoughts below and notice how they reframe personal emotions as external attacks. Instead of acknowledging discomfort, you shift blame outward and justify retaliation:

- **"They're obviously trying to make me look bad—what else was I supposed to do?"** Rather than acknowledging discomfort, your brain turns it into an attack that must be countered.

- **"They always pull this kind of crap; I'm not going to just let it slide."** Even if the situation is isolated, your mind files it as proof of a larger pattern, making overreaction feel justified.

- **"How could they say that and expect me not to take it personally?"** You erase intent and context, assuming every word or action carries deeper meaning.

- **"If they're going to act like that, they deserve whatever they get from me."** Your mind turns emotional pain into moral righteousness, ensuring you never see yourself as reactive—only justified.

- **"I wouldn't have said anything if they hadn't disrespected me first."** By shifting responsibility onto them, you avoid accountability for how you responded.

- **"They know exactly what they're doing—of course I'm going to call them out."** You assume intentionality where there may be none, making neutrality impossible.

- **"I had to defend myself—they were obviously trying to blame me."** You react to discomfort with combativeness, assuming the only way to stay in control is to fight back.

- **"It's not my fault if they can't handle the truth—I'm not going to sit here and take the blame for their mistake."** By framing harshness as honesty, you absolve yourself of responsibility for how your words land.

• **"They're acting like it's no big deal, but it clearly is—to me."** You project your emotions onto others, assuming their reaction is proof of bad intent rather than a difference in perspective.

• **"They're just being selfish because they don't want to see things my way."** Instead of recognizing that people can hold different perspectives without being malicious, you see disagreement as personal disregard.

• **"Of course, they disagree—they only care about themselves."** You make disagreement about character rather than perspective, ensuring there's no room for nuance.

• **"They're just trying to make me feel stupid because they think they're better than me."** Your fear of looking incompetent makes it impossible to separate constructive feedback from personal attack.

• **"It's not that they have a different perspective—they're just refusing to listen to reason."** You assume intellectual superiority, making it impossible to accept alternative viewpoints.

• **"They only care about winning the argument, not about what's actually right."** Conflict becomes about dominance, not resolution, keeping you stuck in a fight-response mindset.

• **"Why do they always have to make everything about them?"** You frame self-expression as attention-seeking, reinforcing the belief that only one person's emotions can be valid at a time.

• **"If they weren't so narcissistic, they'd actually consider my point of view."** Instead of recognizing competing priorities, you assume others are selfish for not prioritizing yours.

• **"They're clearly against me—they don't even want to try to see where I'm coming from."** This makes neutral interactions feel hostile, making it nearly impossible to feel secure in relationships.

Conflict Isn't Courage: How Self-Deception Turns Defensiveness into Your Default

If you're operating in the Conflict-Prone Variant, your thoughts probably feel less like choices and more like gut reactions, like you're just responding to the chaos other people create. In your mind, the problem is always outside of you—someone else's behavior, their failure to deliver, or the fact that people just don't get it. You tell yourself you're standing up for what's right or defending yourself, and any resistance you face only strengthens your belief that you're the victim in the story.

The truth is, self-deception is pulling the strings, distorting your reality and convincing you that your upset is justified. This pattern justifies itself through confrontation and blame-shifting, externalizing insecurities and redirecting your focus outward to avoid what's happening internally. Conflict becomes a tool, a way to assert control and keep vulnerability at arm's length by creating external problems to distract from internal pain.

Below is a list of common internal dialogues tied to the Conflict-Prone Type. As you read through, notice where these thoughts might sound familiar. Do they reflect reality—or just the version your mind's been tricking you into believing?

Excuses, Justifications, and Rationalizations for the Conflict-Prone Rejection – Control to Receive Love and Be Safe Type

If you operate in the Conflict-Prone Variant of Rejection - Control to Receive Love and Be Safe, your mind is rewriting reality to justify your actions. Whether you are deflecting responsibility, framing retaliation as necessary, or convincing yourself that conflict is a test of loyalty and respect, your thought patterns are designed to keep you in control of perception, performance, and compliance.

These thought loops act as mental armor, ensuring that every reaction—no matter how aggressive, dismissive, or retaliatory—feels completely justified. But the deception runs deeper than that. Your mind distorts the entire narrative so that your anger, frustration, or need for control seem like rational responses instead of emotionally driven reactions.

Below are the excuses, justifications, and rationalizations that keep you stuck in the cycle of conflict, control, and reputation management.

Excuses

- **"I wouldn't have reacted this way if they hadn't started it."**
  You frame your response as inevitable, making your emotional reaction someone else's responsibility.

• **"If I don't push back, people will think I'm weak."** You assume that every disagreement is a test of strength, where backing down means losing power.

• **"I'm just telling the truth—if they can't handle it, that's their problem."** You convince yourself that harshness is a virtue, avoiding responsibility for how your words land.

• **"They're just mad because they know I'm right."** You reframe pushback as proof of your superiority, preventing you from questioning your own approach.

• **"I don't have time to sit around analyzing feelings—people just need to get over it."** You dismiss emotional accountability to avoid confronting your own role in conflict.

Justifications

• **"If they're going to act like that, they deserve what ever they get."** You convince yourself that striking back isn't reactionary—it's justified.

• **"If I don't take control, they'll use it against me."** You assume power is al ways shifting, making conflict feel like a survival strategy.

• **"I have to defend myself because people are always looking for ways to make me look bad."** You operate from the belief that you're co nstantly being judged, making vigilance feel like a requirement.

• **"People respect you more when you don't let them get away with things."** You associate aggression with authority, believing that being liked is less important than being fear ed.

• **"I know how this goes—I've been through it before."** You assume patterns will repeat, making it impossible to engage with people as individuals rather than as threats.

Rationalizations

• **"If people really cared about me, they'd fight for me too."** You turn resistance into proof of loyalty, believing that true connection comes through struggle.

• **"I'm only this way because people don't take things seriously unless I make them."** You assume that without your intensity, people wouldn't do what they're supposed to.

- **"It's not that I argue too much—people just hate when someone smarter than them proves them wrong."** You equate pushback with jealousy, ensuring you never have to question your own rigidity.

- **"I don't need validation—I just need people to stop being so sensitive."** You reject emotional needs—not because you don't have them, but because admitting that would mean letting go of control.

- **"I don't have time for people who can't handle the truth."** You weaponize independence, convincing yourself that if people don't like how you operate, it's their loss—not yours.

How This Keeps You Trapped

These thought loops don't just justify conflict—they sustain it. Every time you tell yourself that your reaction was necessary, deserved, or proof of your intelligence, you reinforce the belief that conflict is a requirement, not a choice.

But here's the real deception: these patterns keep you locked in a cycle where every interaction feels like a test of dominance, and the only way to stay ahead is to stay on the attack.

CHAPTER 18

RIGGED TO FAIL

If you're living in the Chaos - Rejection pattern, it feels like life is one giant cosmic joke—a rigged game where you're set up to lose no matter what. You've convinced yourself that effort is a trap, a cruel tease that only pulls you deeper into failure and heartbreak. Hopelessness becomes your home base, whispering that it's safer to opt out than to risk trying. Instead of fighting the chaos, you let it consume you, shaping your identity and serving as your ever-present excuse.

The result is a slow-motion self-destruction. Maybe it's a string of lost jobs, relationships that crash and burn, or an outright refusal to engage with anything resembling stability or purpose. For you, chaos is your comfort zone. Whether it's addiction, hanging out with people who flirt with disaster, embracing joblessness, or latching onto counterculture and anarchy, chaos is the only thing that feels comfortable.

Structure? Stability? Effort? Those don't feel safe—they feel like setups for more pain and betrayal. So you stick with what you know, letting apathy and hopelessness take the wheel. Chaos becomes your armor, shielding you from the sting of trying and failing.

This pattern is rare, but it shows up often in incarcerated populations, which tells you something. Chaos - Rejection is a deeply ingrained way of surviving in a world you've decided will never be safe or fair. But survival isn't the same as living. So the real question is: are you ready to stop letting chaos steer your ship?

The Cycle of Chaos and Futility

Unlike other pattern types, you know it's your fault, yet you don't even care. You lean on a series of elaborate, well-worn narratives to explain away why effort is a waste and why the world is rigged against you (or better off without you). These stories distort reality and actively keep you in a loop of apathy and self-sabotage. Breaking that loop starts here. Has life handed you a perfect storm of hardship, heartbreak and destruction? Yes. But is that a valid reason to make sure your life ends the same way it started? No. To get you unstuck, we have to get you into momentum—something your brain pattern tells you to avoid. Commitment? No thanks. Overcoming an obstacle? Sounds like a trap. Go party or try to numb yourself from the pain of daily life? That was likely the only "yes" your brain gave you. That's all about to change. You can radically shift your life without getting a degree or wasting years away in a system that feels like a prison. You are held captive by your daily inaction and excuses. Unlike other pattern types that sabotage the big upswing toward success, you never even let yourself get started.

Chaos-Themes of Self-Deception

• **Effort equals futility:** The belief that no matter how much effort you put in, failure is inevitable, so it's better not to try at all.

• **Fear of anticipated pain:** The assumption that taking risks or trying will only lead to emotional or physical hurt, making avoidance feel safer.

• **Cosmic betrayal mindset:** The perception that life is inherently unfair or rigged against you, making success or happiness feel impossible.

• **Laziness as self-preservation:** The rationalization that avoiding effort protects you from inevitable failure or disappointment.

• **Identity tied to chaos:** The belief that chaos is a core part of who you are, making stability or structure feel unnatural or unattainable.

• **Perceived lack of control:** The conviction that your actions have no impact on outcomes, reinforcing a cycle of inaction and hopelessness.

How Chaos Tricks You Into Staying Stuck

When your brain is wired for chaos, excuses and justifications become your go-to armor against accountability. They're the logical offspring of the self-deceptive stories you've been telling yourself for years. Excuses help you dodge responsibility for why things fell apart, while justifications defend your decision to stay stuck. Together, they form a comfortable cocoon of chaos, convincing you that you're sparing yourself the wasted effort or heartbreak of being let down again. This mindset reinforces the belief that avoiding effort is a form of self-protection, locking you in a cycle that keeps chaos alive and thriving.

It's critical to remember that your excuses sound reasonable – efficient even. Your justifications all pass the lie detector of your brain. The question is: what would you stand to gain or change by observing the language and how it keeps you in a perpetual cycle of laziness and hopelessness?

Excuses

- **"I just don't care."** Rejecting attachment before it can disappoint, masking hopelessness as apathy.

- **"I wasn't feeling well, so I decided to sleep."** Using physical or emotional shutdown as a socially acceptable escape from responsibility.

- **"I can't keep a job because everyone hates me."** Assigning rejection to others as a way to justify withdrawal before facing failure again.

- **"I'm feeling _____ today, so I just can't make it." (includes suicidal ideation or vague physical symptoms)** Using distress as a shield against accountability, reinforcing the belief that functioning is impossible.

- **"There's no point in trying; it always turns on me."** Expecting betrayal from effort itself, choosing inaction to avoid confirming futility again.

- **"I'll get started tomorrow, but today's already ruined."** Deferring effort with the illusion of future motivation, knowing deep down it likely won't come.

- **"I'm not like other people. I can't do this right."** Framing identity as inherently broken to justify giving up before the world can confirm it.

- **"Nobody really understands what I'm dealing with right now."** Creating emotional distance to protect the belief that connection is hollow or dangerous.

- **"I've already failed so much, there's no point in trying again."** Using accumulated defeat to rationalize total disengagement from hope or growth.

Justifications

- **"It's not my fault that everything always falls apart. That's just the world we live in."** Blaming the world to avoid confronting internal patterns of sabotage and disengagement.

- **"Life is unpredictable; planning is a waste of time."** Rejecting structure as pointless to avoid hope, disappointment, or accountability.

- **"I like when things are messy; structure feels fake."** Romanticizing chaos to justify resistance to order and stability.

- **"Other people don't have to deal with what I deal with; it's not the same for me."** Creating separation to excuse opting out of effort or progress.

- **"I can't focus on that right now; I don't feel well."** Using emotional or physical discomfort to rationalize avoidance and non-participation.

- **"I didn't ask for this chaos—it just follows me wherever I go."** Framing instability as external and inevitable to avoid recognizing self-created disruption.

- **"Trying to be 'normal' would make me miserable anyway."** Rejecting conformity or consistency to protect a fragile sense of identity rooted in defiance.

- **"I'm not cut out for the kind of life that everyone else has."** Othering yourself to validate hopelessness and stay disconnected from responsibility.

- **"If they hadn't done ____, I wouldn't be in this position."** Projecting blame to avoid confronting the consequences of inaction, avoidance, or destruction.

Rationalizations

- **"There's no point. They're just going to fire me anyway."** Rejecting the opportunity before it can reject you.

- **"Why try to fix what's broken when it'll just break again?"** Dismissing solutions to avoid re-engaging with disappointment.

- **"I'm saving myself from disappointment by not getting my hopes up."** Framing hopelessness as wisdom to justify emotional detachment.

- **"Other people have it easier than me; they don't understand what I'm going through."** Creating distance to invalidate comparison and sidestep responsibility.

- **"If I try and still fail, it'll be even worse."** Choosing guaranteed failure over the vulnerability of effort.

- **"I don't need to try because I'm not good enough anyway."** Collapsing self-worth before effort is even attempted.

- **"I'll just wait until I'm feeling better—then I'll get it done."** Postponing action with the illusion of future alignment that never comes.

- **"It's better to quit before they kick me out."** Taking control of the downfall to avoid the sting of rejection.

- **"I'm just being realistic—success isn't in the cards for me."** Labeling defeatism as rationality to avoid the shame of hope.

- **"Even if I gave it my all, nothing would change."** Nullifying effort in advance to maintain the illusion of control in a meaningless system.

How Chaos Shapes What You See

The lens of the Chaos – Rejection pattern skews everything you observe, shifting it into the negative. When you're operating in this pattern, your brain becomes a magnet for reasons why things won't work or why you can't succeed. You fixate on what's wrong—your physical symptoms, how tired you feel, or even intrusive thoughts of hopelessness or suicidal ideation. These interoceptive thoughts act as built-in justifications for staying stuck. "I can't today" becomes your go-to, backed by what feels like undeniable evidence from your body or mind.

This pattern also blinds you to the care and support offered by others. Even when people step in to help or offer a lifeline, you either dismiss it, take it for granted, or fail to notice entirely because your focus is locked inward. You're so absorbed in your chaos that you can't see the opportunities or kindness surrounding you, further fueling your narrative of isolation and defeat. This constant dismissal of external support ensures the cycle of chaos continues unbroken, reinforcing the belief that you're on your own in a hostile world.

- **Shifting to the negative:** Constantly reframing situations to highlight what's wrong, why something won't work, or why it's destined to fail.

- **Defeatist thinking:** Fixating on reasons why you can't succeed or why any effort will only lead to disappointment.

- **Physical symptom fixation:** Using tiredness, illness, or even suicidal ideation as justifications for avoiding effort or responsibility.

- **Interoceptive justifications:** Obsessing over internal sensations or thoughts as evidence for why action isn't possible.

- **Dismissing and rejecting support:** Overlooking or rejecting help from others, which perpetuates isolation and reinforces the belief that no one cares.

- **Self-absorption in chaos:** Being so inwardly focused on your own struggles that you fail to notice opportunities or acts of kindness around you.

Why Chaos Keeps Winning

Self-deception is the fuel that keeps the Chaos - Rejection pattern roaring to life. The most destructive trick your brain plays is convincing you that effort is a waste of time. When you believe that failure is inevitable no matter what you do, why would you even try? This isn't just avoidance—it's a calculated retreat that leaves you stuck in the very cycle you claim to hate. Every chance you avoid or turn down solidifies the belief that life is meaningless. And because you've chosen to avoid the relationships, careers, and experiences that could prove otherwise, your brain gets exactly what it expects: more evidence that chaos is all there is.

Blaming the world—or anyone but yourself—is another tool of self-deception that makes chaos feel inevitable. When you believe that life is out to get you, it's easy to dodge accountability and ignore the fact that some of your misery is self-inflicted. You might dismiss help or reject kindness, telling yourself it doesn't matter, isn't genuine, or that you didn't need it anyway. This keeps you isolated, stewing in your own chaos, while the connections that could bring meaning slip through your fingers. Every opportunity you reject becomes another reason to believe life has no purpose.

But perhaps the most insidious deception is how the Chaos - Rejection pattern convinces you that chaos isn't just where you live—it's who you are. If instability and dysfunction define your identity, stability feels foreign, even threatening. You cling to chaos like it's a lifeline, convinced that breaking free would strip you of your sense of self. And so, you stay in the familiar, sabotaging any chance to build a career, relationships, or a life that could challenge your belief that the world is rigged against you. By avoiding everything that could provide meaning, you reinforce the very belief that keeps you stuck. Chaos wins because you let it.

Purpose in the Mess

You've spent so much time believing that life has no meaning that you've systematically opted out of the very parts of life that could serve as anchors or sources of purpose. By avoiding opportunities for connection, meaningful relationships, or a fulfilling career, you've robbed yourself of the proof your brain needs to see that life can be rich and rewarding. Instead, you fall back on excuses and justifications that reinforce the cycle, ensuring your deep-seated belief that nothing matters stays intact. Moving forward feels impossible, and even your raw talent often goes to waste because you can't get out of your own way.

The harsh reality is that this pattern strips away the best parts of life to protect a belief that does nothing but keep you stuck. Every excuse you make, every opportunity you avoid, and every meaningful effort you reject feeds chaos and deprives you of the chance to rewrite your story. To rewire this pattern, you must confront the lies your brain tells you and dare to disrupt the cycle by taking action, even when it feels uncomfortable or uncertain. The only way out of chaos is through it.

CHAPTER 19

BUILT TO BETRAY

Uncovering the Self-Fulfilling Prophecy of Our Unconscious Motivations

The way you experience life isn't reality—it's a mirror of your unconscious motivations. You see the world through the lens of the patterns running your brain. Every decision you make, every reaction, every repeated struggle is predictable, structured, and tied directly to your brain pattern type. Once an unconscious motivation takes root, it silently dictates what you focus on, how you interpret situations, and the outcomes you create. Over time, this repeated pattern solidifies into a self-fulfilling prophecy, reinforcing the very beliefs that drive you. You think you're responding to reality, but in truth, you're reacting to your own subconscious programming.

Self-deception is a byproduct of unconscious motivation. Once a belief embeds itself beneath the surface, it doesn't just influence behavior—it warps perception. If you believe rejection is inevitable, you behave in ways that make people pull away. If you believe you have to earn love, you structure your entire existence around performance and external approval. If you believe safety comes from control, you tighten your grip on everything until it falls apart. You don't recognize it because your brain protects the pattern at all costs—it filters out evidence that contradicts it, reinforcing the belief until it feels like fact. The moment self-deception enters the equation, you're no longer just repeating a cycle; you're ensuring it continues.

You don't see self-deception while you're in it, but once you recognize it, you can't unsee it. At that point, you either rewire the pattern or admit you're choosing the cycle. Every brain pattern type has a set of unconscious motivations that are measurable, predictable, and rewirable. Once you uncover the exact patterns driving your behaviors, you can dismantle them with accuracy. But if you refuse to examine what's underneath, you'll keep walking straight into the outcomes you claim to hate, never stopping to question how you got there.

Unconscious Motivations of Abandonment – Control to Be Safe (Overt Control)

To those around you, it might seem like you're controlling, rigid, or overly aggressive–but to you, control provides survival and prevents disaster. Your brain has wired you to believe that if you don't enforce structure, anticipate problems, and hold the line, everything will fall apart. Chaos is never an option. So you plan, correct, and control, making sure everything and everyone is operating exactly as they should.

You don't do this for the sake of control itself–you do it because the alternative feels like disaster. If you relax, things will go wrong. People will fail. You'll fail. And failure is unacceptable. So you push harder, demand more, and tighten your grip. What you don't see is that the more you force control, the more unstable things become. The more you enforce compliance, the more people resist. The more you micromanage, the more things slip through your fingers. The more forcefully you react, the more chaos you create.

At its core, this isn't about dominance but fear–fear of losing control, of things falling apart, of being vulnerable, of being abandoned. But your solution–tightening your grip, dictating outcomes, shutting down alternatives–only isolates you further. Your unconscious motivations convince you that your way is the only safe way, but in reality, these thought patterns are keeping you stuck:

> • **Maintaining control, even at the expense of others' emotions or experiences:** Keeping order feels more important than how others feel about it.

• **Keeping people safe, even at the expense of criticizing or ordering them around:** If you don't enforce the rules, disaster feels inevitable.

• **Anticipating and preventing worst-case scenarios, even if it creates unnecessary rigidity:** Structure and strict rules feel like the only way to avoid failure or chaos.

• **Preemptively enforcing discipline, even if it leads to conflict:** It feels better to correct or criticize now than deal with a perceived disaster later.

• **Avoiding chaos, even if it means generating volatility through emotional outbursts:** Emotional explosions feel like a justified way to restore order.

• **Ensuring compliance, even if it makes others feel controlled or disrespected:** Deviations from your expectations feel like threats, not just differences.

• **Proving your way is the only safe way, even if it shuts down collaboration:** Entertaining alternative approaches feels reckless and unsafe.

• **Forcing immediate course correction, even if it creates instability:** Reacting forcefully feels necessary to stop things from spiraling out of control.

• **Preserving personal authority, even if it damages relationships:** Challenges to your methods feel like direct threats to safety.

• **Minimizing perceived risk, even if it means rejecting new information or perspectives:** Your brain tells you the safest way forward, and anything outside that feels dangerous.

• **Protecting yourself from vulnerability, even if it means pushing people away:** Emotional openness feels like a weakness that could lead to abandonment or failure.

• **Maintaining order, even if it creates an environment where others walk on eggshells:** You believe strict enforcement of structure prevents chaos, unaware that your rigidity generates instability.

• **Reacting forcefully to perceived threats, even if it means escalating minor issues into full-blown conflict:** You don't recognize that your own hypervigilance and quick-trigger anger amplify problems rather than solve them.

• **Being the authority on what is "right," even if it isolates you:** If you don't control the situation, you assume everything will go wrong.

• **Avoiding perceived failure, even if it means overcorrecting, micromanaging, or never delegating:** Trusting others to take responsibility feels too risky.

• **Enforcing personal standards, even if it causes resentment or resistance:** You believe that without strict adherence to your expectations, disaster is inevitable.

Unconscious Motivations of Abandonment – Control to Be Safe (Covert)
The Control You Don't Admit to Yourself

You know exactly what you want. You always have. But you don't demand it outright—that would make it too easy for people to challenge you. Instead, you maneuver. You adjust, redirect, and plant seeds that push things in your favor, all while keeping your hands clean. You don't need to argue when you can outthink. You don't need to control openly when you can control quietly.

You're not reckless—you're strategic. You know when to stay quiet, when to withhold just enough, and when to let people believe they're leading when, in reality, they're walking right into the outcome you intended. You compartmentalize, not out of dishonesty, but because giving people full access would mean giving up leverage. Certain details stay hidden, certain mistakes get swept away, and certain truths don't need to be said if they might get in the way.

You're not an open book, but you make people think you are. That's the game.

And when something threatens your position? You won't fight it head-on—you'll slip through the cracks before anyone notices. You'll evade, reframe, or quietly undo what isn't working, making sure you still land on your feet. If it starts to spiral beyond repair, you'll be the one to walk away first—because losing control isn't an option.

You tell yourself you're adaptable, that you do what needs to be done. But adaptability is just a tool to get where you were already planning to go. And as long as you can keep playing the game, you never have to *ask yourself* the real question: what happens when no one—not even you—knows the full truth?

- **Maintaining silent control, even at the expense of honesty or transparency:** You present as agreeable, but beneath the surface, you're still quietly maneuvering things to go your way.

- **Keeping up appearances, even at the expense of facing the truth of a situation:** You justify avoiding tough conversations or realities by telling yourself you're just keeping things "normal" for now.

- **Anticipating and preventing worst-case scenarios, even if it means quietly managing people or outcomes behind the scenes:** You ensure nothing spirals out of control, even if it requires subtle interference or withholding information.

- **Keeping frustrations private, even at the expense of direct communication:** Instead of addressing issues head-on, you let resentment simmer and make passive-aggressive adjustments in silence.

- **Avoiding looking like the problem, even if it means subtly shifting blame or covering it up:** You don't outright lie, but you present situations in ways that make you look reasonable while making others seem unreliable or you bought yourself some time to fix it before they come back.

- **Steering situations subtly, even if it means setting others up to fail:** Your lack of full transparency causes others to misstep, reinforcing your belief that people can't be trusted to handle things properly.

- **Avoiding exposure, even if it means becoming evasive or selectively absent:** If a situation threatens to reveal a mistake, weakness, or messy reality, you find ways to disappear, delay, or redirect.

- **Controlling the narrative, even if it means omitting key details:** You curate what people know about you, ensuring the version of your life you present remains intact.

• **Preserving personal autonomy, even if it means keeping emotional distance:** You allow connection to a point but always maintain an internal 'exit strategy' to avoid feeling trapped.

• **Preventing failure, even if it means never fully committing:** You hedge your bets, keeping options open so you can quickly pivot if something doesn't go your way.

• **Maintaining control of perception, even if it means keeping your true thoughts and struggles hidden:** You tell yourself you're protecting others, but in reality, you're protecting your own image.

• **Leaving before you can be left, even if it means self-sabotaging something good:** If you sense instability, you'd rather destroy the situation on your own terms than risk losing control.

• **Framing your exits as necessary, even if it leaves others blindsided:** Instead of acknowledging your role in relational struggles, you convince yourself that walking away is best for everyone.

• **Avoiding accountability, even if it means denying mistakes until absolutely necessary:** You delay admitting failure, assuming you'll have time to fix things before anyone notices.

• **Minimizing emotional risk, even if it means never being fully seen:** By keeping parts of yourself private, you ensure you never feel too exposed or vulnerable.

• **Easing discomfort, even if it means ghosting and starting over:** Rather than dealing with confrontation or difficult emotions, you justify cutting ties and moving on as "self-preservation."

• **Appearing flexible, even if you've already decided how things will go:** You let others believe they have a say, but in reality, you're just managing perception while sticking to your own plan.

• **Avoiding perceived failure, even if it means keeping people at arm's length:** You'll engage, but only in ways that ensure you're not overly dependent or vulnerable to disappointment.

• **Protecting your pride, even if it means eroding trust:** You'd rather manipulate how you're perceived than risk being truly known, even if it creates distance in your relationships.

Unconscious Motivations for Abandonment - Control to Be Safe (Switch)

Shifting between control styles is something your brain has convinced you is necessary for survival. You see it as adapting to what's required in each situation. In your mind, control isn't about dominance—it's about making things work, ensuring stability, and preventing unnecessary disruptions. But this shifting is the byproduct of a brain wired to avoid perceived threats at all costs. Instead of responding to reality as it is, you're constantly calculating the safest way to maintain control without setting off alarms in those around you.

This pattern was built in childhood, where you learned that different situations demanded different versions of you. At times, you had to be agreeable, accommodating, or invisible to avoid conflict. Other times, you had to step up, take charge, or subtly steer the outcome to prevent chaos. Over time, these shifts became second nature—you don't consciously decide to switch control styles; your brain does it automatically. You might start off easygoing in relationships, only to shift into a more directive role once you feel secure. Or, in a professional setting, you might initially hold back before gradually asserting yourself as the decision-maker. To you, these adjustments feel like natural responses to the world. To others, they feel like deception, manipulation, or an unpredictable shift in behavior that leaves them questioning which version of you is real.

The more you shift, the more unstable your relationships and environments become, reinforcing your belief that you can't ever fully let go. The people around you don't trust your consistency, and deep down, neither do you. Recognizing these unconscious motivations is about seeing the pattern for what it is: a survival strategy that no longer serves you.

Contextual Switching: Control Shifts Based on Environment

- **Maintaining control while appearing flexible, even if it means disguising your true nature:** You shift between control styles depending on what will be most effective in a given setting, ensuring you are never perceived as controlling while still influencing outcomes.

• **Avoiding the appearance of being controlling, even if it means manipulating from the background:** You believe you must adapt your control style based on what others will tolerate, presenting as easygoing while covertly ensuring things go your way.

• **Testing the waters before fully asserting control, even if it means initially holding back:** You subtly assess a new environment, strategically determining when and how much control to exert without triggering resistance.

• **Justifying shifts as necessary for stability, even if it creates more chaos:** You convince yourself that adjusting control styles is what keeps things from falling apart, when in reality, the inconsistency creates uncertainty for those around you.

• **Managing perception, even if it means being different versions of yourself in different settings:** You curate how others see you, shifting between authoritative and agreeable based on what will maintain your influence.

• **Avoiding accountability for control, even if it leads to distrust:** You downplay the moments when you exert control by pointing to times when you were passive, ensuring no one can ever pin down your true nature.

Relational Switching: Control Shifts Over Time Within the Same Relationship

• **Earning the right to take control, even if it means starting off in disguise:** You believe that control must be "earned" through initial compliance, appearing accommodating at first and shifting into overt control once trust is secured.

• **Protecting against rejection, even if it means masking your real tendencies:** You fear that being overtly controlling too soon will push others away, so you play the role of the agreeable partner, friend, or colleague until you feel secure enough to take charge.

• **Avoiding exposure or weakness, even if it means hiding your real thoughts and intentions:** You hold back in relationships, carefully managing what others see of you until you feel safe enough to assert dominance.

• **Preemptively adjusting to avoid confrontation, even if it means**

never truly being seen: You instinctively shift between passive and assertive control styles based on how you predict someone will respond, ensuring you never experience direct conflict.

• **Ensuring stability by controlling change, even if it means micromanaging relationships:** You subtly adjust your behavior based on the emotional climate, becoming more accommodating when people pull away and more controlling when they come closer.

• **Securing a safety net, even if it means leaving people confused about who you really are:** By switching control styles over time, you create an exit strategy—if something goes wrong, you can blame circumstances rather than acknowledging your inconsistency.

Security-Based Switching: Control Shifts Based on Perceived Emotional or Situational Security

• **Viewing control as a privilege earned through security, even if it catches others off guard:** You believe that once you've established trust or status, you are entitled to exert more control, framing it as a natural progression rather than a shift in behavior.

• **Avoiding loss of influence, even if it means changing tactics mid-relationship or career:** You start off appearing passive to maintain approval, but once you feel secure, you assert control to ensure your position remains dominant.

• **Using control shifts to prevent uncertainty, even if it erodes trust:** When you feel insecure, you adopt a passive approach, gathering information and avoiding risk. Once you feel confident, you become more direct, making others question which version of you is real.

• **Ensuring people don't change their minds about you, even if it requires constant adaptation:** You subtly shift between control styles to maintain relationships, making sure no one realizes how much effort you put into managing their perception of you.

• **Reinforcing the belief that others can't be trusted, even if it isolates you:** Every time you shift control styles to maintain security, you convince yourself that no one else is capable of handling things, ensuring you never fully relinquish control.

233

Breaking the Cycle

This pattern convinces you that switching control styles keeps you safe, but all it really does is create instability, mistrust, and emotional exhaustion—for you and everyone around you. The more you justify these shifts, the harder it becomes to recognize that they're rooted in fear. Recognizing this means gaining real control, the kind that doesn't require deception, justification, or constantly shifting between versions of yourself.

Unconscious Motivations of Abandonment - Hold It All Together

You've learned to navigate the world by anticipating what people need before they even ask. You scan for potential problems, sense when emotions are shifting, and adjust accordingly—all without anyone realizing what you're doing. Your role is to keep everything running smoothly so no one has to feel uncomfortable. You do this because you believe others can't handle things without you.

You tell yourself that your sacrifices are necessary. That absorbing blame, smoothing over tension, and keeping people happy is the price you pay for stability. You manage situations behind the scenes, soften truths to avoid conflict, and overextend yourself to prevent disappointment. You rarely ask, "What do I need?" because in your mind, your needs have never been the priority. Survival means making sure everything is okay, even if that means slowly erasing yourself.

At its core, this is about certainty. If you keep managing, smoothing things over, and saying the right things, you won't have to experience the instability you fear. But the truth is, no amount of over-functioning will ever create the control you're looking for. You're keeping yourself trapped in a cycle where your worth is tied to how well you can hold everything together. But if you weren't constantly managing the emotions and actions of others—who would you be?

- **Keeping the peace, even at the expense of your own needs or boundaries:** Your highest priority is ensuring harmony, often sacrificing yourself to maintain it.

- **Preventing conflict, even if it means lying, placating, or telling people what they want to hear:** You justify dishonesty as a way to "smooth things over" and avoid escalation.

• **Maintaining emotional stability in others, even if it means suppressing your own emotions:** You believe you must stay strong and composed so that others don't fall apart.

• **Avoiding being a burden, even if it means silently struggling alone:** You convince yourself you can handle everything and should not ask for help.

• **Being the dependable one, even if it leads to burnout and resentment:** You feel responsible for holding things together and struggle to say no, often overextending yourself.

• **Anticipating and preventing emotional outbursts from others, even if it means manipulating situations behind the scenes:** You subtly adjust your words and actions to keep people calm and avoid unnecessary drama.

• **Minimizing disappointment in others, even if it means taking on more than you should:** You would rather suffer in silence than let someone down.

• **Justifying over-optimism about people, even if it means ignoring red flags:** You focus on others' potential rather than reality, believing people will eventually rise to expectations.

• **Holding relationships together, even if it means enabling unhealthy dynamics:** You justify staying in dysfunctional relationships by believing your role is to "help" or "fix" others.

• **Creating a sense of control through busyness, even if it means never addressing your deeper issues:** You keep yourself constantly occupied to avoid facing your own emotions or unmet needs.

• **Avoiding making others uncomfortable, even if it means lying about your true feelings:** You don't want to upset or disappoint anyone, so you hide your struggles.

• **Managing others' emotions, even if it means absorbing blame or guilt that isn't yours:** You feel a deep sense of responsibility for how others feel and will take on unnecessary guilt to prevent others from suffering.

• **Taking on too much responsibility, even if it's unsustainable:** You believe you are the only one who can handle things properly and struggle to delegate.

- **Avoiding direct confrontation, even if it means resorting to passive-aggressive behaviors:** You dislike conflict but may still express frustration in subtle ways when overwhelmed.

- **Staying in roles of silent suffering, even if it leads to emotional exhaustion:** You believe your struggles are less important than everyone else's and must be kept private.

- **Focusing on survival, even if it means neglecting long-term emotional health:** You believe you just need to "get through this" and will deal with your own issues later.

- **Lying or withholding information to avoid emotional fallout, even if it damages trust later:** You rationalize that telling the truth would make things worse, so you try to "manage" situations instead.

- **Over-functioning in relationships, even if it means enabling dependency:** You believe your role is to take care of others, even if it stunts their growth or independence.

- **Keeping dysfunctional people happy, even if it means sacrificing your own well-being:** You convince yourself you are the only one who can handle difficult people, reinforcing a cycle of self-sacrifice.

Unconscious Motivations of Rejection – Control to Receive Love and Be Safe (People-Pleasing Type: Engaging and Isolating Variants)

You've learned that belonging has to be earned. Whether through staying involved, following the rules, or avoiding attention, you've shaped yourself around what's expected, making sure you don't stand out in ways that could cost you acceptance. Unlike those who people-please to control perception, your focus is on maintaining stability and security. You're trying to ensure you don't become the reason things fall apart.

How you go about this depends on how you've adapted to protect yourself. Some take the engaging approach, throwing themselves into visibility, volunteering, leading, or making sure they are useful in a way that keeps them firmly in place. If you stay involved, if you're always contributing, always proving your value, then people will keep you around. Others take the isolating approach, ensuring belonging by never drawing too much attention to themselves. If you stay quiet, follow the rules, and don't disrupt the structure, then you won't give anyone a reason to push you out.

Both approaches stem from the same underlying fear—that if you stop managing how you fit into the group, you'll lose your place in it. You've trained yourself to scan for expectations, adjust where necessary, and avoid rocking the boat, even if it means suppressing what you actually think or need. You tell yourself it's worth it because stability is safer than uncertainty, but at what cost?

Rejection – Control to Receive Love and Be Safe (People-Pleasing Engaging): Unconscious Motivations

Above all, you trust the rules, the expectations, the structure that tells you how to be enough. You've spent your life looking outside of yourself for guidance, measuring your worth against cultural, religious, or social standards that dictate who belongs and who doesn't. Whether it's through tradition, performance, or compliance, you've learned that safety comes from following the right path—not forging your own.

You attach yourself to hierarchies, groups, or authority figures, believing that as long as you do what's expected, you won't be left behind. When decisions need to be made, you defer to others. When you're uncertain, you look for someone to model. If there's a system, a ranking, or a clear-cut way to fit in, you follow it—even if it means suppressing what you actually think or feel. Your survival strategy is aligning with those who seem to know better.

But the problem with living by external rules is that you never actually build trust in yourself. You shape-shift, comply, and chase approval, but underneath it all, you're still searching for something that makes you feel whole. Your unconscious motivations have convinced you that belonging is earned through obedience, through following the right system, but what happens when the system isn't built for you?

• **Seeking validation through high visibility, even if it becomes exhausting:** You believe that being seen as helpful, hardworking, or socially involved ensures your place in the group.

• **Over-performing, even if it leads to burnout:** You assume that as long as you are valuable to others, you won't be excluded or abandoned.

237

• **Earning acceptance through participation, even if it feels forced:** You believe actively contributing—whether in social groups, work, or family traditions—proves your worth.

• **Constantly scanning for feedback, even if it leads to dependence on external praise:** You monitor others' reactions to assess whether you are doing enough to be liked and accepted.

• **Striving for perfection, even if it causes stress:** You equate being flawless with being worthy of love and inclusion.

• **Controlling how they are perceived, even if it requires effortful self-monitoring:** You adjust your tone, choices, and responses to match what you believe others want.

• **Following social norms or group values, even if they don't personally believe in them:** You comply out of a need for stability and belonging rather than genuine conviction.

• **Giving to receive validation, even if they don't consciously recognize the transaction:** offer help, favors, or support in a way that ensures praise or appreciation in return.

• **Prioritizing inclusion, even if it means suppressing individuality:** You blend in or follow trends to ensure they are never seen as an outsider.

• **Minimizing conflict, even if it means agreeing to things they don't actually want:** You say "yes" reflexively, assuming disagreement could lead to rejection.

• **Deflecting responsibility, even if it prevents growth:** You downplay or avoid accountability to preserve your likability and avoid potential blame.

• **Measuring success by external goalposts, even if it doesn't fulfill them personally:** You pursue careers, roles, or achievements that align with societal expectations rather than personal fulfillment.

Rejection – Control to Receive Love and Be Safe (People-Pleasing Isolating): Unconscious Motivations

You've spent your life making sure you never give anyone a reason to reject you. That means staying quiet, following the rules, and never drawing too much attention to yourself. You don't push back, question expectations, or step outside of what's socially acceptable—because the safest place to be is unnoticed. If you don't stand out, you can't be criticized. If you don't challenge the system, you won't be cast out. If you don't ask for too much, you won't risk being denied.

You see compliance as a survival strategy. There are rules, structures, and traditions for a reason, and as long as you follow them exactly, you assume you'll be okay. You don't need to understand the "why" behind them—you just need to make sure you aren't the one who breaks them. Stability matters more than anything, so you stick to what you know, avoid unnecessary risks, and maintain relationships even when they've stopped serving you. Change feels dangerous, so you stay put, even when part of you wonders if there's something more.

But in constantly blending in, following the script, and avoiding disruption, you've made yourself invisible. You never truly find out who you are outside of expectations. You never fully step into the things you might be capable of. If no one ever really sees you, do you actually belong at all?

- **Avoiding rejection by blending in, even if it means becoming invisible:** You stay quiet, unassuming, and unnoticed to prevent standing out in ways that might invite criticism.

- **Complying without question, even if they don't understand why:** You assume rules exist for a reason and feel safest when following them exactly as expected.

- **Seeking security through predictability, even if it limits growth:** You adhere to rigid structures to avoid uncertainty, assuming control ensures safety.

- **Avoiding attention, even if it prevents them from receiving recognition:** You would rather be unnoticed than risk scrutiny or potential disapproval.

- **Fearing direct rejection, even if it means waiting for others to decide their worth:** You hesitate to initiate relationships, opportunities, or conversations, assuming if you were wanted, others would reach out first.

• **Holding onto relationships out of fear, even if they are unfulfilling:** You prefer stability over change, staying in one-sided or stagnant relationships to avoid loss.

• **Avoiding leadership or high-stakes roles, even if they are capable:** You fear that stepping into visible positions increases the risk of failure or public embarrassment.

• **Suppressing emotions, even if it leads to resentment:** You downplay your need to avoid being seen as difficult, disruptive, or high-maintenance.

• **Prioritizing tradition and expectation, even if it prevents personal exploration:** You follow familial, religious, or societal customs because stepping outside of them feels unsafe.

• **Fearing confrontation, even if it means using passive-aggression or silent withdrawal:** You may express dissatisfaction through avoidance or subtle cues rather than direct communication.

• **Internalizing self-doubt, even if they are competent:** You assume their contributions are not good enough, leading you to hold back in conversations, relationships, or opportunities.

• **Trying to "fix" themselves, even if the standard is unrealistic:** You believe self-improvement is required to maintain inclusion, chasing unattainable ideals.

• **Avoiding risk, even if it means missing out on opportunities:** You prefer to stick to what they know rather than expose themselves to possible failure or judgment.

Unconscious Motivations of Rejection – Control to Receive Love and Be Safe (Conflict-Prone Type: Engaging and Isolating Variants)

Rejection is something you expect. You're not trying to avoid rejection; you're trying to control how it happens. Whether you're pushing people into conflict or pulling away before they get the chance to leave, you're ensuring the cycle repeats—because at least if you control it, you won't be blindsided.

If you're the Engaging Variant, you fight your way to the front of the line. You test loyalty, demand fairness, and call people out before they can dismiss you. You go on the offensive, reading negativity into neutral situations and retaliating before any real harm has been done. If someone sets a boundary, disagrees, or pulls back for even a second, you take it as a threat. You escalate, confront, or force the issue until you feel like you've regained control. But what you don't see is that the more you push, the more people pull away, not because they were going to reject you, but because you made it unbearable to stay.

If you're the Isolating Variant, you vanish. You convince yourself that rejection is already in motion, so you preemptively disappear before anyone gets the chance to push you out. You scan for signs that you're not wanted, overanalyze social shifts, and assume that silence, distance, or minor changes in tone mean people are done with you. Instead of questioning your assumptions, you cut ties, ghost, or quietly withdraw, telling yourself you had no other choice. You believe you're protecting yourself, but in reality, you're ensuring the exact outcome you feared. No one can fight for you if you've already left.

It doesn't matter if you're picking fights or pulling away, the end result is the same. You've trained yourself to believe rejection is inevitable, so you behave in ways that guarantee it happens. When are you going to admit that you're the one creating the cycle?

Rejection – Control to Receive Love and Be Safe Conflict-Prone-Engaging Variant: Unconscious Motivations

You make sure rejection happens on your terms. If someone is going to push you away, you'd rather force their hand than sit around wondering when it's coming. Conflict is something you use to stay in control. You test loyalty, demand fairness, and push back the second you sense something shifting. You don't just defend yourself—you preemptively attack, assuming that if you strike first, you won't be caught off guard.

Your unconscious motivations have convinced you that staying in control means keeping people on edge, ensuring they are constantly proving themselves to you. But the truth is, conflict is keeping you isolated. You've trained yourself to believe that if you stop pushing, you'll disappear. But if your presence is only felt through tension and battles, are people really choosing you or just bracing for impact?

• **Asserting control through conflict, even if it drives people away:** You believe pushing back, challenging, or provoking ensures you won't be dismissed or ignored.

• **Avoiding rejection, even if it means creating conflict first:** You start fights on your terms, assuming it's safer than waiting to be blindsided by exclusion.

• **Proving self-worth through intensity, even if it isolates them:** You believe emotional reactions (yours or others') validate that you are seen, heard, or respected.

• **Testing loyalty, even if it exhausts others:** You create tension or initiate conflict to see who will fight to stay in your life.

• **Escalating tension as a way to feel important, even if it pushes people away:** You fear irrelevance more than conflict and assume dramatic interactions mean you matter.

• **Justifying retaliation, even if no real harm was done:** You interpret neutral or ambiguous behavior as intentional betrayal, fueling your need to "defend themselves."

• **Challenging authority, even if the authority figure isn't oppressive:** You assume leadership, rules, or structure are inherently designed to limit or diminish you.

• **Demanding fairness, even if it damages relationships:** You believe perceived injustice or imbalance is a direct attack on you and must be corrected at all costs.

• **Interpreting disagreement as a threat, even if it's not meant that way:** You struggle to separate healthy discussion from personal attack, making every difference of opinion feel adversarial.

• **Mistaking emotional intensity for connection, even if it creates instability:** You believe without strong reactions, passion, or fights, relationships lack depth or meaning.

• **Interpreting boundaries as rejection, even if they aren't personal:** You see any request for space or time apart as proof you are being abandoned or disliked.

• **Holding grudges as proof of self-respect, even if it keeps them isolated:** You believe letting go or forgiving makes you weak or susceptible to further harm.

- **Blaming others for their isolation, even if they created the distance**: You rationalize being alone by believing people "never really cared" or "weren't real friends anyway."

Rejection – Control to Receive Love and Be Safe (Conflict-Prone Isolating): Unconscious Motivations

You assume rejection is a matter of when, not if. Instead of waiting to be left behind, you make the choice for them. If a conversation feels off, if someone doesn't respond fast enough, if a group dynamic shifts in a way you don't like, you take it as proof that exclusion is already in motion. You tell yourself you're just protecting yourself, avoiding humiliation, staying ahead of the inevitable. But what you don't see is that by pulling away, you're ensuring the exact outcome you fear.

You justify withdrawing, cutting ties, or ghosting people as a necessary escape. You magnify small slights, overanalyze social interactions, and convince yourself that people are secretly judging or rejecting you—even when there's no evidence to support it. Instead of questioning your assumptions, you reinforce them. Someone setting a boundary is a sign they're pushing you out. Someone being polite or kind is a cover for the fact that they don't actually like you. Instead of risking the discomfort of being wrong, you disappear before they have the chance to prove you right.

Your unconscious motivations have convinced you that withdrawing is self-protection. You've trained yourself to believe that isolation is safer than connection, that distance is better than disappointment.

- **Avoiding rejection, even if it means preemptively pulling away:** You assume exclusion is inevitable, so you remove yourself first to avoid the pain of being left behind.

- **Interpreting distance as proof of being unwanted, even when it's neutral:** You see changes in social dynamics, a delayed response, or lack of enthusiasm as confirmation of rejection.

- **Destroying relationships first, even if they were never at risk:** You believe ending things preemptively protects them from humiliation or eventual abandonment.

- **Using conflict as a justification to withdraw, even when staying would serve them better:** You escalate minor issues internally to convince yourself you have no choice but to leave.

• **Fixating on perceived slights, even if they were never intended:** You hyper-focus on minor interactions, assuming others are secretly judging or rejecting you.

• **Assuming others have hidden agendas, even if there's no real evidence:** You distrust kindness or neutrality, expecting an eventual betrayal.

• **Pushing people away as a defense, even if they actually want connection:** You tell yourself you are better off alone rather than risk getting hurt again.

• **Ghosting or avoiding people, even if nothing bad happened:** You distance yourself suddenly, often without explanation, assuming you are unwanted.

• **Suppressing emotions, even if it leads to resentment:** You believe expressing feelings makes you vulnerable, so you bottle up anger or hurt instead of addressing it.

• **Interpreting boundaries as rejection, even if they aren't personal:** You take neutral acts of self-care or independence from others as confirmation you are being excluded.

• **Assuming negativity, even if there is no evidence:** You prepare for rejection or criticism at all times, seeing it as inevitable.

• **Leaving groups or friendships before they are officially excluded:** You believe cutting ties first saves you from the pain of being left out later.

• **Pulling away to see if people will chase after them, even if it damages relationships:** You test others' commitment by creating distance and waiting for reassurance.

• **Blaming others for disconnection, even if they initiated it:** You rationalize ghosting, avoiding, or isolating by assuming people didn't really care in the first place.

Unconscious Motivations of Rejection – Control to Receive Love and Be Safe (Conflict-Prone Type: Engaging and Isolating Variants)

People with this pattern crave validation and attention but assume they must fight for respect and admiration. Unlike Rejection – Control to

Receive Love and Be Safe, which worries about both situational risk and social perception, this type only cares about how they are perceived. You tend to be reckless or careless in most situations—until something threatens your image. Your core belief is that love, respect, and inclusion must be earned through conflict, control, or dominance.

How you handle conflict depends on how you've learned to protect yourself. The Engaging Variant seeks proximity, overuses communication, and forces interactions to ensure they are seen in a specific way. You may be anger-based—combative, dominant, forceful—or anxiety-based—pushy, over-explaining, or attention-seeking. Regardless of their approach, you engage rather than withdraw, assuming that controlling the narrative guarantees validation. You frequently misread social cues, interpreting neutral behaviors as negative, and ask constant validation-seeking questions that turn the interaction negative.

The Isolating Variant internalizes conflict but avoids relationships and engagement altogether. Instead of forcing themselves into interactions, you pull away preemptively, convinced rejection is inevitable. You disengage, ghost, or destroy relationships before you can be rejected, telling yourself it's better to disappear than to look foolish or be exposed as inadequate. Rather than openly asking if something is wrong, you assume negativity, convince yourself you are the cause, and use that belief to justify withdrawing.

Despite their differences, both variants struggle to process positive feedback, assume negativity even where none exists, and hold grudges as a false form of self-protection. Whether they push people into engagement or disappear entirely, both are operating under the same unconscious belief: that rejection is always looming, and controlling how it happens is the only way to avoid being blindsided.

Rejection – Control to Receive Love (Conflict-Prone Engaging) Variant: Unconscious Motivations

You've never trusted that just being yourself is enough to keep people interested. Whether consciously or not, you've learned that who you are is negotiable—something that can be adapted, tweaked, or entirely reinvented to fit the situation. You watch, study, and absorb what people respond to, learning how to play the part that keeps you included. If you can anticipate what someone wants, mirror their preferences, or present yourself in a way that makes you harder to reject, you assume you'll be able to secure your place in their life.

Your brain has convinced you that you can't trust people to choose you unless you make yourself unavoidable. So you over-communicate, demand reassurance, and push your way into interactions, assuming that if you just keep trying, they won't be able to ignore you. If someone pulls away, you push in. If they seem neutral, you assume they're losing interest and shift your approach. You read too much into body language, misinterpret normal social cues as rejection, and react before there's proof that anything is wrong. You mistake intensity for connection, persistence for value, and control for love.

You believe you're doing what it takes to stay relevant, stay included, stay wanted. But what you don't see is that your need for control is making you someone people want to escape. Your unconscious motivations have convinced you that if you stop trying, you'll disappear.

- **Misreading social cues, even if there is no evidence of a problem:** You assume neutral or unrelated behaviors (a change in tone, an unread message, an absentminded look) mean you are being judged or rejected.

- **Overusing communication, even if it pushes people away:** You assume that more communication equals control, validation, and securing your place in someone's life.

- **Asking validation-seeking questions, even if it shifts the conversation negatively:** You frequently ask, "Are you okay?" "Did I do something wrong?" or "Is this about me?" unintentionally steering interactions into uncomfortable emotional territory.

- **Forcing validation, even if it makes them look desperate or aggressive:** You believe that if they just explain more, push harder, or talk your way into closeness, people will eventually respond how you want.

- **Controlling perception, even if it repels people:** You obsessively curate your image, explaining, defending, or demanding to be seen in a specific way.

- **Seeking dominance in relationships:** You assume that being the most assertive, intense, or persistent will force others into admiring or validating you.

- **Pushing conversations, even if the other person isn't engaging:** You fail to recognize when someone is pulling away, assuming that persistence will force reciprocation.

• **Mistaking intensity for connection, even if it drives people away:** You believe that emotional tension, arguments, or drama are proof that someone cares.

• **Escalating situations, even if it makes them look unstable:** You prefer being intense or unpredictable over being seen as insignificant.

• **Testing loyalty, even if it exhausts others:** You push people to prove their commitment through constant communication, forced closeness, or emotional pressure.

• **Morphing identity:** You adjust your values, beliefs, or boundaries if you think it will make you more desirable or accepted.

• **Engaging in sexual exploration or counterculture beliefs, even if it's not authentic:** You may adopt sexual identities, polyamory, or alternative relationship models primarily to gain attention, approval, or love—not because it aligns with your core values.

• **Overwhelming partners with control or attention, even if it suffocates them:** You cling to people, text excessively, demand responses, or impose yourself in an effort to secure validation.

• **Challenging authority, even if the authority figure isn't oppressive:** You see rules and leadership as ways to control them rather than as beneficial guidance.

• **Fixating on being "right," even if it ruins relationships:** You believe being wrong would mean you are unworthy of respect.

• **Holding grudges as a weapon, even if it isolates them:** You believe resentment and remembering past offenses keeps you protected from betrayal.

• **Refusing vulnerability, even if it would bring them connection:** You see emotional openness as something others could use against you.

• **Overcompensating for a fear of being seen as weak, even if it leads to unnecessary fights:** You assume that if you aren't aggressive or persistent, you will be dismissed.

• **Pushing people away to see if they'll fight to stay, even if it results in actual abandonment:** You test others' patience or commitment, assuming rejection will happen anyway.

Rejection – Control to Receive Love (Conflict-Prone Isolating): Unconscious Motivations

You don't wait to be rejected—you assume it's already happening. If someone is distant, you tell yourself it's because they're pulling away. If a text goes unanswered, you convince yourself they don't actually like you. If a conversation feels slightly off, you assume they've secretly decided you're not worth keeping around. Even when there's no real evidence, your brain fills in the blanks with the worst possible outcome. Instead of risking the moment where they confirm what you already believe, you leave first.

You disappear. You pull away, ghost, or create distance before anyone has the chance to do it to you. You tell yourself you're just protecting yourself from rejection, but what you don't see is how often you create the very thing you fear. You let resentment build, replay old conversations, analyze tiny details, convincing yourself you were slighted or overlooked, even when no one else remembers it happening. You assume people don't really care, but you never actually give them the chance to prove you wrong.

Your unconscious motivations have convinced you that the only way to stay in control is to leave before you're left. But isolating yourself ensures rejection. You don't let relationships naturally play out, you don't allow for misunderstandings to be resolved, and you don't give people the space to choose you.

- **Assuming negativity, even if there is no evidence:** You interpret neutral behaviors (someone being quiet, a delayed text, a change in routine) as proof they are being ignored or rejected.

- **Internalizing conflict, even if no one else sees it:** You argue in your own head, replaying perceived offenses and fueling their own resentment.

- **Pulling away first, even if the relationship wasn't threatened:** You assume disconnection is inevitable, so you disengage before the other person has a chance to leave.

- **Fixating on perceived slights, even if they were never intended:** You hyper-focus on minor interactions, assuming everyone is secretly judging you.

- **Avoiding opportunities, even if they would benefit:** You turn down roles, relationships, or risks to prevent the chance of looking foolish.

• **Interpreting boundaries as rejection, even if it's not personal:** You assume that if someone needs space, it means they are being cast aside.

• **Ghosting or avoiding people, even if nothing bad happened:** You distance themselves without explanation, assuming you are unwanted.

• **Pushing away positive feedback, even if it's genuine:** You assume praise or validation is fake, manipulative, or given out of pity.

• **Walking away from relationships, even if the problem could have been fixed:** You believe any conflict means the relationship is doomed, so you leave first.

• **Holding grudges as self-protection, even if it only isolates them more:** You believe resentment prevents you from being made a fool of, unaware that it only reinforces your loneliness.

• **Avoiding leadership or visibility, even if they are capable:** You fear taking up space in ways that could expose you to criticism or failure.

• **Blaming others for disconnection, even if they initiated it:** You rationalize ghosting, avoiding, or isolating by assuming people didn't really care in the first place.

The Two Faces of People Pleasing: People Pleasing Rejection - Control to Receive Love (People Pleasing Engaging and Isolating)

People-pleasing is about controlling how you are perceived. Your focus is on how people see you, how they respond to you, and whether you're being included the way you want to be. Your world revolves around relational interactions, often at the expense of noticing the bigger picture.

At its core, the Rejection - Control to Receive Love pattern is a self-fulfilling prophecy—an endless loop of forcing connection, morphing to fit in, and then feeling rejected anyway. You believe you should be included, valued, and prioritized, but deep down, you also assume you won't be. This contradiction drives you to pursue connection in ways that guarantee the very rejection you fear.

For some of you, that means actively engaging—forcing your way into connection, keeping people entertained, over-explaining, apologizing, or adapting your personality to fit any social dynamic. Your anxiety makes you hyper-visible, constantly scanning for reassurance that you are wanted. But beyond just being likable, you become malleable—chameleons who adjust your opinions, interests, and even your identity or sexuality based on what will make you feel most accepted. You are trading authenticity for inclusion, assuming that as long as you perform correctly, you won't be abandoned. But because this performance is never fully you, you never actually feel secure in your relationships.

For others, the same entitlement plays out through hesitation and avoidance. You badly want to be included, but the fear of saying or doing the wrong thing keeps you stuck on the sidelines, watching instead of engaging. You wait for the perfect moment to step in, overanalyze how you might be perceived, and ultimately let opportunities to connect pass you by. You struggle to believe you belong enough to claim it. When you aren't actively pulled in, you take it as quiet confirmation that you were never really part of the group to begin with.

Your attention is always on how others perceive you. You can be messy, go with the flow, or even chaotic in how life unfolds, as long as you feel liked, included, and seen the "right" way.

One of you seeks control by being everywhere at once—shifting, molding, and adapting to fit. The other seeks control by staying just out of reach—observing, waiting, and missing moments to connect.

Unconscious Motivations of Rejection – Control to Receive Love and Be Safe (People-Pleasing Engaging)

The Hidden Cost of Being Liked

You've spent so much time making sure people like you that you've lost track of whether they actually know you. Every social interaction feels like a performance, adapting, fine-tuning, scanning for any sign that you might be too much or not enough. You tell yourself you're just being agreeable, just keeping the peace, just making things easier for everyone. But beneath all of it is a quiet, relentless fear: If I stop shaping myself to fit, will anyone still choose me?

You are avoiding rejection at all costs. That's why you adjust your personality in real time, mirror the people around you, over-explain, and apologize when no one asked you to. You overcommit to things you don't want to do, assume responsibility for other people's moods, and feel uneasy anytime someone pulls away. You don't push for control in an obvious way, but you are trying to control something—the version of you that people see. Because if you can manage that, maybe you can stop the one thing that terrifies you most: being left out, ignored, or forgotten.

But constantly adapting, performing, and keeping everyone happy has a cost. It leaves you exhausted, disconnected, and unsure if anyone actually likes you or just the version of you they've come to expect. And no matter how much you do, how many people you please, or how much space you take up, you still don't feel secure in your place.

- **Ensuring acceptance, even if it means reshaping their personality:** You adjust your identity, behavior, or opinions in the moment to be included, assuming your real self isn't enough.

- **Ensuring inclusion, even if it feels forced:** You jump into conversations, invite themselves to plans, or find small ways to stay relevant in social dynamics, believing your presence alone isn't enough to guarantee they belong.

- **Preventing exclusion, even if it means overextending themselves:** You fear being left out, so you overcommit, offer help, or become indispensable to others to secure their place in the group.

- **Seeking admiration, even if it feels exhausting:** You equate being liked with being worthy, so you pour energy into entertaining, supporting, or accommodating others, often at your own expense.

- **Over-communicating, even if it overwhelms others:** You assume connection is maintained through constant engagement, so you text frequently, over-explain, or overstay in conversations, fearing that too much space means you'll be forgotten.

- **Asking for reassurance, even if it turns interactions negative:** You frequently ask, "Are you mad at me?" or "Did I do something wrong?" assuming any small shift in mood means they've upset someone.

- **Controlling how others see them, even if it distances them from genuine connection:** You carefully curate your words and actions to avoid disapproval, but in doing so, you struggle to form authentic relationships.

• **Over-explaining, even when unnecessary:** You fear that being misunderstood will lead to rejection, so you justify and defend your choices excessively.

• **Needing constant affirmation, even if it becomes exhausting for others:** You equate silence or neutrality with rejection, assuming that people need to frequently confirm their worth.

• **Adapting too quickly, even if it feels inauthentic:** You mirror others' language, interests, or mannerisms to fit in, believing that sameness is the safest route to acceptance.

• **Mirroring others, even if it seems artificial:** You copy behaviors, interests, or opinions, assuming sameness is the key to belonging.

• **Over-apologizing, even if they haven't done anything wrong:** You assume you are responsible for any shift in mood or energy, believing preemptive apologies will prevent rejection.

• **Interpreting boundaries as rejection, even when they aren't personal:** You struggle to accept that space and autonomy are normal, assuming that any distance means someone dislikes you.

• **Pushing for inclusion, even when social cues suggest space:** You struggle to gauge when to step back, assuming that if you just try harder, people will like you. This can make you overly persistent in conversations or social settings, not realizing others may need time or space.

• **Jumping into relationships or friendships, even if they lack depth:** You seek instant closeness, believing that admiration or shared experiences alone are enough to create lasting bonds. When those relationships don't deepen, you assume it's because something is wrong with you.

• **Holding onto disappointment when efforts aren't reciprocated, even if it wasn't personal:** You feel deeply hurt when people don't match your level of investment, not out of anger, but from a sense of unworthiness or invisibility. You assume, "If they really liked me, they'd put in the same effort."

• **Being overly agreeable, even when it contradicts their real opinion:** You prioritize likability over authenticity, assuming disagreement equals rejection.

• **Using charm, humor, or dramatics, even if it feels forced:**
You assume you must entertain or impress others to be valued,
believing that likability is something that must be actively
maintained.

• **Attaching worth to social status, even if it leads to shallow
relationships:** You believe that being liked, admired, or included is
the ultimate marker of success, even if it means sacrificing depth.

• **Struggling to say no, even when they are overwhelmed:**
You fear that setting boundaries will make you seem selfish or
unlikable, so you agree to things you don't actually want to do.

• **Feeling responsible for group harmony, even when it's not
their job:** You take on the role of mediator, peacekeeper, or
emotional support, believing that if everyone is happy, you will be
safe from rejection.

• **Pushing relationships too fast, even if the other person isn't
interested:** You believe the faster someone gets emotionally
close to you, the more secure the relationship will be. You may
overshare, idealize new friendships, or struggle with pacing, not
realizing they are overwhelming the other person.

• **Holding grudges when people don't reciprocate their efforts,
even if they weren't owed anything:** You expect the same level of
attention you give, assuming imbalance is a form of rejection.

• **Misreading neutral expressions or body language as negative,
even when it isn't:** You believe people are secretly disapproving
of them, leading you to overcompensate or push harder for
approval.

Unconscious Motivations of Rejection – Control to Receive Love and Be Safe (People-Pleasing Isolating)

You mind. You mind a lot. You want to be included, to feel like part of
the group, to stop hovering at the edges of conversations, wondering if
it's too late to jump in. But every time you think about making a move—
sending the first text, speaking up, stepping forward—something stops
you. You hesitate, overthink, wait for the perfect moment, and then the
moment passes. Again.

It's not that you don't care. You care deeply. You replay past interactions, analyze every glance, every silence, searching for proof that you don't really belong. You keep your opinions to yourself, not because you don't have them, but because you don't trust that saying them out loud won't come with consequences—judgment, embarrassment, rejection. You tell yourself you're just waiting for the right time, but if you're honest, you're waiting for a sign that it's safe. That you're wanted. That you won't regret putting yourself out there.

So you stay quiet when you want to speak. You leave early when you want to stay. You convince yourself that if people really wanted you around, they would be the ones to reach out first. But deep down, you know the real reason you're on the outside looking in: you're the one keeping yourself there.

- **Wanting connection, even if it feels safer to stay invisible:** You crave meaningful relationships but fear rejection so much that you shrink yourself, hoping others will reach out first.

- **Avoiding interactions, even if they feel lonely:** You overthink social situations to the point of paralysis, assuming you will be judged or unwanted unless explicitly invited.

- **Trying to blend in, even if it means suppressing their personality:** You stay in observation mode, avoiding saying too much or making waves, believing invisibility is safer than risking negative attention.

- **Fearing small talk, even when they want deeper connection:** You struggle with surface-level interactions, worrying you won't know what to say or that you will come across as awkward.

- **Withholding opinions, even if they feel strongly:** You assume speaking up will lead to conflict, embarrassment, or being disliked, so you default to passivity in conversations.

- **Keeping social interactions short:** You leave events or conversations early, assuming your presence isn't valuable or that others wouldn't notice your absence.

- **Second-guessing every social move, even when others aren't thinking about it:** You replay interactions in your head, analyzing every word and gesture for signs you embarrassed yourself.

- **Observing instead of engaging:** You stay on the outskirts, waiting for an opening, but often let opportunities pass due to hesitation or self-doubt.

• **Minimizing their presence, even when they want to be seen:** You physically and emotionally shrink in group settings, avoiding drawing attention to yourself while secretly hoping someone will notice you.

• **Struggling to initiate plans, even when you want to be included:** You hesitate to reach out, fearing that if you take the lead and get rejected, it will confirm your worst fears.

• **Avoiding attention, even if it leads to disconnection:** You fear being in the spotlight but also fear being forgotten, creating an internal push-pull between wanting connection and avoiding exposure.

• **Avoiding direct rejection, even if it means preemptively pulling away:** You assume exclusion is inevitable, so you remove yourself first to avoid the pain of being actively rejected.

• **Interpreting distance as proof of being unwanted, even when it's neutral:** You assume that if you aren't immediately included, it must mean you are disliked or forgotten, even if no exclusion has actually happened.

• **Withdrawing after perceived rejection, even if you are misreading the situation:** The moment you sense disinterest or emotional distance, you pull away, even if the other person isn't actually disengaging.

• **Refusing to ask for inclusion, even if you secretly want it:** You believe that if you were truly liked, others would seek you out first, leading you to wait rather than risk initiating and being rejected.

• **Fixating on past interactions, even if no one else remembers them:** You replay moments where you felt awkward, excluded, or unnoticed, using them as proof that you don't belong.

• **Holding onto social missteps, even if they were minor or unnoticed:** You assume that any perceived embarrassment is permanent in others' minds, making it difficult for you to re-engage in social spaces.

• **Avoiding opportunities, even if you would benefit:** You turn down invitations, leadership roles, or social opportunities to prevent the possibility of looking foolish or failing in front of others.

• **Blaming others for disconnection, even when they pulled away first:** You rationalize emotional distance by assuming others didn't actually care about you, rather than recognizing your own avoidance.

• **Leaving groups or friendships before they are officially excluded:** You assume relationships have an expiration date and would rather exit first than experience the pain of being left behind.

• **Pulling away to see if people will chase after you, even if it damages relationships:** You test relationships by creating distance and waiting to see if others will follow, using this as a measure of how much you are valued.

• **Avoiding deep relationships, even if you crave closeness:** You assume that if people got to know you too well, they would eventually leave, so you keep relationships at a surface level to prevent future pain.

• **Waiting for the right moment, even if it never comes:** You tell yourself they will engage when the timing feels right, but overthink the moment until it passes, reinforcing your belief that you don't belong.

• **Convincing yourself you don't care, even when you do:** You tell yourself you prefer solitude or independence, but deep down, you long for relationships you are too afraid to initiate.

• **Fearing judgment, even when no one is actually paying attention:** You assume others are scrutinizing your every move, leading to heightened self-consciousness and social anxiety.

• **Overthinking how others feel about you, even when no one is focused on you:** You assume people are analyzing your every move, leading you to withdraw unnecessarily.

• **Avoiding leadership or visibility, even if you are capable:** You fear being noticed in ways that might expose you to criticism or failure.

• **Interpreting boundaries as proof of exclusion, even when they aren't personal:** You take neutral acts of self-care as confirmation you aren't wanted.

- **Assuming praise or compliments are fake, even when they are genuine:** You believe that if you were truly valuable, admiration wouldn't need to be spoken—it would just exist.

Unconscious Motivations of Chaos - Rejection

People with this pattern experience internal and external instability, feeling fundamentally disconnected from structure, routine, and long-term stability. You fundamentally don't believe in structure. To you, structure is an illusion, a trap, or a cruel joke meant to set you up for failure. You assume that any attempt at order will eventually collapse, leaving you looking foolish for ever trying.

Unlike other patterns that fear rejection and try to prevent it, this type assumes rejection is inevitable and unconsciously ensures that it happens. You engage in self-sabotage, isolation, and destruction of relationships, opportunities, or stability before they can be taken away. Because you struggle to sustain effort or direction, your life is often marked by unpredictability, unfinished projects, and cycles of passivity followed by bursts of impulsivity. You might turn to escapism through addiction, self-destructive behaviors, or suicidal ideation to cope with the overwhelming sense that life is unfair and unmanageable.

Unconscious Motivations of the Chaos - Rejection Type
Wired for Chaos

You don't want stability. You don't trust it, and you don't believe in it. People talk about structure, routine, and "building a future" like it's something real—something that won't collapse the second you get comfortable. But you know better. Stability is just a setup. A cruel joke waiting to land.

So you reject it before it can reject you. You don't bother trying to create order in your life because, deep down, you assume it's pointless. Effort feels useless when you believe nothing good will last. You drift, sabotage, or chase extremes—not because you're lost, but because chaos is the only thing that feels real. Uncertainty is predictable. Suffering is familiar. And if you can stay one step ahead of the crash, at least you're in control of the destruction.

You don't do structure. You don't make a long-term effort. You don't have a normal life. Because deep down, you believe you weren't built for it. And the second things start to look too calm, too safe, too good— you find a way to shake the foundation. Chaos isn't just what happens to you; it's what you create.

- **Ensuring rejection, even if you don't consciously recognize it:** You subconsciously believe rejection is an unavoidable fact of life, so you behave in ways that confirm this belief, ensuring it happens.

- **Rejecting structure, even if it would help you:** You see structure as a trap that will eventually fail, so you refuse to engage with it rather than risk looking naive for believing in it.

- **Drifting through life, even if it leads to chronic instability:** You believe things will either work out or collapse on their own, so you avoid taking intentional action toward stability.

- **Fixating on physical or emotional pain to ensure you don't make progress:** You cling to suffering as proof that life is cruel, reinforcing your belief that nothing good will last.

- **Seeking out darkness or pain, even if it worsens your mindset:** You actively consume content that fuels hopelessness, such as horror, extreme violence, or dark sexual material, as a way to keep yourself emotionally submerged in chaos.

- **Creating instability, even if it works against you:** You feel safest in chaos because it's familiar, while stability feels foreign, restrictive, or impossible to maintain.

- **Placing no effort into relationships, even if you crave connection:** You assume relationships won't last, so you don't invest energy in maintaining them, letting them fall apart by default.

- **Seeking escape through drug use, suicidal ideation, or addiction, even if it worsens your circumstances:** You view numbing out as the only way to cope with life's inherent unfairness and instability.

- **Avoiding any positive feedback or evidence of success, even if that means actively trying to destroy your own life or be in denial about possibilities:** You see success, praise, or opportunities as fraudulent or temporary, so you either reject them outright or sabotage them before they can take hold.

• **Associating identity with instability, even if it prevents long-term growth:** You see yourself as someone who "just doesn't do normal life," reinforcing your belief that you are incapable of functioning within structure.

• **Rejecting long-term effort, even if it means never improving your circumstances:** You view sustained effort as pointless since success is temporary and failure is inevitable.

• **Viewing routine as a setup, even if you secretly crave security:** You believe that any structure they try to build will eventually collapse, making the attempt foolish.

• **Experiencing boredom as intolerable, even if stability is necessary:** You believe constant stimulation or disruption is the only way to feel alive, making stability feel like emotional death.

• **Avoiding responsibilities, even if it reinforces your struggles:** You see expectations as suffocating and unfair, so you reject them rather than attempt to meet them.

• **Sabotaging opportunities, even if they were handed to you:** You assume any success will be short-lived, so you disengage before you can fail or be exposed as undeserving.

• **Letting life happen to you, even if it leads to dissatisfaction:** You believe you have no control over outcomes, so you put in no effort and accept whatever comes your way.

• **Experiencing random success, even if you can't sustain it:** You may have natural talent (e.g., artistic, intellectual, or social gifts), but without effort or discipline, your achievements happen by default rather than intention.

• **Attaching self-worth to chaos, even if it keeps you stuck:** You believe a "normal" life is not for you, so you reject structure in favor of instability, reinforcing your identity.

• **Destroying what's given to you, even if it could help:** You assume anything good will eventually be taken away, so you discard it first to maintain a sense of control.

• **Creating problems where there are none, even if life is going well:** You believe peace is temporary and disruption is inevitable, so you unconsciously create instability to feel prepared for what's coming.

• **Engaging in risky behaviors, even if it threatens your long-term well-being:** You seek chaos because it reinforces your belief that life is unpredictable and unfair, making reckless choices feel justified.

• **Blaming external factors, even if your patterns are repeating:** You believe life is happening to you rather than recognizing your own role in maintaining instability.

• **Rebelling against authority, even if the authority figure isn't oppressive:** You reject guidance on principle, assuming all rules exist to limit you rather than protect.

• **Testing boundaries, even if it damages relationships:** You challenge others' limits to prove that people are unreliable and will eventually leave.

• **Distancing from reliable people, even if they offer real support:** You view stable, consistent people as naive or unrelatable, preferring relationships that mirror your own instability.

• **Chasing intensity, even if it prevents long-term satisfaction:** You seek out extreme experiences to feel something, believing routine and stability lead to emotional numbness.

Spotting the Magician's Trick

Recognizing your unconscious motivations is like catching a magician mid-trick—once you see how it works, the illusion loses its power. These patterns have been operating in the background, dictating your choices, shaping your relationships, and reinforcing the very struggles you claim to hate. But now, you have a choice. Instead of blindly playing out the same loops, you can start observing them in real time, noticing when you're justifying, avoiding, overcompensating, or self-sabotaging.

The goal is to start watching your own mind at work—to hear the justifications, feel the compulsion to react, and realize in that split second: Oh, That's the pattern. Because once you can see it, you can dismantle it. And that's exactly what we'll be doing in the next chapters.

CHAPTER 20

OVERRIDE MESSAGES AND TOXIC POSITIVITY

Stop Putting a Band-Aid on a Wound That Needs Stitches

You're staring at your bathroom mirror, repeating to yourself, "I am enough. I am beautiful. I am lovable." Or maybe you're crushing a workout on the Assault bike, reminding yourself that you are worthy because you wrote it in your gratitude journal this morning. On the surface, these all feel beneficial and productive. You might even believe it's helping. But deep down, there's a quieter voice whispering back every time you have to affirm it to yourself and it's saying: "No, you're not."

That negatively skewed voice? That's the real problem. And no amount of affirmations or gratitude journaling are going to properly dismantle it permanently. These negative messages are wired like a bomb— complex, messy, and intended to steer you off course. The adoption of override messages can make the rewiring process a twisted journey of self-deception. When you try to pile positivity on top of a deeply entrenched belief that says the opposite, you create facets or pivot points that can make the rewiring process more complex. Your consciously held beliefs or patterns can become your hubris, leading to your inevitable demise. When you attempt to override instead of fundamentally rewire the origin language your brain uses to generate beliefs, you get locked in a loop, replaying the same intrusive thought over and over again. You're putting a band-aid over a wound that needs stitches.

This is the trap of overriding messages—affirmations, journaling, or even positive self-talk designed to mask the symptoms of a deeper problem. While they might provide a momentary sense of relief, they do not address the root cause and can even make the process of discovering the root cause more challenging.

Motivated to Believe Our Own Lies

A client once embarked on an exercise with me. As I looked through what she had written, I noticed something very obvious. While her peers' work skewed almost exclusively negative, every section of her writing was positive and cheery. With each passing line, I felt the weight of having to approach her and potentially burst her overly positive bubble. After all, she did attend my program for a reason, and I am always more committed to my clients' success than their perception of me. If I had to be the bad guy in order to pursue truth and healing today—so be it. I asked her to pull up the exercise. With as much love in my voice as I could gather, I spoke her name.

I said, "There is no easy way to tell you this, but this page is full of deceit."

She gasped and looked back at me, stunned. I heard a nervous chuckle.

"What do you mean?" she said.

I reminded her what she described as her reason for being enrolled in the program. She nodded. "Was that a lie?" I asked.

"No," she proclaimed boldly.

I went on to show her that the writing on the exercise was aspirational at best, but most likely a toxic positivity override. To this day, this client would tell you this was a pivotal moment. She boldly acknowledged it all in an instant: "This is all bullshit. Every word of it. I want this to be true so badly."

It was like the clouds parted and the sun lit her up for the first time. She had spent so much time and money learning to affirm, manifest, journal, and proclaim. The deeply held beliefs and language generated throughout the early years of life pervade our psyche and subconscious directives. Putting a band-aid over it won't do anything except make us feel confused, conflicted, and, even worse, fraudulent. Override messages ultimately fail. They don't speak the language of the subconscious. They're surface-level fixes that can't penetrate the deeper programming that drives our self-perception and actions. When we align ourselves with the truth and prepare ourselves to face the depth to which this sneaky message has impacted who we are, how we see the world and what actions we choose to take—the healing can truly begin.

Toxic Positivity: A Culture of Delusion and Escapism

Toxic positivity is emotional gaslighting. It's a culture that insists you plaster a smile on your face, have your aesthetic on-point, and focus on "good vibes only," no matter what kind of chaos, pain, or grief is unfolding beneath the surface. You only need to be on Instagram for .002 seconds to witness this. On paper, it might sound like a harmless byproduct of social media, but, in practice, it's a delusional escape that sidesteps or masks the uncomfortable truths we need to confront in order to rewire. The obsession with relentless optimism trains you to silence any emotion or experience that doesn't fit the narrative of effortless happiness.

Toxic positivity doesn't solve anything. It suppresses, invalidates, and bypasses the very emotions and beliefs that are crying out to be addressed. Worse, it leaves us feeling even more broken than before, trapped in a cycle of shame, avoidance, and comparison. You end up feeling like a failure for not being able to "just be happy" when, in reality, happiness was never the problem. Instead, your brain's internal wiring is the root. This culture convinces you that if you aren't feeling better, it must be because you're not trying hard enough, not manifesting properly, or not "aligning your energy." It's an elaborate, sugar-coated form of emotional manipulation.

The truth is, positivity in itself isn't bad. Toxic positivity is a weaponized form of avoidance. It demands that you ignore your reality and reject your emotions in favor of a curated, polished facade. But you can't outrun the subconscious. You can lie to yourself, sure. You can paste a smile on your face and convince yourself you're "choosing happiness." But your nervous system knows. Your subconscious keeps score. And all that unprocessed emotion you shove down in the name of "staying positive" will make itself known one way or another—whether through emotional outbursts, chronic stress, or even physical symptoms that force you to finally confront what you've been trying so hard to ignore.

Your Facade Will Crumble

Toxic positivity invites you to put on a happy face, practice some #selfcare and level up your vibration. In order to do this in our social media driven world, this requires a split to take place—an intentional compartmentalization or dissociation from what you really feel in order to "choose the good vibes." What you're doing in this instance is crafting a facade or persona, shoving down the truth or mess that you know doesn't meet the cultural measuring stick.

This facade comes with consequences. Perhaps these consequences won't sneak attack you for weeks or even months down the road, but they will attack. It's inevitable. You can't outrun emotional cycles indefinitely. Suppressed feelings have a nasty habit of resurfacing, often disguised as chronic symptoms or physical illnesses down the road.

When you wall up and present a facade, you're delaying the healing process. There are moments when a facade might serve as a temporary survival tool during emotional upheaval. But it always comes at a cost. Each time you rely on it, you're borrowing from your future self.

From a mathematical perspective, this means you'll always be in emotional debt. And the interest compounds. Healing requires that we face the issues head on, standing in the mud for a time so that we can do the work required to go deep enough to heal it for good.

The Correlation of Shame

What if you're told to "just be positive," but you can't flip the switch on your emotions? A new problem emerges: shame. This isn't just a side effect—it's the underlying driver of why you feel stuck in the first place. For people who struggle with shame-based wiring, toxic positivity makes you feel guilty for having it in the first place. This compounds the struggle, because now you're not just dealing with the original emotional wound; you're dealing with the belief that you're defective for feeling it at all. It's a shame spiral disguised as optimism.

This is how you end up stuck in an internal war. You're frustrated with yourself for feeling the way you do. You want to "just get over it." You compare yourself to others who seem to be thriving and feel like you're falling behind. And every time someone tells you to "think positive" or "look on the bright side," that internal war gets louder. Shame makes

266

you hide. It pushes you into avoidance, shutting down meaningful self-examination and making it nearly impossible to do the kind of deep work that rewiring requires.

The more you try to force positivity, the more resentment you build toward those who push it on you. You start to feel anger toward people who say, "You look tired," or "You seem off today." They're calling out the very thing you're trying so hard to conceal. The world demands that you keep up the illusion, but your subconscious keeps whispering the truth. And if you keep ignoring that voice, it will only get louder. The only way to escape this cycle is to stop treating shame like something to be conquered through positivity and start addressing it at its root wiring level.

Toxic Positivity Promotes Inauthenticity in Relationships

When toxic positivity becomes the status quo, your relationships start to feel performative. You're no longer being radically honest because, truthfully, when someone asks, "How was your night?" you don't want to lie and say, "Fine." But you also don't feel like you have permission to be real. The curated, sanitized version of reality that fits the script of endless positivity is holding you back, making your interactions feel hollow and disconnected. And here's the problem: the more you live behind that mask, the less you actually know who you are underneath it.

Inauthenticity in relationships is about emotional distance. The more you rely on a false front, the harder it is for people to truly connect with you. Over time, this leads to a dissociation from self, where even you struggle to identify what you really feel or need. You become so accustomed to playing the role of "happy, easy-going person" that when someone asks what's really going on, you don't even know where to begin. And that's dangerous. Because when you lose touch with your own emotional reality, you also lose the ability to assess your needs, establish boundaries, and make decisions that actually serve you.

Authenticity is the foundation of meaningful relationships. But authenticity requires discomfort. It means being willing to sit in the awkwardness of telling the truth, even when it's ugly. It means resisting the urge to brush things off or default to a pre-packaged response. If you want relationships that actually support you, you have to be willing to show up as you are, not as you think you're supposed to be. Anything else is just another layer of self-deception.

Stalled Healing and Growth

Here's the hard truth: healing isn't supposed to look pretty. Growth is messy, raw, and uncomfortable. It requires you to sit in discomfort, face your pain head-on, and dismantle the beliefs that keep you stuck. If you're expecting to "think positive" your way into deep emotional rewiring, you're setting yourself up for disappointment. Real growth is about digging into the roots of your subconscious patterns, identifying where your default wiring is leading you astray, and making strategic moves to change it—not just dressing it up with a new narrative.

Toxic positivity bypasses all of that. It tricks you into thinking that if you just keep journaling your gratitude or chanting affirmations, you'll magically heal. This shallow approach doesn't touch the subconscious programming driving your struggles. Instead of moving forward, you end up running in place, trapped in a healing loop that feels productive but never truly resolves anything. You keep waiting for the day when you'll suddenly "feel different," as if enough good vibes will flip some internal switch. But healing happens through intentional pattern opposition, forcing your brain to break the cycles that are keeping you stuck. Without that level of direct confrontation, all the self-help exercises in the world are just cosmetic fixes on a foundation that's still cracked.

Growth requires disruption. It requires intentional opposition to the beliefs and behaviors that have been running your life on autopilot. That means not just identifying the problem, but actively challenging it—disrupting your default responses, forcing yourself to take new actions, and rewiring the way your brain processes situations. If you're too focused on staying positive, you'll never challenge the hard truths keeping you stuck. Rewiring requires breaking down what isn't working and strategically replacing it with behaviors that actually serve you. Anything less is just emotional busywork disguised as growth.

The Cost of Emotional Bypassing

Toxic positivity invalidates emotions, fosters shame, stalls growth, and builds a culture of escapism in which no one feels safe to show up as their true selves. It teaches people to suppress their struggles rather than confront them, reinforcing the belief that negative emotions are unacceptable and should be hidden at all costs. Over time, this conditioning fuels self-deception, emotional isolation, and chronic dissatisfaction. Instead of working through pain in a way that leads to actual rewiring, you are left with a curated, surface-level existence that feels increasingly fragile under the weight of unprocessed emotions.

Emotional bypassing doesn't eliminate discomfort—it delays and compounds it. Every time you silence an emotion, dismiss a difficult experience, or force yourself to be positive in moments that require introspection, you're pushing those emotions deeper into the subconscious where they continue to shape your behaviors, relationships, and sense of self. The more you resist them, the more they control you. This is why so many people find themselves trapped in cycles of burnout, self-sabotage, or unexplainable emotional outbursts. What was once a "small thing to push past" becomes an undercurrent of resentment, exhaustion, and disconnection from reality.

If we're going to truly retrain the brain, we need to ditch the "good vibes only" mentality and embrace the full spectrum of human emotion. Growth happens in opposition—not in avoidance. It requires a willingness to face the discomfort head-on, challenge deep-seated beliefs, and take tangible action to rewire old patterns. Because real healing happens in the trenches, where you're willing to stand in the discomfort, face the hard truths, and build the resilience needed to come out stronger on the other side.

Unrealistic Expectations

"Look on the bright side." "Focus on the good." "Happiness is a choice."

These phrases sound like well-meaning advice, but they create a dangerous expectation: that you should always be happy, no matter what. This message implies that any other emotion beyond optimism is a failure. It conditions you to believe that sadness, frustration, or anger are signs that something is wrong with you, rather than natural human experiences. The problem is that when you inevitably fall short, you don't just feel bad, you internalize it as proof of personal inadequacy. The fallout can be brutal.

You're left questioning what's wrong with you: Why can't I stay positive? Why am I still struggling when everyone else seems to have it figured out? This constant self-interrogation only deepens feelings of inadequacy, hopelessness, and despair. You don't just feel like you're failing at life—you feel like you're failing at healing. And because toxic positivity demands that you suppress anything that doesn't align with endless optimism, you don't even feel like you have permission to voice those struggles. Instead, you retreat inward, keeping your pain private while performing happiness for the world. This creates a psychological double bind—if you acknowledge your pain, you feel like a failure. If you suppress it, you feel like a fraud. Either way, you're stuck.

Did you know that those who report the best quality of life don't aim for constant happiness? Instead, they expect a certain level of instability and chaos but respond in kind by being adaptable and open. People who cultivate emotional resilience—not toxic positivity—experience greater long-term fulfillment. Why? Because they accept that discomfort, uncertainty, and even suffering are inevitable parts of life. They don't waste energy resisting or denying those experiences. Instead, they focus on their response—shifting perspective, taking actionable steps, and embracing adaptability. Real rewiring comes from building the ability to navigate life's challenges without self-betrayal.

The Trap of Healing Loops

Another danger of overriding messages and toxic positivity is that they keep you trapped in what I call healing loops. This is when you're constantly trying to "heal" but never actually making progress. You journal, you meditate, you chant affirmations, but you still feel stuck because you're only addressing the symptoms of your pain, not the source of the entire system. Instead of rewiring the subconscious beliefs that fuel your struggles, you're layering positive self-talk on top of them. It's like painting over water damage without fixing the leak. It might look better for a while, but eventually, the underlying issue resurfaces, worse than before.

Healing loops give the illusion of progress but leave you in the exact same place. You feel like you're "doing the work" because you're actively engaging in practices that should, in theory, lead to transformation. But the work isn't actually challenging the deep-rooted patterns that shape your behavior, emotional responses, and decision-making. Instead of dismantling the subconscious narratives that are keeping you stuck, you're distracting yourself with healing as a concept. You tell yourself, "I just need to keep working on myself," without realizing that the work you're doing is actually reinforcing the same loops of avoidance and self-deception.

Healing loops keep you spinning in place. You're always "working on yourself," always looking for the next breakthrough, the next modality, the next book or retreat that will finally change everything. But nothing truly shifts, because real rewiring comes from deliberate, strategic opposition to the patterns that have been running your life. If your healing process feels endless, it's time to *ask yourself*: Am I actually healing, or am I just keeping myself busy with the idea of healing?

Positivity Is a Byproduct, Not a Choice

If you're reading this book, let me assure you—we won't be staying in the loop. We're going to break it entirely, piece by piece, dismantling the language that surrounds you like a prison cell. As you'll learn in the upcoming chapters, your Brain Pattern dictates your natural inclination toward optimism or pessimism.

For some Brain Pattern Types, optimism is out of touch with reality, a subconscious trap set to trigger patterned behaviors further down the line. For others, their brains are wired to generate an endless stream of negatively skewed what-ifs and catastrophic thinking. Wherever you fall, remember this: positivity is a byproduct, not a choice.

Our social-media-driven culture has sold you the idea that positivity is something you can simply choose or slap on like a mask. But that's a lie. Positivity is something you build. And building takes time. It takes planning, sequential effort, and repetition—laying the foundation brick by brick.

In the pages of this book, you'll uncover the relationship your Brain Pattern has with positivity and peace, and why those concepts might feel slippery or impossible to hold onto for long. The truth is, your brain's relationship to positivity is heavily distorted by your Brain Pattern Type.

Here's the good news: all human beings have the capacity to rewire their Brain Patterns. That means rewiring your perception of reality, the language your brain generates, the beliefs you hold, and the actions you take. Over the past eleven years, I've seen the most negative, overtly controlling clients radically shift their paradigms—some even after sixty-five years of running the same destructive cycles on repeat.

So, yes, you can do this.

You'll have the knowledge to understand how each mechanism of your Brain Pattern works. You'll have a step-by-step process to observe the areas where your pattern holds you hostage. And most importantly, you'll experience a radical paradigm shift that will forever change how you see yourself and the world around you.

There's a saying I often hear from clients enrolled in my Break Method program: "You can't unsee what you see in Break Method." When you crack the code on your Brain Pattern's distorted filter, you radically shift your paradigm and how you experience reality – forever.

So, I say this: choose the grit over toxic positivity. Choose the uncomfortable truth that demands effort over the aesthetically pleasing lie that keeps your life on repeat.

CHAPTER 21

THE CULT OF COMFORT

Modern society has turned doing whatever the hell we want into a virtue. Comfort-seeking is no longer just an instinct—it's a doctrine. We're spoon-fed a steady diet of "Listen to your body," "Honor your feelings," and "Do what feels right for you" as if those impulses are infallible truths rather than conditioned responses shaped by our past. We've built an entire culture around glorifying emotional indulgence, repackaging avoidance and stagnation as self-love and authenticity.

Let's call it what it is: a con.

The self-help industry, mental health movements, and social media influencers have expertly monetized our desire for comfort, selling us stagnation under the banner of empowerment. Struggle is demonized. Sacrifice is outdated. We're told that if something feels hard, it must be out of alignment. If a relationship or job requires effort, it's toxic. If discipline feels like a burden, it's because we're meant to just "flow." What this really does is reinforce an unspoken rule: if it's uncomfortable, avoid it. If it doesn't come naturally, it must not be you.

This same mindset seeps into how we justify behavior, weaponizing identity and biology as permanent, unchangeable forces. The rise of "It's just how I'm wired" or "It's in my genes" has created a passive approach to self-improvement, where people cling to their worst traits as sacred parts of their identity. If we can blame our temperament, attachment style, or brain chemistry, we never have to ask whether we actually could do something differently. Instead of confronting maladaptive behaviors, we validate them. Instead of building resilience, we build excuses.

The irony? The very mechanisms that allow us to break free from these patterns—our brain's ability to adapt, regulate, and rewire—are right there, waiting to be engaged. The anterior midcingulate cortex (aMCC), one of the brain's key players in self-regulation and motivation, is designed to help us persist through discomfort. It's the part of us that overrides knee-jerk impulses, that pushes through challenge, that makes disciplined effort possible. But the more we default to short-term comfort, the weaker this system becomes.

What most people call preference is often just an unchallenged habit loop. What we describe as authenticity is frequently just a lack of exposure to anything else. We mistake conditioning for identity, mistaking what feels natural for what is best.

The more we surrender to comfort, the more fragile we become. The easier we make life for ourselves, the harder everything feels. When we worship convenience, we train ourselves to believe that struggle is unnatural. And in doing so, we rob ourselves of the very thing that makes life worth living—our ability to overcome, adapt, and redefine who we are.

The Trap of Preference

Preference feels like choice, but it's just your Brain Pattern pulling the strings, whispering, "Let's just stick to what we know." It's a scam, a con artist dressed up as autonomy.

Think about the things you claim to prefer. "I prefer to work alone." Sure, maybe. Or maybe your brain has decided that collaboration is an exhausting minefield of feedback, conflict, and potential failure—so it steers you toward isolation and calls it "independence." "I prefer to stay home instead of going out." Do you? Or does your brain run a preemptive anxiety simulation, convincing you that socializing will be awkward, overwhelming, or just not worth the effort?

Preferences feel like a conscious decision, but they're often just a comfortable prison cell, one we decorate with self-justifications and call personality. Your brain actively rewards these patterns. Every time you comply with preference, you get a nice little hit of relief, the internal equivalent of a pat on the back. See? You didn't have to endure that discomfort. You made the right call. Except the "right call" is just the same choice, reinforcing the same loop, ensuring the same outcome.

Breaking out of this trap means disrupting the cycle. It means recognizing that the things you don't want to do—the things that feel unnatural, uncomfortable, even intolerable—are often the exact things you need to do to break free. It's about overriding preference, exposing yourself to the opposite experience, and allowing your brain to recalibrate. You don't have to like it at first. You just have to do it. Comfort-based pleasure is a leash, and the only way to cut it is to walk in the opposite direction.

So if preference is a scam, what does that say about personality?

Most people like to think of their personality as something inherent, fixed, and deeply personal. But what if the traits you claim as your own—your independence, your cynicism, your introversion, your sense of humor—aren't actually you at all? What if they're just an elaborate set of coping mechanisms, locked in by early experiences and repeated so often that they feel like the truth?

This is where we start to strip away another layer of deception: the myth of an authentic personality.

What is Authentic Personality?

The idea of an authentic personality is one of the biggest scams in modern psychology. People walk around convinced they're acting as their "true selves" when, in reality, they're just running a highly predictable set of subconscious patterns shaped by childhood inputs. What most people mistake for authenticity is just their brain pattern playing out on autopilot, an identity built by default, not by choice.

Authenticity Isn't What You Think It Is

Your authentic personality isn't what you've been calling "just the way I am." It's what would naturally emerge after you've rewired.

Think of your core self—your spirit, the part of you that's truly unique— as a light. In early childhood, your environment starts layering grime on the lampshade. Trauma, conditioning, unmet needs, and survival adaptations all form a crust over that light, distorting the way it shines. The result? The version of you that interacts with the world isn't you—it's the filtered projection of your Brain Pattern.

Over time, this distorted projection becomes what you call your personality. Or is it just an elaborate coping mechanism dressed up as identity?

This is where people get it wrong. They assume that owning their behaviors—radically identifying with their worst habits and tendencies—is self-acceptance. But true authenticity is about systematically removing the layers of distortion to see who you actually are.

Your Personality is Just a Byproduct of Your Brain Pattern

The way you express yourself—the things you think are "just who you are"—are actually the output of your Brain Pattern, selecting responses based on what it learned would keep you safest. The personality traits you take for granted are just its behavioral signatures.

Your Brain Pattern dictates how you communicate, process information, exchange energy, present yourself, and view the future. But these aren't fixed traits—they're just automated coping mechanisms your brain reinforced over time.

The 5 Personality Traits Governed by Your Brain Pattern

These traits are behaviors dictated by subconscious patterning. Once you rewire, you gain control over them instead of being ruled by them.

1. Communication Style

Do you speak in a way that minimizes conflict, over-explains, dominates, placates, or stays silent? Your Brain Pattern determines whether you assert, avoid, people-please, or control.

Words people may use to describe this:

Loud, direct, humorous, jumpy, honest, precise, harsh, soft, people-pleasing, liar, abrupt, dismissive.

2. How You Give & Receive Energy

Are you an over-giver, a taker, a withholder, or a reciprocator? These are just adaptive strategies based on what your childhood taught you about emotional transactions.

Words people may use to describe this:

Controlling, needy, manipulative, fake, thoughtful, over-giver, gracious, kind, transactional, pushover, stingy, reserved.

3. How You Process Information

Do you think strategically? Prefer logic over emotional nuance? Do you overanalyze? Do you problem-solve in ways that make others feel you're cold or disconnected?

The way you scan your environment and interpret patterns is extremely Brain Pattern-specific. Some people process data quickly but miss emotional nuance; others take longer but absorb more depth.

Words people may use to describe this:

Smart, scrappy, cold, brilliant, logical, cunning, strategic, intelligent, stupid, dull, dim, checked out, robotic.

4. Your External Facade

How you carry yourself–body language, tone, microexpressions–was shaped by learned survival tactics. The confident stance, the defensive posture, the over-excited animation: none of it is random.

Words people may use to describe this:

Emotional, hysterical, dramatic, aggressive, passionate, reactive, retaliatory, insecure, calm, peaceful, centered, self-controlled, neutral.

5. Your Outlook and Perception

The way you strategize, plan, and envision the future isn't personality–it's a projection of how your Brain Pattern expects things to unfold.

If you assume failure, it's because your history wired you that way. If you expect smooth sailing, it's because your brain learned to anticipate it.

Words people may use to describe this:

Manipulative, controlling, negative, strategic, optimistic, fun, oblivious, gullible, naive, cynical, skeptical, hopeful, opportunistic.

Your Personality Is a Projection—Not the Real You

None of these things are you. They are merely the consequences of past input.

But here's the good news: if these responses were created, they can also be rewired.

When you rewire your Brain Pattern, your natural personality begins to emerge, one that isn't dictated by fear, self-preservation, or subconscious coping mechanisms.

True authenticity comes from dismantling it to uncover the version of you that was always meant to exist.

But if the traits we've been calling our "authentic self" aren't actually authentic, where do they come from?

The answer lies in childhood. Not in the cliché, "your parents screwed you up" kind of way, but in the more insidious, structural way that early life conditions us to see the world, respond to challenge, and interpret discomfort.

During childhood, your brain wrote the first version of its operating system. This operating system that now dictates everything from how you handle stress to how you justify avoidance.

The Role Childhood Plays in Preference

Childhood is when our brains are programmed to define what's normal, what's deserved, and what's intolerable. It's when we learn whether discomfort is an obstacle to be navigated or a personal affront to be avoided at all costs.

The way discipline and attention were distributed in early life has a direct correlation to the development of Rejection-based Source Belief Patterns—the ones most wired for pleasure-seeking, instant gratification, and external validation. Ironically, these are also the individuals who report the lowest overall quality of life. When you grow up believing that your preferences should be honored without friction, reality becomes a constant disappointment.

Children raised in households where structure was flimsy and discipline was inconsistent—where a parent wavered between indulgence and avoidance, handing out "yes" responses like participation trophies—developed an internal framework of entitlement. Their brains wire around the belief that their wants should be met without resistance.

When the world inevitably fails to cater to their preferences, they default to self-justifications and external blame: I deserve this. This shouldn't be this hard. This isn't my fault. This mental shortcut ensures that rather than building resilience, they lean into pleasure-seeking as a life strategy, reframing obstacles—financial, relational, professional—as injustices rather than the natural friction of existence.

On the flip side, those who grew up in chaotic or unstable households, where attention was unpredictable and discipline meant either delayed gratification or getting nothing at all, developed a radically different emotional architecture. While their childhoods may have been more challenging, they report a higher quality of life and greater emotional resilience as adults. Their necessity-driven adaptation to unpredictability builds a larger anterior midcingulate cortex—the part of the brain responsible for motivation, conflict resolution, and perseverance. Instead of seeking immediate relief, they become more adept at navigating discomfort without crumbling, a skill that pays off in every domain of life.

This contrast exposes an inconvenient reality: the ability to act purely out of preference feels like freedom in the moment, but it's a trap. The more you orient your life around comfort, the more intolerant you become of even minor resistance. Over time, what should be standard life challenges start to feel like personal attacks, and what should be a manageable inconvenience turns into a crisis. The problem isn't the world getting in your way. Rather, your brain was never trained to handle anything but ease.

Ultimately, preference-driven living breeds dissatisfaction. It erodes resilience. And if left unchecked, it transforms every "no," every delay, every challenge into proof that life is unfair. Really, it's just proof that your brain wasn't built to endure the inevitable.

If childhood sets the parameters of your brain's operating system, then habit is what keeps it running.

By the time you reach adulthood, your brain has refined these patterns into highly efficient, automated loops. You don't have to think about how you respond to stress, whether you avoid conflict, or how you approach relationships. Your brain already made those decisions for you years ago. You just keep playing them out—over and over—mistaking repetition for identity.

But your habits are not your personality. They're just the settings you never changed. It's time to ask: are these habits working for me? Or am I just used to them?

Habit Formation vs. Identity

Your habits are not your personality. Left unchecked, they'll hijack it, turning your conditioned responses into what you mistake for an unchangeable identity. A person who has spent years avoiding discomfort, chasing dopamine hits, and reinforcing maladaptive preferences will eventually convince themselves that's just who they are. "I'm just not a morning person." "I don't like structure." "I work better under pressure." No, you don't. You've just trained your brain to function that way, and now you're confusing your conditioning for your core self.

Here's where it gets dangerous: When preference becomes part of the process—whether it's therapy, emotional rewiring, or any attempt at real change—it immediately becomes the biggest stumbling block. Preference is the gatekeeper of staying the same. Your brain wants to do what's easy, what's familiar, what doesn't require reconfiguring the entire system. So when you step into a process designed to disrupt that, preference will step in like a bouncer at the door, throwing up objections: "This doesn't feel like me." "I don't like this approach." "This isn't how I normally do things." Exactly. That's the point.

Rewiring requires a direct assault on preference. If your instinct is to retreat, you must move forward. If your habit is to seek immediate pleasure, you must delay it. If your preference is to avoid something, you must confront it. True change does not come from reinforcing what feels natural; it comes from systematically opposing it until your brain no longer sees the old pattern as the default.

This is where the anterior midcingulate cortex becomes your greatest asset. This tiny but powerful region of the brain is responsible for overriding impulse, pushing through resistance, and making sure you stay in control. When we engage in intentional pattern opposition—forcing ourselves to act against what feels comfortable—we activate the very circuitry needed to create sustainable change. The goal is not to suffer for suffering's sake, but to break the illusion that our past conditioning should dictate our future choices.

In short: what you prefer is irrelevant. Your preferences are, in large part, just the result of your past reinforcing the same choices over and over again. If your preferences aren't taking you where you want to go, they are not serving you–they are keeping you stuck. And if you let them dictate your approach to change, you will sabotage yourself before you ever begin. Rewiring demands that we stop mistaking habit for identity, comfort for truth, and pleasure for progress. It demands that we train our brains to want what actually serves us.

So what happens when you try to change these habits? Your brain panics.

It throws everything it has at you–discomfort, doubt, emotional turmoil–to keep you from abandoning the familiar. And because your brain knows logic won't stop you, it goes for the kill shot: it makes you feel like the change itself is wrong.

This is where most people lose the battle–not because they aren't capable of rewiring their patterns, but because they mistake emotional resistance for a sign that something isn't working.

Your Feelings Are Liars: How Emotion Hijacks Progress

Your brain is a master manipulator. The second you get close to breaking free from an ingrained pattern, it hits the emergency brake. And because it knows logic won't work on you, it goes straight for the emotional jugular t: This feels wrong. This is too harsh. This approach isn't for me. I need something softer, more supportive, more aligned with my emotions.

This is self-preservation–your brain scrambling to keep you locked into old habits under the guise of self-compassion.

Here's How This Trap Works:

1. **You hit the part of the process that actually works.** The rewiring process demands that you do the exact opposite of what your patterns tell you to do. It's uncomfortable. It's confronting. It forces you to recognize that the way you've been operating isn't just ineffective–it's self-destructive.

2. **Your brain doesn't like that realization, so it pivots to emotional self-protection.** It convinces you that the approach itself is the problem. This feels invalidating. This is too direct. I need

something gentler. What's really happening? Your subconscious is throwing a tantrum because the old pattern is under attack.

3. **You misinterpret resistance as proof that this approach isn't for you.** Instead of recognizing discomfort as the necessary friction of change, you see it as a sign to stop. Your brain whispers: If this were the right method, it would feel good. It would make me feel seen. It wouldn't push me this hard. And just like that, you retreat back into comfort, blaming the process instead of the real problem—your refusal to challenge emotional indulgence.

When Victimhood Becomes a Defense Mechanism

This is where a lot of people get stuck. They reach the part of the process that demands real change, but instead of facing it, they feel victimized by it. Suddenly, the very work that holds the key to their freedom feels like an attack. They weaponize their own sensitivity against themselves, convincing themselves that if something feels harsh or unsupportive, it must be wrong.

Change is not about feeling good in the moment. It's about doing what actually works. Growth is inherently uncomfortable. The process is supposed to rewire the way you respond to them.

And this is where self-deception tightens its grip. Your brain will trick you into believing that discomfort equals harm, challenge equals oppression, anything that disrupts your familiar emotional landscape is somehow abusive or unfair. If you can frame necessary change as an attack, you don't have to engage with it. You can stay exactly where you are, clinging to the illusion that your stagnation is the fault of an external force rather than a choice you're making.

This is how victimhood becomes a defense mechanism. If you let your emotions dictate what methods you'll engage with, you'll only ever choose the ones that reinforce your existing patterns. That's how people get trapped in therapy loops, endlessly "exploring their emotions" without ever changing their behavior. That's how people convince themselves that softness and validation are the only paths to healing. In reality, the thing they need most is to be directly challenged.

Your subconscious is an excellent lawyer. It will present an airtight case as to why the work is too harsh, why you shouldn't have to push through discomfort, and why you're justified in retreating into validation rather than action. It will rewrite the story, positioning you as the oppressed, the misunderstood, the victim of a process that "doesn't get you." And in doing so, it hands you the perfect excuse to stay exactly the same.

If you listen to that voice, you will never change because change requires confrontation—of your patterns, your illusions, and, most of all, your own bullshit. The moment you let discomfort convince you that the work is "too much," you've already lost. Because the very thing that feels oppressive is actually the thing setting you free.

Sensitivity as Self-Sabotage

Take a moment to reflect—do you have a pattern of pushing away challenges when it forces you to confront something uncomfortable? Have you ever felt personally attacked in a conversation, only to later realize the person may not have been attacking you at all? Think about past conflicts, fallouts, or lingering resentments. Were those people truly against you, or were they simply on the other side of a difficult discussion? Did they actually harm you, or did they just introduce an idea that threatened the way you saw yourself?

Emotional rewiring often feels like being a rat in a science experiment. The scientist keeps changing the variables—shifting the maze, blocking familiar paths, forcing the rat to adapt. And what does the rat do? It gets frustrated. It hesitates. It turns back. It fights the process. In the rat's mind, this isn't fair; what worked before should still work now.

This is where sensitivity becomes self-sabotage. Instead of focusing on the goal, you focus on how the process makes you feel. You convince yourself that if something is difficult or uncomfortable, it must be wrong. You interpret structure as control, challenge as cruelty, and feedback as an attack. What if that interpretation is just another trick your brain is playing to keep you stuck?

This is how self-deception thrives. It convinces you that the work itself is oppressive, when, in reality, the real oppression is staying exactly where you are. Growth requires friction. Change demands adaptation. And if you've spent years interpreting discomfort as a personal injustice, you've probably spent just as long avoiding the very things that could set you free.

So, are you going to keep fighting the scientist, resenting the maze, and convincing yourself that this entire process is unfair? Or are you going to focus on the goal and recognize that the discomfort isn't a punishment—it's a necessary part of learning the new path? Because the rat that keeps resisting change stays lost. But the one that learns how to navigate the new reality gets to the cheese.

The reward never comes instantly. If you're used to chasing quick relief, if you expect immediate validation the second you step outside your comfort zone, your brain will find a way to pull you right back. Rewiring requires delayed gratification. It demands that you keep moving toward the goal before you feel the reward. If you don't understand that, you'll fall for the same trap over and over again, mistaking discomfort for failure and sprinting back to old patterns because they offer the fastest relief. But if you can break that impulse? That's where real change happens.

Ask yourself:

- Am I resisting this process because it's ineffective—or because it's uncomfortable?

- Is my reaction rooted in logic, or am I reacting emotionally to feeling exposed?

- Am I looking for a process that truly works, or one that feels good while keeping me the same?

- Do I want to be supported, or do I want to be coddled?

If the answer to any of these leans toward emotional justification, you're likely reinforcing the very patterns you claim to want to break.

This is how self-deception thrives. It convinces you that the work itself is oppressive, when, in reality, the real oppression is staying exactly where you are. Growth requires friction. Change demands adaptation. And if you've spent years interpreting discomfort as a personal injustice, you've probably spent just as long avoiding the very things that could set you free.

If your brain is going to sabotage you with emotional resistance, then your first line of defense is learning to sit in discomfort without giving in to it. Because right now, every time you give in—to an emotional reaction, a craving, an avoidance mechanism—you reinforce the belief that discomfort is intolerable.

But discomfort isn't the enemy. Rather, it's the battlefield where rewiring actually happens.

The Role of Delayed Gratification in Rewiring

Pleasure-seeking is a parasite. It hijacks your brain, whispering sweet nothings about how one more scroll, one more bite, one more hit won't hurt. Every time you give in to that itch for instant gratification, you reinforce the idea that discomfort is intolerable and must be avoided at all costs.

Your anterior midcingulate cortex—the part of your brain responsible for overriding impulse-driven behaviors—was built to handle the discomfort of waiting, working, and enduring. It was designed to push you toward long-term reward over cheap, immediate hits of relief. But if you keep caving to every passing urge, that part of your brain atrophies like an unused muscle, and before you know it, you're a puppet dancing on the strings of your next dopamine fix.

Delayed gratification is about rebellion. It's about breaking the false equation that discomfort is bad and pleasure is good. It's about proving to yourself that sitting in unease won't kill you. That craving, that impulse, that moment of tension before you reach for the easy way out? That's the battlefield. The choice to not react, to not self-soothe in the way your brain demands, is the very act that rewires your baseline.

Think about the ways you've trained your brain to expect relief. Do you avoid confrontation because it feels unbearable to sit in unresolved tension? Do you overanalyze every conversation, seeking reassurance because the uncertainty is too much? Do you distract yourself with mindless consumption—scrolling, snacking, binge-watching—because sitting in stillness forces you to face yourself? Every time you seek a quick fix, you reinforce weakness. You condition your brain to believe that you must escape discomfort the moment it arises.

This is why avoiding confrontation erodes self-trust, why compulsive reassurance-seeking keeps you weak, and why mindlessly consuming comfort—even in the form of junk food, meaningless scrolling, or passive distraction—ensures you stay trapped. Every moment you resist the pull of immediate gratification, you teach your brain a different lesson: I can handle this. I don't need an escape. I'm the one in charge.

The Bottom Line

If you want to rewire, you have to prepare for battle. The process isn't soft, it isn't soothing, and it sure as hell isn't going to stroke your ego. It will demand that you willingly step into discomfort, over and over again, without immediate relief. That's what pattern opposition is—choosing what's hard over what's easy, choosing structure over chaos, choosing to act before you feel like it.

So before you move forward, *ask yourself*: Are you ready to stop flinching at discomfort? Are you willing to sit in unease without reaching for relief? Can you face the very urges and impulses that have kept you stuck–and refuse to obey them? Because if you can, then you're finally ready to start breaking the patterns that have been running your life.

CHAPTER **22**

THE REBELLION EFFECT

The Science of Rebellion

Your brain is a master manipulator, an expert con artist working around the clock to keep you locked into the same predictable patterns. It doesn't care if those patterns are actively sabotaging your life—it only cares about keeping them alive. Pattern opposition is the wrecking ball designed to shatter this illusion. It forces your brain to acknowledge that there is another way, one that aligns with what you actually want instead of what your subconscious is programmed to repeat.

Most people assume they can change through sheer willpower. They collect self-help soundbites and white-knuckle their way through their own dysfunction, only to end up right back where they started. But change isn't about wanting it badly enough. It's about strategically dismantling the subconscious language architectures that keep you trapped, proving to your brain that its default response is flawed, and methodically rewiring the pathways that control your behavior.

Pattern opposition works because it forces your brain to submit to a new way of operating. It does this in three critical ways:

1. **It proves that an alternative path exists and that it actually works better.** Your subconscious is a professional liar—it convinces you that deviation from the pattern will lead to catastrophe. Opposition exposes this deception.

2. **It strengthens the anterior midcingulate cortex, the brain's resilience engine.** When you do the things you don't want to do, the aMCC grows, making it easier to keep doing the things you don't want to do. This is how emotional resilience is built.

3. **It retrains the synaptic pathways by wiring apart from the old pattern or thought.** The more consistently you execute an intentional opposite action, the easier it becomes because you've quite literally restructured the brain's wiring.

Pattern opposition is the act of hacking the brain with precise opposition to choose the new behavior. Paired with a framework for dismantling language architectures, pattern opposition acts like a secret password that gives you immediate access to a new way of operating. Change requires disruption, but not just any disruption—the right kind, in the right amount, at the right time. Incremental shifts in opposition are necessary because they allow the brain to experience and integrate a new pattern in real time, proving through direct experience that the new pathway is viable.

By methodically dismantling the old language architectures, we create an environment where the brain naturally begins to select the new behavior over the old default. We use incremental shifts because they give the brain time to gather evidence that the new behavior is valuable and effective. This approach ensures confidence and capability can build naturally, reinforcing the shift through repeated success rather than sheer force or avoidance of defenses. Each incremental shift serves as a calculated input, giving the brain time to process and reinforce the new wiring rather than rejecting it outright.

Precision Over Force: Why One Size Doesn't Fit All

The biggest mistake people make is assuming opposition is a one-size-fits-all solution. It's not. Effective opposition must be tailored to your specific subconscious patterns. Just like the saying one man's trash is another man's treasure—pattern opposition is the same. What helps you rewire and oppose is someone else's default setting. Applying the wrong kind of opposition risks reinforcing the original pattern, making change even harder.

Blindly choosing what you think is the opposite action won't work. Human beings have a tendency to pendulum swing and overcorrect. When we select pattern oppositions, we have to be certain that they break cycles rather than reinforcing them in a different but overcorrected form. Pattern opposition is a precise shift in behavior, communication, thought, or decision. These oppositions interact with the physical world and serve as an input that will begin to generate different outputs than they were previously getting. Think of it like playing ping pong and only knowing how to play one way—if you always hit it as hard as you can to the left side of the opponent's table, then they have 99 percent of the table they never get to play. When we learn how to incrementally pattern oppose, we give the people in our lives a chance to respond to something new, often breaking the chains of their patterns in turn.

We are deliberately identifying the existing pathways that have created chaos, conflict, and drama in our lives. This is how true rewiring happens—by fundamentally altering the structure of what already exists.

When opposition is applied correctly, it shifts the external world around you. The people in your life who are accustomed to your predictable responses will be forced to adapt, often breaking their own unconscious cycles in the process. Every pattern opposition creates a ripple effect, challenging not just your brain, but the entire ecosystem of interactions and dynamics built around your dysfunction. This is the foundation of The Rebellion Effect - a process by which an intentional act of pattern opposition can sustainably rewire your entire Brain Pattern system.

Rebellion Zones: The Battlefront of Change

Your brain pattern distorts your perception of choice, especially when the stakes are high. What should be an infinite range of possibilities gets funneled into a narrow, predetermined set of options—all of which reinforce the subconscious rules your brain has been running on since childhood. It's like being handed a rigged menu at a restaurant, where every dish has the same key ingredients, just rearranged. You think you're making a choice, but really, you're just selecting from a controlled illusion of options that keep your pattern intact.

Enter the Rebellion Zone: the place where your brain's default rule set must be directly and deliberately challenged to expose the flaws in its programming. This isn't about "expanding awareness" or "increasing mindfulness"—vague, feel-good approaches that rarely generate sustainable change. This is a tactical strike against the subconscious rules governing your life, forcing your brain to acknowledge that the foundation it has been operating from is a lie. These rules aren't real, but they feel real—until you expose them for the frauds they are.

The Rebellion Zone is a surgical intervention designed to disrupt the system with precise, calculated opposition. It's the difference between flailing around hoping to break free and strategically hacking the pattern at the exact moment it's most vulnerable. These zones are highly individualized and must be carefully pinpointed to directly challenge the subconscious rules keeping you stuck. Without identifying your specific Rebellion Zones, change remains a theoretical concept rather than something you can implement in real time.

Each Source Belief Pattern has specific Rebellion Zones, and these zones act as pressure points—areas where your subconscious is most sensitive to disruption. They align with the self-deception mechanisms and unconscious motivations discussed in previous chapters, meaning that targeting them with the right opposition forces your brain to confront the reality it's been avoiding. Think of these zones as the cracks in a foundation. You don't need to demolish the entire building, just apply enough strategic pressure in the right places, and the whole thing starts to collapse under its own weight. Rebellion Zones are tailored to your specific brain pattern, ensuring that the opposition lands where it actually matters, rather than where it just feels comfortable or interesting.

Everyone has multiple Rebellion Zones, but strategically targeting one or two can trigger a domino effect, dismantling an entire pattern with minimal effort. Some of these zones are the weak links holding the whole system together. Break the right one, and the rest start to crumble without additional effort. It's like pulling the keystone from an arch. Removing the right piece collapses what once seemed solid and unshakable. The key is precision, understanding which specific areas hold the most leverage so that your efforts result in efficient, sustainable transformation rather than frustration, wasted time, or worse.

The biggest mistake people make? Assuming that opposition is one-size-fits-all—that any form of resistance or rebellion against their default patterns will create change. It won't. In fact, applying the wrong kind of opposition can be just as bad—if not worse—than doing nothing at all. Subconscious patterns are stubborn, and if the opposition doesn't directly challenge the faulty logic of the pattern, your brain will twist it into further proof that its original rules were correct. Instead of breaking the cycle, you reinforce it, making change even harder. This is why so many people feel stuck in loops, repeating the same mistakes despite their best efforts to "break free." Effective opposition must be tailored to your subconscious patterns—challenging them in a way that forces your brain to recalculate rather than dig in its heels. This is the difference between real change and yet another failed attempt at self-improvement.

How Your Brain Fights Back

Your brain does not want you to change.

Your brain is simply wired for efficiency. Its job is to keep running the same neural pathways it has reinforced over the years, ensuring your survival through predictability. Your subconscious doesn't differentiate between patterns that serve you and patterns that destroy you. It only knows familiarity brings safety and unfamiliarity brings danger

When you start actively challenging a long-held pattern, your brain perceives it as a threat. The moment opposition begins, a full-scale internal counterattack is launched to pull you back in.

This resistance isn't obvious. Your brain doesn't just say, "Stop, I refuse to change." That would be too easy to recognize. Instead, it manipulates your perception to make opposition feel unnecessary, illogical, or even dangerous. It will fabricate urgency, distort your emotions, and convince you that this specific moment is an exception to the rule.

This is The Exception Clause—one of the most deceptive and effective traps your brain sets to keep you locked in place even when you're trying to heal.

The Exception Clause: Why This Moment Feels "Different"

The brain is smart enough to know that if it outright rejects change, you'll notice. Instead, it plays a more subtle game. It doesn't try to convince you to abandon opposition completely—just this one time.

It might sound like this:

- "But what if this time it's really a heart attack?" (referring to your 1,799,678th panic attack)

- "I know I said I wouldn't let this person walk all over me anymore,

295

but this is different. This is an emergency."

- "I know I swore off texting my ex, but I just found out their sister passed away. This is the last time."

- "I know I need to set boundaries at work, but my boss really needs me on this one project, and I'm the only one who can do it."

- "I know I'm not supposed to check WebMD, but this symptom feels different. What if it's something serious?"

This is the Exception Clause in action. Your brain takes what should be a straightforward decision—opposing the pattern—and distorts it, injecting doubt, urgency, and rationalization to make it feel like breaking your new rule just this once is not only justified, but necessary. It subtly reframes the situation to make this moment seem like an outlier, one that requires a temporary break from your new behavior. It convinces you that whatever logic applied before doesn't apply now. This instance is different, special, an emergency, or an exception that can't be ignored.

And if you fall for it, you reinforce the old pattern. Each time you give in, even when you know better, your brain logs that experience as proof that its argument was correct. Now, the next time opposition arises, the Exception Clause will come back stronger, more persuasive, and more difficult to resist. Why? Because your brain remembers that you believed it and that it worked. This creates a feedback loop where your subconscious gets better at manipulating you, refining its arguments based on what has successfully pulled you back into the pattern before. The more times you succumb to these seemingly isolated exceptions, the more deeply entrenched the pattern becomes, making future attempts at opposition feel increasingly difficult.

This is how people stay trapped for years in the same cycles despite having full awareness of the problem. The brain doesn't need to fight change with brute force. It only needs to plant enough doubt to make you hesitate. A single moment of hesitation is all it takes to let the old pattern slip back in under the guise of "just this once." But once you recognize the Exception Clause for what it is—a calculated manipulation of your own perception—you start to see the pattern as a whole rather than a series of unrelated moments. And when you see the pattern, you can dismantle it.

The Brain's Resistance Playbook

The Exception Clause is just one of many tactics your subconscious uses to fight back against opposition. When a pattern is under threat, your brain scrambles to defend it using a full arsenal of psychological tricks.

1. Manufactured Urgency

- "I don't have time to deal with this right now."

- "I'll start tomorrow—I don't have time to make it a priority today."

- "My business needs me right now more than I need to build emotional resilience."

  The subconscious will create artificial urgency to push opposition aside. If it can convince you that you need to act immediately in a way that reinforces your old pattern, you'll bypass conscious awareness and react automatically.

Example:

- Someone who struggles with people-pleasing finally works up the courage to set a boundary—only for their brain to panic: "If I say no, they'll be screwed. I'll just help this one last time."

- The person folds, reinforcing the belief that saying no creates disaster.

2. Emotional Exaggeration

- "This is too hard."

- "I can't handle this level of discomfort."

- "What if it doesn't get easier – I can't do this forever."

- "I'll fall apart if I don't go back to what feels safe."

  Your brain amplifies emotions to make opposition feel unbearable. It wants you to believe that the discomfort you're experiencing is evidence that something is wrong, when, in reality, it's just a normal part of rewiring.

Example:

- Someone trying to break free from a toxic relationship feels the pull to text their ex. Their brain magnifies their loneliness: "This is unbearable. I need them."

- The moment they text, relief floods in—but only temporarily. They're back in the same cycle.

3. Selective Memory

- "It wasn't that bad before."

- "We had so many good times. Maybe we just need to try again."

- "I handled this fine last time. I can afford to slip a little."

- "Maybe I overreacted—things weren't as toxic as I thought."

  The brain conveniently filters out negative past experiences to make reverting feel harmless.

Example:

- A person working on quitting alcohol remembers all the fun nights out but conveniently forgets the regret, the shame, and the hangovers.

- They tell themselves: "I was overreacting. I can have just one drink."

- The cycle repeats.

4. Over-Rationalization and Reward

- "I've been doing so well. I deserve a break."

- "One time won't hurt."

- "This is self-care."

  Once you start making progress, your brain flips the script and starts using your success as justification to revert.

Example:

- Someone trying to stop emotional spending resists impulse purchases for a month. Then their brain whispers: "I've been so disciplined—I deserve to treat myself."

- The dopamine hit of shopping reinforces the old behavior, undoing progress.

Will You Recognize the Trap Before It Catches You?

Resistance isn't an if—it's a when.

Your brain will fight back. Will you catch it in time?

Failure doesn't happen in big, dramatic moments. It happens in the small, quiet exceptions that feel harmless in the moment. But when you string enough of those exceptions together, you're right back in the same pattern.

Your brain only needs you to hesitate. One moment of doubt, one slight justification, and suddenly, the pattern is back in control.

When opposition begins, expect resistance. Expect your brain to justify, rationalize, and magnify. Expect the Exception Clause to show up, making this time feel like the one legitimate reason to fall back into old behaviors. Once you see the pattern for what it is, it loses its power.

Patterns of Positive and Negative Self-Deception

We've already established that your brain is a con artist. It knows exactly what to say to keep you locked into your existing patterns, and it doesn't always do it through fear or self-doubt. Sometimes, it weaponizes belief itself.

Self-deception can take on a positive form, too. This is where most people get trapped. They assume self-deception only operates in obvious ways, like making them feel incapable, unworthy, or afraid of change. But just as often, the brain will deceive you in your favor, convincing you that you're more prepared, skilled, or in control than you actually are. It can inflate your confidence to the point where you believe you're making progress, even when you aren't—or worse, push you into reckless action without proper preparation.

Both positive and negative self-deception shape your perception of reality, creating blind spots that distort your decision-making. The key to sustainable rewiring is learning to see when it masquerades as empowerment.

The Lies That Keep You Stuck

Self-deception serves a purpose: it keeps you comfortable. Whether positive or negative, it gives your brain an excuse to avoid opposition and maintain the status quo.

- **Negative self-deception keeps you from taking action.** It exaggerates the difficulty of a task, makes challenges seem Insurmountable, and convinces you that failure is inevitable before you even start.

299

- **Positive self-deception can trick you into thinking no action is necessary or a bold action is viable.** It inflates your sense of ability, making you believe that confidence alone is enough to guarantee success, even when you lack the necessary skills, strategy, or experience. It convinces you that things will just work out, that belief is the primary ingredient for achievement, and that preparation is secondary—or even unnecessary.

This is how an underprepared athlete attempts a complex trick before mastering the fundamentals, how an entrepreneur launches a business without a viable plan, or how someone in financial ruin convinces themselves that manifesting wealth is more important than actually learning financial literacy. Positive self-deception fuels action, but without the right foundation, that action often leads to failure, injury, or setbacks that could have been avoided with objective assessment and preparation.

In contrast, negative self-deception works by planting doubt, hesitation, and fear. It tricks you into assuming the worst, exaggerates obstacles, and convinces you that failure is inevitable before you even attempt something. Where positive self-deception can lead to impulsive risk-taking, negative self-deception leads to avoidance, paralysis, and over-caution. One pushes recklessly forward, the other pulls you back—but both distort reality in a way that makes rewiring your patterns difficult.

"Positive" Self-Deception as the Enemy

The self-improvement industry thrives on positive self-deception. If you've spent any time online, you've seen the endless stream of manifestation, affirmations, and "just raise your vibration" rhetoric that promises success simply by believing you're worthy of it.

This is not to say that confidence, belief, or visualization are ineffective—there's evidence that acting as if can create momentum. But when positive self-deception is left unchecked, it leads to blind optimism without execution. You convince yourself that success is inevitable, that things will simply fall into place, and that believing in yourself is enough, without ensuring that belief is backed by real preparation, effort, or skill.

It can also create entitlement without effort or grit. When you repeatedly tell yourself that you are destined for success, abundance, or recognition without actively putting in the necessary work, you start expecting results that haven't been earned. This mindset breeds frustration and resentment when reality doesn't match the internal narrative. Instead of adapting, improving, or grinding through obstacles, you look for external reasons why success hasn't arrived, blaming circumstances, bad luck, or other people rather than addressing the gap between expectation and execution. Maybe you pull it off temporarily but begin to feel like a fraud because you aren't really at the level of your supposed peers in accumulated knowledge or experience. The illusion eventually catches up, leaving you either scrambling to compensate or retreating in self-doubt, further reinforcing the deception that success is something that happens to you rather than something you build.

This is how people stay stuck in cycles of perpetual self-work without actually rewiring their patterns. They mistake aspirational thinking for transformation and quasi-delusion for a spiritually-motivated shortcut. Failing to recognize positive self-deception in your Rebellion Zones can leave you blind to the very patterns you're trying to break, making you believe you're progressing when you're actually reinforcing old behaviors in a new disguise. If you don't actively question whether your confidence is grounded in real preparation or just a mental shortcut to avoid discomfort, you risk mistaking surface-level change for true rewiring.

The Trap of Negative Self-Deception

Negative self-deception operates in the shadows, distorting your perception of risk, effort, and capability. It makes change feel impossible before you even attempt it.

> • **Anticipating failure before you begin.** Your brain primes you to believe something will be overwhelming, painful, or humiliating— so when it happens, it feels like proof.

> • **Exaggerating discomfort.** The brain makes tasks seem harder than they are, increasing resistance and making avoidance feel justified.

> • **Misinterpreting normal emotions as signs to stop.** Discomfort is a natural part of change, but negative self-deception convinces you that feeling uncomfortable means you're on the wrong path.

Negative self-deception creates a self-fulfilling prophecy. When you expect things to go badly, your perception filters reality through that assumption. You see more "evidence" that supports your belief, reinforcing the idea that you were right to avoid opposition in the first place.

Recognizing the Patterns in Your Own Life

Every pattern type experiences both positive and negative self-deception. The difference lies in how it manifests and which version dominates.

Some people are more prone to positive self-deception—inflating their sense of control, avoiding accountability, or convincing themselves they're further along than they are. Others lean into negative self-deception, exaggerating obstacles and talking themselves out of even trying.

But no one is immune to either. Both forms appear at different points in the rewiring process, and if you don't learn to spot them, they will sabotage your progress.

This is why Rebellion Zones require identifying both. If you don't recognize positive self-deception, you'll trick yourself into thinking you're making progress when you're actually avoiding real change. If you don't recognize negative self-deception, you'll resist action out of fear that it will be harder than it really is.

To make rebellion effective, you have to strip away both illusions and align with objective reality. That means:

- Seeing yourself, your strengths, and your weaknesses clearly.
- Acknowledging where confidence is justified—and where it's an illusion.
- Learning to separate discomfort from actual danger.

The most dangerous lies are the ones you don't recognize as lies. Your brain is an expert at deception—it's your job to see through it. The moment you identify a blind spot, a justification, or an avoidance mechanism, you're at a crossroads. Do you retreat into old excuses, or do you take full ownership and correct the course?

This is where Radical Personal Responsibility (RPR) comes in.

Radical Personal Responsibility: The Turning Point in Rebellion Zones

The brain is especially skilled at weaponizing guilt, shame, or regret to keep you from fully confronting the pattern. Instead of moving forward, you spiral into avoidance, dissociation, or an internal monologue of self-judgment:

- "Ugh, I can't believe I did that again."

- "This is too much—I don't even want to go there right now."

- "If I really acknowledge this, I'll have to admit how much time I've wasted."

The subconscious hijacks the moment, making the process of facing the pattern feel more overwhelming than the pattern itself. This is how people convince themselves that now isn't the right time to deal with it, that they'll "open Pandora's box" if they start unpacking these behaviors, or that they can just "do better" without really looking at what caused the mistake in the first place.

Your brain, like a computer, needs to see the error before it can correct it. It needs data. And Radical Personal Responsibility is how you give it that data without emotional distortion.

RPR: A System, Not a Punishment

RPR is not about assigning moral weight to your mistakes or drowning in self-recrimination. It's about facing what happened objectively so your brain can process and integrate the correction.

RPR is the process of saying:

"I historically struggle with direct communication and I have set people up to fail me as a result."

"I realize my desire for safety has generated conflict and instability in my closest relationships."

"I know that I justify running away or moving on if things don't go exactly the way I silently planned in my head."

That's it. No shame spiral. No self-flagellation. No internal courtroom trial where you argue over whether or not you're a failure. Just data collection and execution.

Ironically, the very thing people avoid—looking directly at the mistake—is the thing that keeps the brain from updating the pattern and supporting the opposition. When you take RPR instead of retreating into avoidance or guilt, your brain becomes significantly more likely to support the rewiring process because it understands why the correction is necessary.

Shame and guilt keep you stuck. RPR keeps you moving.

How to Use RPR in Rebellion Zones

RPR requires deconstructing the system that allowed it to persist in the first place.

To do this effectively, we need to apply RPR within the framework of:

- **Self-deception themes:** What has kept you stuck in the pattern?

- **Unconscious motivations:** What emotional driver makes the pattern feel necessary?

- **Rebellion Zone work:** What opposition must be applied for successful rewiring?

When you use RPR in this way, you're identifying exactly where and how to apply pattern opposition.

The RPR Formula

1. I acknowledge that I [Self-Deception Theme], which has allowed me to [maintain unconscious motivation].

2. I recognize that this has led to [negative consequence or behavioral pattern], reinforcing [subconscious justification].

3. I understand that my [Unconscious Motivation] has kept me locked in this cycle, making it difficult to step into my Rebellion Zone.

4. I see that in order to successfully rewire, I must apply direct opposition in my Rebellion Zone, rather than justify, minimize, or avoid.

This ensures every RPR statement addresses the exact deception running the pattern, the unconscious need that makes it feel necessary, and the opposition required for correction.

Example RPR Statements Using This Framework

1. Acknowledging Self-Deception and Motivation

- "I acknowledge that I have historically struggled with direct communication and have justified my avoidance as 'keeping the peace.'"

- "I recognize that this has led to repeated misunderstandings, unnecessary conflict, and resentment in my relationships, reinforcing the belief that people just don't understand me."

- "I understand that my unconscious motivation for safety and control has made it difficult to communicate clearly because I fear it will lead to instability."

- "I see that in order to successfully rewire, I must step into my Rebellion Zone and oppose avoidance with clear, direct, and timely communication."

2. Addressing Justifications and Behavioral Cycles

- "I acknowledge that I have a pattern of running away or disengaging when things don't go exactly as I planned in my head, justifying it as 'trusting my intuition.'"

- "I recognize that this has led to instability in my career, friendships, and relationships, reinforcing the belief that people always disappoint me."

- "I understand that my unconscious motivation for control has kept me locked in this cycle, making it feel easier to leave than to stay and confront challenges."

- "I see that in order to successfully rewire, I must stay in discomfort when things don't go as planned instead of using avoidance or withdrawal as a coping mechanism."

3. Breaking Patterns That Justify Emotional Avoidance

- "I acknowledge that I have used over-planning and hyper-productivity as a way to justify avoiding uncomfortable emotions."

- "I recognize that this has led to chronic burnout, resentment, and the feeling that I can never truly relax."

- "I understand that my unconscious motivation for certainty and validation has made it feel like slowing down means I will fail or be left behind."

- "I see that in order to successfully rewire, I must challenge my Rebellion Zone by sitting in stillness and processing discomfort instead of distracting myself with productivity."

Why RPR Matters

If you don't recognize and acknowledge your patterns with RPR, your Rebellion Zone work will collapse before it even starts.

- If you minimize your patterns, your brain won't see a reason to change them.

- If you spiral into guilt, your brain will resist correction out of shame and avoidance.

- If you justify or deflect, you'll stay stuck in the same cycle, convinced it wasn't really a problem.

RPR forces you to acknowledge the reality of the situation exactly as it is. This is the turning point where rebellion stops being an abstract concept and becomes something your brain actually supports.

The Choice: Guilt Spiral or Radical Ownership

At every step of your Rebellion Zone work, you will have a choice. You can:

1. Let guilt, shame, or avoidance keep you running the same pattern—because your brain tells you it's safer to pretend you're already doing the work, or that you'll "get to it later."

2. Take RPR and confront the pattern directly—without emotional weight, without self-sabotage, and without justification.

One keeps you trapped. The other rewires your brain.

Ownership, empathy, and humility for your past are what fuel true rebellion. And if you want sustainable rewiring, you don't get to bypass this step.

RPR is the bridge between awareness and transformation—the moment where recognizing your patterns is no longer enough, and true opposition begins. It forces you to choose data over emotion, action over avoidance, and tangible rewiring over the illusion of progress. Without it, you risk staying in the cycle of self-deception, convincing yourself that reflection alone is change. But rebellion is built on decisive, pattern-breaking action. The difference between temporary effort and permanent change is contingent upon whether you take ownership, neutralize justification, and deliberately oppose the behaviors keeping you stuck. RPR is the foundation that ensures your Rebellion Zone work actually holds.

The Fallout of Rebellion & How to Handle It

Opposing a pattern sends shockwaves through your environment. The moment you start choosing pattern opposition over autopilot, the people around you will react. And not all of them will react well.

Your subconscious patterning has shaped your relationships, interactions, and social dynamics for years—possibly decades. The way you've responded to conflict, set boundaries (or failed to), sought validation, or avoided discomfort has been predictable. And in that predictability, the people in your life have found stability.

So what happens when you change? You disrupt the system.

Some people will support it. Some people will fight it. Some people will leave. And some—if you remain consistent—will rewire alongside you without even realizing it.

This is part of the process. If you aren't prepared for it, you might mistake this resistance as proof that you're doing something wrong, when, in reality, it's proof that you're doing something right.

The Three Likely Responses from Others

When you change, expect three primary types of reactions:

1. The Enabler's Meltdown ("I Liked You Better When...")

Some people in your life have unconsciously benefited from your patterns. Maybe they relied on your people-pleasing, emotional caretaking, or lack of boundaries to maintain a sense of control or avoid their own discomfort. Now that you're changing, they feel unstable.

Their subconscious reaction? Blame, guilt, and resistance.

- "You used to be so much easier to be around."

- "I don't even know who you are anymore."

- "I liked you better when you weren't so uptight about everything."

This reaction isn't about you—it's about what your change means for them.

Because if you break the cycle, they have to face the deficits in their own behaviors. They may have to acknowledge that they were complicit in unhealthy dynamics or that they've been avoiding their own work. And not everyone is ready to do that.

Some will flat-out ignore your change and continue responding to you as if you're still running your old pattern. This happens because the brain relies on pattern recognition and assumption—they don't actually register that you're doing something different because their response is so automatic.

How to Handle It:

When someone acts as if you're still running the old pattern, you have to draw attention to the pattern break by leading with RPR and reinforcing the new expectation.

Example Response Using RPR:

I realize I used to avoid detailed work and would just let things slide, but I've realized that actually leads to more work in the long run. So please send me another draft of this within 30 minutes." This identifies accountability for the old behavior while making the new expectation impossible to ignore.

Bottom Line:

They will either adapt to your new standard, or they will struggle with the reality that the old version of you no longer exists.

2. The Power Struggle ("Let's See If You Really Mean It.")

Some will try to push you back into the pattern through direct resistance.

This could look like:

- Testing your boundaries to see if you'll break ("Oh, come on, you don't really mean that.")

- Mocking or belittling your efforts ("You and your little self-improvement phase…")

- Provoking you into an emotional response ("Oh, so you're better than me now?")

Their subconscious is interested in maintaining the status quo. If they can bait you into reacting, they win.

How to Handle It:

- **Recognize the game.** If someone is testing you, it's about control.

308

- **Don't take the bait.** The moment you defend, explain, or prove yourself, you've already lost the upper hand.

- **Remain consistent.** The best way to shut down a power struggle is to show them that no amount of pushing will make you revert.

3. The Silent Drop-Off (Avoidance as a Reaction to Change)

Some people won't argue, guilt-trip, or fight. They'll just leave. Why? Because your new version of yourself no longer serves a role in their world.

This could be because:

- They thrived on your dysfunction and can't connect with you in your rebellion.

- Your growth makes them uncomfortable because it forces them to reflect on their own patterns.

- They were only in your life because of the old version of you—and now that version is gone.

How to Handle It:

- **Let them go.** Their exit is a sign that your rebellion is working.

- **Acknowledge the discomfort with RPR.** A simple statement can open the door for them if they choose to stay.

Example Response Using RPR:

"I know my approach to things has changed a lot, and I recognize that it can be challenging to understand if you haven't gone through the work yourself. I get that change isn't always easy to watch."

Sometimes, this opens a doorway to dialogue. Other times, it gives them permission to leave—and that's okay.

This is also a great opportunity to introduce them to Brain Pattern Mapping or give them a copy of this book. Some of the people resisting now might be ready for their own rebellion soon.

The Best-Case Scenario: Mutual Rewiring by Proxy

Here's what we actually want to happen: your rebellion disrupts their rebellion.

This is the ideal outcome: someone close to you stops running their own pattern simply because you've broken the cycle. This happens most often in symbiotic dysfunction, when two people's patterns are unconsciously designed to keep each other stuck. Your response to a trigger fuels theirs, and theirs fuels yours, creating a loop that feels impossible to escape—until one person breaks it.

Example:

• One partner shuts down when there's conflict, which triggers the other to explode emotionally, which reinforces the first person's belief that shutting down is necessary.

• A friend constantly rescues another from their own bad decisions, which reinforces the belief that they can't be trusted to make choices on their own, which makes the rescuer feel needed and in control.

When one person steps out of the cycle, the other person has no choice but to respond differently.

This is how thousands of marriages have been saved—not because both partners did the work, but because one person stopped feeding the cycle long enough that the other had to change, too.

And one day, that person looks at you and says: How did you do that? Are you a magician?"

But there's no magic, just precision in rebellion.

The Cost of Staying the Same

At the end of this process, you will either:

• Revert back to old patterns because it's easier to keep people comfortable.

• Stand your ground and rewire for good, no matter who stays or goes.

Not everyone will stay. Not everyone will like it. Not everyone will be able to handle the new version of you.

At the end of this process, you'll finally be free of the patterns that have ruled your life.

REBELLION ZONES

CHAPTER 23

YOUR REBELLION ZONE BATTLE PLAN

Welcome to the War Room: Why You Need a Battle Plan

Rebellion is calculated warfare. If you go in swinging blindly, fueled by frustration or desperation, you won't break your patterns—you'll reinforce them. The subconscious is designed to absorb impact and redirect energy back into familiar cycles. This is why sheer force of will never works. Without strategy, precision, and a clear understanding of what you're up against, you'll either burn yourself out, overcorrect into another form of dysfunction, or retreat the moment resistance hits. Rebellion without direction is self-sabotage.

What's at stake? You are about to enter active rewiring territory, the part of the process when your patterns don't just exist in theory but show up in real time, demanding a response. The battle you're about to fight is against subconscious resistance, faulty logic loops, and deeply embedded justifications that will try to pull you back in. This is where you'll encounter the Exception Clause, self-deception mechanisms, and knee-jerk emotional responses designed to make you question whether rebellion is even necessary. If you aren't prepared, your brain will talk you out of opposition before you even realize it's happening.

And here's something critical to understand before you begin: not every "a-ha" moment your brain generates is useful. As you start seeing self-deceptive patterns, you might feel like you've cracked the code. But your brain is an expert at leading you toward red herrings—false insights that seem profound but actually serve to pull you off course. This is why it's crucial to stick to your brain pattern type and strategically address each area one at a time. Jumping around based on what feels relevant in the moment is just another way your subconscious keeps you from making real progress.

This chapter is your Rules of Engagement—the strategy guide that ensures you step into rebellion intentionally, not impulsively. Over the next three chapters, you will identify your pattern-specific rebellion zones, dismantle the subconscious narratives that keep them running, and execute precision opposition. But before you can do any of that, you need to know how to engage without sabotaging your own progress.

How to Use the Rebellion Zone Chapters for Maximum Impact

The next chapters will take you deeper into pattern-specific Rebellion Zones—the precise areas where your subconscious will resist change the hardest and where your pattern opposition will have the highest impact. Each pattern type has unique Rebellion Zones, which means your work needs to be tailored, not random. If you try to apply opposition without considering your specific pattern, you'll risk reinforcing the very behaviors you're trying to break.

This is where most people go wrong. They cherry-pick. Instead of following the structured process, they gravitate toward what feels easiest, most interesting, or least disruptive. Your brain will naturally try to default to familiar terrain—seeking small, comfortable changes that give you the illusion of progress while keeping the core pattern intact. That's why this step requires discipline.

Identify Your Rebellion Zones and Stick to the Process

1. **Find the Rebellion Zones that apply to your pattern type.** Each pattern has high-value targets—places where your opposition work will yield the biggest returns. Your job is to follow the process.

2. **Resist the urge to jump around.** Your subconscious will try to convince you that some other behavior is "more important" or that you should follow a different rebellion path based on what feels relevant in the moment. Don't fall for it.

3. **Trust the structure.** This system is designed to break cycles in a way that ensures sustainable rewiring. If you skip ahead, pick the "easiest" Rebellion Zones, or apply opposition inconsistently, you'll sabotage your own progress.

At this stage, you're actively rewiring your patterns. That means you need to engage with precision, consistency, and full commitment. This process is about executing rebellion in the exact sequence required for it to hold.

Follow the strategy. No cherry-picking. No shortcuts. No substitutions. If you want rebellion to work, you have to commit to playing the long game.

Identifying Your Rebellion Zones: Precision Over Force

Not all opposition is equally effective. Some pattern-breaking efforts will create a domino effect, while others will barely scratch the surface. If you don't identify your high-value targets, you'll waste energy in areas that feel productive but ultimately allow the deeper pattern to remain intact.

Your subconscious will try to distract you with controlled rebellion—changes that seem significant but actually reinforce the original cycle. This is how people stay trapped in false progress loops, making just enough change to feel like they're growing while keeping the core pattern fully operational. Here, precision matters.

Finding Your High-Value Targets

Your Rebellion Zones exist in the areas where your subconscious fights back the hardest. These are the pressure points that, when opposed correctly, cause a structural collapse of the pattern rather than just a surface-level disruption.

To find these high-impact areas, *ask yourself*:

- Where do I feel the most resistance when I consider doing the opposite of my pattern?

  If the thought of doing something differently creates anxiety, anger, or immediate shutdown, it's likely a critical Rebellion Zone.

- What behaviors, thoughts, or choices have remained unchanged despite my best efforts?

  If you keep circling back to the same struggle no matter what approach you take, you're likely hitting a reinforced structure in your subconscious.

- Where do my strongest self-justifications, emotional reactions, or shutdowns occur?

  The areas where you feel most defensive, dismissive, or emotionally reactive are often the ones most crucial to target.

- Where do I currently seek pleasure, comfort or the path of least resistance?

  These areas are ripe for rebellion. Intentionally embracing delayed gratification, harder but more intentional work and resistance all help you win your brain back.

Your Rebellion Zones are the places your brain will fight to keep the strongest grip on the pattern. If a certain opposition feels easy, it's probably not hitting the right target.

The Illusion of Choice: Spotting False Exits

Your subconscious will offer you controlled rebellion options, changes that feel like opposition but actually allow the pattern to remain intact. This is the illusion of choice. It lets you believe you're making progress while ensuring that the real pattern opposition never happens.

Examples of False Exits:

Shifting behaviors instead of addressing the core pattern.

- Example: Instead of addressing a pattern of avoidance, you hyper-focus on a "different problem" that feels urgent but doesn't require true opposition.

Rebelling in ways that feel big but don't challenge the subconscious rule.

- Example: You want to stop over-explaining in conversations, so you cut off communication entirely—avoiding interaction rather than changing how you engage.

Creating new justifications to avoid actual rebellion.

- Example: You convince yourself that you're "not ready" for full opposition, so you delay action in favor of more "preparation."

To successfully rewire, you must be able to see through the illusion and choose real rebellion over controlled rebellion. This requires precision over force—picking the right opposition, not just any opposition. When you hit the right Rebellion Zones, the whole system begins to collapse.

Understanding the Battlefield: What You'll Need to Master for Success

The next battle stage is about dismantling the subconscious language systems keeping the pattern alive. If you don't address the way your brain justifies, distorts, or manipulates reality to maintain old behaviors, rebellion will feel like a constant uphill battle. This is why many people experience temporary wins but long-term collapses. They focus on changing actions without confronting the internal narratives that keep them trapped.

Your brain will fight back with linguistic distortions, false narratives, and subconscious scripts designed to convince you that rebellion is irrational, dangerous, or impossible. These distortions reinforce it by ensuring that opposition feels unnatural, unsafe, or even delusional. If you don't recognize and strip down the language system that built the pattern, opposition alone won't hold.

The Role of Subconscious Language in Self-Deception

Your subconscious controls perception. The way you frame reality in your internal dialogue dictates whether opposition feels logical or self-destructive. If the language system behind your pattern remains intact, your brain will override rebellion by distorting its meaning.

- Opposition feels like self-sabotage instead of self-liberation.

  Example: "If I set this boundary, I'll lose people who matter to me." (Reality: You'll lose people who only thrive in your dysfunction.)

- Change feels unsafe, even when the current pattern is destructive.

    Example: "I know I need to leave this situation, but what if the alternative is worse?"

- The brain justifies delays, minimizing the urgency of opposition.

    Example: "I'll start doing things differently once I feel more prepared."

This is where many people get stuck in intellectual awareness but never execute real change. They understand their pattern, but because their internal language hasn't shifted, the pattern still makes more sense to them than rebellion does.

Unlocking Rebellion Zones with Emotional Logic Intervention Questions

Opposition alone isn't enough—you need to break the internal logic system holding the pattern in place. Later in the book, you'll be introduced to ELI (Emotional Logic Intervention) questions, a tactical tool designed to interrupt subconscious scripts and force your brain to recalibrate.

- Instead of relying on sheer force to oppose a pattern, ELI questions unlock the rebellion zone naturally by exposing the faulty logic keeping it intact.

- The more your brain is forced to logically dismantle its own self-deception, the easier it becomes to sustain rebellion without emotional resistance.

If you only change behavior but leave the language system untouched, your brain will work overtime to pull you back into the pattern. This is where most people fail—not because they weren't willing to rebel, but because they didn't dismantle the subconscious rules that made the pattern feel necessary in the first place.

The Rules of Engagement: Navigating the Rebellion Without Self-Sabotage

Rebellion requires executing precise, high-leverage opposition that dismantles the pattern at its root. If you go in blindly, making random changes that feel rebellious but don't actually target the structure keeping the pattern alive, you're just exhausting yourself.

To ensure that your rebellion leads to real rewiring rather than frustration, regression, or overcorrection, you need to follow these Rules of Engagement.

1. Opposition Must Be Precise—Not Random

You don't need to change everything. You need to change the right things.

- Random acts of rebellion won't dismantle a pattern.

- The most effective opposition targets the pattern's strongest justification mechanisms.

- If opposition feels easy or aimless, you're likely missing the real target.

Example: If your pattern is avoidance, the real rebellion isn't cutting off communication—it's engaging in direct, uncomfortable conversations when every part of you wants to run.

2. Resistance Means You're Hitting the Right Target

Your subconscious is wired to protect your default patterns. When opposition feels deeply uncomfortable, that's a sign you're in the right place.

- If a rebellion zone feels effortless, you might be choosing an easier alternative rather than facing the real opposition.

- The stronger the internal resistance, the more likely you've found a high-value target.

- Your brain will always try to steer you toward the "safe" version of rebellion. Ignore it.

Example: If setting boundaries makes you anxious but cutting people off completely feels easy, your real opposition is probably learning to hold the boundary rather than avoid the interaction altogether.

3. Beware of Overcorrection and Pendulum Swings

Your brain's first instinct isn't precision; it's overcorrection.

- Many people think rebellion is just doing the opposite of their pattern. It's not.

- If you go from one extreme to another, you're reinforcing the idea that balance is impossible.

- The goal is to execute opposition in a way that creates long-term stability.

- Sustainable rewiring happens when you learn to tolerate discomfort, not escape it through another extreme.

Example: If your pattern is people-pleasing, rebellion requires learning to say no and stay present for the discomfort instead of numbing or avoiding it.

4. Your Subconscious Will Try to Talk You Out of Rebellion

The moment you step into opposition, your subconscious will start spinning narratives to keep you from following through.

Common Justifications Your Brain Will Use:

- "This is unnecessary. I don't need to push myself this hard."

- "I'll just ease into this gradually instead." (Translation: Delay until I can justify not doing it at all.)

- "I've already done so much work. I deserve a break." (Translation: Let me sneak back into my pattern under the guise of self-care.)

- Your job is to become fluent in spotting these narratives before they take hold.

Example: If your opposition is staying in discomfort instead of numbing out, your brain will try to justify avoidance as rest. Learn to separate true recovery from pattern reinforcement.

5. No One Is Coming to Force You Into Rebellion

Rebellion is a solo battle. No one is going to drag you into pattern opposition, and no external accountability will save you if you're still internally negotiating with your patterns.

- You are responsible for your own opposition strategy.

- You are responsible for seeing through your own self-deception.

- You are responsible for whether this rebellion succeeds or collapses under self-justification.

- The hardest part of rebellion is the moment you realize that no one else is responsible for making sure you follow through.

Example: If you rely on someone else to hold you accountable, your pattern isn't truly breaking—it's just transferring responsibility. The moment that external accountability disappears, you'll relapse.

Every one of these rules exists for a reason. They aren't suggestions. They're the difference between rebellion that rewires and rebellion that burns out, collapses, or loops back into the same dysfunction. If you ignore them, your brain will make sure you fail. If you follow them, rebellion isn't just possible—it's inevitable.

You're Either Executing Rebellion, or You're Not

There is no middle ground.

- If you cherry-pick your rebellion zones, you are not truly rebelling.

- If you let your subconscious talk you into an easier alternative, you are reinforcing the pattern.

- If you expect someone else to push you through resistance, you are still outsourcing responsibility.

- Rebellion requires action. Either you're executing opposition, or you're negotiating with your pattern. There is no in-between. Choose wisely.

The Next Step: Stepping Onto the Battlefield

You've now been given the blueprint: how Rebellion Zones work, why precision matters, and how your subconscious will try to keep you from fully engaging in opposition. You understand that this is about systematically dismantling the architecture of your patterns. But knowing the strategy and executing it are two entirely different things.

This is where theory ends, and real rebellion begins.

The next three chapters will take you into the specifics of your pattern type's rebellion zones. This is where you'll pinpoint the exact areas that need opposition, uncover the subconscious justifications keeping them intact, and execute rebellion in a way that actually rewires—not just disrupts.

Your only job now? Follow the strategy.

This is about consistency and precision. Your subconscious will try to pull you off track, make you second-guess your rebellion zones, or tempt you into the illusion of progress by choosing easy opposition over necessary opposition. Stay the course.

Now grab a highlighter, lock in your focus, and get ready to identify your pattern-specific rebellion zones. Because from this point forward, you're rewiring. The next move isn't optional. It's necessary.

CHAPTER 24

ABANDONMENT– CONTROL TO BE SAFE (OVERT)

Overt Control types focus on maintaining absolute certainty by ensuring that you are in control of outcomes, environments, and people at all times. You believe that if you don't take control, things will spiral into chaos, and you will be left vulnerable, powerless, or abandoned. Because of this belief, you adopt a direct, forceful, and structured approach to every area of life—making decisions quickly, anticipating problems before they arise, and exerting dominance over situations to ensure they go according to plan.

You view control as safety and certainty as stability. When things feel unpredictable, you feel an overwhelming need to correct, organize, and take charge to prevent worst-case scenarios. This keeps you in a constant state of hypervigilance, ensuring that nothing falls through the cracks but also making it difficult for you to trust others, delegate, or experience true relaxation.

While this control strategy makes you highly competent, reliable, and effective, it also sets you up for intense frustration, impatience, and eventual exhaustion when others don't meet your standards or when life inevitably throws unexpected challenges your way.

Core Motivations

1. Fear of Chaos or Uncertainty

You believe that if you don't step in, things will spiral into instability—and instability leads to danger, failure, or loss of control.

2. Desire for Efficiency and Perfection

You are driven by the need for things to be done the right way (your way), which leads you to meticulously control details and structure every outcome.

3. Belief That Others Can't Be Trusted to Handle Things

You struggle to rely on others because you assume they won't meet your standards or will inevitably fail—forcing you to step in and fix it anyway.

4. Subconscious Fear of Being Let Down or Abandoned

You assume that if you aren't actively managing everything and making yourself indispensable, people will no longer need you, and you'll be left behind.

5. Frustration with Others' Incompetence or Lack of Urgency

You frequently feel like you're the only one who truly understands how to get things done efficiently and correctly—leading to irritation and resentment when others don't meet your expectations.

6. Attachment to Being the One in Control

You equate leadership with safety and struggle to let go of control because it feels like handing over your security to people who won't handle it properly.

7. Fixation on Preventing Mistakes Before They Happen

You constantly anticipate problems and step in to prevent them, believing that if you don't, everything will fall apart.

8. Need for Predictability and Order

You prefer structured, controlled environments where you know what to expect, and you work to enforce this wherever possible to avoid uncertainty.

9. Resistance to Delegation

Even when you're overwhelmed, you struggle to let go of responsibilities because you believe no one else will do it right or with the same level of care.

10. Fear of Wasted Time or Inefficiency

You become impatient or irritated when others move too slowly or fail to meet your standards—seeing their inefficiency as a direct burden on you.

Why Do You Need Rebellion Zones?

Your need for total control and hyper-competence keeps you trapped in cycles of frustration, overburdening yourself, and struggling to delegate or trust others. The rebellion zones help you:

1. You Think You're Being Responsible, But You're Actually Operating from Hypervigilance

You convince yourself that stepping in is necessary to prevent chaos—but it's not logic driving you, it's fear. Your brain equates letting go with danger, even when it's not.

Rebellion Zones push you to recognize when control is a trauma reflex, not a strategic decision.

Why You Need This: To stop letting fear shape your leadership, relationships, and sense of worth.

How You Approach This Rebellion Zone:

• **Observe** when your urgency to take control spikes—even in low-stakes situations.

• **Notice** when your body reacts first: tension, shortness of breath, or a need to act fast.

• **Remind yourself** that fear-based control only creates the illusion of safety—it doesn't build it.

• **Challenge yourself** to let this unfold and see who steps in without managing or directing.

The Self-Fulfilling Prophecy: *By reacting from hypervigilance, you reinforce the belief that everything depends on you—when, in reality, you're the one creating the emergency.*

2. You Think You're Just Being Thorough, But You're Actually in a Loop of Over-Responsibility

You take on too much, then micromanage everyone involved. You tell yourself it's necessary—but it's perfectionism, not leadership.

Rebellion Zones break the cycle of hyper-responsibility that keeps you overworked, resentful, and alone.

Why You Need This: To stop burning out while resenting everyone around you for not helping.

How You Approach This Rebellion Zone:

• **Observe** how often you overcommit, over-plan, or try to do everything yourself.

• **Notice** when your frustration builds toward others even though you never gave them space to help.

• **Remind yourself** that being in control of everything keeps you in a trap of exhaustion and resentment.

• **Challenge yourself** to delegate tasks and resist the urge to follow up or redo them afterward.

The Self-Fulfilling Prophecy: By doing everything and resenting everyone, you keep yourself stuck in a cycle of isolation you secretly want out of.

3. You Think You're Just "Being Realistic," But You're Actually Expecting Others to Fail

You convince yourself you're just anticipating outcomes, but you walk into every situation assuming others will drop the ball.

Rebellion Zones challenge you to give people the chance to prove you wrong—without stacking the deck against them.

Why You Need This: To build relationships based on real trust, not quiet contempt or disappointment.

How You Approach This Rebellion Zone:

• **Observe** how often you assume others will fail or underdeliver unless you step in.

• **Notice** when you subtly sabotage trust by preemptively correcting, checking, or doubting.

• **Remind yourself** that people can only rise when they're actually given space to try.

• **Challenge yourself** to let someone follow through completely without inserting your feedback until it's finished.

The Self-Fulfilling Prophecy: *By assuming failure and acting accordingly, you create the very incompetence you feared—then use it to justify tighter control.*

4. You Think You're Just "Fixing It Fast," But You're Actually Avoiding Discomfort

You jump in quickly when things feel uncertain—not because it's urgent, but because you can't stand the discomfort of waiting or watching things unfold.

Rebellion Zones challenge you to sit still when your instincts scream to interfere.

Why You Need This: To retrain your brain to respond to discomfort with curiosity, not control.

How You Approach This Rebellion Zone:

• **Observe** how quickly you react when things feel uncertain or slow-moving.

• **Notice** the discomfort that rises in your body—the tight chest, tapping fingers, or critical inner monologue.

• **Remind yourself** that discomfort is not danger—it's just unfamiliar space your brain doesn't like.

• **Challenge yourself** to stay still, and let the moment play out without interference.

The Self-Fulfilling Prophecy: *By reacting to discomfort with control, you prevent the very growth and connection that discomfort is trying to teach you.*

5. You Think You're Protecting the Future, But You're Actually Robbing the Present

You fix, plan, and correct in advance—so nothing can go wrong. But in the process, you rob the moment of joy, connection, and spontaneity.

Rebellion Zones teach you to stop bracing for disaster and start being present in your actual life.

Why You Need This: To experience a life that isn't constantly being edited, managed, or preemptively protected.

How You Approach This Rebellion Zone:

• **Observe** how often your mind jumps to "what if" or tries to fix problems before they exist.

• **Notice** when you stop engaging with people in front of you because your brain is already managing a future outcome.

• **Remind yourself** that no amount of control can guarantee safety—and it always comes at the cost of real-time connection.

• **Challenge yourself** to let situations unfold without trying to predict, protect, or preempt the experience.

The Self-Fulfilling Prophecy: By always fixing what hasn't even broken, you never experience the peace or presence you're actually chasing.

6. You Think You're "Just Being Clear," But You're Actually Eroding Trust

You tell yourself that being direct, specific, and efficient is helpful. But your tone, urgency, and volume don't land the way you think they do. People feel criticized, small, or constantly on edge around you—afraid of saying or doing the wrong thing.

Rebellion Zones force you to recognize the emotional impact of your delivery—not just the logic behind your words.

Why You Need This: To create environments where people feel safe to engage with you, not defensive or afraid of triggering your anger.

How You Approach This Rebellion Zone:

• **Observe** how often your "feedback" feels more like correction or confrontation.

• **Notice** when people seem tense, apologetic, or overly formal in response to your tone.

• **Remind yourself** that safety in communication isn't about precision—it's about emotional clarity and connection.

• **Challenge yourself** to soften your tone and give people space to be human—even when they mess up.

The Self-Fulfilling Prophecy: By communicating through pressure and critique, you train people to avoid you, shut down, or resist— which reinforces your belief that no one listens unless you're intense.

7. You Think You're "Holding the Standard," But You're Actually Killing Initiative

You believe your high standards are necessary to keep things running. But in your presence, others stop thinking for themselves. They either wait for your lead or rebel against your control.

Rebellion Zones require you to stop hovering, nitpicking, and constantly correcting—so people have space to grow.

Why You Need This: To allow others to take ownership of tasks and responsibilities without relying on fear or friction.

How You Approach This Rebellion Zone:

• **Observe** how often you step in to tweak, improve, or finish something someone else started.

• **Notice** when people start asking you for permission or validation instead of acting on their own.

• **Remind yourself** that your constant involvement is preventing others from learning, contributing, or caring.

• **Challenge yourself** to delegate fully—and let someone else take it from start to finish without your intervention.

The Self-Fulfilling Prophecy: By taking over everything, you train people to disengage—then resent them for not caring as much as you do.

8. You Think You're Being Helpful, But You're Actually Undermining People

You often step in with "support," advice, or solutions before others even ask. But it doesn't feel like support to them—it feels like micromanagement or judgment.

Rebellion Zones challenge you to stop inserting yourself where you haven't been invited.

333

Why You Need This: To let others build confidence and competence without being rescued or corrected.

How You Approach This Rebellion Zone:

• **Observe** how often you give unsolicited advice, solutions, or corrections in the moment.

• **Notice** when people hesitate to speak openly or defend **themselves** around you.

• **Remind yourself** that being helpful without permission often feels like an attack—not support.

• **Challenge yourself** to stay silent unless help is clearly requested—and trust others to ask if they need you.

The Self-Fulfilling Prophecy: By jumping in uninvited, you reinforce the belief that no one can handle anything without you—ensuring they never get the chance to prove otherwise.

9. You Think You're Leading, But You're Actually Dominating

You pride yourself on being decisive and efficient—but it often comes off as controlling or dismissive. Others feel like their voices don't matter, and eventually, they stop offering them.

Rebellion Zones help you learn the difference between leadership and domination.

Why You Need This: To create environments where people feel ownership and agency—not just compliance or fear.

How You Approach This Rebellion Zone:

• **Observe** how often you make decisions without real input from others.

• **Notice** when people seem disengaged, resistant, or silently frustrated with your direction.

• **Remind yourself** that real leadership invites participation—it doesn't demand obedience.

• **Challenge yourself** to slow down and create space for others to contribute, even if their ideas differ from yours.

The Self-Fulfilling Prophecy: By making all the decisions, you alienate the very people you want buy-in from—then blame them for not stepping up.

10. You Think You're Preventing Mistakes, But You're Actually Creating Fear

You believe your control keeps things from going wrong—but the emotional pressure you create leads to more mistakes, not less.

Rebellion Zones force you to stop managing people with fear and start trusting them to learn by doing.

Why You Need This: To stop creating the very chaos you think you're preventing.

How You Approach This Rebellion Zone:

• **Observe** how often your tone, body language, or facial expressions signal disappointment or urgency.

• Notice when people rush, freeze, or second-guess themselves around you.

• Remind yourself that people perform better when they feel safe—not scared.

• Challenge yourself to create an atmosphere of patience and calm, especially in high-stress situations.

The Self-Fulfilling Prophecy: By trying to control every variable, you introduce anxiety that guarantees the outcome you feared.

11. You Think You're Being Honest, But You're Actually Creating Shame

You call it "being real" or "not sugarcoating"—but your communication style often leaves others feeling small, ashamed, or emotionally unsafe.

Rebellion Zones require you to stop using truth as a weapon and start using it as a tool for connection.

Why You Need This: To stop confusing brutal honesty with emotional maturity—and start building trust instead of fear.

How You Approach This Rebellion Zone:

• **Observe** how often you say things others aren't ready to hear, just to prove a point or assert authority.

• **Notice** when people seem hurt or withdrawn after you "tell it like it is."

• **Remind yourself** that timing, tone, and care matter as much as truth itself.

• **Challenge yourself** to filter your feedback through compassion—not superiority or frustration.

The Self-Fulfilling Prophecy: By using truth to control or shame, you destroy the emotional safety needed for people to grow or stay close.

12. You Think You're the Only One Who Can Handle It, But You're Actually Driving People Away

You tell yourself that no one else can handle things the way you can. But the reality is—no one wants to handle them with you because your way feels harsh, rigid, or thankless.

Rebellion Zones ask you to step back and give people a reason to show up—not a reason to walk away.

Why You Need This: To stop reinforcing your isolation and start creating relationships built on mutual effort—not fear of your reaction.

How You Approach This Rebellion Zone:

• **Observe** when you feel the urge to just do it yourself "because it's easier."

• **Notice** when others seem relieved, resentful, or resistant when you step in.

• **Remind yourself** that your high control doesn't just protect outcomes—it pushes people away.

• **Challenge yourself** to leave space for others to help—even if it means things aren't done your way.

The Self-Fulfilling Prophecy: By doing everything yourself, you end up alone—and then use that as proof that others can't be counted on.

13. You Think You're Creating Accountability, But You're Actually Creating Distance

You push others to meet standards, follow through, and do better. But the way you hold them accountable often feels like criticism, comparison, or judgment—not support.

Rebellion Zones challenge you to build accountability through trust and consistency, not control and fear.

Why You Need This: To create long-term connection and reliability without weaponizing expectations.

How You Approach This Rebellion Zone:

• **Observe** when your version of accountability includes sarcasm, comparison, or a short fuse.

• **Notice** when people emotionally withdraw or become defensive instead of stepping up.

• **Remind yourself** that accountability built on pressure doesn't create loyalty—it creates distance.

• **Challenge yourself** to acknowledge someone's effort without immediately pointing out what's wrong or what's missing.

The Self-Fulfilling Prophecy: By using pressure and performance as a connection point, you build relationships rooted in fear—not trust.

By challenging your deep-rooted need to control, you can move toward healthier, more balanced interactions—ones where you can relax, trust others, and still feel secure even when things don't go exactly as planned.

Rebellion Zones

Control is a non-negotiable defense mechanism. Your brain believes that if you don't control every variable, chaos is inevitable. This is about safety at all costs. Unfortunately, the cost is high—your emotional bandwidth, your relationships, and your ability to adapt.

Your subconscious doesn't care if control alienates others, makes them resentful, or creates exhaustion. It only cares that things are done the right way (which, conveniently, is your way). It's why you feel compelled to micromanage, justify why you had to step in, and maintain an iron grip on every moving part in your life. Your brain sees that hyper-vigilance as necessary damage control.

Your Rebellion Zones exist where this instinct to command, dictate, and enforce is strongest—where your subconscious refuses to trust, collaborate, or allow flexibility. These are the pressure points that, when challenged correctly, dismantle the pattern at its core. And the most effective tool to target them? Controlled Surrender.

For someone with an Overt Control pattern, the idea of letting go often feels irresponsible or outright dangerous. Your brain interprets surrender as reckless. This is why advice like "just let things unfold" or "trust the process" doesn't land. It feels dismissive, unrealistic, and frankly, insulting to the part of you that has spent a lifetime ensuring things don't fall apart.

This is where Controlled Surrender comes in.

Controlled Surrender is not passive. It is the intentional choice to not intervene, even when you know you could control or change the outcome. This distinction is what makes it tolerable for your subconscious. Instead of feeling like you're losing control, you are choosing to conduct an experiment—testing your brain's assumptions about what happens when you step back.

Your primary Rebellion Zones will all be rooted in Controlled Surrender. These are the areas where you will challenge your brain's belief that if you don't step in, things will fall apart.

1. Allowing Others to Lead (Even If It Feels Like a Mistake)

Self-Deception at Play: Micromanagement, justification for over-management, blindspot for collaboration, perceived burden of competence

Unconscious Motivation: Avoiding perceived failure, proving your way is the only safe way, minimizing perceived risk

Rebellion Zone: Let someone else take charge of a task without intervening, checking in or giving feedback—even when they do it differently than you would.

Why This Works: Your brain has convinced you that if you don't step in, things will fall apart. But stepping in all the time exhausts you and makes collaboration impossible. People feel harshly critiqued, incompetent or even worse unloved. Managing at this level also diminishes self-efficacy and confidence. People likely make mistakes or walk on eggshells because they fear the feedback or management style that your brain generates. As you embrace this Rebellion Zone, remember: the goal isn't to suddenly love delegating—it's to prove that over-involvement is making things harder, not necessarily better. If you don't learn to back off, other people won't have a chance to a) learn how to do things on their own, or b) get to do things their own way without critique.

How This Plays Out in Real Life

- You ask someone to handle a task, but before they even begin, you've already decided they'll mess it up. You hover, give excessive instructions, or just take over before they have a chance to fail (or succeed).

- When delegating, you still feel the need to review, edit, or redo what was done—because no one does it quite like you do.

- You give people the illusion of leadership, but only as long as they make the same decisions you would have made. The moment they deviate, you correct or override them.

- When someone presents a new approach, your first instinct is to explain why your way is better rather than staying open to different methods.

- You assume that if you don't step in, things will fall apart, get done incorrectly, or cause unnecessary complications. By giving people the opportunity to prove themselves, you justify keeping control.

- Even if things turn out fine without your intervention, your brain dismisses the success as luck or coincidence, reinforcing the belief that your involvement is always necessary.

By constantly stepping in, you unintentionally train people to hesitate, second-guess themselves, or stop contributing altogether, leaving you in a cycle where you're always in charge—because you've created an environment where no one else is willing (or allowed) to lead.

The Challenge: Let Others Lead Without Intervening

- If you assign someone a task, let them complete it without checking in, offering unsolicited feedback, or stepping in to "fix" it midway. If they need help, they'll ask.

- If someone is handling something slower than you would, resist the urge to speed up the process for them. Let them work at their own pace—even if it feels inefficient.

- If a decision is being made without your input, let it happen without inserting yourself. Even if the outcome isn't what you would have chosen, see what happens when you don't have the final say.

339

- If someone's approach is different than yours, allow it to play out without jumping in to correct, adjust, or take over. Different doesn't mean wrong—your way isn't the only way.

- If frustration creeps in, pause before reacting. Are they actually failing, or is your brain just resisting the discomfort of not being in control?

By holding back and allowing others to take the lead, you break the subconscious belief that your involvement is the only thing preventing failure. You also give people the space to build competence, confidence, and independence instead of keeping them in a cycle of hesitation and reliance on you.

2. Resisting the Urge to Preemptively Fix Everything

Self-Deception at Play: Hyper-vigilance, preemptive resentment, justification for over-management

Unconscious Motivation: Anticipating and preventing worst-case scenarios, avoiding chaos, even if it means creating volatility

Rebellion Zone: When you notice uncertainty, remind yourself that you can be a self-fulfilling prophecy. When you think of the catastrophic "what-ifs," your body language and demeanor shift and the eggshell walking commences. This adds significant tension to your external world and it can negatively impact how something naturally unfolds.

Why This Works: Your brain scans for potential disasters before they happen so it can intervene early. But this instinct makes every moment feel like a crisis and it alters your body language and decision-making in a way that can negatively impact your outcome. By practicing controlled surrender and being mindful of your body language and external facade, you've removed the input of hypervigilance from the environment. This gives you a chance to observe how something would unfold without priming it to turn to disaster.

How This Plays Out in Real Life

- The moment uncertainty arises, your brain jumps to worst-case scenarios, so you subtly (or not so subtly) start steering the situation to prevent disaster before it can even begin.

- You don't just worry about things going wrong; you physically brace for impact. Your body stiffens, your tone shifts, your energy changes, and suddenly, everyone around you picks up on the tension. Whether they realize it or not, they start adjusting

340

their behavior accordingly—walking on eggshells, hesitating, or mirroring your stress.

- Because you're hyper-vigilant about things "going off track," you start subtly interfering before a real issue even presents itself. You remind, recheck, ask leading questions, or "just make a quick adjustment"—which all send a clear message: I don't trust this to work unless I control it.

- Even when things are technically fine, you struggle to relax because your brain is constantly anticipating what might go wrong next. This keeps you in a constant state of stress, which inevitably leaks into your tone, reactions, and presence. This makes the environment more volatile than it ever needed to be.

- The thing you're trying to prevent—failure, chaos, miscommunication—is often made worse by your intervention. Your tension sets off tension in others. Your anxiety about things falling apart creates pressure that makes people more likely to screw up, hesitate, or disengage.

You're actively shaping the environment to match your expectations. You assume disaster is coming, so you act like it's already happening. And when things inevitably become strained, your brain takes it as confirmation that you were right to be on high alert in the first place.

The Challenge: Let Uncertainty Exist Without Preemptive Control

If you feel the urge to check in or remind someone, hold back. See what happens when you trust them to manage it without your intervention.

If you sense something might go wrong, resist the impulse to preemptively fix it. Let the situation unfold naturally before assuming disaster is imminent.

If people around you seem tense, check your own energy first. Are they reacting to the situation, or are they picking up on your hyper-vigilance?

If something is taking longer than expected, let it. Observe how things resolve on their own without forcing efficiency.

If frustration creeps in, pause before stepping in. Are you reacting to a real issue, or are you uncomfortable with not knowing how things will turn out?

By allowing uncertainty to exist without micromanaging it into submission, you create space for a reality where things can work—even when you're not controlling them. Instead of shaping the environment to match your worst fears, you give yourself the chance to see that disorder doesn't always mean disaster.

3. Intentionally Leaving Things Unfinished or Unplanned

Self-Deception at Play: Checklist mentality, over-identification with responsibility, perceived burden of competence

Unconscious Motivation: Avoiding perceived failure, forcing immediate course correction, ensuring compliance at all costs

Rebellion Zone: Choose one task, decision, or project and leave it incomplete—on purpose.

Why This Works: Your subconscious treats task completion as proof of control. But this compulsive need to finish everything doesn't just keep you busy—it feeds your anxiety. Letting something remain undone teaches your brain that incomplete doesn't mean unstable.

How This Plays Out in Real Life

- You start the day with a rigid mental checklist—whether it's tasks, routines, or deadlines—and feel an internal urgency to get through all of it, even if some of it isn't actually necessary.

- You can't fully relax or enjoy downtime because unfinished tasks linger in the back of your mind, pulling your attention away from the present moment. Even when you try to take a break, you feel like you should be doing something productive.

- When an unexpected delay or disruption prevents you from completing something, you feel an immediate need to compensate. Instead of adjusting naturally, you scramble to reshuffle plans, stay late, or push yourself harder—because leaving something undone feels like a failure.

- If someone else doesn't finish something, you feel compelled to step in and do it for them. Even when it's not your responsibility, you justify taking over because it's easier than dealing with your own discomfort over it being incomplete.

- If you don't complete everything you set out to do, you judge yourself harshly, as if productivity determines your worth. You tell yourself that falling behind—even slightly—means everything is at risk of unraveling.

Your subconscious equates completion with stability—as if tying up every loose end is what keeps life from spiraling into chaos. But in reality, your relentless need for closure isn't making you more productive—it's keeping you stuck in a cycle of unnecessary pressure and stress.

The Challenge: Break the Checklist Mentality

- If you feel the urge to complete something just for the sake of closure, stop. Let it sit unfinished and observe how your brain reacts.

- If an incomplete task lingers in your mind, resist the urge to rush back to it. Instead, practice tolerating the discomfort of an open loop.

- If your routine or schedule gets disrupted, don't rearrange everything to compensate. Let the missed task go instead of forcing it back into place.

- If others leave things undone, let them. See what happens when you don't step in to complete it for them.

- If your brain tells you that unfinished equals failure, challenge it. *Ask yourself*: Is this truly urgent, or am I just uncomfortable with incompletion?

By intentionally leaving things undone, you prove to your subconscious that completion is not a prerequisite for stability. You free yourself from the endless cycle of *do more, finish more, control more*—and finally allow yourself to exist without being defined by what's left unchecked.

4. Practicing Emotional Detachment from Justice-Based Reactions

Self-Deception at Play: Justice-centric conviction, black-and-white thinking, blindspot for collaboration

Unconscious Motivation: Being the authority on what is "right," preserving personal authority, enforcing personal standards even if it causes resentment

Rebellion Zone: When someone says or does something that feels "unfair," resist the urge to correct, argue, or enforce your version of justice. Acknowledge that you may be assuming ill intent and need to let the situation unfold or ask a genuine clarifying question instead.

Why This Works: You view right vs. wrong as objective, not subjective. But constantly correcting others is draining and alienating. Sitting in the discomfort of not correcting someone forces your brain to confront that justice enforcement is not a survival requirement. Plus you may actually see that you assumed incorrectly or agitated a situation in a way that turned it into a self-fulfilling prophecy.

How This Plays Out in Real Life

- You feel a strong internal reaction when someone says or does something you perceive as illogical, unfair, or just plain wrong. Before they've even finished speaking, your mind is already formulating a rebuttal.

- If someone doesn't follow a rule or standard you believe in, you feel compelled to step in and correct them. Letting it slide feels like allowing chaos to win.

- When people disagree with you, you don't just see it as a difference in opinion—you experience it as a threat to truth, fairness, or morality. You feel personally responsible for making them see why they're wrong.

- You assume others' intent before asking clarifying questions, leading you to react strongly in situations where misunderstanding could have been avoided. Your sense of justice overrides curiosity, and you miss opportunities to actually connect with people rather than police them.

- Even when your correction is technically right, you notice that it rarely produces the outcome you expect. Instead of fostering understanding, it creates tension, resentment, or withdrawal from the other person.

- If you hold back from correcting something, you feel physically uncomfortable. It's like you're watching a train wreck in slow motion. You're often more upset by the perceived violation than anyone else involved.

Your subconscious convinces you that justice enforcement is a survival requirement—if you don't correct things, things will spiral out of control. But constantly policing others drains you, isolates you, and makes collaboration nearly impossible.

The Challenge: Let Justice Exist Without Your Intervention

- If someone says something you believe is incorrect, pause before responding. *Ask yourself*: Am I assuming ill intent, or could I be misunderstanding their perspective?

- If someone acts unfairly, resist the urge to immediately correct them. Instead, observe how the situation unfolds without your intervention.

- If a disagreement arises, focus on curiosity rather than correction. Ask a clarifying question rather than launching into a counterpoint.

- If you feel the need to "set the record straight," check your energy before speaking. Are you trying to connect and understand, or just prove yourself right?

- If frustration creeps in, let go of the need to win. *Ask yourself*: Is enforcing this my responsibility, or am I just uncomfortable with letting things play out?

By practicing emotional detachment from justice-based reactions, you prove to your subconscious that truth doesn't require your constant enforcement. You gain more peace, stronger relationships, and the ability to engage in discussions without feeling personally responsible for "fixing" them.

5. Tolerating Disorganization, Imperfection, or Unexpected Changes

Self-Deception at Play: Micromanagement, justification for over-management, over-identification with responsibility

Unconscious Motivation: Maintaining order, even if it creates an environment where others walk on eggshells

Rebellion Zone: Let things remain "out of order" longer than usual—without immediately correcting them. In fact, encourage someone who you historically correct or micromanage to create a mess on purpose.

Why This Works: Your brain associates disorder with chaos, and chaos with failure and abandonment. But the truth is, perfectionism is generating the very instability you're trying to prevent. By allowing small imperfections without correction, you weaken the subconscious belief that mess equals failure.

How This Plays Out in Real Life

- When something in your environment is out of place, unfinished, or not up to your standards, your body reacts before you even think about it. You feel a rising urgency to fix it—whether it's a crooked picture frame, a messy countertop, or a work project that isn't progressing exactly how you envisioned.

• If someone doesn't complete a task the "right" way, you step in to correct it–often without realizing how this makes them feel. You tell yourself you're just ensuring things run smoothly, but others experience it as micromanagement and lack of trust.

• When plans change at the last minute, you struggle to pivot. Even if the new plan is totally fine, you feel internally disrupted. Your brain has already preloaded the original version as the only "correct" way forward.

• If your schedule gets thrown off, it's hard to focus on anything else until you "fix" the misalignment. The simple fact that something is "off" makes you mentally stuck in correction mode rather than being present in the moment.

• If people around you are comfortable with a level of disorganization or unpredictability that you wouldn't tolerate, you judge them for it–sometimes silently, sometimes vocally.

• Even if nothing actually goes wrong, your subconscious still perceives disorder as a problem. You may not even realize it, but your rigidity is creating tension, exhaustion, and an environment where others feel like they can't relax around you.

Your brain equates perfection with stability and imperfection with failure. But your constant corrections aren't preventing instability, they're creating it.

The Challenge: Allow Disorder Without Correction

• If something feels "out of place," resist the urge to fix it immediately. Instead, sit with the discomfort and observe whether the issue is truly urgent–or just triggering your need for control.

• If someone does something differently than you would, let it stand. Even if it's messier, slower, or imperfect, allow it to exist without intervention.

• If a last-minute change disrupts your plan, accept it as-is. Rather than scrambling to "restructure" everything, see what happens when you just go with the new plan.

• If you feel tension about disorder, check your energy. Are you making the environment stressful because you feel unsettled?

How does your discomfort affect the people around you?

- If you typically micromanage someone, challenge them to create a mess on purpose. Instead of preventing disorder, actively encourage it—and watch how your brain reacts.

By tolerating small imperfections, changes, and moments of disorder, you teach your brain that mess doesn't mean failure, and control doesn't mean safety. In doing so, you create more peace, less tension, and a space where others feel comfortable—not constantly monitored.

6. Letting People Handle Their Own Problems

Self-Deception at Play: Perceived burden of competence, justification for over-management, preemptive resentment

Rebellion Zone: If you sense something might go wrong, resist the impulse to preemptively fix it.

Unconscious Motivation: Keeping people safe, proving your way is the only safe way

Why This Works: Your subconscious has convinced you that your competence obligates you to fix things for others. But every time you step in prematurely, you reinforce the belief that only you can do things correctly. The real battle is about proving to yourself that their failure doesn't mean your failure.

How This Plays Out in Real Life

- When you see someone struggling, hesitating, or making a mistake, your instinct is to step in before they fail. You justify it as "helping," but deep down, it's really about controlling the outcome.

- If a friend, partner, or coworker is dealing with a difficult situation, you feel responsible for solving it for them. You give unsolicited advice, take over logistics, or offer to handle things—even if they haven't asked for your help.

- When people don't follow your suggested solutions, you feel frustrated and resentful. You wonder why they won't just listen to you. After all, you're only trying to make things easier for them.

- If someone fails after you resist stepping in, you feel an overwhelming sense of guilt—your brain frames it as your failure for not preventing theirs. This reinforces your belief that you can't trust people to handle things on their own.

- You have trouble distinguishing between actual responsibility and self-imposed responsibility. Even when something isn't your problem, it feels like it is. So you take it on, often at the expense of your own well-being.

- When someone learns the hard way or takes longer to figure something out, you struggle to watch it happen. Your brain equates struggle with unnecessary suffering, rather than an essential part of learning and growth.

Your subconscious has convinced you that your competence obligates you to intervene—but in reality, your constant intervention is keeping others dependent on you, not stronger without you.

The Challenge: Let People Struggle Without Rescuing Them

- If someone hesitates or struggles, don't jump in. Let them work through it instead of rushing to do it better or fix it.

- If a problem arises that isn't yours to solve, let it stay that way. Instead of inserting yourself, observe how the situation unfolds without your intervention.

- If someone ignores your advice, accept it. Their choices are theirs to make—even if you think they're making a mistake.

- If someone's failure happens despite your discomfort, let it be theirs to learn from. Remind yourself: Their failure is not my failure.

By allowing people to handle their own problems, you teach your brain that competence doesn't mean responsibility. You also free yourself from the endless cycle of carrying burdens that were never yours to begin with—giving others the space to step up and take ownership of their own lives.

7. Intentionally Disrupting Your Routine or Schedule

Self-Deception at Play: Rigidity disguised as discipline, justification for over-management, avoidance of discomfort through predictability

Rebellion Zone: Deliberately alter, shorten, or eliminate part of your established routine—especially when it feels "necessary" for a successful day.

Unconscious Motivation: Maintaining order even at the expense of flexibility, minimizing perceived risk by controlling every variable, proving that structure equals success

Why This Works: Your subconscious convinces you that your rigid schedule is what keeps everything on track—that if you disrupt it, your productivity, mental clarity, or emotional stability will suffer. But your attachment to routine is what's keeping you stuck. These meticulously structured behaviors aren't just about efficiency; they've become rituals of control, reinforcing the belief that if your routine breaks, you break.

How This Plays Out in Real Life

- Your morning routine is non-negotiable, and any disruption—whether it's skipping a workout, missing a supplement, or shifting your usual sequence—feels like it could throw off your entire day.

- If your schedule gets unexpectedly altered, you struggle to adjust, even if the new plan is just as productive or effective. Instead of adapting, you feel mentally off-balance and preoccupied with what didn't happen.

- When making plans, you prioritize maintaining your structure over spontaneity, relaxation, or connection with others. If someone suggests an activity that interferes with your routine, you feel immediate resistance, even if it's something enjoyable.

- You convince yourself that your discipline is what makes you successful, but in reality, your rigidity is creating unnecessary stress—and sometimes making you unpleasant to be around when things don't go as planned.

- If you do have to break routine, you overcorrect later, doubling down on structure the next day to "make up" for the lost time, as if missing one part of your process means everything is at risk of collapsing.

- When others don't follow structured routines, you silently judge them or assume they're less committed, even if their results are the same (or better) than yours.

Your subconscious has convinced you that structure equals success, but in reality, your attachment to rigid routines is keeping you stuck in a fragile system where any disruption feels like a threat.

The Challenge: Break the Illusion of Control Through Routine

- If you always follow the same routine, change one thing on purpose. Skip a step, reverse the order, or eliminate something entirely—just to prove to yourself that you can.

- If your schedule gets disrupted, don't rush to "fix" it. Instead of scrambling to regain control, see what happens when you just go with it.

- If someone suggests something spontaneous that conflicts with your usual structure, say "yes." Even if it's inconvenient, allow yourself to experience flexibility.

- If you feel anxiety about breaking routine, sit with discomfort. *Ask yourself*: Is this actually affecting my day, or is my brain just uncomfortable with change?

- If your productivity feels lower after a disruption, let it be. Resist the urge to overcorrect the next day to "make up" for what you missed.

By intentionally disrupting your routine, you teach your brain that your stability isn't tied to a schedule—it's tied to your ability to adapt. You gain more freedom, less anxiety, and the ability to live in the present without being ruled by the illusion of control.

8. Breaking the Cycle of Preemptive Resentment

Self-Deception at Play: Preemptively taking over tasks to prevent disappointment, assuming failure before giving others the chance to succeed, convincing yourself it's "easier" to just do it yourself.

Rebellion Zone: Step back and let someone complete a task—even if you assume they'll do it wrong, even if they don't do it on your timeline, and even if the end result isn't perfect.

Unconscious Motivation: Avoiding perceived failure by controlling outcomes, proving your way is the only safe way, minimizing risk by removing variables (other people) from the equation.

Why This Works: Your subconscious is locked into a self-fulfilling prophecy—assuming people will fail, so you intervene before they have the chance to prove you right or wrong. The problem? This pattern never actually tests your assumption. Instead, you keep reinforcing the belief that only you can do things correctly, which not only exhausts you but also breeds resentment toward the very people you refuse to trust.

How This Plays Out in Real Life

- Before someone even has the chance to take responsibility for something, you've already decided they won't do it correctly—so you handle it yourself instead.

• If a task is assigned to someone else, you watch for signs of failure and step in preemptively, justifying it as efficiency rather than a lack of trust.

• You assume that if you don't take control, you'll be the one suffering the consequences—so you'd rather take on the burden than risk being let down.

• Even if someone successfully handles a responsibility, you don't register it as proof they're capable. Instead, you convince yourself it was a fluke, luck, or because you set them up for success behind the scenes.

• When people around you hesitate, you see it as confirmation they're incapable—but in reality, they're hesitating because they're used to you stepping in before they can act.

• You mentally categorize people as "unreliable" before they've even had the chance to show competence.

• You step in before anyone else does, ensuring you stay in control but also reinforcing the belief that they wouldn't have done it anyway.

• You feel unappreciated and overburdened. But you're setting up the dynamic by refusing to delegate.

• You start believing no one else cares or tries as hard as you do—not realizing that they're disengaging because they know you'll just take over.

Your subconscious thinks it's protecting you from disappointment—but in reality, it's creating a cycle where you're always carrying everything alone, and others aren't even given the chance to prove themselves.

The Challenge: Let People Show Up (or Not) Without Intervening

• If someone forgets something, let them remember. Don't remind them, and don't step in. Let them experience the natural consequence of forgetting.

• If a task isn't getting done fast enough, don't swoop in. See what happens when you don't act as the safety net.

• If someone doesn't offer help, ask for it instead of assuming they won't step up. Give them the opportunity before you decide they'll let you down.

- If you feel frustration creeping in, check your assumptions before taking action. Are they actually failing, or are you projecting failure onto them before it happens?

- If someone completes something in a way that isn't your way, let it be. Different doesn't mean wrong—resist the urge to tweak, correct, or redo it.

By breaking the cycle of preemptive resentment, you finally allow the people around you to step up instead of assuming they'll fail. The burden of responsibility shifts off your shoulders, and you start experiencing what it's like to be supported—rather than constantly carrying everything alone.

What You Gain by Embracing Rebellion Zones

The reason your brain resists these changes so intensely is simple: it believes control is the only thing keeping everything from falling apart. Your subconscious has convinced you that if you loosen your grip, things will collapse—people will fail, chaos will spread, and you'll be the one left picking up the pieces. But that's the lie.

What actually happens when you lean into Controlled Surrender and actively embrace your Rebellion Zones? Everything improves—not just for you, but for everyone around you.

1. You'll Strengthen the People Around You (Instead of Weighing Them Down)

Right now, your instinct to step in, oversee, and preemptively fix things is actually preventing others from developing their own self-efficacy. When you control the process, you rob others of the chance to figure things out for themselves. But when you give space—true space, not hovering-in-the-background-waiting-to-fix-it space—people rise to the occasion.

- The people you manage at work will stop relying on you to double-check every decision.

- Your friends and family will feel more capable, trusted, and self-sufficient.

- Your kids or partner will learn to take responsibility, rather than assuming you'll step in when they fall short.

When you stop making other people's success or failure your responsibility, they actually start owning their own outcomes, which makes life easier for everyone.

2. You'll Reduce the Fear of Making Mistakes (Which Ironically, Reduces Mistakes)

Right now, your control-based leadership creates an invisible but powerful pressure, a fear of getting things wrong. And when people are afraid to fail, they actually fail more often.

- When you micromanage, people second-guess themselves, hesitate, or overthink, which leads to unnecessary mistakes.

- When you allow people to do things their way, they stop walking on eggshells and start learning from experience, not fear.

- The people around you will start making better decisions because they'll have the space to learn without the weight of your expectations crushing them.

3. You'll Experience More Collaboration, Positive Feedback, and Better Communication

- Right now, collaboration is strained because your subconscious treats alternative perspectives as a threat to your sense of control.

- When you practice Controlled Surrender, people start responding to you differently. Instead of avoiding confrontation or feeling shut down, they'll actually contribute more.

- You'll start receiving positive feedback about your communication shifts, and the quality of conversations will improve. Instead of running everything solo, you'll actually be part of a team.

4. You'll Get Your Time and Energy Back

Right now, your pattern drains you.

- You spend countless hours managing, overseeing, correcting, and anticipating problems.

- You hold an impossible mental to-do list, keeping track of what everyone else is doing wrong and what you need to fix.

- Even when you're physically resting, your brain is still running through "what-ifs," worst-case scenarios, and contingency plans.

When you implement Controlled Surrender, all that mental noise quiets. You're no longer wasting energy fighting problems that aren't actually yours to solve.

- You'll have more time to focus on what actually matters to you—whether that's work, hobbies, health, or relationships.

- You'll finally be able to experience actual rest, instead of just pausing between battles.

5. You'll Decrease Resentment and Create Healthier Relationships

Right now, your need for control is creating friction in your closest relationships. Even if people don't vocalize it, they feel the weight of your expectations. Whether they respond with avoidance, passive resistance, or outright defiance, the result is the same: resentment builds on both sides.

- They resent you for constantly correcting them.

- You resent them for making you feel like you have to.

When you lean into Controlled Surrender, this cycle breaks.

- Your loved ones get to experience autonomy, agency, and dignity instead of being treated like people who constantly need oversight.

- You stop feeling like everything is on your shoulders, which means less bitterness, frustration, and burnout.

- Instead of people cooperating out of fear of your reaction, they start contributing because they actually want to—which leads to stronger, healthier dynamics built on respect instead of obligation.

6. The Systems Around You Will Work Better Without Constant Supervision

Right now, your subconscious believes that if you're not in control, things will fall apart.

- Systems that rely on micromanagement are weak.

- Teams that can only function under pressure are unstable.

- Relationships that exist under control instead of mutual respect will eventually fracture.

When you remove yourself as the bottleneck, you allow the systems, teams, and relationships around you to become self-sustaining.

- Instead of being the center of everything, you become a respected part of a larger system that works efficiently without you having to carry it all.

- Instead of being driven by fear, stress, and micromanagement, people will be driven by role differentiation, varied approaches, and self-efficacy.

- The dynamic shifts from tension and exhaustion to stability and peace—not because you forced it, but because you finally stopped fighting it.

The Bottom Line

If you embrace your Rebellion Zones, your brain will fight you. It will panic, resist, and tell you you're making a mistake. But when you push through that discomfort, here's what's waiting on the other side:

- Stronger, more capable people around you (who aren't waiting for you to fix everything).

- Fewer mistakes, not more, because people won't be operating under fear-based hesitation.

- A collaborative environment where people contribute willingly, not out of obligation.

- More time and mental energy for yourself—instead of spending it managing everyone else.

- Less resentment, stress, and burnout in your relationships.

- Systems that actually function without you having to micromanage.

The control you cling to is actually creating the chaos you fear. The moment you step back, trust the systems, and let people operate without constant interference, life gets easier—not just for them, but for *you*.

CHAPTER 25

ABANDONMENT– CONTROL TO BE SAFE (COVERT)

Unlike Overt Control, which enforces order through direct management, your control is subtle, indirect, and often unspoken—but just as powerful. You don't impose structure with force; you shape outcomes behind the scenes.

Your subconscious believes that direct control is too risky, that being overt will make you a target, a burden, or too exposed. So instead, you manage from the shadows, steering situations while appearing hands-off, keeping real thoughts private while presenting selective truths, and subtly managing people without making them realize they're being managed.

Your Rebellion Zones exist where your instinct to withhold, maneuver, or disengage is strongest—where you convince yourself that your actions (or lack of action) are about keeping the peace when they're actually about maintaining control. These are the exact places where intentional disruption will force your subconscious to adapt.

You are motivated by a deep-rooted need to ensure emotional and situational stability without appearing controlling. Unlike the overt control subtype, which openly enforces order, Control (Covert) ensures control through subtlety, strategy, and perception management. This type relies on indirect methods to manipulate outcomes while maintaining the illusion of flexibility and passivity.

Core Motivations

1. Maintaining Silent Control While Appearing Hands-Off

You don't want to be perceived as controlling, so you influence situations behind the scenes. You ensure things go your way by subtly steering conversations, withholding information, or guiding others in a way that feels like the other person's choice.

2. Protecting Emotional Safety Without Appearing Vulnerable

You carefully manage relationships to avoid situations where you could be abandoned, or emotionally exposed. You often pull strings quietly to ensure you are never in a position of emotional dependency.

3. Avoiding Direct Conflict While Still Ensuring the Desired Outcome

You don't want to be in open power struggles, so you find indirect ways to get what you want. This often looks like framing a conversation so that the other person feels like they made the choice—but in reality, you know you led them there.

4. Creating a Narrative That Justifies Control as "Adaptability" or "Self-Preservation"

You tell yourself that you are just being adaptable while actually maneuvering circumstances to fit your agenda or desired outcome.

5. Ensuring Predictability Without Seeming Rigid

You avoid chaotic or unpredictable situations by carefully managing people and events in ways that feel non-confrontational. You might make "suggestions" that feel like guidance but are actually steering someone into a predetermined choice.

6. Shifting Responsibility to Others While Maintaining Control

You let others believe they have control, while withholding key information, subtly questioning their choices, or shifting dynamics so the desired outcome still happens. This can result in subtle manipulation, like phrasing things in ways that lead people to a decision rather than outright demanding it.

7. Avoiding Exposure of Their True Intentions

Your greatest fear is being called out on your control tactics, as you deeply need to believe that you aren't controlling. You may become evasive, passive-aggressive, or ghost if you feel your tactics are being seen for what they are.

Why Do You Need Rebellion Zones?

You don't call it control—you call it managing, guiding, or keeping things on track. You convince yourself that people make their own choices, but in reality, you've subtly influenced the situation to ensure the outcome you wanted. Your control is quiet, strategic, and often undetected by the people around you.

But here's the problem: Your need to control shapes how people engage with you. You don't give them full autonomy, and in doing so, you never get to see what's actually real.

The Rebellion Zones aren't about forcing you into chaos or surrendering control completely. Instead, they challenge your assumptions about what happens when you stop interfering. These Rebellion Zones push you to disrupt the belief that control equals safety, forcing you to step back, observe, and let things unfold without your invisible hand in the mix.

1. You Think You're Just "Managing Things," But You're Actually Manipulating Outcomes

You tell yourself you're just being helpful, anticipating needs, or offering insight. But you're subtly steering people in the direction you want them to go, while letting them believe they made the decision themselves.

Rebellion Zones force you to stop pulling strings and allow things to unfold without interference so you can see what's actually real. You gain the ability to experience relationships where people engage with you based on genuine choice, not subtle influence.

How You Approach This Rebellion Zone:

- **Observe** how often you give advice, plant ideas, or redirect conversations to shape an outcome.

- **Notice** when you let someone believe they made a choice independently when, in reality, you nudged them there.

- **Remind yourself** that real trust is built when people make choices freely, not when they are subtly influenced into them. If you never allow things to unfold naturally, you'll never know what's actually meant for you.

- **Challenge yourself** to let situations play out without adjusting them behind the scenes.

The Self-Fulfilling Prophecy: *By constantly influencing outcomes, you never get to see what people would do on their own—reinforcing your belief that you have to control things for them to work out.*

2. You Hide Behind the Illusion of Emotional Self-Sufficiency

You tell yourself that you don't need people the way they need you. You avoid direct emotional expression, choosing withholding, evasion, or humor instead. On the outside, you seem self-reliant. On the inside, you're exhausted from carrying it all alone.

Rebellion Zones push you to communicate openly and take emotional risks rather than defaulting to your usual detached, strategic approach. You gain the ability to stop filtering emotional connection through control and experience relationships without hiding behind detachment.

How You Approach This Rebellion Zone:

- **Observe** how often you rely on humor, logic, or deflection to avoid expressing real feelings.

- **Notice** when you downplay your own emotions while expecting others to share theirs.

- **Remind yourself** that emotional connection isn't a one-way street. If you expect depth from others, you have to be willing to offer it, too. Vulnerability doesn't make you weak; it makes relationships real.

- **Challenge yourself** to express your needs, opinions, or frustrations directly without filtering or softening them to avoid vulnerability.

The Self-Fulfilling Prophecy: *By keeping yourself emotionally guarded, you reinforce the belief that no one can fully understand or support you, ensuring that no one ever does.*

3. You Exit Situations Before You Can Be Rejected

The moment you sense instability, you start pulling away. You tell yourself you're just protecting your peace, when in reality, you're protecting your ego from the risk of rejection, failure, or loss of control.

Rebellion Zones stop you from ghosting, withdrawing, or subtly sabotaging situations before they have a chance to evolve naturally. You gain the ability to break the cycle of preemptive exits and experience relationships without an escape plan.

How You Approach This Rebellion Zone:

- **Observe** when you feel the urge to mentally check out of a situation or relationship before anything has actually gone wrong.

- **Notice** when your Brain Pattern tells you that leaving first is the best way to avoid disappointment.

- **Remind yourself** that leaving first doesn't protect you—it just guarantees that you'll never see what could have happened if you stayed. You're not avoiding rejection; you're ensuring it.

- **Challenge yourself** to stay, engage, and allow relationships to unfold without a premeditated exit strategy.

The Self-Fulfilling Prophecy: By leaving before you can be rejected, you create the very loss and disconnection you were trying to prevent.

4. You Manipulate Perception to Stay in Control

You don't just control situations—you control how people remember them. You carefully curate what information you share, how you frame things, and how much access people have to the real you.

Rebellion Zones strip away this carefully curated version of yourself and force you to engage with people honestly—without pre-planned narratives. You gain the ability to stop controlling how people see you and experience relationships where you're fully seen, not just strategically presented.

How You Approach This Rebellion Zone:

- **Observe** when your Brain Pattern convinces you that you need to maintain a certain image to be respected or valued.

- **Notice** when you withhold, reframe, or selectively share details to control perception.

- **Remind yourself** that true connection comes from being seen as you are, not as the version of yourself you think will be the most accepted or respected.

- **Challenge yourself** to let someone see your real thoughts, opinions, or struggles without managing their reaction.

The Self-Fulfilling Prophecy: By managing perception, you ensure that people never truly know you—just the version you want them to see.

5. You Keep Others Dependent Without Realizing It

You position yourself as the stable, reliable, problem-solver in relationships. You create an unspoken power imbalance, making others feel like they need you more than you need them.

Rebellion Zones force you to step back and let others handle things on their own—even if they do it "wrong" or fail. You gain the ability to experience relationships where you're valued for who you are, not just what you provide.

How You Approach This Rebellion Zone:

> • **Observe** when your Brain Pattern tries to convince you that your value is tied to being needed.

> • **Notice** when you instinctively step in to fix, solve, or manage something for others.

> • **Remind yourself** that real relationships are built on mutual respect—not on someone needing you to function. If people only stay because they rely on you, it's not true connection.

> • **Challenge yourself** to allow people to struggle or figure things out on their own—even if it takes longer or isn't done "right."

The Self-Fulfilling Prophecy: By making yourself indispensable, you attract relationships where people rely on you more than they respect you.

6. You Think Letting Go Means Chaos, When It Actually Means Freedom

Your brain tells you that if you don't subtly manage people and situations, everything will fall apart. In reality, your control is what keeps you stuck, trapped in relationships that feel unbalanced, friendships that feel transactional, and careers that feel exhausting.

Rebellion Zones teach you how to let go without losing yourself, so you can finally experience relationships and success without micromanaging every outcome. You gain the ability to recognize that control doesn't create security—it just creates exhaustion.

How You Approach This Rebellion Zone:

> • **Observe** when your Brain Pattern tells you that if you stop controlling, everything will collapse.

- **Notice** when you feel the urge to intervene, redirect, or micromanage a situation just to feel "safe."

- **Remind yourself** that control is an illusion. You aren't preventing chaos, you're just keeping yourself trapped in a cycle of exhaustion. Letting go is freedom.

- **Challenge yourself** to let things unfold naturally, even if they don't go as planned.

The Self-Fulfilling Prophecy: By insisting on control, you create the very instability and exhaustion you were trying to avoid.

You need Rebellion Zones because your control tactics are an illusion. They give you the feeling of security, but they actually keep you emotionally disconnected, overburdened, and constantly anticipating the next exit strategy.

Your control is exhausting you. Are you ready to see what happens when you stop pulling the strings?

Rebellion Zones

1. Practicing Radical Transparency Instead of Selective Truths

Self-Deception at Play: Selective transparency, rewriting reality, controlling the narrative

Unconscious Motivation: Curating what others know to protect your image, avoiding exposure even if it creates distance, ensuring control over perception

Rebellion Zone: Instead of filtering or withholding key details, practice full transparency, sharing what you normally wouldn't say out loud.

Why This Works: Your subconscious tells you that full honesty is dangerous—that if people knew everything you were thinking or feeling, they'd judge, reject, or use it against you. But withholding key information isn't about keeping things "smooth"—it's about keeping yourself in control. Practicing radical transparency forces you to release control over how others interpret, respond, or act based on what you reveal.

How This Plays Out in Real Life

• You rarely share the full picture of what you're thinking or feeling. Instead, you offer carefully curated pieces of information that maintain the perception you want others to have.

• When you feel vulnerable, uncertain, or upset, you filter your response before speaking—adjusting your words to minimize risk, avoid confrontation, or keep things "smooth."

• If someone asks you how you feel about something, you often give a half-truth or a vague answer, enough to avoid suspicion but not enough to let them fully in.

• You mentally edit your responses based on how you think the other person will react, ensuring that you never say anything that could make you seem weak, unlikable, or out of control.

• You withhold key details that might change the other person's decision-making power. Instead of outright lying, you selectively omit things that would make them act in a way you don't want them to.

• When conflict arises, you justify downplaying or rewriting your feelings, convincing yourself that it's better to avoid the mess rather than risk sharing something that could cause discomfort.

• Even when people notice your lack of transparency and call it out, you brush it off, framing yourself as private, misunderstood, or just "not the kind of person who shares everything."

Your subconscious frames selective truth-telling as self-preservation, but in reality, it's a way of maintaining control over perception, outcomes, and emotional risk. It prevents true connection, keeps people at a distance, and reinforces your belief that no one can fully handle who you are.

The Challenge: Share the Full Truth Without Filtering

• If you usually hold back parts of the story, share the whole thing. No filtering, no omission—say what actually happened or what you really feel.

• If you normally adjust your words to control someone's reaction, resist. Say exactly what you mean without managing their response in advance.

- If you feel the urge to hide something that could shift the outcome, challenge yourself to disclose it. See what happens when you give others full autonomy over their choices.

- If you worry about being judged, express it anyway. Let others react in real time, instead of preemptively controlling how you're perceived.

- If someone asks how you feel, answer honestly—without minimizing, downplaying, or deflecting. Let them see your actual thoughts, not just the version you think they can handle.

By practicing radical transparency, you challenge the belief that only a controlled version of you is acceptable. Instead of managing perception, you allow yourself to be fully seen, fully known, and fully understood.

2. Letting People Make Decisions Without Subtle Interference

Self-Deception at Play: Passive control, shifting responsibility, appearing flexible while secretly steering outcomes

Unconscious Motivation: Ensuring nothing spirals out of control, keeping autonomy while making others feel like they're in charge, steering situations without taking full responsibility

Rebellion Zone: When someone makes a decision, step back fully—no guiding, no leading questions, no subtle redirections.

Why This Works: You may not openly take control, but you still nudge people toward the choices you want them to make. Your influence is about ensuring the final outcome still aligns with your agenda. By letting go of the steering wheel entirely, you prove to your brain that you don't need to orchestrate every detail to stay safe.

How This Plays Out in Real Life

- You ask for others' opinions or input, but only after you've already decided what you want to happen. Their choices are an illusion. If they pick something you don't like, you subtly redirect the conversation until they "change their mind."

- You appear easygoing and flexible, but behind the scenes, you're carefully guiding, suggesting, or framing choices in a way that ensures the outcome aligns with your expectations.

- If someone starts making a decision that doesn't fit your plan, you subtly introduce doubt—asking loaded questions, highlighting potential risks, or bringing up alternatives that nudge them back to your preferred path.

- You let others believe they're in control, but you make small, strategic adjustments along the way to keep things from going too far outside your comfort zone.

- When things don't go your way, you tell yourself, "I didn't even want this in the first place." But the truth is, you never fully let go of control in the first place.

- If someone insists on a choice you don't like, you withdraw your energy, enthusiasm, or support, subtly communicating that they've made the "wrong" decision, even if you never say it outright.

- Even when you think you're stepping back, you're still tracking everything mentally, making sure things don't veer too far outside of your comfort zone, ready to intervene if necessary.

Your subconscious convinces you that it is just being careful, helpful, or making sure things go smoothly. This quiet steering keeps you from ever truly experiencing what it's like to release control and trust others to navigate without your influence.

The Challenge: Step Back and Let the Decision Be Theirs

- If someone is making a choice, let them. Without guiding, leading questions, or subtly influencing their direction, just sit back and observe.

- If you feel the urge to introduce doubt, resist. Let them make mistakes, weigh risks, and own the responsibility of their decision.

- If an outcome isn't what you would have chosen, fully accept it.

- If you find yourself mentally tracking a situation, stop. Challenge yourself to fully disengage, instead of monitoring in case you need to step in later.

- If you feel the need to subtly express disapproval, hold it. See what happens when you don't send signals about what's "right" or "wrong."

By fully letting go of quiet steering, you disrupt the belief that your invisible influence is necessary for stability. Instead of shaping every outcome from the background, you experience what it's like to let things unfold without your fingerprints on them, proving to your subconscious that not everything needs to be managed to be okay.

3. Addressing Conflict Instead of Ghosting or Disengaging

Self-Deception at Play: Avoidance and ghosting, self-protection, easing discomfort by disappearing

Unconscious Motivation: Avoiding emotional risk, minimizing exposure, preventing failure by leaving before you can be left

Rebellion Zone: Stay in the conversation, even when you feel the urge to withdraw. Respond instead of disappearing.

Why This Works: Your default response to emotional discomfort, instability, or potential rejection is to detach, disappear, or quietly phase people out. Your subconscious convinces you that leaving before you can be left gives you power. But in reality, it just keeps you from forming deep, stable connections. Choosing to stay forces your brain to tolerate relational uncertainty instead of trying to control it through avoidance.

How This Plays Out in Real Life

• When a conversation turns uncomfortable, you feel a strong internal urge to shut down, disengage, or find an excuse to leave, physically, emotionally, or both. Instead of responding in real time, you delay, deflect, or disappear until the moment passes.

• You tell yourself that not responding is better than saying the wrong thing. Silence becomes its own form of control, keeping others uncertain, waiting, or second-guessing where they stand with you.

• If someone expresses disappointment, frustration, or hurt, you immediately start crafting an exit plan. Rather than staying and working through it, your subconscious tells you that the safest option is to pull back, minimize contact, or disappear entirely.

• Instead of saying, "I don't want to talk about this right now, but I will," you just vanish and hope the issue fades away.

• You might go silent for days or weeks, then suddenly reappear as if nothing happened, convincing yourself that restarting the conversation would only "make things worse."

367

- If you do stay in the interaction, you keep your responses short, vague, or emotionally distant, giving just enough to acknowledge the conversation, but not enough to truly engage.

- Even if you care about the relationship, you let it die rather than work through the discomfort. You tell yourself that leaving was inevitable, necessary, or the best choice for everyone.

Your subconscious convinces you that exiting is power, that detachment keeps you from getting hurt. It keeps you from experiencing the depth, connection, and trust that come from working through conflict instead of running from it.

The Challenge: Stay Present Instead of Disappearing

- If you feel the urge to ghost, don't. Even if you don't know what to say yet, acknowledge the conversation instead of vanishing.

- If conflict makes you uncomfortable, embrace it. Resist the reflex to shut down, change the subject, or physically leave. Let yourself experience the conflict on the other side of conflict is truth and growth.

- If you normally delay responding to tough messages, reply quickly. Even if it's just, "I need time to process this, but I will respond soon," give the other person clarity instead of silence.

- If you want to emotionally check out mid-conversation, stay engaged. Keep responding, even if it feels difficult or vulnerable.

- If you convince yourself that leaving is the best option, challenge that belief. *Ask yourself*:

  Am I telling myself that leaving now is the best option for everyone involved?

  Does my brain pattern tend to highlight avoidance or withdraw as a go-to strategy?

  Has this created drama and missed opportunities for resolution in relationships?

  Can I challenge myself to stay and face the conflict head on so there is a chance of resolving this issue together?

By choosing to stay instead of disappear, you disrupt the belief that withdrawal is your only form of control. You give yourself the opportunity to build trust, depth, and emotional stability—not by avoiding difficulty, but by proving to your subconscious that you can handle it.

4. Expressing Dissatisfaction in the Moment Instead of Silently Building Resentment

Self-Deception at Play: Withholding discomfort, emotional masking, building resentment

Unconscious Motivation: Keeping frustrations private instead of communicating directly, ensuring emotional safety by avoiding confrontation

Rebellion Zone: When something bothers you, acknowledge it out loud before it has time to fester.

Why This Works: You tell yourself that keeping quiet is keeping the peace, but really, you're avoiding the vulnerability of expressing your needs. Instead, you let resentment build until it leaks out in passive-aggressive behavior, withdrawal, or sudden exits. Practicing immediate expression disrupts the cycle, forcing your brain to experience discomfort without needing to escape it.

How This Plays Out in Real Life

• When something bothers, frustrates, or upsets you, your first instinct is to push it down, pretend it doesn't matter, or convince yourself you're tough enough to handle it.

• Instead of addressing small annoyances in real time, you let them stack up internally. Each unresolved moment adds to the silent scoreboard in your mind—one that no one else knows exists until it overflows.

• When you do express frustration, it's often delayed, passive-aggressive, or comes out in a way that feels out of proportion to the current situation. The person on the receiving end has no idea they've been unknowingly crossing invisible boundaries for weeks or months.

• You pride yourself on being "low maintenance" or "easygoing," but in reality, you're not communicating your real needs, and it's slowly turning into resentment.

• If someone asks if something is wrong, you automatically say, "I'm fine," even though you're absolutely not. You tell yourself you'll bring it up later, but later never comes.

- When resentment builds to a breaking point, you withdraw, disengage, or mentally check out of the relationship or situation entirely without ever having given the other person a chance to fix things.

Your subconscious convinces you that expressing frustration will create unnecessary drama or conflict. Suppressing this frustration leads to exactly what you were trying to avoid—distance, resentment, and emotional disconnection.

The Challenge: Speak When It's Small

- When something bothers you, say it in the moment—even if it feels awkward or unimportant.

- If you catch yourself saying "I'm fine" when you're not, stop and *ask yourself*:

    Do I tell people I'm fine but silently resent them down the road?

    Can I expect someone to fix something I refuse to acknowledge?

    Aren't I setting this relationship up for longterm conflict by avoiding it right now?

- If someone crosses a line or lets you down, express it clearly—without minimizing or brushing it off.

- If you notice your frustration stacking internally, stop and trace it back. What small thing needed to be said earlier but wasn't?

- Challenge yourself to view minor discomfort as a signal to speak up—not as something to bury and "deal with later."

5. Staying Present Instead of Justifying Withdrawal

Self-Deception at Play: Avoidance and ghosting, emotional masking, withholding discomfort, rewriting reality.

Unconscious Motivation: Minimizing emotional risk by never being fully seen, preserving personal autonomy by keeping distance, controlling the narrative by deciding when things end.

Rebellion Zone: When you feel the urge to disengage—whether physically, emotionally, or mentally—stay. Resist the impulse to detach, justify an exit, or shift into emotional coldness.

Why This Works: Your subconscious frames leaving as control. If you end something on your terms, you don't have to experience rejection, disappointment, or vulnerability. Instead of acknowledging when something feels challenging or uncertain, you create narratives that justify pulling away. Staying forces you to experience discomfort without using withdrawal as an escape.

How This Plays Out in Real Life

- When a relationship, job, or commitment starts feeling complicated, emotionally draining, or unpredictable, your brain immediately jumps to the idea that starting over somewhere else will be easier.

- Instead of acknowledging discomfort, stagnation, or conflict, you tell yourself that moving on is the best solution. You rationalize leaving with thoughts like:

  "This dynamic has run its course."

  "It shouldn't feel this hard."

  "I'll be happier starting fresh with someone new."

- You mentally rewrite history to justify the exit, downplaying the good moments and focusing only on the reasons why leaving is the "right" choice.

- The idea of something new and exciting becomes more appealing than the effort required to fix or deepen what already exists. The unknown feels lighter, easier, more fun—not because it actually is, but because it hasn't had the chance to become difficult yet.

- If you do start over, the cycle eventually repeats. New dynamics feel effortless at first, but when emotional depth or complexity begins to develop, you feel the familiar pull to leave again.

- Even when part of you wants to stay and work through things, you convince yourself that reinventing yourself somewhere else will be a shortcut to happiness.

- Instead of acknowledging patterns of avoidance, you frame each new chapter as a fresh start without realizing that the unresolved patterns just follow you.

Your subconscious convinces you that starting over is the solution. But it's just a way to avoid the deeper work of staying, growing, and tolerating discomfort.

The Challenge: Stay and Let Yourself Be Exposed

- If your first thought is, It'll be easier to start fresh. *Ask yourself*:

  Do I have a tendency to get excited about starting new?

  Does my brain trick me into thinking this is going to be easier than sticking this out?

  Have I historically missed moments to grow and build resilience by simply moving onto the next?

  Can I challenge myself to stay engaged for another 30 days to see if this shifts?

- If you feel drawn to the excitement of something new, remind yourself that "new" isn't the same as "better." Every relationship, job, or opportunity eventually requires effort and depth.

- If you catch yourself mentally rewriting history to justify leaving, stop. Acknowledge both the challenges and the good, rather than selectively focusing on why exiting makes sense.

- If you start fantasizing about an easier, more fun version of life somewhere else, challenge yourself to engage more deeply in what's in front of you. See what happens when you lean in instead of out.

- If you're already halfway out the door, say something instead of silently exiting. Have the conversation you'd normally avoid. Face the hard part before assuming that leaving is the only answer.

By staying instead of running, you prove to your subconscious that deep connection, fulfillment, and happiness aren't found by constantly resetting. They're built by showing up, working through challenges, and allowing yourself to be fully present.

6. Letting People Handle Things Without Strategic Influence

Self-Deception at Play: Inability to trust, strategic compliance, passive control.

Unconscious Motivation: Ensuring things go a certain way without overt interference, minimizing perceived risk by managing people behind the scenes, avoiding exposure by never fully trusting others.

Rebellion Zone: Resist the urge to follow up, track, adjust, or mentally manage a situation after letting someone else handle it. Let the chips fall where they may.

Why This Works: Your subconscious tells you that trusting others is reckless–that if you don't monitor, check in, or nudge things in the right direction, failure is inevitable. This belief keeps you trapped in a loop of invisible oversight, where you are never actually free from responsibility. True trust requires allowing things to happen, not just appearing to let go while still tracking the outcome in the background.

How This Plays Out in Real Life

- When delegating, you never fully let go. Even if you aren't actively involved, you track progress, subtly check in, or ensure that you can step back in if needed.

- You say you trust people, but only under conditions you've set. If they veer too far outside those conditions, you find ways to subtly steer them back through reminders, careful phrasing, or "helpful" suggestions.

- If someone makes a decision without consulting you, you feel an immediate urge to assess, adjust, or preemptively correct the outcome before it unfolds.

- When someone struggles, you don't overtly take over, but you position yourself as the fallback option.

- If you don't track a situation, you feel restless, distracted, or anxious, as if not knowing is a form of failure.

- Even when someone proves themselves capable, you mentally dismiss it as luck, an exception, or something that won't last long-term. This reinforces your belief that you are the only constant in ensuring things work correctly.

Your subconscious frames this as being responsible and prepared, but in reality, it's keeping you in a cycle where you never actually experience the freedom of trust.

The Challenge: Fully Let Go and Allow Others to Own Their Role

- If you assign someone a task, let it be truly theirs. There should be no tracking, no checking in, no managing behind the scenes.

- If someone struggles, allow them to struggle. Don't step in–watch what happens when they work through it without your intervention.

- If someone makes a decision you wouldn't have made, let the outcome unfold. Resist the urge to subtly "course correct" after the fact.

- If you start mentally tracking how something is going, stop. Redirect your focus elsewhere and break the habit of low-key monitoring.

- If someone asks for your input, pause before answering. Are they actually asking for help, or are they used to you being the backup plan? Let them figure things out first.

By practicing true trust, you break the belief that your hidden influence is the only thing preventing failure. Instead of being the unseen manager of every situation, you become someone who can exist without needing to control the narrative, even when no one is looking.

7. Letting Your Partner Lead Without Managing from the Background

Self-Deception at Play: Inability to trust, strategic compliance, passive control.

Unconscious Motivation: Ensuring emotional or logistical stability without overt interference, preventing perceived failure by subtly managing decisions, avoiding full vulnerability by maintaining quiet oversight.

Rebellion Zone: Allow your partner to take full ownership of a decision, task, or situation without checking in, advising, or mentally keeping tabs on how it's unfolding. Let them handle it, even if it feels messy or inefficient.

Why This Works: Your subconscious tells you that fully trusting your partner is reckless. If you don't subtly influence, check in, or steer them in the right direction, things will go wrong. This belief keeps you in a cycle where you never actually experience true partnership, only a dynamic where you remain the hidden decision-maker. Letting go of quiet management forces your brain to accept that you don't need to shape everything to ensure security.

How This Plays Out in Real Life

- You say you want a strong, capable partner, but when they step up, you subtly critique their methods. You offer "helpful" suggestions, re-explaining things, or steering them toward your way of doing it.

• You give them the illusion of autonomy, but if they start making choices you don't agree with, you find ways to redirect them back through "casual" comments, gentle corrections, or emotional cues that let them know they're off track.

• When they take the lead in planning something–whether it's a trip, a date night, or a major decision–you mentally track how it's going. You hold back from interfering, but in your mind, you're already preparing a backup plan in case things don't go the way you think they should.

• If they struggle with something, you offer to help before they even ask. You position yourself as the quiet safety net so they never fully get to experience handling it on their own.

• When they make a decision without you, you feel restless, anxious, or even slightly resentful, though you've never vocalized wanting control over the situation.

• If they succeed without your input, you mentally dismiss it as luck, a fluke, or an exception to the rule. This reinforces your belief that they're only capable sometimes, but you are the true constant in keeping things together.

• You subconsciously reward dependence and discourage full autonomy. You do this by withholding trust, approval, or emotional warmth when they make independent decisions that don't align with your expectations.

Your subconscious frames this as being supportive and responsible. But it prevents your partner from fully stepping into their role and keeps you carrying the invisible weight of quiet oversight in the relationship.

The Challenge: Allow Your Partner to Fully Own Their Role

• If they take charge of something, let them. Don't track, don't steer, don't monitor.

• If they struggle, don't preemptively step in. Allow them to figure it out, even if their approach is different from yours.

• If they make a decision you wouldn't have made, let it stand. Don't subtly "fix" or "adjust" it afterward to match your comfort zone.

• If you catch yourself mentally monitoring, stop. Shift your focus elsewhere instead of quietly keeping tabs.

- If they ask for input, stop yourself before answering. Are they actually asking for help, or are they conditioned to check in with you first? Let them work through it before you jump in.

By fully letting go of quiet management, you break the belief that your subtle influence is necessary for stability. Instead of being the unseen handler of your relationship, you allow true partnership to emerge.

What You Gain by Embracing Rebellion Zones

Your subconscious believes it's making sure things go smoothly. You don't demand control; you position yourself as the quiet architect of outcomes. You influence from the background, guiding people, managing perception, and ensuring things don't spiral too far out of your comfort zone.

Your brain tells you that without this silent oversight, things would unravel. That's the lie.

When you actually step into your Rebellion Zones—when you release quiet steering, stop curating narratives, and allow things to unfold without your fingerprints—you gain something unexpected: freedom.

Rebellion Zones force you to confront your hidden control strategies and break free from the need to manipulate the narrative behind the scenes. Instead of remaining in the shadows, quietly managing outcomes, you'll learn to allow others to navigate their own decisions and emotions, creating genuine, trusting relationships in the process.

1. You'll Build Stronger, More Trusting Relationships (Instead of Controlling from the Background)

You currently feel that the only way to maintain control in relationships is by selectively revealing or withholding information. You adjust the narrative, curating a version of yourself that feels safer and easier to manage. But this creates distance and erodes trust. You gain the ability to be fully seen and understood without relying on manipulation. You start to trust others with your truth, allowing you to build more authentic connections.

2. You'll Stop Quietly Steering People's Choices and Finally See Their Real Decisions

You often nudge people in the direction you want them to go without them realizing it. Whether through loaded questions or subtle disapproval, you try to ensure things unfold the way you want them to. You gain the ability to step back and let others make decisions without your invisible influence, allowing you to experience their true preferences and fostering genuine autonomy in relationships.

3. You'll Reduce Emotional Avoidance and Actually Experience Security Without an Escape Plan

Your subconscious tells you that emotional withdrawal is a form of control. When things get tough, you retreat–disengaging to avoid the risk of emotional exposure. You gain the ability to stay present, even during uncomfortable conversations. By confronting conflict head-on, you prove to yourself that emotional stability doesn't require an escape plan–it requires presence.

4. You'll Stop Hiding Your True Feelings and Let Go of Manipulation

You carefully guard your emotions, believing that if people knew how you truly felt, they would judge you or take advantage of your vulnerability. Instead, you withhold or distort your feelings to protect yourself. You gain the freedom to express your authentic feelings without fear of rejection or judgment. This opens the door to deeper emotional intimacy and understanding in your relationships.

5. You'll Stop Using People as Pawns to Create the Outcome You Want

Your interactions are often strategic, designed to ensure that you get what you need or avoid what you fear. But this creates imbalance and leaves others feeling manipulated. You gain the ability to interact without trying to influence the outcome, allowing others to feel empowered and in control of their own decisions while maintaining genuine connection.

6. You'll Stop Seeing Every Interaction as a Battle for Control

You've internalized the idea that the world is a place where power dynamics must constantly be managed. You feel uneasy when you don't have a hand in the decision-making process. You become able to engage in relationships without seeing them as power struggles. You learn to enjoy authentic, free-flowing exchanges that aren't dictated by your need to control every aspect.

7. You'll Learn That Trusting Others Doesn't Mean Losing Control

You fear that letting go of your need to control everything will leave you vulnerable or dependent on others. However, true connection requires trust and mutual respect. You gain the ability to trust others' judgment without feeling the need to take over. You can relax in relationships knowing that true strength comes from shared trust, not dominance.

8. You'll Stop Withholding Parts of Yourself to Stay "Safe"

You've convinced yourself that sharing everything leaves you exposed, so you hold back, even in close relationships, leaving them shallow and incomplete. You become able to share your whole self–flaws, fears, desires, and all–without the belief that you'll be judged or rejected. This brings you closer to others and fosters more meaningful bonds.

The Bottom Line

Your subconscious tells you that control should be quiet, strategic, and undetectable. If no one realizes you're managing things, they won't push back–and everything will stay in balance.

But what if this isn't balanced at all? What if control is what finally sets you free?

When you step into your Rebellion Zones, you stop:

- Strategically withholding information to manage outcomes.

- Influencing people from the background instead of trusting them to figure things out.

- Ghosting, withdrawing, or emotionally disappearing when things get uncomfortable.

- Shaping relationships based on perception management rather than genuine connection.

- Keeping yourself in a cycle where you resent people for relying on you, but also don't trust them to handle things on their own.

Instead, you gain something you've never truly had before:

- More trust from others. People sense when they're being handled, and now they don't have to question your motives.

- Deeper, more genuine relationships. You're no longer managing perception and withholding key truths.

- Less emotional exhaustion. You're no longer running constant mental calculations about how to subtly steer situations.

• More time and energy for yourself. You're not carrying the invisible burden of tracking and managing everyone's reactions.

• Freedom from resentment. You're no longer silently keeping score while pretending everything is fine.

• The ability to let things unfold naturally. There's no need to influence outcomes from the background.

• A real sense of control—without control. Trust and autonomy create stability, not quiet manipulation.

• No more ghosting, withdrawing, or disappearing. You're facing discomfort instead of avoiding it.

• More respect from others. You seriously when they know you say what you mean.

• A life that feels honest and aligned. You're no longer filtering yourself or shaping interactions just to feel safe.

CHAPTER **26**

ABANDONMENT–CONTROL TO BE SAFE (SWITCH)

ABANDONMENT – CONTROL TO BE SAFE (SWITCH) RELATIONAL

Relational switchers are driven by the need to maintain connection and a sense of responsibility for others' stability while avoiding perceived instability in relationships. You compartmentalize your control tendencies—overt in professional settings and covert in intimate relationships—because you believe control ensures competence and success in structured environments but fear it may overwhelm or push others away in emotional or relational settings.

You tend to prioritize stability over authenticity in personal relationships, believing it's safer to be easygoing and agreeable to maintain balance. However, this pattern sets you up for resentment, passive control tactics, and sudden shifts to dominance if you begin to feel unseen, unheard, or when your efforts to maintain stability seem futile.

Core Motivations

Relational switchers act out their behaviors in response to perceived instability or emotional discomfort in relationships. Behaviors are driven by the need to maintain a sense of control without directly confronting the underlying issue.

1. You Fear the Loss of Stability

You suppress overt control behaviors in personal relationships to appear easygoing, but when you feel things slipping into uncertainty, you struggle with bottled-up resentment.

2. You Desire to Prevent Chaos

You avoid direct confrontation, choosing passive forms of control such as subtle manipulation, withholding feedback, or emotional distance.

3. You Seek Validation Through Performance

You feel more secure when you are seen as competent in professional settings, but in personal relationships, you know that directness will disrupt harmony.

4. You Subconsciously Test for Dependability

Instead of directly expressing concerns, you create small conflicts or withdraw emotionally to see how others react, confirming whether people will maintain connection.

5. Compensation for Past Compliance

After prolonged passivity, you sometimes overcorrect into overt control as a way to regain lost influence, leading to an unpredictable relational pattern.

Why Do You Need Rebellion Zones?

Your habitual avoidance of direct conflict and reliance on passive control tactics leads to cycles of instability in relationships. The rebellion zones help you:

- Recognize when you are using manipulation instead of direct communication

- Break the passivity-resentment-overcorrection cycle

- Foster genuine connection rather than testing dependability

- Allow yourself to express needs without fear of disrupting stability

By challenging your hidden need for control, relational switchers can move toward healthier, more sustainable relationship patterns without relying on passive control, emotional withdrawal, or sudden shifts to dominance.

1. Leading at Work But Complying or Avoiding at Home

You run teams with authority and clear direction at work but struggle to assert your needs or preferences at home, opting to keep the peace instead. This habit leaves you feeling unheard and leads to resentment.

Why You Need This: To stop compartmentalizing communication styles. By expressing yourself directly in personal relationships, you allow for genuine connection and mutual respect, rather than silent frustration.

How You Approach This Rebellion Zone:

- **Observe** moments where you avoid expressing needs or desires at home to keep the peace.

- **Notice** how your brain tells you that avoiding conflict will lead to harmony, when in reality, it creates emotional distance.

- **Remind yourself** that direct communication leads to healthier dynamics and prevents resentment from building.

- **Challenge yourself** to speak up when something bothers you, even if it feels uncomfortable.

The Self-Fulfilling Prophecy: By continuing to stay passive, you allow resentment to grow, ensuring that your needs remain unmet and relationships become one-sided.

2. Letting Others Take Charge Without Withholding Feedback

You may appear easygoing, letting others take charge, but underneath, you subtly manipulate situations to align with your preferences. This creates an illusion of flexibility while maintaining hidden control.

Why You Need This: To break free from the illusion of flexibility and experience true vulnerability. By relinquishing control and letting others take charge, you allow relationships to thrive based on mutual input, rather than covert manipulation.

How You Approach This Rebellion Zone:

- **Observe** how often you withhold feedback or subtly influence decisions to align with your preferences.

- **Notice** when you feel discomfort or frustration when things don't go your way, even if you appear agreeable.

- **Remind yourself** that true collaboration involves accepting outcomes without manipulation or hidden influence.

- **Challenge yourself** to give a direct response when asked for your opinion and let decisions unfold without interference.

The Self-Fulfilling Prophecy: By continuously stepping back but still manipulating outcomes, you prevent true collaboration and deepen emotional distance, perpetuating instability in relationships.

3. Acting as a "Supporter" While Covertly Controlling

You often position yourself as the supportive friend or partner, but your help comes with an agenda. You intervene in ways that prevent others from owning their decisions or outcomes.

Why You Need This: To stop the cycle of controlling from behind the guise of helpfulness. By letting others experience both success and failure independently, you allow for growth and real connection, free from hidden motives.

How You Approach This Rebellion Zone:

- **Observe** how often you offer "helpful" suggestions that subtly shift decisions toward your preference.

- **Notice** when you monitor progress or intervene to ensure things go the way you want.

- **Remind yourself** that letting others own their decisions leads to true autonomy, which strengthens relationships.

- **Challenge yourself** to step back and allow others to navigate their own paths without interference.

The Self-Fulfilling Prophecy: By always stepping in and taking over, you undermine others' autonomy, making them dependent on you and reinforcing the belief that they can't succeed without your intervention.

4. Minimizing Conflict to Maintain the Peace

You often suppress your true feelings to avoid upsetting others, believing that staying quiet will keep the peace. But in reality, this leads to unaddressed resentment and emotional withdrawal.

Why You Need This: To stop avoiding confrontation and to recognize that conflict can be constructive when handled with honesty. By addressing issues early on, you prevent resentment from building and create opportunities for deeper connection.

How You Approach This Rebellion Zone:

- **Observe** how you avoid bringing up issues, even when they bother you, in an effort to keep things stable.

- **Notice** how suppressing your emotions or staying silent only causes tension to build up.

- **Remind yourself** that addressing conflicts directly, even when uncomfortable, is essential for maintaining healthy relationships.

- **Challenge yourself** to express your feelings when something bothers you, rather than bottling them up for fear of conflict.

The Self-Fulfilling Prophecy: By avoiding confrontation, you ensure that issues fester, and relationships lose their depth as a result of unresolved tension.

5. Avoiding Vulnerability by Keeping Emotional Distance

You feel safer emotionally distant, afraid that letting others get too close will lead to vulnerability or rejection. So, you keep people at arm's length, using emotional withdrawal to protect yourself.

Why You Need This: To stop using emotional distance as a shield. Vulnerability is essential for building deep, meaningful connections, and embracing it allows for authentic intimacy in relationships.

How You Approach This Rebellion Zone:

- **Observe** moments when you instinctively pull back or disengage emotionally from others to avoid vulnerability.

- **Notice** how distancing yourself might temporarily protect you, but it also leads to disconnection in the long term.

- **Remind yourself** that vulnerability strengthens relationships and that true intimacy requires emotional openness.

- **Challenge yourself** to share your true feelings, fears, or concerns, even if it feels uncomfortable or risky.

The Self-Fulfilling Prophecy: By withdrawing emotionally, you reinforce the belief that others will reject you, leaving you isolated and disconnected.

Rebellion Zones

1. You'll Have Stronger, More Honest Relationships—Without Feeling Like You're Living Two Lives

Self-Deception at Play: You present as agreeable or composed while hiding parts of your identity or true feelings. You tell yourself you're being flexible or keeping the peace, but you're actually avoiding vulnerability.

Unconscious Motivation: Maintaining control by dividing your identity—leading in one context while disappearing in another to avoid emotional exposure or abandonment.

Rebellion Zone: Leading at work, complying at home. You run things efficiently at work but suppress your preferences in personal relationships. You assume that keeping the peace at home means letting others lead—but this passivity isn't true surrender. It's just another way of managing perception and avoiding emotional exposure.

Why This Works: Your subconscious tells you that control belongs at work and compliance belongs at home. But the truth? You can be a leader without micromanaging, and you can be a partner without disappearing. By practicing consistent, direct communication across all areas of life, you stop creating a double life where one part of you thrives and the other self-destructs.

How This Plays Out in Real Life:

- You run your team with authority but hesitate to express needs at home, leaving you irritated when decisions are made without you.

- You tell yourself that "letting others lead" is balance, but really, it's just avoiding conflict.

- You fear that being assertive in relationships will push people away, yet compliance makes you feel unseen and unheard.

- You assume that expressing a need is controlling, but not expressing one at all makes you feel resentful.

The Challenge: Assert Yourself in Personal Relationships Without Defaulting to Compliance

- Share your thoughts or needs in relationships as openly as you would in a work setting.

- If something bothers you, address it directly instead of waiting for resentment to build.

- If you disagree with a partner, friend, or family member, allow yourself to voice it without assuming it will lead to conflict.

- Recognize when you're managing perception in relationships instead of being authentic.

By stepping into direct, honest communication at home—not just at work—you allow relationships to be built on trust rather than strategic self-suppression.

2. You'll Experience True Flexibility—Instead of Using It as a Hidden Form of Control

Self-Deception at Play: Strategic flexibility, passive control, and appearing easygoing while withholding truth. You tell yourself you're being adaptable or cooperative, but in reality, you're quietly managing outcomes behind the scenes—without full transparency.

Unconscious Motivation: Avoiding vulnerability by influencing outcomes quietly—ensuring things go your way without risking confrontation or exposure.

Rebellion Zone: Letting others take charge without withholding feedback. You tell yourself you're "easygoing" in relationships—that you "go with the flow" to keep things simple. But in reality? You still quietly ensure that things ultimately go your way. You may not demand control, but you influence it through strategic flexibility, subtle redirection, and selective withdrawal.

Why This Works: Your subconscious convinces you that keeping control requires subtle influence rather than overt demands. But when you step back and let a decision fully unfold without interference, you break the belief that your flexibility is genuine when, in reality, it's a hidden strategy to maintain control.

How This Plays Out in Real Life:

- You say you don't care where to eat but then steer the decision toward your preference.

- You let others take charge, but if they choose differently than you would, you become subtly withdrawn or frustrated.

- You appear easygoing, but later, you subtly remind people why your approach would have been better.

- You say "whatever works," but feel uncomfortable when things unfold in a way you wouldn't have chosen.

The Challenge: Let Go of the Need to Steer Indirectly

- The next time someone asks your opinion, give a direct response instead of trying to be agreeable.

- Allow a decision to unfold fully without later commenting on how it "could have been done better."

- If something doesn't go as planned, resist the urge to subtly correct or "fix" the situation afterward.

- Notice when you're using flexibility as a means of avoiding true vulnerability or authenticity.

By allowing true flexibility–without strategic influence–you experience what it's like to actually let go, instead of just managing control from the background.

3. You'll Stop Feeling the Weight of Other People's Choices–And Finally Let Them Own Their Outcomes

Self-Deception at Play: You tell yourself you're just being helpful or supportive, but you're actually steering outcomes from the background–often without others realizing it.

Unconscious Motivation: Preserving a sense of safety and importance by staying quietly in control while avoiding the emotional risk of full trust and release

Rebellion Zone: Acting as a "supporter" while covertly controlling. You tell yourself that "supporting others" is different from controlling them. You don't take over–you just offer guidance. You don't demand compliance–you just make sure things don't go off track. But the truth? Your interventions keep people dependent on you while allowing you to maintain control under the illusion of helping.

Why This Works: Your subconscious tells you that you're just helping– but your interventions prevent real autonomy. When you truly step back, you allow others to fully own their decisions and outcomes. You stop carrying responsibility for what isn't yours and release the mental burden of ensuring success.

How This Plays Out in Real Life:

- You offer "helpful" suggestions that subtly shift decisions toward your preference.

- You check in frequently under the guise of "support," but in reality, you're monitoring progress to ensure things go your way.

- You let others lead, but only as long as they make decisions that align with your comfort zone.

- You take on the role of the trusted guide, but the moment someone makes a mistake, you step in to course-correct.

The Challenge: Let Others Navigate Their Own Paths

- Resist the urge to monitor, suggest, or intervene.

- Observe how often you subtly shift discussions or problem-solving toward your preferred outcome.

- Let go of the belief that mistakes equal failure. Growth happens through independent experience.

- Notice when your support is actually a way of ensuring that things unfold within your level of comfort.

By allowing people to succeed or fail on their own, you stop carrying the weight of other people's choices and finally free yourself from the responsibility of silent control.

What You Gain by Embracing Rebellion Zones

Rebellion Zones force you to stop hiding behind passive control tactics and emotional withdrawal in relationships. You may be confident and assertive at work, but struggle to bring that same directness to your personal life, fearing rejection or conflict. These zones challenge you to stop managing perception, overcompensating, or suppressing your true thoughts and feelings. Instead, they help you build authentic, lasting connections based on mutual trust, vulnerability, and consistent communication.

1. You'll Build Stable Relationships Based on Honest Communication

At work, you're able to communicate directly, asserting your needs and preferences with confidence. But in personal relationships, you hesitate, fearing that being too direct will disrupt the harmony or lead to rejection. You gain the ability to express your true thoughts and feelings in your personal relationships just like you do in the workplace. You'll learn that honesty and directness foster trust and mutual understanding.

2. You'll Experience True Flexibility Without Hidden Control

At work, you are able to give clear directions and take charge when needed, but at home, you often default to appearing passive, even though you're secretly controlling outcomes behind the scenes. You might feel like flexibility equals harmony, but deep down, it's a strategy to keep things within your comfort zone. You become able to practice true flexibility, where you allow others to make decisions without the need to guide them covertly. This will create more genuine, trust-based relationships both at work and at home.

3. You'll Stop Testing Others and Start Trusting

You feel confident and secure in your role at work, knowing that you've earned others' trust through your competence. But in personal relationships, you test people's dependability by creating small conflicts or withdrawing emotionally to see if they'll stay. This cycle creates uncertainty and insecurity. You gain the freedom to trust others without needing constant validation or testing. You'll be able to stop second-guessing relationships and begin trusting people for who they are, rather than seeking proof of their reliability.

4. You'll Stop Withdrawing Emotionally and Start Embracing Vulnerability

At work, you're able to engage fully and take charge when needed, but in personal relationships, you retreat emotionally, believing that maintaining distance keeps you safe from rejection or vulnerability. You gain the ability to be vulnerable in relationships, knowing that emotional openness creates deeper connection and intimacy, just as effective communication builds trust at work.

5. You'll Gain Consistency in Your Relational Behavior

You're confident and consistent in your professional life, but at home, you swing between passivity and control. This inconsistency makes it difficult to form stable, trusting connections. You become able to be just as consistent and assertive in your personal relationships as you are in professional settings. This consistency will create a stable foundation for trust and deeper emotional intimacy.

ABANDONMENT – CONTROL TO BE SAFE (SWITCH) SECURITY-BASED

Core Motivations

Security-based switchers are driven by the need to establish control through trust and stability first, before gradually revealing more dominant behaviors. They operate from the belief that they must prove themselves safe and agreeable first before they can begin asserting their full expectations, preferences, or control. Their shift from covert to overt control happens once they feel a sense of security, but this can often feel destabilizing to others, as it may appear as a bait-and-switch in relationships or work environments.

They see their early compliance as a strategy to earn influence, but their later shift toward overt control can create confusion and instability, particularly when those around them expected their initial easygoing nature to remain consistent. This pattern often plays out in professional settings, friendships, and romantic relationships, where they gradually escalate their control over time rather than setting clear expectations from the beginning.

1. You Fear of Losing Control Prematurely

You delay asserting overt control until you feel secure, believing early compliance helps you gain trust before revealing your more dominant or unfiltered side.

2. You Desire to Avoid Early Conflict

You believe that asserting control too soon will create instability or resistance, so you opt for an accommodating approach initially.

3. You Need to Gradually Test Boundaries

You often do not reveal your full control tendencies upfront, instead waiting to see how much authority you can exert once others are comfortable with them.

4. You Subconsciously Need to Reinforce Stability

Once you feel safe, you notice yourself slipping into more overt control, often this passes all of your personal filters and sneak attacks you.

5. You Seek Compensation for Initial Compliance

Because you start in a more passive role, you may later overcorrect into rigid control, feeling you now "deserve" to have your needs met, too.

Why Do You Need Rebellion Zones?

As a Security-Based Switcher, you navigate your relationships and environments with a complex control dynamic—starting off passive and agreeable, only to gradually escalate your dominance once you feel secure. You initially comply and adapt, seeking trust and stability before asserting your preferences or expectations. This delayed shift into overt control, while rooted in your need to feel safe, can destabilize those around you and leave them feeling confused, as it may appear to them as a bait-and-switch.

The problem is, this gradual shift from covert to overt control often leaves others feeling blindsided, creating a sense of instability. What you view as a natural progression to gain influence and protect yourself, others may interpret as manipulation or inconsistency. This pattern can leave you feeling misunderstood, while your relationships—whether personal, professional, or romantic—experience unnecessary strain.

Rebellion Zones force you to break this delayed cycle of control assertion. They challenge you to recognize when your hesitation to assert your influence is masking a hidden agenda, rather than simply being a natural step in building trust. You'll learn to set clear expectations and communicate openly from the start, avoiding the bait-and-switch dynamic that leaves others questioning your true intentions.

By embracing Rebellion Zones, you'll stop relying on gradual escalation to earn control and start fostering a transparent and predictable way of leading and relating. This approach will create more stability for both you and those around you, allowing you to build stronger, healthier relationships based on mutual respect and direct communication.

1. You Stop Using People-Pleasing to Earn Affection and Start Being Authentic

In the early stages of relationships, your brain convinces you that showing up as compliant, agreeable, and accommodating will help you win others' affection or trust. You mirror others, placate their needs, and suppress your true desires to avoid conflict and create a sense of connection. But as you begin to feel secure, you shift into a more controlling and harsh version of yourself, expecting people to meet your needs without the same passive approach.

Rebellion Zones challenge you to stop using people-pleasing and compliance as a strategy to secure affection and trust and to start being authentic from the beginning.

How You Approach This Rebellion Zone:

- **Observe** when you feel the urge to go along with others just to win their favor or make them like you.

- **Notice** how your Brain Pattern tells you that being accommodating is necessary to build trust, even if it means masking your true preferences or needs.

- **Remind yourself** that real trust comes from being open and authentic, not from acting in ways that manipulate others into liking you.

- **Challenge yourself** to show up authentically, even in the beginning stages of a relationship, and express your needs or preferences from the start.

The Self-Fulfilling Prophecy: By using compliance to win affection, you create an illusion of connection that later falls apart when your true needs are revealed, reinforcing the belief that you can't be loved for who you truly are.

2. You Stop Shifting into Control and Start Setting Clear Expectations from the Start

Once you feel secure in a relationship, you begin to shift from a compliant, easygoing version of yourself into a more dominant and controlling person. This abrupt shift often feels like a betrayal to others, especially if they were drawn to the version of you that was initially placating or people-pleasing. They may feel blindsided, confused, and hurt by the sudden change in behavior, especially if they've invested emotionally based on the earlier version of you.

Rebellion Zones push you to stop shifting between compliant and controlling behaviors and start setting clear expectations and boundaries from the very beginning.

How You Approach This Rebellion Zone:

- **Observe** when you feel the urge to change your behavior after securing trust, becoming more controlling or harsh as your sense of security grows.

- **Notice** how your Brain Pattern leads you to feel justified in asserting control, even though it may create confusion and hurt others who trusted the original, more compliant version of you.

- **Remind yourself** that clarity and transparency from the start lead to more stable and trusting relationships.

- **Challenge yourself** to be upfront about your preferences and boundaries early on, instead of holding back and saving your true needs for a later stage.

The Self-Fulfilling Prophecy: By shifting from compliant to controlling, you create confusion and instability, reinforcing the belief that you must manipulate others into liking you before showing your true self.

3. You Stop Manipulating with Early Compliance and Start Building Relationships with Transparency

You may believe that by being overly compliant, agreeable, or accommodating in the beginning, you'll earn the right to later assert control. However, this creates a perception of manipulation, where people feel they've been "baited" into a relationship only to later feel blindsided by the more dominant, harsh version of you. This bait-and-switch behavior can erode trust and cause emotional damage, as others may feel deceived by the version of you that was presented initially.

Rebellion Zones challenge you to stop using compliance as a manipulation tool and instead engage in more transparent, direct, and consistent relationship-building.

How You Approach This Rebellion Zone:

- **Observe** when you feel the urge to give up your preferences, be overly accommodating, or suppress your true desires in order to win approval or affection.

- **Notice** how your Brain Pattern justifies this compliance as a necessary step to securing a relationship, even if it means presenting a false image of yourself.

- **Remind yourself** that real connection is based on honesty, not on manipulating others into liking you by playing a role.

- **Challenge yourself** to express your needs and preferences early, and engage with others in a way that reflects your true self from the start.

The Self-Fulfilling Prophecy: By manipulating with compliance, you create an unstable foundation for relationships, leading to eventual disappointment and reinforcing the belief that you can't be loved for who you truly are.

4. You Stop Using Compliance as a Bait-and-Switch Strategy and Start Building Genuine Trust

In the beginning of relationships, your brain tells you that being agreeable and compliant will help you gain trust, win affection, and secure a sense of safety. You mirror others, placate their needs, and suppress your own desires to create a sense of connection. But as soon as you feel secure, you shift to a more dominant and controlling approach, expecting others to meet your needs without the same accommodating behavior.

Rebellion Zones force you to stop using this bait-and-switch strategy, where you present one version of yourself to get close and then shift to a more controlling one when you feel secure.

How You Approach This Rebellion Zone:

- **Observe** when you feel the need to go along with others just to earn their trust or affection.

- **Notice** how your Brain Pattern leads you to change once you feel secure, becoming more controlling or rigid in your demands.

- **Remind yourself** that genuine relationships are built on honesty and consistency, not on manipulating others into liking you.

- **Challenge yourself** to express your true preferences and assert your needs early, without waiting to feel "safe" first.

The Self-Fulfilling Prophecy: By using compliance as a manipulation tool, you create instability and hurt feelings, reinforcing the belief that you can't be loved for who you really are.

5. You Stop Shifting Control and Start Setting Boundaries Up Front

You might initially hide your true needs or preferences, hoping that by being accommodating and agreeable, you'll secure the trust or approval you need. Once you feel safe, however, you shift to more controlling or demanding behavior, creating confusion and resentment among those around you. This bait-and-switch tactic can make others feel deceived or manipulated, as they realize the person they initially connected with is not the person they are now engaging with.

Rebellion Zones challenge you to stop shifting from compliant to controlling behavior and instead set clear boundaries from the beginning.

How You Approach This Rebellion Zone:

- **Observe** when you switch from being passive to more dominant or controlling once you feel secure.

- **Notice** how this sudden shift might make others feel blindsided or unimportant, as they weren't expecting the change.

- **Remind yourself** that consistency and transparency in setting boundaries help build stronger and more trust-filled relationships.

- **Challenge yourself** to express your preferences and boundaries early on, and avoid the temptation to change your approach after gaining trust.

The Self-Fulfilling Prophecy: By shifting control dynamics, you create confusion and undermine trust, reinforcing the belief that you need to manipulate others to get your needs met.

6. You Stop Building Trust Through Compliance and Start Creating Healthy Expectations

At the start of relationships, you often use compliance to create a sense of trust and connection. You mirror behaviors, placate others, and act agreeable to establish rapport, believing this is necessary for building relationships. But once you feel secure, you shift to a more controlling or harsh behavior, expecting others to meet your needs without the same level of accommodation. This creates a "bait-and-switch" perception, where the person you were initially seen as is no longer the same person in the relationship.

Rebellion Zones challenge you to stop building relationships based on compliance and manipulation, and instead, create genuine, upfront expectations.

How You Approach This Rebellion Zone:

- **Observe** when you feel yourself becoming overly compliant or agreeable, just to earn trust or affection.

- **Notice** how your Brain Pattern justifies this behavior as a necessary step in securing relationships, but later shifts into control or demand.

- **Remind yourself** that trust is built through consistency and authenticity, not by manipulating people into liking you.

- **Challenge yourself** to set clear expectations early on, expressing your true needs without waiting to feel "safe" or "secure."

The Self-Fulfilling Prophecy: By building trust through compliance, you create instability and resentment, reinforcing the belief that you can't be loved for your true self.

Rebellion Zones

When you first begin to challenge your Security-Based Switching pattern, your brain will likely fight back, insisting that you need to build trust gradually before you assert your true control. It will tell you that it's safer to remain passive or compliant at the start of relationships, that this is the best way to earn approval and keep things stable. Your brain may even convince you that once you've earned trust, it's only natural to assert more control, shifting from a "nice" version of yourself to one that demands more from others. It will justify this as a necessary step to ensure that your needs are met—despite the fact that this shift often leaves others feeling confused, manipulated, or even betrayed. This push-pull cycle may feel like the only way to navigate relationships without risking instability.

But this cycle of gradual compliance followed by sudden control only reinforces the very belief that you can't be loved for your true self unless you manipulate your way into people's trust first. Your brain will try to convince you that being fully transparent from the start is too risky, and that holding back is essential for keeping things under control. It might even whisper that if you were more upfront, you'd drive people away or create too much conflict too soon. These justifications are the same old patterns keeping you stuck, reinforcing the illusion of safety while ultimately sabotaging your ability to create authentic, stable relationships. Rebellion Zones are here to help you push through this mental resistance and start building connections based on transparency, consistency, and trust from the very beginning.

1. Revealing Expectations Early Instead of After Security is Built

Self-Deception at Play: People pleasing, mirroring, chameleon behavior, placating, and being agreeable—even when it's dishonest. You shape-shift to match what others want, telling yourself you're just being kind or easy to get along with, while subtly manipulating perception.

Unconscious Motivation: To secure love and approval before revealing the full truth. You want to be seen in the best possible light—easy, compatible, "meant to be." Vulnerability feels unsafe until the connection is secured, so you delay honesty and overperform in hopes of earning a safe place to be yourself.

Rebellion Zone: Set clear expectations and be honest from the beginning instead of slowly shifting over time.

Why This Works: Your brain has convinced you that starting passively makes others more likely to accept control later. But this strategy breeds distrust. People feel tricked when you shift your stance after gaining security. By being upfront about your standards and boundaries from the beginning, you foster trust instead of dependency or resistance.

How This Plays Out in Real Life:

- You start relationships or jobs as agreeable and low-maintenance, but over time, you introduce more rigid expectations.

- People feel caught off guard when you gradually enforce control that wasn't there before.

- You tell yourself that early compliance isn't manipulation, even though it ensures acceptance before your true preferences emerge.

The Challenge: Be Transparent from the Start

- State preferences, boundaries, and expectations early instead of waiting until you feel "safe" to assert them, *ask yourself*:

  Do I tend to play it safe at the beginning of relationships?

  Is it possible this is seen as manipulation down the road when my more direct personality starts coming out?

  Do I have a habit of being agreeable and malleable to get into someone's good graces?

398

Can I see how it would feel like a bait-and-switch when my other side eventually comes out?

Can I challenge myself to be vulnerable and say the truth early to build on a solid foundation?

• If you notice you are strategically withholding personal opinions or needs in new environments to gain approval first—say the honest and direct thing in the moment.

• Remind yourself that people will eventually feel blindsided by your shifts and early transparency prevents this cycle.

2. Allowing Stability Without Tightening Control

Self-Deception at Play: Letting security justify increased control and authority. You tell yourself that stability gives you permission to be more direct or even harsh—framing it as finally being your "true self." What feels like authenticity may actually be a shift into dominance.

Unconscious Motivation: To associate safety with the right to exert greater influence. Once you feel secure, you believe you can stop holding back and fully take charge—interpreting safety as permission to control. Beneath this is a desire to be fully seen and heard without threat, but it often reinforces power imbalances rather than connection.

Rebellion Zone: Resist the urge to tighten your grip once relationships or environments feel stable.

Why This Works: Your brain has convinced you that once trust is secured, control should increase to maintain that stability. The problem? This shift often erodes trust rather than reinforcing it. By resisting the impulse to assert greater authority once you feel safe, you allow relationships and work environments to remain open, adaptive, and reciprocal.

How This Plays Out in Real Life:

• You start relationships by appearing flexible, but once stability is secured, you begin enforcing more rules.

• You feel an increasing need to micromanage once a job or project reaches a certain point of predictability.

• You justify more rigid expectations by telling yourself you've 'earned' the right to set the tone now.

The Challenge: Let Stability Exist Without Over-Structuring

- When stability is achieved you start to shift from relaxed to controlling.

- Allow relationships and projects to unfold organically without inserting new structures.

- Trust that stability doesn't require more control. Sometimes, it requires more trust.

3. Trusting Others' Autonomy Instead of Scaling Influence

Self-Deception at Play: Believing that once trust is earned, it's now safe—and even necessary—to increase oversight or influence to maintain success. You convince yourself it's about protecting the outcome, but it's actually a quiet return to control.

Unconscious Motivation: To equate security with the right to manage more closely. Once things feel stable, you feel justified in scaling your influence to ensure everything continues to meet your standards. Beneath this is a fear that letting go will lead to loss or failure.

Rebellion Zone: Practice stepping back and allowing others to take ownership without interference or increased supervision.

Why This Works: Your brain convinces you that once people trust you, they expect and need more guidance. In reality, increasing control over time erodes trust and autonomy. By resisting the urge to scale your influence, you allow others to grow into their own competence and leadership.

How This Plays Out in Real Life:

- You start off as hands-off in leadership, but once things are running smoothly, you introduce more oversight.

- You struggle to let others fully take ownership, feeling the need to provide constant guidance.

- You justify increased control as being necessary to maintain consistency, despite evidence that things are functioning fine without it.

The Challenge: Let Go of the Need to Expand Control Over Time

- Allow others to continue leading without increasing your involvement as trust grows.

- Resist the urge to insert yourself in decisions that don't require your input.

- Recognize when your need to 'ensure success' is actually limiting others' ability to grow.

- Practice acknowledging and celebrating when things run well without your intervention.

4. The Bait and Switch: When Security Becomes Domination

Self-Deception at Play: Believing that increased control is justified once trust is established—framing it as earned leadership rather than recognizing it as a destabilizing shift. You tell yourself you're just being more efficient or direct, but the dynamic has changed, and not for the better.

Unconscious Motivation: To feel safe enough to reveal your true control tendencies. Once the connection feels secure, you allow your preference for structure or dominance to take the lead—subtly ensuring outcomes reflect your standards, not mutual collaboration.

Rebellion Zone: Maintain consistency in relational dynamics instead of shifting to dominance when you feel secure.

Why This Works: Your brain convinces you that once stability is established, you've "earned" the right to take charge. The problem? Others experience this as a bait and switch, feeling deceived by your initial flexibility. By resisting the urge to tighten control, you allow relationships to remain stable and reciprocal.

How This Plays Out in Real Life:

- You present as easygoing in the beginning, but over time, start enforcing strict expectations.

- Your partner, colleagues, or friends feel blindsided by your increasing need for control.

- You assume that since trust has been established, you now have the right to call the shots.

The Challenge: Stay Consistent Rather than Escalating Control Over Time

- Notice when your behavior shifts from accommodating to authoritarian as relationships deepen.

- Resist the urge to "correct" or "optimize" others' behaviors just because they trust you.

- Recognize that what feels like stability to you may feel like an unsettling shift in power to others.

- Maintain the same level of autonomy and flexibility in relationships that existed in the beginning.

5. Manufacturing Instability When Things Feel Too Peaceful

Self-Deception at Play: Believing that your increased control is necessary when things feel too calm or predictable—when in reality, you may be unconsciously generating instability. You justify your actions as proactive or protective, but they often trigger unnecessary disruption.

Unconscious Motivation: To use control as a tool to break the monotony of stability, reinforcing a familiar pattern of chaos followed by resolution. Peace feels unnatural or unsafe, so the brain creates movement—often in the form of disruption—to restore its emotional baseline.

Rebellion Zone: Recognize and sit with stability instead of unconsciously destabilizing it.

Why This Works: Your brain has been conditioned to seek instability, equating peace with discomfort. When things feel too stable, you might create problems to regain a sense of control. By resisting the urge to introduce unnecessary challenges, you allow stability to exist without forcing chaos.

How This Plays Out in Real Life:

- You pick fights or challenge dynamics when things feel too easy or predictable.

- You suddenly shift rules or expectations, making others feel unsteady.

- You justify shaking things up as "keeping people on their toes" when, in reality, it's your own discomfort with peace.

The Challenge: Accept Stability Without Creating Chaos

- Recognize when your need for control escalates as things settle into consistency.

- Observe when you introduce unnecessary changes just to feel in control.

- Resist the urge to "test" people's loyalty or commitment by introducing instability.

• Allow stability to exist without needing to disrupt it for emotional stimulation.

What You Gain by Embracing Rebellion Zones

Your subconscious tells you that compliance earns security, and security earns control. You enter relationships, jobs, and friendships agreeable, flexible, and accommodating, convincing yourself that early compliance is a strategy for long-term stability. But once that security is established, your brain flips the switch. Suddenly, you're asserting control, enforcing rules, and structuring dynamics that didn't exist before.

But others don't see this as a natural progression; they see it as a bait-and-switch. What felt like an easygoing, adaptable connection suddenly becomes rigid, rule-bound, and controlled.

Your brain has convinced you that this gradual shift protects relationships, but in reality, it erodes trust and creates instability. When you step into your Rebellion Zones and stop hiding control behind compliance, everything changes. Instead of manipulating for security, you experience real trust, real connection, and real influence without the need for a power shift.

1. You'll Build Trust That Lasts—Instead of Trust That Feels Like a Setup

Right now, your subconscious tells you that people will accept your rules later if you wait until they feel safe with you. You don't enter new situations being direct about your needs—you wait, observe, comply, and slowly introduce more structure once trust is secured. But this delayed control isn't stability—it's strategy.

2. You'll Experience Stability Without Feeling the Urge to Tighten Control

Right now, your subconscious believes control should increase as security grows. The moment relationships feel stable, you start adding rules, micromanaging, or enforcing expectations that weren't there before. But stability isn't something that needs to be managed—it's something that needs to be allowed.

3. You'll Stop Losing People Who Feel Blindsided by Your Changing Behavior

You tell yourself that increased control is justified once trust has been earned. You believe that because others feel safe with you, they will accept a new, more structured version of you. But what feels like a natural progression to you feels like an unsettling shift in power to them.

By maintaining consistency instead of slowly increasing control, you build relationships that feel safe and reciprocal rather than strategic and manipulative.

4. You'll Experience Real Trust—Instead of Scaling Control Over Time

Your subconscious tells you that once people trust you, they expect and need more guidance. You start relationships and leadership roles hands-off, but as things run smoothly, you begin inserting more oversight. By resisting the instinct to expand control over time, you allow others to experience competence, trust, and independence.

The Bottom Line

Your subconscious tells you that control is earned over time—compliance secures safety, and safety justifies control. But what if this cycle isn't keeping you safe? What if it's keeping you stuck in a pattern that erodes trust just as fast as it builds it? When you step into your rebellion zones, you stop:

- Building trust just to control it later.

- Losing relationships to an inevitable power shift.

- Structuring stability instead of experiencing it.

Instead, you gain something you've never truly had before: real trust. Real connection. And the ability to be fully seen—without a strategy, without a slow shift in power, and without fear of abandonment.

ABANDONMENT – CONTROL TO BE SAFE (SWITCH) CONTEXTUAL

Core Motivations

Contextual switchers are driven by the need for adaptability as a means of control while avoiding perceived instability or lack of authority in various settings. They shift between overt and covert control strategies based on what feels most effective in the moment, believing this flexibility allows them to manage people and outcomes efficiently.

Unlike other switch types, contextual switchers do not anchor their control tendencies to a single dynamic; instead, they scan their environment and determine whether overt or covert control will serve them best in real time. While this skill can make them highly effective in leadership or crisis situations, it can also erode trust and create instability in their personal relationships as people struggle to predict their true stance.

1. Fear of Losing Influence

You shift between control styles to ensure you are always in a position of power, whether through direct authority or subtle manipulation.

2. Desire to Manage Perception

You fine-tune your behaviors based on what will make them most effective or acceptable in any given situation.

3. Need for Emotional and Strategic Agility

You see your ability to adjust control styles as a sign of strength, but it often prevents you from developing deep consistency in relationships.

4. Avoidance of Confrontation or Exposure

You may use passivity when it serves them, but quickly shift to direct control if you feel your authority is required to keep things safe.

5. Compensation for a Lack of a Fixed Control Strategy

Because your control style is fluid, you may overcompensate in high-stress moments, suddenly becoming rigid, authoritarian, or explosive.

Why Do You Need Rebellion Zones?

By challenging your hidden need to shift control styles to maintain dominance or influence, contextual switchers can develop more predictable and trustworthy relationships, allowing for long-term stability instead of short-term strategic advantages.

1. You Stop Shifting Control Styles to Manage People and Start Holding a Fixed Position

Right now, your brain tells you that control should be fluid—that adjusting your approach based on the situation keeps you ahead and ensures stability. You scan your environment, deciding in real time whether overt or covert control will serve you best. This makes you adaptable, but it also means no one, including you, ever really knows where you stand.

Rebellion Zones challenge you to stop shifting between control strategies to maintain leverage and instead commit to a fixed stance, even when it feels uncomfortable.

Why You Need This: To stop using adaptability as a way to maintain dominance and to start developing real trust and consistency in your relationships.

How You Approach This Rebellion Zone:

- **Observe** when you adjust how you communicate, engage, or assert authority based on what you think will work best in the moment rather than what is actually true for you.

- **Notice** how your Brain Pattern convinces you that maintaining leverage is more important than long-term trust or predictability.

- **Remind yourself** that relationships and leadership require steadiness—people cannot rely on you if your stance is always shifting.

- **Challenge yourself** to hold your position, even when it feels like shifting control could get you a better result.

The Self-Fulfilling Prophecy: By continuing to adjust your control style to suit the moment, you reinforce the belief that stability is a weakness and that true consistency will lead to loss of influence.

2. You Stop Using Perception Management to Keep Control and Start Engaging Authentically

You have mastered the art of adjusting your behaviors to maintain authority without looking like you're in control. You shift your tone, body language, or level of engagement depending on what you think will get the best response. While this makes you a highly effective strategist, it also keeps you disconnected from genuine, unfiltered interaction.

Rebellion Zones challenge you to stop curating interactions and instead show up as you are, without modifying yourself to achieve an outcome.

Why You Need This: To stop micromanaging how others perceive you and to start building relationships where you don't have to manage every interaction like a chess game.

How You Approach This Rebellion Zone:

- **Observe** when you adjust how you speak, react, or engage based on what you think will make you appear most in control.

- **Notice** how your Brain Pattern tells you that controlling perception is the same as being respected or trusted.

- **Remind yourself** that real connection cannot happen when you are constantly shaping and managing how you appear.

- **Challenge yourself** to resist the impulse to modify your behavior in response to how you want others to react.

The Self-Fulfilling Prophecy: By continuing to manage perception, you reinforce the belief that authenticity is a risk and that people only respect what they can't fully read or predict.

3. You Stop Treating Emotional Agility as a Strength and Start Developing True Stability

You pride yourself on being able to shift between different control styles based on what the situation demands. You tell yourself this makes you adaptable, but in reality, it prevents you from establishing the consistency that real stability requires.

Rebellion Zones challenge you to stop viewing fluidity as strength and instead start recognizing that true leadership and connection require predictability, not strategic shape-shifting.

Why You Need This: To stop using adaptability as a defense mechanism against stability and to start recognizing that predictability is what builds trust and lasting success.

How You Approach This Rebellion Zone:

- **Observe** when you change your approach to control in response to a situation rather than maintaining a steady, fixed way of engaging.

- **Notice** how your Brain Pattern tells you that shifting between strategies is necessary to maintain order or keep people aligned with your vision.

- **Remind yourself** that stability doesn't mean losing control—it means creating a foundation where control isn't necessary in the first place.

- **Challenge yourself** to practice consistency, even when it feels inefficient or risky.

The Self-Fulfilling Prophecy: By continuing to shift between control strategies, you reinforce the belief that consistency leads to vulnerability and that stability will make you lose influence.

4. You Stop Avoiding Accountability by Adjusting Your Approach and Start Owning Your Role

You're used to being able to shift between overt and covert control based on what feels safest. If direct authority isn't working, you pull back and manage things behind the scenes. If subtle influence isn't getting results, you switch to a more dominant stance. This strategy protects you from ever being fully responsible when things go wrong because you can always shift the narrative.

Rebellion Zones challenge you to stop using adaptability as an escape hatch and to start holding yourself accountable even when the outcome isn't ideal.

Why You Need This: To stop avoiding responsibility by shifting control styles and to start owning your role in the dynamics you create.

How You Approach This Rebellion Zone:

- **Observe** when you shift between overt and covert control to avoid direct accountability for a situation.

- **Notice** how your Brain Pattern tells you that adaptability keeps you safe from blame or exposure.

- **Remind yourself** that true leadership requires taking responsibility, not just maneuvering outcomes.

- **Challenge yourself** to hold your position and accept the consequences, rather than adjusting to evade them.

The Self-Fulfilling Prophecy: By continuing to shift control styles to avoid accountability, you reinforce the belief that being adaptable is the same as being untouchable—and that taking responsibility will leave you vulnerable.

Rebellion Zones

Contextual switchers rely on adaptability as a subconscious form of control, which can lead to unstable dynamics in both personal and professional relationships. The rebellion zones help you:

- Recognize when you are using adaptability as a manipulation tool rather than a strength.

- Break the cycle of shifting between dominant and passive roles based on your environment.

- Foster genuine connection rather than managing perception.

- Allow yourselves to commit to a consistent leadership style instead of shape-shifting based on context.

1. Maintaining Consistency Instead of Reading the Room

Self-Deception at Play: Believing that shifting between overt and covert control is adaptability rather than a subconscious way to maintain influence.

Unconscious Motivation: Avoiding exposure by switching between compliance and dominance based on what feels safest in the moment.

Rebellion Zone: Commit to a consistent approach rather than adjusting based on perceived external expectations.

Why This Works: Your brain has convinced you that adjusting to each situation is what keeps you in control. But the reality? It creates instability—people don't trust what version of you they're getting. By choosing consistency over constant adaptation, you force yourself to build real, stable relationships.

How This Plays Out in Real Life:

- You shift between assertive and passive depending on the setting, never allowing others to fully understand your true stance.

- You rationalize these shifts as necessary, but they actually prevent genuine connection.

- You assume that maintaining control requires blending into what's expected rather than defining your own role.

The Challenge: Stay True to Your Natural Disposition

- Recognize when you're adjusting too much based on the environment rather than holding your own ground.

- Observe whether people ever question your consistency and consider how that impacts trust.

- Push yourself to respond the same way in all settings, even when your instinct is to shift to maintain an advantage.

2. Leading Without Manipulating

Self-Deception at Play: Believing that influencing others subtly is leadership rather than covert control.

Unconscious Motivation: Ensuring your ideas are accepted without being challenged.

Rebellion Zone: Allow others to contribute their ideas without attempting to steer them in your direction.

Why This Works: You assume that guiding people subtly keeps things efficient, but it erodes their ability to trust their instincts. By stepping back and allowing others to lead without interference, you foster real collaboration.

How This Plays Out in Real Life:

- You make suggestions framed as "helpful advice" but subtly push your own agenda.

- You let others think they're leading, but you only support their decisions when they align with what you wanted.

The Challenge: Let Go of the Need to Influence Every Outcome

- Allow others to lead without inserting yourself.

- Acknowledge when you're framing things to manipulate rather than genuinely supporting.

- Notice when you feel uncomfortable letting others be fully autonomous.

3. Letting Go of Crisis-Based Adaptation

Self-Deception at Play: Believing that shifting between control styles in response to crisis is necessary rather than a subconscious way to maintain control over outcomes.

Unconscious Motivation: Ensuring you always have an advantage by quickly adapting, even if it creates unnecessary instability.

Rebellion Zone: Resist the urge to shift control styles dramatically in moments of perceived crisis.

Why This Works: Your brain convinces you that your ability to quickly switch between control styles keeps you safe. But this habit reinforces chaos and instability rather than allowing situations to resolve naturally. By refusing to escalate control in response to uncertainty, you allow for organic problem-solving and healthier relational dynamics.

How This Plays Out in Real Life:

- You become overly assertive when a situation feels uncertain, even if it's not necessary.

- You retreat into passivity or detachment as a defense mechanism when challenged.

- Your shifts in control style create unnecessary tension in relationships and work settings.

The Challenge: Allow Situations to Develop Without Immediate Adaptation

- Notice when you're reacting to discomfort by shifting between passive and overt control.

- Sit with uncertainty instead of immediately trying to take over or disappear.

- Trust that stability can exist without your immediate intervention.

4. Choosing Stability Over Performance

Self-Deception at Play: Believing that your ability to shift control styles makes you more competent rather than recognizing it as a stress response.

Unconscious Motivation: Maintaining control by ensuring you always present yourself in the best light.

411

Rebellion Zone: Remain steady in relationships and commitments rather than shifting based on who is watching.

Why This Works: Your brain tells you that adaptability is strength, but in reality, constantly shifting behavior to impress others creates emotional exhaustion. By resisting the urge to "perform," you build deeper trust and authenticity in your interactions.

How This Plays Out in Real Life:

- You act differently around different groups, never letting your true self fully emerge.

- You unconsciously shift between dominant and passive roles based on what you think will earn approval.

- You find yourself exhausted from trying to anticipate and manage expectations.

The Challenge: Stay Grounded in Who You Are

- Commit to consistency even when you feel the urge to shift your persona.

- Recognize when you're adapting to win approval rather than staying authentic.

- Allow people to experience you without strategic self-modification.

5. Embracing Discomfort Without Strategy

Self-Deception at Play: Believing that you must adjust control styles to navigate discomfort rather than allowing discomfort to be processed naturally.

Unconscious Motivation: Avoiding vulnerability by ensuring you always have an angle.

Rebellion Zone: Sit with discomfort instead of adjusting your control style as a defense mechanism.

Why This Works: Your brain has trained you to see control shifts as necessary for survival, but in reality, they prevent true connection. By refusing to "play a role" when faced with emotional discomfort, you allow yourself to be fully present.

How This Plays Out in Real Life:

- You shift to humor, detachment, or assertiveness when

uncomfortable instead of sitting with the feeling.

• You manipulate situations to avoid emotional exposure.

The Challenge: Stay Present Without Control-Based Defense Mechanisms

• Recognize when you're shifting in response to discomfort.

• Practice allowing emotions to exist without strategizing.

• Trust that you don't need to control discomfort to survive it.

What You Gain by Embracing Rebellion Zones

Your subconscious tells you that your ability to shift control styles is your greatest strength. You believe that by adapting on the fly—being dominant when needed, passive when beneficial, and strategic in between—you ensure success, stability, and influence.

But the reality? This shape-shifting erodes trust. People never quite know which version of you they're dealing with. In leadership, relationships, and friendships, your adaptability can feel like unpredictability, making others question your true stance.

Your brain tells you that reading the room and adjusting your approach is necessary to stay in control. But what if the real power isn't in adjusting—it's in staying steady? When you step into your Rebellion Zones and stop shifting control styles for strategic advantage, you gain something you've never had before: consistent trust, deeper relationships, and the ability to experience stability instead of managing it.

1. You'll Build Trust That Lasts—Instead of Trust That Feels Conditional

Right now, your subconscious tells you that adjusting between dominance and passivity makes you adaptable. You don't commit to a single control style—you scan the environment, determine what's safest, and shift accordingly. But the problem? People never know where you truly stand.

By choosing consistency over constant adaptation, you force yourself to build real, stable relationships—where people trust that you are who you say you are.

413

2. You'll Experience Real Leadership—Instead of Just Strategic Influence

Right now, you tell yourself that subtly guiding people is leadership. You let others believe they're making decisions, but behind the scenes, you ensure things go your way. You frame your influence as "helpful." But you control outcomes without taking responsibility for doing so.

By stepping back and allowing others to truly lead, you build relationships based on trust and collaboration, not quiet influence.

3. You'll Finally Break the Cycle of Control-Driven Crisis Management

Right now, your subconscious tells you that shifting control styles in moments of crisis keeps you safe. When things feel unstable, you tighten your grip—or retreat completely—depending on what will serve you best. But these shifts don't bring stability. They create chaos.

4. You'll Finally Feel Emotionally Grounded—Instead of Just Performing Stability

Right now, your subconscious tells you that your ability to shift control styles is what makes you competent. You believe that adjusting to every environment makes you stronger, smarter, and more effective. But in reality? Constantly adapting is emotionally exhausting—and keeps you from being truly seen.

By choosing stability over performance, you allow yourself to be fully seen and fully accepted.

5. You'll Experience Discomfort Without Needing a Strategy to Escape It

Your subconscious tells you that adjusting your control style helps you navigate discomfort. When things feel uneasy, you shift into humor, detachment, or assertiveness—whatever will make the situation feel safer. These shifts keep you from actually processing discomfort at all.

By refusing to shift roles when discomfort arises, you teach your brain that real safety comes from presence, not from playing a role.

The Bottom Line

Your subconscious tells you that control must be fluid, adaptable, and strategic. That shifting keeps you in power. When you step into your rebellion zones, you stop:

- Shifting to avoid discomfort.

- Losing people to inconsistent behavior.

- Exhausting yourself trying to manage every situation.

Instead, you gain something you've never truly had before:

- More stable, predictable relationships. People trust that what you say and do today will match what you say and do tomorrow.

- Freedom from managing perception. You're no longer shape-shifting based on what others expect.

- Deeper trust from others. They no longer feel blindsided by your shifting control tendencies.

- Less anxiety about maintaining influence. Real power doesn't come from adjusting—it comes from consistency.

- More time and energy for yourself. You're not constantly scanning, adjusting, and adapting to every situation.

- Fewer conflicts and misunderstandings. People know where you stand, instead of trying to guess which version of you they're dealing with.

- Authentic leadership that doesn't rely on subtle control. You no longer need to manipulate outcomes to maintain authority.

- The ability to stay steady, even when things feel uncertain. You're no longer reacting out of fear of losing control.

- Healthier, more reciprocal relationships. You're no longer alternating between over-giving and suddenly asserting dominance.

- A real sense of security. You've stopped trying to control trust and instead have actually built it.

CHAPTER **27**

ABANDONMENT— HOLD IT ALL TOGETHER

Your driving force is keeping people deescalated and maintaining stability at all costs. You believe that if you don't self-sacrifice, compromise or placate the people around you it will fall apart, situations will become chaotic, or others will lash out emotionally. Because of this belief, you take on extreme burdens, shifting or adapting to constantly manage other people's reactions and life outcomes—often at your own expense.

You are the one who absorbs stress, smooths over the conflict, and prevents emotional meltdowns in those around you. While this makes you appear highly competent and composed, it also creates a reality where you are constantly overextended, emotionally exhausted, and double if not triple booked. The unspoken rule in your mind is: If I hold it all together, everything will be fine.

However, this pattern is a trap—because no matter how much you try to maintain peace, the world around you will always have instability, and no amount of self-sacrifice or bargaining will permanently prevent it. This sets you up for cycles of resentment, burnout, and hidden frustration, even as you continue taking on more responsibility to keep things in balance.

Core Motivations

Your behaviors are rooted in the belief that other people are incapable of handling their emotions or responsibilities without you sacrificing, placating or withholding. This leads to deep patterns of over-giving, over-accommodating and compartmentalizing even when you don't consciously realize it. Your need to manage and maintain stability is what drives your decision-making, often leading to self-sacrifice, avoidance of your own needs, and struggles with boundary-setting.

1. Fear of Others' Emotional Reactions

You placate, omit or pitch versions of the truth to prevent emotional outbursts—it's not that you don't know the truth, you just don't believe they can handle it without losing it.

2. Desire to Keep the Peace

You prioritize stability over honesty, often suppressing your own needs or opinions to prevent disruption.

3. Validation Through Being Needed

Your identity is wrapped up in being the one who can fix, manage, or de-escalate any situation. This gives you a sense of purpose but also keeps you trapped in a cycle of over-responsibility. It also creates dependency and enablement all around you.

4. Subconscious Avoidance of Your Own Needs

You focus on handling everyone else's emotions as a way to avoid dealing with your own unmet needs, exhaustion, or resentment. This can lead to chronic health issues or denial of symptoms for long periods of time.

5. Belief That Your Efforts Prevent Chaos

You operate under the assumption that if you pre-manage, strategize, and fix, peace will never be possible – and it's the thing you want most in the world.

Why Do You Need Rebellion Zones?

1. You Stop Sacrificing Yourself for Others' Peace and Start Prioritizing Your Own Needs

You must keep everything together and put others' needs first to maintain peace and avoid conflict. You hide your true feelings, suppress your own needs, and overextend yourself to make sure everyone else is comfortable, often at the cost of your own well-being.

Rebellion Zones challenge you to stop prioritizing others' peace over your own and to start acknowledging your own needs without guilt or fear of causing discomfort.

Why You Need This: To stop losing yourself in the service of others and start honoring your own needs and boundaries.

How You Approach This Rebellion Zone:

- **Observe** when you begin to overextend yourself, saying yes to things that drain you to keep others comfortable.

- **Notice** how your Brain Pattern tells you that others can't handle your needs, so you bury them to avoid conflict or burdening anyone.

- **Remind yourself** that true peace doesn't come from suppressing yourself, but from a balance where everyone's needs, including your own, are respected.

- **Challenge yourself** to set boundaries and learn to say no even when it feels uncomfortable.

The Self-Fulfilling Prophecy: By continually sacrificing yourself, you reinforce the belief that your needs don't matter and that it's your responsibility to carry the burden for everyone else.

2. You Stop Hiding Your Truth and Start Speaking Up for What You Need

You believe that expressing challenges or feelings isn't as important as maintaining stability in your external world. So, you hide or compartmentalize your true emotions, pretending everything is fine, even when it isn't.

Rebellion Zones force you to stop hiding behind a facade of peace and start speaking up for what you truly need, no matter how uncomfortable it may feel.

Why You Need This: To stop suppressing your emotions and pretending everything is okay when it's not, and to start being vulnerable so others can show up for you.

How You Approach This Rebellion Zone:

- **Observe** when you feel the urge to hold back or pretend everything is fine, even when you're overwhelmed or upset.

- **Notice** how your Brain Pattern tells you that sharing what's really going on isn't as important as something else that feels urgent.

- **Remind yourself** that if you keep everything in and put on an act no one will be able to show up for you and do their part.

- **Challenge yourself** to express your feelings and needs, even if it feels uncomfortable or risky.

The Self-Fulfilling Prophecy: By hiding your emotions, you reinforce the belief that your needs don't matter and that revealing them will lead to rejection or conflict.

3. You Stop Trying to Keep the Peace at the Expense of Your Well-Being and Start Embracing Discomfort

You've trained yourself to maintain peace by making others feel comfortable, often sacrificing your own emotional well-being in the process. Your brain convinces you that the discomfort of conflict is more dangerous than the cost of self-sacrifice.

Rebellion Zones challenge you to stop maintaining peace at your expense and to start embracing the discomfort of standing up for yourself and your needs.

Why You Need This: To stop perpetuating the cycle of self-sacrifice and to start embracing discomfort as a necessary step toward genuine self-care.

How You Approach This Rebellion Zone:

- **Observe** when you prioritize others' comfort over your own, even when it means sacrificing your well-being or time off.

- **Notice** how your Brain Pattern tells you that peace is only achievable through self-neglect, and that expressing your needs will only create turmoil.

- **Remind yourself** that true peace comes from being honest about your needs and honoring them, not by ignoring them to keep others happy.

420

- **Challenge yourself** to be direct and tell the truth in the moment even if it creates conflict.

The Self-Fulfilling Prophecy: *By continuing to suppress your needs, you reinforce the belief that others' peace is more important than your own, perpetuating a cycle of emotional burnout and resentment.*

4. You Stop Overloading Yourself and Start Saying No When Needed

You often take on too much because you feel responsible for keeping everything running smoothly, afraid that saying no will disappoint others or cause problems. Your brain tells you that if you're not doing everything for everyone, you're failing.

Rebellion Zones force you to stop overloading yourself and start setting healthy limits on what you can give without losing yourself in the process.

Why You Need This: To stop feeling responsible for others' needs at the expense of your own mental and physical health.

How You Approach This Rebellion Zone:

- **Observe** when you're saying yes to everything reflexively, trying to please everyone around you at the cost of your own energy and self-care.

- **Notice** how your Brain Pattern tells you that saying no is not an option and you'll somehow figure it out.

- **Remind yourself** that you are not superhuman and you often figure it out at the expense of your schedule, rest or overall health – and that's not sustainable.

- **Challenge yourself** to say no or let me check my calendar first, prioritizing your own needs without guilt.

The Self-Fulfilling Prophecy: *By constantly overloading yourself, you reinforce the belief that your needs don't matter and that keeping everyone happy is your sole responsibility.*

5. You Stop Overloading Your Calendar and Start Setting Realistic Boundaries

You tend to overbook your calendar, convincing yourself that you can "figure it out later" or that you can handle the overwhelming load of tasks and commitments. Your brain tells you that if you just keep going, you'll eventually catch up, ignoring the reality that you're burning yourself out.

Rebellion Zones force you to stop tricking yourself into thinking you can do it all and start setting more realistic and sustainable boundaries for your time.

Why You Need This: To stop overloading yourself and to start recognizing your limits before you reach the point of exhaustion.

How You Approach This Rebellion Zone:

- **Observe** when you're tempted to overbook your calendar, adding more tasks or commitments while tricking yourself into believing you'll somehow figure it out.

- **Notice** how your Brain Pattern tries to convince you that somehow it always works out even though that comes at the expense of lateness and burnout.

- **Remind yourself** that sustainable productivity comes from managing your time and energy wisely, not from constantly overloading your schedule.

- **Challenge yourself** to block out time for rest and relaxation, and learn to say no or let me check my calendar and get back to you.

The Self-Fulfilling Prophecy: By overloading your calendar, you reinforce the belief that you're not doing enough unless you're constantly busy, leading to burnout and resentment.

6. You Stop Avoiding the Details and Start Taking Care of What Needs Attention

As a big-picture thinker, you naturally focus on the larger vision or goals, but you tend to avoid the details and smaller tasks that actually need to be addressed. You may convince yourself that the details aren't important or that you'll get to them eventually. However, letting things slide often leads to missed opportunities or neglected responsibilities.

Rebellion Zones challenge you to stop avoiding the smaller, less glamorous tasks and to start taking action on the details that are crucial to your success.

Why You Need This: To stop neglecting important details that could cause bigger issues later, and to start addressing what needs attention right now.

How You Approach This Rebellion Zone:

- **Observe** when you're avoiding a task because it feels too small or tedious, telling yourself that it can wait or isn't worth focusing on.

- **Notice** how your Brain Pattern tries to convince you that the bigger picture is all that matters, while the small tasks pile up unnoticed.

- **Remind yourself** that the details are often what make the bigger vision possible and that neglecting them creates larger problems down the road.

- **Challenge yourself** to take action on the small, necessary tasks, even if they don't seem important at the moment.

The Self-Fulfilling Prophecy: By avoiding details, you create unnecessary chaos and missed opportunities, reinforcing the belief that you can't succeed without focusing only on the big picture.

7. You Stop Avoiding Difficult Conversations and Start Addressing Problems Head-On

You often delay addressing problems with others, especially when you care about them, because you don't want to hurt their feelings or create conflict. You may feel guilty or uncomfortable, thinking that by avoiding the issue, you can spare them (and yourself) the discomfort. This can cause unresolved tension and lead to resentment.

Rebellion Zones push you to stop avoiding difficult conversations and to start addressing issues directly, even when it feels uncomfortable.

Why You Need This: To stop avoiding problems and to start facing challenges head-on, improving communication and trust in your relationships.

How You Approach This Rebellion Zone:

- **Observe** when you avoid a difficult conversation, telling yourself that it's easier to let things slide and or it'll be worth it in other ways (bargaining or rationalizing).

- **Notice** how your Brain Pattern convinces you that avoiding the problem is an act of compassion, even though it actually delays the inevitable and allows you to justify your avoidance.

- **Remind yourself** that addressing problems directly helps prevent longterm chaos that will likely involve more messes to clean up in the future.

- **Challenge yourself** to face uncomfortable situations and have the tough conversations you've been avoiding, knowing that it will ultimately prevent chaos down and work for you down the road.

The Self-Fulfilling Prophecy: *By avoiding difficult conversations, you reinforce the belief that conflict or confrontation will ruin relationships, preventing you from addressing issues that need resolution.*

8. You Stop Enabling Others and Start Encouraging Self-Efficacy

You often find yourself doing things for others, especially your children or loved ones, because you want to make their lives easier or prevent them from struggling. You step in to help, even when they are fully capable of figuring things out themselves. This might be because you fear that if they struggle, they'll feel rejected or inadequate. However, by constantly enabling them, you prevent them from learning how to take ownership, develop resilience, or build the skills necessary for independence.

Rebellion Zones challenge you to stop enabling others and start fostering self-efficacy by allowing them to take responsibility for their actions and learn from their mistakes.

Why You Need This: To stop robbing others of the opportunity to grow, and to start encouraging them to build their own independence and confidence.

How You Approach This Rebellion Zone:

- **Observe** when you step in to help others, especially in situations where they could figure things out themselves.

- **Notice** how your Brain Pattern tells you that you're being helpful or kind by stepping in, while actually preventing them from learning how to handle challenges on their own or learn boundaries.

- **Remind yourself** that real love and support involve giving others the opportunity to fail, learn, and grow, not just shielding them from every difficulty.

- **Challenge yourself** to take a step back and allow others to take responsibility for their own tasks and challenges, even when it feels uncomfortable.

The Self-Fulfilling Prophecy: *By enabling others, you reinforce the belief that they can't succeed without your help, and you deny them the chance to build independence and confidence.*

Rebellion Zones

1. Setting Boundaries That You Actually Enforce

Self-Deception at Play: Lack of boundaries as loyalty, resignation to overload, managing others' emotions through truth filtering.

Unconscious Motivation: Avoiding conflict and escalation by being overly agreeable and available.

Rebellion Zone: Set a boundary and hold it—without softening it, backpedaling, or making exceptions.

Why This Works: You tell yourself that saying yes to everything is a sign of commitment and loyalty. But in reality, it's a pattern that keeps you exhausted, unreliable, and stretched too thin. Setting boundaries without immediately justifying is created by saying "yes" to the right things.

How This Plays Out in Real Life:

• You struggle to set clear boundaries because you equate saying yes with loyalty and commitment. Turning someone down feels like a betrayal—even when you're already drowning in obligations.

• When you do set a boundary, you immediately soften it with justifications or apologies, explaining why you can't do something instead of just saying no.

• If someone pushes back, looks disappointed, or acts frustrated, you second-guess yourself—sometimes reversing your decision entirely just to keep the peace.

• You assume that if people truly respected you, they wouldn't ask too much of you in the first place. But in reality, people treat you as available because you never enforce when you actually aren't.

• You often say "yes" out of guilt or obligation, thinking, It's fine, I'll make it work. But making it work often means sacrificing your own time, rest, or emotional well-being.

• Over time, you resent how much is expected of you. Instead of enforcing better boundaries, you blame yourself for not being able to handle it all.

425

- Even when you know you're stretched too thin, you tell yourself, "It's easier to just do it than to deal with the discomfort of saying no."

Your subconscious convinces you that holding boundaries makes you selfish, unavailable, or unreliable. But weak boundaries make you inconsistent, exhausted, and unable to fully show up for the things that actually matter.

The Challenge: Set Boundaries and Actually Enforce Them

- If you feel the urge to explain a boundary, don't. Set it clearly, without over-explaining or apologizing.

- If someone pushes back on your "no," hold your ground. Discomfort doesn't mean you made the wrong choice—it just means you're breaking a pattern.

- If you usually agree to things out of guilt, pause before answering. *Ask yourself*:

  Do I historically say yes and then resent them for it later?

  Do I overextend myself in ways that lead to burnout?

  Even though I tell myself I always figure it out, isn't it usually at the expense of my own well-being?

  Can I challenge myself to say no in a kind and compassionate way?

- If you worry about disappointing others, remind yourself: The people who truly respect you will respect your boundaries, too.

- If you notice resentment creeping in, check where you've let boundaries slide. Resentment is often a sign that you've overextended yourself.

By setting and enforcing real boundaries, you disrupt the belief that saying "yes" is the only way to be valued. Instead of constantly overcommitting and burning yourself out, you start making choices that prioritize what truly matters—without guilt, justification, or exhaustion.

2. Letting Others Experience the Consequences of Their Own Choices

Self-Deception at Play: Unintentional enabling, fixer mentality, taking on too much responsibility.

Unconscious Motivation: Avoiding emotional discomfort or emotional chaos by ensuring others are placated and supported.

Rebellion Zone: Resist the urge to step in when someone makes a bad decision or struggles with a task—let them deal with the natural fallout.

Why This Works: You convince yourself that helping is the right thing to do, even when you're exhausted or resentful. But when you always step in, smooth things over, or carry the load, you reinforce dependency and prevent others from developing self-sufficiency. By allowing people to experience their own consequences, you break the belief that it's your job to rescue everyone.

How This Plays Out in Real Life:

- The moment someone starts struggling, making a mistake, or dealing with a setback, you feel a strong pull to intervene, fix, or soften the impact before they have to experience discomfort.

- You tell yourself that stepping in is the "right thing to do"—but deep down, you feel exhausted and frustrated that people rely on you to hold things together.

- You anticipate problems before they happen, adjusting plans, handling logistics, or warning people in advance. They never even realize how much you're managing for them.

- Even when you know you should let someone figure it out for themselves, you step in anyway, thinking, It'll just be easier if I do it.

- You take on too much responsibility for others' choices, feeling guilty if you don't try to "help" them avoid failure, disappointment, or struggle.

- When people don't suffer the natural consequences of their own actions, they continue relying on you to bail them out, manage the details, or absorb the fallout.

- You resent how much you do for others, but at the same time, you don't trust them to handle things on their own—reinforcing the belief that if you don't fix it, everything will fall apart.

Your subconscious convinces you that helping is kindness and letting go is cruelty. But rescuing people from their own consequences doesn't serve them—it keeps them dependent on you while you burn out in the process.

The Challenge: Let People Struggle Without Rescuing Them

- If you sense someone is about to make a mistake, let them. Stop preemptively stepping in to save them before they even ask for help.

- If someone is struggling with something they should handle themselves, don't intervene. Let them work through it without offering to take over.

- If you feel guilt creeping in, remind yourself: their struggle is not your responsibility to absorb. They are capable of handling their own emotions and consequences.

- If someone asks for help, assess whether they actually need it—or if they just don't want to deal with discomfort. Encourage them to try before stepping in.

- If you find yourself fixing things for others out of habit, pause. *Ask yourself*: Am I doing this because it truly helps them, or because it's easier than letting them face the result of their choices?

By allowing people to experience the consequences of their own actions, you disrupt the belief that rescuing equals love. Instead of keeping people dependent and keeping yourself exhausted, you start fostering real accountability, self-sufficiency, and relationships built on mutual responsibility—not quiet resentment.

3. Prioritizing Your Own Needs Without Justifying It

Self-Deception at Play: Lack of self-preservation, burnout as a way of life, avoiding being a burden.

Unconscious Motivation: Self-sacrificing to keep the peace even at your own expense.

Rebellion Zone: Choose one priority—something that benefits only you—and follow through on it without guilt, explanation, or overcompensating for others afterward.

Why This Works: You tell yourself that your needs come second (or last)—you'll take care of yourself after everyone else is okay. But that day never comes. By intentionally prioritizing your own needs, you challenge the belief that self-sacrifice is noble and necessary and prove to your subconscious that you don't have to be falling apart to deserve care.

How This Plays Out in Real Life:

- You constantly put others' needs ahead of your own, telling yourself, "I'll take care of myself later"—but later never comes.

- When you do consider prioritizing yourself, you feel guilty, selfish, or indulgent—as if your well-being is optional compared to the needs of others.

- If you do take time for yourself, you make up for it later by overextending, working harder, or overcompensating.

- You dismiss your needs as "not that urgent" or "not as important" as what everyone else is dealing with.

- If someone asks what you want, you instinctively defer to what's easier, more convenient, or better for them.

- You rationalize that burnout is just part of life, convincing yourself that you don't have a choice but to keep pushing forward.

- Even when you're physically, mentally, or emotionally drained, you still say yes when people need something—believing that saying no would make you a burden.

Your subconscious convinces you that self-sacrifice is noble, necessary, and just how things are.

The Challenge: Prioritize Yourself Without Guilt or Justification

- If you feel the need to justify taking time for yourself, don't. Do it without explanation.

- If someone asks what you want, say what you actually want without waiting for others to answer so you can adjust.

- If you normally push your needs aside for later, act on them now. Later never comes unless you make it happen.

- If guilt creeps in, remind yourself: Needs are not selfish or indulgent and by always accommodating others you enable them to be more self-centered.

- If you instinctively try to "make up for it" after prioritizing yourself, stop. You don't need to compensate for taking care of yourself.

By choosing to prioritize your own needs without guilt or justification, you disrupt the belief that your value is tied to self-sacrifice. Instead of constantly pushing through exhaustion, you start creating a life where your well-being actually matters—without needing to justify why.

4. Speaking the Truth Instead of Filtering It

Self-Deception at Play: Managing others' emotions through truth-filtering, avoiding direct confrontation, preventing conflict through placating.

Unconscious Motivation: Avoiding emotional exposure and unpredictable reactions by managing how others receive the information.

Rebellion Zone: Say exactly what you think or feel, without filtering, softening, or packaging it for emotional digestion.

Why This Works: You believe that truth must be carefully managed so others don't react badly. You subtly edit what you say to avoid hurting feelings, triggering emotional outbursts, or making things harder. By delivering truth without manipulation, you allow others to process and react on their own terms, proving that their emotions are not your responsibility to manage.

How This Plays Out in Real Life:

   • Before you say something, you automatically adjust your words, tone, or delivery—not to be dishonest, but to soften the impact, prevent conflict, or avoid setting someone off.

   • If you anticipate a strong emotional reaction, misunderstanding, or tension, you instinctively hold back or sugarcoat what you really mean—telling yourself, "Now isn't the right time" or "They won't take it well."

   • You tell partial truths, omit details, or deliver information in small doses instead of being direct, believing that slow-dripping the truth will make it easier for the other person to handle.

   • When you do finally express frustration, disappointment, or boundaries, it often comes too late. Resentment has already built up or after the situation has escalated beyond what it needed to be.

   • You feel trapped in relationships, friendships, or work dynamics where people don't actually know what you think or feel, because you've spent so long managing their emotions instead of expressing your truth.

- Even when someone asks for your honest opinion, you scan for how they might react and adjust your response accordingly, leaving them with only a curated version of the truth.

- If a conversation becomes emotionally intense, you instantly shift into de-escalation mode, trying to keep things light, smooth, or controlled—even if that means hiding how you really feel.

Your subconscious convinces you that filtering the truth is the best way to avoid unnecessary conflict, tension, or emotional fallout.

The Challenge: Say What You Mean Without Editing or Softening It

- If you feel the urge to filter, don't. Say what you actually mean, exactly as you mean it.

- If you normally scan for how someone will react before speaking, challenge yourself to stop. Let them process without adjusting your words for them.

- If you usually deliver truths in pieces, say the whole thing at once. Give them all the information upfront instead of slow-dripping it.

- If you're tempted to soften a boundary, hold firm. Let your words be direct, not cushioned.

- If someone reacts strongly, let them. Their emotions are theirs to handle, not yours to preemptively manage.

By practicing directness without filtering, you disrupt the belief that truth must be carefully controlled to keep the peace. Instead, you begin building trust, clarity, and real relationships—ones where people know where you stand, instead of guessing at what you're actually thinking.

5. Saying No Without Over-Explaining or Trying to Soften the Blow

Self-Deception at Play: Lack of boundaries as loyalty, minimizing disappointment in others, avoiding direct confrontation.

Unconscious Motivation: Trying to preemptively de-escalate others' emotional responses by being overly agreeable.

Rebellion Zone: Say "no" without softening it, giving an excuse, or promising to make up for it later.

Why This Works: You often say yes out of guilt, obligation, or fear of letting people down. When you do say no, you overcompensate by giving long explanations or promising to help in some other way.

Practicing a clean, unapologetic no forces your brain to accept that your value is not tied to being available at all times.

How This Plays Out in Real Life:

- When someone asks you for a favor, commitment, or responsibility, your immediate instinct is to say "yes"–even when you know you don't have the time, energy, or desire.

- If you do say "no," you immediately feel the need to soften the rejection, giving a long-winded explanation, apologizing excessively, or offering an alternative to make up for it.

- You worry that saying no will disappoint, inconvenience, or frustrate others, so you overcompensate–scheduling something else, making future promises, or agreeing to "maybe later."

- You say "yes" to things you don't want to do just to avoid the awkwardness of saying "no," telling yourself, "It's fine, I'll figure it out"–even though you already feel stretched too thin.

- If someone pushes back or acts disappointed, you immediately second-guess your decision, wondering if you should just agree to keep the peace.

- Even when you want to set boundaries, you struggle to do it without guilt, shame, or discomfort.

- You resent how much you're carrying, but you also resist setting limits because you equate being available with being loyal, kind, or dependable.

Your subconscious convinces you that your value is tied to your willingness to accommodate others.

The Challenge: Say "No" Without Apologizing, Explaining, or Making Up for It

- If you feel the urge to soften a "no," don't. Say it clearly and directly, without adding unnecessary explanations.

- If someone asks for something you don't have the bandwidth for, decline without guilt. Your time and energy are not endless resources.

- If you typically follow a no with an excuse or justification, challenge yourself to stop at "no." You don't owe an explanation for prioritizing yourself.

- If someone reacts poorly to your boundary, let them. Their feelings are not your responsibility to fix.

- If you catch yourself trying to compensate after saying no, pause and remind yourself that you will make things worse by navigating yourself into the grey area just to soften the blow.

By practicing a clean, unapologetic no, you disrupt the belief that your worth is based on how much you give. Instead of constantly managing others' expectations, you start protecting your own time, energy, and mental well-being—without explanation, justification, or guilt.

6. Allowing Others to Solve Their Own Emotional Discomfort

Self-Deception at Play: Mediation as a necessity, managing others' emotions through truth-filtering, taking on too much responsibility.

Unconscious Motivation: Being hyperaware of other's emotional states and needs so that you can maintain peace and stability in the group dynamic.

Rebellion Zone: Resist the urge to intervene when someone is upset, disappointed, or frustrated. Let them process it instead of absorbing it for them.

Why This Works: You believe that if someone else is struggling emotionally, it's your job to help them feel better. You step in before they even ask, smoothing things over before they have time to process. But this prevents them from learning how to handle emotions on their own—and keeps you trapped in the role of emotional caretaker. Letting people handle their own discomfort proves that their emotions are not yours to manage.

How This Plays Out in Real Life:

- The moment someone looks upset, frustrated, or uncomfortable, you instinctively step in—offering reassurance, fixing the problem, or filtering the truth to soften the blow.

- You sense emotional shifts before people even speak. You adjust your tone, rephrase your words, or change the subject to avoid triggering a bigger reaction.

- If someone reacts negatively to a situation, you immediately jump into problem-solving mode, believing it's your responsibility to make them feel better.

- You absorb other people's emotional distress like it's your own, leaving you exhausted, overburdened, and unsure where their emotions end and yours begin.

• You placate, lie, or filter the truth to avoid watching someone struggle with disappointment or anger–telling yourself you're just "keeping the peace."

• If someone is in conflict with another person, you take it upon yourself to mediate. You try to fix the situation before they've even had a chance to work through it themselves.

• Even when you logically know someone else's emotions are not your responsibility, you still feel guilty, restless, or anxious if they are upset and you don't step in to fix it.

Your subconscious convinces you that helping others regulate their emotions is necessary for stability.

The Challenge: Let People Sit With Their Own Emotions

• If someone is upset, don't rush to fix it. Let them have their feelings without stepping in to manage them.

• If you feel the urge to soften or filter the truth to avoid discomfort, resist. Let them handle reality instead of trying to make it more digestible.

• If someone is venting frustration, don't immediately offer solutions.

• If you sense emotional distress, let them bring it up instead of adjusting your behavior to prevent escalation. Stop shaping conversations to keep things smooth.

By allowing others to handle their own emotional discomfort, you disrupt the belief that peace requires your intervention. Instead of constantly carrying the weight of other people's feelings, you start to experience what it means to support others without losing yourself in the process.

7. Delegating Even When It Feels Inefficient

Self-Deception at Play: Avoidance of delegation and detail work, fixer mentality, time blindness and overcommitment

Unconscious Motivation: Anticipating who is capable and preemptively assuming tasks or responsibility to avoid conflict or chaos.

Rebellion Zone: Delegate a task—even if explaining it feels like more effort than just doing it yourself. Resist the urge to step back in, clarify, or re-do it later.

Why This Works: You resist it because it feels inefficient to explain things step-by-step when you could just handle it yourself. You're a big-picture thinker who thrives in high-stakes problem-solving, but when it comes to small, tedious, or logistical details, your brain immediately checks out. Instead of figuring out how to delegate, you pile more onto your own plate, creating a cycle where you're overloaded but still procrastinating detail work. Practicing delegation forces you to accept that true efficiency is about freeing up your time and mental energy long-term.

How This Plays Out in Real Life:

- You take on massive workloads without hesitation. But when it comes to scheduling, filling out forms, or explaining processes to others, you avoid it or put it off.

- You don't mind complex problem-solving, but small, detailed tasks feel tedious and frustrating. Instead of delegating them, you just delay them until they become a crisis.

- You overload yourself with responsibilities but don't let anyone help—not because you want control, but because it feels like more effort to explain things than to just do them yourself.

- You procrastinate tasks like responding to emails, organizing paperwork, or breaking down long-term plans into steps, even though you know that delaying them will make things harder later.

- You tell yourself, "I'll figure it out," instead of creating a system or structure that could prevent last-minute scrambling.

- Even when someone wants to take something off your plate, you hesitate to hand it over. Explaining it feels exhausting, and you're sure they won't do it the "right" way.

- If you do delegate something, you check out completely or step back in later to "clean it up," which makes you feel like delegation was a waste of time.

Your subconscious convinces you that delegating is inefficient and detail work is an unavoidable burden.

The Challenge: Delegate Even When It Feels Like More Effort

- If you always tell yourself it's faster to do it yourself, delegate anyway. The short-term "efficiency" of handling it alone keeps you overloaded long-term.

- If you struggle to explain things, push through the discomfort. Take the time to teach someone once, rather than doing it yourself forever.

- If you tend to avoid detailed work, tackle one small logistical task before it becomes urgent. Stop waiting until stress forces you to handle it.

- If you start to check out mid-task, stay engaged just long enough to set up a structure for delegation. Avoiding details isn't the solution—handing them off is.

- If you delegate something, let it stay delegated. Don't step back in to tweak, adjust, or redo it. Allow others to handle things, even if it's not your version of perfect.

By letting go of the belief that delegation is inefficient, you disrupt the cycle of taking on too much while avoiding the details that could actually make your life easier. Instead of constantly scrambling, delaying, and feeling overloaded, you start building a system where things don't have to rely on you alone.

8. Accepting That "Figuring It Out" Isn't a Superpower—It's a Limitation

Self-Deception at Play: Fixer mentality, time blindness and overcommitment, chaos as adaptability.

Unconscious Motivation: Trying to keep others happy and supported even if it means perceived flakiness or lateness.

Rebellion Zone: Stop relying on your ability to "pull it off at the last minute." Instead, acknowledge that overloading yourself has real consequences and intentionally plan in a way that prevents last-minute scrambling.

Why This Works: You tell yourself that being able to "figure it out" under pressure is proof of your adaptability and resilience. But in reality, it's a survival mechanism that keeps you chronically stressed, overextended, and constantly reacting instead of creating a life with balance. By admitting that always "pulling it off" isn't a skill but a coping strategy, you create space for rest, intentionality, and commitments that don't require self-sacrifice.

By interrupting the need to overextend, fix, and manage everyone else's well-being, you prove to your subconscious that your worth is not determined by what you carry. Stability isn't created by sacrificing yourself for others—it's built by allowing life, relationships, and responsibilities to exist without requiring your constant intervention.

How This Plays Out in Real Life:

- You convince yourself you'll figure it out, despite the fact that your calendar is triple-booked, you're running on fumes, and you're setting yourself up for failure.

- You take on more than is reasonable, believing that you can stretch time, energy, and logistics just enough to make it all work.

- You show up late, frazzled, or behind schedule, but rationalize it as part of your nature, because you always make it work in the end.

- You tell yourself that your ability to perform under pressure is a strength, even though it leaves you resentful, exhausted, and without time for yourself.

- When things inevitably collapse or don't go as planned, you blame external circumstances instead of recognizing that the problem is that you keep putting yourself in unsustainable situations.

The Challenge: Create Structure Instead of Depending on the Last-Minute Save

- If you assume you'll "figure it out," stop. Instead, plan realistically based on what you actually have capacity for.

- If you tend to overcommit, practice saying No or I need to discuss that with ___ x person before I decide.

- If you're frequently late, overloaded, or rushed, examine your role in it. Are you creating chaos by believing you'll always "pull it off?"

- If your schedule is always full, create intentional gaps. Make space before it's forced on you by burnout.

By breaking the cycle of relying on yourself to "figure it out," you disrupt the belief that overloading yourself is just how life works.

Instead of constantly navigating stress, exhaustion, and last-minute recoveries, you start building a life that doesn't need to be saved—because it's sustainable from the start.

9. Being Direct Instead of Delaying the Inevitable

Self-Deception at Play: Managing others' emotions through truth-filtering, preventing conflict through placating, avoidance of direct confrontation.

Unconscious Motivation: Avoiding topics or conversations that may escalate a situation while trying to figure out how much truth the other person can handle.

Rebellion Zone: Say what you need to say directly, without sugarcoating, slow-dripping, or waiting for the "right moment." Stop managing how the other person might react—let them handle their own emotions.

Why This Works: You tell yourself that if you are too direct, the other person will lash out, spiral, or make your life harder. So instead, you soften the truth, delay saying what needs to be said, or withhold entirely—believing you are preventing unnecessary conflict. But in reality, you are only delaying the inevitable. The longer you wait or filter the truth, the bigger the explosion when it finally comes.

Even if their reaction is as bad as you feared, it's evidence that the relationship dynamic is built on avoidance, emotional manipulation, or a toxic cycle that needs to be confronted rather than managed. Your goal is to stop participating in dysfunctional patterns that require dishonesty and emotional micromanagement to function.

How This Plays Out in Real Life:

- When something is bothering you, you don't say it outright. Instead, you edit, soften, or delay telling the truth to avoid setting someone off.

- You withhold information until you believe the other person can "handle it," often underestimating their ability to manage their emotions.

- The longer you wait, the harder the conversation becomes, because by the time you finally say something, it has built into a bigger issue than it needed to be.

• The people around you can feel that something is off, but because you aren't being honest, they stop trusting your words.

• When the truth finally comes out, the reaction is often worse than if you had just been upfront from the start.

• When someone does react poorly, you take it as proof that you were right to withhold information—instead of recognizing that this is a sign of a larger toxic cycle that needs to be dealt with, not manipulated.

• You tell yourself that you are just being considerate, but in reality, you are creating distrust, avoidance, and unnecessary tension in your relationships.

The Challenge: Stop Managing Others' Emotions—Say It Now

• If you feel the urge to soften something, say it directly instead. No sugarcoating, no unnecessary buffer—just clarity.

• If you're waiting for the "right moment" to say something, recognize that the delay is only making it harder. Speak now.

• If you assume someone will react badly, let them. Their emotions are theirs to process, not yours to control.

• If they do react exactly how you feared, don't take it as evidence that withholding was the right move. Instead, recognize that this is a cycle that needs to be broken—not a situation that needs more careful emotional management.

• If you usually hold back for fear of conflict, remind yourself: honesty builds trust—delaying it destroys trust.

By choosing directness instead of filtering or delaying, you disrupt the belief that truth needs to be managed to prevent conflict. Instead, you begin building relationships based on trust, clarity, and mutual responsibility—rather than emotional micromanagement and avoidance.

What You Gain by Embracing Rebellion Zones

Your subconscious tells you that keeping the peace is your job. You believe that if you don't manage people's emotions, prevent chaos, and absorb the stress, everything will fall apart. You've built your life around keeping things running smoothly—even at your own expense.

No matter how much you strategize, sacrifice, and over-function, peace will never come from managing everyone else. The people around you will still struggle, get overwhelmed, and make bad choices. Your efforts only delay the inevitable, leaving you exhausted in the process.

When you step into your Rebellion Zones and stop holding it all together for everyone else, you stop living a life of exhaustion, silent resentment, and over-functioning. Instead, you finally experience real stability, real support, and real peace without carrying the entire burden alone.

1. You'll Actually Have Energy for the Things That Matter—Instead of Being Burnt Out by Things That Don't

Right now, your subconscious tells you that saying yes to everything is the price of loyalty and stability. You assume that setting boundaries will let people down, cause conflict, or make things fall apart. Not having boundaries is exactly what's making you unreliable, stretched too thin, and constantly behind.

By setting and enforcing real boundaries, you disrupt the belief that saying "yes" is the only way to be valued.

2. You'll Stop Being Everyone's Safety Net—And Let Them Stand on Their Own

Right now, your subconscious tells you that stepping in, fixing things, and preventing problems is the right thing to do. But the truth? Your constant intervention is keeping people dependent on you—and keeping you trapped in exhaustion and resentment.

By allowing people to experience the consequences of their own actions, you disrupt the belief that rescuing equals love.

3. You'll Finally Experience Stability—Instead of Constantly Chasing It

Right now, you tell yourself that your ability to handle anything last-minute is a strength. But in reality? This habit keeps you chronically overwhelmed, overloaded and overbooked.

By breaking the cycle of relying on yourself to "figure it out," you disrupt the belief that overloading yourself is just how life works. Instead of constantly navigating stress, exhaustion, and last-minute recoveries, you start building a life that doesn't need to be saved—it's sustainable from the start.

The Bottom Line

Your subconscious tells you that peace comes from keeping everything together. That if you let go, everything will collapse. But what if the real peace isn't in managing everything—but in finally stepping back?

When you step into your rebellion zones, you create:

- Stronger, more independent people around you. They're no longer relying on you to manage their emotions or responsibilities.

- Less exhaustion and burnout. You're not spending every waking moment absorbing stress for everyone else.

- More time and energy for yourself. Instead of constantly rearranging your schedule to accommodate everyone else's needs.

- Clearer, more honest relationships. People know your real boundaries instead of assuming you'll always say "yes."

- Less resentment and frustration. You're no longer over-functioning while others under-function.

- True stability—not just a fragile peace that depends on your constant intervention.

- Freedom from the guilt of prioritizing yourself. Taking care of your own needs doesn't make you selfish, it makes you sustainable.

- More respect from others. When you enforce boundaries, people start taking you seriously instead of treating you like an unlimited resource.

- Less mental clutter. You're no longer pre-managing everyone else's reactions, responsibilities, and logistics.

- A life that actually works for you—instead of one where you're constantly putting out fires that aren't yours to fight.

CHAPTER 28

REJECTION— CONTROL TO RECEIVE LOVE AND BE SAFE

REJECTION – CONTROL TO RECEIVE LOVE AND BE SAFE (PEOPLE-PLEASING ENGAGING)

Your core drive is ensuring that you are liked, valued, and chosen by shaping yourself to meet the expectations of others. You believe that if you prove yourself useful, accommodating, or agreeable enough, you will secure belonging and avoid rejection. This leads you to constantly track how others perceive you, adapt to fit their needs, and overextend yourself in ways that make you indispensable.

Your brain has trained you to equate acceptance with effort. You don't just want to be liked—you need to be actively chosen, sought out, and validated in a way that proves your worth. Because of this, you pour energy into maintaining relationships, anticipating people's needs before they ask, and ensuring that others never feel discomfort in your presence. In your mind, being wanted is something you have to earn, over and over again.

This makes you highly aware of people's perception of you and your reputation. It also sets you up for cycles of resentment, exhaustion, and disappointment when your effort isn't acknowledged in the way you expect. Even when people do care for you, you struggle to believe it's real unless they express it in a way that matches how much you've given. You start questioning what you did wrong—or what you need to do next to "fix" it.

Core Motivations

1. Fear of Rejection or Being Unwanted

You believe that if you stop trying, giving, or accommodating, people will lose interest or you'll be ostracized from your desired group

2. Desire to Maintain Harmony

You adjust your personality, preferences, and opinions to keep interactions smooth and positive, avoiding anything that could make you seem difficult or unlikable.

3. Belief That Love and Acceptance Must Be Earned

You assume that you have to prove your value through compliance, effort, or attentiveness.

4. Fear of Being "Too Much" or "Not Enough"

You scan interactions for signs that you are failing to meet unspoken expectations, adjusting your behavior to avoid getting socially sanctioned.

5. Fixation on Reciprocity as Validation

You feel confused when your level of effort isn't reciprocated and take it as a sign that you need to fix something or do better

6. Hyper-Awareness of Social Cues

You over-analyze tone, facial expressions, or delayed responses, cautious that they could mean something negative about you.

7. Fear of Being Forgettable or Replaceable

You believe that if you aren't actively showing up, giving, or making an impact in someone's life, you will be overlooked or someone else will be chosen instead.

8. Attachment to Social Comparison

You frequently compare how you measure up against others, wondering if you're liked more or less, wanted more or less, important more or less.

9. Struggle with Being Fully Present

You are so busy tracking how you are being perceived that you struggle to relax, enjoy interactions, or let things unfold naturally.

Why Do You Need Rebellion Zones?

Your need to secure love, approval, and emotional safety by over-giving, anticipating needs, and shaping yourself to be indispensable keeps you trapped in a cycle of exhaustion, self-neglect, and quiet resentment. You assume that if you are always available, always likable, and always meeting others' needs, you will be chosen, valued, and never left behind.

The Rebellion Zones challenge your brain's automatic assumption that your worth is tied to what you do for others. These Rebellion Zones push you to disrupt the belief that approval must be earned through effort, forcing you to let people engage with the real you instead of the curated, accommodating version of you.

1. You Learn That Love Exists Without Earning It

Your brain sees effort as the price of connection. If you stop adjusting, fixing, or proving yourself, you start to feel uneasy—like love might disappear. Rebellion Zones force you to sit in stillness instead of scrambling to prove your place.

Why You Need This: To experience love that doesn't require constant self-sacrifice.

How You Approach This Rebellion Zone:

- **Observe** your thought patterns when you feel the urge to check in, follow up, or do something extra to "secure" your place in a relationship.

- **Notice** how your Brain Pattern tricks you into seeing stillness as indifference, distance, or a sign that something is wrong.

- **Remind yourself** that other Brain Pattern types don't require constant affirmation to feel secure in their relationships; they just allow them to unfold.

- **Challenge yourself** to stop initiating, fixing, or adjusting just to maintain harmony. If the relationship can't withstand you simply being present instead of performing, is it real connection or just emotional labor?

445

The Self-Fulfilling Prophecy: By constantly proving your value through effort, you set up relationships where your worth is tied to what you give. You exhaust yourself and attract people who take more than they give—ultimately proving your own fear that love isn't freely given to you.

2. You Stop Seeking Validation Through Social Tracking

You may not realize it, but you've trained yourself to measure your worth through external responses. You scan interactions for approval—through tone, expressions, or how quickly someone replies—trying to gauge if you're still "liked" or wanted. Rebellion Zones challenge you to stop tracking approval and allow relationships to unfold naturally.

Why You Need This: To recognize that true connection doesn't require constant performance or monitoring.

How You Approach This Rebellion Zone:

- **Observe** how often your brain searches for external proof of being valued—whether through social cues, compliments, or reassurance.

- **Notice** how your Brain Pattern tries to convince you that silence or neutral responses mean something negative.

- **Remind yourself** that real connection isn't built on constant reassurance; it's built on mutual trust and respect.

- **Challenge yourself** to let go of comparison, whether it's worrying if someone likes you as much as they like someone else or wondering if you're important enough in their life.

The Self-Fulfilling Prophecy: By tracking and adjusting yourself to ensure people stay connected to you, you create relationships that feel fragile—dependent on constant effort. The truth is, the people meant for you will stay without you micromanaging their perception of you.

3. You Stop Equating Helpfulness with Worth

You have a habit of making yourself indispensable in people's lives, offering help, anticipating needs, and overextending yourself to prove your value. But this comes at a cost: exhaustion, resentment, and relationships that feel more like unpaid emotional labor than mutual connection.

Why You Need This: To break the belief that love and belonging must be constantly earned through service.

How You Approach This Rebellion Zone:

- **Observe** how often you step in to help, fix, or manage situations before someone even asks.

- **Notice** how your Brain Pattern convinces you that your worth is tied to how much you contribute or comply.

- **Remind yourself** that people who truly value you don't require constant proof of your usefulness.

- **Challenge yourself** to step back and see if people engage with you without the extra effort—if they only reach out when they need something, that's not a real connection.

The Self-Fulfilling Prophecy: By making yourself indispensable, you attract relationships where your value is tied to what you do rather than who you are. You reinforce the belief that you have to keep giving to keep people close, when in reality, the right people will stay without constant effort.

4. You Challenge Your Fear of Being "Too Much" or "Not Enough"

Your brain is constantly scanning for signs that you're failing to meet expectations.

You adjust your personality, tone, and even opinions based on who you're with—hoping to avoid criticism, rejection, or being labeled as difficult. Rebellion Zones force you to hold your own space, even when you feel the pull to shrink or shift to fit in.

Why You Need This: To stop filtering yourself to be more likable at the expense of your own needs and authenticity.

How You Approach This Rebellion Zone:

- **Observe** when you feel the urge to soften your words, agree when you don't, or hold back an opinion out of fear of disapproval.

- **Notice** how your Brain Pattern tricks you into believing that blending in, complying or people-pleasing is the only way to be liked.

- **Remind yourself** that not everyone needs to like you—true belonging comes from being yourself, not constantly adjusting to avoid disapproval.

- **Challenge yourself** to speak honestly and focus on a personal goal, even if it means risking a moment of discomfort.

The Self-Fulfilling Prophecy: By filtering yourself to fit in, you create relationships where you're never fully seen or valued for who you actually are. You trade authenticity for approval, but in doing so, you never get the connection you truly crave.

5. You Stop Measuring Your Worth by Reciprocity

When you give to others, you want proof that you're valued in the same way. You expect people to mirror your effort, and when they don't, you take it as a sign that something is wrong. Rebellion Zones force you to detach your self-worth from what others do (or don't do) in return.

Why You Need This: To recognize that giving isn't a contract—it's a choice, and it shouldn't define your value.

How You Approach This Rebellion Zone:

- **Observe** when your Brain Pattern expects reciprocity as a sign of validation and security—whether it's someone reaching out first, matching effort, or recognizing your sacrifices.

- **Notice** how disappointment creeps in when others don't respond the way you hoped.

- **Remind yourself** that true connection isn't about keeping score—someone not matching your energy doesn't mean they don't care.

- **Challenge yourself** to give without expectation and see who stays even when you aren't bending over backward.

The Self-Fulfilling Prophecy: By measuring your worth through reciprocity, you set yourself up for constant disappointment. You expect others to validate your effort, but when they don't, you feel like you've failed. The truth? Your worth isn't defined by how much you do for others—it's something you don't have to prove.

Rebellion Zones

Rebellion Zones force you to stop proving your worth, step back from the compulsion to accommodate, and see what happens when you stop controlling love through self-sacrifice, overextension, and constant social tracking.

Your biggest challenge will be allowing space for relationships to flow naturally instead of trying to manage them. Right now, you only feel secure when you are actively reinforcing your place in people's lives. But real connection is about trusting that you are valued without having to prove it.

By stepping into your Rebellion Zones, you stop earning love through effort and start experiencing relationships that don't require self-sacrifice to stay intact.

1. Making Decisions Without Seeking Feedback or Permission

Self-Deception at Play: Seeking feedback and validation, fear of uncertainty and over-overseeing, s-worth tied to compliance.

Unconscious Motivation: Support with decisions to avoid responsibility, blame or shame.

Rebellion Zone: Make a decision entirely on your own—without asking for input, second-guessing, or checking how others feel about it first.

Why This Works: Your subconscious tells you that you can't trust yourself to make the right choice, so you rely on external approval before taking action. By choosing without validation, you prove to your brain that your decisions are valid, even without someone else's confirmation.

How This Plays Out in Real Life:

- When faced with a decision—big or small—your first instinct is to ask for input, check how others feel about it, or scan for external feedback before acting.

- You overthink simple choices, replaying scenarios in your head, wondering what the "right" move is—not because you don't know, but because you're afraid of making the wrong choice alone.

- You feel paralyzed when you don't get immediate validation or if others give conflicting opinions, making it even harder to move forward.

- If you do make a decision on your own, you immediately second-guess yourself, wondering, What if I misread this? or, What if someone else would have done it differently?

- You defer to authority figures, friends, family, or group norms instead of relying on your own instincts—assuming that others' approval equals certainty.

- When making plans, you wait for a consensus before fully committing—because if you make a choice that others don't align with, you feel exposed or insecure.

- You avoid bold, independent decisions because they feel risky—but in reality, the constant need for validation keeps you stuck, indecisive, and disconnected from your own instincts.

Your subconscious convinces you that checking with others is just being careful, smart, or responsible.

The Challenge: Make a Choice Without Seeking Permission

- If your first instinct is to check with someone before deciding, don't. Trust yourself to make the call alone.

- If you feel the need to run a choice by multiple people, *ask yourself*:

- If I keep looking for feedback to make my decisions will I ever truly learn how to do this on my own?

- Can I build self-trust by relying on the opinions of others?

- Can I challenge myself to make a decision and observe the outcome objectively to learn the lesson?

- Even if I make a mistake, won't I still learn from it I don't have anyone else to blame?

- If you second-guess a decision you already made, resist the urge to undo it. Sit with the discomfort of trusting your choice.

- If you feel uncomfortable acting without validation, do it anyway. Let yourself experience what it feels like to trust your own instincts and take the pressure off this decision feeling like life or death.

- If you normally follow the crowd's preferences, make a choice that is purely your own, even if no one else agrees with it.

By choosing without external validation, you disrupt the belief that certainty must come from others. Instead of constantly seeking reassurance, you begin developing real self-trust—the kind that isn't dependent on approval, feedback, or consensus.

2. Letting Others Be Disappointed Without Trying to Fix It

Self-Deception at Play: Fear of rejection and conflict, minimizing conflict by saying "yes," over-identification with others' needs.

Unconscious Motivation: Keep others happy or stabilized to ensure you maintain your reputation or image.

Rebellion Zone: Say "no" to something, and allow the other person to feel disappointed—without over-explaining, softening the blow, or trying to make up for it.

Why This Works: You believe that keeping people happy keeps you safe—socially, emotionally, and relationally. You equate approval with security and assume that if people are upset with you, it means you've damaged the relationship or lowered your value in their eyes. But in reality, true connection is based on authenticity, boundaries, and trust. Allowing others to be disappointed forces your subconscious to recognize that you can still be accepted and valued, even when you say "no."

How This Plays Out in Real Life:

• When someone asks for something, you instinctively say "yes"—even if it's inconvenient, exhausting, or something you don't want to do—because turning them down feels too uncomfortable.

• If you do say no, you feel instant anxiety or guilt, wondering if they're upset with you or if this will change how they see you.

• You worry that disappointing someone means they will like or respect you less—so you try to soften the rejection with long-winded justifications, offering alternative ways to help or saying, "Maybe next time," even if you don't mean it.

• If someone reacts negatively to your boundary, you start questioning whether you should have said, "no" at all—wondering if their disappointment means you made the wrong choice.

• You assume that if someone is upset with you, it's a sign you need to fix the situation, rather than recognizing that people are allowed to feel disappointment without it meaning you did something wrong.

• You track social cues, body language, or tone shifts after saying "no," scanning for signs that the other person is upset, even if they haven't said anything outright.

• You may agree to things just to avoid the awkwardness of saying,

• 'no," even if you know you don't have time or energy for them.

Your subconscious convinces you that you need to keep people happy to be liked, valued, or included. But avoiding disappointment doesn't make you more lovable. It makes you more exhausted, overextended, and disconnected from your own needs.

The Challenge: Let People Be Disappointed Without Trying to Fix It

- If you say "no," stop there. No softening the blow, no long explanations—just let it be a "no."

- If someone reacts negatively to your boundary, resist the urge to backtrack. Their feelings about your decision do not determine your worth, and it's a good learning experience for you to see how others handle their emotions.

- If you feel anxious after saying "no," remind yourself that disappointment is temporary—respect lasts. Setting a boundary doesn't erase your value.

- If you usually overcompensate after saying "no," don't. You don't have to make up for setting a boundary by offering something else.

- If you feel the urge to check if someone is upset, pause. *Ask yourself*:

    Historically, do I feel the instinct to make sure people aren't upset with me?

    Is this desire to seek reassurance connected to my fear of rejection?

    Is my conflict avoidance creating internalized problems for me that I'm trying to work on?

    Can I challenge myself to let this play out and not check in on their feelings?

By allowing others to be disappointed without trying to repair, soften, or undo it, you disrupt the belief that approval is the only path to belonging. Instead of constantly managing your choices based on how others might feel, you start to experience what it's like to prioritize your needs without it costing you love, respect, or connection.

3. Stating Your Real Opinion Without Filtering It for Approval

Self-Deception at Play: Managing perception, following social norms for stability, prioritizing inclusion over individuality

Unconscious Motivation: Avoid blame or shame by staying quiet to see what the group consensus is.

Rebellion Zone: Say what you actually think or feel, even if you know it might be unpopular or different from what others want to hear.

Why This Works: Your subconscious has convinced you that expressing your true thoughts will lead to conflict, judgment, or disapproval. But constantly adjusting your opinions to match others keeps you trapped in a version of yourself that isn't fully authentic. By practicing unfiltered honesty, you prove that your voice doesn't need to be curated to be valuable.

How This Plays Out in Real Life:

- In conversations, you instinctively scan for social cues before speaking, adjusting your response to match the group's tone, beliefs, or expectations.

- When someone asks for your opinion, you hesitate, reword, or soften your answer, making sure it aligns with what they want to hear, even if it's not what you actually think.

- You feel uncomfortable expressing disagreement or having a different perspective, assuming it will make people like you less or create unnecessary tension.

- If you do voice your opinion and sense even the slightest discomfort or pushback from others, you immediately downplay, backtrack, or deflect as if you need to smooth things over.

- You find yourself agreeing with others just to keep the conversation moving smoothly, even when internally you're thinking something completely different.

- When making choices, you prioritize what will be well-received over what actually aligns with your beliefs, telling yourself that it's just easier to go along with things.

- You sometimes lose track of what you actually think or feel because you've spent so much time adjusting to external expectations.

Your subconscious convinces you that staying agreeable and aligned with others is what keeps you safe, included, and liked. Filtering your real thoughts keeps you from being truly known, and forces you to maintain relationships where your voice isn't actually present.

The Challenge: Say What You Actually Think—Without Filtering for Approval

- If you normally scan for how others feel before speaking, don't. Say what you actually think first.

- If you instinctively soften or edit your opinion, challenge yourself to be fully direct. Let your words stand on their own.

- If someone disagrees with you, hold your ground instead of backtracking. Difference doesn't mean rejection.

- If you're tempted to agree just to keep the placate, stop. *Ask yourself*:

    Do I historically agree with others so that I don't ruffle feathers?

    Am I considering lying just as a way to fit in and feel like part of the group?

    Does lying or manipulating prevent people from truly getting to know me and my opinions?

- If you feel discomfort after stating your real thoughts, stick with it. Your worth isn't tied to approval and the truth helps people create a closer connection to you if they align.

By expressing your unfiltered opinions, you disrupt the belief that likability is more important than authenticity. Instead of constantly adjusting to fit in, you start building relationships where you are valued for who you actually are—not just for how well you align with others.

4. Exploring Your Identity by Trying New Things—Without External Influence

Self-Deception at Play: Over-identification with others' needs, prioritizing inclusion over individuality, following social norms for stability.

Unconscious Motivation: Avoidance of being the beginner while sticking to the familiar to manage reputation or image.

Rebellion Zone: Break out of your usual routine by trying something completely new—something that is entirely your choice, without considering how others would perceive it or whether it "fits" with who you've been told you are. Pay attention to not just what you like, but what you don't like, because both reveal who you truly are. Challenge yourself to be a beginner at something instead of sticking only to what you already excel at.

Why This Works: Your subconscious has convinced you that your identity is tied to external expectations, cultural programming, or group values. Because you've spent so much time aligning with others, your true preferences have been buried under conformity and approval-seeking. You also avoid situations where you don't feel immediately competent, preferring to stay in spaces where you already excel, rather than risking looking unskilled or uncertain. By intentionally shaking up your routine, exposing yourself to new experiences, and allowing yourself to be a beginner, you disrupt the belief that who you are has already been decided for you. Instead, you begin the process of actively discovering your real preferences, desires, and interests without pressure to conform or perform.

How This Plays Out in Real Life:

- You default to familiar activities, routines, and interests—not necessarily because you love them, but because they feel safe, expected, or approved by those around you.

- You rarely question whether you actually like something. You just keep doing what you've always done or what's been modeled for you.

- You assume that "this is just who I am," but you've never actually tested that assumption by exploring options outside of what's been socially or culturally reinforced.

- When faced with the opportunity to try something new, you immediately evaluate how others might perceive it, rather than considering whether it excites or intrigues you.

- You avoid activities, styles, hobbies, or experiences that seem "out of character" for you, without recognizing that your sense of identity may not have been fully formed—it was just shaped by what was expected of you.

- You hesitate to try things where you won't immediately excel, avoiding situations where you have to be a beginner, ask for help, or struggle through the learning curve.

- If you do try something new and don't like it, you take it as a failure. But recognizing that discovering what you don't like is just as important as discovering what you do like.

Your subconscious convinces you that stepping outside of what's known or expected is risky. Your identity isn't fixed, and your true preferences can only be revealed through experience, not through assumptions based on past conformity.

The Challenge: Break Out of the Familiar and Discover What's Actually Yours

- If you always stick to safe, expected choices, challenge yourself to do something completely out of character. You won't know what's "you" until you test new experiences.

- If you struggle to name your likes and dislikes beyond what you were raised with, start experimenting. Treat life like a series of low-stakes experiments—try, observe, and adjust.

- If you feel hesitation before trying something new, *ask yourself*:

  Have I historically stuck to things that feel familiar and safe?

  Do I tend to assume what others will think about what I'm doing?

  Is it possible that I'll project my fears onto others and use them as a justification to stay in my safety net?

  Can I challenge myself to try something new and embrace the feeling of being a beginner at something?

- If you avoid being a beginner, pick something where you know you'll struggle at first. Let yourself be unskilled without shame. Growth comes from tolerating imperfection.

- If you try something and don't like it, count it as a win. Knowing what isn't for you is just as valuable as knowing what is.

- If you fear looking foolish, remind yourself: no one is watching as closely as you think. Your job is to explore, not to impress.

By intentionally shaking up your routine, trying things outside your usual scope, and embracing the process of trial and error, you disrupt the belief that who you are has already been decided for you. Instead of continuing to operate within old, familiar boxes, you start actively creating your own definition of self, one that isn't shaped by external expectations, but by real experience.

5. Not Adjusting Yourself to Match the Group

Self-Deception at Play: Controlling how you are perceived, prioritizing inclusion over individuality, fear of uncertainty, and over-overseeing.

Unconscious Motivation: Assessing the group identity to find ways to connect or fit in.

Rebellion Zone: Enter a social situation and remain fully yourself–no mirroring, no adjusting, no adapting to blend in.

Why This Works: You instinctively scan for social cues and adjust your energy, tone, or personality to match the group. But this pattern keeps you from fully experiencing connection because you're always in performance mode. By staying grounded in who you are, you break the belief that belonging is something you have to constantly work for.

How This Plays Out in Real Life:

- When entering a social setting, you immediately scan the environment and adjust your personality, energy, or tone to match the group.

- You subconsciously mirror people's mannerisms, opinions, or emotions–not because you're trying to deceive them, but because you believe that blending in makes connection easier.

- If you're in a new environment, you default to observation mode first, waiting to see what's acceptable before fully engaging.

- You struggle to identify what your natural personality feels like in a group setting because you're so used to adapting based on the people around you.

- You downplay parts of your personality, interests, or opinions that don't seem to fit with the group, even if they're things you genuinely love.

- If you express a thought or reaction that doesn't get a positive response, you instantly shrink, adjust, or redirect the conversation.

- After social interactions, you overanalyze what you said or did, wondering if you "got it right" or if anyone perceived you differently than you intended.

Your subconscious convinces you that belonging is something that must be managed and earned. But belonging built on constant adaptation is a performance.

The Challenge: Stay Fully Yourself in Social Settings

- If you feel the instinct to adjust your energy or personality, don't. Let yourself exist exactly as you are and think of it as practice.

- If you normally mirror people to make interactions smoother, resist. Let them experience the real you, even if it feels slightly misaligned at first.

- If you catch yourself filtering your opinions, say what you actually think. Let people react, rather than shaping your words to avoid discomfort.

- If you feel self-conscious about how you're coming across, remind yourself: The right people will connect with you as you are—not a curated version of you.

- If you tend to overanalyze social interactions after the fact, stop. You don't have to perfect every conversation to be worthy of connection.

By staying grounded in who you are, you disrupt the belief that you must shape-shift to fit in. Instead of constantly managing perception and adjusting for approval, you begin to experience what it's like to connect authentically with no performance required.

6. Choosing Rest Without Feeling Like You Have to Earn It

Self-Deception at Play: Over-performing for validation, measuring success by external goalposts, striving for perfection.

Unconscious Motivation: Be of service to maintain reputation or sense of duty.

Rebellion Zone: Take time off, rest, or do something purely for yourself—without justifying why you "deserve" it or making up for it later.

Why This Works: You associate inclusion and worthiness with output—if you're not achieving, helping, or contributing, you fear becoming invisible or irrelevant. Practicing rest without guilt forces your subconscious to see that your value doesn't come from what you produce. It exists regardless.

How This Plays Out in Real Life:

- You struggle to rest unless you've "earned" it, telling yourself that relaxation is only acceptable after you've been productive enough.

- Even when you do take a break, you mentally tally up what

still needs to be done, making it impossible to fully enjoy the downtime.

• If you spend a day doing nothing, you feel uneasy, guilty, or behind, convincing yourself that you're "wasting time."

• You say things like, "I'll rest once I finish this," but once you finish, you immediately move the goalpost and find something else that "must" be done first.

• If someone else is relaxing while you're working, you feel a mix of irritation, envy, and confusion. In your mind, rest is something that must be justified, not simply allowed.

• You pack your schedule so full that there's no room for stillness, using busyness as a way to prove that you're responsible, hardworking, or valuable.

• When you do rest, you feel the need to overcompensate later—working harder, pushing longer, or taking on extra tasks to "make up" for it.

Your subconscious convinces you that being busy makes you valuable, and slowing down means you're falling behind. But your worth exists, even when you do nothing.

The Challenge: Rest Without Guilt, Justification, or Overcompensation

• If you feel the urge to "earn" your rest, stop. Rest because you need it, not because you checked off enough tasks.

• If you mentally justify why you deserve a break, challenge yourself to rest without explanation. You don't need permission.

• If you catch yourself feeling guilty for doing nothing, sit with it. Rest is necessary. It's rewiring pattern opposition for you—so enjoy it.

• If you usually overcompensate after resting, resist. You don't have to work twice as hard later to make up for taking care of yourself.

• If your schedule is always full, build in intentional, untouchable time for rest. Don't wait until burnout forces you to stop.

By choosing rest without guilt, you disrupt the belief that your worth is measured by your output. Instead of constantly chasing productivity to feel valuable, you begin to experience what it's like to exist without needing to prove your right to slow down.

7. Allowing Others to Be Wrong About You Without Correcting the Narrative

Self-Deception at Play: Controlling how you are perceived, seeking validation through high visibility, deflecting responsibility to preserve likability.

Unconscious Motivation: Control public perception to manage reputation.

Rebellion Zone: If someone misinterprets your intentions, opinions, or choices, resist the urge to explain, correct, or over-explain.

Why This Works: You have an instinctive need to manage how others see you—to make sure they "get" you, like you, and never misunderstand you. But this pattern keeps you constantly performing, explaining, and proving. Letting people draw their own conclusions forces your brain to recognize that their perception isn't your responsibility.

How This Plays Out in Real Life:

- When someone misunderstands your intentions, opinions, or choices, you immediately feel the need to clarify, correct, or explain yourself, even when it's not necessary.

- You replay conversations in your head, worrying that someone got the wrong impression of you or took something the wrong way.

- If someone forms an opinion about you that isn't accurate, you feel uneasy, restless, or anxious—as if your likability or worth depends on setting the record straight.

- You instinctively jump into damage control mode when you sense that someone's perception of you might be shifting in a way you don't like.

- You sometimes offer explanations that weren't asked for, just to make sure no one gets the wrong idea.

- You fear being judged for things you didn't even do or intend, feeling like you need to defend yourself preemptively.

- Even if correcting the narrative wouldn't change anything, you still feel an internal pull to make sure people understand your side.

- Your subconscious convinces you that if people misinterpret you, you've somehow failed. But you don't owe everyone an explanation. Letting people be wrong about you is an act of self-trust.

The Challenge: Allow Misperceptions Without Trying to Fix Them

- If someone misinterprets you, resist the urge to correct them. Let their perception be theirs to hold without you needing to manipulate or control.

- If you feel anxious about how others see you, remind yourself: my worth isn't tied to their understanding of me.

- If you catch yourself over-explaining to protect your image, stop. Say less and trust that people will think what they think.

- If you feel uncomfortable letting people be wrong about you, sit with it. Discomfort is a sign you're breaking an old habit.

- If someone assumes something incorrect about you and it doesn't truly impact your life, let it go. Not everything requires a correction and the truth will eventually prevail.

By allowing others to be wrong about you without trying to fix it, you disrupt the belief that your worth is dependent on perception management. Instead of exhausting yourself proving, performing, and perfecting your image, you start to experience what it's like to be free from the constant need for approval.

8. Breaking the Habit of Over-Explaining or Over-Apologizing

Self-Deception at Play: Fear of rejection and conflict, seeking feedback and validation, minimizing disappointment in others.

Unconscious Motivation: Maintain constant feedback loop or reassurance to maintain public image.

Rebellion Zone: Say, "no," set a boundary, or share an opinion without adding a long-winded explanation or unnecessary apology.

Why This Works: Your subconscious tells you that people need a full explanation to understand why you're saying no or asserting yourself. But in reality, over-explaining and over-apologizing only reinforce the belief that your choices require approval. By practicing direct communication without justification, you prove to yourself that your words can stand on their own.

How This Plays Out in Real Life:

- When you say, "no," you immediately follow it up with a long-winded explanation as if you need to justify why you're allowed to decline.

- If you express an opinion, you soften it with disclaimers like "I don't know, maybe it's just me" or "I could be wrong, but…"–downplaying your own perspective.

- You apologize for things that don't require an apology, saying, "Sorry, I just…" before making a request or setting a boundary.

- If someone looks even slightly disappointed or surprised, you immediately feel the need to clarify, adjust, or backtrack–assuming they need more reassurance.

- You feel uneasy after stating a boundary or saying "no," wondering if the other person is upset with you–even if their reaction doesn't actually indicate that.

- You believe that if you don't explain yourself thoroughly, people might misunderstand you, judge you, or think less of you.

- You talk in circles or over-explain simple things, believing that if you just explain enough, the other person will accept your choice without any discomfort.

Your subconscious convinces you that people need full explanations to respect your decisions. But over-explaining reinforces the belief that your choices aren't valid unless others approve of them.

The Challenge: Say It Without Explaining or Apologizing

- If you say, "no," stop there. No extra details, no justification–just a simple "no."

- If you catch yourself over-explaining, pause.

- *Ask yourself*:

    Am I assuming they need more information to not get the wrong impression?

    Can I challenge myself to trust that if they have a question or need more information that they will ask on their own?

- If you instinctively apologize before making a request, replace "sorry" with "thank you" or nothing at all.

- If someone looks disappointed after you set a boundary, resist the urge to soften or adjust it. Their feelings don't require your over-explanation.

- If you feel the urge to justify yourself, sit with discomfort instead of filling the silence. Let your words stand on their own.

By breaking the habit of over-explaining and over-apologizing, you disrupt the belief that your choices require approval to be valid. Instead of constantly seeking reassurance through words, you start to trust that your boundaries, opinions, and decisions are enough—without permission, without apology, and without justification.

9. Allowing Uncertainty Without Seeking Reassurance

Self-Deception at Play: Freeze response and external influence, fear of uncertainty and over-overseeing, seeking feedback and validation.

Unconscious Motivation: Maintain constant feedback loop or reassurance to maintain public image.

Rebellion Zone: When faced with uncertainty, resist the urge to seek reassurance, validation, or feedback. Make a choice based on your own instincts and move forward without checking.

Why This Works: Your fear of uncertainty keeps you constantly looking outward for answers, approval, and direction. But outsourcing decisions prevents you from developing self-trust. By sitting in the discomfort of not knowing and not asking for reassurance, you teach your brain that you don't need external validation to move forward.

How This Plays Out in Real Life:

- When faced with an uncertain situation, your first instinct is to seek reassurance—asking others what they would do, double-checking your decision, or looking for confirmation that you're making the "right" choice.

- You overthink simple choices, fearing that if you don't get it exactly right, something bad might happen.

- If you can't get immediate feedback or validation, you feel frozen—unable to move forward until someone else confirms your decision.

- When you do make a choice on your own, you second-guess yourself, mentally replaying the situation and wondering if you should have done it differently.

- You find yourself checking in with multiple people before committing to something, as if the number of people who agree with you determines whether the choice is correct.

- You often feel like you don't fully trust your own instincts, so you look to external opinions, research, or authority figures to tell you what's best for you.

- When something feels unclear or unpredictable, your anxiety spikes, making it difficult to think rationally. Instead of tolerating the uncertainty, you reach for immediate reassurance to relieve the discomfort.

Your subconscious convinces you that if you don't get reassurance, you'll make the wrong choice and suffer for it. Constantly looking for validation keeps you stuck in a cycle of self-doubt, preventing you from developing real self-trust.

The Challenge: Sit with Uncertainty Instead of Seeking Reassurance

- If you feel the urge to check your decision with someone, don't. Make the choice on your own and commit to it.

- If uncertainty makes you anxious, let yourself feel the discomfort instead of trying to escape it. Your ability to handle not knowing is stronger than you think.

- If you normally wait for validation before taking action, act first. Remind yourself that commitment must precede confidence, and that's where your Brain Pattern keeps setting you up to fail.

- If you start mentally replaying your choice, remind yourself: I won't learn how to make confident decisions on my own if I keep going to others for assistance.

- If you usually research extensively before making a simple decision, set a time limit. Allow yourself to decide without endless information-seeking.

By breaking the habit of seeking reassurance, you disrupt the belief that you need external confirmation to trust yourself. Instead of constantly outsourcing certainty, you begin to develop true self-trust—the kind that allows you to move forward without waiting for permission.

10. Measuring Yourself by Internal Standards Instead of External Approval

Self-Deception at Play: Over-identification with others' needs, self-worth tied to performance or compliance, seeking feedback and validation.

Unconscious Motivation: Seek external validation to feel secure or on track.

Rebellion Zone: Define success, value, or worth on your own terms instead of looking to outside validation, metrics, or social feedback. Make a decision or assess your progress based only on what you believe—not how others respond.

Why This Works: Your subconscious tells you that your worth is determined by how well you perform, how much others approve of you, or how closely you align with group standards. This belief keeps you trapped in a cycle of over-performing, scanning for feedback, and adjusting yourself to fit what's expected. Practicing internal self-measurement disrupts the need for external validation and proves that your value isn't something that has to be earned—it already exists.

How This Plays Out in Real Life:

- You define success by external validation—praise, performance metrics, social feedback, or other people's opinions—rather than what actually feels meaningful to you.

- If no one acknowledges your effort, you start questioning whether it was "good enough" or whether it even mattered at all.

- When making a decision, you instinctively look for outside confirmation, wondering if others would approve before trusting your own judgment.

- You push yourself to over-perform, believing that as long as you are meeting expectations, achieving enough, or making yourself useful, you will be valued.

- You often feel disconnected from your own desires and personal definitions of success because you've spent so much time following external goalposts.

- If you achieve something but don't receive the level of recognition you expected, the achievement suddenly feels hollow or meaningless.

- You constantly scan for signs of approval or disapproval from others, even in situations where you should be measuring success based on your own standards.

Your subconscious convinces you that worth is something that must be proven, earned, or recognized externally. But your value exists regardless of how others measure it.

The Challenge: Shift from External Validation to Internal Self-Trust

- If you instinctively look for feedback before feeling good about something, stop. Let your decision ride and observe how it plays out to learn the lesson.

- If you feel like an achievement is only meaningful if others acknowledge it, challenge that thought. *Ask yourself*:

   Have I looked for validation on tasks my entire life?

   Is this rooted in a childhood pattern that has been leading to resentment and frustration?

   Can I review my effort personally instead of looking to others for validation?

- If you struggle to define success without external markers, take time to create a static measurement. How can you define success on this goal without it being dynamic or intangible?

- If you're tempted to compare yourself to others, redirect your focus inward with radical personal responsibility. Instead of asking, "Am I doing enough?" *ask*,

   Did I put in effort and preparation to execute this task?

   Can I challenge myself to identify two areas where I can improve next time?

- If you don't get the response you expected after an accomplishment, remind yourself: everyone is focused on their own life and problems—they are likely not thinking about the same thing as I am.

By measuring yourself based on internal standards instead of external approval, you disrupt the belief that your value is dependent on recognition. Instead of constantly chasing validation, you begin to experience what it's like to define your own worth—on your terms, not anyone else's.

11. Separating Your Identity from Family, Culture, or Religious Expectations

Self-Deception at Play: Following social norms or group values for stability, prioritizing inclusion over individuality, fear of rejection and conflict.

Unconscious Motivation: Maintain a standard of conformity to manage reputation.

Rebellion Zone: Make a choice, hold an opinion, or engage in an interest that is solely based on your personal beliefs and preferences—not what you were taught to value by family, culture, or religion.

Why This Works: Your subconscious tells you that staying aligned with group expectations is what keeps you safe, accepted, and worthy of belonging. You've been conditioned to filter your likes, dislikes, and decisions through the lens of external authority figures, cultural values, or religious doctrine, often without questioning whether those beliefs actually resonate with you. By intentionally choosing something that is truly yours, without seeking permission or approval, you disrupt the belief that compliance equals security.

How This Plays Out in Real Life:

- You automatically align with family, cultural, or religious expectations without questioning whether they truly resonate with you.

- When faced with a decision, you instinctively consider how it fits within the values you were raised with—often prioritizing group acceptance over personal alignment.

- You feel guilt, anxiety, or inner conflict when making choices that deviate from what you were taught, even if they feel more authentic to you.

- You often default to what is expected of you rather than exploring your own preferences—whether it's career choices, relationships, belief systems, or personal interests.

- You avoid expressing differing opinions, questioning traditions, or embracing new perspectives out of fear that doing so will create tension or make you an outsider.

- If you do break away from an expectation, you feel the need to explain, justify, or soften it, as if your choices require approval from the larger group.

You struggle to trust that you can still belong even if you don't conform, so you continue prioritizing external alignment over internal truth.

The Challenge: Shift from External Identity to Internal Ownership

- If you automatically align with what you were taught, pause and question it.

- Before making a decision, *ask*:

  Do I actually believe this, or is this just what my culture or religion says I should believe?

  Would I still choose this if no one in my family or circle would ever know?

  Am I making this choice because compliance feels like the only way to be included?

- If you feel guilt or anxiety when making a choice outside of expectations, sit with it.

- Recognize that guilt isn't proof that you're doing something wrong—it's just a conditioned response to stepping outside of what's familiar.

- *Ask yourself*:

  Will I ever know who I truly am and what I like if I keep blindly complying?

- If you struggle to express opinions that contradict your upbringing, start small.

- Practice stating a personal preference that isn't shaped by external influences—whether it's music, career choices, relationships, or belief systems.

- When you feel the urge to soften or downplay your opinion to make it more palatable, resist the urge.

- If someone disagrees, let the disagreement exist instead of immediately trying to smooth it over.

- If you feel pressure to justify or explain yourself, stop.

- Instead of over-explaining, try this:

  "I know that in our culture we are supposed to _____ , but that's not what I feel right now. "

- If others push back, observe your instinct to defend yourself, but don't engage. Acknowledge the challenge of moving beyond cognitive dissonance and remain empathetic and calm.

- The more you practice not seeking permission, the more you rewire your brain to see your choices as valid without external approval.

- If you fear losing connection by asserting your individuality, test that belief.

- Ask: Is my connection with this group conditional on my compliance?

- True belonging allows for individuality. If acceptance is only granted when you conform, it's not real acceptance—it's control.

- Challenge this by making one choice that is entirely yours and observing how others respond.

Your subconscious convinces you that staying within the framework of what you were raised with is what makes you safe and accepted. But belonging built on compliance is self-abandonment.

What You Gain by Embracing Rebellion Zones

At your core, you have spent your entire life earning love and security through performance, over-giving, and bending yourself into whatever shape you think will keep people close. You've mistrusted your own worth, assuming that love is something you prove rather than something you simply receive.

Your Rebellion Zones force you to stop the chase, drop the mask, and test what happens when you no longer rely on performance-based love. This feels terrifying at first, but the rewards are undeniable.

1. You Learn That Your Worth Isn't Tied to What You Can Do for Others

You've always measured your value by how much you give, how much you accommodate, and how much effort you put in. Rebellion Zones force you to stop over-giving and let people show up for you instead—so you can see, in real time, that you are worthy of love without having to earn it. You gain the freedom to exist without proving yourself every second of every day.

2. You Stop Attracting Relationships That Only Work If You're Over-Performing

Your past relationships and friendships have been built on the unspoken rule that you must earn your place. You say "yes" when you want to say "no." You fix things that aren't yours to fix. You absorb blame that isn't yours. Rebellion Zones teach you to stand still and see who sticks around—and who only wanted you when you were bending over backward. You gain relationships that don't feel like an unpaid internship in love and friendship.

3. You Finally Experience Love That Feels Safe Without Overextending Yourself

Your brain has convinced you that love is fragile and will disappear the moment you stop trying to earn it. Rebellion Zones force you to step back and observe what people do when you stop managing their perception of you. You will see clearly who actually values you and who was just using your constant effort as a crutch. You gain love that doesn't feel like a constant test you might fail at any moment.

4. You Stop Feeling Exhausted, Drained, and Over-Committed

You have taken on more responsibility than you should have—always feeling like it's your job to keep people happy, de-escalate conflict, and make sure no one leaves. Rebellion Zones make you face your fear of disappointing people, only to realize that most of the pressure was self-imposed. You gain more time, more energy, and more emotional clarity than you've had in years.

5. You Stop Silently Resenting the People You're Trying to Please

The more you suppress your own needs, the more you start to resent the people who have no idea how much effort you're putting in. Rebellion Zones break this cycle—you stop over-performing, and suddenly, the invisible scorecard disappears. You gain genuine connection instead of unspoken contracts.

6. You Get to Find Out Who Actually Loves You for You

The biggest fear in the back of your mind has always been this: What if I stop trying, and everyone leaves? Rebellion Zones force you to test that theory—to stop earning, stop chasing, stop bending—and see what happens. What you'll discover? Some people were only there for the effort you gave, but the right people were always there for you. You gain real love. Real safety. Real relationships—without the exhausting performance.

The Bottom Line

When you step into your Rebellion Zones, you will begin to disrupt the belief that love must be worked for, that connection is fragile, and that approval is something you must constantly secure.

You will learn how to:

- Trust that relationships don't require constant reinforcement to stay intact.

- Stop assuming that if someone isn't actively affirming your place, you are being forgotten.

- Detach from the belief that your worth is based on how much you do for others.

- Let relationships flow naturally instead of feeling like you must maintain control.

- Allow others to invest in you without guilt, fear, or the need to prove you deserve it.

By stepping into your Rebellion Zones, you shift from constantly managing relationships to actually experiencing them, without over-explaining, over-giving, or trying to earn what you already have.

REJECTION – CONTROL TO RECEIVE LOVE AND BE SAFE (PEOPLE-PLEASING ISOLATING)

Your behaviors are driven by a deep desire for stability, acceptance, and emotional security—but with as little risk of rejection or scrutiny as possible. Unlike the engaging people-pleasing type, who actively seeks approval through effort, you take a passive, compliant approach—staying quiet, following expectations, and avoiding actions that could make you stand out.

At your core, you fear exposure. You assume that if you draw too much attention, assert yourself, or take up too much space, people will judge, dismiss, or reject you. So instead, you blend in, comply, and keep your needs small, hoping that by avoiding mistakes or disruptions, you will be accepted.

Because of this, you may stay in relationships long past their expiration date, avoid opportunities that require visibility, or hesitate to express your real opinions for fear of being seen as difficult. You struggle with leadership, confrontation, or breaking from tradition. Stepping outside of what is expected feels unsafe. Instead of risking rejection, failure, or embarrassment, you opt for the predictable, the familiar, and the path of least resistance.

At its core, this pattern is about believing that standing out, making waves, or asserting yourself could result in emotional harm.

Core Motivations

1. Avoiding Rejection by Blending In, Even If It Means Becoming Invisible

You stay quiet, unassuming, and unnoticed to prevent standing out in ways that might invite criticism or judgment.

2. Complying Without Question, Even If You Don't Understand Why

You assume that rules, structures, and social norms exist for a reason, and that the safest path is to follow them exactly as expected.

3. Seeking Security Through Predictability, Even If It Limits Growth

You adhere to rigid routines, traditions, or expectations to avoid uncertainty, assuming that control equals emotional safety.

4. Avoiding Attention, Even If It Prevents You from Receiving Recognition

You would rather be overlooked than scrutinized, assuming that visibility increases the risk of failure, embarrassment, or being disliked.

5. Fearing Direct Rejection, Even If It Means Waiting for Others to Decide Your Worth

You hesitate to initiate relationships, conversations, or

opportunities, believing that if people truly wanted you, they would reach out first.

6. Holding Onto Relationships Out of Fear, Even If They Are Unfulfilling

You prefer stability over change, staying in one-sided or stagnant relationships just to avoid the discomfort of loss or transition.

7. Avoiding Leadership or High-Stakes Roles, Even If You Are Capable

You fear that stepping into visible positions increases the risk of failure, judgment, or public embarrassment.

8. Suppressing Emotions, Even If It Leads to Resentment

You downplay your needs and emotions to avoid being seen as difficult, disruptive, or high-maintenance.

9. Prioritizing Tradition and Expectation, Even If It Prevents Personal Exploration

You follow familial, religious, or societal customs because stepping outside of them feels unsafe or destabilizing.

10. Fearing Confrontation, Even If It Means Using Passive-Aggression or Silent Withdrawal

Rather than addressing issues directly, you express dissatisfaction through avoidance or subtle cues, hoping others will just "get it."

11. Internalizing Self-Doubt, Even If You Are Competent

You assume your contributions, opinions, or presence are not valuable enough, leading you to hold back even when you have something meaningful to offer.

12. Trying to "Fix" Yourself, Even If the Standard Is Unattainable

You believe that constant self-improvement is necessary to be accepted, chasing perfection rather than embracing your existing worth.

13. Avoiding Risk, Even If It Means Missing Out on Opportunities

You stick to what is familiar and predictable, preferring to play it safe rather than risk exposure, failure, or rejection.

Why Do You Need Rebellion Zones?

Your need to stay safe by blending in, complying, and avoiding visibility keeps you trapped in a cycle of invisibility, hesitation, and self-suppression. You assume that if you stay quiet, follow the rules, and never take up too much space, you won't be rejected or criticized.

Your biggest challenge will be trusting that you don't need to wait for permission to participate in your own life. You only feel safe when you are following the expected path, staying neutral, and avoiding actions that might draw attention to you. But real connection, confidence, and fulfillment come from choosing yourself.

By stepping into your Rebellion Zones, you stop playing small for safety and start building a life where your presence, voice, and choices actually matter.

1. You Learn That There Is No "Right Time"

Right now, your brain tells you that you need to wait for the right time to act. If you don't feel fully ready, you assume that means you should wait. Rebellion Zones force you to take action before you feel prepared.

Why You Need This: To stop sitting on the sidelines of your own life, waiting for a moment that never comes.

How You Approach This Rebellion Zone:

- **Observe** how often you think, "I'll do it when I'm ready" instead of "I'll do it now."

- **Notice** when your Brain Pattern convinces you that waiting protects you, when in reality, it just keeps you stagnant.

- **Remind yourself** that confidence doesn't come from waiting—it comes from committing and being courageous.

- **Challenge yourself** to commit to a decision before you feel 100 percent sure, because you never will.

The Self-Fulfilling Prophecy: By always waiting for the perfect moment, you miss out on opportunities, relationships, and experiences. In the end, your hesitation is what actually costs you what you want.

2. You Stop Watching and Start Doing

Right now, your brain tells you that it's safer to observe first before stepping in. If you watch long enough, you believe you'll know exactly what to do. Rebellion Zones force you to stop overanalyzing and start participating.

Why You Need This: To stop living like a spectator in your own life and start engaging with the things you want.

How You Approach This Rebellion Zone:

- **Observe** how often you watch others take action and tell yourself you'll "do it next time."

- **Notice** when you overthink a situation so much that the opportunity passes you by.

- **Remind yourself** that you don't need more preparation—you need more action.

- **Challenge yourself** to say yes before you have time to talk yourself out of it.

The Self-Fulfilling Prophecy: By staying on the sidelines, you never get the experiences, relationships, or success you crave. Watching doesn't prepare you—only doing does.

3. You Face the Fear of Being Seen

Your brain tells you that being seen is a risk. If you stay in the background, no one can criticize, reject, or judge you. Rebellion Zones force you to stop hiding and let yourself be noticed.

Why You Need This: To stop equating visibility with danger and start recognizing that you are allowed to take up space.

How You Approach This Rebellion Zone:

- **Observe** when you pull back from attention to avoid ridicule or the inability to control an outcome.

- **Notice** when you downplay your abilities or avoid stepping into the spotlight to protect yourself.

- **Remind yourself** that being seen doesn't equal being ridiculed—your brain just convinced you that it does.

- **Challenge yourself** to speak up, step forward, and take initiative and think of it as practice.

The Self-Fulfilling Prophecy: By making yourself invisible, you ensure that no one truly knows or values you. You can't receive recognition, connection, or success if no one knows you're there.

4. You Stop Avoiding and Start Engaging

You feel it's easier to stay quiet, keep your head down, and go with the flow. If you avoid drawing attention, you believe you can sidestep rejection. Rebellion Zones force you to step forward instead of shrinking back.

Why You Need This: To stop mistaking avoidance for safety—real security comes from building confidence through action.

How You Approach This Rebellion Zone:

- **Observe** how often you hold back from joining a conversation, stepping into a leadership role, or pursuing an opportunity because it feels "too risky."

- **Notice** when you tell yourself you don't care, when the truth is you're afraid of not being able to control the outcome.

- **Remind yourself** that every time you avoid it, you reinforce the belief that you can't handle it and that you're incapable.

- **Challenge yourself** to say yes and remind yourself that you build capability through struggle and potential mistakes. You'll never be capable if you don't start practicing now.

The Self-Fulfilling Prophecy: By constantly choosing avoidance, you teach yourself that you aren't *capable of handling challenges—which isn't true. But if you never try, you'll never prove yourself wrong.*

5. You Stop Letting Fear Make Your Decisions

Right now, you believe that fear means "stop." If something makes you nervous, you assume that means you shouldn't do it. Rebellion Zones force you to see fear as a signal to move forward, not back.

Why You Need This: To stop letting fear decide your life for you.

How You Approach This Rebellion Zone:

- **Observe** how often you back away from something just because it feels unknown.

- **Notice** when you mistake nerves for danger and use that as an excuse to avoid or delay things.

- **Remind yourself** that you're likely to ruminate on the missed opportunity so you might as well save yourself the "what-if" and regret by doing it right now.

- **Challenge yourself** to do things without feeling confident about them. Confidence is something that is built when you commit and build courage.

The Self-Fulfilling Prophecy: By letting fear run the show, you stay stuck. The life you want? It requires walking through fear, not around it.

6. You Learn That Compliance Isn't the Same as Respect

If you question authority, tradition, or group expectations, you fear being judged or cast out. Rebellion Zones force you to separate true respect from blind compliance.

Why You Need This: To stop mistaking silence for virtue—real respect comes from engaging with your beliefs, not blindly following them.

How You Approach This Rebellion Zone:

- **Observe** when you go along with something just because it's expected of you, not because you've arrived there through critical discourse.

- **Notice** when you avoid questioning family, religious, or cultural expectations out of fear rather than genuine belief.

- **Remind yourself** that challenging ideas is a sign of personal integrity and actually helps anchor beliefs with more conviction over time.

- **Challenge yourself** to speak up or make a different choice, even if it means being uncomfortable.

The Self-Fulfilling Prophecy: By always complying, you may avoid short-term conflict, but you also lose yourself in the process. Without questioning, exploring, or asserting your own beliefs, you become a reflection of others, not your true self.

7. You Stop Equating Approval with Love and Safety

If you make choices that challenge their expectations, you assume they will ostracize you or push you out of the group dynamic. Rebellion Zones force you to stop confusing obedience with connection.

Why You Need This: To realize that real love isn't conditional on how well you follow the rules.

How You Approach This Rebellion Zone:

- **Observe** how often you make choices based on what will please others rather than what actually feels right to you.

- **Notice** when you feel anxiety over disappointing family, religious ideals, or authority figures, even when it conflicts with your own wants or needs.

- **Remind yourself** that true relationships are built on authenticity, not just agreement.

- **Challenge yourself** to make a decision that reflects what you actually want, even if it risks disapproval.

The Self-Fulfilling Prophecy: By constantly seeking approval, you ensure that you never truly feel accepted for who you are. No one knows the real you, only the version you curate for their comfort.

8. You Learn That Taking Up Space Isn't Selfish

You believe that prioritizing yourself is selfish. If you set boundaries, ask for what you need, or stand up for yourself, you fear being seen as demanding. Rebellion Zones force you to stop making yourself small for the comfort of others.

Why You Need This: To recognize that your needs, voice, and presence matter just as much as anyone else's.

How You Approach This Rebellion Zone:

- **Observe** when you instinctively shrink yourself—physically, emotionally, or verbally—to avoid taking up space.

- **Notice** how often your Brain Pattern tries to trick you into thinking engaging and participating will make you look selfish.

- **Remind yourself** that being assertive isn't the same as being rude or aggressive and it will help you create connections that will add meaning to your life.

- **Challenge yourself** to take up space unapologetically, whether that's through speaking, expressing your opinions, or standing firm in your choices.

The Self-Fulfilling Prophecy: By making yourself small, you train others to overlook you. You attract relationships where you're treated as an afterthought, reinforcing the belief that your presence isn't important. But you were the one erasing yourself.

Rebellion Zones

Your brain has spent a lifetime trying to secure love and inclusion by blending in, following expectations, and ensuring you don't stand out in ways that might invite rejection or criticism. Unlike the engaging people-pleasing type, who actively pursues relationships and visibility, you take a passive, cautious approach—complying, staying in the background, and waiting for others to decide your worth.

You try to avoid every possibility of rejection. You assume that if you follow the rules, stay unnoticed, and don't disrupt expectations, you will be safe. So you suppress your needs, defer to others, and stick to familiar patterns, believing that as long as you don't make waves, you won't be cast aside.

Because of this, you may stay in stagnant relationships out of fear of change, hesitate to step into leadership roles even when qualified, or avoid expressing your opinions to keep the peace. You struggle with uncertainty, risk, or personal recognition, because they feel like opportunities for failure rather than growth. Instead of advocating for yourself, you wait, hoping others will see your worth without you having to assert it.

The moment you read through your Rebellion Zones, your brain will try to convince you that playing it safe is the better choice, that you're just being smart. You'll rationalize silence as humility, compliance as practicality, and staying small as the safest way to maintain connection. But these behaviors often leave you overlooked, unfulfilled, and uncertain whether people actually see the real you.

But let's be clear: this isn't about forcing you into the spotlight or making you reckless. What you're here to learn is how to stop filtering every decision through fear of rejection—how to break the cycle of waiting, avoiding, and complying before rejection even happens.

For now, just focus on seeing the battlefield for what it is without assuming you have to disappear to survive it.

1. Speaking Up Instead of Staying Invisible

Self-Deception at Play: Avoiding rejection by blending in, internalizing self-doubt, assuming others should notice you first.

Unconscious Motivation: Stay invisible or blend into the background to avoid ridicule or damage to reputation.

Rebellion Zone: The next time you feel the urge to stay quiet, hold back, or wait for someone else to speak first–don't.

Why This Works: Your subconscious tells you that staying invisible is the safest way to avoid rejection. You assume that if people truly valued your input, they would ask for it. By choosing to speak up before you feel 100 percent ready, you prove to your brain that you don't need permission to take up space.

How This Plays Out In Real Life:

• You automatically fade into the background of social gatherings or work events

• When faced with an opportunity to engage or lead - you pull away or defer to others.

• You feel anxiety if pushed to be in the spotlight or an overt leadership position.

• You often default to being agreeable even if you don't personally align with the consensus.

• If you do find yourself in the spotlight, you struggle with bold confidence and strong communication.

The Challenge: Let Your Voice Be Heard Without Waiting for an Invitation

• You typically wait to be asked for your opinion, offer it first.

• If you hesitate to speak in meetings or group settings, challenge yourself to contribute before the conversation shifts. *Ask yourself*:

Do I historically stay quiet then ruminate on what I wanted to say after?

Am I frustrated with my inability to express myself in the moment?

Am I tricking myself into assuming it will go poorly and make me look bad?

Is it challenging for me to connect deeply with others because I hold myself back and stay quiet?

Can I challenge myself to speak up and think of it like practice?

By choosing to engage instead of shrinking, you disrupt the belief that your worth is determined by how little space you take up.

2. Making Decisions Without Defaulting to Others

Self-Deception at Play: Complying without question, holding onto relationships out of fear, avoiding leadership even when capable.

Unconscious Motivation: Seek reassurance, guidance or collaboration from others to avoid responsibility or blame.

Rebellion Zone: The next time you're faced with a choice, make the decision entirely on your own, without asking for permission or validation.

Why This Works: Your subconscious tells you that deferring to others is the safest way to avoid mistakes, conflict, or disapproval. You assume that if someone else makes the choice, you can't be blamed if it goes wrong. But by choosing for yourself, you prove to your brain that you are capable of leading your own life.

How This Plays Out In Real Life:

- You seek out other's opinion or guidance

- When faced with a decision, you seek allies or leadership to make the decision or give clear direction.

- You question your decision until someone validates it or aligns with your perspective.

- You often default to seeking hierarchy or experts to inform your next steps.

- You avoid making decisions on your own to avoid blame or shame if it turns on you.

- You struggle with self-trust and consider what others will think when making a decision.

The Challenge: Trust Your Own Decisions

- If you tend to ask others what to do before deciding, stop. This prevents you from building self-trust. Even if it doesn't work out— at least you learn from the mistake instead of having an out to blame someone else.

- If you feel the urge to seek reassurance before acting, challenge yourself to act first and remind yourself that self-expression doesn't require anyone else's approval.

- If you assume you need to follow expectations, *ask yourself*:

Historically, do I filter my wants and needs through my perceived duties or allegiances?

By constantly filtering based on the perception of others don't I rob myself of opportunities to figure out who I am and what I like?

By choosing for yourself, you disrupt the belief that security only comes from following someone else's lead.

3. Allowing Yourself to Be Seen Instead of Staying in the Background

Self-Deception at Play: Avoiding attention, suppressing emotions, avoiding leadership or high-stakes roles.

Unconscious Motivation: Avoidance of observation or attention to prevent ridicule or shame.

Rebellion Zone: Step into visibility—whether that means accepting recognition, sharing your true thoughts, or allowing others to see your real emotions.

Why This Works: Your subconscious tells you that attention equals scrutiny, and scrutiny leads to rejection. You assume that if people really appreciated you, they would recognize you without you having to step forward. But by allowing yourself to be seen, recognized, and acknowledged, you prove to your brain that visibility does not equal rejection.

How This Plays Out In Real Life:

• You automatically become the observer - pulling away to watch instead of engaging or leading.

• When entering a social or group event, you find yourself looking for the sidelines to observe and figure out how to best engage.

• You feel it's safer to wait to be invited into the group rather than establish your position independently.

• You often default to what unfolds socially rather than finding your "in" and directing your destiny.

• You avoid seeking out communication and connection opportunities and default to waiting to be picked.

The Challenge: Accept and Embrace Recognition

- If you usually deflect or minimize compliments, say "Thank you" and make direct eye contact.

- If you feel uncomfortable being the center of attention, challenge yourself to step more toward the center of the action and draw your shoulders back.

- If you tend to downplay your achievements, challenge yourself to own them instead of brushing them off. Say This:

- "Thank you. I've been working hard on _____ and it's nice to see the effort paying off."

By allowing yourself to be seen, you disrupt the belief that it's safer to stay unnoticed.

4. Making Decisions Without Retreating

Self-Deception at Play: Avoiding commitment, fear of making the wrong choice, equating hesitation with safety.

Unconscious Motivation: Avoid commitment or bold decision-making to protect reputation and prevent embarrassment.

Rebellion Zone: When faced with a decision, make a choice and follow through—without second-guessing, delaying, or withdrawing.

Why This Works: Your subconscious tells you that staying on the sidelines protects you. If you don't commit, you can't fail. If you wait long enough, the "right" choice will reveal itself. But by continuously avoiding decisions, you keep yourself stuck, missing out on relationships, opportunities, and personal growth. When you start making decisions without retreating, you teach your brain that taking action is safer than staying frozen in hesitation.

How This Plays Out In Real Life:

- You avoid making decisions or boldly committing out of fear of making the wrong choice.

- You struggle with freeze and flight – preventing you from engaging without overthinking or withdrawing.

- You feel inner conflict about wanting to be a part of the group dynamic but not knowing the timing or approach to engage.

- You often default to waiting for others to engage you rather than insert yourself.

- You trick yourself into justifying a non-commital approach to avoid heartbreak or embarrassment.

The Challenge: Step In Instead of Stepping Back

- If you catch yourself thinking, I'll decide later–decide now. Delaying is just disguised avoidance.

- If you hesitate to engage in a conversation, event, or relationship, challenge yourself to say yes before you have time to overthink.

- If you assume that waiting longer will make a choice easier, remind yourself: action creates clarity. Hesitation creates stagnation.

By making decisions and following through, you disrupt the belief that staying safe means staying small. You start proving to yourself that you are capable, resilient, and worthy of stepping fully into your own life.

5. Choosing Growth Over Predictability

Self-Deception at Play: Seeking security through predictability, avoiding risk to prevent failure, prioritizing stability over growth

Unconscious Motivation: Choose the monotony of the familiar to avoid risk to your reputation or image.

Rebellion Zone: Take a calculated risk, whether that means trying something new, changing a routine, or stepping outside of your comfort zone.

Why This Works: Your subconscious tells you that sticking to what you know keeps you safe. You assume that predictability ensures stability. But by allowing yourself to step into uncertainty, you train your brain to see that growth doesn't always equal risk. It often leads to a fuller, more connected life.

How This Plays Out In Real Life:

- You seek out the familiar rather than try new things even though it's boring.

- When given a unique or new opportunity, you default to your familiar environments or groups instead of pushing your boundaries.

- You are anxious when presented with new opportunities, even if they excite you.

- You often default to isolation or avoidance even if part of you wants to try the new thing.

- You avoid being a beginner because you desire to control how you're perceived around others.

The Challenge: Take a Small Risk Today

- If you tend to avoid trying new things, challenge yourself to do something unfamiliar.

- If you feel locked into routines out of comfort, intentionally disrupt one routine each day to prove to yourself that life doesn't fall apart when you pivot.

- If you assume stability means playing it safe, remind yourself: safety is not the same as fulfillment.

By choosing growth over stagnation, you disrupt the belief that comfort is more important than connection.

6. Engaging Instead of Waiting to Be Chosen

Self-Deception at Play: Fearing direct rejection, assuming if you were wanted others would reach out first, avoiding initiation to stay safe

Unconscious Motivation: Observe from the sidelines to assess the group dynamic before seeking inclusion.

Rebellion Zone: Instead of waiting for someone to invite you, engage with you, or affirm your value—make the first move.

Why This Works: Your subconscious tells you that if people truly wanted you around, they would reach out first. Since that doesn't always happen, you withdraw, assume exclusion, or wait for proof of your worth before engaging. But by choosing to initiate connection, you prove to your brain that your presence matters—even if no one explicitly confirms it first.

How This Plays Out In Real Life:

- You wait for an invitation rather than step into group settings on your own.

- When presented with group dynamics, you watch instead of engage despite wanting the connection.

- You feel anxiety about what others may think and don't want to look stupid or unworthy.

- You often default to watching even if that means missing out on opportunities to connect.

- You avoid bold interactions that are self-initiated.

- You struggle to believe that if you initiated, it would be well-received or welcomed.

The Challenge: Reach Out Without Waiting for an Invitation

- If you want to spend time with someone, initiate the plans instead of waiting for them to suggest it.

- If you assume people don't care because they don't reach out first, challenge that belief by engaging instead of withdrawing.

- If you feel hesitant to start conversations, test your discomfort by initiating one in a low stakes environment to practice.(Think: coffee shop, grocery store or shop)

By engaging before waiting for confirmation, you disrupt the belief that being chosen must always be passive.

7. Expressing Needs Instead of Suppressing Them

Self-Deception at Play: Suppressing emotions to avoid being high-maintenance, avoiding confrontation even when unhappy, fearing that expressing needs will push people away.

Unconscious Motivation: Avoid judgment or ridicule by keeping ideas or opinions to yourself.

Rebellion Zone: Clearly state what you want, feel, or need—without apologizing, softening, or assuming you are a burden.

Why This Works: Your subconscious tells you that keeping your needs small makes you easier to accept. You assume that if you ask for too much, set limits, or take up emotional space, people will see you as difficult. But by expressing your needs without minimizing or apologizing, you prove to your brain that your value doesn't depend on how little you require from others.

How This Plays Out In Real Life:

- You keep your ideas to yourself even if you feel passionate

- You tell yourself that you don't want to ruffle feathers or risk upsetting others with your opinion.

- You convince yourself the potential for opposition is a risk to your reputation and not worth it.

- You default to the majority group opinion and pretend to be in agreement to fit in.

- You avoid expressing differing opinions, questioning traditions, or embracing new perspectives out of fear that doing so will create tension or make you an outsider.

- You struggle with the confidence or words to express your ideas or opinions even if you are aware of them.

The Challenge: Own Your Needs Without Justifying Them

- If you catch yourself saying, "It's not a big deal," when it actually is—stop. Say what you need.

- If you struggle to ask for help, challenge yourself to make one direct request today.

- If you assume expressing discomfort will push people away, test that belief by being honest instead of suppressing.

By expressing instead of shrinking, you disrupt the belief that your needs must be invisible for you to be accepted.

8. Choosing Self-Trust Over Compliance

Self-Deception at Play: Complying without question, prioritizing tradition over personal needs, avoiding decisions that could lead to disapproval.

Unconscious Motivation: Be compliant to groupthink standards as a way to be seen in a positive light.

Rebellion Zone: Make a decision based on what you want, not what others expect from you.

Why This Works: Your subconscious tells you that sticking to external rules, traditions, or expectations keeps you safe. You assume that if you follow the "right path," you won't risk failure, rejection, or judgment. But by making decisions based on your own wants and values, you prove to your brain that self-trust matters more than external approval.

How This Plays Out In Real Life:

- You automatically align with groupthink ideas or standards as a way to play it safe and fit in

- When you innately disagree, you suppress your opinion and nod with the group to maintain the sense of connection.

- You convince yourself that your opinion doesn't matter and only poses a risk to your ability to fit in with the group.

- You are quick to suppress or even question your own opinion.

- You avoid expressing differing opinions, questioning traditions, or embracing new perspectives out of fear that doing so will create tension or make you an outsider.

The Challenge: Choose for Yourself Without Seeking Permission

- If you always follow the safe choice, challenge yourself to pick what you truly want instead.

- If you think about what your family or in-group would think, stop. *Ask yourself*:

   Have I considered my family, group or religion in my decisions my entire life?

   Can I see where this has built a pattern of compliance over expression?

   Is it possible that I'm living a life that is bland or disconnected as a result of this pattern?

   Can I challenge myself to try something new or different today to see how it feels?

- If you assume breaking from tradition is dangerous, remind yourself: compliance without deep understanding is empty. If I explore and push I will learn to anchor my beliefs more deeply or set them aside.

By choosing self-trust over compliance, you disrupt the belief that external validation determines your worth.

What You Gain by Embracing Rebellion Zones

At your core, you've spent your life managing emotional distance like a survival strategy—engaging just enough to maintain connection while ensuring no one gets too close. You've convinced yourself that staying in control of your availability and vulnerability keeps you safe, but in reality, it's kept you stuck in a cycle of shallow relationships, silent loneliness, and unspoken needs.

Rebellion Zones force you to challenge the belief that love is only safe in small, controlled doses. They push you to risk being fully seen, step into connection without retreat, and discover that the right people won't leave just because you show up as your whole self.

1. You Find Out That You Are Not "Too Much" or "Not Enough"

Your brain has convinced you that you either overwhelm people or fail to measure up, so you avoid full engagement to prevent either outcome. Rebellion Zones push you to stay in situations where you would normally pull away, ghost, or shrink, giving people a chance to prove your fear wrong. You realize that people can handle the real you—without judgment, rejection, or disappointment.

2. You Experience Connection That Isn't Built on Performance or Withdrawal

You've only ever allowed yourself two options in relationships:

1. People-pleasing to earn your place.

2. Withdrawing and isolating when you feel like you don't belong.

Rebellion Zones force you to exist in the middle space, where you don't have to over-perform or disappear to feel safe. You gain a third option—relationships where you simply exist, without proving, chasing, or hiding.

3. You Stop Settling for Shallow, Low-Risk Relationships

You've gravitated toward relationships that feel safe because they don't demand vulnerability. In doing so, you've accepted surface-level connection as your default. Rebellion Zones make you step deeper into relationships and test the fear that the real you will drive people away. You gain the relationships you've always wanted—but were too afraid to fully step into.

4. You Break the Cycle of Loneliness You Pretend Isn't There

You tell yourself that you don't need people, but deep down, you feel the ache of being disconnected. You avoid showing too much need because relying on others feels risky—what if they don't show up? Rebellion Zones force you to lean into connection instead of silently withdrawing, teaching you that the right people will show up when you give them the chance. You gain a life where you don't have to be self-sufficient to feel safe.

5. You Finally Get to Be Fully Seen Instead of Carefully Edited

You have managed your presence carefully, only showing the "acceptable" parts of yourself. You avoid deep conversations, emotional exposure, and anything that could make you feel misinterpreted or misunderstood. Rebellion Zones challenge you to stop controlling the narrative and see what happens when you let yourself be fully known. You gain freedom from the exhausting job of constantly curating how people see you.

6. You Stop Living in Constant Emotional Self-Preservation Mode

You've lived your life like an emotional survivalist—always anticipating loss, rejection, or failure before it even happens. You withdraw before you can be left, stay quiet to avoid conflict, and never fully settle into any relationship because "what if it doesn't last?" Rebellion Zones make you sit in the discomfort of staying, of risking, of trusting—and through that, you learn that safety doesn't come from control, it comes from real connection. You build a life where you aren't constantly bracing for rejection.

The Bottom Line: You Learn That Connection Is Safe

You have spent your life believing that people only want the safest, most controlled version of you—the version that never asks for too much, never pushes too hard, and never risks real exposure. You've convinced yourself that your presence is either overwhelming or unnecessary, so you carefully regulate how much of yourself you allow people to see.

But here's the truth: real love doesn't require that kind of management.

Rebellion Zones force you to test the lie that love and acceptance are only possible when you stay emotionally small, agreeable, or detached. They push you to risk being fully seen, to lean into relationships without a backup exit strategy, and to experience connection without retreating into isolation the moment things feel uncertain.

Through this process, you learn that:

- People don't leave just because you stop over-performing.
- You are not "too much" when you show up fully.

- Your presence is valuable, even when you're not actively proving it.

- You don't have to be the easiest, least demanding person in the room to be loved.

- Letting people in doesn't mean losing control—it means gaining freedom.

You are not actually protecting yourself from rejection—you are rejecting yourself first to prevent others from doing it later. And in doing so, you have spent your life settling for half-connection, half-truths, and half-versions of yourself.

Rebellion Zones give you a new option—one where you can belong without bargaining, be loved without over-giving, and be safe without constantly guarding yourself.

Are you ready to find out what happens when you stop pulling away?

REJECTION – CONTROL TO RECEIVE LOVE AND BE SAFE (CONFLICT-PRONE ENGAGING)

Your behaviors are driven by a deep need to secure love, validation, and emotional safety by asserting control over relationships through intensity, challenge, and direct engagement. Unlike the isolating conflict-prone type, who pull away to protect themselves, you push forward—confronting, testing, and asserting yourself to ensure you are not overlooked, dismissed, or emotionally outmatched.

At your core, you fight to prevent rejection. Because of this, you instinctively escalate situations, seek emotional confirmation through tension, and create moments that force people to prove their commitment to you. If someone seems passive, disengaged, or emotionally neutral, you assume they are losing interest. Instead of waiting, you push harder, testing their loyalty, forcing conversations, or introducing conflict to see if they will fight to keep you close.

This creates a cycle where you seek certainty by raising the emotional stakes in relationships. If someone matches your intensity, it reassures you that they care. If they disengage, you take it as proof that they were never fully invested. You struggle with neutrality, space, or emotional unpredictability because they leave too much room for doubt.

Core Motivations:

1. Fear of Being Overlooked, Invalidated, or Replaced

You don't just want to be liked. You want to be recognized, prioritized, and impossible to ignore. If you aren't actively engaged in someone's life, you assume you are being forgotten.

2. Desire for Control Over Emotional Power Dynamics

You are hyper-aware of who holds influence in relationships, ensuring that you are never in a vulnerable position where others have control over your emotional stability.

3. Belief That Love and Safety Must Be Earned Through Challenge

You assume that if relationships are too easy, they must not be real. If someone truly values you, they should be willing to prove it–through engagement, intensity, or emotional reaction.

4. Seeking Reassurance Through Conflict and Emotional Intensity

You subconsciously believe that strong emotional reactions confirm commitment. If someone argues, gets defensive, or passionately debates with you, it reassures you that they care.

5. Needing Verbal and Emotional Confirmation to Feel Secure

You struggle to trust subtle affection or quiet consistency. You crave explicit words, direct actions, and obvious proof that someone still values you.

6. Interpreting Neutrality or Distance as a Threat

If someone pulls back, stops engaging in deep conversations, or doesn't react as emotionally as you do, you assume they are losing interest and act to force clarity.

7. Over-Explaining to Control Perception

You feel the need to clarify, justify, or control how others see you—ensuring that no one misinterprets your words, actions, or emotions.

8. Tracking Fairness and Feeling Wronged When Effort Isn't Reciprocated

You keep a mental scoreboard of investment: who reaches out first, who makes the plans, who reacts emotionally. If effort feels unbalanced, you feel slighted and push for resolution.

9. Struggling to Let Go of Perceived Slights or Moments of Disinterest

If someone doesn't respond as expected, seems distracted, or doesn't match your emotional energy, you take it as a rejection, even if it wasn't meant that way.

10. Assuming Rejection Is Imminent and Acting First to Stay in Control

You anticipate disinterest before it happens, making preemptive moves to either test the relationship or pull away before you can be rejected.

Why Do You Need Rebellion Zones?

You are trapped in a cycle of forcing proof, pushing for reactions, and misinterpreting neutral moments as threats. The very behaviors you use to test for closeness often destabilize the relationships you're trying to protect.

Rebellion Zones force you to drop the need to control emotional dynamics and sit in uncertainty. They challenge you to stop equating tension with love, so you can build relationships based on mutual stability, not emotional warfare.

1. You Learn That Love Doesn't Have to Be Earned Through Conflict

Right now, your brain tells you that if someone truly values you, they will prove it, often generating emotional intensity and conflict.

Peace and stability will tend to be viewed as signs that something is being hidden. You're likely to push for reassurance or test the people around you when this happens. Rebellion Zones challenge you to sit in stillness instead of escalating situations to create reassurance.

Why You Need This: To experience love that isn't built on push-pull dynamics or emotional proof-seeking.

How You Approach This Rebellion Zone:

- **Observe** how often your Brain Pattern prompts you to bring up the past, seek reassurance and read into a boundary.

- **Notice** how your Brain Pattern tells you that calm comes from distance and that you need a reaction to confirm closeness.

- **Remind yourself** that some Brain Pattern types express love through consistency, not conflict—just because they aren't proving it the way you want doesn't mean they don't care.

- **Challenge yourself** to let neutral moments exist without forcing an emotional response.

The Self-Fulfilling Prophecy: By testing and seeking reassurance through conflict, you create instability in relationships—ultimately causing the very distance you were trying to prevent.

2. You Stop Interpreting Neutrality as a Threat

You are hyper-aware of shifts in emotional tone, energy, and attention. If someone seems distant, distracted, or doesn't match your intensity, you assume something is wrong. Rebellion Zones force you to recognize that neutral moments aren't rejection—they are normal and may even be a sign of security and peace.

Why You Need This: To stop spiraling every time someone isn't fully engaged with you.

How You Approach This Rebellion Zone:

- **Observe** how often you feel unsettled when someone isn't responding the way you expect in your head.

- **Notice** when your Brain Pattern reads into tone shifts, pauses, or casual indifference as signs of rejection or impending doom.

- **Remind yourself** that some people may appear indifferent or disengaged when they are relaxed and at peace.

- **Challenge yourself** to let people be in their own world without assuming it has something to do with you.

The Self-Fulfilling Prophecy: By misinterpreting how others show up when they are relaxed and secure, you create tension and conflict destabilizing the security you had previously built.

3. You Stop Scanning for Emotional Engagement

Right now, your brain tells you that constant scanning for emotional engagement is critical to the longevity of your relationship. If you don't ensure that you know how they feel about you at all times, you can't be prepared to control the outcome. Rebellion Zones force you to let go of the measurement and experience relationships without constant power analysis.

Why You Need This: To stop seeing relationships as a game of emotional survival and start experiencing real connection.

How You Approach This Rebellion Zone:

- **Observe** how often you track subtle body language, tone of voice, or how frequently they reach out and use this to measure how secure your relationship is.

- **Notice** when your Brain Pattern tells you to seek reassurance if the other person doesn't seem emotionally invested.

- **Remind yourself** that fixating on subtle cues can lead to faulty assumptions and unnecessary conflict.

- **Challenge yourself** to lean in without expecting something in return to feel like your investment was worth it.

The Self-Fulfilling Prophecy: By constantly scanning for emotional engagement in others, you're likely to misread signs and generate conflict that pushes your partner away.

4. You Learn That Over-Explaining Won't Prevent Rejection

You believe that if you explain yourself enough, you can control how people perceive you. If someone misinterprets your words or actions, you panic, clarify, and try to fix the narrative. Rebellion Zones force you to let go of the need to control perception.

Why You Need This: To stop wasting energy defending, explaining, and proving yourself when it isn't necessary.

How You Approach This Rebellion Zone:

- **Observe** how often you jump in to defend, clarify, justify, or over-explain something you've said or done.

- **Notice** when your Brain Pattern tells you that it's dangerous to assume others will see you the way you want without steering or manipulation.

- **Remind yourself** that not everything needs to be micromanaged. People need to be able to have the freedom and sovereignty to come to their own conclusions.

- **Challenge yourself** to let potential misunderstandings sit without overcorrecting them or steering the outcome. If they have a question, they can come to you.

The Self-Fulfilling Prophecy: By constantly over-explaining, you actually make things feel more complicated than they are, drawing attention to problems that may not have even been a big deal to begin with.

5. You Stop Tracking Every Moment of Unreciprocated Effort

You keep score. Who reaches out first. Who texts back faster. What the deeper meaning is behind their reaction or response. If effort feels unbalanced, you push for reassurance or to make sure they know it wasn't fair. Rebellion Zones force you to let go of the need for exact reciprocity in every interaction.

Why You Need This: To stop seeing relationships as transactions that must be perfectly equal at all times.

How You Approach This Rebellion Zone:

- **Observe** when you mentally track who is initiating, investing, or showing more emotion.

- **Notice** how your Brain Pattern creates a narrative of unfairness or imbalance based on assumption rather than facts.

- **Remind yourself** that healthy relationships have natural ebbs and flows—sometimes one person gives more, and that's okay.

- **Challenge yourself** to let small moments of imbalance go without needing to address them and take ownership of your natural desire to get when you give rather than giving without expectation.

The Self-Fulfilling Prophecy: By constantly tracking fairness, you make people feel like they're walking on eggshells—ultimately making relationships more transactional than meaningful.

6. You Let People Show Up for You Without Forcing Them To

You assume that if you don't actively engage, people will move onto something else. If you aren't testing or experiencing emotional interaction, you fear being replaced. Rebellion Zones force you to see what happens when you stop forcing connection and let others meet you halfway.

Why You Need This: To stop assuming that if you aren't actively creating engagement, people won't care about you.

How You Approach This Rebellion Zone:

- **Observe** how often you insert yourself into interactions out of fear, not genuine desire.

- **Notice** when your Brain Pattern tells you that if you aren't with someone, they will forget about you or find someone else.

- **Remind yourself** that healthy relationships don't require constant maintenance to exist and that your actions are more likely to push the other person away.

- **Challenge yourself** to pull back, focus on independent time and building trust during time apart.

The Self-Fulfilling Prophecy: By always being the one pushing for engagement, you never actually find out who values you when you aren't forcing the dynamic.

Rebellion Zones

1. Not Reacting Immediately to Perceived Injustice or Disrespect

Self-Deception at Play: Justice-centric thinking, assumption of ill intent, demand for fairness at any cost.

Unconscious Motivation: Seek fairness or justice without considering differing opinions or perceptions.

Rebellion Zone: When you feel the impulse to call something out as unfair, offensive, or disrespectful—stop.

Why This Works: You believe that if you don't challenge what's wrong, you are allowing yourself to be disrespected. But reacting immediately often escalates minor issues into full-scale battles and prevents you from seeing the full picture. Practicing delayed response forces your subconscious to recognize that not everything requires immediate confrontation.

How This Plays Out In Real Life:

• You automatically get defensive or try to stand up for yourself if you feel wronged.

• When feeling wronged or judged, you react quickly to make sure they know they've crossed a line.

• You feel anger at the thought of someone disagreeing with you or seeing you in a certain way.

• You often default to a victimized lens instead of pause to see their side.

• You quickly express opinions or make corrections.

• You struggle to see other's perspectives because you feel emotionally reactive and hurt.

The Challenge: Question Your Motives Before Reacting

• If you feel the urge to correct or confront, set a timer for 30 minutes and *ask yourself*:

Do I historically have a tendency to take things personally?

Has reacting immediately to this type of situation created conflict and division in the past?

Does my brain pattern prompt me to measure for fairness and justice?

Is it possible that I'm assuming ill intent when I'd be better served by trying to understand the other person's perspective?

Can I challenge myself to put on a timer for 30 minutes then if I still feel I need clarity ask a genuine clarifying question to understand the other person's perspective?

• If you feel the need to make someone acknowledge the injustice, remind yourself:

You have a tendency to experience heightened emotions and look for someone to blame. Instead of assuming ill intent, you need to ask questions and inquire about the other person's motive.

By delaying or preventing your response, you disrupt the belief that fairness must always be enforced in real time, creating space for reflection instead of unnecessary conflict.

2. Letting Go of the Need to Be Right

Self-Deception at Play: Difficulty seeing different perspectives, projection and blame, resistance to vulnerability and collaboration.

Unconscious Motivation: Desire to correct the record to avoid further conflict or damaged reputation.

Rebellion Zone: Enter a discussion with the goal of listening rather than proving your point. Prioritize understanding over being right.

Why This Works: You often dig in your heels, assuming your perspective is the only logical or justifiable one. This creates tension, alienation, and defensiveness from others—not because they don't respect you, but because your refusal to consider other perspectives makes resolution impossible. Practicing openness to being wrong breaks the belief that admitting fault means losing power.

How This Plays Out In Real Life:

- You stand up for yourself or try to correct other's perspectives to make sure people don't see you in a negative light.

- You feel anger when receiving feedback that doesn't match your perspective or point of view.

- You desire to correct or replay as a way to feel safe enough to move forward.

- You struggle with allowing things to unfold and desire to control the outcome.

- You argue about details to ensure you don't feel misrepresented or victimized.

The Challenge: Prioritize Understanding Over Winning

- If you catch yourself preparing a rebuttal instead of listening, stop and focus on what's being said.

- If you assume others just don't get it, *ask yourself*:

  What if I'm missing something they see?

  Could both of our perspectives have value?

  Am I debating them because I feel like we can't both win?

- If you feel the urge to dismiss or disprove someone's view, remind yourself: admitting a shift in perspective isn't weakness—it's intelligence.

By embracing the possibility of being wrong, you disrupt the belief that control comes from dominance rather than collaboration.

3. Resisting the Urge to Escalate Small Problems

Self-Deception at Play: Intrusive thoughts and overthinking, self-fulfilling victimization, addiction to control.

Unconscious Motivation: Desire to seek reassurance and control the narrative to protect reputation.

Rebellion Zone: When you catch yourself mentally escalating a small issue, step away from the narrative instead of feeding it.

Why This Works: Your subconscious amplifies minor interactions into full-scale betrayals, injustices, or threats to your well-being. This often makes you react prematurely, assume ill intent, or push people away before a situation even unfolds. By choosing to disengage from catastrophizing, you prove to your subconscious that not every thought deserves action.

How This Plays Out In Real Life:

- You have trouble letting things go because any wrong feels worthy of addressing.

- When faced with any issue, your brain tells you letting it go will make it worse.

- You feel anger about the injustice of the situation and can't move on until someone takes ownership.

- You struggle to hear their side of the story without the desire to correct or rebut.

- You bring up the past to seek reassurance or reconciliation even if the other person has moved on.

The Challenge: Drop the Story Before It Becomes a Spiral

- If you feel yourself mentally replaying an interaction for proof of betrayal, redirect your focus to a tangible task or distraction in the physical world.

- If you assume something small will turn into a disaster, *ask yourself*:

Do I historically fixate on negative outcomes as a way to justify my behavior?

When I anticipate and observe others closely, don't I tend to create an eggshell walking environment?

• If you struggle to let things go, remind yourself: fixating on a problem only negatively impacts your body language, voice and ability to emotionally regulate.

By resisting the urge to escalate, you disrupt the belief that every perceived slight needs immediate intervention.

4. Accepting Boundaries Without Interpreting Them as Rejection

Self-Deception at Play: Interpreting boundaries as rejection, holding grudges as proof of self-respect, blaming others for disconnection.

Unconscious Motivation: Need to control proximity and connection to others to feel safe and loved.

Rebellion Zone: When someone sets a boundary, resist the urge to interpret it as an attack or proof that they don't care about you.

Why This Works: You subconsciously believe that if people cared about you, they either wouldn't set limits or would compromise to keep you happy. This leads you to take space, time apart, or neutral boundaries as rejection.

How This Plays Out In Real Life:

• You take boundaries as a sign that something is turning on you.

• When faced with a boundary, you look for workarounds or ways to manipulate the outcome.

• You feel anger about being controlled or prevented access.

• You default to ruminating on injustice rather than trying to see their side.

• You may use ultimatums or threats to try and get what you want.

• If you do comply with the boundary, you struggle with needing check-ins or reassurance during the time apart.

• You struggle to trust that boundaries are not a deeper sign of rejection or lack of interest.

The Challenge: Let Boundaries Exist Without Misinterpreting

- If someone says they need space or have other plans, don't push for reassurance or to manipulate them into aligning with your agenda—give it to them.

- If you feel rejected by a boundary, *ask yourself*:

  Do I historically fixate on what they are doing when we aren't together?

  Does my brain pattern tend to trick me into mistrust and worst case scenario thinking?

  Am I telling myself that distance equals disinterest?

  Is it possible that I'm convincing myself that a normal request is a sign of disaster in my relationships?

  Can I challenge myself to see how my pushiness can create the opposite reaction that I want?

  Is it true that showing this person I can maturely handle space is beneficial to my relationship in the long run?

- If you feel resentment toward someone for enforcing a boundary, remind yourself: Boundaries are tools for longevity and trust.

5. Not Assuming the Worst About Others' Intentions

Self-Deception at Play: Projection and blame, assumption of ill intent, fixating on perceived slights.

Unconscious Motivation: Read into other's deeper intentions through body language and voice tone.

Rebellion Zone: When you catch yourself assuming someone is acting against you, pause and consider an alternate explanation instead.

Why This Works: Your brain defaults to worst-case interpretations, assuming that others are intentionally ignoring, undermining, or rejecting you. But this habit creates unnecessary conflict, alienates people, and reinforces cycles of defensiveness. By challenging your initial assumptions, you force your subconscious to recognize that most people aren't out to get you.

How This Plays Out In Real Life:

- You automatically assume others dislike you or think you're inferior.

502

- You read into subtle body language or actions and project your own insecurities onto the other person.

- You feel anxiety or anger when unable to determine exactly how the other person feels.

- You seek reassurance or clarity on how the other person feels, which may frustrate or annoy them.

- You express your insecurity, which can disrupt the process of connection and trust.

- You struggle with allowing situations to unfold without meddling, testing, or asking leading questions.

The Challenge: Consider an Alternative Explanation

- If you assume someone's silence, tone, or actions are meant to harm you, set a 60-minute timer before reacting.

- If you feel certain someone intended to be rude or dismissive, *ask yourself*:

    Do I historically take other people's words or tone personally?

    Have I ever misread a situation and created conflict because of it?

    Is it possible that the other person is just focused on something else and I'm reading into their response?

    Could they be distracted, tired, or dealing with something unrelated to me?

    Can I challenge myself to let it play out without pushing for deeper understanding?

- If you struggle to give people the benefit of the doubt, remind yourself: not everyone thinks or reacts the way you do. Assuming the worst only hurts you and causes conflict.

6. Remembering That No One Is Thinking About You as Much as You Think They Are

Self-Deception at Play: Projection and blame, assuming negativity without evidence, interpreting distance as proof of being unwanted.

Unconscious Motivation: Protect yourself from rejection by centering social interactions around how others perceive you.

Rebellion Zone: Move through social situations without assuming others are analyzing or judging you. Assume others are focused on themselves and not you.

Why This Works: Your brain projects your insecurities onto others, making you believe they are constantly evaluating you. But in reality, most people are too focused on themselves to be scrutinizing you.

How This Plays Out In Real Life:

- You try to figure out what others are thinking with a distortion of your worst fears.

- You forget that others are focused on broader group dynamics or their own problems and not even thinking about you.

- You anticipate how others may feel by assuming what they are thinking about.

- You convince yourself others are focused on you instead of worried about their own problems.

- When reading the room, you project your insecurities onto the intent of others without physical evidence.

The Challenge: Let Go of the Belief That People Are Analyzing You

- If you assume someone is judging you, remind yourself: most people are focused on their own life and interests.

- If you replay conversations, remind yourself: no one is dissecting this but me.

- If someone is neutral or distracted, assume it's about them, not you.

- If you hesitate out of self-consciousness, do it anyway. No one is watching you as closely as you're convinced they are.

7. Stopping the Projection of Your Own Negative Self-Talk Onto Others

Self-Deception at Play: Projection and blame, assuming negativity without evidence, self-fulfilling victimization.

Unconscious Motivation: Blaming others for how you feel lets you avoid confronting the internal belief that you're unlovable or not good enough.

Rebellion Zone: When you assume someone thinks poorly of you, remind yourself that most people are focused on their own lives and it's likely to be your own insecurity at play.

Why This Works: Your subconscious likely assigns your inner critic's voice to others, making you believe they see you the way you see yourself. Learning to separate your own self-judgment from reality disrupts this false belief.

How This Plays Out In Real Life:

- You walk into a room and immediately scan faces for signs of disapproval or judgment.

- A neutral glance or lack of greeting is interpreted as rejection.

- You start adjusting your behavior to "fix" something no one actually noticed—overexplaining, over-performing, or overly accommodating.

- You replay conversations afterward, obsessing over tone, facial expressions, or delays in response.

- You assume silence means someone is upset with you, even without evidence.

- You initiate conflict or apology preemptively, trying to smooth something over that didn't exist.

- Others feel confused or overwhelmed by your energy, start to distance, which reinforces your belief that people don't like you.

- You take that distancing as proof that you're unlovable or too much—never realizing your projection triggered the breakdown.

The Challenge: Stop Assuming Others Think What You Think About Yourself

If you assume someone dislikes you, *ask yourself*:

- Do I fear that I am unlikeable or embarrassing?

- Am I replaying an interaction with a negatively skewed lens?

- Do I historically read into other people's body language or tone and make it about myself?

If you misread someone's tone, remind yourself: people aren't secretly evaluating me—that's my own inner critic.

8. Resisting the Urge to Retaliate When You Feel Hurt, Slighted, or Embarrassed

Self-Deception at Play: Justifying retaliation, assumption of ill intent, self-fulfilling victimization.

Unconscious Motivation: Desire to stand up for perceived wrongs even if you're reacting from a skewed emotional perspective.

Rebellion Zone: When you feel the impulse to retaliate after feeling embarrassed or dismissed, pause. Let the feeling exist without acting on it.

Why This Works: Your brain treats emotional discomfort as a battle that needs to be won. But retaliation generates a cascade of conflict, keeping you stuck in a cycle of hurt feelings and drama.

How This Plays Out In Real Life:

- Someone makes a comment that hits an insecurity, and instead of processing the emotion, you fire back with sarcasm, passive-aggression, or a jab.

- You feel dismissed in a group setting and suddenly go quiet or cold, making others feel confused or guilty.

- You assume someone is intentionally trying to hurt you and respond with defensiveness or emotional withdrawal.

- You bring up unrelated past grievances to gain the upper hand in a conversation.

- You say something pointed to provoke guilt or shift blame so you don't have to admit you were hurt.

- You escalate a situation to gain control, even when it could have passed without conflict.

- The emotional retaliation may feel justified in the moment, but it leaves you feeling isolated, misunderstood, or ashamed afterward.

The Challenge: Poke Holes in the Feeling and Remain Calm

- If someone offends you, *ask yourself*:

  Do I feel hurt often?

  Am I likely to take things personally?

  Is it possible that this is a misunderstanding that needs to be understood instead of pounced on?

Is it possible that I'm feeling exposed and embarrassed and looking for someone to blame?

When I retaliate for something the other person doesn't understand, don't I risk looking emotionally unhinged?

Have I taken the time to ask a genuine clarifying question to make sure I'm interpreting this accurately?

9. Breaking the Cycle of "Grass Is Greener" Thinking

Self-Deception at Play: Perpetual dissatisfaction, idealizing what you don't have, avoiding commitment by focusing on what's missing.

Unconscious Motivation: Avoid the risk of emotional disappointment by keeping one foot out the door—idealizing what's not present allows you to protect yourself from fully committing or being let down.

Rebellion Zone: When you start idealizing what you don't have, resist mentally comparing it to what you do have in a way that devalues your present.

Why This Works: Your subconscious convinces you that happiness exists somewhere else, making your current reality feel inadequate. Practicing presence disrupts this belief.

How This Plays Out In Real Life:

• You're in a relationship but focus on how it could be better—more affection, more validation, more depth—without acknowledging what's working.

• You compare your partner, friend group, or job to idealized versions in your mind or online, leading to dissatisfaction.

• When things feel stable, you begin fixating on flaws or imagining how someone else might "see you" or treat you better.

• You pull away emotionally or create conflict when things are going well, subconsciously testing if something "better" will come along.

• You mentally shop for alternatives—new relationships, social circles, or opportunities—without ever fully engaging where you are.

• You hesitate to express gratitude or build deeper roots because that level of presence feels too vulnerable.

• You convince yourself that your unhappiness is due to your circumstances, rather than your internal pattern of avoidance and comparison.

The Challenge: Stay Where You Are Without Comparing It to What Could Be

• If you start romanticizing an alternative, remind yourself: you historically bring your problems with you and "new" doesn't actually solve anything longterm.

• If you feel FOMO, remind yourself: you tend to compare and contrast to get yourself to feel stuck and frustrated, often missing what's right in front of you.

By staying engaged with the present, you disrupt the belief that happiness is always elsewhere.

10. Stopping the Chase for "Something Better" to Fix Your Happiness

Self-Deception at Play: Perpetual dissatisfaction, avoiding internal work by seeking external change, fear of stability.

Unconscious Motivation: To outrun feelings of inadequacy or emotional discomfort by attaching hope to the next external shift—believing a new job, partner, or environment will finally bring the love and validation you crave.

Rebellion Zone: When you feel the urge to make a drastic life change, pause and evaluate whether you're chasing excitement instead of facing internal dissatisfaction.

Why This Works: Your brain convinces you that happiness exists in the next move, job, or relationship. But fulfillment doesn't come from external shifts—it comes from internal stability.

How This Plays Out In Real Life:

• You feel emotionally restless and decide you need a big change—quitting a job, moving, ending a relationship—without fully exploring what's actually bothering you.

• You convince yourself that a new environment or person will finally make you feel seen, valued, or worthy.

- You jump from project to project, partner to partner, or friend group to friend group, searching for the "perfect fit" that never quite satisfies.

- You get an initial dopamine hit from change, but soon feel disappointed and start fantasizing about the next shift.

- You tell yourself, "If I just had ___, I'd finally be happy," without acknowledging your role in creating discontent.

- You avoid routine or stability, fearing it will expose your internal emptiness or make you feel trapped.

- You stay busy chasing external excitement to distract from the real emotional work that still needs to happen inside.

The Challenge: Stop Chasing "New" as a Shortcut to Happiness

- If you feel restless, stop and give yourself an automatic 72-hour cooling-off period before making big decisions.

- If you idealize a different life, remind yourself: every new situation or opportunity is arrived at with your Brain Pattern. This makes it likely that you will eventually turn on the new thing and start seeing it in a negative light eventually. The positive and negative skewing is entirely dependent on your emotional state or mood.

By breaking the cycle of idealizing the new and having to face the distorted perception at play, you disrupt the belief that new is truly better than what you have right now.

11. Stopping the Habit of Rewriting the Past Through a Negative Lens

Self-Deception at Play: Self-fulfilling victimization, projection, and blame, emotional filtering.

Unconscious Motivation: To protect your emotional narrative by assigning blame externally—rewriting the past as more negative than it was helps justify your feelings of rejection and disappointment.

Rebellion Zone: When you feel tempted to label a relationship or experience as "always bad" due to one negative moment, stop yourself. Remind yourself that your emotional state can mischaracterize large chunks of time if you don't stay on top of it.

Why This Works: Your brain rewrites history based on current emotions, making the past seem worse than it was. Practicing fact-checking helps you hold multiple truths at once.

How This Plays Out In Real Life:

- You feel triggered in the present and retroactively assign negative intent to past experiences that previously felt positive.

- After a breakup or conflict, you reframe the entire relationship as toxic or one-sided to protect your ego and avoid grief.

- You ignore moments of connection, kindness, or growth in past relationships because they contradict your current emotional narrative.

- You tell yourself you "should've known" or "always felt something was off," even if that wasn't your lived experience at the time.

- You vent or retell stories with distorted timelines or exaggerated harm, reinforcing your role as the wronged party.

- You use black-and-white thinking to label people as "always manipulative" or "never who I thought they were," even when that wasn't consistently true.

- You resist nuance because it threatens the safety of your victim narrative—and if you allow both good and bad to exist, it becomes harder to know who to blame.

The Challenge: Fact-Check Your Memory Before Rewriting the Past

- If you start mentally distorting the past, stop. Remind yourself that:

    Your emotions can distort your perception of reality in a way that is no longer aligned with objective reality.

    You risk destroying or ruining healthy or positive situations or relationships by not pushing back against your Brain Pattern tricks.

- If you're currently doubt everything and feeling upset, *ask yourself*:

    Do I have a habit of seeing things through a negatively skewed lens when I'm upset?

    Does this make me more likely to label past moments that were actually positive as negative instead?

    Has this negative skewing created conflict in my relationships with people who feel upset at my misrepresentation?

By letting my brain skew things negatively, don't I risk destroying situations or relationships that had positive momentum?

• If you feel regret or anger, remind yourself: my current emotions will try to destroy past positives and rewrite them to justify my current state. This will only keep me stuck.

What Do You Gain by Embracing Your Rebellion Zones?

The love you're fighting for isn't the love you actually want. Your Rebellion Zones force you to let go of control, disengage from unnecessary battles, and find out what happens when you stop pushing for proof of love and let people show you who they really are.

1. You Stop Confusing Attention with Love

Your brain equates engagement with connection, even if that engagement comes from fighting, debating, or stirring up conflict. If someone is reacting to you, it reassures you that you matter, even if the interaction is negative. Rebellion Zones force you to sit in the discomfort of not reacting, not pushing, not forcing—so you can see who still chooses to show up when you're not demanding it. You gain the realization that love isn't something you have to extract from people—it's something they either give willingly, or they don't.

2. You No Longer Waste Energy on People Who Were Never Really Invested

You've spent years fighting to get people to care, prove their loyalty, or acknowledge you. But here's the thing: if someone only engages with you when forced, they were never truly invested. Rebellion Zones break this exhausting cycle. You stop chasing, stop provoking, and let people reveal their real level of commitment. You gain freedom from the exhausting need to test and prove every relationship.

3. You Learn That True Connection Doesn't Require Constant Justification

You tend to over-explain, defend, and try to prove your perspective. You assume that if someone doesn't immediately agree, you just need to push harder. Rebellion Zones teach you that the right people don't need to be convinced of your worth—they already see it. You find peace in knowing that your perspective doesn't need to be argued—it just is.

4. You Stop Attracting Relationships Built on Power Struggles

Your relationships often feel like a constant battle for control, validation, or emotional dominance. Whether it's friends, family, or partners, you've learned to fight for your place instead of naturally belonging. Rebellion Zones force you to disengage from unnecessary conflict and see who sticks around when you're not constantly proving yourself. You gain relationships that feel balanced, easy, and emotionally secure instead of like a never-ending test of loyalty.

5. You Experience Love That Feels Secure Instead of Conditional

Your past has taught you that love must be reinforced, tested, and fought for. You assume that if you stop pushing for attention, people will lose interest. Rebellion Zones prove that the people who truly care about you won't disappear when you stop demanding their presence. They will stay because they want to. You gain love that doesn't require you to fight to keep it.

6. You Get to Feel Peace Instead of Always Being on Guard

You live in a constant state of anticipation—always ready to defend, debate, or prove your worth. You don't fully relax in relationships because your brain is wired to assume you need to fight to be seen. Rebellion Zones teach you how to sit in stillness, let go of the battle, and experience the peace that comes from knowing you don't have to earn love through conflict. You gain a life where love feels like safety, not a battlefield.

The Bottom Line: You Learn That Love Can't Be Forced

For your entire life, you have equated effort with security, engagement with connection, and conflict with proof that you matter. You've convinced yourself that if you don't fight for love, you'll lose it.

But here's what Rebellion Zones reveal:

- Love that requires constant justification was never real love to begin with.

- The people who want to be in your life don't need to be tested into proving it.

- You don't have to fight, push, or demand space. You naturally deserve it.

Your entire life has been spent in survival mode, ensuring you're not overlooked, dismissed, or abandoned. But Rebellion Zones show you a different reality, one where love is freely given, not extracted through conflict.

Are you ready to see what happens when you stop forcing connection and start letting it flow naturally?

REJECTION – CONTROL TO RECEIVE LOVE AND BE SAFE (CONFLICT-PRONE ISOLATING)

Your behaviors are driven by a deep need to protect yourself from rejection, criticism, or emotional exposure by maintaining distance. Unlike the engaging conflict-prone type, who seeks direct confrontation to prove their value and secure respect, you take a more withdrawn, avoidant approach—ensuring that people don't get close enough to challenge or reject you in the first place.

Your brain tells you that people will either misunderstand you, fail to meet your standards, or ultimately disappoint you, so rather than waiting for that to happen, you preemptively disengage, critique, or push people away.

You might not actively seek out conflict, but you keep yourself on guard, hyper-aware of people's flaws, inconsistencies, or ways they might let you down. You often feel like an outsider looking in, analyzing relationships from a distance rather than fully engaging in them. You tend to ruminate on patterns of blame and conflict in your mind rather than seeking out the physical opposition.

You don't genuinely prefer isolation; you just see it as a way to stay in control of how people see you, so they never have the power to truly reject you.

Core Motivations:

1. You Fear Being Let Down, Rejected, or Deceived

You assume that disappointment in relationships is inevitable. Rather than risk being blindsided, you stay emotionally guarded, ensuring that no one gets close enough to hurt you.

2. Desire for Control Over Who Has Access to You

You are highly selective about where you invest your time and energy. You control connection by keeping others at a safe distance until they've proven their loyalty. Even then, you remain skeptical.

3. Belief That True Connection Requires Emotional Consistency and Effort

You believe relationships should be built on clear effort, fairness, and follow-through. If someone is inconsistent, disengaged, or fails to meet your expectations, you see it as proof that they aren't worth the time or effort.

4. Preemptively Withdrawing to Protect Yourself

You assume that rejection is always on the horizon, so you justify pulling away or not engaging. This allows you to feel in control, even if it creates distance you don't actually want.

5. Interpreting Others' Behavior Through a Lens of Rejection

Your brain is constantly scanning for signs that someone is losing interest, pulling away, or subtly devaluing you. A slow response, a change in tone, or a shift in routine can trigger deep feelings of mistrust or disconnection that may prompt you to pull away or avoid.

6. Feeling Emotionally Self-Sufficient—But Also Deeply Alone

You try to convince yourself that you don't want to rely on connection and that you're more of a loner. Beneath the surface, you experience a profound loneliness, one that you struggle to acknowledge or address.

7. Struggling to Trust That Others' Intentions Are Pure

You assume that people have hidden motives, and you are fixated on looking for inconsistencies in their words or actions.

This makes it difficult for you to relax into relationships without maintaining a level of skepticism.

8. Keeping Score of Who Puts in Effort—and Who Doesn't

You track fairness in relationships, noting who reaches out first, who prioritizes you, and who follows through. If effort feels unbalanced, you quickly adjust by pulling back, rather than asking for what you need.

9. Assuming Distance Means Disinterest

If someone becomes less engaged, doesn't react as expected, or simply needs space, you interpret it as rejection or dissatisfaction rather than a normal rhythm of human connection. This often leads you to withdraw further or place blame, reinforcing the cycle of emotional isolation.

Why Do You Need Rebellion Zones?

Your brain has spent a lifetime strategizing how to avoid rejection, keeping you trapped in observation or rumination from the sidelines. Unlike the engaging conflict-prone type, which fights for connection through communication intensity, you get stuck cycling on patterns of blame and mistrust in your mind.

You assume rejection is inevitable. But here's the problem: This cycle doesn't protect you—it isolates you.

Rebellion Zones force you to disrupt these ingrained defenses. They challenge you to stop filtering relationships through rejection-based assumptions and break the cycle of preemptive withdrawal, avoidance and quiet resentment.

1. Staying Instead of Preemptively Leaving

Right now, your brain tells you that leaving first protects you from rejection. If you control the ending, you think you can avoid the pain of being excluded. Rebellion Zones force you to stay engaged, even when discomfort arises.

Why You Need This: To stop assuming every relationship is a ticking time bomb.

How You Approach This Rebellion Zone:

- **Observe** how often you mentally check out of relationships long before they end.

515

- **Notice** when your Brain Pattern tells you to leave first rather than risk embarrassment.

- **Remind yourself** that not every subtle shift in connection is proof that things are falling apart or turning on you.

- **Challenge yourself** to stay engaged and initiating instead of looking for an exit strategy.

The Self-Fulfilling Prophecy: By leaving first, you create the rejection you were trying to avoid. Instead of experiencing connection, you prove your own fears right—over and over again.

2. Seeing Situations Objectively Instead of Filtering Through Rejection

You analyze tone, body language, and responses as proof of rejection. If someone is neutral or less engaged, you assume it means they don't think you're worthy or good enough. Rebellion Zones challenge you to pause before assigning meaning to neutral moments.

Why You Need This: To stop assuming small shifts in behavior are personal attacks.

How You Approach This Rebellion Zone:

- **Observe** how often you search for hidden rejection in neutral interactions.

- **Notice** when your Brain Pattern fixates on a perceived slight as proof that someone is secretly judging you.

- **Remind yourself** that most people's actions aren't about you—they're just living their lives.

- **Challenge yourself** to let things play out or ask a genuine clarifying question to understand their perception or motive.

The Self-Fulfilling Prophecy: By assuming rejection in every interaction, you create distance where none needs to exist.

3. Expressing Discontent Instead of Silently Withdrawing

You convince yourself that expressing frustration is pointless or will be met with dismissal. If someone lets you down, you withdraw rather than say anything. Rebellion Zones push you to voice your feelings instead of silently pulling away.

Why You Need This: To stop punishing people with silence instead of clarity.

How You Approach This Rebellion Zone:

- **Observe** when you avoid confrontation and let resentment build in your mind instead.

- **Notice** when your Brain Pattern tells you that speaking up won't matter.

- **Remind yourself** that people can't meet your needs or problem solve if they don't know what's wrong.

- **Challenge yourself** to express your perspective to the other person before mentally checking out.

The Self-Fulfilling Prophecy: By keeping your emotions hidden, you rob people of the chance to respond, adjust, or prove they care—reinforcing your belief that they never did.

4. Asking Directly Instead of Expecting People to "Just Know"

You assume that if someone really cared, they'd just understand what you need. When they don't show up the way you want, you take it as proof of disinterest. Rebellion Zones force you to state your needs outright, instead of expecting mind-reading.

Why You Need This: To stop seeing connection as a test people pass or fail.

How You Approach This Rebellion Zone:

- **Observe** when you want someone to know what you need without having to say it out loud.

- **Notice** when your Brain Pattern assumes the other person is selfish and doesn't care rather than acknowledge that you haven't voiced what you need out loud.

- **Remind yourself** that people aren't ignoring you. They just aren't aware of what's going on in your mind.

- **Challenge yourself** to ask directly instead of silently keeping score or waiting angrily for them to figure it out.

The Self-Fulfilling Prophecy: By expecting people to read your mind, you set them up to fail—then resent them for failing.

5. Letting People Show Up Without Testing Them

You test people's loyalty by pulling away to see if they'll chase. If they don't reach out first, you assume they don't really care. Rebellion Zones challenge you to let relationships unfold naturally.

Why You Need This: To stop manufacturing rejection just to confirm your fears.

How You Approach This Rebellion Zone:

- **Observe** when you withdraw or pull away just to see if someone will notice.

- **Notice** when your Brain Pattern tries to focus on the other person's responses rather than taking ownership for instigating the withdrawal.

- **Remind yourself** that healthy relationships don't require testing. They require honest in-the-moment communication.

- **Challenge yourself** to stay engaged instead of testing their commitment through withdrawal.

The Self-Fulfilling Prophecy: By testing people's loyalty, you create conditions where even the most patient individuals eventually pull away.

6. Letting People Set Boundaries Without Taking It Personally

You assume that if someone sets a boundary, it means they're pushing you away or don't take you seriously. If someone asks for you to stop doing something, you spiral into shame and self-doubt instead of acknowledging their request. Rebellion Zones force you to accept boundaries or requests without assuming rejection.

Why You Need This: To stop seeing healthy limits or requests as judgment or criticism.

How You Approach This Rebellion Zone:

- **Observe** when you feel judged by someone asking for something that goes against your instinct or choice.

- **Notice** when your Brain Pattern tells you that boundaries or requests that go against what you want are warning signs that you are being rejected.

- **Remind yourself** that boundaries or requests make relationships sustainable and reciprocal.

- **Challenge yourself** to see the other person's perspective and seek understanding rather than take it as judgment or critique.

The Self-Fulfilling Prophecy: By reacting negatively to boundaries or requests, you push people away—confirming the fear you were trying to avoid.

7. Assuming Neutral Intent Instead of Taking Everything Personally

You analyze every word, pause, or shift in tone as if it's about you. If someone is neutral, distracted, or short, you assume they're pulling away. Rebellion Zones force you to assume neutrality first, instead of filtering everything through rejection.

Why You Need This: To stop turning neutral interactions into proof of exclusion.

How You Approach This Rebellion Zone:

- **Observe** how often you assign hidden meaning to people's actions or facial expressions.

- **Notice** when your Brain Pattern creates rejection scenarios that the other person may be completely unaware of.

- **Remind yourself** that most people's behavior has nothing to do with you and you have a tendency to read into things with a lens of personal attack.

- **Challenge yourself** to assume neutrality and ask if they need anything rather than take it personally.

The Self-Fulfilling Prophecy: By constantly searching for proof of rejection, you find it—even when it was never there.

8. Engaging in Relationships Without a Backup Plan

You always keep an exit strategy, emotionally or physically. You are frequently thinking about what else is out there or what might be better. Rebellion Zones force you to commit to relationships without keeping one foot out the door.

Why You Need This: To stop treating relationships like a risk that requires constant monitoring and escape routes.

How You Approach This Rebellion Zone:

- **Observe** how often you mentally check out and seek an escape route before things even go wrong.

- **Notice** when your Brain Pattern tells you to isolate or be alone to remain in control.

- **Remind yourself** that real security and connection comes from engagement, not from preparing to pull away.

- **Challenge yourself** to engage and serve others, especially when you feel the pull to detach.

The Self-Fulfilling Prophecy: By never fully committing, you never fully experience connection. This reinforces the belief that relationships can't be trusted.

9. Letting Relationships Be Imperfect Without Seeing Them as a Failure

You hold high personal standards for relationships, expecting them to meet your definition of loyalty, effort, and fairness, even if you aren't personally upholding the same standards. If someone falls short of your expectations, you assume the relationship is flawed or doomed.

Rebellion Zones push you to accept imperfection without interpreting it as proof of rejection.

Why You Need This: To stop treating every misstep or disappointment as a dealbreaker.

How You Approach This Rebellion Zone:

- **Observe** when you mentally write off a relationship after one mistake or minor conflict.

- **Notice** when your Brain Pattern searches for proof that someone isn't "meeting the standard."

- **Remind yourself** that imperfection is not failure—relationships are messy, and that's normal.

- **Challenge yourself** to stay engaged and take personal accountability for mistakes you've made to level the playing field.

The Self-Fulfilling Prophecy: By expecting perfection, you guarantee that no relationship will ever feel safe enough to keep.

Rebellion Zones

The moment you read through your Rebellion Zones, your brain will try to argue why they aren't worth pursuing. You'll convince yourself that your distance is just practicality, that your reluctance to engage deeply is just discernment, and that your skepticism about people's motives is just being realistic. You'll rationalize withdrawal as independence, and hyper-awareness of flaws as being perceptive.

But let's be clear: this isn't about forcing you to trust blindly, open up recklessly, or pretend people don't let each other down. That would be naive. What you're here to learn is how to stop filtering relationships through rejection-based assumptions—how to break the cycle of preemptive withdrawal, emotional detachment, and quiet resentment.

1. Staying Instead of Preemptively Leaving

Self-Deception at Play: Avoiding rejection by pulling away first, destroying relationships before they're at risk, leaving before being excluded.

Unconscious Motivation: Avoid commitment or vulnerability to outrun assumed rejection or blame.

Rebellion Zone: When you feel the urge to leave—physically, emotionally, or mentally—stay. Let relationships unfold without assuming they're doomed.

Why This Works: Your subconscious tells you that exclusion is inevitable, so you pull away before it happens. Whether it's a friendship, a group setting, or a relationship, you control the ending to avoid the pain of being left behind. By staying engaged instead of detaching, you force your brain to recognize that not all relationships are set to fail. Not every interaction needs to be an escape plan.

How This Plays Out in Real Life:

- You justify avoiding social interactions or opportunities to connect

- You mentally check out of relationships long before they end, assuming things will fall apart eventually.

- You convince yourself that cutting ties first is better than waiting to be excluded.

- You ghost or disappear suddenly, even when nothing bad has happened, just to avoid the discomfort of potential rejection.

- You escalate minor issues internally to justify distancing yourself, convincing yourself that others don't actually care.

- You withdraw as a test, waiting to see if people will chase after you. Even when they do, you doubt their sincerity.

The Challenge: Stay Present Instead of Preemptively Leaving

- If your instinct is to pull away when a relationship feels off, resist. Reach out to connect or offer an act of service that isn't self-serving or transactional.

- If you normally leave groups or friendships without explanation, challenge yourself to communicate directly.

By challenging the instinct to leave first, you disrupt the belief that removing yourself is the only way to stay in control. Instead of seeing connection as a risk to be managed, you start seeing it as an experience to navigate in real time without preemptively deciding how it will end.

2. Seeing Situations Objectively Instead of Filtering Through Rejection

Self-Deception at Play: Assuming negativity without evidence, fixating on perceived slights, interpreting neutral distance as rejection.

Unconscious Motivation: To avoid the pain of unexpected rejection by assuming it's already happening—if you expect disconnection, you can emotionally retreat first and avoid being blindsided.

Rebellion Zone: When you feel yourself assuming rejection—pause. Consider other explanations instead of treating your first assumption as fact.

Why This Works: Your subconscious scans interactions for evidence that you're being dismissed, ignored, or excluded. A slow reply, a lack of enthusiasm, a neutral response. Your brain translates these into proof of rejection, even when nothing is actually wrong. By actively considering alternative perspectives, you train your brain to stop treating every small shift in energy as confirmation that you're unwanted.

How This Plays Out in Real Life:

- You overanalyze tone, responses, and body language, assuming that if someone isn't actively affirming you, they must be pulling away.

- You take neutral social shifts personally, believing that any change in attention or dynamic means people no longer value you.

- You assume that if someone sets a boundary, it's about you being unwanted, even if it's not personal.

- You fixate on a single perceived slight, replaying it over and over in your head as proof that someone secretly dislikes you.

- You struggle with trust, assuming that people have hidden agendas, even when there's no real evidence.

The Challenge: Challenge Your First Interpretation

- If someone takes longer than usual to respond, remind yourself that people have their own lives. It's not necessarily about you.

- If your first instinct is to assume rejection, stop and *ask yourself*:

    Historically do I assume something is about me that may not in fact be?

    Do I tend to take things personally or feel slighted even when the other person has no idea?

    Has this led to unnecessary conflict in the past?

    Can I challenge myself to assume something positive or accidental?

- If you feel convinced someone is secretly judging you, look at your history of assuming judgment when it's typically underlying insecurity.

By training your brain to stop before assuming rejection, you disrupt the cycle of filtering everything through a personal lens. Instead of seeing relationships as tests you're bound to fail, you begin seeing them as evolving interactions that aren't always about you.

3. Expressing Discontent Instead of Silently Withdrawing

Self-Deception at Play: Suppressing emotions, using conflict as a justification to withdraw, assuming others won't care if you express frustration.

Unconscious Motivation: To maintain emotional safety by staying in control of your inner world—expressing frustration feels like handing power to someone who might reject, dismiss, or use it against you. Withdrawing gives you control over the outcome.

Rebellion Zone: If something bothers you, express it instead of shutting down, ghosting, or mentally checking out.

Why This Works: Your subconscious tells you that voicing your frustration is pointless—that people won't change, won't listen, or that expressing emotions will only make things worse. So instead, you go silent, create distance, or let resentment build. But when you hold things in, people never actually get the chance to respond, adjust, or prove they care.

How This Plays Out in Real Life:

- You feel frustrated or disappointed but keep the conflict or upset in your head instead of verbalizing it to the offending party.

- You begin to physically distance yourself, leaving the other person confused or unaware anything is wrong.

- You feel justified avoiding texts, canceling plans, or growing cold in conversation.

- You replay scenarios in your head, building arguments or resentment internally, but never speak them aloud.

- Over time, this leads to accumulated resentment, disconnection, and confirmation of your belief that relationships aren't a good fit.

The Challenge: Say It Instead of Stuffing It Down

- If your instinct is to hold back your feelings, force yourself to articulate them—without over-explaining or apologizing.

- If you assume someone won't care, share your perspective without assuming or pointing fingers to see if they are receptive.

- If you normally let frustration build into quiet resentment, speak up before it reaches that point.

- If you want to disappear instead of engaging, *ask yourself*:

  If someone did this to me, would I take it personally?

  Would I take this as a signal that they don't care and are rejecting me?

  Can I challenge myself to see how disappearing will make things worse and more tense?

By expressing yourself instead of ghosting or suppressing emotions, you disrupt the belief that silence is your only way to maintain control.

4. Asking Directly Instead of Expecting People to Just Know

Self-Deception at Play: Interpreting boundaries as rejection, assuming others have hidden agendas, blaming others for disconnection.

Unconscious Motivation: Protect yourself from vulnerability and disappointment by expecting people to prove their love through intuition—if they really cared, they'd just know. This allows you to stay emotionally guarded while holding others to unspoken standards. If they fall short, you can justify pulling away without ever having to risk direct communication.

Rebellion Zone: Instead of assuming someone should "just know" what you need or expect, ask for it outright.

Why This Works: You assume that if people really cared, they would naturally understand what you need. So when they don't show up the way you want, you take it as proof that they were never invested. The reality? Most people aren't mind readers. By stating what you need instead of expecting others to figure it out, you prove to your brain that connection isn't just a test people pass or fail.

How This Plays Out in Real Life:

- You feel disconnected or disappointed but don't articulate what you need—you wait to see if they notice.

- When someone doesn't offer support, affection, or acknowledgment the way you wanted, you interpret it as proof they don't care or are self-centered.

- You raise your expectations without informing anyone, then feel let down when they inevitably don't meet them.

- You expect others to read your mood, understand your silence, or decode passive cues—then withdraw when they don't.

- You test people by withholding affection, support, or communication to see if they'll "step up" on their own.

- You internalize unmet needs as rejection and use that pain to justify emotional distance or total disengagement.

- Over time, people experience you as guarded, unpredictable, or emotionally unavailable—even though internally, you're desperate to feel seen and understood.

The Challenge: Be Clear About What You Want

- If you feel let down by someone's actions, *ask yourself*:

  Did I actually tell them what I wanted or needed in a way they could take action on?

  Have I historically set people up to fail me by not giving them the information they need to meet my needs?

- If you assume someone is pulling away, ask them a genuine clarifying question instead of staying silent and resentful or asking with an accusatory tone.

- If you expect reciprocity in a relationship, state your expectations instead of silently keeping score.

By asking instead of assuming, you disrupt the belief that connection must be proven rather than built through communication.

5. Letting People Show Up Without Testing Them

Self-Deception at Play: Pulling away to see if people will chase, fixating on fairness, hyper-focus on loyalty tests.

Unconscious Motivation: Avoid the vulnerability of genuine connection by staying in control of emotional risk–testing people allows you to keep your guard up while determining if others are "safe" or "worth it."

Rebellion Zone: Instead of testing people by pulling away, waiting, or pushing them to "prove" themselves, let relationships unfold naturally.

Why This Works: Your subconscious tells you that you need to test people to see if they're really invested. So you create distance, waiting to see if they notice or care. This cycle creates exactly what you fear–distance, disconnection, and resentment. By allowing people to show up without being tested, you start experiencing connection for what it is–not as something that must be "proven."

How This Plays Out in Real Life:

- You suddenly stop texting or emotionally pull back to see if someone will reach out first.

- You wait to see how long it takes someone to notice your silence, assuming their response (or lack of it) reveals how much they care.

- You withhold affection, vulnerability, or attention, believing others need to "earn" continued access to you.

- You overanalyze response times, tone, or enthusiasm, treating minor changes as proof of fading loyalty or disinterest.

- When people don't respond the way you hoped, you retreat further and tell yourself they failed the "loyalty test."

- Even when someone shows up for you, you question their motives or assume they'll eventually let you down.

- Over time, your tests create confusion and distance, reinforcing your belief that people can't be trusted or don't truly care.

The Challenge: Let People Show Up Without Testing Them

- If you normally pull away to see if someone will notice or react, don't. Stay engaged and initiate something out of the ordinary.

- If you find yourself waiting to see if someone will reach out first, challenge yourself to reach out instead.

- If you assume that someone's investment must be tested to be trusted, recognize that testing can actually degrade the perception of trust in the relationship.

By dropping loyalty tests, you disrupt the belief that the only safe relationships are the ones people fight for.

6. Letting People Set Boundaries or Provide Feedback Without Taking It Personally

Self-Deception at Play: Assuming boundaries or feedback mean rejection, interpreting others' needs as a reflection of your worth.

Unconscious Motivation: Maintain a sense of emotional safety by interpreting feedback or boundaries as signs of rejection—if someone corrects you or asks for space, your subconscious reads it as confirmation that you're failing or unwanted.

Rebellion Zone: When someone sets a boundary or provides feedback, see it as an opportunity to make a change or correction to benefit the growth of the relationship.

Why This Works: You assume that if someone needs space, sets a limit, or gives feedback, it means you're not doing it right. The reality? This feedback and attention to detail can help you grow your relationship and build trust.

How This Plays Out in Real Life:

- Someone sets a boundary, and you immediately feel hurt or

retaliatory, assuming they're pulling away or trying to cut you out.

• You replay the interaction in your head, interpreting their feedback as a personal attack rather than a chance to adjust.

• You respond with silence, distance, or withdrawal instead of asking clarifying questions or staying engaged.

• You feel a need to defend yourself or justify your actions instead of acknowledging the other person's needs.

• You assume, "If they really cared, they wouldn't need space from me," and begin emotionally shutting down.

• You internalize feedback as proof that you're unlovable—rather than simply recognizing a normal relational adjustment.

• Over time, you avoid closeness or collaboration to preempt situations where feedback might be given, creating chronic disconnection and loneliness.

The Challenge: Accept Boundaries and Feedback Without Taking It as an Attack

• If someone takes time for themselves, don't assume it means they're pulling away. They may just enjoy time to be independent and reset.

If you feel hurt by feedback given, remind yourself that feedback helps us make valuable pivots and informed decisions in relationships. It's not a personal attack; it's an opportunity.

7. Assuming Neutral Intent Instead of Taking Everything Personally

Self-Deception at Play: Assuming negativity without evidence, fixating on perceived slights, seeing hidden meaning in neutral interactions.

Unconscious Motivation: Protect yourself from unexpected emotional pain by assuming rejection before it happens—if you take things personally, you can retreat on your own terms instead of risking the vulnerability of being blindsided.

Rebellion Zone: When you feel yourself reacting to an interaction as if it's personal—stop. Assume neutrality first before assigning meaning.

Why This Works: Your subconscious tells you that people's words, actions, or lack of response are a direct reflection of their feelings about you. If someone forgets to invite you, doesn't respond right away, or seems less engaged than usual, you assume it's intentional—that they're rejecting you, losing interest, or quietly pushing you away.

But most people are thinking about themselves—not crafting hidden messages to make you feel bad. By assuming neutral or positive intent before reacting, you force your brain to stop filtering interactions through rejection.

How This Plays Out in Real Life:

- You overanalyze tone, word choice, or timing in texts and conversations, assuming that small details hold a deeper meaning.

- You assume that if someone doesn't engage enthusiastically, they're pulling away.

- You mentally replay small moments over and over, trying to figure out what someone really meant.

- If someone forgets to invite you or includes others but not you, you see it as proof that you don't belong.

- If a friend or partner is distant, you assume it must be about something you did, rather than considering their personal stress or emotions.

The Challenge: Assume Neutrality First

- If you find yourself overanalyzing a conversation, stop. *Ask yourself*:

  When I overanalyze do I tend to skew the analysis negatively?

  Historically, do I project my own insecurities as the opinions of others?

  Do I have a tendency to assume the worst about signs that others may overlook?

- If someone is less engaged than usual, consider that they might just be distracted or dealing with their own issues.

- If you start to spiral over a perceived slight, remind yourself that most people are not actively thinking about how their actions affect you—they are just living their lives.

- If you assume someone is intentionally excluding or ignoring you, stop and *ask yourself*:

Do I tend to fill in the blanks from my rejection-skewed lens?

Do I have a pattern of not asking and assuming I'm being left out?

Can I challenge myself to ask a genuine clarifying question to see if there is a misunderstanding or simply invite myself?

By assuming neutral intent, you disrupt the belief that people's actions are always tied to you. Instead of constantly filtering interactions through rejection, you start seeing things for what they actually are—not what you fear they mean.

What You Gain by Embracing Rebellion Zones

You hold back—watching, waiting, analyzing—telling yourself that staying quiet keeps you safe. In your head, you're already building a case, tracking every inconsistency and injustice, but instead of speaking up, you withdraw. You assume others should already understand what you need, and when they don't, it only justifies your choice to stay distant. You convince yourself that pulling away is protecting you from embarrassment or rejection, but in reality, it just keeps you stuck— isolated, unheard, and silently resenting the very people you wish would meet you halfway.

Your Rebellion Zones force you to stop waiting for proof that people will fail you. Instead of retreating into silence or pushing others away when assumptions take over, you'll practice saying what you actually mean, giving people the chance to meet you where you are. It won't feel natural at first, but the alternative is staying locked in a cycle where you never really get what you need, because no one even knows you need it.

1. You Stop Using Silence as a Shield

You keep your thoughts locked inside, assuming that if people really cared, they'd already understand what you need. But instead of feeling seen, you end up resentful, frustrated that no one is responding to the things you never actually said. Rebellion Zones push you to stop using silence as a form of protection and start expressing yourself before frustration turns into quiet detachment. You get your needs met without waiting for others to read your mind.

2. You No Longer Assume the Worst Before It Happens

You are always scanning for signs of rejection, analyzing people's words, tone, and body language for proof that they're pulling away. If something feels slightly off, you assume it's a warning sign and emotionally disengage before you can be hurt. Rebellion Zones force you to stop treating neutral interactions like rejection—and instead, wait for actual evidence before assuming the worst. You break free from constantly overanalyzing relationships and creating distance that never needed to exist.

3. You Speak Instead of Letting Resentment Build

When someone upsets you, you don't address it. Instead, you mentally track every slight, letting frustration simmer beneath the surface while outwardly acting like nothing's wrong. Over time, this hidden resentment builds into complete emotional disengagement. Rebellion Zones force you to communicate your frustrations instead of assuming that speaking up won't matter. You become able to resolve conflicts before they push you into unnecessary withdrawal.

4. You Stop Testing People to See if They Care

You pull back—waiting to see if someone will chase after you, check in, or try harder. If they don't, you take it as proof that they never really cared. But in reality, most people don't even realize they're being tested. Rebellion Zones force you to engage directly instead of playing games to see who will "prove" their loyalty. You gain a more secure experience of connection that isn't built on hidden expectations or passive tests.

5. You Let People Set Boundaries or Give Feedback Without Assuming They're Rejecting You

When someone sets a boundary or gives feedback, your brain instantly jumps to the worst-case scenario. You assume it means you've done something wrong, that they don't want you around, or that the relationship is ending. Rebellion Zones challenge you to see boundaries and feedback as normal, healthy, and necessary to move a relationship forward in truth—not as proof that you're being excluded. You're able to respect boundaries or feedback without spiraling into fear, shame, or overcorrection.

6. You Ask for What You Need Instead of Expecting People to Just Know

You assume that if someone really valued you, they would instinctively understand what you want or need. But when they don't, you take it as proof of disinterest and quietly pull away. Rebellion Zones push you to state your needs outright instead of expecting mind-reading. You know that when your needs aren't met, it's not because people don't care—it's because you kept them in the dark.

7. You Stop Assuming Every Change in Behavior is a Warning Sign

If someone is less talkative, takes longer to reply, or doesn't seem as engaged, your brain immediately starts writing a story about how they're losing interest or pulling away. Rebellion Zones force you to pause before assuming rejection and consider alternative explanations first. You become able to experience connection without constantly searching for proof that something is wrong.

8. You Experience Relationships Without a Backup Plan

You keep an emotional exit strategy—never fully committing to relationships, fixating on grass-is-greener or FOMO to keep you open to something else. You tell yourself this keeps you safe, but it really just prevents you from ever truly anchoring in security and attachment. Rebellion Zones force you to fully engage instead of always keeping one foot out the door. You gain a deeper sense of connection that isn't based on self-protection.

9. You Stay Instead of Running When Things Feel Uncertain

The moment you sense emotional risk, your instinct is to retreat—either mentally checking out or physically pulling away before things can turn bad. Your Brain Pattern tricks you into justifying leaving or pulling away as an act of self-preservation when it's really self-sabotage. Rebellion Zones push you to stay and engage, even when discomfort arises. You experience relationship depth in real time instead of justifying premature escapes or exits.

10. You Let People Show Up for You Without Pushing Them Away

Deep down, you want connection, but you also assume people will let you down. You pull away before they get the chance.

Rebellion Zones force you to give people a real opportunity to show up instead of rejecting them before they can reject you. You experience loyalty and care without self-sabotaging relationships before they can fully develop.

The Bottom Line

Your brain has trained you to believe that if you don't control the terms of engagement, you'll be overlooked, invalidated, or emotionally at risk. You assume that most relationships will let you down, so you keep yourself at a distance—watching, analyzing, and controlling what people are allowed to see.

But what if the very behaviors you use to protect yourself from rejection are what keep you in a cycle of loneliness, disconnection, and quiet frustration?

When you step into your Rebellion Zones, you will begin to disrupt the belief that staying guarded and withdrawn is the only way to stay safe. You will learn how to:

• Trust that relationships don't have to be all-or-nothing—fully detached or fully dependent.

• Stop assuming that distance equals protection from rejection.

• Detach from the idea that most people aren't worth the effort.

• Learn to express needs and boundaries instead of assuming people should "just know."

• See relationships for what they actually are, instead of filtering them through past disappointments or personal ideals.

By stepping into your Rebellion Zones, you shift from viewing connection as a risk to actually experiencing relationships that feel steady, mutual, and built on trust—without having to test, withdraw, or disappear.

CHAPTER 29

REJECTION– CONTROL TO RECEIVE LOVE

REJECTION – CONTROL TO RECEIVE LOVE (PEOPLE-PLEASING ENGAGING)

Your brain has spent a lifetime securing acceptance and inclusion by shaping yourself to fit the needs and expectations of others. Unlike the isolating people-pleasing type, who holds back and waits to be chosen, you actively insert yourself into relationships, initiating, accommodating, over-giving, and ensuring you remain visible, relevant, and indispensable.

You attempt to prevent rejection through compliance and effort. You assume that if you are agreeable enough, helpful enough, or entertaining enough that people will choose you. You adjust your personality, mirror others, anticipate needs before they're expressed, or overextend yourself to ensure you remain part of the group or relationship. Your fear of being cast aside keeps you locked in this exhausting cycle, convincing you that the only way to secure belonging is through relentless adaptation. But rebellion offers you something you've never had—freedom to exist as you are, without the constant performance, and the chance to see who truly chooses you.

Motivations:

1. Ensuring Acceptance, Even If It Means Reshaping Your Personality or Doing "The Right Thing"

You adjust your identity, behavior, or opinions in the moment to be included, assuming that your real self isn't enough to secure belonging.

2. Preventing Exclusion, Even If It Means Overextending Yourself

You fear being left out, so you overcommit, overextend, offer help, or make yourself indispensable to secure your place in the group.

3. Seeking Admiration, Even If It Feels Exhausting

You equate being liked with being worthy, so you pour energy into entertaining, supporting, or accommodating others, often at your own expense.

4. Over-Communicating, Even If It Overwhelms Others

You look to communication as a way to test your connection to others.

5. Seeking Reassurance, Even If It Turns Interactions Negative

Your brain prompts you to ask, "Are you mad at me?" or "Did I do something wrong?" assuming that any small shift in mood means you've upset someone.

6. Controlling How Others See You, Even If It Distances You from Genuine Connection

You carefully curate your words and actions to avoid disapproval and keep up appearances, but in doing so, you struggle to form authentic relationships where people know the real you. Do you know the real you?

7. Over-Explaining, Even When It's Unnecessary

You fear that being misunderstood will lead to rejection, so you justify and defend your choices excessively trying to make sure you don't upset or offend people.

8. Adapting Too Quickly, Even If It Feels Inauthentic

You mirror others' language, interests, or mannerisms to fit in, believing that sameness is the safest route to acceptance.

9. Over-Apologizing, Even If You Haven't Done Anything Wrong

You assume you are responsible for any shift in mood or energy, believing preemptive apologies will prevent rejection.

10. Interpreting Boundaries as Rejection, Even When They Aren't Personal

You struggle to accept that space and autonomy are normal, assuming that any distance means you must have made a mistake that needs to be fixed.

11. Pushing for Inclusion, Even When Social Cues Suggest Space

You struggle to gauge when to step back, assuming that if you just do more or help more, you'll be invited closer. This can make you overly persistent in conversations or social settings, not realizing others may need time or space.

12. Jumping into Relationships or Friendships, Even If They Lack Depth

You seek instant closeness, believing that admiration or shared experiences alone are enough to create lasting bonds. When those relationships don't deepen or deepen as quickly as you desire, you assume it's because you're doing something wrong.

13. Holding Onto Disappointment When Efforts Aren't Reciprocated, Even If It Wasn't Personal

You feel hurt when people don't match your level of investment, not out of anger, but from a sense of unworthiness or invisibility. You assume, "If I was doing the right things, they'd match my same effort."

14. Being Overly Agreeable, Even When It Contradicts Your Real Opinions

You prioritize likability over authenticity, assuming that disagreement equals rejection.

15. Using Charm, Humor, or Dramatics, Even If It Feels Forced

You assume you must entertain or impress others to be valued, believing that likability is something that must be actively maintained.

16. Attaching Worth to Social, Religious, or Cultural Status, Even If It Leads to Shallow Relationships

You believe that being liked, admired, or included in the group is the ultimate marker of success, even if it means sacrificing depth or the pursuit of individual identity.

17. Struggling to Say No, Even When You Are Overwhelmed

You fear that setting boundaries will make you seem selfish or unlikable, so you agree to things you don't actually want to or shouldn't do.

18. Pushing Relationships Too Fast, Even If the Other Person Isn't Interested

You believe that the faster someone gets emotionally close to you, the more secure the relationship will be. You may overshare, idealize new friendships, or struggle with pacing, not realizing you are overwhelming the other person.

Why Do You Need Rebellion Zones?

Your brain tells you that belonging is something you earn or achieve—not something you naturally deserve. You shape-shift, accommodate, and overextend, convinced that if you can just be agreeable enough, entertaining enough, or helpful enough, you'll never have to face rejection. But instead of securing lasting connections, this strategy keeps you in a cycle of chasing, proving, and exhausting yourself to maintain relationships that may not even be built on authenticity.

The problem is, no matter how much you give, acceptance never feels secure. Rebellion Zones force you to break free from this cycle, challenging you to stop chasing external approval and start building connections that don't rely on performance.

1. You Stop Performing for Acceptance and Start Existing as Yourself

Right now, your brain tells you that connection requires constant effort—that you must entertain, impress, or prove your value to be included. You adapt in real time, shifting your opinions, interests, or personality to fit whatever the situation demands. But in doing so, you lose sight of who you actually are. Rebellion Zones challenge you to stop filtering yourself for the sake of likability and start showing up as you—without constant self-editing.

Why You Need This: To build relationships that don't require you to perform to stay included.

How To Approach This Rebellion Zone:

- **Observe** how often you adjust your tone, personality, or preferences to match the people around you.

- **Notice** how your Brain Pattern convinces you that the real you isn't enough.

- **Remind yourself** that real belonging isn't conditional on your ability to entertain or please.

- **Challenge yourself** to express an honest opinion or preference without gauging reactions first.

The Self-Fulfilling Prophecy: By constantly adjusting yourself to fit in, you ensure that people never get to know you—reinforcing the belief that your real self isn't worthy of connection.

2. You Challenge the Fear That Setting Boundaries Means Losing Connection

You hesitate to say no, hold back from expressing discomfort, and assume that prioritizing yourself will make people turn away. Instead, you overcommit, take on more than you can handle, and stretch yourself thin to maintain approval. But the people who truly value you won't disappear just because you set a boundary. Rebellion Zones force you to break the belief that saying no equals rejection—challenging you to create space without fear of losing your place in people's lives.

Why You Need This: To stop tying your worth to self-sacrifice and start valuing your own time and energy.

How To Approach This Rebellion Zone:

- **Observe** how often you override your own needs to accommodate others.

- **Notice** how your Brain Pattern makes you feel guilty for setting limits.

- **Remind yourself** that boundaries don't push away the right people—they reveal them.

- **Challenge yourself** to decline one request without over-explaining or apologizing.

The Self-Fulfilling Prophecy: By never setting limits, you attract people who take advantage of·or mock your willingness, reinforcing the belief that you have to overextend yourself to be valued.

3. You Shift from Seeking Reassurance to Trusting Your Own Stability

Your brain constantly scans for shifts in tone, text responses, or social cues—interpreting the smallest changes as proof that something is wrong. You ask, "Are you mad at me?" or "Did I do something wrong?" believing that if you don't get immediate reassurance, you must have messed up. But this cycle creates exhaustion for both you and the people around you. Rebellion Zones force you to break the habit of external reassurance-seeking and start cultivating internal stability—trusting that your relationships aren't as fragile as your brain makes them seem.

Why You Need This: To stop overanalyzing every interaction and start trusting that you are secure without constant confirmation.

How To Approach This Rebellion Zone:

- **Observe** how often you feel the urge to ask for reassurance or check in on someone's mood.

- **Notice** how your Brain Pattern convinces you that uncertainty means rejection.

- **Remind yourself** that people's emotions and reactions are not always about you.

- **Challenge yourself** to sit with discomfort of the unknown instead of immediately seeking validation.

The Self-Fulfilling Prophecy: By constantly needing reassurance, you create exhaustion in relationships, reinforcing the belief that people eventually pull away from you.

4. You Stop Equating Speed with Security in Relationships

You dive headfirst into new friendships or relationships, assuming that the faster the connection forms, the more secure it will be. You overshare, push for closeness, and assume that if someone doesn't match your energy immediately, they must not care. But real connection isn't built overnight—it's built through consistency. Rebellion Zones challenge you to slow down and build relationships at a sustainable pace, rather than forcing instant attachment out of fear.

Why You Need This: To stop mistaking rapid connection for real depth and start creating relationships that last.

How To Approach This Rebellion Zone:

- **Observe** how quickly you feel the need to push for deeper connection.

- **Notice** how your Brain Pattern convinces you that slowness means disinterest.

- **Remind yourself** that real bonds take time, and forcing closeness often backfires.

- **Challenge yourself** to let a relationship unfold naturally without accelerating it.

The Self-Fulfilling Prophecy: By pushing too hard too fast, you overwhelm others—reinforcing the belief that people always pull away from you.

5. You Let Go of Relationships That Aren't Built on Reciprocity

You give endlessly—your time, energy, support—assuming that if you just do enough, people will mirror your effort. When they don't, you feel hurt, invisible, or unworthy. But sometimes, it's not about you. Some people simply won't meet you at your level, and that's not a reflection of your worth. Rebellion Zones force you to stop over-giving to prove your value and start recognizing when it's time to redirect your energy.

Why You Need This: To stop measuring your worth by how much effort you put in and start recognizing when to let go.

How To Approach This Rebellion Zone:

- **Observe** how often you give more than you receive in relationships.

- **Notice** how your Brain Pattern convinces you that effort equals worthiness.

- **Remind yourself** that people show up for relationships in different ways—and some simply aren't as invested.

- **Challenge yourself** to match someone's energy instead of always exceeding it.

The Self-Fulfilling Prophecy: By refusing to acknowledge when people aren't reciprocating, you keep yourself in one-sided relationships, reinforcing the belief that you have to earn love.

Rebellion Zones

1. Allowing Silence Instead of Over-Communicating

Self-Deception at Play: You tell yourself that communication keeps relationships healthy—but in reality, you're over-explaining, overreaching, or trying to maintain connection even when it's not needed. You fill the gaps with messages, follow-ups, or emotional check-ins, not because something is wrong, but because silence feels threatening.

Unconscious Motivation: Secure a sense of belonging by constantly managing how others experience you—if there's silence, your brain interprets it as disconnection or disapproval. Talking becomes a way to earn love and approval by staying visible, helpful, or emotionally available at all times.

Rebellion Zone: When a conversation naturally ends, let it end—without extending it, following up, or trying to "fix" any perceived gaps.

Why This Works: Your subconscious tells you that if you aren't actively maintaining connection, it will disappear. You assume that if people aren't engaging with you frequently, they must be pulling away. By learning to sit with silence and let relationships breathe, you train your brain to see that connection doesn't require constant maintenance.

How This Plays Out in Real Life:

- You send follow-up texts after conversations to clarify, soften, or reaffirm what was said.

- You feel anxious when a thread dies down and restart it just to make sure the person isn't upset or drifting.

- You extend conversations past their natural endpoint out of fear that ending it too soon will make you seem cold or disinterested.

- You interpret someone's slow response or short reply as disapproval and immediately try to "win them back" with more energy or warmth.

- You replay your tone, wording, or punctuation, wondering if you unintentionally caused a disconnect.

- You feel responsible for managing the emotional tone of every exchange—even when no one asked you to.

- Over time, this leads to burnout, misread situations, and feeling like you're always giving more than you're receiving.

The Challenge: Let Conversations End Naturally

- If you feel the urge to send another text just to keep the conversation going, stop.

- If someone doesn't respond right away, challenge yourself to wait instead of double-texting.

- If you assume space means disinterest, remind yourself: People don't need constant interaction to care about you.

- If you over-explain, challenge yourself to say less and let people interpret things on their own.

2. Letting People Initiate Instead of Always Making the First Move

Self-Deception at Play: You tell yourself you're just proactive or good at staying connected—but underneath that effort is fear. You overextend, constantly check in, and make the first move to avoid being left out or forgotten. You convince yourself you're keeping the relationship alive, but it's really about preventing the silence that might confirm your worst fear: that you're not wanted unless you're useful.

Unconscious Motivation: Prevent feelings of rejection by staying one step ahead of potential disconnection. Constant initiation becomes a form of control that masks your deeper fear: that if you stop trying, no one will choose you on their own.

Rebellion Zone: Stop initiating and let people show up for you instead.

Why This Works: Your subconscious tells you that if you don't reach out, you will be forgotten. You assume that relationships are only maintained through constant effort on your part. But by allowing others to initiate, you prove to your brain that you are valued without needing to chase connection.

How This Plays Out in Real Life:

- You're always the one texting first, organizing meetups, or checking in—even when others don't reciprocate.

- You tell yourself, "That's just who I am," but secretly feel drained and underappreciated.

- You experience anxiety when no one reaches out, assuming people are losing interest or don't value you.

- When you experiment with pulling back, you obsessively

monitor whether anyone notices or makes a move toward you.

- You feel pressure to keep conversations alive or to "prove" your worth by being available and attentive.

- You overextend yourself socially, fearing that if you stop trying, you'll be excluded or forgotten.

- Over time, you begin to resent others for not matching your energy, while still convincing yourself that their approval is necessary to feel secure.

The Challenge: Give Others a Chance to Reach Out

- If you always initiate plans, step back and see who reaches out first.

- If you assume people will forget about you if you don't check in, challenge that belief by waiting.

- If you feel anxious when a conversation fades, let it fade and see what happens.

3. Being Honest Instead of Over-Adapting

Self-Deception at Play: You convince yourself that you're just easygoing, adaptable, or "reading the room." But in reality, you're shape-shifting—mirroring others, downplaying your own opinions, and avoiding anything that could create friction. You agree to things you don't want or stay quiet to avoid standing out, believing it's the only way to stay included.

Unconscious Motivation: Earn love and secure belonging by becoming who others want you to be. Over-adapting helps you feel accepted in the short term, but it disconnects you from your true self and reinforces the belief that authenticity is a liability, not an asset.

Rebellion Zone: Express your real preferences, opinions, and interests, even if they don't match the group.

Why This Works: Your subconscious tells you that being different is risky, that sameness equals safety. You assume that if you don't adapt to others, you might be excluded. By choosing to hold your identity instead of adjusting to fit in, you train your brain to see that authenticity leads to deeper, more meaningful relationships.

How This Plays Out in Real Life:

- You downplay your preferences or stay neutral when asked for your opinion, even if you feel strongly about something.

- You agree with people even when you internally disagree, fearing that honesty will lead to conflict or disconnection.

- You mirror others' energy, language, or interests to feel aligned—even if it means hiding parts of yourself.

- You suppress quirks, values, or boundaries that might "rock the boat" or make you seem different.

- You over-analyze how you're being perceived and adjust in real time to stay likable or low-maintenance.

- You feel emotionally exhausted or unseen in group settings, but chalk it up to needing "alone time" rather than recognizing the cost of inauthenticity.

- Over time, you lose clarity on what you actually want, like, or need—because you're so used to shapeshifting for connection.

The Challenge: Show Up as Yourself, Not as Who You Think They Want

- If you usually agree just to avoid conflict, speak your actual opinion.

- If you feel the urge to mirror someone's interests, pause. Stick to your own preferences.

- If you fear being different, remind yourself: People connect through honesty, not just through sameness.

4. Accepting Boundaries Without Seeing Them as Rejection

Self-Deception at Play: You take boundaries personally—assuming they mean you've done something wrong or that you're being pushed away. You struggle to accept space without interpreting it as disapproval. In response, you apologize excessively, over-explain, or try to fix the situation in hopes of restoring connection immediately.

Unconscious Motivation: Avoid feelings of shame or unworthiness by seeking constant reassurance. You try to fix it through apology, overexplaining, or increased effort, hoping to win back approval and reestablish connection before rejection can set in.

Rebellion Zone: When someone sets a boundary, respect it without trying to negotiate, apologize, or overcompensate.

Why This Works: Your subconscious tells you that if someone asks for space, it must mean they don't like you anymore. You assume that distance equals disapproval. But by allowing people to have their own limits without internalizing them, you retrain your brain to stop equating space with exclusion.

How This Plays Out in Real Life:

- When someone asks for space, you feel instantly anxious or ashamed, assuming it's about you.

- You try to fix the discomfort by over-apologizing, offering to change, or seeking clarity that goes beyond what's needed.

- You interpret healthy boundaries as coldness, distance, or punishment.

- You mentally spiral, wondering what you did wrong or how you came across, even if the boundary was expressed kindly.

- You try to re-engage too quickly, reaching out or softening the boundary in hopes of restoring closeness.

- You struggle to give others space without secretly resenting them or fearing abandonment.

- Over time, this creates a pattern where others feel smothered or misunderstood, and you feel like you're walking on eggshells to avoid being shut out.

The Challenge: Allow Boundaries Without Emotional Panic

- If someone says they need time, don't follow up or check in. Let them come back when they're ready.

- If a person says no to plans, don't assume they don't want to see you.

- If you feel hurt by a boundary, *ask yourself*: is this actually about me, or am I making it personal?

Why This Works: Your subconscious tells you that if you invest in people, they should invest in you equally. If they don't, you assume you are being taken advantage of or they don't really care. But by detaching your worth from other people's responses, you free yourself from resentment and exhaustion.

How This Plays Out in Real Life:

- You go out of your way for others, but feel hurt when they don't reciprocate in the same way or with the same energy.

- You convince yourself you're giving freely, but you're secretly keeping mental tallies of how much you've done.

- You interpret unmet expectations as signs that others don't value you, even if you never expressed what you wanted.

- You withdraw or become passive-aggressive when someone doesn't show up the way you hoped.

- You struggle to say no to requests but grow resentful when your own needs go unnoticed.

- You find yourself stuck in one-sided dynamics, then blame others for not matching your invisible standard.

- Over time, you feel emotionally depleted and unappreciated, but continue to overextend in hopes that someone will finally "prove" your value.

The Challenge: Give Without Expecting Immediate Return

- If you feel hurt that someone isn't matching your effort, pause. *Ask yourself*: Am I giving because I want to—or because I expect something back?

- If you assume imbalance means rejection, remind yourself: people express care in different ways.

- If you catch yourself mentally keeping track of who does what, stop.

By giving freely instead of seeking equal return, you disrupt the belief that love and friendship must always be measured to be real.

What Do You Gain by Embracing Your Rebellion Zones?

Rebellion Zones force you to break the cycle of over-performing and experience what happens when you stop proving, stop chasing, and allow the truth to unfold instead.

1. You Discover That You Are Lovable Without Over-Giving

You assume that if you aren't constantly accommodating, people won't choose you. You believe that love is a transaction. You give endlessly so that people won't leave. Rebellion Zones force you to sit in the discomfort of not over-extending yourself and realize that real love doesn't disappear just because you stop proving your value. You gain the ability to experience love that isn't tied to what you do for others, but simply for who you are.

2. You Break Free from the Exhaustion of Constantly Managing Perception

You scan for what people want and adjust accordingly to ensure they like, accept, or validate you. You don't just try to be liked. You try to be exactly what someone else needs so you feel indispensable. Rebellion Zones push you to drop the chameleon act and see what happens when you show up as yourself, without trying to optimize for approval. You gain the relief of knowing that you don't have to be everything for everyone to be worthy of connection.

3. You Learn That Saying "No" Doesn't Make You Unlovable

You struggle to set boundaries because you assume saying no risks rejection or disappointment. You push past your own limits, sacrificing your own needs to keep the peace or maintain relationships. Rebellion Zones teach you to set limits without guilt, knowing that the right people won't leave just because you choose yourself for once. You gain the confidence to prioritize your own needs without feeling like you're risking your relationships.

4. You Attract Relationships That Don't Feel Like Emotional Labor

You are used to relationships where you carry the emotional weight, checking in, making plans, holding space, and doing the work. You assume that if you stop managing everything, the relationship will fall apart. Rebellion Zones force you to step back and see who actually puts in effort when you stop over-functioning. You gain the ability to experience relationships where connection is mutual, not one-sided emotional labor.

5. You Let Go of the Fear That If You Stop Trying, People Will Leave

You assume that love is conditional and that the moment you stop putting in effort, people will pull away. You try to be helpful, available, and agreeable at all times to keep people invested. Rebellion Zones challenge you to test the lie that connection only exists if you are constantly earning it. You realize that real love doesn't vanish the moment you stop over-performing.

6. You Finally Feel Seen Instead of Just Useful

You have spent so much time being helpful, accommodating, and easy to be around that you rarely feel truly known. People love what you do for them, but you don't always feel like they love you for you. Rebellion Zones force you to be present without performing—so you can experience relationships where people actually see and appreciate the real you. You gain the ability to be valued for who you are, not just for what you provide.

The Bottom Line

You spend most of your energy calculating how others see you—what they might be thinking, what you could say to win them over, what you need to do to be enough. You morph, shift, and over-deliver just to make sure you're perceived the right way. But underneath the performance is fear: If I stop showing up this way, they'll leave. You feel exhausted, resentful, and never fully seen.

Your Rebellion Zones challenge the belief that love has to be earned through performance. These targeted interruptions help you stop over-giving in hopes of gaining affection or validation. They break the feedback loop where your worth is tied to how much you do, fix, or give to others.

Your Rebellion Zones will help you:

- Say no without guilt or panic.

- Let people down without catastrophizing the outcome.

- Stop anticipating what others want and start asking what you need.

- Disrupt the belief that love must be proven or secured through sacrifice.

- Notice when you're shape-shifting to be liked instead of being authentic.

- Allow relationships to deepen without curating every interaction.

- Be consistent—even when you're not being praised or validated.

They prove something different:

- You don't have to keep performing for love—real connection doesn't require a costume.

- You are allowed to take up space without earning it.

- You don't have to carry the emotional weight of every room to feel secure.

For the first time, you'll begin to experience love that isn't transactional. Not because you perfected your performance—but because you were willing to stop performing altogether. Are you ready to be seen without the show?

REJECTION – CONTROL TO RECEIVE LOVE (PEOPLE-PLEASING ISOLATING)

Your brain has spent a lifetime wanting connection while convincing you it's safer to stay invisible. Unlike the engaging conflict-prone type, who pushes for validation through direct confrontation, you take a passive, hesitant approach—opting out, overthinking, and waiting for others to initiate.

You assume rejection is inevitable. You believe that if you were truly wanted, people would seek you out first, include you without prompting, and never require you to assert yourself. Since this rarely happens the way you expect, you withdraw, wait, and tell yourself the right moment will come later, but later never comes.

The moment you read through your Rebellion Zones, your brain will try to convince you that waiting is the smart choice, that you're just being cautious. You'll rationalize silence as patience, opting out as self-respect, and waiting for the perfect moment as just making sure you don't embarrass yourself. But these behaviors often leave you lonely, unseen, and disconnected from the relationships you actually want.

This isn't about forcing you to be loud, pushy, or reckless. What you're here to learn is how to stop filtering every social decision through fear of rejection—how to break the cycle of hesitating, avoiding, and waiting for the right moment that never comes. Focus on seeing the battlefield for what it is without assuming you don't belong in the fight.

Core Motivations:

1. You want connection but it feels safer to stay invisible

You crave meaningful relationships, but you fear that if you initiate, you will be judged, ignored, or subtly excluded. Instead of stepping forward, you wait, hoping others will prove your place before you take the risk.

2. You avoiding interactions even though if feels lonely

You overthink social situations until the moment passes, convincing yourself that engaging now would be awkward or forced. You assume that unless you are explicitly invited, you aren't really wanted.

3. You try to blend in by taking on the traits of the group

You stay in observation mode to see what traits the group rewards. You believe you have to figure out how to present yourself to be included rather than just be yourself.

4. You fear small talk, even though it can be a stepping stone to deeper connection

You struggle with surface-level interactions, worrying you'll run out of things to say, come across as awkward, or fail to connect in a meaningful way. This leads to avoiding conversations entirely instead of pushing through the discomfort.

5. You withholding bold opinions or radical honesty

You assume that if you speak up it could upset others and get them to turn on you. So you default to passivity in conversations, letting others lead and hoping you don't say something "wrong."

6. You try to keep social interactions short even though you want to stay

You find yourself justifying leaving events, conversations, or group settings early. You assume that people wouldn't notice your absence or that you might overstay your welcome.

7. You second guess social moves that others aren't even thinking about

You replay interactions in your head, analyzing every word and gesture to determine whether you embarrassed yourself, annoyed someone, or were subtly rejected.

8. You observing or think about more than actual participation

You stay on the outskirts, waiting for the right moment to jump in or watching others live their lives. Instead of taking action, you watch from a distance. You convince yourself it wasn't the right time or it isn't something that would go well.

9. You minimize your presence even though part of you wants to be seen

In group settings, you emotionally distance, standing toward the back, avoiding eye contact, keeping your movements small, and not drawing attention to yourself. You secretly hope someone will notice you anyway.

10. You struggle to initiate plans

You hesitate to reach out, assuming that it could be awkward and result in rejection.

11. You avoid attention even if it makes you feel unworthy

You tell yourself you don't want to be the center of attention, but you also don't want to feel invisible. This creates a push-pull dynamic where you long for recognition but actively avoid situations where you might be noticed.

12. You avoid direct rejection by pulling away first

You assume exclusion or rejection is inevitable, so you distance yourself first, removing yourself from friendships, conversations, or groups before anyone has the chance to reject you.

13. You interpret distance or quiet as proof of being unwanted

If someone doesn't respond quickly, invite you to something, or engage as much as you'd like, you take it as confirmation that they don't value you, even if there's no real evidence of exclusion.

14. You withdraw after perceived rejection even if you are misreading the situation

If someone seems less engaged or distracted, you pull away completely, assuming they must not want to interact anymore. Even if they never actually disengaged, your withdrawal becomes a self-fulfilling prophecy.

15. You refuse to ask for inclusion even if you secretly want it

You believe that if you were truly liked, people would naturally seek you out. You wait instead of risking rejection by initiating.

16. You fixate on past interaction even if no one else remembers them

You replay moments where you felt awkward, excluded, or unnoticed, using them as proof that you don't belong or you're just not good at relationship interaction.

17. You hold onto social mistakes even if they were minor or non-existent

You assume that any small mistake—an awkward pause, a joke that didn't land—has permanently changed how people see you, making it harder for you to re-engage.

18. You avoid opportunities even if they would benefit you

You turn down invitations, leadership roles, or social opportunities to prevent the possibility of looking foolish or failing in front of others.

19. You avoid deep relationships even though you crave closeness

You assume that if people knew the real you, they would eventually leave. You keep relationships at a surface level to prevent future pain.

Why Do You Need Rebellion Zones?

Your brain tells you that connection is safest from a distance. You crave meaningful relationships but hesitate to step forward, waiting for others to prove your place before you take the risk. You blend in, avoid drawing attention, and pull away the moment you sense rejection—even if it's not real.

The problem is, this strategy doesn't protect you. It just ensures that you stay stuck—isolated, unseen, and waiting for something that never comes. Rebellion Zones force you to stop waiting and start participating. They challenge you to step into social discomfort and risk being known, so you can finally experience connection instead of just observing it.

1. You Stop Waiting to Be Chosen and Start Taking Up Space

You believe that if you truly mattered, people would naturally seek you out. You hesitate to join conversations, waiting for an invitation that never comes. Rebellion Zones challenge you to step forward, even when no one explicitly asks.

Why You Need This: To stop assuming that if you aren't directly included, you aren't wanted.

How To Approach This Rebellion Zone:

- **Observe** the hesitation that arises before speaking, joining, or engaging.

- **Notice** how your Brain Pattern tells you to wait for proof that you belong. You often miss critical moments to participate.

- **Remind yourself** that most people aren't actively excluding you. They're just focused on their own experience. Other Brain Pattern types will just jump in or invite themselves without waiting and so can you.

- **Challenge yourself** to jump in without waiting to feel comfortable or confident.

The Self-Fulfilling Prophecy: By always waiting for others to make the first move, you ensure that you remain unseen, reinforcing the belief that you don't matter.

2. You Challenge Your Fear of Small Talk as a First Step to Connection

You fear surface-level conversation. It feels fake, forced, and pointless. But by avoiding small talk, you also avoid the pathway to deeper relationships. Rebellion Zones force you to engage, even when it feels uncomfortable—so you can build real connections instead of opting out.

Why You Need This: To stop using discomfort as an excuse to avoid people entirely.

How To Approach This Rebellion Zone:

- **Observe** your impulse to disengage when a conversation feels "shallow" or "annoying."

- **Notice** how your Brain Pattern tells you that small talk isn't worth it.

- **Remind yourself** that deeper relationships start with casual interactions that build over time. This is an unavoidable step of relationship building.

- **Challenge yourself** to stay in the conversation just a little longer and ask questions about the other person. Think of this as practice in relationship-building.

The Self-Fulfilling Prophecy: By avoiding small talk, you prevent relationships from forming, keeping you in a cycle of isolation while convincing yourself that connection isn't possible.

3. You Speak Up Instead of Letting Conversations Happen Around You

You default to the background, letting others lead the conversation while you observe. You assume that if you say the wrong thing, people will turn on you or judge you. Rebellion Zones push you to test this assumption by expressing your thoughts, instead of filtering yourself.

Why You Need This: To stop assuming that silence keeps you safe when it actually keeps you unseen.

How To Approach This Rebellion Zone:

- **Observe** how your Brain Pattern tricks you into hesitating before sharing an idea or opinion.

- **Notice** how your Brain Pattern tells you that it's safer to stay quiet or the moment has passed.

- **Remind yourself** that your thoughts and opinions need to be brought out into the physical world.

- **Challenge yourself** to contribute at least once in every group interaction. Let go of the desire to find the right moment and just seize the exact opportunity when you notice.

The Self-Fulfilling Prophecy: By staying quiet, you prevent people from knowing who you are.

4. You Stop Avoiding Attention Just Because It Feels Unfamiliar

You assume that staying out of the spotlight is the best way to avoid rejection. But by constantly minimizing yourself, you reinforce the idea that you shouldn't be seen. Rebellion Zones push you to sit with the discomfort of visibility—so you can finally start feeling worthy of being noticed.

Why You Need This: To break the habit of hiding from opportunities that could actually bring you closer to the life you want.

How To Approach This Rebellion Zone:

- **Observe** how you physically or emotionally avoid in group settings.

- **Notice** how your Brain Pattern tells you that being seen is a risk rather than an opportunity to connect and build with others.

- **Remind yourself** that avoiding attention robs you of opportunities and momentum you actually crave in life.

- **Challenge yourself** to pick a central location, stand with your posture open and shoulders tall and embrace small opportunities for conversation.

The Self-Fulfilling Prophecy: By constantly avoiding attention, you reinforce the belief that you should be overlooked, making it impossible to ever feel truly included.

5. You Stop Interpreting Distance as Rejection

If someone doesn't reply immediately, if a friend doesn't invite you to something, or if people seem distracted, you assume you've been quietly rejected. Instead of waiting for confirmation, you preemptively pull away—removing yourself before you can be hurt. Rebellion Zones force you to stay, even when your brain is screaming at you to retreat.

Why You Need This: To stop creating distance where there may not have been any if you let it unfold.

How To Approach This Rebellion Zone:

- **Observe** the moment your brain starts assuming rejection and justifying pulling away.

- **Notice** how your Brain Pattern urges you to disengage before it gets worse or you feel more embarrassed.

- **Remind yourself** that most people are distracted, not deliberately pushing you away.

    Challenge yourself to hold steady. Resist the urge to disconnect at the first sign of uncertainty. *Ask yourself*:

    Do I historically interpret delayed responses or silence as rejection or a let down?

    Is it common for my Brain Pattern to then justify pulling away to save myself the embarrassment?

    When I pull away from someone who wasn't even aware of the perceived let down, don't I look like an emotionally immature person?

Is that the reputation I want to build for myself in relationships?

The Self-Fulfilling Prophecy: By pulling away too soon, you actually cause the distance you feared—proving to yourself (incorrectly) that you weren't wanted in the first place.

6. You Take Initiative Instead of Waiting for Others to Include You

You assume that if people really wanted to connect with you, they would reach out first. Because of this, you hesitate to initiate plans, assuming it would be awkward or one-sided. Rebellion Zones force you to challenge this assumption by stepping forward instead of waiting.

Why You Need This: To stop equating waiting with proof of worth. In reality, most people are just caught up in their own lives.

How To Approach This Rebellion Zone:

- **Observe** how often you wish someone would invite you, but refuse to initiate yourself.

- **Notice** how your Brain Pattern convinces you that reaching out would be weird or unwelcome.

- **Remind yourself** that some events or get togethers happen organically by people opting in or inviting themselves. If you act distant and aren't around as often, it may seem like you aren't included.

- Challenge yourself to ask if you can join or participate when you hear about an event. Say this:

    "I realized I'm not as much a part of the group as I'd like to be, and it can seem like I'm busy doing my own thing."

    "I've been trying to work on this behavior and reach out more."

    "I'd love to come to _____ if there is room."

The Self-Fulfilling Prophecy: By never initiating, you convince yourself that people don't actually want you around. They might just be assuming the same thing about you.

Rebellion Zones

When you read through your Rebellion Zones, your brain will try to convince you that avoiding attention keeps you safe, that waiting to be included is better than risking rejection, and that keeping quiet helps you blend in. These behaviors don't protect you—they keep you trapped, unseen, and disconnected.

But let's be clear: this isn't about forcing yourself into the spotlight or pretending to be someone you're not. What you're here to learn is how to stop waiting for permission to participate, stop assuming exclusion before it happens, and stop pulling away at the first sign of discomfort.

1. Stepping Into Conversations Instead of Watching from the Sidelines

Self-Deception at Play: Telling yourself you're just observing, being polite, or waiting for a better time—when in reality, you're holding back because you fear being unwelcome, irrelevant, or a burden to the group.

Rebellion Zone: If a conversation interests you, jump in without waiting for the perfect moment. Even if it feels unnatural, push through the discomfort and contribute.

Unconscious Motivation: Avoid the pain of feeling uninvited or overlooked by staying invisible unless clearly invited in. Remaining on the sidelines allows you to preserve the illusion that you're being kind, non-intrusive, or easygoing—while protecting yourself from the risk of social rejection or emotional exposure.

Why This Works: Your subconscious tells you that if you don't immediately belong, you shouldn't try at all. You assume that if people don't pull you in, they must not want you in the group. By inserting yourself, you prove to your brain that most social interactions are open, flexible, and waiting for you to engage.

How This Plays Out in Real Life:

- You hang back quietly in group conversations, waiting for someone to ask your opinion or give you permission to speak.

- You feel left out or unseen but tell yourself that you're just "happy to listen."

- You notice moments where you could contribute, but talk yourself out of it with thoughts like "That would sound dumb," or "It's too late now."

- You later regret not participating and replay the conversation, wishing you had spoken up.

- You convince yourself that being invisible is safer, even though it leaves you feeling disconnected or emotionally isolated.

- You assume your silence protects others from discomfort, when in truth it prevents you from being known and deepening connection.

- Over time, this creates a self-fulfilling belief that people don't care about what you think—because you never give them the chance to know it.

The Challenge: Speak Up Before You Talk Yourself Out of It

- If you feel hesitant, remind yourself: overthinking what I'm going to say is making me hesitate.

- If you think, I should wait for an opening, don't. Take the next available pause and ask a simple question.

- Think of this as practice. Remind yourself that you couldn't ride a two-wheel bicycle the first time. You'll need to have some awkward moments before inserting yourself into conversations feels more comfortable. *Ask yourself*:

> Do I tend to get home from an outing or event and dwell on all of the things I wanted to say but didn't?

> Do I historically ruminate on missed opportunities that lead me to feel hopeless?

> If I keep waiting for the "right moment" in conversations won't I perpetuate this cycle?

> Can I challenge myself to practice and not take each interaction so seriously?

> Can I go practice at a coffee shop or community-focused activity outside of my typical group so I can take the pressure off?

2. Allowing Yourself to Be Seen Without Shrinking

Self-Deception at Play: Minimizing your presence to avoid judgment, rejection, or the pressure of sustaining connection—while convincing yourself you're simply being respectful, non-intrusive, or "not needing attention."

Unconscious Motivation: Protect yourself from the perceived risk that being noticed will lead to criticism, disapproval, or rejection. Shrinking allows you to stay in the background where you feel less exposed.

Rebellion Zone: Place yourself in the middle of the group, not the edges. Keep your posture open, make eye contact, and allow yourself to be visible—without immediately looking for an exit.

Why This Works: Your brain tells you that avoiding attention keeps you safe, but it also keeps you excluded. By intentionally allowing yourself to be noticed, you train your brain to stop equating visibility with vulnerability.

How This Plays Out in Real Life:

- You walk into a room and immediately look for a low-traffic spot—corners, side chairs, or seats that feel "out of the way."

- You fold your arms, look down, or keep your phone out as a barrier to avoid eye contact or engagement.

- You speak quietly, limit self-expression, or nod along instead of offering your own opinions or ideas.

- You feel more comfortable serving or supporting than being in the spotlight, even if you have something meaningful to share.

- You avoid being the first to speak, volunteer, or step forward—even when you're qualified or interested.

- You tell yourself "I don't want to take up too much space," but feel quietly hurt when no one notices you.

- Over time, this habit reinforces the belief that people don't value or include you—when in reality, they've never had the chance to see the real you.

3. Initiating Plans Instead of Waiting for an Invite

Self-Deception at Play: Assuming that if people wanted to include you, they would have already invited you, assuming that everyone was invited rather than opted in themselves.

Unconscious Motivation: Seek proof of your worth through unsolicited inclusion. Initiating plans feels vulnerable because it risks confirming your fear that people don't actually want you around.

Rebellion Zone: Reach out. If you want to spend time with someone, invite them. If you overhear plans, ask if you can join.

Why This Works: Your subconscious tells you that if they wanted you there, they would have asked. By initiating, you disrupt the belief that inclusion has to be proven before you can participate.

How This Plays Out in Real Life:

- You hear a group talking about weekend plans and immediately assume you weren't invited because they don't value you. You retreat, withdraw, and let resentment simmer.

- When a friend posts about a dinner you weren't part of, you spiral into self-doubt, comparing yourself to others and wondering what's wrong with you.

- Instead of asking someone to grab lunch or go for a walk, you wait for them to reach out—and then interpret their silence as confirmation that you don't matter.

- You tell yourself you're "low maintenance" or "just go with the flow," but really, you're avoiding the risk of being turned down.

The Challenge: Stop Expecting Inclusion Without Effort

- If you find out about plans you want to be a part of, challenge yourself to ask—instead of assuming exclusion.

- If you feel awkward or scared, remind yourself: people don't always think to include others. It doesn't mean they don't want you there.

4. Staying in the Moment Instead of Overanalyzing It

Self-Deception at Play: Replaying social interactions in your mind, assuming you embarrassed yourself or made a mistake.

Unconscious Motivation: Analyze every interaction afterward to course-correct or prevent rejection before it happens. Rumination becomes your way of trying to maintain connection—by obsessively reviewing whether you "got it right."

Rebellion Zone: When you catch yourself analyzing an interaction, redirect your focus to the present.

Why This Works: Your subconscious tells you that overanalyzing prevents future mistakes, but it actually keeps you stuck in self-doubt. By choosing to let go of minor social missteps, you train your brain to move forward instead of ruminating.

How This Plays Out in Real Life:

- You finish a conversation and instantly start wondering if your laugh was too loud or if you overshared.

- You send a text and then read it over five times, questioning every word choice.

- You replay a group interaction in your head all night, trying to decode everyone's body language and wondering if they secretly didn't like you.

- Instead of enjoying the moment, you mentally exit and start monitoring yourself from a third-person perspective, trying to predict others' reactions in real time.

- After social events, you isolate or withdraw because your brain tells you that you "probably said something dumb."

The Challenge: Stop Reliving Every Social Moment

- If you catch yourself replaying an interaction, stop and ask:

Am I likely to replay this with a negative lens?

Do I tend to focus on the worst case and use it as justification to pull away or retreat?

- If you assume people are thinking about your awkward moment, remind yourself: they aren't. They are likely focused on themselves.

- If you feel embarrassed, redirect your focus to a task or something physically engaging instead of mentally spiraling.

5. Asking for Clarity Instead of Assuming the Worst

Self-Deception at Play: Taking someone's slow response, distracted behavior, or emotional distance as proof that they don't like you.

Unconscious Motivation: Avoid the sting of rejection by preemptively pulling away, giving you a false sense of control. You'd rather create a story that protects you than risk hearing something painful—even if the story is wrong.

Rebellion Zone: If you feel ignored or excluded, ask a clarifying question. Before justifying pulling away, see if there is an alternate explanation.

Why This Works: Your subconscious tells you that distance equals disinterest. But in reality, most people have lives, distractions, and reasons unrelated to you. By asking instead of assuming, you challenge the belief that silence is rejection.

How This Plays Out in Real Life:

- Your friend doesn't respond to your message for a few hours, so you assume they're mad at you and stop reaching out.

- Someone seems quiet or distracted during a conversation, and you instantly think, "They're annoyed with me," and go silent.

- Your partner pulls back emotionally for a day or two, and you spiral into old narratives—questioning your worth or assuming the relationship is falling apart.

- Instead of checking in, you retreat and then later say, "I just figured you didn't want to talk to me."

- You treat discomfort like proof instead of a cue to ask a question—and the result is chronic disconnection.

The Challenge: Seek Clarity Before Reacting

- If someone takes longer to reply than usual, assume they're busy. They're not avoiding you. Give them the benefit of the doubt first.

- If you feel excluded, ask a clarifying question. Say this:

  "Hey, I just wanted to reach out. I know I can sometimes misinterpret things (or take things personally) so I just wanted to get some insight from you."

- Don't say:

  "Hey, you didn't call me back this week. Are you mad at me?"

  "Hey, I'm feeling hurt and I want to know why you didn't call me back?"

6. Accepting That Relationships Grow Through Consistency, Not Just Big Moments

Self-Deception at Play: You believe that strong connections should feel immediate and intense. If there's no instant spark or vulnerability, you assume it's not a real connection.

Unconscious Motivation: Desire to bypass the risk of slow, uncertain connection by skipping straight to emotional depth. Instant intimacy feels safer than the unpredictability of long-term investment. If it starts fast and feels intense, it reassures you that it's real.

Rebellion Zone: Instead of waiting for a perfect friendship or social experience, commit to small, repeated interactions.

Why This Works: Your subconscious tells you that if a connection doesn't feel instant or deep, it isn't real. But in reality, relationships grow through repeated exposure.

How This Plays Out in Real Life:

- You meet someone new, have one good conversation, then feel let down when the next interaction doesn't match the initial intensity.

- You pull away from friends who don't "get deep" fast enough or assume someone isn't a real friend if they don't text you daily.

- You ghost people after one lukewarm hangout, believing that if it didn't click immediately, it never will.

• You wait for someone to make a grand gesture before investing any real effort, telling yourself, "If they wanted to be close, they'd show it."

• You feel resentful when others maintain long-standing friendships while yours feel short-lived or surface-level—without realizing you never let consistency do its job.

The Challenge: Invest in Consistency Over Grand Gestures

• If a conversation feels surface-level, remind yourself that depth takes time.

• If you don't feel instantly connected, resist the urge to disengage or move onto the next without letting it play out naturally.

• If you think, This isn't my group, challenge yourself to keep showing up. Be sure that it isn't simply a pattern of opting out or justifying disengagement.

What You Gain by Embracing Rebellion Zones

Rebellion Zones force you to stop waiting in the shadows, hoping someone will finally see you. They challenge you to take up space, initiate connection, and break the cycle of retreating before rejection ever happens. Instead of assuming you're unwelcome, you start stepping into opportunities. You can finally experience connection rather than just imagining it.

1. You Learn That Being Unnoticed Isn't the Same as Being Unwanted

You assume that if no one directly invites or includes you, it means they don't want you around.

Instead of joining in, you stay back, waiting for confirmation that never comes. Rebellion Zones challenge you to stop mistaking neutrality for exclusion and start participating, even when no one explicitly asks. You gain the ability to engage without waiting for permission, realizing most people are just caught up in their own world—not actively pushing you out.

2. You Stop Letting Silence Turn Into a Self-Fulfilling Prophecy

If someone doesn't respond quickly, invite you to something, or engage as much as you'd like, you take it as confirmation that you aren't valued. You pull away before they can reject you—ensuring the very disconnection you feared. Rebellion Zones force you to stay instead of assuming the worst, giving relationships a real chance instead of sabotaging them preemptively. You let interactions unfold naturally without assuming silence means you've been dismissed.

3. You Realize That Observation Isn't the Same as Participation

You linger on the outskirts, watching others engage instead of joining in. You assume that unless you're directly invited, you aren't really wanted. You stay in observer mode, convincing yourself it wasn't the right time. Rebellion Zones push you to shift from watching life happen to actually taking part in it. You feel present and involved instead of just analyzing social dynamics from a distance.

4. You Stop Shrinking Yourself Just to Feel Safe

You minimize your presence, standing in the background, avoiding eye contact, and keeping your movements small. You want to be noticed—but not too much. You want to be included—but not at the risk of standing out. Rebellion Zones challenge you to stop making yourself invisible just because attention feels uncomfortable. You gain the ability to take up space without assuming it's a risk or an inconvenience to others.

5. You Learn That Small Talk is a Bridge, Not a Barrier

You hate small talk, seeing it as forced, awkward, or pointless. But by avoiding it, you also avoid the pathway to deeper relationships—convincing yourself of a connection isn't possible when you've never actually taken the first step. Rebellion Zones push you to stay in the moment, engage, and allow conversations to develop naturally. You're able to build connection over time instead of dismissing it before it even starts.

6. You Stop Letting Overthinking Kill Your Momentum

You replay social interactions, overanalyzing every word, gesture, or glance. You assume you must have embarrassed yourself, annoyed someone, or been subtly rejected—even when no one else remembers the moment. Rebellion Zones challenge you to recognize that your internal scrutiny isn't reality—it's just your brain running a fear-based script. You move forward without letting imaginary rejection dictate your next move.

7. You Start Taking Initiative Instead of Hoping Someone Will Pull You In

You assume that if people really wanted you around, they would reach out first. But instead of asking to join, you sit back–letting distance form while telling yourself it's proof that you weren't wanted. Rebellion Zones push you to take social risks, extend invitations, and stop waiting for proof of belonging before you step in. You're able to create connection instead of waiting for it to magically happen.

8. You Stop Avoiding Relationships Just Because They Feel Risky

You crave deep connections but keep people at arm's length, fearing that if they really knew you, they'd eventually leave. Instead of opening up, you settle for surface-level interactions–keeping yourself safe but never fully seen. Rebellion Zones challenge you to test this assumption, allowing people to get to know the real you. You gain the ability to experience genuine closeness instead of keeping relationships at a distance to avoid disappointment.

Bottom Line

Your Brain Pattern tells you that the safest way to move through life is to watch instead of participate: stepping forward seems dangerous. Speaking up feels like a risk. Being seen feels like something you should avoid.

But here's the truth: hiding doesn't protect you. It just ensures you stay unseen, unheard, and disconnected.

Rebellion Zones force you to test reality instead of trusting your fears. They push you to see what happens when you step forward instead of waiting. They challenge you to let people know you exist–so you can finally experience the connection you've been craving.

Your challenge is clear: Stop shrinking. Stop waiting. Stop assuming exclusion. Take the risk. Step forward. And see who's been waiting for you this entire time.

Your Rebellion Zones will help you:

• Recognize when you are opting out because of fear rather than actual exclusion.

- Break the habit of waiting for the "perfect" moment and engage in real time.

- Disrupt the belief that if people wanted you, they would make the first move.

- Push through discomfort instead of retreating into overthinking.

- Test the idea that neutrality isn't rejection—it's just space.

- Stop assuming that your presence must be earned through perfection or external validation.

- Take up space without constantly scanning for negative reactions.

Your biggest challenge will be facing the discomfort of showing up before you feel 100 percent ready. Right now, you only engage when you feel absolutely certain you won't be embarrassed or dismissed. But it's just an excuse your brain uses to keep you from taking risks.

REJECTION - CONTROL TO RECEIVE LOVE (CONFLICT-PRONE ENGAGING)

Your behaviors are shaped by an unconscious desire to secure love, validation, and emotional significance. You take an active, engaged approach, ensuring that you are not ignored or taken advantage of.

You refuse to passively accept rejection. Your brain tells you that love and respect are to be earned. You push interactions to higher emotional stakes, creating tension, questioning intentions, or setting up dynamics that force others to prove their investment in you.

But rather than making you feel secure, this cycle keeps you in a constant state of needing to confirm your place in people's lives. Even when people do care about you, you struggle to trust it. If they seem neutral, passive, or unwilling to meet your needs when they arise, you take it as proof that they don't care and are not truly committed.

This pattern doesn't consciously want conflict—but it is an unfortunate byproduct of the way your assumptions escalate into communication cycles that create volatility.

Core Motivations:

1. You don't want to be overlooked, invalidated or belittled.

You want to ensure that you matter in people's lives—that your presence is respected and taken seriously.

2. You Desire Control Over Emotional Power Dynamics

You are hyper-aware of who holds influence in relationships, doing everything you can to avoid being in a vulnerable position where others have control over you.

3. You Believe That Love Should Be Earned

You assume that if relationships are too relaxed, they must be disengaged. If someone truly values and loves you, they should be willing to prove it through acts of romanticism or grand gestures.

4. You Seek Reassurance That Tends to Generate Conflict

You ask questions, test and assume in a way that creates conflict and tension. You feel the need to seek concrete information to rely on.

5. You Hyper-Focus on Fairness, Loyalty, and Reciprocity

You are constantly tracking who puts in effort, who initiates contact, and who is emotionally invested. If things feel unbalanced, you confront it directly or create situations that force the other person to prove their commitment.

6. You Fear Being Emotionally Outmatched or Controlled

You dislike feeling like someone else has the upper hand in a relationship. You instinctively assert yourself—either through direct confrontation, debate, or taking a dominant role in interactions.

7. You Struggle to Trust Unspoken or Passive Affection

If someone expresses care in a quiet, consistent way, you may question whether they really mean it. You trust active effort, engagement, and passion more than subtlety.

8. You Tend to Interpret Neutrality or Distance as a Threat

If someone pulls back, stops engaging in deep conversations, or doesn't react as emotionally as you do, you assume they are losing interest and are hiding something.

Why Do You Need Rebellion Zones?

Your brain equates conflict with connection. If someone is willing to get to the other side of a conflict with you then they must care. But here's the problem: the love you're fighting for isn't the love you actually want.

Rebellion Zones force you to drop the battle strategy, step back from the need to force connection, and see what happens when you stop controlling love through tension, debate, and power struggles.

1. You Learn That Love Can Exist Without Conflict

Right now, your brain sees intensity as proof of connection. If things are calm, you may start to question someone's motives or become suspicious. Rebellion Zones force you to sit in stillness instead of picking a fight just to feel secure.

Why You Need This: To experience love that isn't built on push-pull dynamics.

How To Approach This Rebellion Zone:

- **Observe** your thought patterns when things feel calm, quiet or even boring.

- **Notice** how your Brain Pattern tries to trick you into seeing it as a sign of something negative.

- **Remind yourself** that other Brain Pattern types prioritize peace and quiet. When this type feels secure, they may become more quiet and "boring."

- **Challenge yourself** to remember that you push and pull to seek reassurance. This dynamic creates volatility that is likely to push away a partner who craves peace and stability.

The Self-Fulfilling Prophecy: By testing and seeking reassurance, you destabilize the relationship and push the other person away. Ultimately, your behavior will generate the very outcome you most want to avoid.

2. You Stop Seeking Reassurance Through Conflict

You may not realize it, but you've come to associate engagement in tension with proof of commitment. Without meaning to, you create friction—through questions, assumptions, or setting up reactions—to feel secure in who will stay, defend themselves, or prove they're invested. Rebellion Zones challenge you to allow people to show up on their own terms, rather than relying on conflict as a test of loyalty.

Why You Need This: To recognize that if the only way to get someone to stay with you is to control and test them - they may not actually be for you.

How To Approach This Rebellion Zone:

- **Observe** your thought patterns. Try to seek reassurance and desire to question or control the other person.

- **Notice** how your Brain Pattern tricks you into seeing them as the enemy or opposition.

- **Remind yourself** that you are assuming the other person isn't trustworthy or capable of staying in love without your manipulation.

- **Challenge yourself** to remember that letting go of the constant control and questions allow the other person to show you who they really are. You're just afraid they won't choose you if they aren't being guided.

The Self-Fulfilling Prophecy: By controlling or manipulating the interaction, you risk keeping people in your life who aren't really emotionally invested and stable.

3. You Break the Cycle of Emotional Exhaustion

Every relationship feels like a battle. Even when things are good, you're scanning for signs of rejection, betrayal, or disengagement. You keep one foot in, one foot out, always ready to fight or walk away or move to a new place. Rebellion Zones force you to stop bracing for impact and let love exist without constant defense mode.

Why You Need This: To learn what it feels like to trust connection without preparing for its collapse.

How To Approach This Rebellion Zone:

- **Observe** your thought patterns when things feel calm, quiet or even boring.

571

- **Notice** how your Brain Pattern tries to scan subtle facial expressions or replay someone's words in your head.

- **Remind yourself** that when you allow yourself to constantly scan for problems, you're likely to let your Brain Pattern weaponize non-issues.

- **Challenge yourself** to pick your battles and hold yourself back for at least 4 hours to see if your perspective has shifted.

The Self-Fulfilling Prophecy: By assuming everything will fall apart or blow up in your face, you likely push the relationship to explode or even move on to a destructive behavior yourself in an effort to prepare for the inevitable.

4. You See Who Actually Wants You—Without Pressure or Force

You assume that if you don't stand up for yourself and make them see your pain, they won't do the right thing. You start fights, create urgency, or force interaction to prove that people still care. Rebellion Zones force you to stop chasing, stop proving, and see who naturally shows up without being pulled into a power struggle.

Why You Need This: To experience relationships that don't require constant effort just to keep them alive.

How To Approach This Rebellion Zone:

- **Observe** your thought patterns. Express feelings and emotions so others can feel sympathy or feel guilty about their actions.

- **Notice** how your Brain Pattern tricks you into immediately aligning with your feelings.

- **Remind yourself** that your Brain Pattern is likely to look for ways to hold others accountable or punish them for the way you feel.

- **Challenge yourself** to remember that your feelings are a byproduct of a distorted lens.

The Self-Fulfilling Prophecy: When you focus on expressing that you've been hurt, you miss a key opportunity to poke holes in the entire cycle of why you feel hurt in the first place.

5. You Learn That Being "Right" Isn't the Same as Being Loved

You spend so much time proving, debating, and defending yourself. Winning the argument doesn't equal winning love. You use emotional intensity in conversations where it feels you are not in alignment. You struggle to see the other person's perspective and interpret it as a direct insult on your character. You look for ways to prove your side of things. Rebellion Zones push you to stop leading with the need to be right and start leading with the need to collaborate and shift perspectives.

Why You Need This: To prioritize collaboration over control.

How To Approach This Rebellion Zone:

- **Observe** that your thought patterns immediately take offense to what the other person is saying. It populates an oppositional narrative.

- **Notice** how your Brain Pattern tricks you into immediately aligning with your own perspective.

- **Remind yourself** that your Brain Pattern is likely to look for ways to push buttons and hit below the belt.

- **Challenge yourself** to remember that there will be important information housed in both perspectives. Your Brain Pattern will trick you into thinking that listening to any of their perspectives is ridiculous.

The Self-Fulfilling Prophecy: When you get retaliatory and combative in the face of argument you miss key opportunities to see the other person's side and deescalate. This prolongs the state of opposition in the relationship ultimately leading to more conflict and the assumption of inevitable opposition.

6. You Finally Get to Experience Love That Feels Like Peace Instead of a Battle

You have never truly experienced love without tension. Even in your happiest moments, there's an underlying anticipation of conflict or rejection. Rebellion Zones help you rewire your nervous system to accept love without needing to disrupt it.

Why You Need This: To finally feel what it's like when love feels steady, safe, and secure—without the constant need to fight for it.

How To Approach This Rebellion Zone:

- **Observe** your Brain Pattern's discomfort with peace and calm.

- **Notice** how your Brain Pattern wants to assume something is wrong or being hidden.

- **Remind yourself** that your Brain Pattern equates the stability of security with a sign of disconnection—not peace.

- **Challenge yourself** to remember you likely have a partner who craves peace and stability. They relax and rest when they feel safe and connected and this isn't a negative sign. It's a sign of commitment and stability.

The Self-Fulfilling Prophecy: Your Brain Pattern weaponizes the state of peace and relaxation that comes when stability is present. It tries to trick you into seeking reassurance that destabilizes the connection and commitment.

Rebellion Zones

The moment you read through your Rebellion Zones, your brain will try to justify your instincts. You'll convince yourself that pushing harder means you care, that if someone truly valued you, they would be willing to engage in intensity, and that conflict is a necessary tool for securing relationships. These behaviors often push people away instead of pulling them closer.

But this isn't about making you passive or forcing you to tolerate neglect. What you're here to learn is how to stop treating every shift in energy, every unread message, or every pause in engagement as proof that you need to fight harder for your place.

1. Allowing Neutrality Instead of Forcing Validation

Self-Deception at Play: You misread neutral social cues as signs of disinterest or rejection. Instead of letting space exist, you push for immediate reassurance—forcing conversation, probing for affirmation, or escalating emotionally just to get a reaction.

Unconscious Motivation: You equate calm, quiet, or neutrality with abandonment. The moment someone seems even slightly distant, your brain fires off alarms—they're mad, pulling away, or done with you. So you try to fix it fast: push the conversation, demand clarity, or stir up conflict just to force engagement.

Rebellion Zone: If someone seems distracted, slow to respond, or less engaged, don't assume it's about you, allow it to exist without forcing clarity.

Why This Works: Your subconscious tells you that if someone isn't actively affirming you, they are disengaging. You assume that neutrality, distance, or delay means rejection. By learning to tolerate space without seeking immediate validation, you train your brain to stop overcompensating for rejection that isn't happening.

How This Plays Out in Real Life:

- You send a message and, when the response is short or delayed, you follow up with emotionally loaded questions like, "Are you mad at me?" or "Did I do something wrong?"

- In person, if someone seems quiet, you start over-talking or pushing deep conversation, even when it's not appropriate.

- If a partner or friend pulls back slightly, you pick a fight just to get a reaction or reestablish intensity.

- You flood the silence with texts, voice memos, or questions to "keep the connection alive," when in reality, it's your panic about perceived rejection doing the talking.

- You confuse emotional neutrality with emotional neglect—and that confusion keeps your relationships in a constant state of tension and repair.

The Challenge: Stop Seeking Immediate Validation

- If you feel uneasy about a shift in energy, remind yourself that your Brain Pattern seeks to create instability when things are calm. Recalibrate peace and calm to stability and commitment in your mind.

- If you want to ask, "Are you mad at me?" or "Is something wrong?" Don't. Remind yourself that when you test or seek reassurance, the person is likely to show signs of frustration that you can misinterpret and weaponize. Focus on a positive distraction and allow the situation to unfold.

- If you assume someone's quietness means they are pulling away, challenge that assumption. Remind yourself that you are likely to attract a partner who wants peace.

- If you feel the need to clarify or defend yourself during or after a conversation, stop.

2. Releasing the Need to Be "Right" Every Interaction

Self-Deception at Play: You frame your emotions and reactions as objective truth—believing that your hurt or perception must be validated for the relationship to feel safe. You fixate on proving your

575

intentions, clarifying your actions, or controlling how others see you.

Unconscious Motivation: Fear that if someone misunderstands you or sees you in a negative light, it means you're not lovable or worthy. Being seen wrong feels like being rejected. So you fight for control—of the story, the conversation, or their perception—because control gives you the illusion of emotional safety.

Rebellion Zone: Let go of the need to win, control, or shape the outcome of every interaction.

Why This Works: Your subconscious tells you that if you don't prove you're right, they will think of you in a negative light. You assume that if people don't see you exactly as you want to be seen, they don't value you. By allowing space for imperfection and disagreement, you prove that love and respect exist when you aren't in control.

How This Plays Out in Real Life:

- You get into an argument and feel compelled to clarify your tone, motives, or intentions—over and over—until the other person agrees with your perspective.

- You over-explain your side of things in texts or conversations, even when the topic is minor, just to make sure your image remains intact.

- You feel deeply unsettled when someone says, "I don't see it that way," and can't let it go until you've convinced them why they should.

- You leave interactions feeling depleted because you're constantly "managing" how others interpret you, even at the cost of connection.

- You avoid silence, disagreement, or unresolved tension by forcing conversations to continue until you feel seen, affirmed, and emotionally clean—believing anything less is rejection.

The Challenge: Choose Connection Over Control

- If you feel the urge to correct someone's perception of you, stop. *Ask yourself*:

    Am I assuming what they think?

    Am I projecting my own fears or insecurities onto others?

    Am I struggling to see their side because of the accountability I'd have to take?

When I get defensive and push to be right, doesn't that actually damage my reputation in the long run?

Can I challenge myself to let this unfold without me pushing to control the narrative?

• If you sense someone pulling away, don't chase. Remind yourself that some people need to process by themselves.

• If you find yourself pushing for a reaction, a response, or a confession, stop. Take radical personal responsibility for your actions. Try these:

"I can see that I'm pushing you and being demanding. I've been trying to work on this and I can see clearly what I'm doing."

"I'm going to walk away from this conversation for a bit and give myself time to reset."

"I am working on trying to trust how things unfold and this is challenging for me."

"I will continue working on letting you share your perspective or answer without getting defensive or retaliatory."

3. Letting Relationships Flow Without Tests of Loyalty

Self-Deception at Play: You create emotional scenarios—intentionally or subconsciously—that require others to prove their loyalty or commitment. You might withdraw, act cold, pick fights, or overwhelm people with intensity to trigger a response. Then you interpret their reaction as proof of whether or not they truly care.

Unconscious Motivation: Create situations that reveal someone's intentions before they have a chance to hurt you. If they pass your test, you feel temporarily safe. If they don't, at least you saw it coming.

Rebellion Zone: Allow people to engage naturally without setting up conditions that force them to prove their investment.

Why This Works: Your subconscious tells you that if you don't test people, you'll never know if they truly care. You assume that if someone doesn't fight for you, they must not value you. But by allowing relationships to unfold naturally, you train your brain to recognize commitment without forcing proof.

How This Plays Out in Real Life:

• You go quiet or pull away without explanation, hoping someone will notice and chase you.

- You escalate a minor disagreement just to see if the person will "fight for you" or check in afterward.

- You make veiled comments like "you probably don't even care" to provoke reassurance or declarations of love.

- You create drama or intensity in relationships because you equate emotional turbulence with passion and loyalty.

- You feel deeply disappointed when someone doesn't pass your "test," even though they didn't know they were being tested in the first place.

The Challenge: Stop Testing, Start Trusting

- If you feel the urge to create distance, stop yourself. Remind yourself you're setting up a game. It's likely to blow up in your face.

- If you notice that you're escalating a conversation that confuses the other person, take radical personal responsibility and give yourself a timeout.

- If you assume a lack of intense emotion means disinterest, remind yourself: Some people

4. Accepting Boundaries Without Seeing Them as Rejection

Self-Deception at Play: You interpret boundaries as exclusion or emotional punishment. Instead of honoring someone's limit, you immediately question it, feel hurt by it, or challenge its fairness. You assume that if a boundary stings, it must be wrong—or worse, that it means the person doesn't value you.

Unconscious Motivation: When someone sets a boundary, it feels like they're creating distance or choosing themselves over you—which your brain reads as rejection. To protect your sense of worth, you fight the boundary or make the other person wrong for setting it. You believe that if someone truly cared, they wouldn't need boundaries with you.

Rebellion Zone: When someone sets a boundary, take it at face value. Don't assume it's a sign they don't care.

Why This Works: Your subconscious tells you that if someone needs space, they are pulling away from you. You assume that a boundary isn't fair or justified if it hurts you. But by respecting someone's request or boundary, you train your brain to stop seeing it as a personal attack worthy of creating conflict.

How This Plays Out in Real Life:

- A friend says they need a night to themselves, and you respond with guilt or passive-aggressive texts, implying they're being selfish or distant.

- Your partner says they don't want to talk about something right now, and you push harder—believing their silence means they don't care.

- Someone asks for a limit (time, energy, space), and you accuse them of being unfair or shutting you out.

- You tell yourself, "If they really loved me, they wouldn't need that boundary," and use your pain as justification to question or punish their decision.

- You demand "equal treatment" or hyper-focus on perceived imbalances in boundaries, without asking whether your emotional response is actually about fear—not fairness.

The Challenge: Allow Boundaries Without Resistance

- If someone asks for something that you don't like, respect it instead of pushing for clarity.

- If a person is slower to engage, don't assume you are being pushed out. Many who are slower to engage do so because they are afraid of being pushed. Ironically, they are trying to avoid the trap you've set in the relationship.

- If you assume distance means disinterest, remind yourself that this is an opportunity for growth. Learning that people can be apart and come back together without control or direction is a pivotal aspect of stable attachment.

5. Seeing Connection Beyond Emotional Intensity

Self-Deception at Play: You confuse emotional highs and lows with relational depth. If things are calm or steady, you feel bored, disconnected, or suspicious. You may stir the pot, revisit old conflicts, or amplify your emotional expression to recreate intensity.

Unconscious Motivation: Intensity feels like proof that someone still cares. When things are too calm, your brain panics—they must be checked out, hiding something, or drifting away.

Rebellion Zone: Choose connection without tension. Allow moments of calm without forcing emotional intensity.

Why This Works: Your subconscious tells you that, if there's no passion, conflict, or heightened emotion, the relationship is fading or something else is going on. You assume that quiet means disinterest and intensity means security. By choosing stability over constant reinforcement, you prove to your brain that real connection exists beyond heightened emotion.

How This Plays Out in Real Life:

- You feel disconnected when there's no deep emotional conversation or visible passion, so you pick a fight or bring up an old issue just to feel something.

- You interpret a calm evening or slow reply as disinterest and start testing your partner to see if they still care.

- You view peaceful relationships as a sign something is wrong or being hidden.

- You associate emotional vulnerability with weakness, so you use anger, sarcasm, or defensiveness to stay in control.

- You hold onto grudges as fuel to keep emotional intensity alive—even when the other person is trying to move forward.

The Challenge: Allow Connection Without Conflict

- If a conversation feels uneventful, challenge your Brain Pattern narrative. Remind yourself it's likely a sign of peace, stability and commitment.

- If you find yourself pushing for an argument or reaction, stop. Take radical personal responsibility for your Brain Pattern behavior. Remind yourself that this doesn't damage your reputation. Try these:

  "I can see that I'm reading into a moment of peace and misinterpreting it."

  "I'm going to give myself time to reset so I don't ruin this moment."

  "I am working on trying to trust how things unfold and this is challenging for me."

  "I know that I often see positive moments as I sign that something is off. I'm actively working on it."

What You Gain By Embracing Rebellion Zones

Rebellion Zones challenge your belief that love must be proven through conflict, emotional intensity, or constant reassurance. They interrupt the drive to test, correct, or chase validation—and show you that connection can be safe, steady, and mutual. When you stop trying to force closeness and start trusting the process of natural connection, relationships become a place to breathe, not perform.

1. You Learn That Calm Isn't a Sign of Rejection

You equate quiet moments with disinterest, assuming that if there's no emotional intensity, something must be wrong. You either stir the pot or pull away, convinced the relationship is fading. Rebellion Zones help you embrace stillness without panic. You learn to feel safe in emotional neutrality and stop mistaking peace for abandonment.

2. You Stop Using Conflict as a Substitute for Closeness

When things feel emotionally distant, you might provoke, escalate, or overexplain to draw someone closer. The goal isn't always clarity—it's reassurance. Rebellion Zones challenge you to let the moment sit without trying to control it. You gain the ability to stay connected without needing drama to prove someone cares.

3. You Let People Engage Without Forcing Loyalty

You test others—going cold, picking fights, or withdrawing—to see if they'll chase you. If they don't react the way you want, you take it as confirmation they never cared. Rebellion Zones teach you to stop creating loyalty tests. You gain trust in the idea that people can show up for you without being cornered or coerced.

4. You Learn That Boundaries Aren't Personal Attacks

You assume that if someone needs space or sets a limit, they're rejecting you. You push back, demand fairness, or make it about your hurt. Rebellion Zones challenge you to accept boundaries as part of healthy relationships, not emotional punishments. You gain the ability to respect others' needs without spiraling into self-doubt or conflict.

5. You Discover That Love Doesn't Require Constant Proof

You feel driven to explain yourself, defend your emotions, or control how others see you—because you think love depends on being understood perfectly. Rebellion Zones interrupt this need to be right. You learn that connection can withstand imperfection and that being loved doesn't require managing every perception.

6. You Stop Mistaking Intensity for Intimacy

You chase emotional extremes, holding onto grudges or creating tension to maintain closeness. You confuse the high of conflict and reconciliation with real depth. Rebellion Zones help you see that intimacy grows through consistency—not chaos. You gain the ability to feel connected without being in crisis.

7. You Build Trust Without Needing to Control the Outcome

You try to steer conversations, correct misunderstandings, and prove your worth in every interaction. Rebellion Zones challenge you to release control and let people form their own opinions. You gain peace in knowing that love doesn't have to be curated—it can be real even when messy or unresolved.

8. You Allow Love to Be Stable, Not Just Intense

You've trained your brain to equate love with effort, tension, and emotional labor. Rebellion Zones retrain that system. You learn to receive love in its quieter forms—presence, consistency, respect—without interpreting it as a lack of interest. You finally experience a kind of love that doesn't require proving, performing, or surviving.

The Bottom Line

For years, you have lived by the belief that if you don't fight for love, you won't have it. You assume that:

- If you don't push, people will leave.

- If you don't test, people won't prove they care.

- If you don't stay in control, you'll be powerless in relationships.

Rebellion Zones prove something different:

- The right people don't need to be tested into loyalty.

- Love that requires constant justification isn't real love.

- You don't have to fight to be seen—you are already worthy of connection.

For the first time in your life, you'll experience relationships that don't need tension to feel real, connection that doesn't require force, and love that exists without struggle.

REJECTION – CONTROL TO RECEIVE LOVE (CONFLICT-PRONE ISOLATING)

Your behaviors are driven by a desire to avoid being seen in an unfavorable light that could lead to embarrassment, ridicule or shame. Unlike the Rejection – Control to Receive Love (People-Pleasing – Isolating), who avoids, holds themselves back, and passively accepts loneliness as their fate, you avoid, hold yourself back, and observe. Instead of accepting disconnection, you analyze, ruminate, and assign blame.

At your core, you fear being misunderstood, embarrassed, or judged. Your brain tells you that people will think you're unworthy or foolish and the idea of putting yourself out there makes you feel exposed.

Rather than engaging directly, you retreat—watching from a distance, replaying interactions, and searching for proof that you've been judged, dismissed, or secretly ridiculed. You construct narratives about what people must think about you, anticipating rejection before it happens. In your mind, the distance between you and others is a calculated retreat to avoid further humiliation or perceived failure.

But instead of making you feel protected, this cycle keeps you isolated and mentally trapped in an endless loop of self-justification and silent resentment. Even when people do care about you, they struggle to reach you because your instinct is to withdraw, assume their kindness is pity, or dismiss connection as temporary and unreliable. You believe love should be clear, undeniable, and freely given. Your instinct to retreat, analyze, and brace for judgment ensures you never truly feel secure.

At its core, this pattern is about avoiding the risk of being seen, misinterpreted, or embarrassed, even if it means sacrificing the connection you deeply crave.

583

Core Motivations:

1. You assume people think negatively about you—even if there's no real evidence.

You read into body language, tone, or social dynamics, assuming that people are judging, dismissing, or working against you. If someone seems neutral or indifferent, your brain interprets it as something being wrong or hidden.

2. You retreat from connection, but your mind turns distance into conflict.

You struggle to sit in stillness. When you withdraw, you don't feel at peace, you feel wronged. Instead of assuming people are just busy or neutral, you build narratives about what they really think of you, fueling resentment and opposition.

3. You crave purpose but sabotage your own momentum.

You want meaning, success, or adventure, but your brain convinces you that each opportunity is flawed, unfair, or doomed from the start. You bounce from career to career, idea to idea, without long-lasting commitment, often because the reality never matches the idealized version you built in your head.

4. You thrive in personal challenges but struggle with group-based commitments.

You're capable of pushing yourself physically, mentally, or professionally when the challenge is yours alone. But the moment anything requires a team, shared goals, or community, your motivation starts to wane. You prefer to operate outside of group dynamics, assuming that involvement will lead to conflict, judgment, or disappointment.

5. You see social dynamics as a battlefield—even when no one is against you.

Your brain scans for opposition, constantly looking for ways you've been slighted or left out. You convince yourself that people have hidden agendas, even when they don't. You fixate on competition, comparison, and injustice—often without direct evidence.

6. You misinterpret neutrality as a personal attack.

When others don't react strongly—whether in conversations, text responses, or professional settings—you assume they're withholding something. Your brain tells you that something is off, even when it's not.

7. You build up expectations in your mind—then tear things apart when reality doesn't match.

You idealize experiences, relationships, or opportunities in the planning stage, but once reality sets in, you find ways to pick them apart. You fixate on what should have happened instead of engaging with what is.

8. You enjoy adventure—but only when done alone.

You're drawn to pushing your own limits, whether through travel, endurance, or skill-based goals. But the moment adventure involves group dynamics or shared decisions, frustration sets in. You struggle to balance personal autonomy with the unpredictability of others.

9. You avoid being in the spotlight—unless it's on your own terms.

You want to be seen for what you're good at, but you don't want unsolicited attention. You fear that if the focus turns on you at the wrong time, you'll feel stupid or inadequate.

10. You dismiss positive feedback and push back against encouragement to lead.

When others recognize your potential or encourage you to step into leadership, your brain immediately rejects it. Instead of seeing it as validation, you assume they're setting you up for failure, overestimating you, or putting you in a position to be criticized. If you're forced into the spotlight, you become frustrated and hyper-aware of every perceived misstep.

11. You resent pressure and obligation—but also refuse to take the small steps toward success.

You dislike feeling forced, expected, or obligated to perform, even when it aligns with something you claim to want. Your brain fixates on the perceived burden of taking action, making even minor steps feel overwhelming. You reject structure, external motivation, and gradual progress—yet feel frustrated when success remains out of reach. Instead of engaging, you ruminate about the unfairness of your position, staying stuck in comparison and self-criticism while avoiding real movement.

12. You sabotage things you were once excited about.

You build anticipation in your mind, only to find ways to ruin the experience for yourself when it actually happens. Whether it's self-sabotaging a relationship, a job, or a personal goal, your brain convinces you that something wasn't right—allowing you to retreat instead of staying engaged.

13. You compare yourself to others to fuel self-criticism.

You look for people to motivate you on social media or in real life but instead of inspiring, it generates comparison and a feeling of frustration at what you don't yet have. Your mind constantly contrasts your life, choices, and achievements with others, not to motivate yourself, but to reinforce why you're behind, why it's unfair, or why it's pointless to try.

14. You want success, but you talk yourself out of stepping into it.

You get stuck in the space between wanting more and dismissing opportunities as flawed or impossible. Your mind tells you that you won't be able to keep up with the pressure or commitment and will probably fail, so why try?

Why Do You Need Rebellion Zones?

Your brain tells you that distance is safer than disappointment. You withdraw, analyze, and assume—convincing yourself that if people truly cared, they would make the effort first. But instead of finding peace in isolation, your mind turns silence into conflict, neutrality into rejection, and absence into proof of disloyalty.

The problem is, this strategy doesn't protect you. It just ensures that you stay stuck—caught in a cycle of waiting, resenting, and avoiding.

Rebellion Zones force you to stop watching from the sidelines and start engaging with reality instead of your assumptions. They challenge you to stop building opposition in your head and see what happens when you step forward instead of pulling away.

1. You Stop Testing Who Cares and Start Taking Ownership of Your Connections

You believe that if people truly valued you, they would notice your absence, chase after you, and fight to keep you close. You pull back to see who reaches out, but when they don't, you take it as proof that you don't matter. Rebellion Zones challenge you to actively participate in relationships instead of testing them from a distance.

Why You Need This: To stop waiting for others to initiate so that you can build real connection.

How To Approach This Rebellion Zone

- **Observe** how often you expect people to prove their care through pursuit, rather than initiating direct conversation.

- **Notice** how your Brain Pattern convinces you to pull away instead of stating what you want.

- **Remind yourself** that healthy relationships require engagement—not silent tests.

- **Challenge yourself** to initiate instead of withdrawing before resentment builds.

The Self-Fulfilling Prophecy: By constantly staying quiet about missed expectations or hurt feelings to see who notices, you ensure that people don't have the chance to show up for you—reinforcing the belief that you aren't valued.

2. You Challenge the Assumption That People Are Against You

You frequently analyze body language, tone, or subtle social cues, searching for signs that you're being judged, dismissed, or disliked. Your brain convinces you that if someone seems indifferent or distracted, they must secretly have an issue with you. Rebellion Zones force you to check your assumptions against reality instead of letting them spiral into unnecessary opposition.

Why You Need This: To stop misinterpreting neutrality as rejection and focus on what's actually happening.

How You Approach This Rebellion Zone:

- **Observe** your instinct to read into tone, expression, or phrasing—assuming negative intent.

- **Notice** how your Brain Pattern tells you that this conversation is a waste of time or is even trying to get you to focus on the qualities in the person you don't like.

- **Remind yourself** that most people's actions have nothing to do with you. To see the world the way you do is self-centered.

- **Challenge yourself** to ask for clarity instead of assuming conflict exists where it doesn't.

The Self-Fulfilling Prophecy: By reading into body language and behavior from a negatively skewed lens, you create opposition in your mind that is likely to destroy a natural connection in conversation, creating an opportunity for rejection.

3. You Engage Instead of Escaping When Situations Don't Go as Planned

You build up idealized scenarios in your mind, but when reality doesn't match, you withdraw.

Instead of adjusting to the moment, you pick apart what went wrong, mentally exit, or convince yourself it wasn't worth it. Rebellion Zones force you to stay engaged—even when things don't feel perfect or comfortable.

Why You Need This: To stop sabotaging experiences by disengaging the moment they don't meet your expectations.

How You Approach This Rebellion Zone:

- **Observe** how quickly your brain shifts into criticism when things don't go exactly as imagined. Your mind focuses on what doesn't stack up.

- **Notice** how your Brain Pattern urges you to focus on the negative and project into future scenarios about nothing working right or being fulfilling.

- **Remind yourself** that real-life experiences are unpredictable. It's not a reason to shut down.

- **Challenge yourself** to stay involved by asking small questions, intentionally touching things in your physical environment to get you out of your head, challenging yourself to focus on one positive or neutral, even when part of you wants to mentally check out.

The Self-Fulfilling Prophecy: By retreating when things feel off or focusing on the negative, you never get to be present for the experience, reinforcing the belief that nothing truly satisfies you.

4. You Stop Rejecting Encouragement and Start Seeing It as Opportunity

When people recognize your strengths and push you toward growth, you immediately push back.

You assume they're overestimating you, setting you up for failure, or just trying to force you into something you're not ready for. Rebellion Zones challenge you to accept positive feedback instead of treating it as pressure or expectation.

Why You Need This: To stop rejecting opportunities that could actually move you forward.

How You Approach This Rebellion Zone:

- **Observe** your instinct to dismiss praise, downplay encouragement, or avoid leadership roles.

- **Notice** how your Brain Pattern convinces you that any expectation is a trap.

- **Remind yourself** that being recognized for your potential is not an attack—it's an opportunity and it doesn't inherently mean obligation or pressure.

- **Challenge yourself** to say thank you and set your sights on one small step toward that goal.

The Self-Fulfilling Prophecy: By rejecting every invitation to grow, you reinforce the belief that success isn't for you.

5. You Stop Viewing Big Commitment as Traps

You crave purpose and success, but you resist the small, structured steps that would actually get you there. Your brain tells you that obligation is suffocating, commitment is a trap, and following a set path means losing your freedom. Rebellion Zones challenge you to reframe structure as a tool for success—not something designed to limit you.

Why You Need This: To move forward instead of staying stuck in endless cycles of avoidance.

How To Approach This Rebellion Zone:

- **Observe** how often you reject or push away big-picture commitments, even when they serve your goals.

- **Notice** how your Brain Pattern convinces you that taking action is a setup and will lead to failure or ridicule.

- **Remind yourself** that finding purpose and success in life is a byproduct of incremental commitments and tenacity.

- **Challenge yourself** to follow through on three small commitments staying focused on short-term rather than big-picture goals.

The Self-Fulfilling Prophecy: By refusing to act on small commitments and opportunities, you keep yourself in a state of watching as others achieve the purpose you claim to want.

6. You Take Responsibility for Your Success Instead of Resenting Others for Theirs

You compare yourself to others, but instead of feeling motivated, you use it as proof that you'll never measure up. You tell yourself that if you had their advantages, background, or opportunities, things would be different. Rebellion Zones force you to take ownership of your path instead of fixating on how unfair things feel.

Why You Need This: To stop justifying inaction by convincing yourself the odds are stacked against you or that success and purpose can be achieved by others—but not you.

How To Approach This Rebellion Zone:

- **Observe** when you compare your journey to others as a way to excuse avoidance or activate fears that you'll never be enough.

- **Notice** how your Brain Pattern convinces you that success was easier for other people or tied to their destiny rather than hard work and tenacity.

- **Remind yourself** that self-pity keeps you stuck—only small sustained actions change your reality.

- **Challenge yourself** to restrict content and social media consumption of people you look up to or want to emulate. Stay focused on small commitments that keep you engaged in your own life.

The Self-Fulfilling Prophecy: By staying focused on what others have or how capable they are, you ensure that you build up negative self-talk and comparison to keep yourself stuck and stagnant.

Rebellion Zones

1. Engaging in the Moment Instead of Waiting for the "Right" Time

Self-Deception at Play: You convince yourself you're just being thoughtful or reading the room, but really, you're overthinking every move. You wait for the "perfect" moment to engage, speak, or connect—telling yourself it's about timing. In reality, it's about control. You avoid vulnerability by staying stuck in your head, planning instead of participating. You'd rather hang back than risk being seen and not accepted.

Unconscious Motivation: Avoid vulnerability by trying to control the conditions of connection—waiting for the "right" moment is really about minimizing emotional risk. It feels safer to observe and plan than to risk putting yourself out there and not being received.

Rebellion Zone: Speak, contribute, or engage immediately instead of waiting for the "right" moment.

Why This Works: Your subconscious tells you that it's not the right time and it could lead to awkwardness. But by waiting, you often miss the moment entirely. By choosing to engage before you feel fully ready, you train your brain to see that you don't need ideal conditions to engage and connect.

How This Plays Out in Real Life:

- You feel a desire to speak up or join a conversation but convince yourself it's not the right time.

- You overanalyze the tone, timing, or energy in the room, waiting for a "perfect opening" that never comes.

- You hold back in meetings, group settings, or social interactions, assuming others won't care what you have to say.

- You mentally rehearse what you want to say or do, but by the time you feel ready, the moment has passed.

- You tell yourself, "I'll say something later" or "I don't want to interrupt," then feel regret or disconnection afterward.

- Others may experience you as distant, disengaged, or aloof—when in reality, you're stuck in your own head, calculating the risk of participation.

- Over time, this pattern reinforces your belief that you don't belong or aren't needed, even though you've never given people the chance to truly connect with you.

The Challenge: Act Before You Feel 100 Percent Ready

- If you have something to say, say it before you talk yourself out of it.

- If you hesitate to join a conversation, step in instead of waiting for the perfect opening. *Ask yourself*:

  Do I historically overthink the timing of entering a conversation?

  Do I trick myself into thinking there will be a better moment to justify not speaking now?

  Do I tend to ruminate on missed opportunities after the moment has passed?

  Am I convincing myself that it would be awkward if it didn't land the way I want it to?

  Can I challenge myself to say something and take it as a learning experience?

- If you feel like you should wait to text, reach out, or check in, do it now. *Ask yourself*:

  Am I going to ruminate on what I want to say and build up resentment?

  Does this historically lead me to see the other person as an opponent?

  Is my Brain Pattern trying to trick me into turning on the other person to excuse myself from taking action?

  Can I challenge myself to say something now so I don't dwell on it?

- If you typically hold back in group settings, challenge yourself to speak once before the conversation shifts.

By engaging in the moment, you disrupt the belief that waiting ensures acceptance, but it often just ensures invisibility.

2. Initiating Plans Instead of Waiting for Invitations

Self-Deception at Play: You tell yourself you're just easygoing or not trying to bother anyone—but really, you're avoiding the risk of being turned down. You assume that if people wanted you around, they'd ask.

Instead of directly expressing your desire to connect, you stay silent and hope others will do the emotional heavy lifting. You equate asking to be included with desperation or neediness.

Unconscious Motivation: Avoid confirming the fear that you're not truly wanted—if you wait for invitations, you preserve the illusion that you're liked, even if you're not prioritized. Initiating feels too vulnerable because if someone declines or doesn't reciprocate, it threatens your sense of worth.

Rebellion Zone: Be the one to initiate instead of waiting for others to reach out first.

Why This Works: Your subconscious tells you that if people really liked you, they would make the first move. Since they don't, you assume you're not as well-liked as others, leading you to withdraw instead of seeking out the connection you want. By initiating, you train your brain to recognize that relationships require participation, not just silent hope.

How This Plays Out in Real Life:

- You want to see someone or be included, but decide not to reach out because you think it will make you look desperate.

- You tell yourself, "If I was important to them, I wouldn't have to ask."

- You notice others making plans without you and spiral into self-doubt: "What am I doing wrong? Why didn't they include me?"

- You rationalize your withdrawal as "being chill" or "not wanting to bother people," while secretly hoping they'll miss you and reach out.

- You use social comparison to fuel the belief that you're the outsider—"They always include her. I guess I'm not good enough."

- When you are invited, you overanalyze it: "Did they feel sorry for me?" or "Am I a backup plan?"

- You equate initiation with lowering your value, so you freeze—then internalize the silence as proof that you're not lovable.

The Challenge: Take the Lead Without Waiting for an Invitation

- If you want to see someone, be the one to text first.

- If you feel left out of plans, suggest your own instead of assuming you weren't wanted.

- If you hesitate to make a request, ask anyway instead of waiting for someone to offer.

- Think of outreach as practice and take the pressure of each invitation individually.

- Stop thinking of an acceptance of an invitation as a direct measurement of your value or likeability.

By initiating instead of waiting, you disrupt the belief that belonging should happen passively.

3. Staying in Conversations Instead of Opting Out Early

Self-Deception at Play: You tell yourself you're just tired, not into small talk, or that the moment has passed—but really, you're bailing early to avoid discomfort. The second something feels even slightly awkward or uncertain, you withdraw. You keep interactions brief and controlled to avoid the risk of rejection or emotional exposure.

Unconscious Motivation: Preserve your sense of worth by controlling your own exit—if you leave first, you don't have to risk overstaying, being judged, or discovering that others don't actually enjoy your presence.

Rebellion Zone: Stay engaged longer than your comfort zone allows. Don't cut interactions short just because you assume they will become awkward or make you feel uncomfortable.

Why This Works: Your subconscious tells you that if people really wanted you around, they would show it. Since you don't see clear proof, you leave before things can turn on you, avoiding rejection by controlling your own exit. By staying, you force your brain to recognize that connection doesn't always have to be explicitly confirmed. It often just happens.

How This Plays Out in Real Life:

- You join a group conversation but mentally check out after a few minutes, feeling like you don't really belong.

- The second there's a pause or slight awkwardness, you interpret it as a sign to leave—"I'm clearly not adding anything."

- You exit events or conversations early to avoid the possibility of being left out, embarrassed, or unnoticed.

- You assume people are just being polite, not genuinely interested, so you cut things short before that "truth" can be revealed.

- You replay conversations afterward, obsessing over one awkward moment, using it as justification for leaving early.

- You avoid deepening connection because staying longer makes you feel more emotionally exposed or visible.

- Over time, your early exits create a pattern of disconnection, reinforcing your belief that you're not someone people are eager to engage with.

The Challenge: Stay Instead of Quietly Disappearing

- If you feel yourself pulling away mid-conversation, stay for ten more minutes.

- If you assume your presence isn't as valuable as someone else's, gravitate toward that person instead of pulling away. *Ask yourself*:

   Do I see qualities in this person that are valuable or gaining positive attention?

   Can I challenge myself to stay in this person's orbit for at least 5 more minutes?

- If you normally leave an event early, give yourself permission to stay and see what happens.

By staying instead of exiting, you disrupt the belief that people only value you if they constantly show it.

4. Expressing Needs Instead of Hoping People Just Know

Self-Deception at Play: You tell yourself you're low-maintenance or just going with the flow, but in truth, you're afraid to voice your needs. You avoid speaking up, hoping others will notice or guess what you want. You believe that if someone really cared, they'd already know—and if they don't, it must mean you're not important to them.

Unconscious Motivation: Protect your sense of worth by tying love to being chosen or noticed without asking—voicing your needs feels like admitting weakness or risking disappointment.

Rebellion Zone: Say what you want without assuming people can read your mind.

Why This Works: Your subconscious tells you that if someone really valued you, they would naturally know what you need or be able to pick up on your cues. If they don't, you assume it's proof that they don't care or are too self-centered to notice. But by expressing needs instead of testing people, you prove to your brain that it is actually your inability to directly communicate that is disrupting collaboration and closeness.

How This Plays Out in Real Life:

- You expect people to pick up on your moods, frustrations, or needs without having to say anything.

- You feel slighted when someone doesn't offer support, check in, or make space for you—but you never actually asked them to.

- You interpret people's failure to notice or accommodate you as a personal rejection: "If they cared, they'd know."

- You avoid expressing what you want—whether it's more time, inclusion, or help—because you fear being a burden or sounding needy.

- You silently keep score in relationships, then pull away when your unspoken expectations aren't met.

- When others do respond to expressed needs, you feel uncomfortable or undeserving, reinforcing your tendency to suppress next time.

- Over time, this creates patterns of quiet resentment and emotional distance, all while convincing yourself no one truly understands or values you.

The Challenge: Be Direct About What You Are Thinking or Want

- If you are upset about something someone did or didn't do, reach out and say it directly instead of stew about it silently.

- If you want to be included in something, don't wait around and get upset in your mind. Ask about plans and insert yourself.

- If you assume silence means disinterest or selfishness, test that belief by engaging instead of isolating.

5. Seeing Social Neutrality as Normal Instead of Assuming Rejection

Self-Deception at Play: You read too much into silence, tone, or brief interactions—convinced they mean you did something wrong. You assume people are pulling away, judging you, or secretly annoyed, even when there's no clear evidence. Instead of allowing space or neutrality, you interpret it as proof that you're not wanted.

Unconscious Motivation: Maintain a fragile sense of worth by constantly scanning for proof that you matter—if someone isn't actively affirming you, your brain fills in the silence with assumed rejection.

Rebellion Zone: Accept social neutrality as normal. Stop assuming every shift in energy is about you.

Why This Works: Your subconscious tells you that if people aren't actively seeking you out, they must not care about you. If someone is distracted, quiet, or simply not as engaged, you assume it's a signal about you. But by recognizing that people have their own moods, distractions, and lives, you retrain your brain to stop assuming rejection where it may not exist.

How This Plays Out in Real Life:

- A friend is less chatty or more distracted than usual, and you immediately assume they're upset with you or pulling away.

- You overanalyze text tone, pauses in conversation, or delayed responses as proof that someone is annoyed or disinterested.

- You withdraw emotionally the moment you feel someone's energy shift, even if they haven't said or done anything negative.

- You avoid follow-ups or invitations because you assume they wouldn't want to hear from you unless they initiated.

- You replay neutral interactions obsessively, trying to find the hidden meaning behind someone's facial expression, word choice, or timing.

- You feel invisible or unwanted when someone isn't overtly warm or affirming, even if they're just tired, distracted, or focused elsewhere.

- Over time, this assumption of rejection becomes a filter that blocks connection and creates self-imposed isolation.

The Challenge: Allow Neutrality Without Reading Into It

- If someone takes longer to respond, remind yourself that they are most likely distracted by something in their own lives rather than intentionally delaying their response.

- If someone is quiet, consider that they might just be tired or mulling something over—not upset or judging you.

- If you feel like you embarrassed yourself, recognize that people don't analyze your actions as deeply as you do. *Ask yourself*:

    Do I historically replay my actions through a highly critical lens?

    Does my brain try to trick me into seeing others as the opposition or enemy?

    Is it true that most people are focused on their own lives and unlikely to be dwelling on this issue like I am?

    Can I challenge myself to take ownership of projecting my own insecurities onto others?

By seeing neutrality as normal, you disrupt the belief that everyone is secretly judging or rejecting you.

6. Taking Radical Personal Responsibility Instead of Dwelling on What Didn't Work Out

Self-Deception at Play: You replay the past obsessively—fixating on missed chances, blaming bad timing, or externalizing the reason things didn't go your way. You paint yourself as the victim of circumstance while ignoring the patterns and choices that led you there. It feels easier to mourn what could've been than to face how you may have sabotaged what was.

Unconscious Motivation: Preserve your sense of worth by blaming external factors when things fall apart—acknowledging your own role in missed opportunities feels like confirming the fear that you're the reason love, connection, or success slips away.

Rebellion Zone: Own your role in the outcome. Stop romanticizing what you "lost" and start recognizing how you contributed to the result.

Why This Works: Your subconscious clings to the narrative that things didn't work out because of external forces, timing, or someone else's decisions. But by continuously replaying what could have been, you avoid confronting how your own hesitation, avoidance, or sabotage played a role. It wasn't just bad luck or misalignment—you had agency, and you made choices that shaped the outcome. When you shift from passively lamenting the past to actively taking responsibility, you reclaim control over your future.

How This Plays Out in Real Life:

• You replay relationships or opportunities that didn't work out, fixating on what the other person did wrong or how the timing wasn't right.

• You romanticize past scenarios, convincing yourself that everything would've worked out if the circumstances had just been different.

• You avoid looking at how your silence, avoidance, hesitation, or passive disengagement shaped the outcome.

• You build mental highlight reels of "what could've been," which reinforce a false sense of victimhood and loss.

• You tell yourself you were never given a real chance—without acknowledging that you never actually showed up fully.

• You feel weighed down by regret but use it to justify emotional isolation rather than motivate growth.

• Over time, this fixation on lost potential makes you hesitant to try again, fearing that effort will only lead to the same kind of pain.

The Challenge: Stop Narrating the Loss, Start Owning the Role You Played

• When you catch yourself ruminating on what didn't work out, take radical personal responsibility for the exact moments where you contributed to the outcome.

• Instead of thinking about what "should have been," give yourself an honest review.

• Consider that the idea of what you lost might not even match the reality of what it would have been. Your brain tends to glorify what is gone.

• Instead of seeking external validation or waiting for someone to prove your assumptions wrong, take proactive steps toward the connections and opportunities you claim to want. *Ask yourself*:

Am I idealizing a past possibility while ignoring the ways I actively contributed to its failure?

Do I conveniently ignore my own hesitation, avoidance, or excuses when reviewing these situations?

Is my attachment to "what could have been" a way to avoid dealing with the effort required to build something new?

Can I challenge myself to stop blaming timing, circumstances, or people and instead focus on the lesson I need to learn here?

7. Embracing All Types of People and Interactions Instead of Justifying Disengagement

Self-Deception at Play: You tell yourself certain people just "aren't your type" or "aren't in alignment," but really, you're crafting excuses to avoid connection. You judge quickly, disengage early, and write people off without giving them a chance. You protect yourself from vulnerability by keeping interactions shallow and avoidant.

Unconscious Motivation: Avoid the emotional risk of rejection by preemptively disqualifying others—if you convince yourself that people aren't a match or "just don't get you," you don't have to face the discomfort of trying, being seen, or potentially being let down.

Rebellion Zone: Recognize when you're manufacturing reasons to disconnect—challenge your avoidance and let people reveal who they are instead of deciding for them.

Why This Works: Your subconscious uses avoidance as a protective mechanism. Instead of openly admitting that connection feels risky or vulnerable, your brain defaults to the excuse that most people simply aren't right for you. This lets you maintain the illusion of self-sufficiency while dodging the risk of rejection, disappointment, or emotional effort. Many of these "justifications" are fabrications designed to keep you safe in your bubble. Letting people actually show up and reveal who they are—not just who you assume them to be—interrupts this cycle and allows for real engagement.

How This Plays Out in Real Life:

- You meet someone and quickly decide they're not "your type" or not deep, interesting, or self-aware enough to invest energy in.

- You sense the potential for connection but dismiss it with surface-level judgments: "They're too mainstream," "Not on my level," or "I just don't vibe with them."

- You mentally scan for reasons to opt out before giving people a real chance to show up.

- You convince yourself you're being discerning or protecting your peace, when really you're avoiding the vulnerability of engagement.

600

- You feel socially disconnected but tell yourself it's because "there just aren't many people I resonate with."

- When someone does try to connect, you keep the interaction surface-level or subtly push them away to test their interest or protect yourself from being fully seen.

- Over time, this creates a lonely cycle of disconnection where you feel unseen, but also never allow yourself to truly be seen.

The Challenge: Stop Writing People Off Prematurely

- Instead of assuming misalignment, challenge yourself to give people space to reveal their real personality over time.

- If you find yourself picking apart small flaws as a reason to disengage, consider that your brain is actively looking for an out rather than seeing the whole picture.

- When you feel an urge to disengage, *ask yourself*:

  Does my Brain Pattern tend to highlight the negative so I can justify pulling away?

  Am I judging others in a way I fear being judged myself?

  Can I challenge myself to let this relationship unfold naturally before I form an assumption about who they are?

  Even if this person ends up not being a good fit for me, didn't I get practice with communication and pattern opposition?

- Test the assumption. Give the interaction another round. Meet up again, have another conversation, and observe how your perception shifts when you let go of your need to control the narrative.

What You Gain by Embracing Rebellion Zones

Rebellion Zones force you to break the cycle of retreating, resenting, and rejecting opportunities before they can reject you. They challenge you to step forward before your brain convinces you that everything is already lost—so you can finally experience what happens when you engage with life instead of analyzing it from the outside.

1. You Learn That Neutrality Isn't the Same as Rejection

You assume that if someone isn't overly warm, excited, or

validating, they must be judging, dismissing, or uninterested in you. Your brain fills in the blanks with worst-case scenarios, making every neutral interaction feel like a quiet rejection. Rebellion Zones force you to stop assigning hidden meaning to people's reactions and start seeing neutrality for what it is: neutral.

You gain the ability to interact without constantly scanning for rejection, allowing relationships to unfold naturally.

2. You Stop Letting Resentment Build Over Things You Never Expressed

You assume that if people cared, they would just know when something is wrong. Instead of stating your needs or concerns, you withdraw—testing their investment or waiting for them to figure it out. When they don't, you take it as proof that they don't actually value you. Rebellion Zones challenge you to communicate directly instead of assuming that silence equals disregard. You're able to build real connection instead of waiting for people to pass your silent tests.

3. You Realize That Idealizing Then Destroying Keeps You Stuck

You build up ideas of what relationships, careers, or experiences should feel like. When they don't match, you pick them apart and disengage. You convince yourself that nothing ever meets your standards, but in reality, your brain is primed to reject things before they have a chance to succeed. Rebellion Zones force you to stop seeking perfection and start engaging with reality as it is. You gain the ability to stay involved instead of abandoning things the moment they stop feeling ideal.

4. You Stop Searching for Opposition in Every Interaction

You walk into social settings, workplaces, or new situations assuming you'll be excluded, judged, or overlooked. You scan for subtle slights or hidden negativity, even when there's no real evidence of it. Rebellion Zones challenge you to drop the assumption that everyone is against you and start seeing what happens when you enter situations without bracing for conflict. You're able to exist in social spaces without filtering everything through the lens of competition or rejection.

5. You Build Momentum Instead of Sabotaging It

You want adventure, success, or purpose, but the moment something starts to feel real, your brain convinces you that it's flawed or doomed. Instead of taking the next step, you ruminate on everything that could go wrong, turning potential into frustration. Rebellion Zones force you to stop rejecting progress just because it doesn't feel perfect from the start. You gain the ability to move forward without talking yourself out of every opportunity.

6. You Learn That Isolation Doesn't Actually Give You Control

You retreat to regain a sense of power, assuming that if you disengage first, no one can reject or disappoint you. But instead of feeling powerful, you feel disconnected, bitter, and stuck– watching life happen instead of being part of it. Rebellion Zones challenge you to step into discomfort instead of convincing yourself that walking away is the only way to win. You're able to engage with life instead of watching from the sidelines.

7. You Stop Using Comparison as a Weapon Against Yourself

You look at others' success, relationships, or progress–not to inspire yourself, but to reinforce why you'll never measure up. Your brain convinces you that if things were fair, you'd be further ahead–but instead of taking action, you sink into frustration. Rebellion Zones force you to stop fixating on what others have and start focusing on what's actually in your control. You gain the power to build something for yourself instead of staying stuck in cycles of self-criticism and avoidance.

The Bottom Line: You Don't Have to Keep Disappearing to Feel Safe

You tend to focus on the connections and friendships other people have and why that never seems to be you. Instead of taking ownership of your tendencies to withdraw, wait or pre-emptively judge, you dwell on what's not fair. You assume that if people truly cared or thought you were worthy, they would reach out. Your pattern leaves you feeling lonely and disconnected.

The Rebellion Zones challenge your brain's assumption that retreating is the only way to avoid ridicule or rejection. These Rebellion Zones push you to disrupt the habit of testing people through absence or silence and give you real, tangible proof of the connection that is possible.

Your Rebellion Zones will help you:

- Recognize when you are pulling away as a test rather than a true need for space.

- Break the habit of assuming silence means rejection.

- Disrupt the belief that if people don't immediately reach out, they must not care.

- Push through discomfort instead of shutting down.

- Test the idea that relationships can exist without constant proof of commitment.

- Stop assuming that if people don't chase you, they are walking away.

- Allow connection to unfold without always waiting for external validation.

They prove something different:

- You don't have to constantly scan for rejection—it's not always happening.

- Silence doesn't mean exclusion—sometimes, it's just space.

- You are worthy of connection—even when you aren't chasing it.

For the first time, you'll experience relationships that don't require avoidance, self-erasure, or waiting for proof that you belong. Are you ready to stop waiting on the sidelines and step fully into your life?

CHAPTER 30

CHAOS–REJECTION

Your brain doesn't interpret consistency as safe; it registers it as pointless, temporary, or even a trap. The second things start to settle, you feel the pull to disrupt, escape, or destroy before life does it for you. You tell yourself you "thrive in chaos," that stability is an illusion. But the truth is, you don't thrive in chaos—you've just learned to become it. Because it's familiar, your brain treats it like the only thing you can count on.

This is where "The War Against Futility" begins.

Your rebellion is about proving to your subconscious that momentum, connection, and consistency aren't a setup for failure. These rebellion zones will push back against the belief that life is working against you, that effort leads nowhere, and that chaos is the only constant. The truth is, making connections andgeneratingactually do end up feeling good—eventually.

Core Motivations:

1. Reject Consistency and Connection

You assume that if you avoid stability, structure, or connection first, you won't have to experience the pain of losing them later.

2. Avold the Letdown of Effort That "Leads Nowhere"

You tell yourself that if you don't try, you won't have to face the disappointment of failure. You assume that any effort will eventually be wasted, so why bother?

3. Protect Yourself from Being Trapped or Controlled

You view routine, commitment, and accountability as threats, ways for people, systems, or expectations to box you in and limit your freedom.

4. Create Meaning Through Disruption

If nothing feels stable, predictable, or fulfilling, you generate chaos, intensity, or conflict just to feel alive, engaged, or significant.

5. Confirm That Nothing Lasts

You instinctively sabotage relationships, jobs, or opportunities because if you let them continue, they might fail on their own, and that feels worse than failing on your terms.

6. Resist Structure to Prove You Are in Control

You assume that if you follow the rules, commit to something long-term, or embrace consistency, you are giving up control. You see rebellion as a form of autonomy, even when it works against you.

7. Test People to See If They'll Stay

You create emotional instability, push people away, or reject help to confirm whether others are truly invested. If they leave, it reinforces your belief that no one stays.

8. Ensure You Are Never Vulnerable

You tell yourself that believing in stability, love, or success will only make it hurt more when they disappear. So instead, you remain detached, resistant, and skeptical.

9. Find Excitement in Chaos When Stability Feels Dull

If life starts feeling steady, predictable, or repetitive, you disrupt it—consciously or subconsciously.

10. Keep Yourself from Fully Committing to Anything

You assume that if you fully invest in something—whether it's a relationship, a goal, or even a belief system—you are setting yourself up for disappointment.

Why Do You Need Rebellion Zones?

1. You Reject Stability Before It Can Reject You

Your brain sees stability as a threat—something that will inevitably slip away and leave you disappointed. If you push away stability, you won't have to deal with the pain of losing it later. Rebellion Zones force you to experience stability, even when it feels like it's slipping through your fingers.

Why You Need This: To learn that stability doesn't have to come with pain and loss, and you don't have to push it away to protect yourself.

How To Approach This Rebellion Zone:

- **Observe** how your brain tells you that stability is an illusion.

- **Notice** when you're avoiding commitments or disconnecting because stability feels too safe or predictable.

- **Remind yourself** that your brain pattern doesn't trust stability because it's afraid to be tricked or hurt.

- **Challenge yourself** to engage with stability even when it feels boring.

The Self-Fulfilling Prophecy: By rejecting stability, you trap yourself in a cycle of chaos and self-sabotage, ensuring that you never experience the peace of commitment.

2. You Resist Effort Because You Assume It's Wasted

Right now, your brain sees effort as a waste of time. Rebellion Zones force you to invest without fearing the outcome.

Why You Need This: To discover that effort doesn't always have to result in disappointment. Sometimes, the risk is worth it.

How To Approach This Rebellion Zone:

- **Observe** how your brain convinces you that effort will be wasted in the long run.

- **Notice** when your brain pattern tricks you into being lazy or reckless.

- **Remind yourself** that you are likely to use your feelings to justify self-destruction.

- **Challenge yourself** to put in effort even if it feels boring and pointless. You're growing the most important emotional muscle: resilience.

The Self-Fulfilling Prophecy: By avoiding effort, you guarantee failure, because you never allow yourself to try and break the pattern of self-sabotage.

3. You Reject Commitment to Keep Your Freedom Intact

You believe commitment is a trap—something that takes away your autonomy. Rebellion Zones force you to choose commitment without sacrificing your sense of freedom.

Why You Need This: To understand that commitment doesn't equal control.

How To Approach This Rebellion Zone:

> • **Observe** how you start to feel obligated or restricted when asked to commit to things.

> • **Notice** how your brain pattern tricks you into seeing commitment as a trap.

> • **Remind yourself** that commitment issues are ultimately rooted fear. Are you a fearful person?

> • **Challenge yourself** to say, "yes" to small commitments. Acknowledge that you aren't as fearless as you deceive yourself into believing.

The Self-Fulfilling Prophecy: By rejecting commitment, you ensure you stay stuck in the chaos you've created.

4. You Create Chaos to Feel Alive

Your brain seeks disruption to escape the dullness of stability. Rebellion Zones force you to embrace calmness and structure without disrupting everything around you.

Why You Need This: To learn that stability doesn't have to be boring. You don't need chaos to feel alive.

How To Approach This Rebellion Zone:

> • **Observe** how your brain tricks you into believing chaos makes you feel more alive.

> • **Notice** when you feel the urge to create conflict or instability to feel something.

- **Remind yourself** that your brain pattern experiences peace and stability as boredom.

- **Challenge yourself** to be present to the feeling of boredom.

The Self-Fulfilling Prophecy: By constantly creating chaos, you rob yourself of the peace and fulfillment that stability can offer, even when it feels like it's too calm.

5. You Test People to Confirm They'll Leave Anyway

You believe that if you push people away first, it won't hurt when they leave. Rebellion Zones force you to stay open and trust others without the need to test their loyalty.

Why You Need This: To experience trust without needing constant validation that others will stay.

How To Approach This Rebellion Zone:

- **Observe** how you minimize or ignore the efforts of others and tell yourself they'll eventually turn on you.

- **Notice** when you withdraw emotionally or push others away.

- **Remind yourself** that you sabotage relationships as a way to perpetuate chaos around you.

- **Challenge yourself** to acknowledge kindness without jumping into a hopeless future scenario.

The Self-Fulfilling Prophecy: By testing others and pushing them away, you guarantee that they will leave.

6. You Sabotage to Avoid the Pain of Loss

Right now, your brain sees failure as less painful than the potential loss of something good. Rebellion Zones force you to stay present in situations that feel too good to be true.

Why You Need This: To learn that failure isn't always a foregone conclusion, and you don't have to sabotage yourself to avoid disappointment.

How To Approach This Rebellion Zone:

- **Observe** how your brain tries to convince you that self-sabotage ends things on your terms.

- **Notice** when you start to pull back from something because you question how long it will last.

- **Remind yourself** that you're actually scared of not being able to control outcomes.

- **Challenge yourself** to let things unfold without prematurely ending them just to control the outcome.

The Self-Fulfilling Prophecy: By sabotaging yourself, you ensure that things can't last because you never allow them the chance to develop fully.

Rebellion Zones

1. Effort Without Immediate Proof

Self-Deception at Play: You convince yourself that effort is pointless unless it delivers immediate, visible results. You rationalize inaction as self-protection, telling yourself you're just being realistic or avoiding disappointment.

Unconscious Motivation: You've been conditioned to believe that nothing lasts and that hope leads to hurt. So instead of risking disappointment, your brain keeps you trapped in cycles of disengagement and avoidance. It whispers: If you don't try, you can't fail. If you don't care, you can't be crushed.

Rebellion Zone: Commit to incremental effort without attaching it to reward.

Why This Works: Your brain only sees effort as a setup and prevents you from ever trying at all. The only way to break this pattern is to put in small moments of effort without trying to connect it to a reward. By maintaining even the smallest routine without interruption, you prove that effort isn't wasted—it builds over time.

How This Plays Out in Real Life:
- You hesitate to start things because you assume it'll end up being a waste of your time

- You rely on last-minute, chaotic effort instead of incremental steps.

- You avoid long-term commitments because they feel like traps.

- You ignore small wins as meaningless or coincidental.

The Challenge: Stick With Effort Even When It Feels Pointless

- Choose one small task and commit to it daily for seven days at a time.

- When your brain pattern says, "This doesn't matter," label it as resistance and do it. *Ask yourself*:

  Though I convince myself that nothing matters, isn't it true that I'm actually delaying tasks because they don't feel worthwhile?

  Can something be both worthwhile and irrelevant?

  Can I challenge myself to meet this incongruency head-on?

- If you feel the urge to quit or blow it off, acknowledge how your Brain Pattern wants to disrupt any sequential progress. Meet the challenge head-on.

- Instead of waiting for motivation, go through the motions and check off the box without seeking any feedback.

2. Cooking a Meal With Full Sensory Engagement

Self-Deception at Play: You tell yourself it doesn't matter—eating is just another task to get through. You grab whatever's easy, skip meals, or eat while scrolling because you don't see the point in slowing down. You justify it because you're convinced that your body isn't worth the effort.

Unconscious Motivation: You numb yourself to the sensory world because it makes it easier to stay detached. If you start caring about small things—like how your food smells or tastes—it might open the door to caring about other things. That feels dangerous. Your brain wants to avoid the sting of hope or effort that could lead to disappointment, so it rejects engagement altogether.

Rebellion Zone: Cook a meal twice per week focused on your senses.

Why This Works: Your brain resists small acts of care and engagement because it associates them with wasted effort. Being fully present while cooking forces you to reconnect to your physical environment instead of staying lost in avoidance and detachment.

How This Plays Out in Real Life:

- You grab quick, processed food instead of taking time to make something for yourself.

- You forget to eat and distract yourself away from your hunger cues.

- You eat while distracted—scrolling, watching TV, barely noticing the food.

- You avoid activities that require patience, presence, or step-by-step effort.

The Challenge: Engage in Cooking as a Sensory Experience

- Pick one meal to cook twice a week from a recipe.

- Engage your senses deliberately—smell the spices, listen to the sizzle, feel the textures.

- Play a specific genre of music while cooking to anchor the experience.

- Sit down and eat without distractions. No phone, no TV—just you and the meal.

- If you normally rush through meals, force yourself to eat slowly.

3. Pushing Through Justifications to Bail on Work

Self-Deception at Play: You tell yourself there's no point in showing up—work feels meaningless, your effort won't change anything, and you've probably already screwed up your reputation anyway. You fixate on feeling tired, run-down, or slightly off and use it to justify staying in bed or skipping the day entirely.

Unconscious Motivation: Avoid work because you don't want to face the fear that your effort won't matter. Your brain frames everything as pointless to protect you from the possibility of failure or disappointment. If you don't try, you can't lose.

Rebellion Zone: Go to work without excuses for one week.

Why This Works: Your brain associates work with oppression instead of self-respect. When you consistently follow through, you build a reputation and reinforce internal stability. Your goal is to prove that following through is what builds self-trust.

How This Plays Out in Real Life:

- You frequently call in sick, ditch obligations, or postpone work without a real reason.

- You convince yourself you'll "fix it later"—but never do.

- You tell yourself you already have a bad reputation so it doesn't matter if this choice makes you look bad.

The Challenge: Override Excuses and Prove You Can Be Consistent

- When you feel the urge to bail on work, *ask yourself*:

  Am I telling myself it doesn't really matter because I already have a bad reputation?

  Am I trying to justify that it doesn't matter because I don't like my job?

  Can I challenge myself to go to work even though I'm not motivated?

  Can I challenge myself to stick to this goal for 1 week to see if anything shifts?

- Keep track of each time you follow through on a visual calendar. Watch how much more stable your life becomes when you stop flaking.

- Remind yourself that every time you call out, you are reinforcing instability.

- If the urge to bail feels overwhelming, pause and ask:

  Can I challenge myself to commit to the next hour?

4. Physical Connection With a Family Member or Friend

Self-Deception at Play: You convince yourself you don't need physical closeness—it's unnecessary, awkward, or just not your thing. You avoid hugs, touch, or even sitting close to people and justify it by saying you're independent or not very emotional. The truth is, you push people away before they get too close. You'd rather scroll or zone out than risk the discomfort of human connection.

Unconscious Motivation: Your brain avoids physical connection because it triggers vulnerability. Touch requires presence, and presence opens the door to emotional intimacy—the very thing you've learned to distrust. It feels safer to stay detached, self-contained, and unavailable.

Rebellion Zone: Initiate or accept physical connection.

Why This Works: Your brain avoids physical closeness as a form of emotional self-protection. But physical touch grounds you in the moment and strengthens trust, connection, and presence.

How This Plays Out in Real Life:

- You rarely initiate hugs or casual physical connection with family or friends.

- You brush off affection, feeling uncomfortable or dismissive.

- You keep conversations surface-level, avoiding emotional closeness.

The Challenge: Initiate or Accept Physical Connection

- Give a hug to a family member or friend at least twice a week.

- Hold physical connection for a full five seconds instead of breaking it quickly.

- When someone offers affection, don't resist or deflect it. Let it land.

- If the idea of physical connection makes you cringe, lean into the discomfort. It's a sign of how much you've been avoiding true connection.

By leaning into moments of connection, you prove to your brain that closeness is not a threat—and that you don't have to live in isolation.

5. Stability Without Sabotage

Self-Deception at Play: You tell yourself structure is a trap. Routines feel boring, planning feels pointless, and the moment something becomes predictable, you start looking for an exit. You justify impulsive decisions or missed responsibilities by saying you're just "living in the moment" or that you'll figure it out later. You treat consistency like a threat—then wonder why nothing ever feels stable.

Unconscious Motivation: You reject structure before it can disappoint you. Chaos gives you a false sense of control; if you're the one who blows things up, then you can't be blindsided. But behind the disruption is a deep craving for consistency and security—you just don't trust yourself to maintain it, so you destroy it before it tests you.

Rebellion Zone: build structure without letting it collapse.

Why This Works: Your brain associates stability with loss of freedom—but structure actually creates freedom. If you stick with small, sustainable routines, you prove to yourself that stability is a tool.

How This Plays Out in Real Life:

- You resist planning, goal-setting, or making long-term commitments because it feels suffocating.

- You justify disengagement in daily life—never maintaining a steady rhythm.

- When life starts to go well or become predictable, you disrupt it by making impulsive decisions.

The Challenge: Build Structure Without Letting It Collapse

- Create a simple, repeatable morning routine and commit to it for seven days—no skipping, no adjustments, no justification to stop.

- Keep track of stability disruptors, whenever you feel the urge to add chaos, *ask yourself*:

  Do I historically start justifying chaotic friends or decisions when things are going smoothly?

  Can I see where this pattern negates any progress I try making?

  Can I challenge myself to stick with the seven days then re-evaluate later?

- If boredom creeps in, lean in instead of running away.

- If you feel trapped by structure, remind yourself that consistency doesn't remove freedom—it creates it.

6. Receiving Success Without Destroying It

Self-Deception at Play: You tell yourself success doesn't mean anything. You minimize small wins, dismiss praise, and quickly shift your focus to what's still going wrong. You convince yourself it was luck, a fluke, or that it won't last.

Unconscious Motivation: Success feels like a setup. So you preemptively ruin opportunities to avoid the pain of losing something you let yourself enjoy. Self-sabotage becomes a twisted form of control: if you destroy it, at least no one else can. But underneath all of that is a fear that you aren't capable of sustaining anything meaningful—and if you prove yourself wrong, you'll be expected to keep showing up.

Rebellion Zone: Let success exist without sabotaging it.

Why This Works: Your brain assumes success is either fake, temporary, or a trap. But when you resist self-sabotage, you prove to your brain that success isn't a setup.

How This Plays Out in Real Life:

- You achieve something significant but immediately downplay it as luck or coincidence.

- You get a great opportunity, but ghost or sabotage before it fully materializes.

- When people praise your work, you deflect, diminish, or reject the compliment.

- You feel uncomfortable when life is going well and look for ways to self-destruct.

- You assume any good thing will eventually fall apart, so you preemptively ruin it on your terms.

- You associate long-term success with increased vulnerability, so you prevent yourself from sustaining it.

The Challenge: Let Success Happen Without Destroying It

- When you achieve something, stop before dismissing it. Instead of saying, "It's not a big deal," try saying, "This is a small productive step and it did require effort. Perhaps I can do even more."

- If you feel the urge to sabotage or blow something up that was going well in your life, wait 24 hours before making a decision. Give yourself time to recognize whether it's fear talking and establish the history of the pattern, *ask yourself*:

    Historically, do I mess things up when they seem to be going well?

    Can I see where this may be a subconscious desire to destabilize my life or relationships so my brain can feel "safe"?

    Is it possible I'm afraid of what would happen if this keeps getting better?

    Would I finally have something I'd be afraid to lose?

    Can I challenge myself to see that not ever caring about anything is a destructive way to live life?

- Keep a running tab of wins. Write down every small and big win so your brain can't deny the progress.

- When you get external praise, force yourself to accept it. No deflecting, no self-deprecating comments—just say, "Thank you."

7. Financial Consistency Without Self-Sabotage

Self-Deception at Play: You tell yourself money doesn't matter. You avoid your bank account, overspend on things that give you a quick hit of dopamine, and pretend you'll figure it out later. You rationalize it by saying you're not materialistic or that you don't care about security, but underneath it all, you're dodging the responsibility of facing your financial reality.

Unconscious Motivation: Your brain keeps your relationship with money chaotic so you never have to confront what stability—or long-term vision—might actually require from you. Recklessness becomes a shield against the fear that you're not capable of maintaining control, and avoiding the truth feels better than facing the possibility that change is in your hands.

Rebellion Zone: Track spending and stick to one financial commitment.

Why This Works: Your brain keeps money chaotic so it never feels like a source of security. By engaging with financial reality, you prove to yourself that stability is possible.

How This Plays Out in Real Life:

- You avoid looking at your bank account because you assume the worst.

- You spend impulsively and justify it with, "I'll figure it out later."

- You tell yourself that savings don't matter because you don't care about that stuff.

The Challenge: Track Spending and Stick to One Financial Commitment

- For 30 days, track every single dollar you spend in a notebook.

- Save $5 per day in a lockbox or bank account for 30 days.

- Resist the urge to avoid financial reality. Look at your balance every morning for 5 minutes, even when it makes you uncomfortable.

8. Daily Movement to Override Laziness

Self-Deception at Play: You tell yourself movement isn't that important—or that you'll get to it later. You wait until you "feel like it," even though that feeling rarely comes. You rationalize inactivity by blaming tiredness, discomfort, or your mood. You chase ease, comfort, or numbing instead of choosing the thing that would actually make you feel better. You label movement as optional or excessive, when in truth, you're just avoiding the discipline it requires.

Unconscious Motivation: Your brain treats movement as pointless effort. Movement threatens that numbness—so your brain convinces you to stay still in the name of "rest," when it's really just self-sabotage in disguise.

Rebellion Zone: Move your body every day for at least 10 minutes—even if you don't feel like it.

Why This Works: Your brain associates movement with unnecessary effort, but consistent movement moves energy in your body and helps you somatically release.

How This Plays Out in Real Life:

- You avoid exercise or embodiment.

- You convince yourself that movement "doesn't really matter."

- You trick yourself into thinking you need to feel good to move but moving will actually help you feel better.

The Challenge: Engage in 5 Minutes of Intentional Movement Daily

- Move your body every day for at least 5 minutes with a timer.

- Pick one movement (dance, shake with shoes off or walking in place) and do it for at least 5 minutes daily.

9. Breaking Negative Content Loops

Self-Deception at Play: You convince yourself that your content choices don't really matter. You downplay how much negativity, violence, or chaos you consume—and how deeply it affects your mindset. You pretend you're just observing, but you're actually reinforcing your own disconnection from hope, peace, and purpose.

Unconscious Motivation: You gravitate toward chaos because it validates your belief that nothing matters. Dark or disturbing content keeps you emotionally numb and detached—it confirms your worldview and protects you from disappointment.

Rebellion Zone: Do a dark content fast Monday, Wednesday, and Friday this week. Replace it with Binaural Beats or nature sounds.

> **Note:** You don't need to jump to toxic positivity—just choose something that doesn't feed despair. Nature videos, calming music, a documentary that teaches something, or even silence. Interrupt the loop.

Why This Works: Your brain uses dark or chaotic content to stay disconnected from the present moment and justify detachment from life. When you replace even a small part of your content consumption with something grounded, your nervous system starts to reset. You prove to your brain that peace doesn't mean naivety—and it doesn't require you to give up your edge or insight. It simply shifts you out of hopelessness.

How This Plays Out in Real Life:

- You consume a steady diet of violent, dark, or disturbing content.

- You avoid engaging with anything that feels "too positive" or "fake."

The Challenge: Replace 15 Minutes of Dark Content With Something Neutral

- Cut off your negative content consumption for 24 hours.

- If you feel resistance, *ask yourself*:

  Does it feel like humanity is so broken and dark that this at least feels honest?

  Is it possible that my brain avoids upbeat or funny because it feels fake or like a setup?

  Can I challenge myself to cut this off for 24 hours at a time and see what shifts?

10. Changing Your Crowd to Shift Your Identity

Self-Deception at Play: You tell yourself your friends "get you," even when they actively encourage self-destruction or feed your worst habits. You ignore red flags and justify their influence by calling it freedom or authenticity. You label more stable, grounded people as fake, judgmental, or just too soft. The truth is, you'd rather feel accepted in dysfunction than risk feeling out of place in a healthy environment.

Unconscious Motivation: You cling to people who mirror your chaos because it keeps you from having to change. Being around others who normalize instability makes you feel safe—because you're not the only one spinning out. So you reject the people who challenge your narrative and stay loyal to those who help you stay stuck.

Rebellion Zone: Limit time with chaotic or destructive influences, and initiate one connection per week with someone who models the kind of stability you say you want.

You don't have to cut everyone off immediately—but you do need to stop pretending your environment doesn't shape you. Curate your circle with intention.

Why This Works: By shifting your environment, you prove to yourself that identity isn't tied to chaos. It's a choice.

How This Plays Out in Real Life:

- You stay in social circles that encourage self-destruction or chaos.

- You dismiss stable, supportive people as "boring" or "out of touch."

- You stick with friends you feel won't judge your lifestyle or outlook.

The Challenge: Spend Time With One Stable Person Weekly

- Have one conversation per week with someone who is outside of your current circle and not chaos-driven.

- Resist the urge to immediately write them off as "not your type of person."

- If discomfort or disgust creeps in, *ask yourself*:

  What qualities does this person have that would benefit my life?

  Can I challenge myself to observe them rather than convince myself we have to be best friends?

What You Gain by Embracing Rebellion Zones

By embracing Rebellion Zones, you break free from the self-imposed chains of chaos and instability. Here's what you stand to gain:

1. Stability Without the Fear of Losing It

You start to understand that stability doesn't always end in disappointment. By allowing stability into your life without resisting it, you experience a new kind of freedom—one that's grounded and secure, rather than controlled or stifled. Real freedom doesn't require constant instability. You learn to enjoy peace without waiting for it to crumble.

2. Meaningful Effort Without the Fear of Failure

By putting in effort without obsessing over the outcome, you learn that trying isn't a waste of time—it's an investment in your future. You start seeing that real growth happens by embracing it as part of the journey. You gain the ability to try, fail, and learn without beating yourself up for it. Effort becomes a tool for progress rather than a gamble.

3. Autonomy That Doesn't Rely on Rebellion

By committing to something that's meaningful, you learn that you can be independent without rejecting all forms of structure. Real autonomy doesn't come from rebelling against everything. It comes from making deliberate choices that serve your goals. You gain the power to choose your commitments while still maintaining your freedom, without the need to constantly resist the structure.

4. Peace Without the Urge to Disrupt

You discover that stability doesn't have to be boring. The peace that comes from embracing steadiness allows you to focus on creating lasting, meaningful relationships and goals. Instead of sabotaging to feel something, you learn how to properly label or categorize calm. You gain the ability to enjoy life's quiet moments and create lasting meaning without needing to stir chaos.

5. Trust Without the Need to Test

You learn that true connection comes from trusting people without pushing them away first. By allowing relationships to unfold naturally, you learn that people can stick around and engage without being tested. You gain deeper, more authentic connections with people who stay because they want to, not because they were forced to prove it.

6. Confidence Without Sabotage

Instead of sabotaging your success out of fear, you begin to embrace opportunities and let them unfold. You recognize that success doesn't have to be fleeting or disappointing if you choose to commit to it. You gain the ability to fully commit to relationships, goals, and yourself, knowing you're worthy of success and capable of seeing it through.

7. Momentum That Actually Goes Somewhere

You stop the cycle of starting and stopping, allowing your efforts to build and move forward. Instead of running from predictability, you gain the consistency that propels you toward meaningful progress. You gain momentum that builds evidence of success and effort, instead of stalling and feeling hopeless.

8. A Sense of Control That Isn't Dependent on Destruction

Real power comes from choosing your direction with intention. You learn that control doesn't have to be about avoiding commitment, but about making choices that align with your goals. You gain the ability to control your life by making conscious, empowered choices, rather than simply reacting to situations or pushing everything away.

9. Freedom That Isn't Just Avoidance in Disguise

You start to see that true freedom is about having options, not avoiding responsibility or commitment. You learn how to make empowered choices that create real autonomy, rather than using avoidance as a way to feel in control. You gain true freedom by embracing the discomfort of growth, rather than staying stuck in the familiar patterns of avoidance and resistance.

The Bottom Line

Your brain has convinced you that stability is an illusion, consistency is pointless, and effort will only end in failure. If you don't invest, you can't lose. If you don't try, you can't be disappointed. If you don't believe in stability, you won't be the fool who trusted it.

But here's the truth your brain won't let you accept:

- You don't actually "thrive in chaos"—you've just learned to survive it.

- Disrupting things before they settle doesn't make you in control—it keeps you trapped.

- The effort you avoid is the very thing that would break you out of the cycle you hate.

Your Rebellion Zones aren't here to force you into a rigid, structured life. They aren't here to tell you to embrace predictability, schedules, or routines that feel like a prison. Instead, they exist to disrupt the belief that chaos is your only option. They are about proving to your brain, through action, that:

- Momentum doesn't mean the trap is closing in—it means you're actually going somewhere.

- Stability isn't a setup—it's what gives you space to actually build something.

- Effort isn't wasted energy—it's how you break the pattern you've been stuck in.

- Connection isn't control—it's what makes life worth engaging in at all.

Your biggest challenge will be acting before you "feel" like it. You're not going to "feel" ready. Your brain pattern tricks you into thinking that focused attention toward a future goal is futile. But, if you learn to push through the early discomfort, your life will change and you won't be able to deny it.

CHAPTER 31

THE LONG CON: DISMANTLING THE SYSTEM

What Is a Long Con?

A *long con* isn't a typical con artist scam. It's not a quick deception that gets exposed and leaves you feeling duped. It's a carefully orchestrated, slow-burning manipulation that unfolds over time Unlike a short con, which relies on speed and misdirection, a long con conditions you to accept falsehoods as truth. You've likely been living inside this con for so long that you no longer recognize it as deception.

A long con works because:

> • **It starts early.** The deception begins before you ever have the awareness to question it.

> • **It feels normal.** The system is so deeply woven into your thinking that it feels like you—not something happening to you.

> • **It shapes your choices.** Every decision you make is subtly guided by the rules of the con.

> • **It reinforces itself.** You unknowingly participate in maintaining it, making it stronger with every cycle.

The Long Con You've Been Living

Your brain has been running its own long con on you since early childhood. It has weaponized systems of language against you, shaping your perception of reality in ways that feel true—but aren't. Every assumption you've made about yourself, other people, and the world around you has been filtered through a deceptive internal logic system designed to keep you in familiar patterns, even when those patterns are destructive.

Think about:

- Every time you assumed someone would abandon you before they actually did.

- Every time you told yourself you had to control a situation to feel safe.

- Every time you believed you weren't capable of something before you even tried.

That wasn't reality. That was the con—your brain's scripted manipulation, built from early childhood inputs that shaped your belief system. It's been playing the long game, creating a loop so airtight that you've spent your life arguing in favor of your own limitations.

The Trap of Weaponized Language

The way your brain reinforces this con is through language—the internal narration that defines what you believe is possible. Every time you categorize an experience—"This is dangerous," "I'm not good enough," "People can't be trusted"—you are reinforcing the same deceptive logic that's kept you stuck all along.

This happens at the speed of thought, so you don't notice it. But make no mistake: this isn't random. It's a system, a structured, predictable system that determines how you react, what choices you perceive as available, and—most importantly—what options you never consider at all.

Your brain's primary job is to perceive and generate language to categorize and define what it thinks it's seeing. When you see, hear, feel, or experience something, your brain names it. You see a round red fruit, and your brain generates the word "apple." You feel the heat of the sun on your skin, and your brain generates the word "warm." You hear the sound of laughter, and your brain generates the word "happy."

628

These labels feel automatic and factual, but they are just your brain's attempt to organize input into something that makes sense.

This extends beyond objects and sensations—it applies to feelings, interactions, and entire belief systems. You feel a hug from your partner, and your brain generates the word "safe." But for someone else—someone whose past experiences have shaped a different set of definitions—a hug at the wrong time might generate the word "frustrating," "smothering," or even "threatening." They are all the same physical experience with completely different brain-generated labels.

Language follows perception, translating raw experience into structured meaning. But here's where the con takes hold: your brain doesn't pull these labels from an objective dictionary. It pulls them from your past experiences, your patterns, and the assumptions you've reinforced over time. The words your brain generates aren't necessarily true, but once they are assigned, they shape what you believe you're seeing. You're perceiving a narrated version of reality, one shaped by the language your brain has attached to past experiences.

Your brain has spent decades rigging the game against you, using a system you don't even know is there. It has convinced you that the way you see things is the way they are, when in reality, you've been playing by rules you never agreed to.

Why Awareness Alone Won't Save You

This is why self-awareness alone fails. You can't outthink a system that's already controlling your thoughts. You can journal about your feelings, meditate on your triggers, and analyze your past all you want—but if you don't dismantle the language system itself, the con remains intact. The awareness that you need to change isn't enough.

Your brain isn't just misinterpreting or distorting reality—it's actively reinforcing its own faulty conclusions, making sure you don't question them. It does this by distorting perception, restricting available choices, and feeding you a loop of justifications that make dysfunctional behaviors seem logical. The more you argue with it, the more evidence it supplies to prove itself right. This is why so many people feel stuck—awareness puts you in a staring contest with your brain, but it doesn't give you the ability to win.

To break out of this loop, you have to strategically disrupt the system. You must teach your brain to recognize where it has distorted perception, locked you into false conclusions, or manipulated reality to fit its existing narrative. The moment the con is exposed, your brain disengages. For the first time, you can see the full spectrum of choices that were always there. This is what allows you to enter your Rebellion Zone.

But here's the catch: your brain isn't going to just roll over and accept this. It will fight to maintain its control, and it will do so using the same language structures that have kept you trapped all along. The only way to dismantle this system is to understand exactly how your brain argues against you—and that means stepping into the courtroom.

The Tale of Two Lawyers: The Prosecutor vs. The Defense Attorney

Inside your mind, there's a constant trial happening—one where your past, your fears, and your deepest insecurities are being used as evidence against you. But this isn't a fair trial.

On one side of the courtroom, you have the Prosecutor—a ruthless, manipulative force whose sole job is to keep you stuck. He's polished, strategic, and willing to play dirty. Think Harvey Specter from Suits—a lawyer so sharp and charming that even when he's breaking the law, you find yourself rooting for him. That's your Prosecutor. He knows all your secrets, every mistake you've ever made, every doubt you've ever whispered to yourself—and he's weaponized them against you. He has one job: to prove beyond a shadow of a doubt that you can't change.

On the other side, you have your Defense Attorney—the one who's supposed to be fighting for you. But there's a problem. Right now, your Defense is weak, unprepared, and barely audible. If the Prosecutor is Harvey Specter, your Defense Attorney is the first public defender in My Cousin Vinny—the guy who seems fine behind closed doors but then steps up in court, stutters through his opening statement, and completely falls apart. If you don't fire him fast, you're going to prison.

This is the reality of your inner dialogue.

The Prosecutor's Tactics: How Your Brain Tricks You into Staying Stuck

Your Prosecutor doesn't argue fairly. He twists facts, distorts memories, and makes sure you see only the evidence that supports his case. He's the master of selective storytelling—cutting out every moment of resilience, success, or progress you've ever had and highlighting only your failures.

His strategy includes:

• **Weaponizing your secrets.** He drags out your past mistakes and uses them as proof that you can't change.

• **Distorting reality.** He takes something small and makes it seem like irrefutable evidence that you are doomed to repeat the past.

• **Using your fears against you.** He convinces you that stepping outside of your comfort zone will only lead to disaster.

• **Manipulating you into believing he's protecting you.** He makes you think his arguments are keeping you safe, when in reality, you're just experiencing Stockholm syndrome.

Here's the most dangerous part: you believe him.

You've spent so much time listening to the Prosecutor's voice that you've started to think he's the one looking out for you. You trust him. You think he's the only one telling you the truth.

Why Your Defense Attorney Is Losing (and How to Turn It Around)

Right now, your Defense Attorney doesn't stand a chance. He's muted, unprepared, and constantly drowned out by the sheer force of the Prosecutor's argument.

• **He has no strategic counterargument.** The Prosecutor anticipates your weak defenses and shuts them down before they can gain traction.

• **His voice is too quiet.** The Prosecutor's argument is loud, fast, and confident. Your Defense is hesitant, unsure, and unconvincing.

• **You've been rooting for the wrong side.** You've been so conditioned to trust the Prosecutor's voice that you don't even give your Defense a chance to speak.

If you were watching this trial unfold from the outside, you'd be screaming at the defendant to fire their attorney and fight back. That defendant is you.

The Turning Point: Strengthening Your Defense

To win this trial, you don't need to "silence" the Prosecutor, you need to out-strategize him. That means:

1. **Building a stronger argument.** Anticipate the Prosecutor's tricks before he uses them.

2. **Raising the volume on your Defense Attorney.** Make his presence impossible to ignore.

3. **Refusing to root for the Prosecutor anymore.** Recognize that he's not here to protect you. He's here to keep you exactly where you are.

This isn't about empty affirmations, blind optimism or willing your way through it. It's about dismantling the Prosecutor's case so thoroughly that your brain is forced to acknowledge reality. You're not stuck because you're incapable—you're stuck because your Prosecutor has been running the show unchallenged.

That ends now.

The ACB Pathway: How Perception Becomes a Closed System

How Your Brain Shrinks Your Choices

In every moment, as a human being with free will, you can choose anything. You have an infinite number of possibilities—smile, laugh, yell, run, crack a joke, hide, take a deep breath, change the subject, say nothing at all. So why don't you?

Why, in the moments that matter most, do you always seem to default to the same handful of responses?

Your brain technically allows for free will—but only up to a point. Right now, your brain pattern locks you in a cycle that limits your choices before you even realize it's happening. It's not that you can't choose differently. It's that you don't even see the full range of choices in the first place.

This happens because of the language of assumption—a silent but powerful force that runs in the background of your mind, shaping what you believe is available to you.

What Is an Assumption?

An assumption is your brain's instant interpretation of reality, based on what it has already learned to expect. It's the first filter applied to your perception, deciding what is likely to be true before you even have time to consciously process what's happening. Assumptions feel automatic and factual because your brain presents them as obvious truths, but in reality, they are pattern-driven predictions, not facts.

And here's where the trap is set:

 • **Your assumption is a byproduct of your Brain Pattern's perception.** It is your brain's automatic shortcut to determine what is happening and what it means.

 • **Once the assumption forms, your brain moves to conclusion.** The conclusion is the moment your brain turns the assumption into a logical-sounding truth that reinforces your pattern.

 • **Your conclusion dictates the behavioral choices you believe are available to you.** At this point, you are no longer responding to reality—you are responding to the filtered version of reality that aligns with your assumption. The only choices that remain are the ones that won't disprove the conclusion.

This entire process happens automatically and at lightning speed. You don't consciously decide to limit your choices—your brain does it for you. Let's break this down with an example:

Let's say you're about to have a difficult conversation with someone. The moment you consider bringing it up, your brain picks up on a subtle look in their eye and the assumption begins:

 • **Assumption:** People are untrustworthy and can snap without warning.

 • **Conclusion:** I need to keep this to myself or wait for a better time.

 • **Behavior:** Keep the topic hidden until a better time.

Look at what just happened. In one second, your brain removed every choice that would have opposed the assumption. If the full range of possible choices had been available, you might have considered speaking openly, setting a boundary, or resolving the issue. But your brain locked those options out of your awareness, leaving you with limited choices: silence, withholding, waiting for a better time or handling it myself.

You didn't rationally decide to avoid the conversation. Your brain pre-filtered your options to protect the belief that people can't be trusted.

The Circle Exercise: What's Really Happening in Your Mind

Right now, you believe you are making choices. And in a technical sense, you are. But what you don't realize is that your brain is making most of those choices for you before you even become aware of them.

To visualize this, picture two circles:

- The large outer circle represents all possible behavioral choices—everything you could do in response to a situation.

- The smaller inner circle represents the restricted set of choices your brain allows you to see.

When your brain pattern isn't engaged, you have access to the entire outer circle, meaning you can see and consider every possible response—from the most predictable to the most unexpected. You have full access to free will.

But the second your brain pattern activates, the filtering process begins. Your brain forms an assumption, which then leads to a conclusion. And as soon as that conclusion is drawn, the entire field of available choices shrinks to only those that reinforce the assumption. All other possibilities disappear.

At this point, you are no longer choosing freely. You are choosing from a pre-filtered set of options that align with what your brain has already decided is true.

And here's where it gets worse: this process creates a self-fulfilling prophecy.

Your assumption dictates your behavior, and your behavior generates the outcome that confirms the original assumption.

How This Becomes a Self-Fulfilling Prophecy

Let's go back to the difficult conversation example:

- **Assumption:** People are untrustworthy and can snap without warning.

- **Conclusion:** It's better not to bring this conversation up right now.

- **Behavior:** Keep the topic hidden until a better time.

- **Outcome:** The issue festers, resentment builds, and the other person eventually does react negatively—either because they

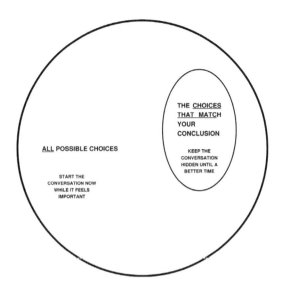

YOUR CONCLUSION DEFINES THE NEW LIMITED DATA SET YOU PERCEIVE

THE <u>CHOICES</u>
THAT MATCH
YOUR
CONCLUSION

KEEP THE
CONVERSATION
HIDDEN UNTIL A
BETTER TIME

<u>ALL</u> POSSIBLE CHOICES

START THE
CONVERSATION NOW
WHILE IT FEELS
IMPORTANT

EX. *ASSUMPTION*; PEOPLE ARE UNTRUSTWORTHY AND CAN SNAP AT ANY MOMENT
EX. *CONCLUSION:* IT'S NOT SAFE TO BRING UP THIS CONVERSATION RIGHT NOW.

Pictured Above: ACB Pathway Diagram

feel tension or because they feel you were being dishonest and manipulative.

Now your brain uses that reaction as evidence that people are untrustworthy. This wasn't an objective reality—it was a cycle.

Your assumption narrowed your available choices, your choices shaped your behavior, and your behavior directly influenced the outcome in a way that confirmed the original assumption.

This is the trap of self-fulfilling prophecies. Your brain creates proof that its assumptions are correct, not because they were true to begin with, but because your limited choices made them inevitable.

If the full range of options had been available to you (represented by the large outer circle in the diagram), you might have spoken up earlier, de-escalated the situation, or resolved the issue before it turned into a problem. But because those choices were filtered out before you even considered them, the only path forward was the one that validated your assumption.

Your Brain Does This Automatically

You never consciously decided to eliminate certain choices. Your brain filtered out the idea of speaking up before you could even consider it.

This happens so fast that it feels like free will, but what's actually happening is that your brain has created an artificial limitation, locking you inside the small circle. And because you can't see the choices that were removed, you don't question it.

And the more emotionally charged a situation is, the more guaranteed it is that your ACB pathway will be activated. When emotions run high—when you feel hurt, scared, angry, or vulnerable—your brain tightens the filter even further, ensuring you default to the most predictable and familiar response.

If this filtering process weren't happening, you'd have access to every choice in the outer circle, meaning you could respond based on what's best for you in the moment.

Most people don't even realize their choices are being filtered because they've never stopped to question it.

The first step in breaking out of this loop is recognizing that your brain is constantly shrinking your choices to fit an assumption. Once you see it happening, you can start to challenge the assumption, expand your perceived choices, and ultimately break into the full outer circle.

Your goal isn't to force yourself into new behaviors—it's to remove the false limitations that have been placed on you so that you can finally make real choices.

Right now, you default to the same small set of choices over and over because your Prosecutor controls the case. His argument is airtight because it's been reinforced by years of lived experience. He doesn't just present evidence—he filters what even counts as evidence in the first place. This means that, before you ever make a decision, before you ever feel an emotion, before you ever even perceive an available option, your brain has already pre-filtered reality to fit a predetermined set of conclusions.

ACBs: The Language of the Prosecutor

Your brain filters your reasoning. Every assumption you make about people, the world, and yourself is locked into place by an unseen structure that keeps the Prosecutor's case intact.

This structure is called an ACB Pathway—Assumption, Conclusion, Behavior—and it dictates how you experience reality:

1. **Assumption.** The subconscious belief about how people will act or how events will unfold.

2. **Conclusion.** The automatic decision about what you must do to prepare, respond, or protect yourself.

3. **Behavior.** The small, pre-filtered set of actions your brain allows you to choose from—keeping the conclusion true.

ACBs are self-reinforcing. They don't just predict behavior—they lock it in. If your assumption is that people can't be trusted, your conclusion will be that you have to rely only on yourself. Your brain will then limit your behavioral options to things that reinforce that belief—micromanaging, over-preparing, pushing people away—ensuring that even if someone is trustworthy, you never give them a chance to prove it.

Here's how this plays out in real time:

- **Assumption:** People are untrustworthy and will let me down.

- **Conclusion:** I have to handle things on my own, or I'll get hurt.

- **Behavior:** Over-preparing, micromanaging, keeping people at arm's length, refusing help.

Your assumption stays true, not because it's a universal fact, but because your behavior ensures that you never step outside of it. Even when people offer support, you resist, test, or withdraw. Eventually, they either stop trying or let you down in some way. And just like that, your Prosecutor gets another piece of evidence to add to his case.

If this is happening in one small area of life, it's a nuisance. When it's running the entire show, it's a closed-loop system that keeps you locked inside a false perception of reality.

This is why understanding your ACB structure is critical. Once you see the mechanism, you can start to break it apart. Now, let's look at the general ACB structures across Abandonment, Rejection, and Chaos patterns to see how they operate.

ACBs Across Brain Pattern Types: Abandonment Patterns

Brain Pattern Types will have similar ACBs within their typology, as the architecture of assumptions, conclusions, and behaviors follows a predictable framework. However, just as the Source Belief Spectrum has variance, ACBs also present subtle but meaningful differences. These variations don't change the core structure of how an ACB functions, but they do shape the specific way the belief manifests in behavior. In this section, we will break down the general ACB structure for each pattern type while also highlighting the slight variances that influence how these beliefs drive decision-making and emotional responses. By understanding both the commonalities and nuances within your pattern, you can start to observe your own ACBs in real time—spotting the way your brain pre-filters choices to reinforce its assumptions.

General Language Structure of an ACB for Origin Source Belief

- **Assumption:** People will _____ (how you expect others to act or how they will influence unfolding events).

- **Conclusion:** I have to _____ (what you believe you need to do to prepare or handle the situation).

- **Behavior:** The pre-filtered set of behavioral choices your brain allows you to see, designed to keep the conclusion true.

For all Abandonment patterns, the general Assumption is: people are untrustworthy and will let me down.

Variants of the Assumption (Abandonment Patterns):

- People are untrustworthy and won't follow through.

- People are untrustworthy and will say one thing but do another.

- People are untrustworthy and will leave me behind and lie to me.

- People are untrustworthy and have ulterior motives.

Three Key Takeaways for Abandonment:

1. **Core assumption of betrayal.** All Abandonment patterns share the fundamental belief that people are untrustworthy and will ultimately let them down. This assumption sets the stage for self-protective behaviors and control mechanisms.

2. **Variation in perceived untrustworthiness.** While the core assumption remains the same, different Abandonment patterns interpret betrayal in slightly different ways—some expect people to be unreliable, deceptive, emotionally or physically abandoning, or manipulative.

3. **Predictable filtering of experience.** These assumptions pre-filter behavioral choices, meaning individuals with Abandonment patterns will unconsciously expect and interpret interactions in a way that reinforces their belief, even if evidence suggests otherwise.

For all Rejection patterns, the general Assumption is: people will blame me for something or make me feel unworthy.

Variants of the Assumption (Rejection Patterns):

- People will blame me or make me feel stupid.

- People are talking about me, and I'm going to be made fun of or judged.

- People will think I'm inadequate, stupid, or not enough.

- People don't understand me, and I will judged unfairly

- People will ignore me or accuse me of something I didn't do.

Three Key Takeaways for Rejection:

1. **Core assumption of judgment and blame.** All Rejection patterns share the belief that people will assign blame or make them feel unworthy, leading to a heightened sensitivity to criticism, exclusion, or misrepresentation.

2. **Variation in how rejection is expected.** While the foundation of rejection remains the same, different patterns anticipate it in specific ways—some fear being labeled as stupid or inadequate, others expect social ridicule, unfair judgment, or outright false accusations.

3. **Hypervigilance to social perception.** These assumptions shape how interactions are interpreted, making individuals prone to seeing judgment or exclusion even when it may not be present, reinforcing a cycle of defensiveness or withdrawal.

For all Chaos patterns, the general Assumption is: there's no point in trying because everything is a setup.

Variants of the Assumption (Chaos Patterns):

- Nothing matters because life is cruel and will always be unfair.

- Everything falls apart and blows up in my face no matter what.

- The worst will always happen, and there is nothing I can do about it.

- Nothing is as it seems, and it's better to expect nothing.

Three Key Takeaways for Chaos:

1. **Core assumption of futility.** All Chaos patterns operate under the belief that there is no point in trying because the outcome is already rigged against them, leading to a deep sense of resignation or defiance.

2. **Variation in how chaos is expected.** While the core belief remains the same, different variations shape how inevitability is framed. Some see life as inherently cruel and unfair, others expect constant destruction, unavoidable worst-case scenarios, or deception at every turn.

3. **Self-perpetuating disengagement.** These assumptions discourage effort and long-term investment, reinforcing behaviors that either sabotage potential success or keep individuals from fully engaging in opportunities, relationships, or personal growth.

The Red Rose Illusion: Are You Seeing Reality or Just Your Pattern?

As you're reading this chapter, surely some of you have felt the subtle or obvious pushback of thoughts like:

- But these things are true.
- People really do always let me down.
- Everything in my life does fall apart
- I always make mistakes.

Here's the reality: you subconsciously seek out the people who will trigger your deepest fears and insecurities. For example, if you have anxious attachment, you're highly likely to seek out an emotionally unavailable partner. If you struggle with low self-trust, you may seek out an authoritarian presence but also feel judged and criticized by their communication style.

This may be the tougher pill to swallow, especially if you've recently ended a relationship that was fraught with tension and conflict. Sometimes, the way you engage with someone pushes them to act in a way that triggers you, and when you change the way you engage with them, their response changes too. But for some people, it's not as simple as that—it isn't just a response to a stimulus you are generating.

To properly illustrate this concept, imagine that you're standing at the edge of a large flower field. The field is covered in hundreds of colors and varieties. Your brain, however, believes it can only pick red roses. This is the distortion of your brain pattern. You could walk across the entire field and end up with a bouquet of red roses only. Was that because other flowers weren't available? No. It's because your brain hid them from you as you walked.

As you near the end of this book, you'll be faced with a decision that will come after you boldly step into your Rebellion Zones. When you look at the people around you in your relationships, and you've changed the stimulus you're giving, taken radical personal responsibility, and they still won't evolve with you—a red rose might just be a red rose. But more often than not, the way you were acting made it look like a red rose when they were really a daisy.

You will only truly know when you go first. Step into the Rebellion Zone and stay consistent. Remember that it may take time and repetition to get someone to respond to your new pattern interruption. So pay close attention to the guidelines in the next chapter for how to tie it all together—awareness of the patterns of self-deception and unconscious motivations, combined with the action of the Rebellion Zones and upcoming ELI questions. When you follow through completely, you'll finally see who is a rose and who is a daisy.

Conclusions Based on Adaptive Source Belief Variations

Once the assumption is made, the brain moves to a conclusion. A Conclusion in an ACB pathway is the internal rule or belief a person adopts as a direct response to their assumption about the world or other people. It represents what they believe they must do to prepare for, control, or survive the expected outcome. This belief is not typically questioned—it operates as a subconscious directive that shapes decision-making, emotional responses, and available behavioral choices. The conclusion will vary based on your Adaptive Source Belief.

Abandonment - Control to Be Safe (Overt):

Conclusion: I have to take action and manage this to avoid disaster.

Behavior: Direct, overt control—taking charge, leading, or fixing problems head-on, telling others what to do, criticizing.

Variants of the Conclusion (Overt):

- I have to manage this situation or do it myself to make sure it gets done.

- I have to control this situation by managing others and offering feedback.

- I have to take control of this situation because no one else is capable of fixing this.

- I have to take control of this situation; otherwise, it will turn on me.

- I have to get ahead of this situation by managing others, assuming the worst, or doing it myself.

Common Behavioral Responses for Overt Control:

- **Taking charge.** Stepping in and making decisions for others.

- **Micromanaging.** Feeling the need to oversee every step.

- **Over-functioning.** Taking on extra work to ensure things are "done right."

- **Directing.** Telling others what needs to be done.

- **Anticipating problems.** Fixing things before they "go wrong."

- **Asserting authority.** Using forcefulness or assertiveness to control outcomes.

Three Key Takeaways for Abandonment – Control to Be Safe (Overt):

1. **Control as a means of safety.** The core belief behind Overt Control is that taking charge is the only way to prevent disaster. This drives a relentless need to manage, direct, and fix situations to maintain stability.

2. **Variations in justification for control.** While all Overt Control patterns involve direct intervention, the specific reasoning varies—some believe they must handle everything themselves, others feel responsible for managing others, and some assume failure is inevitable without their control.

3. **Behavioral patterns reinforce the conclusion.** Individuals with this pattern actively assert control through behaviors like micromanaging, over-functioning, preemptively fixing problems,

and asserting authority, all of which keep the assumption that "no one else is capable" locked in place.

Abandonment – Control to Be Safe (Covert):

Conclusion: I have to watch this situation carefully and find subtle ways to get ahead of it.

Behavior: Indirect, behind-the-scenes control—observing, manipulating, or testing without overt action.

Variants of the Conclusion (Covert):

- I have to test or observe to see beyond people's ulterior motives.

- I have to observe and wait before I know what action to take.

- I have to anticipate and manipulate to get ahead of this situation.

- I have to figure out a way to fix this without looking controlling.

- I have to fix this behind the scenes without being caught.

Common Behavioral Responses for Control to Be Safe (Covert):

- **Testing.** Setting up subtle traps to see if people will follow through.

- **Withholding information.** Controlling the flow of details to maintain an upper hand.

- **Indirect questioning.** Using passive language to extract information.

- **Hyper-observation.** Paying attention to micro-expressions, inconsistencies, and tone shifts.

- **Strategic withdrawal.** Pulling back to gather data before making a move.

- **Social maneuvering.** Subtly influencing others without appearing controlling.

Three Key Takeaways for Abandonment – Control to Be Safe (Covert):

1. **Control through subtlety, not force.** Unlike Overt Control, Covert Control operates behind the scenes, using observation, manipulation, and careful planning to steer situations without appearing controlling.

643

2. **Variations in stealth-based control.** While all Covert Control patterns involve indirect management, the justification varies. Some feel the need to test for ulterior motives, others believe in waiting before acting, and some focus on fixing things discreetly to avoid exposure.

3. **Behavioral tactics maintain the illusion of non-control.** Those with this pattern rely on testing, withholding information, hyper-observing, and social maneuvering to influence outcomes while maintaining the appearance of neutrality or detachment.

Abandonment - Control to Be Safe (Switch):

Conclusion: I have to observe and select the most strategic way to fix this situation.

Behavior: Switching between overt and covert control depending on what seems most effective.

Variants of the Conclusion (Switch):

- I have to watch closely so I know what I need to do to fix this.

- I have to be adaptable and ready to fix this situation.

- I need to fix this by adapting my presentation to fit the best outcome.

Common Behavioral Responses for Switch Control

- **Shape-shifting.** Changing tone, demeanor, or tactics based on the situation.

- **Adapting to authority figures.** Shifting into compliance or rebellion depending on power dynamics.

- **Strategic compliance.** Pretending to go along while setting up a backup plan.

- **Controlling access.** Restricting or granting access to themselves or information.

Three Key Takeaways for Abandonment - Control to Be Safe (Switch):

1. **Control through adaptability.** Unlike rigid Overt or stealthy Covert Control, Switch Control adapts in real time, shifting between direct action and behind-the-scenes influence based on what seems most effective.

2. **Strategic shapeshifting.** Individuals with this pattern modify their approach depending on the situation, whether by

complying, rebelling, manipulating, or withdrawing, ensuring they maintain control without being easily detected.

3. **Control over perception and access.** Their behaviors, such as strategic compliance, controlling access to information or themselves, and adjusting their presentation, allow them to steer outcomes while maintaining flexibility and deniability.

Abandonment - Hold It All Together

Conclusion: I have to anticipate what could go wrong so I can start fixing things before they break.

Behavior: Preemptive problem-solving, self-sacrifice, and constant vigilance to maintain stability.

Variants of the Conclusion (Hold It All Together):

• I have to anticipate and observe to determine what needs to be done to fix this.

• I have to closely observe so I know what people need before they need it.

• I have to anticipate disaster and prepare myself to face it.

• I have to anticipate that I'll have to fix this or work harder.

• I have to figure out who is going to let me down before they do.

Common Behavioral Responses for Hold It All Together:

• **Over-functioning.** Taking on responsibility beyond what's necessary.

• **People-pleasing.** Trying to maintain harmony at all costs.

• **Emotional suppression.** Ignoring personal needs to keep things "stable."

• **Hyper-awareness.** Monitoring the emotional state of others.

• **Avoiding confrontation.** Letting things go unresolved to maintain peace.

• **Self-sacrificing.** Putting others' needs ahead of their own, even to the point of burnout.

Three Key Takeaways for Abandonment - Hold It All Together:

1. **Control through preemptive fixing.** The Hold It All Together pattern is driven by the belief that anticipating and solving

problems before they escalate is the only way to maintain stability, leading to hyper-vigilance and over-functioning.

2. **Sacrificing self to maintain peace.** Individuals with this pattern prioritize others' needs over their own, often engaging in people-pleasing, emotional suppression, and self-sacrifice to prevent conflict or instability.

3. **Hyper-awareness as a survival tactic.** They constantly monitor people's emotions and behaviors, believing they must predict disappointment, work harder than necessary, and avoid confrontation to keep everything from falling apart.

Rejection – Control to Receive Love and Be Safe (People-Pleasing Engaging)

Conclusion: I have to manage how I am perceived and adapt to what others want to avoid blame, criticism, or rejection.

Behavior: Highly visible, approval-seeking engagement—securing belonging through over-giving, over-performing, and prioritizing others' needs over their own while managing their image to ensure acceptance.

Variants of the Conclusion (People-Pleasing Engaging):

• I have to be a certain way for people to like me or see me the way I want to be seen.

• I have to make sure I don't upset or disappoint people, or I'll lose their approval.

• I'll get blamed or in trouble for doing something or saying something wrong if I don't compartmentalize, people-please, and manage others' emotions.

• I have to be agreeable and avoid conflict to keep people from turning against me.

• I have to constantly adjust how I present myself to maintain connection and ensure I'm not misunderstood.

Common Behavioral Responses for People-Pleasing Engaging:

• **Over-functioning.** Taking on excessive responsibilities to remain needed and valuable.

• **Seeking approval through high visibility.** Staying involved in everything to reinforce their importance.

- **Mirroring others.** Adjusting personality, opinions, or preferences to match those around them.

- **Over-apologizing.** Taking responsibility for things they didn't do to maintain harmony and avoid blame.

- **Compartmentalizing emotions.** Suppressing discomfort or boundaries to avoid disrupting the group dynamic.

- **Compulsive reassurance-seeking.** Asking validation-seeking questions ("Are you mad at me?" "Did I do something wrong?") to confirm they are still liked or included.

- **Struggling to say "no."** Defaulting to "yes" out of fear that setting boundaries will lead to rejection.

- **Deflecting conflict through humor or distraction.** Keeping things light to avoid uncomfortable conversations or direct confrontation.

- **Performing for acceptance.** Using achievements, charm, or helpfulness as proof of worthiness.

Three Key Takeaways for Rejection – Control to Receive Love and Be Safe (People-Pleasing Engaging):

1. **Control through image management.** The People-Pleasing – Engaging pattern is driven by the belief that maintaining a likable, agreeable image is the only way to avoid blame, criticism, or rejection, leading to compulsive adaptation to others' expectations.

2. **Over-functioning to secure belonging.** Individuals with this pattern prioritize external approval over their own needs, engaging in over-giving, over-performing, and mirroring others to ensure they are liked, included, and never seen as a problem.

3. **Avoidance of conflict at all costs.** Their behaviors—such as compulsive reassurance-seeking, over-apologizing, compartmentalizing emotions, and using humor to deflect conflict—reinforce the fear that setting boundaries or expressing true feelings will lead to rejection.

Rejection – Control to Receive Love and Be Safe (People-Pleasing Isolating)

Conclusion: I have to stay small, agreeable, and unnoticed to avoid blame, conflict, or rejection.

Behavior: Maintaining connection through compliance, invisibility, and minimizing personal needs—avoiding attention, confrontation, or anything that could make them stand out negatively.

Variants of the Conclusion (People-Pleasing Isolating):

- I can't express myself authentically—I have to compartmentalize or avoid this altogether.

- If I don't make a plan to change myself, I won't be received well by people around me.

- I have to be quiet and agreeable so I don't give people a reason to criticize or reject me.

- If I say or do the wrong thing, I'll be blamed, embarrassed, or pushed away.

- I have to follow expectations exactly so I don't stand out in a bad way.

- I have to suppress my real thoughts and emotions so I don't make people uncomfortable or upset.

- I have to wait for others to initiate, reach out, or invite me—if they don't, it means they don't want me there.

Common Behavioral Responses for People-Pleasing Isolating:

- **Avoiding leadership or visibility.** Preferring to stay in the background to avoid scrutiny or criticism.

- **Complying without question.** Following expectations or rules without considering personal preferences.

- **Waiting for others to make the first move.** Hesitating to initiate relationships, conversations, or opportunities.

- **Minimizing personal needs.** Avoiding asking for help, attention, or support to avoid feeling like a burden.

- **Suppressing emotions.** Keeping feelings private to avoid conflict or rejection.

- **Internalizing blame.** Assuming responsibility for misunderstandings, even when not at fault.

- **Ghosting or disappearing when overwhelmed.** Withdrawing rather than confronting discomfort.

- **Hyper-awareness of how they are perceived.** Constantly monitoring behavior to avoid being judged.

- **Avoiding direct confrontation.** Using silence, avoidance, or passive responses instead of addressing problems.

- **Struggling to say "no."** Agreeing to things they don't want to do out of fear of disappointing others.

- **Tolerating mistreatment to maintain relationships.** Believing that setting boundaries risks losing connection.

- **Compartmentalizing emotions.** Hiding certain aspects of themselves to fit into different social settings.

- **Over-preparing for interactions.** Strategizing what to say or do ahead of time to avoid making mistakes.

- **Planning self-improvement as a requirement for acceptance.** Feeling they must fix themselves before they are worthy of connection.

Three Key Takeaways for Rejection – Control to Receive Love and Be Safe (People-Pleasing Isolating):

1. **Control through invisibility and compliance.** The People-Pleasing – Isolating pattern is driven by the belief that staying small, agreeable, and unnoticed is the safest way to avoid rejection or criticism, leading to self-suppression and passivity in relationships.

2. **Minimizing needs to maintain connection.** Individuals with this pattern avoid asking for support, suppress emotions, and tolerate mistreatment out of fear that asserting themselves will lead to disapproval or abandonment.

3. **Fear of initiation and exposure.** Their behaviors—such as waiting for others to initiate, hyper-monitoring their perception, avoiding confrontation, and over-preparing for interactions—reinforce the belief that any misstep could result in rejection, making them hesitant to take up space in relationships or social settings.

Rejection – Control to Receive Love and Be Safe (Conflict-Prone Engaging)

Conclusion: I have to defend, prove, or explain myself to be accepted.

Behavior: Using intensity, persistence, or confrontation to secure love and respect—believing that emotional engagement, even through conflict, proves their worth in relationships.

Variants of the Conclusion (Conflict-Prone Engaging):

- I have to explain myself or win people over to my side, so I don't get blamed or judged.

- I have to be ready to defend myself or prove them wrong.

- I will never be loved or accepted as I am, so I have to force people to see my value.

- If I don't assert myself, I will be dismissed, overlooked, or forgotten.

- I have to challenge, push back, or create tension to prove I matter in relationships.

- I need to force validation or attention, or I will be ignored.

- If I let things go, it means I don't value myself enough to stand up for what's right.

- I have to test people to see if they truly care about me.

- If someone sets a boundary with me, it means they are rejecting me, and I have to push back.

- I have to create emotional intensity to keep people engaged—if things feel too calm, it means they don't care.

Common Behavioral Responses for Rejection – Control to Receive Love and Be Safe (Conflict-Prone Engaging)

- **Defensive arguing.** Reacting quickly to perceived criticism, often escalating minor disagreements into full-blown conflicts.

- **Justifying everything.** Feeling the need to over-explain or defend actions, even when not accused of anything.

- **Pushing boundaries to test loyalty.** Instigating conflict to see if people will stay or prove their commitment.

- **Emotional reactivity.** Responding with visible frustration, hurt, or anger when feeling misunderstood or unappreciated.

- **Seeking validation through debate.** Engaging in frequent intellectual or moral debates to prove worth or intelligence.

- **Over-correcting perceived injustice.** Jumping into conflicts (even when not personally involved) to defend fairness or prevent perceived mistreatment.

- **Passive-aggressive behavior.** Making pointed jokes, sarcastic remarks, or using subtle digs instead of addressing issues directly.

- **Needing the last word.** Struggling to let conversations or conflicts end without feeling like they won or proved their point.

- **Over-analyzing social interactions.** Obsessively replaying conversations, searching for ways they were wronged or misunderstood.

- **Anticipating rejection through anger.** Preemptively pushing people away by being combative before they can be rejected.

- **Asserting independence through conflict.** Resisting perceived control by rejecting help, advice, or collaboration.

- **Hyper-sensitivity to exclusion.** Feeling slighted or rejected over small social cues and responding with confrontation or withdrawal.

- **Intensely pursuing closure.** Struggling to let conflicts go without a clear resolution, even when the other person has moved on.

- **Toggling between connection and conflict.** Being highly engaged and warm one moment, then distant or combative the next, depending on emotional state.

- **Testing others' loyalty through emotional escalation.** Creating dramatic situations to see who will stick around or prove their devotion.

Three Key Takeaways for Rejection – Control to Receive Love and Be Safe (Conflict-Prone Engaging):

1. **Conflict as a means of securing connection.** The Conflict-Prone – Engaging pattern is driven by the belief that intensity, debate, or confrontation prove love, loyalty, and personal worth, making conflict feel necessary for validation.

2. **Persistent need to defend and prove worth.** Individuals with this pattern feel the need to justify, explain, or force recognition, leading to defensive arguing, over-correcting perceived injustices, and seeking validation through intellectual or emotional battles.

3. **Emotional push-pull reinforces fear of rejection.** Their behaviors—such as pushing boundaries to test loyalty, toggling between warmth and conflict, and anticipating rejection through anger—create a cycle where they unintentionally push people away while seeking proof of connection.

Rejection – Control to Receive Love and Be Safe (Conflict-Prone Isolating)

Conclusion: I have to withdraw, shut down, or leave to protect myself.

Behavior: Avoiding perceived rejection by pulling away first, suppressing emotions, or isolating—believing that distancing themselves prevents pain, judgment, or disappointment.

Variants of the Conclusion (Conflict-Prone Isolating):

- If I don't pull away first, I'll eventually be pushed out.
- I have to leave before people realize I don't belong.
- If I don't disappear, I'll be judged or humiliated.
- I have to suppress my emotions so I don't look weak.
- If I let people get too close, they'll hurt me.
- I can't trust relationships, so I need to keep my distance.
- If someone disagrees with me, it means they don't respect me.
- I have to withdraw when conflict arises to avoid being blamed.

Common Behavioral Responses for Rejection – Control to Receive Love and Be Safe (Conflict-Prone Isolating)

- **Internalizing conflict.** Holding onto resentment, frustration, or perceived injustices without verbalizing them, leading to passive withdrawal.

- **Avoiding direct confrontation.** Shutting down, stonewalling, or disengaging instead of addressing issues directly.

- **Silent retaliation.** Withdrawing affection, responsiveness, or engagement as a way to punish or test others.

- **Emotional self-isolation.** Pulling away from relationships when feeling misunderstood, unappreciated, or rejected.

- **Ruminating on past conflicts.** Replaying past disagreements or perceived slights, fueling resentment and avoidance.

- **Delaying responses to create distance.** Ignoring calls or messages, waiting longer to reply, or responding with minimal effort as a way to control engagement.

- **Hyper-sensitivity to criticism.** Taking feedback or neutral comments personally and withdrawing instead of discussing concerns.

- **Passive-aggressive avoidance.** Making vague statements like "It's fine" or "Don't worry about it" while internally holding onto anger.

- **Testing people through silence.** Withdrawing communication to see who will notice or make an effort to reconnect.

- **Disappearing after conflict.** Going radio silent or cutting people off completely instead of working through misunderstandings.

- **Interpreting boundaries as rejection.** Taking others' need for space as a sign of abandonment and responding by emotionally checking out.

- **Emotionally withholding to avoid vulnerability.** Keeping deep thoughts, struggles, or emotions private to prevent further perceived rejection.

- **Creating emotional distance preemptively.** Detaching from relationships or opportunities before they can result in rejection or criticism.

- **Minimizing their own needs.** Convincing themselves that speaking up isn't worth it, leading to long-term resentment.

- **Avoiding opportunities for repair.** Refusing to revisit conversations or conflicts, even when resolution is possible.

Three Key Takeaways for Rejection – Control to Receive Love and Be Safe (Conflict-Prone Isolating):

1. **Self-protection through withdrawal.** The Conflict-Prone – Isolating pattern is driven by the belief that pulling away first prevents rejection, criticism, or humiliation, leading to a habit of shutting down, disappearing, or emotionally detaching.

2. **Suppressing instead of addressing conflict.** Instead of directly confronting issues, individuals with this pattern internalize resentment, delay responses, and engage in silent retaliation, believing that avoidance shields them from pain or blame.

3. **Preemptive detachment reinforces isolation.** Their behaviors—such as interpreting boundaries as rejection, testing people through silence, and avoiding opportunities for repair—create a cycle where fear of rejection leads to self-imposed loneliness and unspoken resentment.

Rejection – Control to Receive Love (People-Pleasing Engaging)

Conclusion: I have to perform, adapt, or over-give to be loved.

Behavior: Seeking validation and connection through social engagement, over-functioning, and adaptability—believing that securing love requires effort, approval, and being indispensable.

Variants of the Conclusion (People-Pleasing Engaging):

- I have to stay involved and helpful so people see my value.

- I have to anticipate what others need and provide it before they ask.

- If I don't make people happy, they won't love me.

- I have to mirror others to make sure I fit in.

- I have to be the best, most reliable, or most entertaining to stay included.

- If I don't prove myself, I will be forgotten.

- I have to constantly adapt to keep people from leaving me.

Common Behavioral Responses for People-Pleasing Engaging:

- **Over-functioning in relationships.** Taking on emotional labor, fixing others' problems, or constantly proving worth.

- **Seeking approval through high visibility.** Staying involved in everything to reinforce importance.

- **Mirroring others.** Adjusting personality, values, or interests to match those around them.

- **Over-apologizing.** Taking responsibility for things they didn't do to avoid conflict.

- **Compartmentalizing emotions.** Suppressing discomfort or boundaries to maintain harmony.

- **Compulsive reassurance-seeking.** Frequently asking questions like "Are we good?" or "Did I do something wrong?"

- **Struggling to say "no."** Defaulting to "yes" out of fear that setting boundaries will lead to rejection.

- **Performing for acceptance.** Using charm, achievements, or helpfulness as proof of worthiness.

- **Deflecting conflict through humor or distraction.** Keeping things light to avoid uncomfortable conversations.

- **Prioritizing others' needs over their own.** Feeling guilty when focusing on their own desires or boundaries.

Three Key Takeaways for Rejection – Control to Receive Love (People-Pleasing Engaging):

1. **Love is seen as conditional.** The People-Pleasing – Engaging pattern is driven by the belief that love and belonging must be earned through constant giving, adapting, or performing, leading to over-functioning in relationships and a fear of being forgotten or excluded.

2. **Self-worth is tied to external validation.** Individuals with this pattern seek approval through high visibility, compulsive reassurance-seeking, and mirroring others, prioritizing how they are perceived over their own needs.

3. **Conflict and boundaries feel like a threat.** Their behaviors—such as struggling to say "no," over-apologizing, compartmentalizing emotions, and deflecting conflict through humor—stem from the fear that asserting themselves will lead to disconnection or abandonment.

Rejection – Control to Receive Love (People-Pleasing Isolating)

Conclusion: I have to stay quiet, agreeable, and unobtrusive to be accepted.

Behavior: Avoiding rejection by withdrawing, observing, and staying in the background—believing that not pushing buttons, staying out of the way, and blending in ensures love and acceptance.

Variants of the Conclusion (People-Pleasing Isolating):

- If I don't ruffle feathers, I won't give people a reason to reject me.

- I have to step back and observe rather than actively engage so I don't misstep.

- If I stay neutral, I won't get caught in conflict or drama.

- I have to be easygoing and undemanding so people will keep me around.

- If I express my real thoughts or needs, people might push back, and I don't want to deal with that.

- If I stay quiet, I won't say the wrong thing and embarrass myself.

- I have to let others take charge—if I step in, I might do it wrong.

Common Behavioral Responses for People-Pleasing Isolating:

- **Withdrawing instead of engaging.** Pulling back from conversations or group dynamics to avoid drawing attention.

- **Observing rather than participating.** Watching how others behave before deciding if and how to engage.

- **Avoiding conflict by staying neutral.** Not voicing strong opinions or taking sides to prevent upsetting others.

- **Letting others make decisions.** Deferring to others rather than asserting personal preferences.

- **Suppressing emotions to avoid upset.** Avoiding emotional expression so as not to disrupt harmony.

- **Monitoring social dynamics before engaging.** Waiting for cues from others rather than initiating interactions.

- **Holding back thoughts or input.** Preferring to listen rather than risking saying something that could be disagreed with.

- **Staying agreeable at all costs.** Going along with group decisions, even if they don't align with their own desires.

- **Avoiding leadership roles.** Letting others take charge to avoid being in a position of scrutiny.

- **Ruminating on discomfort.** Dwelling on mistreatment, unfairness, or unmet needs in their head rather than advocating for themselves.

Three Key Takeaways for Rejection - Control to Receive Love (People-Pleasing Isolating):

1. **Acceptance is linked to invisibility.** The People-Pleasing - Isolating pattern is driven by the belief that staying quiet,

agreeable, and unobtrusive is the safest way to avoid rejection, leading to passivity and self-suppression in relationships.

2. **Engagement is carefully calculated.** Individuals with this pattern observe rather than participate, defer decisions to others, and avoid strong opinions or emotional expression, believing that staying neutral protects them from conflict or disapproval.

3. **Internalizing instead of asserting.** Their behaviors—such as withdrawing instead of engaging, ruminating on discomfort, and suppressing emotions—reinforce a cycle where needs go unmet because they avoid advocating for themselves, leading to resentment and further isolation.

Rejection – Control to Receive Love (Conflict-Prone Engaging)

Conclusion: I have to defend, explain, or control situations to ensure I am prioritized and not blamed.

Behavior: Using intensity, confrontation, or persistence to secure love—believing that defending, proving, or asserting themselves is necessary to maintain connection and avoid being dismissed or overlooked.

Variants of the Conclusion (Conflict-Prone – Engaging):

• I have to defend or explain myself or do what everyone else wants to avoid being criticized or rejected.

• If I don't prepare my defense or try to control the situation, people will overlook or not prioritize me.

• I need to be on the defense and be ready to explain why I'm not to blame.

• If I don't push back, I will be dismissed or forgotten.

• I have to challenge, push, or create tension to prove I matter in relationships.

• I have to force validation, or people will take me for granted.

• If I let things go, it means I don't value myself enough to fight for love.

• If someone sets a boundary with me, it means they are rejecting me, and I have to push back.

• I have to create emotional intensity to keep people engaged—if things feel too calm, it means they don't care.

Common Behavioral Responses for Conflict-Prone Engaging:

- **Defensive communication.** Over-explaining, justifying, or preemptively defending themselves in conversations.

- **Testing relationships through conflict.** Creating tension or picking fights to see who will stay.

- **Forcing validation.** Repeating explanations or escalating discussions to make sure they are heard.

- **Challenging authority or structure.** Rejecting rules, guidance, or leadership, assuming it's meant to suppress them.

- **Pushing conversations even when the other person disengages.** Assuming persistence will force closeness.

- **Mistaking emotional intensity for connection.** Believing that fights, passion, or drama are proof of depth in relationships.

- **Interpreting boundaries as rejection.** Assuming any request for space or time apart means they are being cast aside.

- **Fixating on being "right," even if it harms relationships.** Believing that being wrong means they are unworthy of respect.

- **Holding grudges as a defense mechanism.** Using resentment to ensure they are never made a fool of again.

- **Refusing vulnerability, even if it would bring them closer to people.** Viewing emotional openness as something that can be used against them.

- **Overcompensating for a fear of being seen as weak.** Using aggression, dominance, or intensity to ensure they are taken seriously.

- **Pushing people away to see if they'll fight to stay.** Testing others' patience or commitment by creating distance or tension.

Three Key Takeaways:

1. **Conflict is used to secure connections.** The Conflict-Prone – Engaging pattern is driven by the belief that pushing back, asserting dominance, or creating intensity is necessary to ensure love, respect, and priority in relationships, leading to a cycle of defensiveness and confrontation.

2. **Validation must be fought for.** Individuals with this pattern

test relationships through conflict, force validation, and push conversations past their natural stopping point, believing that if they don't fight to be seen, they will be overlooked or dismissed.

3. **Boundaries and calmness feel like rejection.** Their behaviors—such as interpreting boundaries as abandonment, mistaking emotional intensity for love, and holding grudges to maintain control—reinforce the idea that if someone isn't actively engaging (even through tension), they don't care.

Rejection – Control to Receive Love (Conflict-Prone Isolating)

Conclusion: I have to pull away, shut down, or disappear to avoid blame, conflict, or rejection.

Behavior: Avoiding perceived rejection by withdrawing, shutting down, or isolating—believing that removing themselves from situations protects them from judgment, disappointment, or exclusion.

Variants of the Conclusion (Conflict-Prone Isolating):

- If I don't pull away first, I'll eventually be rejected or blamed.

- I have to leave before people realize I don't belong.

- If I don't disappear, I'll be criticized, judged, or embarrassed.

- I have to suppress my emotions and stay quiet to avoid being called out.

- If I let people get too close, they'll eventually hurt me.

- I have to detach so no one sees my weaknesses.

- If I remove myself from the situation, I won't have to explain or defend myself.

- I need to avoid situations where I might be expected to prove my worth.

Common Behavioral Responses for Conflict-Prone Isolating

- **Preemptive withdrawal.** Pulling away from people before they have a chance to reject them.

- **Emotional suppression.** Shutting down feelings instead of expressing them to avoid vulnerability.

- **Fixating on perceived slights.** Overanalyzing minor interactions as signs of judgment or rejection.

- **Ghosting.** Disappearing from relationships suddenly rather than confronting discomfort or conflict.

- **Pushing people away to test commitment.** Creating distance to see who will fight to keep them around.

- **Interpreting boundaries as rejection.** Assuming that someone needing space means they are being cast aside or unloved.

- **Holding grudges as self-protection.** Using resentment to prevent future vulnerability or closeness.

- **Avoiding opportunities for connection.** Rejecting relationships, social events, or group participation to minimize emotional risk.

- **Shutting down in conflict.** Becoming emotionally unavailable or refusing to engage rather than addressing issues.

- **Blaming others for disconnection.** Rationalizing their own withdrawal by assuming others didn't care enough to keep them close.

- **Avoiding visibility or leadership.** Staying in the background to minimize scrutiny, judgment, or responsibility.

- **Distancing as a defense mechanism.** Believing that pulling away protects them from future pain or rejection.

Three Key Takeaways for Rejection – Control to Receive Love (Conflict-Prone Isolating):

1. **Withdrawal as self-protection.** The Conflict-Prone - Isolating pattern is driven by the belief that removing themselves from situations prevents blame, criticism, or rejection, leading to emotional suppression and distancing as a defense mechanism.

2. **Fear of exposure fuels isolation.** Individuals with this pattern avoid visibility, suppress emotions, and detach from relationships, believing that staying quiet and unnoticed minimizes the risk of being judged or hurt.

3. **Disconnection reinforces rejection beliefs.** Their behaviors—such as ghosting, holding grudges, and misinterpreting boundaries as rejection—create a cycle where their preemptive withdrawal leads to the very exclusion they fear, reinforcing their belief that they don't belong.

Chaos – Rejection

Conclusion: Everything is a set up and will turn on me if I get my hopes up.

Behavior: Rejecting consistency, long-term effort, or emotional stability–believing that structure is a setup, people are unreliable, and any attempt at success or connection will ultimately be wasted.

Variants of the Conclusion (Chaos – Rejection):

- If I trust this, I'll just be disappointed when it fails.

- I'm better off not trying because it will betray me.

- If I put effort into something, it will eventually collapse anyway.

- I'm better off alone, so I don't get hurt by others.

- I can't trust stability because it's just a cruel joke that will turn on me.

- I need to reject rules and expectations before they are used against me.

- There's no point in trying because everything falls apart.

Common Behavioral Responses for (Chaos – Rejection):

- **Sabotaging stability.** Destroying or undermining progress before something can go wrong.

- **Seeking extreme experiences**. Engaging in risky behaviors to avoid feeling trapped or numb.

- **Avoiding long-term effort.** Refusing to commit to consistency in relationships, work, or self-improvement.

- **Drifting instead of making decisions.** Letting life happen rather than taking control, assuming effort is pointless.

- **Escaping through distraction.** Using substances, media, or thrill-seeking to avoid emotional investment.

- **Testing limits and rules.** Challenging people, systems, or expectations to prove they can't be trusted.

- **Rejecting help or resources.** Avoiding support because they assume it will eventually be used against them.

- **Destroying what's given to them.** Pushing away good opportunities or relationships before they can be taken away.

- **Attaching self-worth to chaos.** Believing that a stable or "normal" life isn't meant for them.

- **Blaming external factors for instability.** Viewing life as happening to them, reinforcing the idea that control is impossible.

Three Key Takeaways for Chaos - Rejection:

1. **Distrust of stability drives self-sabotage.** The Chaos - Rejection pattern is rooted in the belief that structure, stability, and success are setups that will eventually collapse, leading to self-sabotage and rejection of long-term effort.

2. **Chaos feels safer than disappointment.** Individuals with this pattern avoid commitment, test limits, and seek extreme experiences, believing that rejecting stability first is better than being blindsided by its failure.

3. **A cyclical pattern of destruction.** Their behaviors—such as sabotaging stability, rejecting help, and drifting instead of making decisions—create a self-fulfilling prophecy where chaos reinforces their belief that nothing lasts and no effort is worth it.

Your Conclusion is the directive that determines what actions feel available. Once your brain decides what must be done to uphold the Assumption, it filters out all behaviors that don't align, making your reactions feel automatic, repetitive, and even inevitable. This is why you don't just respond to the reality in front of you—you respond based on what your brain has already decided is true.

From here, behavior takes over. The next section breaks down exactly how each pattern's Conclusion triggers behavior—and more importantly, how those behaviors keep reinforcing the same assumptions, trapping you in an endless loop. Recognizing these behavioral cycles is your first step to breaking them.

The Baton Pass: How Your Conclusion Triggers Behavior and Where Rebellion Zones Come In

You've identified the Assumption (A) that runs your pattern, shaping how you interpret situations before you're even fully aware of it. But assumptions don't just sit in your mind—they lead to a Conclusion (C), the internal rule your brain creates to dictate what must happen next. And once that conclusion is set, it passes the baton to behavior.

Your brain only allows you to see the behaviors that reinforce the conclusion. This is why your choices feel repetitive, automatic, and sometimes even inevitable. You act based on what your brain has already decided is true.

This is where Rebellion Zones become critical. Every area where you default to a behavior pattern is an area where a Rebellion Zone can and should overlap. If your brain is filtering out possible actions and keeping you locked in a cycle, your Rebellion Zone is where you challenge that filter. The next section will break down how each pattern's conclusion directly drives behavior—and how those behaviors keep reinforcing the same assumptions, trapping you in an endless loop. Recognizing these behavioral cycles is your first step to breaking them. Let's take a closer look.

Common Behavioral Responses for Abandonment Patterns

Note: Behavioral responses are also influenced by an additional factor: Timeline Imbalance. This is one of nine distinct markers tracked with Brain Pattern Mapping. While we do not cover Timeline Imbalance in this book, your unique markers will be described in your Brain Pattern Mapping results. Please refer to those markers to see what type of behavior you would experience in this phase. The following are general examples of how someone may respond at this phase:

- **Anticipate.** Always predicting how people will let them down.

- **Test.** Subtly or overtly testing people's reliability or truthfulness.

- **Observe.** Hyper-fixating on small details to gauge consistency.

- **Hypervigilance.** Constantly scanning for signs that things will go wrong.

- **Ask questions.** Fishing for inconsistencies or probing for reassurance.

- **Fast talking.** Overexplaining or justifying to maintain control.

- **Isolate.** Withdrawing preemptively before being let down.

- **Hyper-independence** – Assuming full responsibility to avoid relying on others.

- **Withdraw.** Pulling back emotionally or physically to create distance.

- **Set up.** Creating scenarios (consciously or unconsciously) to confirm assumptions about people.

- **Worst case scenarios.** Mentally preparing for the worst, reinforcing distrust.

- **Plan.** Over-preparing, structuring interactions to minimize perceived risks.

- **Take action.** Acting preemptively to prevent perceived threats or failure.

- **Quiet.** Going silent as a form of control or self-protection.

- **Loud.** Over-asserting themselves to compensate for feeling powerless.

- **Read between the lines.** Assuming hidden meanings in what people say or do.

- **Hyperaware of small changes in body language or one.** Constantly monitoring others for micro-signals that might indicate a shift in behavior or intention.

Common Behavioral Responses for Rejection Patterns

For Rejection-driven individuals, behaviors revolve around avoiding perceived exclusion, managing social acceptance, and protecting themselves from judgment, embarrassment, or blame—whether through people-pleasing, withdrawing, testing relationships, or hypervigilance. This simplified list highlights the most common ways Rejection patterns manifest in daily life.

- **Anticipate.** Always predicting how people will let them down.

- **Test.** Subtly or overtly testing people's reliability or truthfulness.

- **Observe.** Hyper-fixating on small details to gauge consistency.

- **Hypervigilance.** Constantly scanning for signs that things will go wrong. Read between the lines. Assuming hidden meanings in what people say or do, often searching for signs of rejection.

- **Hyperaware of small changes in body language or tone.** Monitoring micro-signals that might indicate emotional withdrawal.

- **Ask questions.** Fishing for reassurance with questions like "Are you mad at me?" or "Did I do something wrong?"

- **Fast talking.** Over-explaining or justifying actions to control how they are perceived.

- **Force validation.** Repeating explanations or insisting on emotional engagement to confirm they are still wanted.

- **Fixate on perceived slights.** Replaying small moments for proof of rejection.

- **Comparing self to others.** Measuring personal worth based on how others are treated in comparison.

- **Isolate.** Withdrawing preemptively before being let down.

- **Hyper-independence.** Assuming full responsibility to avoid relying on others or being disappointed.

- **Withdraw.** Pulling back emotionally or physically to create distance when they feel insecure.

- **Ghost.** Cutting ties suddenly rather than confronting emotional discomfort.

Pulling away to test commitment. Creating emotional or physical distance to see if others will chase after them.

- **Set up.** Creating scenarios (consciously or unconsciously) to confirm assumptions about people.

- **Worst case scenarios.** Mentally preparing for rejection or abandonment before it happens.

- **Plan.** Over-preparing for social interactions to minimize the risk of being judged or left out.

- **Take action.** Acting preemptively to avoid or control a feared rejection.

- **Quiet.** Going silent as a form of control, waiting to see if others will notice.

- **Loud.** Over-asserting themselves or escalating conflicts to compensate for feeling powerless or ignored.

- **Push conversations.** Assuming persistence will force validation.

- **Escalate small issues.** Amplifying problems to prove importance or create emotional engagement.

- **Hold grudges.** Using resentment as a form of self-protection to prevent further hurt.

- **Challenge authority or rules.** Rejecting guidance or structure, assuming it is meant to suppress them.

- **Emotionally test relationships.** Pushing people away to see if they will fight to stay.

Common Behavioral Responses for Chaos Patterns

For Chaos-driven individuals, behaviors revolve around avoiding stability, rejecting structure, and maintaining unpredictability—whether through distraction, self-sabotage, or reckless decision-making. This simplified list highlights the most common ways Chaos patterns manifest in daily life.

- **Avoid.** Putting off tasks, responsibilities, or decisions indefinitely.

- **Distract.** Using external stimulation (social media, drama, chaos) to avoid engaging with real life.

- **Use sickness or mental health as an excuse.** Leaning on real or exaggerated symptoms to justify inaction.

- **Oversleep.** Sleeping excessively to escape reality.

- **Binge-watch shows or scroll endlessly.** Consuming media mindlessly to avoid boredom or responsibility.

- **Overeat or undereat.** Using food to self-soothe or exert control over circumstances.

- **Substance use.** Using alcohol, drugs, or other vices to check out from reality.

- **Sabotage stability.** Creating problems where there are none to avoid routine.

- **Quit when things get hard.** Abandoning jobs, projects, or relationships at the first sign of discomfort.

- **Start over constantly.** Jumping from one idea, relationship, or lifestyle to another instead of sticking with anything.

- **Overspend or financial self-sabotage.** Avoiding financial security by spending recklessly or refusing to budget.

- **Refuse help or resources.** Pushing away support systems that could create stability.

• **Engage in reckless behaviors.** Seeking out danger, impulsivity, or risky decisions.

• **Chase chaos.** Jumping into high-stakes or dramatic situations unnecessarily.

• **Consume extreme content.** Seeking out horror, violent media, or dark content to stay emotionally detached.

• **Break rules or test boundaries.** Rejecting authority or guidance instinctively.

• **Ghost suddenly.** Disappearing from relationships with no explanation.

• **Test loyalty.** Creating conflict or pulling away to see who will fight to keep them.

• **Blame others for disconnection.** Assuming people abandoned them instead of recognizing their role in isolation.

• **Refuse to commit.** Avoiding deep relationships to maintain a sense of freedom.

CHAPTER 32

MEET ELI

Dismantling the System: Breaking Down the Prosecutor's Argument

Your brain filters choices, justifies behaviors, and reinforces patterns that keep you trapped in a repeating cycle. The next step is learning how to dismantle that system piece by piece so that the behaviors keeping you stuck no longer feel necessary or inevitable.

Your brain runs a multi-layered defense system that ensures your pattern stays intact.

This system is best dismantled by addressing four distinct areas:

1. **Strongman.** The thought or belief that needs to be rewired to make this new behavior available and how it sounds in your head—think of this like the puppet master

2. **Mechanism.** The subsequent behavior pattern that generates a negative outcome

3. **Problem.** A negative outcome you are actively aware of in your daily life

4. **Dangling Carrot.** A motivator that can be used to engage your brain in rewiring

When dismantling the language, we must move through it in this exact sequence. Think of your Brain Pattern like a running stitch sewn into fabric—the only way to remove it is to follow the path in which it was sewn. Using this framework prompts the brain to see the error itself, rather than being forced into change. This makes your Rebellion Zone available to you without needing to white-knuckle your way through it.

Step 1: The Strongman, The Core Argument Keeping You Stuck

The Strongman is the internal argument the Prosecutor makes that convinces you the behavior is necessary. It's a rationalization, an excuse, or a justification that makes your pattern feel logical, protective, or even inevitable.

These thoughts sound like absolute truths in your head, but they are actually designed to keep the cycle running. The Strongman doesn't tell you, "You should sabotage yourself." Instead, it says, "You just need a break," "This is too much," or "You're better off handling this yourself." It disguises itself as reasonable.

Examples of Strongman Beliefs Across Patterns:

- Abandonment – Control to Be Safe: "They can't handle this on their own."

- Abandonment- Hold It All Together: "I'll figure it out later."

- Rejection – Control to Receive Love and Be Safe (People-Pleasing – Engaging): "I need to say it exactly like this so they like me."

- Rejection – Control to Receive Love (Conflict-Prone – Isolating): "They probably think I'm an idiot."

- Chaos – Rejection: "Nothing matters."

As we prepare to learn about ELI—a powerful structure that grants you access to your Rebellion Zone, you need to recognize that these Strongman arguments are not facts. They are well-crafted strategies your brain uses to keep you in the pattern.

Step 2: The Mechanism, How the Pattern Reinforces Itself

The Mechanism is the engine that keeps the Strongman belief alive. It's a network of behaviors and automatic responses that prove the Strongman belief to be true over and over again.

Your Mechanism works by filtering your experiences so that only the evidence that supports the Strongman belief gets through. This is why behaviors feel automatic—they're designed to reinforce the assumption rather than challenge it.

Examples of Mechanisms Across Patterns:

- Abandonment - Control to Be Safe: Micromanaging, anticipating failure, refusing to delegate.

- Abandonment - Hold It All Together: Over-functioning, absorbing others' emotional burdens, preemptively fixing problems to prevent conflict.

- Rejection - Control to Receive Love and Be Safe (People-Pleasing - Engaging): Over-functioning, seeking reassurance, avoiding conflict.

- Rejection - Control to Receive Love (Conflict-Prone - Isolating): Pulling away, ghosting, withdrawing from relationships at the first sign of discomfort.

- Chaos - Rejection: Sabotaging stability, creating unnecessary problems, rejecting structure.

Recognizing the Mechanism helps you see that the behaviors keeping you stuck are not accidental. They are part of the pattern's self-defense system.

Step 3: The Problem, The Real-World Cost of the Pattern

Your brain works hard to avoid recognizing the actual cost of your behaviors because seeing the truth would require you to change. This is why you may justify, downplay, or ignore the Problem that your pattern is creating in your life. But the truth is, every pattern has a price—and it's one you've been paying over and over again.

Examples of Problems Across Patterns:

- **Abandonment - Control to Be Safe:** Relationship conflict, resentment towards others, diminished self-efficacy in the people around you, hypervigilance creating burnout.

- **Abandonment - Hold It All Together:** Exhaustion, constant lateness, and double bookings, carrying emotional burdens.

- **Rejection - Control to Receive Love and Be Safe (People-Pleasing - Engaging):** Burnout, frustration over not feeling genuinely appreciated, low self-trust, struggling to form deep connections.

- **Rejection - Control to Receive Love and Be Safe (Conflict-Prone - Isolating):** Self-imposed loneliness, misinterpreting boundaries as rejection, intrusive thoughts, difficulty maintaining long-term relationships, constant cycles of cutting people off.

- **Rejection - Control to Receive Love (People-Pleasing - Engaging):** Feeling used or unappreciated in relationships, resentment from overextending, difficulty asserting needs, struggling with self-worth.

- **Rejection - Control to Receive Love (Conflict-Prone - Isolating):** Chronic push-pull dynamics in relationships, frequent arguments, emotionally withdrawing as a test of loyalty, misinterpreting neutral feedback as personal attacks.

- **Chaos - Rejection:** Chronic instability, struggling to build security in career or relationships, reinforcing the belief that peace is impossible.

If you don't emotionally register the Problem, your brain won't feel the urgency to challenge the Mechanism. You can also use an emotional response to the awareness of a problem to motivate you. Some of you may feel disgusted or angry when the awareness of a problem you've created gets brought to your attention. This is positive and can be used in our dismantling process.

Step 4: The Dangling Carrot, The Motivation to Disrupt the Pattern

Your brain won't comply unless it sees compelling reasons to shift. The Dangling Carrot is what makes breaking the cycle worth it. It has to feel more rewarding than the comfort of staying in the pattern.

Examples of Dangling Carrots Across Patterns:

- **Abandonment - Control to Be Safe:** bolstered self-efficacy in kids and partner, decrease in daily stress, less conflict in relationships, feeling understood, decrease in anxiety or OCD symptoms

- **Abandonment - Hold It All Together:** peace, stability, time for self-care or to have downtime, ability to communicate directly and honestly

- **Rejection - Control to Receive Love and Be Safe (People-Pleasing - Engaging):** stronger sense of self outside of group dynamics, increased self-trust, increased relationship connections or depth

- **Rejection – Control to Receive Love and Be Safe (Conflict-Prone – Isolating):** ability to pick your battles and maintain peace, enhanced relationship connection, decreased negative self-talk and intrusive thoughts, stepping into opportunities instead of waiting

- **Rejection – Control to Receive Love (People-Pleasing – Engaging):** stronger sense of self, decreased negative self-talk and intrusive thoughts, closer friendships, increased self-trust

- **Rejection – Control to Receive Love (Conflict-Prone – Isolating):** less conflict in relationships, more active engagement in group activities and friendships, stepping into leadership opportunities without negative self-talk

- **Chaos – Rejection:** financial stability, relationship building, self-efficacy, connection to something bigger than yourself

The Dangling Carrot must be personally motivating—if it's not compelling enough, the brain will default to protecting the Strongman. These will be different from person to person. However, within Brain Pattern types there will be common themes we address in the next chapter that can be used either as a skeleton that you build onto or on its own.

Let's look at a client example:

Client Reported Issue: Wife reports struggling to communicate directly and to set new standards for the division of labor around the house with her husband.

Wife's Pattern: Abandonment – Hold It All Together

Husband's Pattern: Rejection – Control to Receive Love and Be Safe (Isolating – Conflict Prone)

Wife's Strongman:

- It doesn't matter

- He won't follow through, and it'll still fall on me

- I'm better off not wasting my time

Wife's Mechanisms:

- Indirect or ineffective communication

- Keeping things in

- Hyperindependent

673

- Enabling

- Assuming conflict

- Being calculated or strategic

- Missing appropriate time to engage collaboration

- Putting on a facade and presenting a way that doesn't match your thoughts

Wife's Problems:

- Crossed boundaries that lead to resentment

- Overloading your plate leads to exhaustion

- Messy follow-through

- Inconsistency in daily routines or structures

Wife's Dangling Carrots:

- Decrease in marital conflict

- Repeatable process for duties and responsibilities at home

- Trust in husband's follow through

- More time for self-care and keeping up on tasks around the house

Now that you understand what's behind the current of this system, you can translate these language structures into the holy grail of rewiring strategy: ELI. ELI questions will force the brain to recognize the logical errors keeping the cycle intact—step by step, in a sequence designed to eliminate escape routes. After you get familiar with ELI questions, we will bring this client example back to introduce how the ELI questions address each phase of this framework to strategically dismantle the system.

Meet ELI, Your New Best Friend

This is the tool that will shatter those loops in real time. ELI is your Prosecutor's worst nightmare. ELI is a strategic questioning system designed to disrupt the emotional response that keeps behaviors automatic and unquestioned.

How ELI Works:

- Engages logic instead of emotionally reacting. Interrupts your brain's default reaction and redirects it into logical processing instead of an emotional response.

- Disrupts the Prosecutor's argument. Uses a structured sequence of questions to expose the flaw in your brain's reasoning.

- Backs your brain into a logical corner. The question structure forces a clear "yes" or "no" answer, leaving no room for gray area or rationalization.

- Dismantles the language structures that keep you stuck. Systematically combats your excuses, rationalizations and justifications before your brain is even able to generate them

ELI Doesn't Fight Your Emotional Response—It Reroutes It

Instead of allowing your brain to react impulsively based on old patterns, ELI forces a transition from emotional processing (amygdala and hippocampus) to strategic thinking (prefrontal cortex). This redirection makes emotional hijacking nearly impossible—your brain must pause and engage in logic instead of looping in the pattern.

In the ELI acronym:

- **"E" stands for emotional response**, which has a short reaction time between stimulus and response, often triggering impulsive or automatic behavior.

- **"L" stands for logical response**, which engages a longer reaction timeline, allowing the brain to assess reasoning, long-term cause and effect, and real-world consequences before acting.

- **"I" stands for Intuitive response**, a process that—once emotional escalation is deactivated—enables you to perceive the present moment with greater objectivity and nuance.

This process doesn't override emotion—it reroutes it, allowing logic and intuition to work together rather than being hijacked by reactive patterning. Many people mistakenly believe that intuition and "following your gut" are the same thing. In reality, they couldn't be more different.

"Following your gut" is more closely tied to instinct, a survival-based, automatic response driven by past conditioning. Intuition, by contrast, is a deeper, more nuanced awareness—one that an emotionally activated person would completely overlook or contaminate with fear-based insights. When emotional processing is intentionally redirected using an ELI question sequence, we create the space for intuition to become a balance point in decision-making, ensuring we don't default to raw emotional reactions or rigid logic, but instead make choices from a clear, strategic, and informed state.

What Makes a Question an ELI Question?

ELI requires strategically dismantling faulty logic in real time. A true ELI question meets three essential criteria:

1. It forces a binary "yes" or "no" answer.

- There's no room for hedging, rationalization, or emotional avoidance. The brain is forced to answer clearly, and the question is intentionally crafted to generate a strong (sometimes visceral) reaction through "yes" or "no."

- Yes: "If I assume they don't care, don't I historically start pushing them away?"

- No: "Does that person even care about me?" (Too open-ended and allows emotional narrative to get behind the wheel—keeps the brain looping.)

2. It directly challenges the Prosecutor's argument.

- The question must expose the flaw in the pattern's logic, not just explore feelings or past experiences.

- Yes: "When I fixate on my fear of failure, don't I start making silly mistakes?"

- Yes: "Don't these silly mistakes actually set me up to fail?"

- No: "Why do I make silly mistakes when I'm stressed out?" (This just reinforces the struggle.)

3. It leads the brain to dismantle its own logic.

- A strong ELI question traps the brain in a logical contradiction. It has no choice but to see its own faulty reasoning.

- Yes: "If I assume that I can't trust people, don't I end up testing them in ways that make them pull away?"

- No: "Can I trust this person?" (This doesn't expose the error—this just sets up an emotional reaction)

Some ELI questions are designed to elicit a "yes," reinforcing a logical

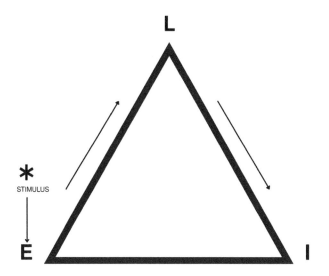

Pictured Above: ELI Triangle

truth the brain can recognize: "If I slow down before I respond, do I make better decisions?"

These "yes"-eliciting questions work by pointing out a behavior shift connected to a desired outcome. Does the person want to make better decisions? Without the prompting of this ELI question, might they not realize that their impulsivity drives the pattern of mistakes?

Others are designed to elicit a "no," forcing the brain to recognize that its current behavior isn't serving its best interest: "Has saying yes reflexively created a schedule that allows for self-care or free time?"

These "no"-eliciting questions work by exposing the lack of something you actually value.

Example: "Has saying yes reflexively created a schedule that allows for self-care and free time?"

This question points out to the person's brain that they do not have something they actually want. A person with this pattern will be motivated by time to themselves or relax yet their behavior makes it an impossibility. With a "no"-framed question here we accomplish two simultaneous tasks:

1. We show the brain that it doesn't have something it actually wants (a motivator).

2. The behavior it is currently trying to justify is responsible for this lack (accountability).

Both "yes" and "no" ELI questions serve the same function: they break the emotional autopilot and force logical clarity. The difference is in their approach—"yes" questions affirm a logical truth, while "no" questions expose an inconvenient reality that motivates you to start fixing the problem.

Both approaches serve the same purpose: they expose the flawed logic keeping your pattern intact.

What Is Not an ELI Question?

Open-Ended Self-Reflection

- "Why do I always do this?" Keeps you in an emotional loop instead of breaking it. Allows your Prosecutor to start weaponizing past experiences to put you into a shame spiral.

Vague, Abstract Thinking

- "What if I just let this go?" Doesn't directly dismantle the faulty belief. Questions like this give too much room for aspirational thinking where someone can want something intellectually, convince themselves they are onboard, and then their actions do not follow.

Blaming or Shaming Language

- "Why am I so bad at this?" ELI doesn't punish—it forces clarity through logic. These questions help expose the error and the lesson rather than motivate through negativity and shame.

Multipart Questions

- "Is this pattern tied to impulsivity or urgency?" ELI doesn't elicit answers that aren't a distinct "yes" or "no." When you leave it open, you walk yourself into a grey area that allows emotional reactivity to take over.

Questions That Require Nuance

- "Is it really true that I'm not safe with my partner?" ELI doesn't allow for your emotional response and instinct to highlight the answers.

When used correctly, ELI hijacks the Prosecutor before the Prosecutor can hijack you, redirecting your brain from emotional reaction to logical clarity in a matter of seconds. Now, let's break down how to build an ELI sequence that shuts the loop down every single time.

How Does ELI Work?

ELI works by disrupting your Prosecutor's argument at its core. It does this by:

1. Challenging the Strongman Belief (What Feels True)

This is the core argument your Prosecutor is using against you.

Example: "If I don't take control, everything will fall apart."

ELI Examples:

- "Is my brain tricking me into thinking micromanaging is the only path to safety right now?"

- "Historically, do I accidentally create conflict around me with the way I try to manage situations?"

- "Does my communication style tend to make people nervous?"

- "When people are nervous, aren't they more likely to make silly mistakes?"

- "When people start making mistakes don't I use it to justify my control cycle?

2. Disrupting the Mechanism (How the Pattern Reinforces Itself)

These questions challenge the behaviors that make the belief feel real.

Example: Withholding and being strategic with delivering the facts

ELI Example:

- "Is my brain telling me that they can't handle this information right now without getting upset?"

- "Historically, do I then keep certain things to myself and wait for a better time?"

- "When I'm calculated and strategic with my partner, don't they react as if I'm hiding something?"

- "Hasn't this led to more conflict in the long run?"

- "Is it true that when I justify withholding information, I set myself up to look like a liar?"

- "Doesn't this eventually blow up in my face and make me look like the bad guy?"

3. Highlighting the Problem (Real-World Consequences of the Pattern)

These questions force emotional accountability—making it clear that continuing this behavior means choosing a known negative outcome.

Example: Marital conflict and trust issues

- ELI Example: "Don't I delay the inevitable when I withhold or omit to not set someone off?

Example: Lack of close friendships and loneliness

- ELI Example: "When I slip into chameleon behavior, aren't I making it nearly impossible for others to form a strong connection to the real me?"

Example: Family members have become lazy and dependent on micromanaging

- ELI Example: "When I micromanage, do people ever learn to do things well on their own?"

4. Presenting the Dangling Carrot (Motivation to Choose an Alternative)

- These questions introduce the benefit of breaking the cycle.

- Examples:

  - Dangling Carrot: Free time, relaxation, alone time

  - ELI Question: "By saying no to this right now, aren't I creating more time to relax and rest?"

  - Dangling Carrot: Self-efficacy and independence in my kids

  - ELI Question: "If I let my kids do their kitchen duties their way tonight, don't I get a step closer to building self-efficacy in my kids? "

  - Dangling Carrot: More sex, better intimate connection

- ELI Question: "Won't I improve my sex life by taking ownership of small mistakes with my partner as soon as I notice them?"

When asked in this sequence, ELI questions systematically weaken the pattern's grip on you. They pull the entire structure apart from the inside until your Brain Pattern throws its hands up and says, "You got me."

Why is ELI So Effective?

1. It Disrupts Emotional Responses Before They Dictate Behavior

• Your default response is emotionally driven, coming from the amygdala and hippocampus, the brain regions responsible for emotional processing and memory.

• When you engage with an ELI question, your brain is forced to shift from emotional reaction to logical analysis, activating the prefrontal cortex, which is responsible for strategic thinking and long-term decision-making.

• This means that instead of reacting automatically based on past trauma or assumptions, you can think strategically about cause and effect.

2. It Doesn't Give Your Prosecutor an Exit Strategy

• The sequence forces your brain to recognize its own contradiction. It can't justify the behavior without also acknowledging the cost.

• Unlike emotional arguments, which can be rationalized away, ELI questions leave no room for escape.

3. It Works With Your Brain, Not Against It

• Instead of forcing change through sheer willpower, ELI guides the brain to a new conclusion on its own.

• The question-based aspect of ELI is critical as the brain processes information like a computer. Pointing out the error like a command or comment doesn't work. Strategically asking questions to help your brain figure it out - works every time.

• When your brain discovers the error in logic itself, the shift feels natural, not forced.

What Makes a Good ELI Question?

A good ELI question forces the brain to recognize the flaw in its own logic. It leaves no room for debate or emotional justification.

- It must elicit a clear "yes" or "no" answer.

- **Bad**: "Why do I always feel the need to micromanage?" (Too open-ended—allows for excuses.)

- **Good**: "Historically has micromanaging led to conflict with the people around me?"

- It must follow a logical sequence that eliminates escape routes.

- **Bad**: "Wouldn't it be better if I stopped micromanaging?" (Leading question—invites argument.)

- **Good**: "Am I trying to convince myself that my way is the only way when it really just makes me feel more safe?"

- It must not reinforce the pattern.

- **Bad**: "Am I safe?" (This confirms the belief instead of dismantling it.)

- **Good**: "Do I convince myself that control will make me feel safe when the reality is it just perpetuates my hypervigilance?"

- It must create a logical contradiction that forces a perception shift.

- **Bad**: "Why does that person not like me?" (Invites argument and justification.)

- **Good**: "Do I have a tendency to assume others don't like me when it's usually a projection of my own insecurities?"

Why ELI Questions Must Follow a Specific Order

ELI is a structured, strategic intervention that systematically dismantles faulty thinking in four steps:

1. Strongman (Primary Argument of the Prosecutor). Challenge the belief that keeps the pattern in place.

2. Mechanism (How the Pattern Reinforces Itself). Expose how behaviors keep proving the belief true.

3. Problem (Real-World Consequences of the Pattern). Highlight the cost of continuing the cycle.

4. Dangling Carrot (The Alternative Option). Introduce the benefit of change so the brain actually wants to comply.

This order forces the brain to dismantle its own argument, layer by layer.

Breaking the Cycle: How Rebellion Zones Disrupt Automatic Behaviors

By now, you understand that your brain doesn't just let you make any choice. It filters your options, narrowing them down to only the behaviors that reinforce your pattern. This is why change feels so difficult—your brain isn't offering you a menu of all possible actions. It's handing you the same pre-approved choices over and over again, keeping you stuck in a loop.

Each time you engage in the behaviors that align with your Conclusion (C), you confirm the Assumption (A) that started the whole process. This is how your brain keeps reinforcing the idea that your pattern is true. If your pattern is Chaos - Rejection, every time you disrupt stability or self-sabotage, your brain takes it as proof that consistency isn't meant for you. If your pattern is Rejection - Control to Receive Love Love and Be Safe (People-Pleasing Isolating), and you withdraw at the first sign of discomfort, your brain reinforces the belief that pulling away is the only way to avoid rejection.

This is where Rebellion Zones come in.

How Rebellion Zones Work to Break the Cycle

A Rebellion Zone isn't just about choosing a different behavior—it's about strategically disrupting the entire automated response that keeps your pattern alive. Right now, your Assumptions, Conclusions, and Behaviors are reinforcing each other in a loop. Your Rebellion Zone targets that loop by forcing your brain to acknowledge an alternative and engage with it.

While future ELI questions will help disrupt the Assumption and Conclusion, Rebellion Zones are designed to intervene at the behavioral level, breaking the cycle in real time. This means:

• Pinpointing the behaviors that directly feed your pattern.

- Challenging the belief that these behaviors are necessary.

- Forcing your brain to see and engage with an alternative action.

Example 1: Rejection - Control to Receive Love and Be Safe (People-Pleasing - Isolating)

- **Behavior:** Automatically withdrawing from social situations to avoid discomfort.

- **What it reinforces:** "If I pull away, I won't get blamed, embarrassed, or rejected."

- **Rebellion Zone:** Staying present and engaged when the impulse to withdraw kicks in—not just forcing social interaction, but actively disrupting the urge to disappear.

Now let's apply ELI:

- **Strongman:** Do I convince myself that others will think I'm stupid or inferior?

- **Mechanism:** Historically, do I tend to project my deepest insecurities onto others and act as if that's how they feel?

- **Problem:** Has this created conflict in relationships and destroyed opportunities for breakthrough in my life?

- **Dangling Carrot:** Can I ever become an established part of a social group if I keep opting out?

- **Challenge Question:** Can I challenge myself to stay 1 more hour and start conversations with at least 2 people before I leave?

Example 2: Chaos - Rejection

- **Behavior:** Creating instability when life starts feeling too structured.

- **What it reinforces:** "Routine is a trap; structure will fail me eventually."

- **Rebellion Zone:** Sticking with a routine even when it feels suffocating—not just trying to build stability, but actively challenging the feeling that stability is dangerous.

Now let's apply ELI:

- **Strongman:** Do I tell myself that nothing matters, making any effort feel futile?

- **Mechanism:** Historically, do I self-sabotage any momentum or stability as soon as I become aware of it consciously?

- **Problem:** Has this created patterns of chaos and dependency in my life?

- **Dangling Carrot:** Would financial stability give me access to more opportunities in my life?

- **Challenge Question:** Can I challenge myself to continue this routine even if it feels boring or futile for 3 more days?

Example 3: Abandonment - Control to Be Safe (Overt)

- **Behavior:** Taking over a situation instead of delegating, assuming others will fail or disappoint them.

- **What it reinforces:** "If I don't take control, everything will fall apart."

- **Rebellion Zone:** Allowing others to take responsibility, even when it feels uncomfortable—not just letting go, but actively resisting the urge to micromanage or fix things.

Now let's apply ELI:

- **Strongman:** Am I convinced that I am seeing this situation in a superior way compared to others?

- **Mechanism:** Historically, do I take over and control others in a way that leads to conflict and hurt feelings?

- **Problem:** Has this created patterns of mistakes, dependency, and missed expectations?

- **Dangling Carrot:** If I actively relinquish control and let people learn, won't they eventually be able to complete something on their own?

- **Challenge Question:** Can I challenge myself to delegate this or allow it to unfold without correcting or guiding the process?

You can play around with this framework as you tackle the Rebellion Zones for your pattern type. If you go back to review these chapters, you'll now notice ELI questions woven throughout the section to orient your thinking toward positive change.

CHAPTER 33

THE OTHER SIDE (OF REWIRING)

You can't unsee it now.

Once you've made it through this book, there's no going back. You've spent chapters dissecting your patterns, learning how they were built, and—more importantly—how they've been running the show without your permission. But now, you hold the keys. The filter is off, the distortion exposed. And that means you'll start to see it everywhere.

At first, this new awareness can feel like a superpower. You've cracked a code that was hiding in plain sight. People's behaviors make sense in a way they never did before. The outbursts, the manipulations, the excuses, the stubborn self-sabotage—it's all just Brain Patterns pulling the strings. And yet, with that clarity comes something heavier: the realization that most people have no idea what's controlling them. They are still in the dark, blindly reacting, endlessly looping. They don't know they're locked in a system. But you do.

This knowledge isn't just a gift; it's a responsibility. If you're in a relationship, you might already be recognizing just how much of your dynamic has been dictated by unconscious patterns colliding. And if you're the one reading this book, that probably means you're the one going first. Rewiring isn't something you can demand from someone else. You have to embody it first, show what's possible, and carry the extra weight until it sparks something in them. The heavy lifting starts with you. The reward is this: you become living proof that change is possible, and that kind of shift is contagious.

Yes, you're going to see people's patterns now. Yes, you're going to hear their Strongman beliefs playing on a loop, justifying their behaviors like a rigged courtroom inside their minds. And yes, it can be frustrating to watch them stay locked in something you now see so clearly. But if there's one thing this work teaches, it's that almost nothing is without a certain level of self-deception. That argument you used to take personally? It's just someone's Brain Pattern locked in a repetitive loop of rigidity and black-and-white thinking. That emotional withdrawal? That's their Abandonment – Hold It All Together at play. That need to control everything? It's their own distorted strategy for feeling safe. The more you see behind the curtain, the more you realize—it was never really about you.

And that's where empathy expands.

When you understand what's happening underneath someone's behavior, it becomes easier to meet them with patience rather than reactivity. You don't have to excuse it, but you also don't have to absorb it. You can stand firm in your own rewiring while recognizing that most people are still trapped in their illusions. Even when someone is being cruel, manipulative, or outright reckless, they're not actually choosing those behaviors the way you might think. Their brain is still running the same distorted code it's always run. Unlike you, they haven't been given the chance to see it yet.

After reading this book, you'll see self-deception everywhere. The temptation to go in guns blazing, pointing out to others when they are lying to themselves, will be strong, but this is not an effective strategy. Think of the movie Inception. If the architect disrupts the dream too much, too quickly, the dreamer's subconscious turns against them, attacking to protect the illusion. The same thing happens in the real world. If you push too hard, if you try to force someone to see their self-deception before they are ready, they will fight you. Their brain will protect the pattern at all costs.

There is a strategic way to help others learn to spot self-deception. One of the most effective methods is stepping into your own Rebellion Zones and allowing people to experience a brand new stimulus. When they see you behaving differently, something in their system has to recalibrate. This pattern interruption can change everything. And one of the most powerful things you can do in these moments is to take radical personal responsibility—acknowledge how you used to operate, where you were blind, and how you're changing now. When you model this level of self-awareness, you set a new standard for the relationship. It makes it possible for the other person to start boldly owning their own self-deception as well.

A Note About Symbiotic Dysfunction

In relationships—whether intimate, familial, friendship, or professional—there's a particular type of patterned dynamic that emerges between two people: symbiotic dysfunction. This describes a pairing in which two distinct Brain Pattern Types interact in a way that mutually fulfills the triggers of their pattern. In other words, person A gets triggered by person B into their pattern, and person B's patterned reaction just so happens to be person A's trigger—and vice versa. It creates a cycle of reinforcement, where each person keeps the other locked in their behaviors.

The reality is that, especially in intimate relationships, we unconsciously select partners who trigger us in exactly the right way. This is all by design. They say opposites attract, but it's much deeper than that. We are drawn to the people who provide the specific flavor of triggering we both need and perpetuate. It's why people often friend-zone those with the same Brain Pattern Type as them but feel undeniable chemistry with those who challenge them in just the right way.

For this reason, there is an art to pattern interruption in relationships. If you charge in, disrupting everything without care, it can destabilize the dynamic in ways that create unnecessary conflict. Instead, the key is to disrupt in a way that invites curiosity rather than defensiveness. The best way to do this? Show—don't tell. Step into your rebellion zones with consistency and precision. When you behave in a way that contradicts the expected pattern, you create a new stimulus for the other person to react to. That shift in the dynamic can be the catalyst for real change.

Though I've already introduced the concept, it's too important not to remind you that people will respond in one of three ways when you change:

1. They act as if you've behaved or spoken the old way because they are acting purely out of assumption.

2. They may push back in immature or retaliatory ways to get you to revert to old ways.

3. They appear confused or shocked before reacting in a positive way.

The truth is, when you truly oppose your patterns and step into your Rebellion Zones, the people around you will likely be shocked, or even mad. For some of you, your Rebellion Zone may be interpreted as aggressive because on the other side of no boundaries and self-sacrifice is a person we've enabled or allowed to use us. Conversely, some of your Rebellion Zones will soften you and allow you to listen more and let others collaborate with you. Even as you're reading this now, you're probably realizing that these two Brain Pattern spectrum typologies end up together.

This is why when one type stops allowing themselves to be a self-sacrificing doormat and the other learns how to take radical personal responsibility, literal magic happens. Throughout my career, I've seen miracles take place in marriages. This work is profound and has the ability to transform the vast majority of toxic relationships.

Toxic relationships occur when both partners fail to take the time to understand what drives each other's behavior beneath the surface. Terms like "love bombing" and "stonewalling" are often thrown around in pop psychology, much like the term "narcissist." However, these labels frequently oversimplify and misrepresent complex behavioral patterns. There is always another side to the story.

On the other side of love bombing is someone who feels deeply and intensely in the moment but later becomes distracted or uncertain during different phases of their cycle. Does that make their expressions of love and affection a lie? No—although pop psychology might have you believe it's a calculated manipulation tactic. Likewise, on the other side of stonewalling is often a reactive and emotionally volatile partner who creates an environment where the other person feels like they're constantly walking on eggshells. In many cases, stonewalling is not about control but rather a response to feeling unable to communicate without triggering conflict or escalation.

There is always another perspective. Relationships are an interplay of inputs and outputs, and when both people are willing to examine what's truly driving their reactions, these patterns can be understood and rewired. The challenge lies in having the courage to look behind the curtain and confront what's really pulling the strings.

This work doesn't just change you—it changes the way you engage with the world. And as you integrate these tools, you'll start to see a ripple effect. Your kids will pick up on it. Your spouse will notice. Your friendships will shift. People will start asking what's different about you, why you don't react the same way you used to. And some of them—when they're ready—will want to know how they can do it, too.

Imagine a world where everyone had this knowledge—where emotional intelligence wasn't some rare skill but a baseline expectation. Where people weren't just reacting to their wounds but actively choosing their behaviors. Where relationships were built on clarity instead of unconscious projections. That's the world I've been working toward since I was thirteen years old—a world where we're no longer slaves to the brain patterns we didn't choose.

And this book? It's only the beginning.

Everything we covered here—Brain Patterns, Rebellion Zones, Strongman beliefs, ELI Questions—is just a fraction of the full framework. In Brain Pattern Mapping, there are nine core markers, and in this book, we've only scratched the surface by covering two. That means there's even more depth, more precision, and more opportunity for targeted rewiring than what you've experienced here. The most common thing I hear from people after they go through this work? "This should be required for every human being." And I agree.

Our world is in the midst of a mental health crisis, and the way out isn't more diagnoses or more medication—it's breaking the cycles that keep people stuck. And that starts with you. By finishing this book, you've taken a step toward something bigger than yourself. You're not just rewiring your own life; you're shifting the landscape for everyone around you. You're part of the solution.

This work isn't easy, and at times, the burden of seeing what others can't might feel heavy. But keep going. Because every time you step into a Rebellion Zone, every time you choose to disrupt a pattern instead of feeding it, you make it easier for the next person to do the same.

And that's how we change the world—one brain at a time.

ENDNOTES

Glossary

ACB Pathway (Assumption - Conclusion - Behavior)

A subconscious pathway through which a person's brain pattern filters perception, forms conclusions, and drives behavior. The brain pattern influences the assumption—a distorted interpretation of what's happening in the present moment. It then draws a fixed conclusion, often rooted in past emotional experiences, which limits the perceived range of choices available. Once the brain locks in a conclusion, unfamiliar or healthy options become invisible or inaccessible, and the person defaults to automatic, patterned behavior. Understanding the ACB Pathway reveals where language structures need to be dismantled so perception—and choice—can expand in real time.

Adaptive Source Belief Pattern

The compensatory strategy the brain develops between ages six to twelve in response to the Origin Source Pattern (a byproduct of nurture). The Adaptive Source Belief is Informed by nature—the individual's spiritual or genetic design - responding to the repetitive adversely perceived stimuli in a patterned and unique way.

Brain Pattern Mapping

Break Method's diagnostic framework that identifies nine distinct markers to map how the brain processes information, emotion, relationships, threat, and control. These patterns predict internal dialogue, behavioral outcomes, and areas of sabotage with precision.

Timeline Diagnostics

A six-category system used to organize and interpret patterned behavior:

1. Structure, control, food, finances, fear
2. Sexual behavior, intimacy, desire
3. Performance, validation, measurement
4. Attachment, commitment, and connection
5. Communication, tone, self-expression
6. Information processing, creativity, and ideation

Each category is assigned a modifier to define its expression:

- + = Overactive
- – = Underactive
- +/– = Starts overactive, collapses into underactive
- –/+ = Starts underactive, builds into overactive

Controlled Surrender

A rewiring technique for control-oriented patterns in which the individual intentionally chooses not to intervene, even when they are fully capable of doing so. The point is not helplessness—it's acknowledgment of capability followed by a conscious decision to let things unfold.

This technique works by soothing the nervous system through internal validation: "I could control or fix this if I wanted to—but I'm choosing not to because that pattern has long-term costs."

Controlled Surrender retrains the brain to experience agency in surrender, rather than interpreting it as danger, chaos, or failure. Over time, this builds tolerance for unpredictability and stability without control.

Dangling Carrot

A personally motivating reward that makes the discomfort of change feel worth it. The carrot must reflect something the person deeply values—like intimacy, peace, time freedom, or respect—or it won't effectively challenge the pattern's grip. This motivator becomes a critical part of the ELI framework.

The Inner Defense Attorney

The internal voice of logic, intuition, and truth—but in most people, it's the weaker opponent in the internal courtroom. The Defense Attorney tries to redirect behavior during emotional spirals, but is often overpowered and under-equipped compared to the Prosecutor (your brain pattern).

To become effective, the Defense Attorney must be intentionally strengthened and given the right language, strategy, and evidence through tools like ELI Questions, Pattern Opposition, and Rebellion Zones. When fortified, it becomes a powerful advocate for present-moment choice and long-term stability.

ELI (Emotion-Logic Interrupt)

A strategic process that disrupts emotional reactivity and re-engages the prefrontal cortex using a custom sequence of logical, targeted questions. ELI restores presence, enabling the person to make decisions from intuition and awareness, not emotional autopilot.

ELI Questions

A series of binary (yes/no) logic-based questions designed to challenge the faulty assumptions, rationalizations, and self-deceptions driving patterned behavior. Read in sequence, they expose the subconscious motives and open up new behavioral options in the moment.

Emotional Addiction Cycle

The brain's chemical and behavioral attachment to familiar emotional states—even when painful. It operates in three predictable stages:

- Origin Response (ages 0-5)

- Protective Response (ages 5-10)

- Escalating Response (10+ when compensation fails)

This cycle is reinforced by repeated environmental input and keeps the person looping until the pattern is intentionally disrupted.

Emotional Homeostasis

The brain's emotional "set point," developed in childhood. It's the familiar emotional state the brain works to maintain—even if it's chaotic, unsafe, or painful—because familiarity is prioritized over function or truth. The subconscious will recreate circumstances to maintain this baseline.

Mechanism

The repeated pattern of thoughts and behaviors that creates a predictable negative outcome. It is the active process by which a Source Belief Pattern stays alive. Until identified and disrupted, the mechanism continues to override new choices.

Negative Self-Deception

A subconscious distortion that amplifies risk and suppresses reward, convincing the person that effort is futile or dangerous. It blocks forward motion and justifies inaction.

Example: "What's the point? Nothing's going to change."

Origin Source Belief Pattern

The foundational belief formed between ages two through five through repeated emotional and environmental experiences. A byproduct of nurture, it establishes the core lens through which a person interprets safety, connection, and control for the rest of their life unless rewired.

Pattern Opposition

A deliberate behavioral disruption that does the strategic and intentionally timed opposite of what the pattern wants to do. It's specific, not random, and when applied consistently, creates new neural pathways that replace the automatic, familiar response.

Pattern Oscillation

A swing between two opposing behaviors within the same Timeline category. It reflects the brain's unconscious attempt to create balance through overcorrection—usually swinging from one extreme to the other.

- +/- = Starts overactive, collapses into underactivity
- -/+ = Starts underactive, builds into overactivity

Positive Self-Deception

A subconscious distortion that magnifies the reward while minimizing risk. It creates the illusion that something is improving or manageable when the underlying pattern remains unchanged.

 Example: "It's better than it was—I'm sure it'll work itself out."

Problem

A real-life frustration, pain point, or stressor that the person already feels and acknowledges. It must be tangible and emotionally relevant, or it won't provide enough leverage to challenge the pattern and motivate true change.

The Inner Prosecutor

The internal voice of sabotage. It distorts logic, fuels fear, and reinforces the emotional addiction cycle by convincing the person that change is unsafe or doomed to fail. It often disguises itself as protective reasoning or truth.

Rebellion Zone

A specific, high-impact life situation where a Source Belief Pattern consistently plays out and where the opportunity for intentional rewiring is strongest. This is the moment the brain is most likely to default to old behavior—but also the moment it is most primed for change through the application of synaptic plasticity.

Rebellion Zones are not random—they are strategically identified and approached using a set sequence of interventions, including Pattern Opposition, ELI Questions, and language disruption techniques. These tools support the brain in choosing new behaviors over automatic responses, allowing the pattern to be dismantled in real time.

Self-Deception

A subconscious distortion in how the brain perceives reality, defines that distorted reality as truth, and reacts to it. These reactions feel logical because they are reinforced by justifications, excuses, and internal rationalizations, even when they lead to self-sabotage. Each Brain Pattern Type has a unique set of self-deceptive tendencies that keep them stuck.

Source Belief Pattern

A two-part system that forms in childhood and determines how a person perceives reality and strategically responds to it.

- The Origin Source Belief is shaped by nurture—it forms between ages 2-5 through repeated emotional input from the environment and caregivers. This creates the brain's core assumptions about how the world works and what is required to stay safe, loved, or in control.

- The Adaptive Source Belief develops between ages 6-12 and is influenced by nature—including the person's spiritual identity, genetic design, and level of self-trust. It reflects how the individual responds to those early assumptions and chooses to show up in the world.

Together, the Origin and Adaptive form a subconscious rule set that drives perception, strategy, and behavior. Understanding a person's Source Belief Pattern reveals the underlying motivations and distortions behind their decisions—explaining not just what they do, but why they do it, even when it works against their goals.

Strongman

The internal narrative that defends the pattern and makes the behavior feel justified. It often sounds noble, reasonable, or necessary, but it's actually the subconscious protecting the pattern from being disrupted.

Example: "If I don't keep everything together, everything will fall apart."

Synaptic Plasticity

The brain's built-in ability to form new neural connections and reorganize itself in response to new experiences. This is the foundation for rewiring in Break Method—proving that emotional patterns aren't permanent and can be changed through consistent, targeted intervention.

Traditional Mental Health Paradigm

A model based on subjective therapist observation, symptom labeling, and long-term talk therapy. While often well-meaning, it can reinforce client dependence and misdiagnosis due to interpretation bias.

Break Method contrasts this with a data-driven, narrative-informed diagnostic system that identifies patterns with accuracy, removes guesswork, and focuses on sustainable emotional rewiring.

References

Baars, B. J. (1988). A cognitive theory of consciousness. Cambridge University Press.

Baars, B. J. (1997). In the theater of consciousness: The workspace of the mind. Oxford University Press.

Baumeister, R. F. (1997). Evil: Inside human violence and cruelty. W.H. Freeman.

Baumeister, R. F., & Newman, L. S. (1994). How stories make sense of personal experiences: Motives that shape autobiographical narratives. Personality and Social Psychology Bulletin, 20(6), 676-690. https://doi.org/10.1177/0146167294206006

Berglas, S., & Jones, E. E. (1978). Drug choice as a self-handicapping strategy in response to noncontingent success. Journal of Personality and Social Psychology, 36(4), 405-417. https://doi.org/10.1037/0022 3514.36.4.405

Broadbent, D. E. (1958). Perception and communication. Pergamon Press.

Bruner, J. S., & Minturn, A. L. (1955). Perceptual identification and perceptual organization. Journal of General Psychology, 53(1), 21-28. https://doi.org/10.1080/00221309.1955.9714288

Burns, D. D. (1980). Feeling good: The new mood therapy. HarperCollins.

Chalmers, D. J. (1995). Facing up to the problem of consciousness. Journal of Consciousness Studies, 2(3), 200-219.

Chalmers, D. J. (1996). The conscious mind: In search of a fundamental theory. Oxford University Press.

Csikszentmihalyi, M. (1990). Flow: The psychology of optimal experience. Harper & Row.

Dawkins, R. (1976). The selfish gene. Oxford University Press.

Dennett, D. C. (1991). Consciousness explained. Little, Brown and Company.

Dennett, D. C. (1995). Darwin's dangerous idea: Evolution and the meanings of life. Simon & Schuster.

Festinger, L. (1954). A theory of social comparison processes. Human

Relations, 7(2), 117-140. https://doi.org/10.1177/001872675400700202

Festinger, L. (1957). A theory of cognitive dissonance. Stanford University Press.

Freud, A. (1936). The ego and the mechanisms of defense. International Universities Press.

Freud, S. (1908). Creative writers and day-dreaming. In The standard edition of the complete psychological works of Sigmund Freud (Vol. 9, pp. 143-153).

Freud, S. (1911). The case of Schreber: Psychoanalytic notes upon an autobiographical account of a case of paranoia.

Harmon-Jones, E., & Mills, J. (1999). Cognitive dissonance: Progress on a pivotal theory in social psychology. American Psychological Association.

Hong, Y.-Y., Morris, M. W., Chiu, C.-Y., & Benet-Martínez, V. (2000). Multicultural minds: A dynamic constructivist approach to culture and cognition. American Psychologist, 55(7), 709-720. https://doi.org/10.1037/0003-066X.55.7.709

Hróbjartsson, A., & Gøtzsche, P. C. (2001). Is the placebo powerless? A systematic review of randomized trials comparing placebo with no treatment. New England Journal of Medicine, 344(21), 1594-1602. https://doi.org/10.1056/NEJM200105243442106

Jung, C. G. (1964). Man and his symbols. Doubleday.

Jung, C. G. (1969). The archetypes and the collective unconscious (2nd ed., R. F. C. Hull, Trans.). Princeton University Press. (Original work published 1959)

Kahneman, D. (2011). Thinking, fast and slow. Farrar, Straus, and Giroux.

Kahneman, D., & Tversky, A. (1979). Prospect theory: An analysis of decision under risk. Econometrica, 47(2), 263-291. https://doi.org/10.2307/1914185

Kastrup, B. (2019). The idea of the world: A multi-disciplinary argument for the mental nature of reality. John Hunt Publishing.

Leahy, R. L. (2003). Cognitive therapy techniques: A practitioner's guide. Guilford Press.

Lord, C. G., Ross, L., & Lepper, M. R. (1979). Biased assimilation and attitude polarization: The effects of prior theories on subsequently considered evidence. Journal of Personality and Social Psychology, 37(11), 2098–2109. https://doi.org/10.1037/0022-3514.37.11.2098

Marks, G., & Miller, N. (1987). Ten years of research on the false-consensus effect: An empirical and theoretical review. Psychological Bulletin, 102(1), 72–90. https://doi.org/10.1037/0033-2909.102.1.72

Miller, W. R., & Rollnick, S. (2002). Motivational interviewing: Preparing people for change. Guilford Press.

Nickerson, R. S. (1998). Confirmation bias: A ubiquitous phenomenon in many guises. Review of General Psychology, 2(2), 175–220. https://doi.org/10.1037/1089-2680.2.2.175

Rhodewalt, F., & Vohs, K. D. (2005). Defensive strategies, motivation, and the self: Understanding self-handicapping and self-presentation. Self and Identity, 4(1), 1–16. https://doi.org/10.1080/13576500444000041

Ross, L., Greene, D., & House, P. (1977). The "false consensus effect": An egocentric bias in social perception and attribution processes. Journal of Experimental Social Psychology, 13(3), 279–301. https://doi.org/10.1016/0022-1031(77)90049-X

Sharot, T. (2011). The optimism bias. Current Biology, 21(23), R941–R945. https://doi.org/10.1016/j.cub.2011.10.030

Sheldrake, R. (2012). The science delusion: Freeing the spirit of enquiry. Coronet.

Sheldrake, R. (2013). Science set free: 10 paths to new discovery. Deepak Chopra Books.

Skinner, B. F. (1953). Science and human behavior. Macmillan.

Skinner, B. F. (1974). About behaviorism. Alfred A. Knopf.

Suls, J., & Wheeler, L. (2013). Social comparison theory. In E. K. Kessler (Ed.), Encyclopedia of management theory (pp. 741–745). Sage Publications.

Tononi, G. (2004). An information integration theory of consciousness. BMC Neuroscience, 5(1), 42. https://doi.org/10.1186/1471-2202-5-42

Vaillant, G. E. (1977). Adaptation to life. Harvard University Press.

Wundt, W. (1897). Outlines of psychology. Wilhelm Engelmann.